SCM CORE TEXT

Religion and Modern Thought

Victoria S. Harrison

D0522464

scm press

British Library Cataloguing in Publication data

A catalogue record for this book is available
from the British Library

978 0 334 04126 9

First published in 2007 by SCM Press
9–17 St Alban's Place,
London N1 0NX

www.scm-canterburypress.co.uk

SCM Press is a division of
SCM-Canterbury Press Ltd

Typeset by Regent Typesetting, London
Printed and bound in Great Britain by
William Clowes Ltd, Beccles, Suffolk

Contents

Preface

This book is unusual both in what it covers and in how the material is treated. Unlike most books penned by Western academics, this book does not focus exclusively on Christianity but covers Islam and Judaism as well. And unlike many treatments that do cover several faiths, it presumes neither the standpoint nor the superiority nor the correctness of any one of them. Moreover, in dealing with Judaism, Christianity and Islam, this book is avowedly interdisciplinary. It ranges from the philosophy of religion, through the history of ideas, to theology and religious studies, while nevertheless retaining a philosophical perspective. It might, perhaps, be most succinctly characterized as applied philosophy of religion.

The explanation for the interdisciplinary approach adopted here is as follows: I was initially trained in philosophy and theology at Heythrop College, University of London. Since then I have taught: philosophy of religion at Birkbeck College, University of London; history of ideas at Kingston University, London; philosophy and world religions at the Muslim College, London; theology at the University of Notre Dame, London Centre; philosophy at the University of Colorado at Boulder; and, most recently, philosophy at the University of Glasgow. Thus, in writing this book I have been able to draw upon my experience as a philosopher, a historian of ideas and a theologian.

I am grateful to all the students I taught at the above-named institutions for their enthusiastic participation in discussions about many of the ideas considered in this book. I am particularly grateful to those students who took my course 'Religion and Modern Thought' at Kingston University between 1997 and 2001. Thanks are also due to two of my former colleagues at Kingston University, John J. Clarke and MaryAnne Perkins, who first introduced me to the history of ideas. Both were a great source of inspiration and encouragement.

Particular thanks also go to my former colleagues and students at the Muslim College, London. I am grateful for the insight into the British Muslim community afforded by my two years of work and friendship with them. Many ideas gleaned from conversations in and outside the classroom have found their way into this book.

I owe a debt of gratitude to the many colleagues and friends, too numerous to mention, who have stimulated and encouraged me, and thus made a contribution to this book. My mother, Marjorie Harrison, has been an eager critic since the inception of the project. Thanks are also due to Alan Carter for his comments on an earlier draft.

My interest in comparative monotheism was aroused during a year spent living in and around Jerusalem – a notoriously troubled centre of pilgrimage for Jews, Christians and Muslims. My hope is that this book will contribute to greater understanding between adherents of the Abrahamic faiths, as well as between those in our society who profess religious faith and those who do not. It is my belief that increased sensitivity to the religious dimensions of the intellectual, political and cultural debates prominent in the twentieth century is a precondition to understanding, and perhaps to ameliorating, the conflicts that threaten to polarize even further our global community in the third millennium of the common era.

Victoria S. Harrison
University of Glasgow
March 2007

1

Introduction

Don't bother about being modern. Unfortunately it is the one thing that, whatever you do, you cannot avoid.[1]

Not very long ago, people were announcing the death of God, and predicting that religious belief would die out in the face of modernity. However, although traditional religions are no doubt under considerable strain as a result of their adherents' efforts – and their failures – to adapt to the times, we are nevertheless witnessing what looks more like a religious revival than a terminal decline. Indeed, in the twentieth century, religious belief systems proved themselves to be remarkably resilient and highly adaptable to new circumstances. The striking resilience of religious beliefs led some to suggest that it must come naturally to us to hold them.[2] This suggestion derives some plausibility from the observation that as far back in time as there is evidence of human culture, there also appear to be traces of religion. The apparent ubiquitousness of religious convictions has sometimes been taken to indicate that religiosity is deeply embedded within the structure of human consciousness.[3]

Karen Armstrong, author of the provocative best-seller *A History of God*, argues that being human and being religious are intimately connected. As she puts it: '*Homo sapiens* is also *Homo religiosus*'.[4] She continues:

> Men and women started to worship gods as soon as they became recognisably human; they created religions at the same time as they created works of art. This was not simply because they wanted to propitiate powerful forces but these early faiths expressed the wonder and mystery that seems always to have been an essential component of the human experience of this beautiful yet terrifying world.[5]

Although the true nature of prehistoric humans and their culture is extremely difficult to establish decisively, it does seem plausible that all known human societies have developed hand in hand with some form of religion. In fact, much of how societies have developed would seem to have been shaped by religious beliefs. Moreover, key periods of human history have been dominated by religion and, often tragically, by religious disagreements. Thus, as the renowned twentieth-century scholar of religions, Ninian Smart, remarks, in order to 'understand human history and human life it is necessary to understand religion ...'.[6]

But while few would deny that in the past religion had a tremendous influence on people's lives, many now assume that other ideas, which have recently gained currency, are now the real driving force behind human history, and that the influence of religion pales in the face of the power of these new ideas. And although this latter claim would appear to be at best an exaggeration, as any examination of the social and political impact of religion in the twentieth century would reveal, it is nevertheless true that religion no longer has the same sway over world events that it formerly held. But even if their importance has waned, it would clearly be exceedingly premature to deny that religious beliefs still exert considerable influence on the lives of many in the modern Western world.

On the other hand, it is beyond dispute that the encounter with modernity has significantly transformed the main religions practised in the West. This change is apparent in the outward form, or institutional aspect, of those religions, as well as, perhaps more importantly, in the way they are understood, and their core claims interpreted, by their adherents. While each religious tradition has always harboured a rich array of theological opinions, these have never been as available, to those who are fortunate enough to be religiously literate, as they are today. Moreover, modern technology has made a range of theological views accessible through television, radio and, more recently, the internet.[7] One result of the increased accessibility of such information is that people are exposed to a much broader range of possible interpretations of their own tradition than was formerly the case when their religious ideas were mediated exclusively through their local rabbi, priest or mullah. Another result is that, nowadays, few adults in the West are entirely ignorant of religious traditions other than the one dominant within their own culture.[8] However, while the breadth of knowledge may well have increased in many quarters, whether or not the same is true of the depth of knowledge is another matter.

Clearly, as the effects of the intellectual and cultural movement set in motion by the European Enlightenment are still being felt and assimilated, the encounter of religion with modernity is an ongoing one.[9] Even today, this encounter is capable of arousing passion. And strong emotions are displayed not only by religious believers but also by those whose commitment to modernity would seem to pit them against everything traditional – especially religious ideas. To many traditionally minded religious thinkers, it can seem that authentic religion and modern thought are diametrically opposed, with no common ground between them. One such thinker is the well-known Muslim philosopher Seyyed Hossein Nasr (born 1933). He argues that an intrinsic feature of modern thought is its lack of a sense of the sacred, and such a sense is, in his view, precisely what is most characteristic of religious thought.[10] Nasr goes on to define a modern man or woman as someone who lacks this sense of the sacred. And according to his view, modern men and women are incapable of appreciating the value of religious ideas unless they acquire this sense; and until they do, they are likely to be highly antagonistic towards religion. However, any such perspective that describes modernity and religiosity as mutually exclusive is likely to overlook the very substantial changes that traditional religious belief systems are currently undergoing as a result of their encounter with modernity.

It is precisely certain of these changes that this book examines in detail by investigating the encounter between the Abrahamic religions and modern thought, focusing on intellectual developments particularly within Western Europe and North America since the closing years of the nineteenth century. Hence, the focus of what follows is not monotheisms *per se*, otherwise Sikhism and Zoroastrianism would be included. Rather, the concern is with those monotheisms that have profoundly impacted modern Western culture and society. Consequently, this book concentrates on Judaism, Christianity and Islam because they are the most influential religions practised in the West today,[11] as well as being those that have enjoyed the most influence on Western thought. Despite the fact that the largest proportion of the world's Christians and Muslims, as well as almost half of the world's Jews, reside outside the West, in the following chapters I do not examine the major monotheistic religions within a global context; this is because I am principally interested in the transformations undergone by these religious traditions within the West.[12] On occasion, however, I do discuss particular movements and thinkers from outside the West (such as Latin American liberation theology), but only insofar as they have exerted some significant influence upon the Abrahamic faiths within the West.[13]

This study, then, focuses on those intellectual trends that look set to have a long-term impact upon Judaism, Christianity and Islam as it is practised in North America and Western Europe, as well as focusing on certain thinkers and movements within the State of Israel, which has been seen as an integral part of 'the West' since the mid-twentieth century. But, it might be asked, why bother to focus on all three monotheisms rather than just on one: namely, Christianity, which is the one traditionally dominant in the West? The short answer is that, whereas many parts of the world have in the past sought cultural homogeneity (and some still do when they embark on the horrors of ethnic cleansing), most of the West has become progressively more pluralist. And if, in the twenty-first century, we are to bridge the most important of the deep divisions forming within our society, then we require a greater understanding of our common cultural wealth.[14] Moreover, our historical debt is to all three of the Abrahamic religions, and not just to Christianity (the latter view being widely and mistakenly presumed). Islam, for example, exerted a profound influence on Western culture during the Middle Ages, and was responsible for reintroducing Aristotle into Western philosophy (Aristotelian conceptions occupying a central role within Roman Catholicism). In addition, a more comprehensive understanding of the encounter between religion and modern thought than would otherwise be possible can only be attained by examining all three of the Abrahamic religions. For, as we shall see, while these religions are in many respects very different they are in other important respects strikingly similar. These similarities and differences are thrown into relief through consideration of the impact of modern thought on each of these traditions, and by close analysis of the variety of ways in which their adherents have reacted and adapted their beliefs to this impact.

It should be noted that by 'modern thought' I mean thought which has distinctively 'modern' characteristics; such as the rejection of tradition or the refusal to accept religious authority simply because it is based on tradition. These characteristics burst dramatically onto the stage in the Enlightenment,[15] and they became increasingly entrenched in Western culture as time passed. Towards the close of the eighteenth century, Immanuel Kant (1724–1804), a leading figure in the European Enlightenment and the harbinger of the new epoch, astutely observed:

> Our age is, in especial degree, the age of criticism, and to criticism everything must submit. Religion through its sanctity, and law-giving through its majesty, may seek to exempt themselves from it. But they then awaken just suspicion, and cannot claim the sincere respect which reason accords only that which has been able to sustain the test of free and open examination.[16]

The rejection of tradition has been ongoing at least since the Enlightenment. Two distinct intellectual currents have contributed to this rejection. The first, represented by Kant, avers that tradition should be rejected in favour of a rational, scientific approach to the world. The second, advocated by the romantic Jean-Jacques Rousseau (1712–78), stresses that rejecting tradition is a means to attaining individual authenticity. Both of these currents have contributed to what is now commonly described as a process of detraditionalization.[17] In this process the locus of authority shifts from outside individuals to within, as critical reason (or, in some versions, conscience) supersedes tradition. While detraditionalization has no doubt occurred in the modern West, I shall nevertheless argue that it is a more complex process than many have assumed. As we shall see, it is a mistake to regard tradition and modernity as necessarily mutually exclusive, with the former always giving way to the latter. In modernity, traditional ideas are critically assimilated into new patterns of thought, and both old and new ideas flourish simultaneously. What we

4

shall observe is perhaps best described as the creative reformulation of religious traditions in response to modern thought.

There is another reason which suggests that we should not hastily conclude that tradition and modernity are opposed and mutually exclusive. The substance of tradition is what has been handed down from the past (the Latin verb *tradere* means 'to hand over'), and this has suggested to some that modernity may have developed its own traditions to which we are now heir. As John B. Thompson argues, tradition can be viewed

> as a set of background assumptions that are taken for granted by individuals in the conduct of their daily lives, and transmitted by them from one generation to the next. In this respect, tradition is an interpretative scheme, a framework for understanding the world. For, as hermeneutic philosophers such as Heidegger and Gadamer have emphasized, all understanding is based on presuppositions, on some set of assumptions which we take for granted and which form part of a tradition to which we belong. No understanding can be entirely presuppositionless. Hence the Enlightenment critique of tradition must, in Gadamer's view, be qualified. In juxtaposing the notions of reason, scientific knowledge and emancipation to those of tradition, authority and myth, the Enlightenment thinkers were not dispensing with tradition as such but were rather articulating a set of assumptions and methods which formed the core of another tradition, that of the Enlightenment itself. In the hermeneutic sense of tradition, the Enlightenment is not the antithesis of tradition but is, on the contrary, one tradition (or cluster of traditions) among others – that is, a set of taken-for-granted assumptions which provide a framework for understanding the world.[18]

Nevertheless, what we ordinarily mean by 'tradition' is not simply 'a set of background assumptions'. When we talk of a person accepting a tradition we also imply that he or she accepts a set of beliefs, institutions or practices that have prevailed within their community for a considerable length of time. Hence, we must distinguish between accepting traditional ways of thinking and starting a new tradition, and not conflate them by reducing both to merely 'a set of background assumptions'.

Interestingly, however, whereas Enlightenment thinkers may have begun a new tradition, most so-called 'modern' thinkers now conceptualize the problems they face within that, now established, Enlightenment tradition. Thus, while it may be the case that much modern thought claims to be inimical to traditional authority, modern thinkers should grant that tradition has a significant and, arguably, essential role in the modern world. For modern thought is now no less fed by tradition than was the pre-modern thought which it sought to replace.

In beginning to explore the relationship between modern thought and the Abrahamic religions, there are two difficulties that need to be confronted. These are difficulties that plague any study of religion: namely, there seems to be no unproblematic definition of 'religion', and, furthermore, scholars disagree about what should qualify a person to be counted as religious. Some claim that religions are principally composed of patterns of ritualized behaviour that fulfil a social function – for example, ceremonies such as circumcision – and that being religious just means that a person participates in such behaviour. Others prefer to regard religion as primarily a matter of ideas, beliefs and worldviews. Being religious would then consist in having certain ideas and beliefs, and, perhaps, subscribing to an elaborate worldview of the appropriate sort. Still others claim that religion is principally a matter of faith, and that being religious consists in having certain feelings. In short, we might attempt to define religion, and to specify who is to count as a religious person, either functionally, intellectually or affectively. How this fundamental issue is treated will colour any subsequent analysis of religion in relation to modern thought. As we shall see, how religion is defined, and how religious persons are to be identified, also has significant social and political consequences. In Chapter 2, therefore, I consider some contrasting definitions of religion, and discuss some recent attempts at stipulating who is to count as a religious person.

But, clearly, while defining 'religion' and 'religious person' is a necessary prerequisite for studying any religion (as we need to be able to identify the object of study), it is only the beginning. For if we are to acquire even a cursory appreciation of any specific religion, it is essential that we be cognizant of the circumstances in which it arose, its core beliefs and the main changes it has undergone through time. This is particularly important when considering Judaism, Christianity and Islam because of their long and intertwined histories. Consequently, Chapter 3 briefly outlines the origins, historical development and core beliefs of these traditions in order that the impact of modernity upon them may be better assessed. These short accounts of the fundamental features of the Abrahamic religions are, of course, by no means exhaustive; they aim simply at providing sufficient information to prepare the ground for the more detailed thematic treatment that follows. For modern thought has not merely impacted on some abstract notion of 'monotheism' or 'religion', but on particular religions as they are practised in specific historical circumstances.

Each of the subsequent chapters concentrates on a different theme germane to the encounter between the traditional Abrahamic religions and modern thought. The themes have been selected because they are focal points of the challenge modern thought poses to traditional religious ideas, as this challenge has taken shape in Western Europe and North America. Wherever possible, the focus remains on intellectual and cultural developments that have emerged since the closing years of the nineteenth century. Occasionally, however, it has proven necessary to consider ideas from an earlier historical context in order to throw light on more recent intellectual trends.

Modern philosophy and modern thought are tightly connected. In fact, it may be no exaggeration to claim that philosophical developments gave rise to much of what is distinctive in modern thought. Hence, the first theme to be considered is the relationship between religious faith and modern philosophy or, what is usually regarded as its prime component, 'reason'. Clearly, the critical appraisal of religious beliefs and institutions that had previously been uncritically accepted by the majority of the population had dramatic effects on those beliefs and institutions. Few with any awareness of twentieth-century intellectual history would doubt that one of the major challenges posed to religious faith in this era came from academic philosophers. A school of philosophy known as 'verificationism' was extremely influential, and certain philosophers committed to its tenets mounted a seemingly devastating attack on the belief systems of traditional religions. Strict verificationists hold that the meaning of a statement consists in the kinds of empirical observations one would need to make in order to show the statement in question to be true. The implication is that all strictly religious propositions are meaningless because they cannot, even in principle, be verified through observation. Chapter 4 thus considers various issues connected with the verification of religious knowledge claims. It also examines the quintessentially modern demand that religious belief has a rational basis, and the diverse and creative ways in which those sympathetic to religion have responded to this demand.

We return to philosophical problems raised by religious language in Chapter 5. Judaism, Christianity and Islam each developed around a set of texts regarded by believers as sacred Scripture. Philosophical inquiry into the nature and limits of language caused a fundamental change in the way that many modern believers understood the significance of these sacred texts. As philosophers of religion explored different ways of explaining how our all-too-human languages could convey information about the divine, many religious believers struggled to come to terms with new ways of interpreting the ancient texts of their traditions. Chapter 5 examines some of the ways that changing views about language have affected traditional religion, while also appraising some of the most important theories about how religious language is thought to function. In particular, it examines some views of religious language that were developed in an effort to move thought about language beyond the framework established by verificationism. We shall see that what on the surface may appear to be a technical debate about the nature and proper function of language has had a profound impact on the way many modern religious people interpret core religious claims.

Abstract reasoning, in the form of philosophy, was not alone in exerting a huge impact on twentieth-century religious ideas. Practical reasoning, in the form of natural science, also impacted traditional religions to an unprecedented degree. The theme of Chapter 6, then, is the impact that natural science has exerted upon traditional religion since the late nineteenth century. During much of the twentieth century, many thinkers simply assumed that as science advances, religion retreats. Lately, however, this simple picture has been cast into doubt. Chapter 6 discusses various ways of construing the relationship between the claims of modern scientists and those of religious believers. As we shall see, various positions have been defended. Some claim that science and religion are irreconcilable worldviews, and that a person must choose one or the other. A rival view holds that no genuine conflict between the claims of science and those of religion is possible because they do not share a single subject matter about which they could disagree. Yet others argue that science and religion are not only compatible, but should both contribute to a unified and coherent worldview. To illustrate this last perspective, I examine a set of arguments which, by the end of the twentieth century, had come to play a prominent role within the project of arriving at such a worldview: namely, new design arguments for the existence of God.

Both science and religion are concerned with truth. Twentieth-century philosophy problematized the notion of truth, even scientific truth. Moreover, influenced by the philosopher Ludwig Wittgenstein (1889–1951), one popular response to the uncertainty about the foundations of scientific, philosophical and religious claims has been to tie the notions of truth and language to a 'form of life'. An implication of this idea is that knowledge-claims are neither true nor false in themselves, but are only so within the context of a form of life. The twentieth century saw increased contact between people of different cultures and faiths to such a degree that it is no exaggeration to claim that religious diversity now characterizes much of the West, raising the question of how the mooted truths of different forms of religious life relate to one another. This has given birth to an important theoretical movement – namely, religious pluralism. Chapter 7 considers the challenge that religious diversity poses to traditionally minded believers, while examining some of the ways in which more progressive religious thinkers attempt to accommodate religious diversity. It does so by outlining the three main theories currently available to religious thinkers for explaining the relationship between the various religions: religious exclusivism, religious inclusivism and religious pluralism.

In our increasingly multicultural and environmentally threatened world, it would be dangerous to ignore the global political impact of religion. The relationship between politics, religion and the environment is thus the theme of Chapter 8. As well as considering the impact of two world wars on religious ideas, this chapter examines some of the distinctive types of religious thought that were inspired by the new political awareness that many religious believers acquired in the second half of the twentieth century. It also analyses some rival views of the relationship between politics and religion. As we shall see, some think that religious ideas should be kept completely separate from politics. Liberation theologians, drawn from the ranks of Judaism, Christianity and Islam, disagree; many going so far as to argue that the distinction between politics and religion is a false one. The so-called 'theology of liberation' became one of the most influential movements within Western religion in the last few decades of the twentieth century. In this chapter, I also consider black theology, which developed in the United States in conjunction with the civil rights movement in the 1960s. Chapter 8 concludes with an examination of eco-theology, which is one of the most recent forms of religious thought to emerge. It first appeared in nascent form in conjunction with the environmental awareness that initially arose in the late 1960s. The rapid growth of eco-theology is a direct response to the threat of environmental catastrophe, a threat which many theologians not unreasonably believe to be a genuine one.

Whereas liberation theologians focus on the plight of the poor, feminists contend that there are inequalities which cut across class divides. In their view, liberation theologians do not go far enough, and special attention needs to be paid to the situation of women in traditional forms of Judaism, Christianity and Islam. The twentieth century saw massive changes in the way women's roles in, and contribution to, society were perceived and evaluated. The difference can hardly be underestimated between the lifestyle and social expectations of the majority of women in the West at the close of the nineteenth century, on the one hand, and those of their counterparts at the end of the twentieth, on the other. We shall see that this transformation within secular society has also been accompanied by demands for change in the religious domain. Chapter 9 concentrates on the challenges that the attitudes and expectations of modern women pose to religious beliefs and institutions. It considers the way that feminist challenges have shifted from a demand for equal opportunities within their religious communities to the call for a radical reinterpretation of the concept 'God'. It also looks at some responses to feminists' arguments from their more conservative co-religionists. We shall see that some religious feminists have come to believe that it is not enough simply to challenge traditional forms of monotheism for promoting attitudes that are damaging to women. They argue that the dominant conception of God has led not only to the de-valuing of women but also to a widespread disregard for the natural world. Ecofeminist theology, a sub-branch of eco-theology, was consolidated after feminist theologians began to confront the problems posed by the environmental destruction that became increasingly evident as the twentieth century drew to a close.

Chapters 4 to 9 focus on what might be seen as the more progressive dimensions of the religious response to modernity. But this, of course, is only one side of the story. Another strategy, employed by many religious believers, is to resort to religious fundamentalism. Presently, there are fundamentalist tendencies in Judaism, Christianity and Islam; and some of them are powerful enough to exert a significant impact on Western culture. Chapter 10 examines the character of religious fundamentalism, as well as the worldviews that motivate it. It further considers some of the key similarities and differences between fundamentalist movements within the three Abrahamic traditions. This chapter also addresses the 'secularization thesis' – that is, the thesis that there is an inverse relation between secularization and commitment to religion in any society, and, hence, that as Western societies become increasingly secular they will become correspondingly less religious. After arguing that the secularization thesis does not account for the pattern of religious resurgence apparent recently in the West, it concludes by considering what I propose is best seen as the parasitic relationship between religious fundamentalism and modernity.

Without doubt, during the twentieth century, Western culture in general, and religion in particular, changed immeasurably. And while most of the twentieth century is perhaps best characterized as 'modernist', we now appear to find ourselves in what is frequently termed 'the postmodern world'. Chapter 11 concludes this study by examining how Judaism, Christianity and Islam look in this seemingly postmodern world. It analyses some of the characteristics of postmodernity, while considering some reinterpretations of religion proposed by Western thinkers in an attempt to accommodate religion to the ostensibly postmodern world. Finally, I consider the state of the Abrahamic monotheisms in the West at the start of the third millennium. Arguing that it would be a mistake to regard these traditions as mere vestiges of the lost world of pre-modernity, I assess the extent to which they have, nevertheless, been seriously undermined by the intellectual and cultural forces that shaped the twentieth century.

It should now be apparent that this book tackles a variety of subjects that are not usually approached in one volume. Some of the themes treated are more often encountered in books on the philosophy of religion, whereas others are more usually found in religious studies or in sociology of religion texts. However, all of these apparently disparate themes have something in common. Each addresses an important aspect of the relation between religion and modern (or postmodern) thought and culture; and the fact that they are not usually examined within the same discipline prevents us from gaining a fuller appreciation of their combined significance. Hence, the broader, inter-disciplinary treatment provided here reveals important connections that are frequently missed – connections which it is vitally important to understand if we are even to begin making sense of the possible trajectories of the new century lying before us.

It is my hope, moreover, that this book will prove of use to scholars within a range of disciplines, but particularly to philosophers of religion whose work often tends to presuppose an essentialist conception of religion far removed from religions as they are understood and practised in the real world. The danger of such a conception is that it can render one insensitive to the nuances of religious traditions and the transformations that religious ideas undergo, as religious thinkers creatively respond to diverse and changing cultural situations. As I demonstrate in this book, during the twentieth century many radical transformations of key religious concepts, such as the concept 'God', have been proposed by adherents of the Abrahamic faiths. Philosophers of religion may prefer to remain unacquainted with some of these ideas because they rightly perceive that bad ideas flourish alongside good ones. However, by ignoring these new ideas they run the risk of their work being considered irrelevant by those who, perhaps, stand to benefit from it the most.

Finally, in writing this book I hope to acquaint the reader not only with the kinds of conclusions that various thinkers have arrived at in response to some of the challenges posed to religion by modernity but also, and most importantly, with the kinds of arguments that have been adduced in support of these conclusions. This volume cannot pretend to comprise a comprehensive survey. It focuses only upon what I take to be some of the more interesting and representative responses to modernity.

This book should provide readers with some feel for the extremely wide variety of forms of religious thought, many of which to date remaining relatively unknown to all but a few specialists. For there is a far, far greater variety of religious thinking than most people, who are usually only familiar with their own faith, and who, even then, are often unfamiliar with important aspects of their own tradition, often realize. If this book better acquaints the reader with the luxuriant plurality of modern and postmodern religious thought, then it will have served its purpose.

Study questions

1 What might it mean to claim that holding religious beliefs comes naturally to humans? Is this claim plausible?

2 How much influence do religious beliefs currently have on the lives of the majority within the West?

3 What effects have modern technologies, such as the internet, had on the way that religious ideas are transmitted?

4 What reasons might be given to support the view that authentic religious belief and modern thought share no common ground? Do you find any of these reasons convincing?

5 Is the distinction between modern thought and pre-modern thought a useful one to draw? What are the characteristics of modern thought that distinguish it from pre-modern thought?

6 Must 'tradition' and 'modernity' be held to be mutually exclusive, or can one consistently embrace both?

Select bibliography

Barnett, S. J., 2003, *The Enlightenment and Religion: The Myths of Modernity*, Manchester: Manchester University Press.

Blumenberg, H., 1983, *The Legitimacy of the Modern Age*, trans. by R. M. Wallace, Cambridge, Massachusetts: MIT Press.

Heelas, P. (ed.), 1998, *Religion, Modernity, and Postmodernity*, Oxford: Blackwell.

Heelas, P., S. Lash and P. Morris (eds), 1996, *Detraditionalization: Critical Reflections on Authority and Identity*, Oxford: Blackwell.

Milbank, J., 1993, *Theology and Social Theory: Beyond Secular Reason*, Oxford: Blackwell.

Smart, N., 1977, *The Religious Experience of Mankind*, Glasgow: Collins.

Tarnas, R., 1996, *The Passion of the Western Mind: Understanding the Ideas that Have Shaped our World View*, London: Pimlico.

Notes

1 Salvador Dali, 1976, *Diary of a Genius*, London: Pan Books, p. 52.

2 Talcott Parsons seems to suggest this in his 'Introduction' to Max Weber, 1963, *The Sociology of Religion*, Boston: Beacon Press, see p. xxviii.

3 See, for example, Mircea Eliade, 1978, *A History of Religious Ideas*, vol. 1, trans. by W. R. Trask, Chicago: University of Chicago Press, p. xiii.

4 Karen Armstrong, 1999, *A History of God: From Abraham to the Present: the 4000-year Quest for God*, London: Vintage, p. 3.

5 Armstrong, *A History of God*, p. 3.

6 Ninian Smart, 1977, *The Religious Experience of Mankind*, Glasgow: Collins, p. 12.

7 One striking and novel feature of life in the twentieth century, which has contributed enormously to the spread of knowledge about other cultures and religious traditions, was the prominence of cinema and, later, television. In the second half of the century, people were just as likely to be exposed to new ideas through these media as through books, especially scholarly books. Consequently, cinema provides one important key to understanding modern culture. There is no doubt that it facilitated the reception of modern ideas on the part of many people in the West, and that it has also shaped their perception of modernity.

Hence, in the following chapters, I provide several references to popular films where they are particularly relevant to the issues discussed.

8 Increased awareness of a range of faith-traditions has, moreover, been facilitated by the rise of global tourism in the second half of the twentieth century.

9 In taking modernity as a 'given', this book presumes no stance on the relation between its origin and the Judaeo-Christian tradition. Therefore, I do not discuss the debate between those who hold that modernity is an estranged product of this tradition and those who argue, to the contrary, that modernity should be regarded as an independent development. For the former view, see John Milbank, 1993, *Theology and Social Theory: Beyond Secular Reason*, Oxford: Blackwell. And for a defence of the latter position, see Hans Blumenberg, 1983, *The Legitimacy of the Modern Age*, trans. by R. M. Wallace, Cambridge, Massachusetts: MIT Press.

10 Seyyed Hossein Nasr, 'Reflections on Islam and Modern Life', *Al-Serat*, 6 (2000) at http://www.al-islam.org/al-serat/reflect-nasr.htm.

11 It goes without saying that there are significant minorities in the West practising other religions (Hinduism, for example). And while the impact that such minorities have had on modern Western culture and society is considerable, it is significantly weaker than that of the Abrahamic religions. My focus on monotheism should, however, by no means be taken to imply that I regard this form of religion as paradigmatic. Nor does my choice to study Judaism, Christianity and Islam in the West imply that the forms of these religions practised there are paradigmatic for Jews, Christians and Muslims in other parts of the world.

12 It should be noted, of course, that ideas do not respect geographical boundaries, and some intellectuals work on both sides of the ideological frontiers between 'East' and 'West' and between 'North' and 'South'.

13 The strategy of focusing upon developments within the West is, surprising as it may seem, especially helpful with respect to Islam. Most studies that deal with Islam focus on the 'Muslim world' and ignore or underestimate the significant transitions that Muslim thought has undergone at the hands of Western Muslims. It is those transitions that I hope to emphasize in this book. In refusing to regard Islam exclusively as an element of 'Eastern culture', I argue that the common perception that Islam is inevitably in conflict with the West is deeply misleading. In short, the characterization that I question portrays a dichotomy between 'the East' and 'the West', and aligns Islam firmly on the side of the former. The power of this portrayal is a result of the orientalist scholarship, which gained currency in the modern world, that subsequently shaped the image of Islam. Such a portrayal is premised upon the view that 'Islam is the complete negation of Europe' (Ernest Renan, 1947, *Oeuvres complètes*, Paris: Calmann-Livy, vol. 2, p. 333), thereby distorting the common history of the Abrahamic faiths, which unfolded in a shared territory (the Mediterranean basin). It also distorts the current reality in which, given that Christian and Muslim faith communities increasingly share overlapping territories, it is an anachronism to refer to the 'Muslim world' and the 'Christian West'.

14 Ninian Smart observes that 'in the contemporary world one must understand other nations' ideologies and faith in order to grasp the meaning of life as seen from perspectives often very different from our own' (Smart, *Religious*, p. 12). Clearly, with the spread of religious and cultural plurality, we need to

understand the ideologies and faith of other communities within our own society, and not just in other countries.

15 The origins of modernity, however, undoubtedly lie much further back in time. Many, such as Richard Tarnas, claim that modernity began to emerge in the late Middle Ages, especially during the Renaissance. See Richard Tarnas, 1996, *The Passion of the Western Mind: Understanding the Ideas that Have Shaped our World View*, London: Pimlico.

16 Immanuel Kant, 1933, Preface to the 1st edition of the *Critique of Pure Reason*, trans. by Norman Kemp Smith, London: Macmillan, p. 9, Axi, note a. The rejection of traditional authority was as strong a motivation for the Utilitarians in the nineteenth century as it was for Immanuel Kant in the eighteenth.

17 See Paul Heelas, Scott Lash and Paul Morris (eds), 1996, *Detraditionalization: Critical Reflections on Authority and Identity*, Oxford: Blackwell.

18 John B. Thompson, 1996, 'Tradition and Self in a Mediated World' in Heelas, *Detraditionalization*, pp. 91f.

2

Defining Religion and the Religious Person

Our world contains a striking diversity of religious traditions. Given that most of us probably have no trouble recognizing such traditions as religious, it is perhaps surprising that there is little agreement about what religion is or, indeed, if 'it' is anything distinctive at all. Scholars have sought to define religion so as to identify both what makes something a religion and what, if anything, distinguishes religions from secular social organizations like clubs. Elementary though this task may seem, it has proven difficult to formulate a definition of religion that can command wide assent. Many rival definitions have been proposed, most of which can be classified as examples of one of three basic types: intellectual definitions, affective definitions and functional definitions.

Rival definitions of religion

Intellectual definitions stipulate that the defining, or essential, feature of religion is belief about a particular sort of object. The following definition, proposed by James Martineau, is of this type: 'Religion is the belief in an ever living God.'[1] While definitions of this type highlight something important about religions – the undeniable fact that propositional beliefs typically play a significant role within them – nevertheless, they take no account of other, equally prominent, features of religion. They fail to recognize, for example, the centrality of 'religious' emotions like piety, the importance of faith and the key role of traditional practices. Yet each would seem to constitute typical features of many religions. A further problem is that defining religion in terms of belief that has a particular kind of object, such as God, entails that certain belief systems which are routinely regarded as religions – Theravada Buddhism, for example – would have to be classed as non-religious; an entailment which strikes many as counter-intuitive. To avoid this problem, one might insist that any kind of belief would suffice, as long as it was held with sufficient seriousness and intensity. However, building into intellectual definitions conditions about the way a belief is held is tantamount to admitting that intellectual definitions by themselves are inadequate. It would also allow any kind of belief system to be a candidate for the label 'religious', provided only that it was held with sufficient passion.

Moreover, we do not need to look to non-monotheistic religions to see the inadequacy of intellectual definitions. For they would not even seem to be applicable to Judaism. As Eugene Borowitz claims: 'for the Jew, religion cannot be so easily identified with the affirmation of a given content of belief'.[2] As Borowitz further points out, such definitions would seem to be particularly suited to Protestant forms of Christianity, which do tend to portray religion as essentially the affirmation of a set of beliefs. Indeed, those who propose intellectual definitions would seem to regard Protestant Christianity as the paradigmatic form of religion, and such a standpoint is clearly inadequate today in an increasingly multicultural world. Let us therefore consider another type of definition, and see if it is any less problematic.

Affective definitions of religion regard faith, and the emotions that characteristically accompany it, as the defining, or essential, features of religion. George Lindbeck refers to this type of definition as 'experiential–expressive' because definitions of this type focus on 'the "experiential–expressive" dimension of religion', and interpret 'doctrines as noninformative and nondiscursive symbols of inner feelings, attitudes, or existential orientations'.[3] As Lindbeck observes, despite their considerable dissimilarities, intellectual and affective definitions are akin insofar as they are both *religious* types of definition. In other words, they describe religion from a perspective that focuses on features of religion that are important to believers. Thus, these two approaches, or combinations of them, are typically adopted by theologians and other religiously committed scholars.[4]

The most well-known affective definition was proposed by a foundational figure within modern Protestant theology, Friedrich Schleiermacher (1768–1834). Schleiermacher stipulated that the 'essence of religion consists in the feeling of absolute dependence'.[5] This definition is clearly a product of Schleiermacher's conception of religion as, primarily, a way of experiencing reality rather than a set of doctrinal formulations. Useful though his definition may be, it is clearly a reaction against intellectual definitions. As such, it is, perhaps, too one-sided to serve as an objective definition. By defining religion purely in terms of a certain kind of feeling – the feeling of absolute dependence – Schleiermacher ignores the important intellectual component of religions, and thus gives a distorted picture of them. Moreover, his definition appears to be biased towards his own religious tradition. It may well be that the kind of feeling he focuses upon is the defining feature of Lutheran Christianity (or, at least, was so during his lifetime). However, such a feeling would not appear to be central to, for example, most forms of Buddhism or, to take another example, to Daoism. If that is the case, then the feeling of absolute dependence cannot be the defining feature of *all* religions.

Another criticism of Schleiermacher's definition is that the feeling of absolute dependence may be experienced by both religious people and self-avowedly non-religious people – which, again, suggests that such a feeling does not constitute a defining feature of religion. For example, environmentalists can have a feeling of absolute dependence upon the natural world without thereby holding a religious attitude (although some do hold one). Schleiermacher himself, however, saw this as an advantage of his theory. He believed that people mistakenly perceived themselves as non-religious because they rejected formalized religious doctrines and official religious institutions; but rejecting these and rejecting religion were in his opinion two quite distinct activities.[6] Thus, Schleiermacher is quite happy to insist that a necessary and sufficient condition for being religious is that one experience the feeling of absolute dependence. It was precisely this kind of view that the founder of psychoanalysis, Sigmund Freud (1856–1939), criticized in his influential work *The Future of an Illusion*. Freud claimed that it was a mistake to describe 'as "deeply religious" anyone who admits to a sense of man's insignificance or impotence in the face of the universe'.[7] Rather, only those who seek a remedy for this feeling are genuinely religious. In his view: 'The man who goes no further, but humbly acquiesces in the small part which human beings play in the great world – such a man is, on the contrary, irreligious in the truest sense of the word.'[8] Indeed, in Freud's account, religion is a remedy for the kind of feeling referred to by Schleiermacher. On this view, religious practices such as ceremonies and rituals, if successful, function to remedy the disturbing sensation of 'man's insignificance or impotence in the face of the universe'. Hence, Schleiermacher might be accused of confusing the cause of religion with the meaning of 'religion'.[9]

This brings us to the third type of definition of religion: functional definitions. These concentrate on the function of religion as its defining, or essential, feature. The particular function that religion is thought to serve is not always, however, the one that Freud identified. Rather, the purported function of religion is sometimes construed more broadly. Consider, for example, the anthropologist J. G. Frazer's definition: 'By religion, then, I understand a propitiation or conciliation of powers superior to man ...'[10] Frazer, then, defines religion in terms of its supposedly propitiatory or conciliatory function. But do all religions serve such a function? It would seem not. For yet again, Buddhism constitutes a clear counter-example. It is even questionable whether the various monotheisms should be seen as fulfilling this function. Moreover, it seems implausible to hold that religions as diverse as Lutheran Christianity, Advaita Vedanta Hinduism and Daoism all serve the same function – however broadly this function is conceived.

This brief survey might suggest that what each type of definition regards as the defining, or essential, feature of religion should be incorporated into a comprehensive definition: one that would give due weight to the intellectual, the affective and the functional components of religion. Unfortunately, such a comprehensive definition would be problematic because, like the various types of definition examined above, it would either encompass too much or too little. For example, there would be nothing to exclude secular humanism or Marxism from counting as religions. Moreover, one could not respond to the problem of including too much by building the notion of a religious ultimate, or God, into the definition. That strategy would certainly exclude secular humanism and Marxism, but it would also exclude 'religions' like Theravada Buddhism and Daoism (in which the notion of God does not play a significant role). Clearly, any definition of religion that failed to include these principal forms of religion would be severely inadequate.

In addition, not only does each type of definition considered above fail to apply to mainstream forms of Eastern religious traditions, but each also seems inapplicable to Judaism. Some argue that a definition of religion inclusive of Judaism would have to acknowledge that being Jewish involves a relationship to the Jewish community.[11] Yet no prominent intellectual, affective or functional definition emphasizes the religious person as part of a community. But surely, this consideration would also apply to Christianity and Islam. Most, if not all, forms of Christianity conceive individual Christians to be intrinsically part of the ecclesial community. Likewise, Muslims do not stand alone but are part of the *umma* – the Muslim community. The importance of this dimension of religiosity is apparent if one considers what takes place when a person converts to one of the Abrahamic religions: they are welcomed into the community of the Jewish People, the Church, or the *umma*. Because the types of definition surveyed above fail to acknowledge this important dimension of Abrahamic monotheisms, many find them inadequate.

Clearly, though, any assessment of the adequacy of a definition of religion is likely to be influenced by the kind of theory of religion one presupposes. Definitions are, it might be claimed, miniature versions of the theories which inspire them. And there is an important difference between *religious* theories of religion and *naturalistic* ones.[12] Typically, theories of the former type are developed by thinkers belonging to some particular religious tradition. They usually presuppose a religious interpretation of ourselves and our world, and they attempt to justify that interpretation by providing an account of the divine origin of the religion in question. A religious theory might, for example, appeal to the role of prophets or angels as divine messengers instrumental in the formation of a particular historical religious tradition. Or, more generally, religion may be conceived as a response to revelation in the form of divine word or deed. James Thrower claims that religious theories can be identified by the way they regard religion as ontologically primary; that is, by viewing religion as capable of explaining other phenomena and in no need of explanation itself.[13] Naturalistic theories, on the other hand, regard the phenomena of religion to be in need of some explanation. In contrast to religious theories, they attempt to explain religion by appealing to natural facts. Freud's theory of religion, for example, is a naturalistic theory that tries to explain religion by appeal to facts about human psychology.[14] Influential forms of naturalistic theory have been proposed by Karl Marx, Émile Durkheim, Max Weber and, more recently, the sociobiologist E. O. Wilson.[15] Such theories were especially prominent in the second half of the nineteenth century and in the first half of the twentieth. Their popularity seems to rise and wane in accordance with the success or failure of the more general psychological, political, economic, social or biological theory within which they are embedded.

In line with this distinction between religious and naturalistic theories of religion, definitions of religion can be categorized as either *religious* or *naturalistic*. Clearly, a non-sectarian scholar will be likely to find many of the available religious definitions of religion unacceptable. This is because many of them presuppose the truth of certain key religious claims – such as, for example, that there 'are manifestations of a Power which transcends our knowledge'.[16] Nevertheless, many scholars remain cautious of naturalistic definitions of religion. This is because, as we have seen, they are derived from naturalistic theories of religion which are themselves part of highly controversial theories of much broader scope. While naturalistic theories remain influential, they have not been widely accepted because they rely on assumptions about religion which are highly contested – and, for the same reason, naturalistic definitions also fail to achieve widespread support.

Given the difficulties of both religious and naturalistic theories of religion, some scholars have attempted to stipulate a definition that presupposes neither a religious nor a naturalistic theory. Keith Yandell argues that the following definition is neutral between religious and naturalistic theories:

> [A] religion is a conceptual system that provides an interpretation of the world and the place of human beings in it, bases an account of how life should be lived given that interpretation, and expresses this interpretation and lifestyle in a set of rituals, institutions and practices.[17]

While Yandell may well have succeeded in maintaining a neutral stance between religious and naturalistic definitions of religion, his definition nevertheless exhibits the now familiar problem of including too much. Maoism, for example, is 'a conceptual system that provides an interpretation of the world and the place of human beings in it' and which 'bases an account of how life should be lived given that interpretation' and, moreover, 'expresses this interpretation and lifestyle in a set of rituals, institutions and practices'. Yet most people would want to say that Maoism is most accurately classified as a political ideology and not as a religion.

The failure of a definition such as Yandell's to demarcate the religious from the non-religious domain, without taking a stance on the religious versus naturalistic issue, might suggest that we should consider religion from another perspective. It may be that religions fall under the wider concept 'culture'. Indeed, this view has been proffered by the famous anthropologist Clifford Geertz (1926–2006), who argues that religions should be analysed as cultural systems.[18] Geertz took the concept 'culture' to denote a 'historically transmitted pattern of meanings embodied in symbols, a system of inherited conception expressed in symbolic forms by means of which men communicate, perpetuate, and develop their knowledge about and attitudes toward life'.[19] Clearly, both religious and secular 'patterns of meaning' would fit under this definition of culture. Nevertheless, Geertz offers a definition of religion that aspires to identify religions as a sub-class of cultures. According to Geertz, a religion is:

(1) a system of symbols which acts to (2) establish powerful, pervasive, and long-lasting moods and motivations in men by (3) formulating conceptions of a general order of existence and (4) clothing these conceptions with such an aura of factuality that (5) the moods and motivations seem uniquely realistic.[20]

There is no doubt that this definition of religion has provided scholars with a useful perspective from which to study religions.[21] Nevertheless, it is not unproblematic. First, adherents of Marx's historical materialism, especially when they wave red flags, may well be counted as religious on this definition. And second, religions in which symbols appear to play a relatively minor role – Quakerism, for example – do not seem to register on Geertz's theory. Indeed, religions would seem to be more diverse and complex than his theory allows. While telling us part of the story, he inevitably leaves much untold. Indeed, every theory presupposes some account of what data will be relevant and what must be explained. With a limited definition of 'religion', theorists, in focusing on this data, will inevitably draw attention away from other aspects of religion – aspects that another brand of theorist may regard as of key importance. Each theory we have considered, then, comes with its own peculiar biases. Perhaps for this reason, theories of religion would seem to rival religions in the diversity they exhibit, and the prevailing definitions of religion they have generated seem to have shed little light on what – if anything – all and only religions have in common.

An alternative approach

Given the difficulty of arriving at a satisfactory definition, the suspicion arose that the attempt to define 'religion' is futile. In the early 1960s,

Wilfred Cantwell Smith argued that the attempt was misguided, and could not succeed, because the term 'religion' does not pick out phenomena that are naturally grouped together. In other words, religions do not possess some common defining feature that the term 'religion' picks out. According to Smith, 'religion' is a concept created by modern Western scholars and superimposed upon a variety of phenomena; the superimposition serving to create the impression that 'religion' is a unified thing. This superimposition gradually began to take place, Smith believes, in the eighteenth century. At that time there was a sudden swell of interest in other cultures on the part of Western scholars. Prior to the introduction of the concept 'religion', Smith argues, there were simply a variety of interconnected practices and beliefs embedded in the various cultures of the world. Moreover, these beliefs and practices could not be neatly parcelled into either of the two, mutually exclusive, categories of 'religious' and 'secular'. Smith further claims that there was no need for the term 'religion' until the various cultures of the world began to have prolonged encounters with one another, particularly during the colonial period.[22] One result of the superimposition of the new concept was, Smith opines, that people increasingly viewed themselves as members of ideologically opposed communities. Moreover, in many cases, they came to regard themselves as in exclusive possession of both truth and the promise of salvation.

In Smith's view, then, 'religion' is a divisive concept that stimulates ideological confrontation. Thus, he counsels that the concept be abandoned, pointing out that people

> throughout history and throughout the world have been able to *be* religious without the assistance of a special term, without the intellectual analysis that the term implies. In fact, I have come to feel that, in some ways, it is probably easier to be religious without the concept; that the notion of religion can become an enemy to piety. One might almost say that the concern of the religious man is with God; the concern of the observer is with religion. ... In any case, it is not altogether foolish to suggest that the rise of the concept 'religion' is in some ways correlated with a decline in the practice of religion itself.[23]

Persuasive as this position has seemed to many, it is nevertheless deeply problematic. The theory does not, for example, enable us to understand how the wars of religion, which ravaged Western Europe in the transition from the medieval to the modern period, were *religious* wars. Nor does it seem able to account for the persecution of Jewish people that was a persistent feature of European history long before the modern era. Moreover, there is evidence that a major force in the extremely lengthy development of certain religious traditions has been their awareness of rival traditions.[24] It may be that Smith's theory provides a more accurate characterization of the indigenous belief systems of India and Africa, many of which to this day remain localized and lack a trans-geographical organizing body, than it does of the religions of Europe – particularly as they developed in the common era. It may be, though, that such criticisms miss the main point of Smith's argument. In the passage quoted above, Smith characterizes the concept 'religion' as the enemy of religion. He thus appears to accept that there is such a thing as religion. Perhaps we should, therefore, interpret him as denying that the concept 'religion' appropriately latches onto that thing. But if Smith's concerns are solely about the limitations of our present conception of religion, then surely they can be allayed by refining the concept. And the attempt to refine our concept better to reflect what religions actually are is surely what motivates scholars to seek definitions of religion.

Despite these problems, many late twentieth-century scholars agreed with Smith that the search for a defining feature of religion was futile. Moreover, there was widespread recognition that the problems encountered in attempting to define religion might not originate from anything unusual about the phenomenon of religion, but rather from the assumption that concepts represent things that are grouped together by virtue of having a common defining feature, or essence. Perhaps the various religions do not have any defining features, or essence, in common? The argument that, contrary to surface appearances, certain concepts do not have a single, essential, defining feature was advanced in the twentieth century by the influential Austrian philosopher of Jewish descent, Ludwig Wittgenstein.[25]

Wittgenstein illustrates his theory of language by means of the word 'game', claiming that it is fruitless to search for a single feature that all games have in common.[26] Prior to reflection, most of us probably assume that if things are games, then there must be some feature they all possess that makes them all games. But as Wittgenstein asks:

> What is common to them all? – Don't say: 'There *must* be something in common, or they would not be called "games"' – but *look and see* whether there is anything common to all. – For if you look at them you will not see something that is common to *all*, but similarities, relationships, and a whole series of them at that.[27]

Wittgenstein shows that if we consider any feature that some games possess, we will find some other game that does not possess it. Competitive activity, for example, may at first sight appear to be a feature possessed by all games. However, counter-examples are easy to come by: certain card games, solitaire for instance, are not competitive. As no feature is possessed by all games, no single feature can be used to define what games are.

What games as a class possess, argues Wittgenstein, are a number of different features, and no game displays all of them. Nevertheless, for something to be a game, then some of these features must be present. We can imagine four different kinds of games displaying the following properties:

Game 1: W, X, Y
Game 2: X, Y, Z
Game 3: W, Y, Z
Game 4: W, X, Z

Game 1 has features W, X and Y. Game 2 has features X, Y and Z. Game 3 has features W, Y and Z. And Game 4 has features W, X and Z. Notice that no single game has all the features and that there is no single feature that is common to all the games. But, clearly, the first game resembles the second game in a number of respects (they both possess features X and Y), the second resembles the third (they both possess features Y and Z), the third resembles the fourth (they both possess features W and Z), and so on. Wittgenstein described this pattern of resemblance as being rather like a natural family.[28] Different members of the same family resemble each other, but not always in the same way. The daughter might have her mother's eyes and her father's nose. The son might have his mother's hair and his father's eyes. Wittgenstein suggested that we think of certain concepts as analogous to families. Just as family resemblances enable us to recognize the various members of a natural family even though there may be no trait that all the family members have in common, the diverse things covered by a single concept also exhibit 'family resemblances' that enable us to recognize them as belonging to the same class. Different games exhibit family resemblances, and it is by virtue of these family resemblances that something is a game.

Wittgenstein's analysis of the word 'game' is meant to show that concepts are not necessarily as simple as they might at first appear. A single concept, like 'game', can be used to refer to things that do not share any defining feature. He claims that we are misled by such concepts if we assume that there must be some feature possessed by everything falling under one of them. In Wittgenstein's view, many of our concepts are like this. Later thinkers, inspired by his approach, have proposed that one reason why religion is so difficult to define might be because 'religion' is one of these concepts that do not refer to things possessing a single defining characteristic. Perhaps, instead, 'religion' is a complex concept used to refer to things with a number of features – a number of family resemblances – not all of which need be present.

Consider Theravada Buddhism and Christianity: both revere a holy founder, but Theravada Buddhists, unlike Christians, do not believe in a

God. So these religions exhibit a family resemblance as well as an important difference. Contrast these religions with Shaivite Hinduism, whose adherents do not revere a holy founder but who do believe in a God. Were we to compare and contrast all religions, we may well find nothing that they all have in common, but we might nevertheless discover many overlapping resemblances between them. In fact, increased knowledge of world religions seems to many to support this assessment. The study of religions discloses an enormous diversity of beliefs and practices interwoven with striking resemblances. The diversities can be so extreme that even two forms of the 'same' tradition might seem to have little important in common (never mind one common defining feature). Nevertheless, both can be recognized as bearing a family resemblance to one another. Such observations, combined with the many difficulties involved in the search for a definition of religion which is neither too inclusive nor too exclusive, have led many to adopt a 'family resemblance approach' to religion; John Hick being one prominent twentieth-century scholar to advocate this approach.[29] Hick advises us to abandon the search for a definition of religion and instead recognize that religions have family resemblances that allow us to identify them as falling under the concept 'religion'.

This approach, however, is not unproblematic. If we regard as a member of the 'religious family' everything that has some feature in common with standard examples of religion, the concept 'religion' will have such a wide scope that it may well be analytically useless. Moreover, there would seem to be a host of resemblances between 'religious' and 'secular' belief systems.[30] Given so many resemblances, how could we determine which of them allow us to identify something as a member of the religious family? To decide which resemblances are relevant and which are not would seem to require additional criteria. Hick, in recognizing this need, suggests that, because religious beliefs and practices characteristically have a deep importance for those who hold them, Paul Tillich's notion of 'ultimate concern' might stand as our central criterion. In other words, beliefs and practices are to be recognized as part of the 'religious family' by virtue of being invested with 'ultimate concern'. Hick claims that this 'quality of importance pervades the field of religious phenomena. Not everything that has more than transient importance to us is religious; but all authentic as opposed to merely nominal religiousness seems to involve a sense of profound importance.'[31] Notice that this is not offered as a definition of religion but as a criterion by which we can rule out certain things as excluded from the family of religions. It seems, then, that without the help of an additional criterion, the family resemblance approach is a blunt analytical tool that cannot distinguish between cases of religion and cases of non-religion. However, a new problem is raised by the attempt to provide a supplementary criterion. Any criterion will reflect its proponent's assumptions about the nature of religion; this is clearly true, for example, of Hick's criterion. But the family resemblance approach was offered in order to avoid such assumptions.

At this point it appears that we have come full circle. What one is prepared to regard as a religiously relevant family resemblance will depend upon what one means by 'religion'. Given certain assumptions, one might include belief systems such as humanism and Marxism; given certain others, one might not. One way out of this impasse might be to resist the urge to supplement the family resemblance approach with a separate criterion, and to accept that in some cases there will be no clear answer to the question of whether something is part of the family of religions or not. Hick concedes this much even while advocating his additional criterion. For he claims that in some cases – Confucianism and Christian Science, for example – there may not be a clear answer. In such cases, he opines, one can merely note 'their positions within a complex, ramified network of related phenomena' and '[h]aving done this we have resolved – or perhaps dissolved – the problem of the definition of "religion"'.[32]

Some have held, however, that the fact of there being no clear answer to the question whether or not something is a religion or religious is symptomatic of a deeper problem afflicting the concept 'religion' and its cognates. Timothy Fitzgerald argues that the fact that 'religion' has no clear meaning implies that there is no such thing as religion.[33] According to Fitzgerald, people have failed to define religion because there are no genuine religious phenomena to identify. Purported religious phenomena are, he argues, the result of our imposing an artificial conceptual division between the 'religious' and the 'secular' onto a world that does not exhibit any such distinction. It is to this conclusion that the existence of the borderline cases discussed above points, in his view. Consequently, Fitzgerald proposes that '[r]eligion cannot reasonably be taken to be a valid analytical category ...'.[34] And he concludes that, because it has no legitimate object, religious studies should be assimilated to cultural studies, and scholars of religion, as a distinct species of academic, should be retired. Thus, he claims, the concept 'religion' and its cognates should be withdrawn from circulation.

Is it the case, however, that terms with no clear meaning are not analytically useful and should be eliminated from our discourse? Inspection will reveal that many of our terms lack a clear meaning. Perhaps, then, 'religion' is 'open textured' or an example of what philosophers call a vague concept. A vague concept typically has a range of applications that are undisputed alongside other possible applications in which there is no clear answer to the question of whether or not the concept is appropriately applied. While such concepts are philosophically interesting, they are by no means rare. Natural languages contain a large number of vague concepts, many of which are mundane. 'Bald', for example, is a vague concept. How much hair must you have lost in order for the concept 'bald' to apply appropriately to you? Many cases of hair-loss seem to be borderline cases in which it is neither definitely right nor definitely wrong to call a person bald. This is not usually taken to imply that there is something mysterious about baldness, or that we should drop the concept 'bald'. Nor does it raise doubts about whether there is such a thing as baldness. If we can accept that some of our concepts are like this, and that their vagueness does not make them unduly problematic, then why not regard 'religion' as such a concept? Other examples of terms that lack a clear meaning, but which are analytically important nevertheless, are 'species' and 'mind'. These have no clear or undisputed meaning, yet they are both central to their respective disciplines of biology and psychology. That such terms have no clear meaning generates questions which fuel research within these disciplines. It is not usually taken to suggest either that the terms be dropped or that the disciplines be assimilated into others that do not employ them. It seems open to us to view 'religion' in the same way. That it has no clear undisputed meaning may be what contributes to its ability to stimulate research programmes. Such a lack of clear meaning would not, then, seem to constitute a good reason for phasing out the term; just as dispute about the meaning of 'species' or 'mind' is not usually taken as sufficient grounds for dropping both the terms and the areas of study in which they are central. Fitzgerald's conclusion, then, does not seem to be entailed by his premises.

There is a further, more practical, reason, though, why we should resist the idea that religion does not constitute a distinct phenomenon. Consider again the question: Why should we try to define religion? As we have seen, whether or not Marxism is a religion is one example of the type of question that has given rise to the search for a definition of religion. An appropriate definition of religion would enable us to determine what we can legitimately count as being covered by the term 'religion'. And this matters because there are a number of well-documented cases in which great significance is attached to the question of whether some particular belief system should be classified as a religion or not. In the twentieth century, it was not uncommon, for example, for governments to call upon their citizens to fight in wars. But the governments of many countries exempted those citizens whose conscientious objection to participation in war was based on a religious belief – say, one that committed them to pacifism. Clearly, whether or not one's beliefs were counted as 'religious' was of great importance in these circumstances. To take a concrete example, during the Second World War, the government of the United States called upon its citizens to fight. Many claimed exemption on the grounds of religious beliefs that committed them to pacifism. However, certain of the 'religions' adhered to by would-be conscientious objectors were not recognized by the US government as religions. As a result, many found themselves denied the status of conscientious objectors, and were incarcerated for refusing to fight. Quakers as well as Hopis were denied conscientious-objector status, and were imprisoned because their respective belief systems were not officially recognized as religions.[35] In short, these pacifists were imprisoned simply because the definition of religion adopted by the government of the United States excluded their 'religion' from official recognition.

Such religious discrimination runs counter to the trend, dominant throughout much of the twentieth century, to accord greater value to religious freedom. Indeed, freedom of religion is identified as a significant human right in a landmark document of the twentieth century, the Universal Declaration of Human Rights, which states that

> [e]veryone has the right to freedom of thought, conscience and religion; this right includes freedom to change their religion or belief, and freedom, either alone or in community with others and in public or in private, to manifest their religion or belief in teaching, practice, worship and observance.[36]

Definitions of religion that are too limited in scope can be a serious impediment to the success of efforts to claim, or to protect, this right. So the debate about the best way to define 'religion', which at first sight may have appeared purely academic, turns out to have wide ramifications with respect to vitally important human concerns. For this reason, we should be cautious of Fitzgerald's claim that there is no such thing as religion; a hard-won right to religious freedom will not elicit much respect if the existence of religion is seriously questioned.

This notwithstanding, if we consider what originally motivated the search for a definition of religion, we may find that there is some truth to Fitzgerald's claim. The search for a definition of religion can be seen as quintessentially modern insofar as modernity was the first era in which a firm distinction between religion and the rest of human activity was presupposed. As previous eras made no such distinction, they had no need of the concepts 'religious' and 'secular'. Such concepts can be seen as a product of the modern impulse to separate 'religion' from the rest of cultural life,[37] in order to underwrite the independent autonomy of the 'secular' realm of the social and political world. As Joseph D. Bettis comments:

> The attempt to describe religion as a separate and independent sphere of human activity did not appear until the nineteenth century. Schleiermacher's *On Religion* was one of the first books to regard it as an isolable subject. Prior to that a religious tradition was identified with the cultural tradition that provided the fundamental means of individual

and social identification. Traditionally, religion referred to the basic guiding images and principles of an individual and a culture. Religion was identical with style of life.[38]

Given the provenance of the peculiarly modern attempt to distinguish 'religion' from other areas of human activity, it is not surprising that religion should elude concise definition and, hence, appear to some as a fictional entity created by modern intellectuals. In a sense, then, we might argue that 'religion' is a fictional entity: it seems not to be a ready-made feature of the world but rather a construction generated by a powerful desire to impose firm conceptual distinctions on a world that, perhaps, does not in itself exhibit them. However, in another sense, religion does not seem merely to be a fictional entity, for the result of projecting 'religion' onto the world may well be that our world has come genuinely to exhibit it. Like a self-fulfilling prophecy, the desire to separate a 'religious' from a 'secular' realm may have led to the emergence of two distinct realms – a sphere of identifiable religious practices and institutions, on the one hand, and a sphere of secular practices and institutions that explicitly exclude the religious, on the other. To complicate matters further, though, the creation of distinct 'religious' and 'secular' realms would not appear to have taken place at the same speed throughout all parts of the world.

It may seem that the problems we have been discussing are not likely to affect our understanding of the major religious traditions that constitute the focus of this book. However, issues often arise regarding what counts as Judaism, Christianity or Islam. It may be that these ancient and established religious traditions can best be seen as constituted by sub-traditions united by family resemblances – resemblances, moreover, that often appear to be obscured from the view of religious practitioners themselves. Religious traditionalists tend to opt for an essentialist view of their religious tradition, arguing that those who have let go of some particular beliefs or practices should not be considered genuine adherents of the faith. Analysing religious traditions and sub-traditions in terms of family resemblances might have the advantage of granting us a perspective from which to examine a religion without having to accept uncritically the interpretation of that religion advanced by any one group within its family. It may also facilitate awareness of both the similarities between the different sub-traditions of one religion and the important differences between them. Moreover, this approach might also be fruitfully applied to portray the relationship between the three Abrahamic faiths. For Judaism, Christianity and Islam may be seen as diverging traditions within the extended family of Abrahamic monotheism. This approach thus provides a vantage point from which to study the three faiths simultaneously, without being compelled to make evaluative judgements concerning which is the 'best' or the more authentic form of monotheism.

Criteria of religiosity

While philosophers of religion have attempted to define religion, some sociologists of religion have focused on a different, albeit related, task. They have sought to answer the question: What criteria should we employ to classify a person as religious? This question was asked with increasing frequency in the late twentieth century, as criteria that had proven adequate in the past came to appear incapable of providing an appropriate standard for judgement. Debate over criteria intensified apace with the growing perplexity regarding just what 'religion' means. Until late in the twentieth century, two criteria of religiosity were widely regarded as individually necessary and jointly sufficient: if a person was, first, affiliated to a religious institution, and second, held religious beliefs, then he or she could be classified as 'religious' as opposed to 'non-religious'.

Over the twentieth century, as societies became increasingly secular, there was a huge drop in the percentage of the population of the developed world that claimed affiliation to a religious institution. Thus, an increasing number of people failed to meet the first criterion. Recent surveys suggest, however, that a surprising number of these people not only held on to their religious beliefs but also typically retained a sense of religious identity. This surely indicates that the relationship between religious affiliation and religiosity is much more complex than was formerly assumed. And it further suggests that it is now inappropriate to regard such affiliation as a necessary condition for a person to be classified as religious, for it seems counter-intuitive – indeed, quite bizarre – to regard a devout believer as irreligious simply because she eschews membership of a religious institution. Because of this reason, the adequacy of the first criterion has come into serious question.

Moreover, the second criterion – possession of religious beliefs – has also come to be regarded with suspicion. This is because whether or not a person holds religious beliefs might not always be obvious to an observer. And it may not be obvious because a person might express his or her beliefs in idiosyncratic, untraditional terms.[39] One result of doubt about the adequacy of these criteria is that many scholars have come to believe that, in a large number of cases, there may be no clear answer to the question of whether or not a person is religious, and hence whether or not he or she should be categorized as such. Many have concluded that the only possible criterion of whether a person is religious or not is whether or not that person says that she is. (Indeed, this is the criterion that has been adopted by many of those who carry out censuses.)

All of this suggests that a deep problem may lie in the continued use of the outmoded categories of 'religious' and 'non-religious' that are presupposed by the two standard criteria of religiosity. At the very least, it would seem mistaken to insist that both criteria should be met if a person is to be regarded as religious. It is certainly clear that we can no longer assume that anyone who holds religious beliefs will be affiliated to some religious institution or other. Let us consider in more detail, then, some reasons for dropping the claim that affiliation to a religious institution is a necessary condition of religiosity. Sociologists of religion Jacques Janssen and Maerten Prins have studied the relationship between religious belief and institutional affiliation among Dutch youth.[40] They chose Dutch youth as the subjects for their study because, as is well known, the Netherlands was in the forefront of the Western European secularization process in the last quarter of the twentieth century.[41] Janssen and Prins believe that the Dutch youth constitute that segment of the Western European population with the highest level of secularization. Hence, they hold that the complex relationship between a lack of commitment to a religious institution and the possession of religious beliefs can be clearly illustrated by studying this group.

Surprisingly, Janssen and Prins found that, although many of the Dutch youth remain unaffiliated with any religious institution, only a very small number of them 'reject religion explicitly or prefer atheism'.[42] The Dutch youth, Janssen and Prins claim, 'do still show a religious identity, but it has become a private affair, insecure, non-specific and abstract'.[43] While the Dutch youth had the lowest level of affiliation to religious institutions among the youth of the 16 European countries that formed the original study, nevertheless when religiosity was measured absent the conventional criterion of institutional affiliation, they emerged as remarkably religious. Janssen and Prins argue that this pattern also holds good for the youth of other European countries. The young people of England, Germany, France and Belgium have all been found to have little interest in religious institutions, but neither do they seem particularly drawn to atheism. This research suggests that regarding affiliation to a religious institution as a necessary condition for being religious is seriously to misrepresent the real level of religiosity in any given population.

Moreover, a French sociologist of religion, Pierre Bréchon, conducted a survey of religious attitudes in France at the close of the twentieth century,[44] which corroborates the findings of Janssen and Prins. Bréchon found that, although France has been a traditional stronghold of Roman Catholicism, a large percentage of the population have come to view institutional Roman Catholicism with considerable distrust. Bréchon's research, however, indicates that this low appraisal of institutional Roman Catholicism is not correlated with a widespread rejection of religious belief and identity. Rather, Bréchon found that a large number of people describe themselves as Roman Catholic – thus admitting to having a religious identity – even though they have very little, or nothing, to do with institutional Roman Catholicism. Reflection on the data collected during this study left Bréchon with

> the impression that Roman Catholicism – as a system – has lost its homogeneity, and that it is actually lived in an extremely individual way. Moreover, those who have detached themselves from institutional Roman Catholicism have nevertheless managed to retain, or reconstitute, elements of the older belief system. Religion today is less regulated than previously, being more diffuse and disseminated, more composite and heterodox. Those who claim to be without a religion comprise an even less homogenous group, vacillating between a commitment to rationality and science and an adhesion to belief in life after death or other similar beliefs. They are united as a group only in their opposition to religious systems. Religious meaning has become an individual affair. The grand systems of meaning, which in early times came as pre-assembled packages, are now nothing but repositories of ideas from which one can freely take whatever one chooses and leave the rest. However, religiosity continues to be an important dimension in the construction of individual identity, and a person's entire intellectual framework will be marked by the position he or she takes on religious matters. Despite their continued importance, religious identities have become increasingly complex and nuanced.[45]

Bréchon would seem to agree with Janssen and Prins, then, that, given the complex texture of religious identity in the late twentieth century, it has become inappropriate to regard institutional affiliation as a necessary condition of religiosity. Moreover, both of the studies considered above suggest that, when we ask what enables us to identify a person as 'religious', we should be sensitive to the diverse forms that religiosity can take. Given this diversity, it would seem that there is no clear and uncontroversial method that can be used to determine whether or not someone is religious. Furthermore, even an outright denial of religious identity may not constitute decisive evidence that a person is irreligious. Bréchon claims that a significant number of those who declared themselves to be without a religion nevertheless claimed to be committed to such quintessentially religious objects of belief as the existence of God, life after death, and miracles. In the light of this confusing data, Bréchon concludes that it is no longer helpful to categorize people as belonging to one of only two possible groups: the 'religious' or the 'non-religious'. Instead, he advocates employing a tripartite scheme demarcating: those affiliated to a religious institution, who hold the conventional beliefs of that institution; those not affiliated to a religious institution, but who, nevertheless, hold religious beliefs; and, finally, those unaffiliated to a religious institution, who lack religious beliefs.

However, it seems that Bréchon's tripartite scheme fails to incorporate another significant group: namely, those who are affiliated to a religious institution without holding the conventional beliefs of that institution. Many argue that this group comprises a significant proportion of the 'religious' population. Eugene Borowitz, for example, claims that this category is particularly relevant to Judaism, where synagogue affiliation would often seem to be motivated by social reasons.[46] But surely we would not wish to call a person religious simply because she joins a religious institution for a wholly non-religious reason. To do so seems quite counter-intuitive. Hence, the existence of this fourth group shows that the first criterion of religiosity – affiliation to a religious institution – is not a sufficient condition for being a religious person.

Notwithstanding the large membership of this fourth group, of the three groups that Bréchon identified, those in the second group comprise, in his opinion, the fastest growing group in France. Moreover, there is evidence that this pattern holds in the United States,[47] and it may well be that this would prove true of many other European countries – which suggests that any assessment of religion and modern thought would do well to bear this important group in mind.

So, whereas throughout much of the twentieth century many scholars recorded that church attendance was declining in Western Europe, thereby concluding that Western Europeans were becoming less religious, Bréchon's research suggests that this analysis misses something important. For the fact that religion is becoming increasingly de-institutionalized does not necessarily entail that people are becoming less religious. Religiosity, it would seem, can survive de-institutionalization. Indeed, this idea is supported by a growing number of scholars of religion.

Despite the plausibility of this view, it may be that those who support the de-institutionalization thesis have tended to overstate their case. For they often fail to acknowledge that, by the end of the twentieth century, many Christian denominations seemed to be flourishing – Roman Catholicism and Pentecostalism, for example, were growing at a significant rate. Moreover, at this time, an estimated 20,000 Christian denominations competed for adherents. It can be argued, nonetheless, that this situation indirectly supports a qualified form of the de-institutionalization thesis. The range of denominations available may have contributed to the decreased importance that affiliation to a particular denomination has in the religious life of many Christians. Research seems to indicate that the trend is for Christians to be less committed to particular denominations, and to switch their ecclesial allegiance frequently and readily, depending on the quality or convenience of specific ecclesial communities.[48]

But do the notions of 'de-institutionalization' and 'affiliation to a religious institution' tie the research reviewed above too closely to Christianity (with its traditional focus on church attendance)? After all, traditionally, neither Judaism nor Islam has given membership of religious institutions the importance that Christianity has done. It may seem, then, that the debate we have considered is of more relevance to Christianity than to the other two Abrahamic monotheisms. However, while evidence suggests that Christianity has been becoming increasingly de-institutionalized, other evidence suggests that religious institutions are coming to play a greater role in Judaism and Islam in the modern West than they have typically done in other times and places. Many mosques in North America, for example, are structuring themselves on the model of the mainstream Protestant parish. And membership of such mosques is taking on greater importance in the lives of many Western Muslims. With regard to the changing role of mosques in North American Muslim life, Michael Wolfe, himself a North American Muslim, observes:

> The mosques of America have had to provide, in addition to floor space for prayer, the fabric of a community that Muslims in the traditional homelands of Islam take for granted. If practising Islam means something more than carrying out the rites of the religion, then American Muslims practice it differently from other places in the world, and one of the chief ways they differ is in their multipurpose mosques. ... Mosques are now beginning to play a similar role in America to churches and synagogues.[49]

Despite this development, there is a crucial disanalogy between institutionalized Christianity and what we might call institutionalized Judaism and Islam. Traditionally, membership of a particular Christian institution implied subscription to the version of Christian belief embraced by that institution. This is an aspect of institutional religion to which most forms of Judaism and Islam have never been committed. Many Jews and Muslims who choose to affiliate to a particular religious institution nevertheless retain considerable latitude concerning the content of their personal religious beliefs. Furthermore, despite the trend toward an increasing role for synagogues and mosques in the Western religious context, it seems likely that many Jews and Muslims hold religious beliefs without feeling any need to join such congregations. Thus, they would be classifiable under Bréchon's second category (that is, the category of those who are not affiliated to a religious institution, but, who, nevertheless, hold religious beliefs).

It might seem, however, that the somewhat amorphous, often de-institutionalized, religiosity that many Jews, Christians and Muslims exhibit in the twentieth century will have strayed too far from the traditional forms of Abrahamic monotheism to be of interest to us. Such a judgement, however, may be too hasty. Perhaps the innovative and private form of religion exhibited by that large number of people who fall into Bréchon's second category, far from constituting a complete break with the traditions of the past, is in creative continuity with those traditions. Moreover, it would surely be one-sided to emphasize the discontinuities while ignoring the many, striking continuities. In every age, inherited traditions are handled creatively, and the tendency for older generations to view their juniors as departing violently and illegitimately from the past is not uncommon. This implies that when, in the following chapters, the impact of twentieth-century cultural and intellectual movements on religion is considered, it would be a mistake to focus exclusively on the responses of representative religious figures or organizations. Consequently, in what follows I seek to avoid grand generalizations about what religious people do or should believe. Instead, I aim to provide a fuller picture by attending to the work of a range of thinkers, including independent scholars (some of whom, perhaps, holding forms of religious belief that would not be regarded as entirely orthodox by more conventional 'religious' people).

Conclusion

In this chapter I have indicated some of the problems involved in defining 'religion', and I have discussed some of the difficulties arising from attempts to stipulate who is to count as a 'religious person'. We have seen that the terms 'religion' and 'religious person' are both highly contentious and could be viewed as 'essentially contested'.[50] The debates generated by these terms suggest that an essentialist understanding of either religion or religious people should be avoided. An essentialist claims that there are certain essential features that make a thing what it is, and these features allow us to define it as such. According to an essentialist about religion, religion is *one thing*, and all religions are instances of that thing in virtue of possessing the same essential property or properties. What should we conclude from the implausibility of essentialism about religion? Surely not that there is no such thing as religion. Rather, we should embrace the more limited conclusion that it would be mistaken to assume that all religions exhibit the same essential features. This conclusion encourages us to take seriously the real differences that exist between religious traditions. Moreover, just as 'religion' would not seem to be one thing, there is no good reason to suppose that Judaism, Christianity or Islam are each one homogeneous entity. Each of these religious traditions can itself be analysed using the family resemblance approach. If these traditions are thought of as composed of sub-traditions possessing family resemblances, there will be less of an inclination to search for a homogeneous tradition that is, itself, highly contested. Nor will we be inclined to ex-

34

pect all those who adhere to any one of the major monotheisms to accept exactly the same set of beliefs. This approach thus allows us to be sensitive to the diversity of religious belief and practice commonly found even within the 'same' tradition, while simultaneously providing a framework for appreciating such diversity as part of richly textured and continuously evolving traditions. In a nutshell, while debates in the philosophy of language are ongoing,[51] there are pragmatic grounds for our deploying a family resemblance approach within this study. For, surely, in a multicultural world we need a theoretical approach to the study of religions that is not from the outset prejudicial to any religion. And a family resemblance approach seems most suited to this requirement.

Bearing in mind the diversity within each religious tradition, we are now in a position to consider the three traditions that comprise the focus of this book. In the following chapter, I provide an overview of the core features of Judaism, Christianity and Islam.

Study questions

1 Why attempt to define religion? What are some of the dangers of failing to define religion?

2 In your view, what makes something a religion, and what, if any thing, distinguishes religions from secular social organizations like clubs?

3 Is there anything wrong with the suggestion that any kind of belief system could be 'religious', provided only that it is held with sufficient passion?

4 Why did F. D. E. Schleiermacher believe that rejecting formalized religious doctrines and official religious institutions and rejecting religion were not the same thing? Do you agree?

5 What is the difference between *religious* theories of religion and *naturalistic* ones? Which type of theory seems likely to have more explanatory power?

6 Are there features that we may expect to find in all instances of religion?

7 What is the family resemblance approach to defining religion? What problems is it meant to solve? Does it solve them?

8 Is 'religion' a vague concept? If so, does that imply that it isn't a useful concept?

9 What does Wilfred Cantwell Smith mean by the claim that there is no such thing as religion? Is his view plausible?

10 Should we regard affiliation to a religious institution as a necessary condition for a person to be classified as religious? If so, why?

11 Are the categories of 'religious' and 'non-religious' outmoded, and, as such, inapplicable within the West today?

Select bibliography

Borowitz, E. B., 1968, *A New Jewish Theology in the Making*, Philadelphia: The Westminster Press.

Davie, G., 1994, *Religion in Britain since 1945: Believing without Belonging*, Oxford: Blackwell.

Fitzgerald, T., 2000, *The Ideology of Religious Studies*, New York and Oxford: Oxford University Press.

Geertz, C., 1973, *The Interpretation of Cultures: Selected Essays*, New York: Basic Books.

Greeley, A. M., 2003, *Religion in Europe at the End of the Second Millennium: A Sociological Profile*, New Brunswick and London: Transaction Publishers.

Hick, J., 1989, *An Interpretation of Religion: Human Responses to the Transcendent*, London: Macmillan.

Lindbeck, G. A., 1984, *The Nature of Doctrine: Religion and Theology in a Postliberal Age*, Philadelphia: The Westminster Press.

McCutcheon, R. T., 2001, *Critics not Caretakers: Redescribing the Public Study of Religion*, Albany: State University of New York Press.

McCutcheon, R. T., 1997, *Manufacturing Religion: The Discourse on Sui Generis Religion and the Politics of Nostalgia*, New York: Oxford University Press.

McGrath, A. E., 2002, *The Future of Christianity*, Oxford: Blackwell.

Phillips, D. Z. (ed.), 1996, *Can Religion be Explained Away*, London: Macmillan.

Schleiermacher, F. D. E., 1928, *The Christian Faith*, Edinburgh: T. & T. Clark.

Smith, W. C., 1978, *The Meaning and End of Religion: A Revolutionary Approach to the Great Religious Traditions*, London: SPCK.

Thrower, J., 1999, *Religion: The Classical Theories*, Edinburgh: Edinburgh University Press.

Wittgenstein, L., 1959, *Philosophical Investigations*, trans. by G. E. M. Anscombe, Oxford: Blackwell.

Wolfe, M., (ed.), 2002, *Taking Back Islam: American Muslims Reclaim Their Faith*, Emmaus, Pennsylvania: Rodale.

Notes

1 Martineau's definition is cited in William Alston, 1967, 'Religion' in P. Edwards (ed.), *The Encyclopaedia of Philosophy*, vol. 7, London: Macmillan, p. 143.

2 Eugene B. Borowitz, 1968, *A New Jewish Theology in the Making*, Philadelphia: The Westminster Press, p. 44.

3 George A. Lindbeck, 1984, *The Nature of Doctrine: Religion and Theology in a Postliberal Age*, Philadelphia: The Westminster Press, p. 16.

4 Functional definitions, in contrast, as we shall see below, are *non-religious* definitions of religion. In seeking to define religion in naturalistic terms, those adopting this approach arrive at definitions that will inevitably seem inadequate to the vast majority of religious people. This type of definition, as Lindbeck points out, is typically adopted by scholars of religion who are not themselves commit-

ted to any faith, and who seek to explain religion from one of the perspectives offered by the social sciences. Lindbeck himself finds all of these approaches inadequate and, consequently, seeks to develop an alternative 'cultural-linguistic' approach. The key to Lindbeck's analysis is the idea that 'religions resemble languages together with their correlative forms of life and are thus similar to cultures'. Lindbeck, *Nature*, p. 18.

5 Cited in Alston, 'Religion', p. 141. And see F. D. E. Schleiermacher, 1928, *The Christian Faith*, Edinburgh: T. & T. Clark, pp. 16f.

6 As we shall see, below, Schleiermacher's claim that rejecting religious doctrines and religious institutions is not the same as rejecting religion altogether seems to have been borne out by studies of late twentieth-century attitudes towards religion.

7 Sigmund Freud, 1962, *The Future of an Illusion*, trans. by W. D. Robson-Scott, London: The Hogarth Press and the Institute of Psycho-Analysis, pp. 28f.

8 Freud, *Future*, pp. 28f.

9 Freud, *Future*, pp. 28f.

10 Cited in Alston, 'Religion', p. 140.

11 See, for example, Borowitz, *New*, pp. 44f.

12 For a survey of prominent examples of these rival theories, see James Thrower, 1999, *Religion: The Classical Theories*, Edinburgh: Edinburgh University Press. Remarking on the sudden appearance of these theories in the West from the mid-eighteenth century, Thrower suggests that 'it is only when religion has ceased to be at the living heart of a culture, that is, when its status has become problematic, that explanations to account for its existence come to the fore'. Thrower, *Religion*, p. 3.

13 Thrower, *Religion*, p. 3.

14 Naturalistic psychological theories typically suggest that religion originally arose out of a primitive mental state such as fear or guilt, with Freud being the most famous exponent of such a view. Alternatively, sociological theories, which are also naturalistic, typically propose that religious beliefs and practices arose to fulfil a social function. One such function could have been to stabilize society through encouraging people to conform to social norms. The French sociologist Émile Durkheim (1858–1917) went so far as to suggest that religions originated in primitive human beings who worshipped society. See Émile Durkheim, 1995, *The Elementary Forms of the Religious Life*, trans. by Karen E. Fields, New York: Free Press.

15 I discuss Wilson's theory in Chapter 6.

16 Herbert Spencer, cited in Alston, 'Religion', p. 140.

17 Keith Yandell, 1999, *Philosophy of Religion: A Contemporary Introduction*, London: Routledge, p. 16.

18 Geertz's work is voluminous. However, see, for example, Clifford Geertz, 1973, *The Interpretation of Cultures: Selected Essays*, New York: Basic Books, chapter 4.

19 Geertz, *Interpretation*, p. 89.

20 Geertz, *Interpretation*, p. 90.

21 Geertz's perspective continues to be developed by, among others, Russell T. McCutcheon and Timothy Fitzgerald. See, for example, Russell T. McCutcheon,

2001, *Critics not Caretakers: Redescribing the Public Study of Religion*, Albany: State University of New York Press; and Timothy Fitzgerald, 2000, *The Ideology of Religious Studies*, New York and Oxford: Oxford University Press.

22 Smith's thesis is taken even further by Timothy Fitzgerald when he claims that '[t]he construction of "religion" and "religions" as global, crosscultural objects of study has been part of a wider historical process of western imperialism, colonialism, and neocolonialism. Part of this process has been to establish an ideologically loaded distinction between the realm of religion and the realm of non-religion or the secular. By constructing religion and religions, the imagined secular world of objective facts, of societies and markets as the result of the free association of natural individuals, has also been constructed.' Fitzgerald, *Ideology*, p. 8.

23 Wilfred Cantwell Smith, 1978, *The Meaning and End of Religion: A Revolutionary Approach to the Great Religious Traditions*, London: SPCK, p. 19.

24 This dynamic seems to have had a profound effect on the development of both Christianity and Islam, as these rival forms of monotheism were often perceived by their adherents as mutually threatening.

25 Although Wittgenstein came from a Jewish family, it would probably be a mistake to regard him as a 'Jewish philosopher'. For a discussion of this distinction, see Yuval Lurie, 'Jews as a Metaphysical Species', *Philosophy*, 64 (1989), pp. 323–47.

26 See Ludwig Wittgenstein, 1959, *Philosophical Investigations*, trans. by G. E. M. Anscombe, Oxford: Blackwell, paragraph 66.

27 Wittgenstein, *Philosophical*, paragraph 66.

28 Wittgenstein: 'I can think of no better expression to characterize these similarities than "family resemblances"; for the various resemblances between members of a family: build, features, colour of eyes, gait, temperament, etc. etc. overlap and criss-cross in the same way.' *Philosophical*, paragraph 67.

29 See John Hick, 1989, *An Interpretation of Religion: Human Responses to the Transcendent*, London: Macmillan, pp. 3–5. Ninian Smart's popular book *The Phenomenon of Religion*, London: Macmillan, 1973, was also instrumental in promoting the family resemblance approach.

30 For a discussion of this and other problems arising from the family resemblance theory, see Fitzgerald, *Ideology*, chapter 4.

31 Hick, *Interpretation*, p. 4.

32 Hick, *Interpretation*, p. 5.

33 Fitzgerald, *Ideology*, p. 6.

34 Fitzgerald, *Ideology*, p. 4.

35 For the case of the Hopis, see Frank Waters, 1977, *The Book of the Hopi*, London: Penguin Books, pp. 317–21.

36 Article 18 of the Universal Declaration of Human Rights (1949).

37 It has been argued that the modern academic study of religion serves to reinforce the projection of these concepts onto the world, and is thereby collusive in distorting the phenomena. See Russell T. McCutcheon, 1997, *Manufacturing Religion: The Discourse on Sui Generis Religion and the Politics of Nostalgia*, New York: Oxford University Press.

38 Joseph D. Bettis, 1975, *Phenomenology of Religion*, London: SCM Press, p. 170.

39 One problem is that, for many people, traditional religious beliefs no longer have a clear, uncontested meaning. Many people today reject the traditional religious concepts that figure in formulations of these beliefs. The word 'God', for example, has become extremely problematic. One study has shown that, although young people frequently use the word 'God', when asked 'who this God is they talk about, they use all kinds of words and metaphors. It seems as if they construct their own definitions on the spot. ... [Y]oungsters reported that they were unable to give answers to the well-known Vergote/Tamayo questionnaire on the image of God because, in their view, the items were not suitable (any more) to describe God. Traditional images of God have lost credibility. Young people prefer a vague and abstract representation of God. They devoutly practice the mission from Jim Morrison's "An American Prayer: 'Let's reinvent the Gods'".' Jacques Janssen and Maerten Prins, 'The Abstract Image of God: The Case of the Dutch Youth', *Archives de Sciences Sociales des Religions*, 109 (2000), pp. 42f.

40 See Janssen and Prins, 'Abstract Image'.

41 As Janssen and Prins claim: 'The figures seem clear and unambiguous. In 1945, 40% of the Dutch population were Catholics; in the year 1992 this was 22% and in the year 2020 this percentage is predicted to be 15%. For the Protestant denominations the figures are even more telling. In 1945, their percentage was above 40; in the year 1992 this was 18, and in the year 2020 it will be below 10. The percentage of non-Church-members was 15 in 1945, in 1992 it was 57 and it is predicted to rise to 73 in 2020.' 'Abstract Image', p. 31.

42 Janssen and Prins, 'Abstract Image', p. 32.

43 Janssen and Prins, 'Abstract Image', p. 32. Moreover, according to Janssen and Prins, even those young people who are affiliated to a religious organization have a religious identity that is no less private, insecure, non-specific and abstract.

44 See Pierre Bréchon, 'Les attitudes religieuses en France: Quelles recompositions en cours?', *Archives de Sciences Sociales des Religions*, 109 (2000), pp. 11–30.

45 Bréchon, 'Les attitudes', p. 29. My translation.

46 See Borowitz, *New*, p. 33. See also, p. 46.

47 See Richard H. Taylor et al. (ed.), 2002, *Religious Congregations and Membership in the United States 2000: An Enumeration by Region, State and County Based on Data Reported for 149 Religious Bodies*, Glenmary Research Center.

48 Alister E. McGrath (2002), for example, argues thus in *The Future of Christianity*, Oxford: Blackwell.

49 Michael Wolfe, 2002, 'Mosques Take Root in American Soil' in M. Wolfe (ed.), *Taking Back Islam: American Muslims Reclaim Their Faith*, Emmaus, Pennyslvania: Rodale, pp. 194f.

50 For the notion of 'essential contestability', see W. B. Gallie, 'Essentially Contested Concepts', *Proceedings of the Aristotelian Society*, 56 (1955–6), pp. 167–98.

51 It should be noted that many philosophers now reject the Wittgensteinian approach to meaning, especially with regard to natural kinds (such as water). The impetus for this rejection has come from the work of Saul Kripke and Hilary

Putnam. See Saul Kripke, 1980, *Naming and Necessity*, Oxford: Blackwell; and Hilary Putnam, 'The Meaning of "Meaning"' in H. Putnam, 1979, *Mind, Language and Reality*, Cambridge: Cambridge University Press, pp. 215–71. On the Kripke-Putnam theory of meaning, 'water' is taken to mean H_2O. However, religion would not seem to be a natural kind with a causally efficacious underlying structure *à la* water, with its specific molecular structure that is presumed to be causally responsible for its observable properties. Hence, the family resemblance approach might be thought to remain viable in the case of a number of concepts, such as 'religion', that do not refer to those features of the world ordinarily studied by natural scientists.

3

The Three Abrahamic Faiths

Attempts to provide an account of any religious tradition that is free from the distinctive outlook, and interpretation of history, associated with any particular branch of that tradition are fraught with difficulty. Moreover, disagreements concerning what constitutes the objective facts of the matter seem endemic to discussions of religion. Difficulties are compounded when the history of the religious tradition under examination is as long and complex as that of Judaism, Christianity or Islam. Nevertheless, in this chapter I seek to provide an objective account of the origins and subsequent evolution, up to the modern period, of the three Abrahamic faiths. While aspiring to be sensitive to the way in which these faiths are interpreted by many of their more traditional adherents, I make use of the resources and critical perspectives available to any early twenty-first-century scholar.

Let me begin, then, with Judaism, the first of the Abrahamic faiths to emerge from the Near East. After a brief account of Judaism's origins, I explain the key developments that occurred in the rabbinic period. I then discuss what I regard as some of the most significant features of Judaism in the medieval period. Finally, I provide a brief description of the three forms of Judaism that emerged during the nineteenth century – a time in which major changes began to appear within traditional Judaism.

Judaism

The Hebrew Scriptures, or the Tanakh,[1] a collection of short books held sacred by the Jews, are our primary source of knowledge regarding the origins of the tradition that today we call 'Judaism'. These texts contain ancient tales, familiar to many in the West, about the Israelites – who later became known as the Jews. The earliest books mention the activities of a semi-nomadic tribe from Mesopotamia (that is, modern Iraq).[2] The events purportedly referred to in the stories told about this tribe cannot be dated accurately. Historians estimate a date falling sometime between the twentieth and thirteenth centuries BC – in other words, between the middle and late Bronze Ages. Despite this uncertainty, many believe that the Judaic tradition began between 1900 and 1800 BC, when one of the semi-nomads, named Abram, left Mesopotamia for the land of Canaan (which is currently part of the State of Israel).[3] The Hebrew Scriptures relate that God spoke to Abram, informing him that he was to be the father of a nation, and instructing him to change his name to Abraham. They further claim that Abraham's response was to build an altar so that his people could worship God. Traditional Jews regard this encounter between God and Abraham as the beginning of the Jewish religion.

The Hebrew Scriptures also recount that Abraham's relationship with God was sealed with a covenant (in other words, a special agreement). Many texts emphasize that the covenant includes all the descendants of Abraham – the Israelites. It is pointed out in the Scriptures that Abraham's descendants were instructed by God to distinguish themselves from other peoples by the practice of male circumcision. Thus, circumcision came to be regarded as the outward sign that a man was included in the covenant. Even today, many Jews look upon circumcision as a necessary condition of a man's membership in the Jewish community.

Given how long ago the Israelites are said to have accepted the covenant, it is not surprising that people disagree about what happened to them next. According to the account provided by the Hebrew Scriptures, Abraham's descendants remained in Canaan for some time, eventually migrating to Egypt in an effort to escape a famine that was making life impossible in their adopted land. In Egypt they were enslaved by the reigning Pharaoh, from whose power Moses liberated them – but only with the help of the direct intervention of God. Most Jews and Christians have long accepted this traditional account, and have done so largely uncritically. Moreover, though with some variation, so have most Muslims. It is only fairly recently that, supported by certain archaeological discoveries, critical examination of the Hebrew Scriptures has led to the increasing acceptance of a slightly more complex account, which nowadays a significant number of people accept (and for which there seems to be more extra-Scriptural evidence than there is for the traditional one). According to this alternative account, in the thirteenth century BC, another group, who also claimed to be descendants of Abraham, joined Abraham's descendants in Canaan. This new group came from Egypt, from whence they had recently been liberated from slavery under the leadership of Moses. When the second group arrived in Canaan, they merged with the original group of Abraham's descendants. Together this ethnically diverse group came to form 'the people of Israel'.

Despite the fact that a growing number of Jews have come to accept some version of the non-traditional account, the traditional one remains influential within all forms of Judaism. Its influence is tangible in many of the practices that characterize Jewish lifestyles today. But perhaps the continuing influence of the traditional account is most pronounced in connection with the belief that God revealed the Torah – his law – during the exodus from Egypt. According to the traditional account, this revelation occurred while the Israelites were taking temporary refuge on Mount

Sinai. Traditional Jews believe that, through Moses, God revealed how they were expected to live up to their side of the covenant by respecting Ten Commandments.[4] This version of Moses' encounter with God on Mount Sinai has traditionally been regarded as the foundational event of Judaism. Remembrance of these purported events still bears huge significance within Judaism, and the veracity of the traditional account in respect of this has only relatively recently been seriously questioned by some Jews.

The traditional account of the history of the people of Israel continues with a series of tales about Joshua, a descendant of Moses. The Hebrew Scriptures relate that after almost 40 years, Joshua succeeded Moses. Under Joshua's leadership the land of Canaan was conquered and occupied. There followed a lengthy period of prophets and then kings. Despite an abundance of stories and legends, the history of these times is difficult to reconstruct accurately. Modern methods of textual analysis seem to show that in the early books of the Hebrew Scriptures many layers of tradition and myth are superimposed on one another.[5] Modern scholarship has also revealed that the Scriptures were written long after the events they purport to refer to ostensibly occurred. The story of the formation of the people of Israel and their movement into Canaan, for example, seems to have been written down in the eighth century BC. Moreover, the version of the Pentateuch[6] that we have today appears to have only been finalized in the fifth century BC. Fortunately, we are on firmer historical ground when it comes to the history of the Jewish people from the time of the incorporation of the land of Canaan into the Roman Empire.

Some 60 years before the beginning of the common era, the Jewish territories were conquered by Pompey, thereby falling under Roman rule. There was no large-scale revolt until that of AD 66–70, the climax of which came in AD 70 when the centre of Israelite worship, the Temple in Jerusalem, was destroyed by the occupying forces. The Roman occupation had brought with it not only political subjugation but also religious persecution. The prolonged occupation, along with the destruction of the Temple, rendered the practice of Judaism, as it had been known before, impossible. The events of AD 66–70 thus ushered in a new era of Judaic history – an era that would be dominated by the far-reaching and charismatic influence of rabbis (male Jews who formed part of a loosely defined class of religious teachers and scholars).

Consequently, what is now known as 'rabbinic Judaism' developed in direct response to the destruction of the Temple. Prior to this, Judaism had been a cultic religion revolving around a hereditary priesthood and an ancient system of animal sacrifice. In one blow, the destruction of the Temple made the sacrificial system impossible to administer, leaving the priestly caste redundant. Many Jews interpreted these events as God's way of punishing their people for their collective failure to live up to the covenant. In the face of this disaster, the rabbis ingeniously moulded

Judaism into a religion that focused on the family, the community and the sacred text, rather than on the priesthood, the sacrificial system and the Temple. There is no doubt that this innovation facilitated Judaism's survival as a diasporic religion – that is, as a religion whose adherents were dispersed throughout the known world.

The rabbinic period saw the popularization of many practices that are now widely regarded as characteristic of traditional Judaism. The rabbis, for example, established the widespread use of phylacteries. Phylacteries are small leather containers which Jewish men strap to their left arms and foreheads during prayer. The reason for this practice is to be found in the Book of Deuteronomy:

> Hear, O Israel! The LORD is our God, the LORD alone. You shall love the LORD your God with all your heart and with all your soul and with all your might. Take to heart these instructions with which I charge you this day. Impress them upon your children. Recite them when you stay at home and when you are away, when you lie down and when you get up. Bind them as a sign on your hand and let them serve as a symbol on your forehead; inscribe them on the doorposts of your house and on your gates.[7]

It is unclear how this text would have been understood in its original context, before the development of phylacteries as we know them today.[8] Nevertheless, on the strength of this biblical text, the rabbis made the use of phylacteries – which was previously a minority practice – widespread. The rabbis' promotion of this practice is a typical example of their strategy for developing a distinctive lifestyle by extrapolating from the core texts of their tradition. And they were successful in making the use of phylacteries one of the defining practices of the Jewish people. A similarly successful application of this strategy occurred when the rabbis took the basic food laws stipulated in the Pentateuch and systematically codified them into a rigorous system, the following of which characterizes traditional Jewish life to this day.

Ultimately, the lasting achievement of the rabbis was to have shaped a lifestyle that stood out starkly from non-Jewish ones. The rules that regulated this lifestyle also served to keep the Jewish community separate from the gentile, or non-Jewish, community. This is because it would have been impossible within a mixed community to follow all the rabbinic stipulations. From the rabbinic period onwards, a Jew was easily recognizable on account of his or her adherence to a specific lifestyle. Whether or not a person was a Jew was not decided principally on the basis of that person's beliefs. Rather, the key issue was whether or not the person in question was a member of the Jewish community. And that issue could largely be settled by examining his or her lifestyle.

In addition to codifying Jewish law ('*halakah*'), and establishing practices such as the use of phylacteries, the rabbis shaped Judaism in other ways that took it further away from its roots in a Temple-based, cultic religion.[9] The rabbis seem to have made no effort to keep the priesthood going. After the destruction of the Temple in Jerusalem, the priesthood was regarded as redundant, and rabbis themselves took on a more central role within the Jewish community. In line with this development, increasing importance was given to synagogues – local places of meeting and prayer. Synagogues had existed before the destruction of the Temple, but they had not occupied a particularly important place in the everyday life of the Jewish people. However, once the Temple was destroyed, synagogues became crucial because of their role in binding together local Jewish communities and providing a focus for their common religious life. This shift of emphasis from Temple to synagogue heralded another key change in Judaism: as sacrifice in the Temple became impossible, emphasis was put instead on prayer and study. The rabbis encouraged all male Jews to study their religious texts – principally the Torah; but in time the texts came to include the growing body of literature that developed during the rabbinic period.

Nevertheless, the primary religious text of rabbinic Judaism remained the Torah: namely, the first five books of the Tanakh. However, the rabbis must have come to believe that the Torah alone was insufficiently detailed to meet the needs of an increasingly diverse community. In response to this conviction, they began to compile the text known as the Mishnah in order to supplement the Torah. The earliest Mishnah is thought to date from about AD 200. It is not the work of a single author, but the product of multiple writers, compilers and editors. None of the rabbis ever claimed responsibility for the Mishnah. The received view was that, along with the written revelation given to Moses on Mount Sinai, there was also an oral revelation – a revelation thought to have been passed from generation to generation by word of mouth. However, after the destruction of the Temple, the rabbis felt that it was necessary to commit the oral revelation to writing so that it could better serve as a guide for the dispersed community.

In time it must have become too cumbersome to keep adding to the Mishnah, so the rabbis compiled another text – the Talmud.[10] The Talmud was to the Mishnah what the Mishnah was to the Torah: namely, a commentary and elaboration. Actually, two forms of the Talmud emerged. The earliest was the Jerusalem Talmud; and the Babylonian Talmud followed around a century later. Finally, the rabbis developed yet another level of textual tradition – the Midrash. This comprises a collection of inspiring sermons by popular rabbis. It also contains their interpretations of certain passages from the prophetic and other later writings included in the Tanakh. The date of the material that forms the

Midrash is uncertain – the earliest sections probably originating between the third and the sixth centuries AD.

By the end of the rabbinic period, then, Judaism had developed into a tradition that was supported by a four-tiered sequence of texts. This sequence, and its chronology, may be represented as follows:

Torah	>	Mishnah	>	Talmud	>	Midrash
		circa AD 200		Jerusalem		*circa* AD 200–500
				circa AD 400		
				Babylonian		
				circa AD 500		

These four texts formed the backbone of the Jewish community, providing it with the support that it had previously received from the Temple cult and its system of sacrifices and priests.

The sense of having a covenant with God that all Jews shared was another crucial aspect of the Judaism of this period. It buttressed a feeling of communal identity strong enough to carry the Jewish tradition through the centuries following the destruction of the Temple. It is difficult to determine how important the idea of living in a special relationship with God was within pre-rabbinic Judaism. But it is certain that it became especially prominent during the rabbinic period. We can conjecture that the rabbis needed some rationale to explain why the Jewish community alone had to bear the burden of a lifestyle that, under the close control of the rabbis, was becoming increasingly codified and, perhaps, onerous. The rabbis provided the required rationale by appealing to the old idea of the Lord's covenant with Israel, which was thought to have been passed on matrilineally through the generations since the time of the first patriarch, Abraham. The rabbis emphasized that, while the sign of the covenant was male circumcision, living according to the covenant required that a person keep the Law (that is, the Torah) as well as the oral law. In practice, obeying the Law meant that adult males were required to keep a covenant consisting of 613 commandments. And keeping these commandments was facilitated by the carefully regulated life of communal worship and prayer devised by the rabbis.[11]

Clearly, then, the rabbis did much to shape Judaism as a way of life. They emphasized the idea of the Lord's covenant with the Jewish people and went into explicit detail about how it ought to be fulfilled. However, beyond a staunch commitment to monotheism, the rabbis were not greatly concerned with the content of Jewish belief. They seem to have revelled in rivalling each other in interpretations of the Scriptures, and, on the whole, were remarkably tolerant of diverse theological opinions. The formal elucidation of Jewish beliefs had to wait until the post-rabbinic period (that is, until after the close of the sixth century AD). Ironically, in the post-rabbinic period – precisely when the core features of the Jewish belief system were being consolidated – various distinctive forms of Judaism began to evolve.[12]

From the beginning of the seventh century AD, Jewish communities rapidly formed in the urban centres of Europe. They were, however, often disadvantaged, as their members were not protected by the laws of the lands in which they resided. Rehearsing the troubled history of Europe's Jewish communities would take us too far afield. Suffice it to say that these communities often fell victim to sporadic outbreaks of anti-Semitism. Not infrequently, entire Jewish communities would be forced to evacuate the place that they had settled and move to a new environment that seemed to promise more security.[13] Such forced migrations peaked in the fifteenth century AD, when Jewish communities were compelled to leave a host of places where they had become established.

It is widely held that Jewish communities in Europe fared better in the Muslim territories than in the Christian ones, because Islamic law offered protection to Jews resident within Muslim countries.[14] Jews in Muslim Spain, for example, were part of an intellectually and economically flourishing community. When Granada finally fell to the Christians in 1492, this hitherto flourishing community was hit by what was to become one of the most notorious expulsions of Jews in European history. The persecution of Jews in Europe continued throughout the medieval period – one result being the invention of the ghetto, or walled-in Jewish quarter, which became a standard feature of many European urban centres.

Against the background of this traumatic history, European Judaism developed considerably during the Middle Ages. The outstanding intellectual motivating this development was the philosopher Moses ibn Maimon, better known as Moses Maimonides (AD 1135–1204). Maimonides spent the first part of his life in Muslim Spain – in the city of Cordoba, to be precise – where he was a slightly younger contemporary and an avid admirer of the great Muslim philosopher ibn Rushd.[15] Maimonides experienced religious persecution at first hand, having to flee Cordoba along with his family in 1148. After wandering from town to town in Spain for several years, in 1160 they arrived in Fez (in North Africa). However, they failed to find peace and security in Fez, and had to flee after Maimonides' teacher Judah ha-Kohen ibn Susan was assassinated. Eventually, the family settled in Fostat (now known as Cairo), where Maimonides was to write his most famous work, *The Guide of the Perplexed*.[16]

Maimonides' principal interest lay in the elusive connection between faith and reason. By means of philosophy, he attempted to provide rational grounds for adhering to Jewish beliefs. In other words, he aimed to demonstrate that Judaism was a rational religion, intellectually superior to the superstitious religion of his contemporary Christians. Although much of Maimonides' philosophy is now of only historical interest,[17] he still stands as the intellectual authority behind the 13 principles of belief which all 'Orthodox' Jews are supposed to accept. Under the influence of ibn Rushd – who had attempted to establish a similar list for Muslims – Maimonides set out to capture the essence of Jewish belief in a system of propositions. According to Maimonides, all Jews should believe:[18]

1 In the existence of God.
2 In the unity of God.
3 In the incorporeality of God.
4 In the eternity of God.
5 That worship is due to God alone.
6 In prophecy.
7 That Moses was the greatest of the prophets.
8 That the Torah is divine.
9 That the Torah is unchangeable.
10 That God is omniscient (all-knowing).
11 In post-mortem retribution or reward for one's actions in this life.
12 In the future coming of the Messiah.
13 In the resurrection of the dead.[19]

Furnished with Maimonides' 13 principles, Judaism entered modernity. The French Revolution of 1789 was a landmark for European Jewish communities as it set in motion the slow process of social and political integration in countries that had for centuries regarded Jews as aliens. The new intellectual trends that swept across Western Europe during the Enlightenment had a profound effect on Judaism. In fact, the Jewish people experienced an Enlightenment of their own, known as the *Haskalah*.[20] From this time on, the already fragmented Jewish community began to splinter further, as sections of the community responded to modernity in a host of different ways. Three distinctive forms of Judaism arose in the nineteenth century, and these were to exert a huge impact on the shape of Judaism in the twentieth century.

Reform Judaism, a foundational figure of which being Abraham Geiger (1820–74), was the first of these new forms of Judaism to develop. It began modestly as some Jews, belonging to synagogues in Germany, sought to modernize their liturgy. The early Reform Jews wanted to replace the customary use of ancient Hebrew (which few of them understood) with the vernacular as the language of prayer, and to incorporate a choir and an organ into their synagogue meetings. The movement quickly developed and spread from Germany to England – where the West London Reform Synagogue was founded in 1841 – and to the New World. As time passed, its programme for reform became more far-reaching. The definitive expression of the mature movement was issued in 1885 at a meeting of Reform rabbis in Pittsburgh. A key part of the defining statement of Reform Judaism issued at Pittsburgh reads:

> We recognize in the Mosaic legislation a system of training the Jewish people for its mission during its national life in Palestine, and today we accept as binding only its moral laws and maintain only such ceremonies as elevate and sanctify our lives, but reject all such as are not adapted to the views and habits of modern civilization. ... We hold that all such Mosaic and rabbinical laws as regular diet, priestly purity, and dress originated in ages and under the influence of ideas entirely foreign to our present mental and spiritual states. ... Their observance in our day is apt rather to obstruct than to further modern spiritual elevation. ... We recognize in the modern era of universal culture of heart and intellect the approaching of the realization of Israel's great messianic hope for the establishment of the kingdom of truth, justice, and peace among all men. We consider ourselves no longer a nation but a religious community and therefore expect neither a return to Palestine nor a sacrificial worship under the sons of Aaron not the restoration of any of the laws concerning the Jewish state. ...[21]

This statement provides a succinct account of the main principles of Reform Judaism. Jewish law, sacrosanct and unchangeable according to previous Jewish tradition, is to be selectively discarded. All laws that are unsuited to life in the modern world are to be cast aside in the interests of making Judaism into a religion suitable for modern men and women.

In practice, those laws which tended to reinforce the separation of Jews from gentiles were the first to be rejected. Moreover, the idea that Judaism was an expression of universal culture was vigorously promoted. Thinkers associated with this movement thus strove to reduce Judaism to a few, supposedly universal, principles: in effect, they sought to represent Judaism as ethical monotheism. The traditional hope of Judaism for the return of the people of Israel to their ancient homeland thus came to be represented as a hope for all humankind: for a kingdom of 'truth, justice, and peace'. Gone was the eschatological desire to return to Palestine and to restore the ancient Temple and the associated systems of priesthood and sacrifice. Reform Jews were aware of the incongruity between their traditional prayer, in which they expressed desire to return to their homeland, and the reality of their commitment to their lives within their adopted countries. They chose, therefore, to abandon the former,[22] and to commit themselves fully to their European (and, later, North American) homelands. And they embraced the consequence of this choice when they agreed to stop regarding Israel as a 'nation' and, instead, to portray it as a 'religious community'. The implication of this was that Judaism was to become a self-conscious 'religion', rather than simply a way of life – moreover, a religion that was to be on a par with the various forms of Christianity, a religion fully at home in the pluralist, liberal democratic cultures of the modern Western European nations.

Modern Orthodox Judaism, by contrast, and key to whose formation was Samson Raphael Hirsch (1808–88), initially developed as a reaction to what was perceived as the excesses of Reform Judaism. Despite this, like Reform Judaism, it sought the integration of Jews within broader society and culture. As Jacob Neusner explains:

> The formation of [Modern] Orthodox Judaism as an articulated Judaic system took place when integrationists proposed an alternative to Reform Judaism. They concurred with the Reformers on the basic social policy of integration, but they differed from them on how integration was to be worked out.[23]

Reacting to the Reformer's apparent willingness to concede the provisionality of even those elements of the tradition that previously had been regarded as most sacrosanct, the Modern Orthodox reiterated the traditional view that Judaism derived from God's revelation at Sinai, and hence could not be changed. But this appeal to tradition was a highly self-conscious one, and, arguably, that is what distinguishes the Modern Orthodox Judaism that emerged in nineteenth-century Europe from the traditional form of Judaism that existed prior to this time.

Another, related feature of Modern Orthodox Judaism both reveals its affinity with Reform Judaism as well as divergence from previous Judaism. Namely, Modern Orthodox Judaism, like Reform Judaism and unlike previous Judaism, was premised upon a distinction between the religious and the secular domains. Acceptance of this distinction entailed that Judaism was now seen as a 'religion', having to do explicitly with the religious realm rather than with the secular realm, and that, as such, it paralleled other religions such as Christianity and Islam. Neusner argues that acceptance of this distinction is symptomatic of the wide conceptual gulf separating Modern Orthodox Judaism (and, indeed, other nineteenth-century Judaisms) from the tradition prior to this point in time. For prior to this, Jews had perceived the whole of their lives as regulated by the Torah – a regulated lifestyle that was not regarded as a 'religion', but simply as a 'given' way of life.[24] In accepting the distinction between the religious and the secular, Modern Orthodox Jews were able to distinguish a part of life which was Jewish from a part which was secular. They could then, Neusner argues, retain traditional attitudes and lifestyles with respect to the former, while living just like everyone else in modern society with respect to the latter.

Clearly, with regard to their different views on the susceptibility of Judaism to change, Reform Judaism and Modern Orthodox Judaism stand at opposite ends of the currently prevailing spectrum of interpretations. Not surprisingly, then, some thinkers felt unsatisfied with these alternatives, and sought to create a form of Judaism that took a stance mid-way between the seeming extremes of Reform and Modern Orthodoxy. The result was Conservative Judaism, a foundational figure of which being Louis Ginzberg (1873–1953). In brief, Conservatives wished to retain a higher level of observance of Jewish Law than did the Reformers but without commitment to what was perceived as the unduly rigid standpoint of the Modern Orthodox. The Conservative movement was thus led to emphasize orthopraxy (orthodox behaviour) over orthodox belief. Conservative Jews thus managed to retain the veneer of a traditional Jewish lifestyle without commitment to those theological beliefs that struck many moderns as increasingly untenable. Thus, Ginzberg declared that Judaism 'teaches a way of life and not a theology'.[25] The result of this view was a seemingly paradoxical indifference to the worldview that nourished the tradition, combined with a staunch commitment to the lifestyle that developed alongside that worldview.

One key difference between these three forms of Judaism that developed in the nineteenth century, as well as between these and the previous tradition, concerns their respective views of revelation. As Neusner explains, prior to the nineteenth century, the tradition

> maintained that not only the Hebrew Scriptures ('Old Testament') but also the entire canon of rabbinic writings constituted that one whole Torah that Moses received at Sinai. The three Judaisms of the nineteenth century met that issue head on. Each of the possibilities – only Scripture, everything, some things but not others – found proponents. The consequent theory of revelation had to explain the origin and authority of each of the components of the received canon. And, further, that theory of revelation had to explain what, precisely, revelation meant. The position of [Modern] Orthodoxy on this matter takes on significance only in the larger context of the debate with Reform. Reform through Geiger took the view that revelation was progressive. The Bible derived from 'the religious genius of the Jewish people'. [Modern] Orthodoxy through Hirsch as the example saw the Torah as wholly and completely God's word. A middle position, represented by Conservative Judaism, espoused both views. God revealed the written Torah, which was supplemented by 'the ongoing revelation manifesting itself throughout history in the spirit of the Jewish people'.[26]

These three forms of Judaism, characterized by their distinctive views of revelation, were bequeathed to the twentieth century by the thinkers of the nineteenth. Indeed, Jews at the beginning of the twenty-first century have inherited a religious tradition that is defined according to the terms established by these three nineteenth-century systems of Judaism.

Let us now turn to the origins and development of the next form of Abrahamic monotheism to emerge from the Near East: Christianity.

Christianity

Jesus of Nazareth, a Jew who lived in Palestine under the Roman occupation at the beginning of the common era, stands as the founder of the Jewish movement that evolved into Christianity.[27] A carpenter by profession, Jesus appears to have led an unremarkable life until he was about 27 years old. At this time he began a career of public preaching, attracting a small but dedicated following from among his contemporary co-religionists. However, after only three years, his preaching career was suddenly cut short due to his execution by crucifixion in Jerusalem by the Roman authorities.

Christians typically believe that Jesus was the Son of God, and that he was the agent chosen by God the Father to save humanity. Typically, they further believe that during his life he performed a number of miracles, which revealed his divine nature. But most importantly, Christians typically believe that three days after his execution, he returned to life before ascending to heaven, where he reigns at the right-hand side of God. The belief in the resurrection is especially important, for if Jesus had returned from the dead, then this event shows the possibility of an afterlife.

So little has been established with any certainty about the historical figure of Jesus that some scholars have entertained serious doubts about whether or not he existed.[28] Our lack of knowledge is compounded by the fact that Jesus, himself, wrote nothing. Consequently, what is known about him has to be gleaned from what remains of the short texts that were composed and circulated by his admirers after his death. These texts, which are not extant in their original form, purport to describe Jesus' words and deeds as people who had known him remembered them. Eventually, these texts were collected together and substantially edited to form the first part of what was to become the Christian Scriptures (known to later Christians as the 'New Testament'). These Scriptures constitute our primary source of historical knowledge about early Christianity. Within them, the development of the movement begun by Jesus can be traced as it grew further apart from Judaism, and finally broke away completely. The core of these Scriptures comprises four Gospels that are known by the names Matthew, Mark, Luke and John.[29] Mark is probably the oldest, dating from within about ten years of Jesus' death (c. AD 40). Matthew and Luke probably reached their final form 20 to 30 years later (c. AD 60–70). Finally, John was compiled perhaps 60 years after the death of Jesus (c. AD 90). The histories of the various Christian communities, during their formative years, are partially recorded in several letters that also form part of the Christian Scriptures.[30]

The religious titles that Christians gave to Jesus, such as 'Messiah' and 'Christ',[31] betray Christianity's origins in the Judaism of the first century of the common era. Not only was early Christianity infused with Jewish religious concepts, it appears that many early Christians soon came to believe that the Christian community was the 'new Israel'. A large number of early Christians seem to have thought that, because the Jewish people had failed to recognize the Messiah, God had rejected his former people and chosen a new one. This negative appraisal of Judaism did not, however, prevent the new Christian movement from adopting the Hebrew Scriptures as their own, thereby preserving for posterity Christianity's link with the Judaism of the past. Indeed, for many early Christians, the Scriptures simply were the Hebrew Scriptures. This has meant that, even today, the Hebrew Scriptures remain an important part of most Christian religious ceremonies, and the stories they contain continue to colour the imagination of many Christians.

Despite the many similarities between the new Christian movement and contemporary Judaism, members of the former rapidly came to hold some quite distinctive beliefs. Most of these beliefs concerned Jesus, his relationship to God, and his role in God's plan for the world. In the Christian Scriptures, Jesus is referred to in a number of ways. In addition to the titles mentioned above, other titles are introduced – for example, 'Lord', 'Word of God', and 'Son of God'. However, the most striking and distinctive claim made about Jesus in the New Testament is probably this: 'For God so loved the world that he gave his only Son, so that everyone who believes in him may not perish but may have eternal life.'[32]

This claim raises a question that vexed many in the early stages of Christianity's evolution into a world religion, and which continues to be debated by Christians to this day: How can Jesus be a human being and at the same time be the Son of God? This was no mere academic issue to the fledgling Christian community, as its members were often accused of blasphemy because they appeared to be worshipping a man rather than God. Blasphemy was a serious charge in the ancient world, and it often resulted in the accused person being severely punished. In the face of this, early Christians strove to refine their conception of the relation between God and Jesus. A lively, and often passionate, debate ensued about these matters, and at an early stage of the debate, it became clear that what many Christians wanted to say about Jesus was incompatible with the claims most Jews would accept. This divergence of views precipitated the break between the new Christian movement and Judaism. Another factor contributing to this break was a dispute about whether or not converts to the new movement ought to obey Jewish Law. Christians came to be identified as the group who held, against other Jews, that converts need not follow Jewish Law, and that Jesus was the Messiah whom God had sent to the Jewish people.

Once the Christian movement had broken away from Judaism – a break facilitated by the destruction of the Temple and the subsequent scattering of the Jewish community – it entered what is now known as its patristic period. This period began after the various books and letters which form the Christian Scriptures were completed (about AD 100), and it is conventionally thought to have ended in AD 451 – the year in which an important Church Council took place in Chalcedon (in present-day Turkey). Some key theological developments occurred during this period, and they culminated in the formulation of the foundational doctrines of Christianity.[33] If one is to understand Christianity as it exists today, it is essential to possess some familiarity with these developments. As we shall see below, during this period, theologians, monks and politicians defined what was to count as orthodox Christian belief.

The first concern of Christian thinkers in the patristic period was apologetics – that is, the reasoned defence and justification of the Christian faith against it critics. *Apologia* was perceived to be vitally important because, in the second and third centuries of the common era, Christians often fell victim to brutal persecution. At times, the persecution was so severe that the continued existence of the Christian movement was threatened.[34] It is no surprise, then, that intellectually inclined Christians were concerned to explain and defend their faith. The most famous theologians from this apologetic period are Justin Martyr (*c.* AD 100–65), Irenaeus of Lyons (*c.* AD 130–200), and Origen (*c.* AD 185–*c.* 254). The apologetic works from this time can often be recognized by their titles – Justin Martyr's most famous work, for example, was simply called *Apology*.[35] Irenaeus of Lyon contributed a book called *Against the Heresies*. This was a tract against Gnosticism – an esoteric cult, which grew into a powerful rival to orthodox Christianity in the ancient world. Origen's most famous apologetic work is called *Against Celsus*. (Celsus was a pagan philosopher, and the author of the first known hostile critique of Christianity.)

The apologetic period ended in AD 311, when Christianity was given the status of a legal religion within the Roman Empire. Shortly afterwards, the Emperor Constantine converted to Christianity. Once Christianity became not only tolerated but also legally protected, its intellectuals no longer had to devote their energy to apologetics. They were able to turn their attention to the substantive content of Christian beliefs, and begin the process of clarification. In so doing, they defined the boundaries of orthodoxy. The centuries following AD 311 consequently saw a series of Church Councils that proposed and ratified doctrines regarding core aspects of the Christian faith – principally doctrines concerning the nature of God and the identity of Jesus.

Prior to these Councils, there was no one standardized set of beliefs that all Christians were expected to hold. Ideas had been developed by different theologians and accepted by different communities as the need for them arose. But there had been little attempt to systematize all the diverse things that people believed. Individual theologians had simply taken whichever early Christian texts were available to them, and elaborated on the hints and suggestions they found in them about the identity of Jesus and his role in God's plan. However, it is notable that, even at this early stage, two views concerning the nature of Jesus had already been condemned: ebionitism (the view that Jesus was an ordinary human being);[36] and docetism (the view that Jesus was totally divine, and only appeared to be human). Ebionitism and docetism are clearly opposite views, and both approaches were condemned as heretical in the second century AD. In other words, people holding either of these views were no longer regarded as part of the Christian community. But apart from the condemnation of ebionitism and docetism, there was a marked lack of consensus about what Christians were supposed to believe about Jesus and his relation to God. Moreover, this lack of consensus increasingly led to outbreaks of violence within the Christian community – making travel through the Empire difficult, particularly in Palestine.

Constantine appears to have found this incendiary situation intolerable. Consequently, on becoming Emperor, he prioritized the formulation of doctrines that as wide a swathe of the Christian community as possible could agree on. He probably regarded Christian doctrine as politically important because consensus among Christians would likely contribute to a social stability that would, in turn, facilitate political unity. Thus, Constantine's desire for theological consensus ushered in the second – the post-apologetic – phase of the patristic period. During this phase, *apologia* was no longer the principal concern of theologians. Instead, their efforts were geared towards reaching theological agreement on doctrinal issues. In short, this was a time characterized by extensive theological debate, as rival views were explored and assessed.

Two Church Councils stand out in this period; both of them having a monumental impact on Western and Eastern Christianity. Constantine, himself, convened the first, the Council of Nicea, in AD 325. The second, the Council of Chalcedon, was convened in AD 451.[37] The principal aim of those attending these Councils was to clarify the orthodox Christian conception of the person of Christ. Although the two Councils shared this aim, there was a significant difference in their approach. At the Council of Nicea, the debate was about whether, and in what sense, Jesus was divine. In other words, the principal issue concerned the *relation of Jesus to God*. By contrast, the debate at the Council of Chalcedon presupposed

Jesus' divinity, and focused instead on clarifying the *relation between the human and the divine within Jesus*.

Three hundred and eighteen bishops and theologians gathered at the Council of Nicea, and together they produced the Nicene Creed – one of the earliest known official Christian testaments of faith. In its most important section, the Creed announces that Christians believe

> in one Lord Jesus Christ, the Son of God, begotten of the Father as only begotten, that is from the reality of the Father, God from God, Light from Light, true God from true God, begotten not created, of the same reality as the Father, through whom all things came into being, both in heaven and in earth; Who for us humans and for our salvation came down and was incarnate, becoming human.[38]

The Nicene Creed, however, does not stop with this positive statement of what Christians believe. It also contains a list of propositions that it is unacceptable for a Christian to hold: 'those who ... assert that he, the Son of God, is of a different subsistence or reality, or that he is created, or changeable, or mutable, the Catholic and Apostolic Church anathematises them [i.e., excludes them from the community]'.[39]

Those present at the Council of Nicea thus endorsed the claim that Jesus was co-equal to God the Father. In other words, they declared Jesus to be of the same reality as God. However, and not surprisingly, this claim heralded considerable confusion in the period following the Council. To understand why the members of the Council agreed to this way of describing Jesus' relation to God, we need to consider the view they rejected.

When the Council of Nicea was convened, there was a particular controversy rattling the foundations of the young Church: the Arian controversy. Moreover, the controversy surrounding Arianism is now widely regarded as one of the most momentous in the history of Christianity. And there is no doubt that, from the standpoint of the Church, it was the main heresy of the fourth century. Arianism was perceived as such a serious threat to the Church that the Council of Nicea was summoned precisely in order to refute it. Arius (*c.* AD 250–336), the thinker behind the controversy, was a Christian theologian and a popular preacher. By no means a figure on the margins of Christianity, he was in charge of one of the main churches in Alexandria, which was one of the most important centres of Christianity at this time. Arius seems to have thought that, with respect to their beliefs about Jesus, many Christians had, in effect, lost touch with reality. He regarded this as acutely dangerous to the faith because it rendered Christianity absurd in the minds of those pagan intellectuals who might otherwise have found it attractive. By freeing Christianity from the more incredible claims made on its behalf, he hoped to enhance its appeal to the educated pagan public of his day. In order to do so, he began by arguing that the titles used of Jesus in the

Scriptures were merely titles of honour, or courtesy titles, that were not meant to suggest that Jesus was divine. Taking it for granted that God is the *one* source of all created things, he reasoned that God cannot be *both* Father and Son. He therefore concluded that, contrary to what many Christians believed, the 'Son' was a creature, and therefore should not be referred to as 'God'.

Controversy raged over Arius' claim that Jesus was not divine. Athanasius (*c.* AD 296–373), a contemporary Alexandrian, passionately rose to the challenge, and set about discrediting Arius' views. Athanasius' main counter-argument was a simple one, although it proved to be remarkably persuasive. It is based on two premises that he holds all Christians should agree with. The first premise is that only God can save creatures; the second premise is that Jesus saves creatures. From the first premise, Athanasius deduced that if Jesus is not God, then he cannot save us. But the second premise states that he can. Thus, Athanasius arrived at the conclusion that the Son – Jesus – must therefore be God. Athanasius' view proved to be more successful than that of Arius – so much so, in fact, that Arius was disgraced, while Athanasius was elected Bishop of Alexandria in AD 328. The story did not end there, however; for Athanasius was eventually deposed from his bishopric on account of his opposition to Arianism, only to have his views declared orthodox after his death. The turbulent fortunes of Athanasius demonstrate how changeable was the perception of what was, and what was not, acceptable theology during this period. Nowadays, Athanasius is generally regarded as the foremost interpreter of the position endorsed at Nicea. His view – namely, that the Son can be distinct from the Father without being any less the divine being – came to be regarded by many later generations of Christians as the position agreed upon at the Council of Nicea.

As opinion had swayed towards Athanasius' view and against Arius, those present at the Council of Nicea chose to describe Jesus and God as sharing 'the same reality' (*homoousios*). However, despite their agreement on this way of putting things, there is little reason to think that all present had the same understanding of what '*homoousios*' meant. Indeed, virtually as soon as the Council of Nicea closed, debate ensued about the meaning of what had been agreed upon. This debate became so fractious that, well over a century after the Council of Nicea, another Council was called to try to settle the matter again. At the Council of Chalcedon, in AD 451, a group of Church leaders managed to agree on the following statement, which, although it did not settle all the disagreements,[40] subsequently became the benchmark of Christian orthodoxy:

> Therefore, following the holy Fathers, we all with one accord teach to acknowledge one and the same Son, our Lord Jesus Christ, at once complete in Godhead and complete in humanity, truly God and truly

human, consisting also of a rational soul and body; of the same reality as the Father as regards his Godhead, and at the same time of the same reality as us as regards his humanity; like us in all respects, apart from sin; as regards his Godhead, begotten of the Father before the ages, but yet as regards his humanity begotten, for us and for our salvation, of Mary the Virgin, the God-bearer; one and the same Christ, Son, Lord, Only-begotten, recognized in two natures, without confusion, without change, without division, without separation; the distinction of natures being in no way annulled by the union, but rather the characteristics of each nature being preserved and coming together to form one person and subsistence, not as parted or separated into two persons, but one and the same Son and Only-begotten, God the Word, Lord Jesus Christ; even as the prophets from earliest times spoke of him, and our Lord Jesus Christ himself taught us, and the creed of the Fathers has handed down to us.[41]

While these doctrinal debates were taking place, many of those involved in them were also busy solidifying the institutional structure of the Church. The first Christians had believed that Jesus would return very soon, and that this would signal the end of the world. Many found it quite shocking when the first generation of Christians had passed away, and yet Jesus had not returned. In time, most Christians abandoned the belief that the end of the world was imminent.[42] Given their situation, it seemed to many Christians that their community was destined to preserve the content of the faith that had been passed from the original followers of Jesus so that it could be transmitted from generation to generation. The idea quickly gained ground that the genuine content of faith could only be preserved for posterity if it was personally handed down from one person to another in an unbroken succession traceable back to Jesus. This core idea – that the content of faith must be transmitted through a succession of people – led to the formation of a special category of Christians who were regarded as key players in this succession. Those in this category became known as bishops. Consecration as a bishop signified that a man had received the genuine content of the faith, and was now, himself, in a position to pass it on.

As Christianity attracted a growing number of adherents, Christian communities proliferated in the Eastern and Western parts of the Roman Empire. In order to ensure that the members of these communities all had access to the genuine content of the faith, many felt that it was necessary to organize them into geographical groupings, and put each group under the leadership of a bishop. Thus, incrementally, the institutional machinery of Christianity was put in place. Originally 12 principal centres of Christianity were recognized. Each was a place associated with one of Jesus' 12 earliest followers. Gradually, however, throughout the fourth and fifth centuries, Constantinople and Rome emerged as the two main centres of Christianity. When the Emperor Constantine moved the centre of the Roman Empire away from Rome to the small city of Byzantium, which he re-named Constantinople,[43] this city naturally became the administrative centre of the Christian Church. Ironically, just at the time when Christianity began to enjoy importance in Rome, Rome ceased to be important to the Empire: the centre of both the Empire and Christianity was now Constantinople.

From this time on, relations between those in power in the Western and Eastern parts of the Empire became increasingly strained. This was largely due to the difficulty of administering the western part of the Empire from Constantinople. One side-effect was that the leaders of the Western Church, who were still in Rome, became less dependent on the authority of the Church leaders in Constantinople. The origin of the subsequent split between the Eastern and Western branches of Christianity lies here. Despite the fact that the Patriarch in Constantinople was recognized as the leader of the whole Church by Christians in the East and the West, the Christian leader in Rome gradually became the *de facto* leader of Christianity in the West. Less than a century after the relocation of Constantine's government from Rome to Constantinople, the leader of the Church at Rome had adopted the title 'supreme pontiff'.

During the Middle Ages, the power of the Roman papacy spread throughout Western Europe. Those groups who refused to acknowledge the papacy were effectively excluded from shaping Western Europe's history. A landmark in the weakening relations between the Eastern and Western branches of Christianity came in AD 800 when Pope Leo III crowned Charlemagne Emperor of the Holy Roman Empire, despite the fact that the Empire still had an emperor in the east. Thus the stage was set for Western Europe to break away politically from Eastern Europe. (Formally, the separation occurred several centuries later. But the significant event was the installation of an independent Western emperor.)

The fracturing of Christianity in Eastern Europe was spurred along by its encounter with Islam, as well as by the scandalous fourth crusade in which Christians from the West pillaged and sacked Constantinople. In Eastern Europe, the political influence of Christianity drained away – a slow process culminating in AD 1453 when Constantinople was conquered by the Ottoman Turks, and officially became an Islamic city. Although the political influence of the Christians in Constantinople was drastically reduced as a result of the Muslim takeover, the ecumenical Patriarchate of Constantinople continued to be honoured by Eastern Orthodox Christians – and this has continued into our time.[44] The other feature that has continued into our time is, of course, the split between Eastern and Western Christianity. There has been no significant progress towards reconciliation. Recently, however, the ecumenical movement

– which is a movement to facilitate discussion across church boundaries – has helped to increase mutual understanding.

The Reformation of Western Christianity in the sixteenth century further contributed to the schism between the two estranged branches of the Christian tradition. Throughout the Middle Ages, reform movements sporadically emerged and faded within Western Christianity. The most significant of these periods of reform is, retrospectively, simply called 'the Reformation'. Until the Reformation proper, reform movements had come predominantly from within the papal hierarchy or from within monastic communities, and had aimed to reform these structures from within. This changed during the Reformation, when the zeal of the reformers was turned against the papacy and monasticism themselves. The Reformation was, at root, directed against internal corruption, chiefly that of the bishop of Rome (the pope), the monastic orders and the clerics. The reformers, principal among whom being Martin Luther (1483–1546) and John Calvin (1509–64), wanted to recover what they saw as the original message of the Bible. Although the reform movement began *within* the established Western Church, it soon became clear that the reformers' ideals demanded a radical break from the old ecclesial structures and teaching of the past. Thus Protestantism was born.

'Protestant' is a term that has come to be applied to a variety of quite distinct Christian churches, all emerging in the period of Reformation or in response to ideas popularized in this period. These churches embrace a diverse range of beliefs and practices. Some Protestant churches are ideologically closer to the pre-Reformation Church than to other Protestant groups. Mainstream Protestant churches continue to hold the core beliefs of pre-Reformation Christianity – specifically, beliefs about the nature of God and the identity of Jesus. But they differ from traditional Western Christianity in their conception of the Church, particularly regarding the role of the papacy. The crux of the difference between Protestant churches and the pre-Reformation Church, however, lies in their different convictions concerning who has authority over religious beliefs and practices. Protestants typically do not allow any authority, be it papal or that of the tradition, to determine how they should live – only the Bible can do that, they maintain.

It would be a mistake, however, to regard the Reformation as having no impact on what remained of the original pre-Reformation Western Church. This Church is identified by many today as the 'Roman Catholic Church'[45] – a name that reflects the fact that its administrative and spiritual centre is still located in Rome. Less well known is the extent to which the Roman Catholic Church was itself transformed during the period of Reformation. In 1545, its leaders convened the Council of Trent. The aim of those attending this Council was to formulate a response to the reformers' criticisms of the established Christian belief-system and ecclesial institutions within Western Europe. The results of this Council were far-reaching, to say the least. In fact, the form of Roman Catholicism practised today is no less a product of the Reformation than are the various Protestant churches.

The radical transformation that Christianity underwent in this period was accompanied by a wave of religious persecutions in which many Protestants and Catholics died on account of their beliefs. Unlike the persecutions experienced in former times, these were inflicted on the Christian community by those within its ranks against their co-religionists who interpreted the faith differently. Thus, Roman Catholics persecuted Protestants, Protestants persecuted Roman Catholics, and different groups of Protestants persecuted each other. Not surprisingly, religious persecution in Western Europe encouraged emigration to the New World. Thus, both Protestant and Catholic forms of Christianity became established in the Americas.[46]

Arguably, the reformers' rejection of the authority of the leaders of the Roman Church served as a precedent for the wholesale rejection of authority that swept Western Europe in the Enlightenment. The term 'Enlightenment' signifies the historical period, following the Reformation, in which a significant number of leading thinkers felt that humanity had lived under superstition and mystification for too long.[47] The enlightened thinkers of this age wished to subject all beliefs to critical appraisal. Everything, they declared, was to be illuminated by the light of reason.

During the Enlightenment, Christian texts and traditions were re-examined from the perspectives opened up by newly developed methods of historical criticism.[48] The notion that the Scriptures contained revelation that had come directly from the mouth of God was radically undermined. This challenge to the authority of the sacred texts led many to question the legitimacy of the unique place that Christianity, as the official religion of the Roman Empire, had come to occupy in Western society. Consequently, belief in Christianity's special status gradually eroded. Church and state became recognized as separate entities, and Western society began to be more tolerant of non-Christian religions as well as of the many varieties of Christianity that had developed by this time. Religious liberty became a social and political ideal towards the end of the eighteenth century. This process was facilitated by the proliferation of different Christian denominations in the wake of the Reformation. The main non-Roman Catholic forms of post-Reformation Christianity were Lutheranism, Calvinism (the Reformed Church) and Anabaptism. Each of these forms of Christianity claimed that the ultimate court of appeal in religious matters was the judgement of the individual Christian. One consequence of their commitment to this claim was that each of these congregations was vulnerable to division. Every theological disagreement could, potentially, spawn a new church – and many did. Thus, an increasing number of Christian denominations competed for adherents, and thereby embarrassed the desires of many for Church unity. Moreover, as we shall see in Chapter 10, this process of fragmentation continued unabated into the twentieth century, when it was given new momentum by the explosion of Christian fundamentalism.

While the fragmentation of Christianity in the modern period was unprecedented in its extent, the Christian tradition, as we have seen in this chapter, has been no stranger to change. Throughout its nearly 2,000 year long life-span, Christianity has taken on a wide variety of forms. Not surprisingly, then, the content of Christian belief has changed considerably over time, and nowadays one looks in vain among different groups of Christians for agreement about the content of the Christian faith. Nevertheless, despite the lack of agreement, there are some key beliefs and practices that mark people out as Christian. For example, as we have seen, early Christians placed a great deal of importance on the figure of Jesus of Nazareth, and Christians today continue to regard Jesus as central to their faith. Most Christians still hold that Jesus is the Son of God. And many, but not all, hold the doctrine of the Trinity, according to which the one God is, in an important sense, three persons: Father, Son and Spirit. Many Christians regard the doctrine of the Trinity as the central teaching of the Christian faith.

Over the last century, at least, the percentage of the population of Europe confessing Christian faith has fallen dramatically. But, despite falling numbers, Christianity still remains the religion with the largest following within Europe and North America. However, a new phenomenon has sprung up in the West over the past century: Islam has now become the religion with the second largest following within Western Europe. This is mainly due to immigration from Islamic countries, but there are also a growing number of Western converts. France is the country in Western Europe with the highest proportion of Muslims relative to the total population; some three million Muslims are estimated to reside there. Germany and the United Kingdom also both have a strong Muslim presence. Similarly, there is a growing Muslim community in North America.[49] In the United States, the Muslim population is currently on the verge of outnumbering the Jewish population, and many believe that this has already happened in Canada.[50]

Of course, Christianity did not undergo its evolution in total isolation either from Judaism, its 'mother-tradition', or from Islam, its 'sister-tradition'. As we have seen, in the earliest days of the Christian movement, Christians began to define themselves in a way that distinguished them from Jews. A similar process began to take place as Christians encountered the Muslim faith in the early Middle Ages. So let us now turn to Islam – the last of the family of Abrahamic monotheisms to emerge from the Near East.

Islam

In the early seventh century AD, the religious movement that we now know as Islam began to take shape in Arabia. This movement, set in motion by Muhammad (c. AD 570–632),[51] developed out of the predominantly pagan indigenous culture of the region. At this time, most of the population of Arabia belonged to nomadic tribes. There were, however, some non-nomadic tribes in small towns, such as Mecca. Despite its size, Mecca had recently developed into a lively commercial centre. It was also a site of religious pilgrimage, hosting an important shrine called the Ka'ba that still stands today. Through Mecca's role as a commercial and religious centre, Arabians came into contact with Jews and Christians, whose beliefs had a significant cultural impact.

In the midst of this lively environment, Muhammad was born into a merchant family of the clan of Hashim. Until about two generations prior to his birth, his family had probably been travelling nomads. They had recently become relatively successful traders, and had settled down in Mecca. Despite this prosperity, it is unlikely that Muhammad's youth was an easy one, as his father died before he was born, and his mother also died while he was very young. Upon the death of his mother, his grandfather took charge of him. Several years later, when his grandfather died, his upbringing fell to his uncle, Abu Talib. Little else is known about Muhammad's childhood and youth up to the time of his marriage, at age 25, to a wealthy widow named Khadijah.

The first half of Muhammad's life does not seem to have been extraordinary – a fact that many Muslims view as evidence of the transformative power of the religious experiences he began to have when he was in his forties. Muslim tradition tells us that each year Muhammad retreated to a cave on Mount Hira, near Mecca, for meditation – a practice that was quite common among Meccans at the time. During one of these retreats, he had a religious experience in which he felt that Allah was speaking to him through the angel Gabriel. According to Muhammad's own account of this experience, he received a clear instruction from Allah to

Recite: In the Name of thy Lord who created,
 created Man of a blood-clot.
Recite: And thy Lord is the Most Generous,
 who taught by the Pen,
 taught man that he knew not.[52]

This passage captures the beginning of the religious movement now known as Islam, as that beginning is represented in Muslim tradition. Muhammad was about 40 years old when he had the experience that he claimed to have recorded in this passage. Throughout his life he continued to have religious experiences similar to this first one, with the verses he claimed he was instructed by Allah to recite being recorded in the Qur'ān.[53] These verses amount to a body of literature which became the core text of the new religion. According to Muslim tradition, Muhammad was an illiterate who consistently maintained that he was not the author of the Qur'ān, but simply remembered what was dictated to him. The conviction that the Qur'ān, in its original Arabic form, is the eternal and unalterable speech of Allah, eventually became a hallmark of traditional Muslim belief.[54] Indeed, the vigorous debate that took place in the young Muslim community about the Qur'ān and its relationship to Allah closely paralleled the debate among Christians about whether Jesus was divine, human or both.[55]

At about AD 613, Muhammad began to preach in public, and a dedicated group of companions began to gather around him. But Muhammad met opposition from the merchant aristocracy, who probably felt that their financial interests and social privileges were threatened by his message. In AD 622,[56] increasing opposition in Mecca prompted Muhammad and his companions to move to the nearby town of Medina, where Muhammad established his spiritual and political leadership of the community. This dual role set the precedent for the refusal of traditional Muslims to separate religion and politics.[57]

While in Medina, Muhammad frequently encountered members of the Jewish community. Initially, it seems that he was enthusiastic about collaborating with monotheists from an ancient and well-established religious tradition. He was also eager to incorporate the Jewish community into the polity that he was in the process of consolidating. However, during the course of his stay in Medina, he became increasingly disillusioned with the Jews that he met there. While he appears to have learnt much from them, ultimately he drew sharp boundaries between his religion and Judaism.

In AD 624, Muhammad sent a clear signal to his companions and to the Jews of Medina when he declared that henceforth Mecca was to be the direction which Muslims would face when they prayed. Until this time, Jerusalem had been the direction of prayer. The switch to Mecca indicates that the young Muslim community was eager to distance itself from the older Jewish faith. From this time on, relations between Muhammad's community and the Medinan Jews quickly deteriorated; several of the Jewish tribes being forced to leave the city. The nadir of this increasingly strained relationship came in 627, when Muhammad ordered the massacre of the adult males of the one Jewish tribe that had remained in Medina: the Banu Qurayza. In addition, the tribe's women and children were subsequently sold into slavery.

During this period, the story of Ishmael acquired a special significance for Muhammad. It was well known at the time that the Jews claimed to be descended from Abraham through his son Isaac. Isaac was believed to be the child of Abraham's wife, Sarah, who had conceived and given birth in fulfilment of a promise made by God. However, according to the Hebrew Scriptures, Isaac was not Abraham's firstborn son. He had an elder brother: Ishmael. Ishmael was thought to be the son of Hagar, Abraham's concubine. When Sarah gave birth to Isaac she resented Hagar and Ishmael, and insisted that Abraham send them away – a request to which Abraham regretfully complied. The story does not end there, however, for the Hebrew Scriptures contain the startling claim that God would also make Ishmael the father of a great nation. Legend added that Hagar and Ishmael had been exiled to Arabia, where Ishmael became the father of the Arabs.

Muhammad employed this story, with great effect, to convince many that the God of the Jews was involved in the history of the Arabs. This enabled him to portray his religious movement as a legitimate alternative to, and equal partner of, Judaism and Christianity. He thus gave his companions new confidence in their unique religious heritage and relationship to God, while simultaneously undermining the view that God especially favoured the Jews. Muhammad believed that the claim made in the Hebrew Scriptures about Ishmael's descendants had been fulfilled in his community. Thus, there is nothing inconsistent in the incorporation of significant portions of the Hebrew Scriptures into the Qur'ān.[58]

Muhammad's message was, in effect, that Muslims and Jews (as well as Christians) came from a single stream of religious history that had diverged with Abraham's two sons. Thus, in the Qur'ān we find the following statement:

> We believe in God, and that which has been sent down on us, and sent down on Abraham and Ishmael, Isaac and Jacob, and the Tribes, and in that which was given to Moses and Jesus, and the Prophets, of their Lord; we make no division between any of them, and to Him we surrender.[59]

Thus, Muhammad claimed that his religious movement was not an innovation, but had been destined for the Arab people from the beginning of their ancestry. Moreover, Islam was not perceived to be an independent 'religion', but rather another variation on the theme of Abrahamic monotheism. In time, many Muslims came to believe that Islam was monotheism in its pristine form – a form of which Judaism and Christianity were corrupted versions.

Muhammad and his companions conquered Mecca in AD 630, gaining control of almost the entire Arabian Peninsula. Even at this stage, however, Muhammad was still actively giving shape to his religious movement. One of the last things that he did before his death was to require each member of his community to make Mecca the goal of a pilgrimage.

It was an ancient Arabian custom to embark on a pilgrimage to the site of the Ka'ba. Muhammad incorporated this custom into Islam, thus giving the ancient pagan tradition a new significance. Even today this pilgrimage, or *hajj*, as Muslims know it, is an important feature of the Islamic year.

By the time of his death, Muhammad had consolidated a religious and political community around a distinctive set of beliefs and practices.[60] He had also left the community a substantial body of literature that was taken to have come directly from Allah. Allah is described in the Qur'ān as the all-knowing creator of heaven and earth. The Qur'ānic image of Allah is encapsulated in this passage:

He is the All-creator, the All-knowing.
His command, when he desires a thing, is to say to it
  'Be,' and it is.
So glory be to Him, in whose hand is the dominion
  of everything,
and unto whom you shall be returned.[61]

The Qur'ān repeatedly emphasizes that each of us will be 'returned' to Allah when we die. This is to impress upon us that we are responsible for our good and bad deeds, and will be held accountable for them after death. Not surprisingly, then, the Qur'ān also has a great deal to say about how we ought to behave in order to live in a way that is pleasing to Allah. Socially responsible behaviour is counselled. We should be attentive to the weak and exploited, such as orphans, elderly widows and slaves. Muhammad instituted a community-based tax which everyone who could was expected to pay – the money collected being used to benefit the least well off in the community.[62] The injunctions to behave morally in the Qur'ān are given an interesting twist with the further claim that if you wrong somebody you simultaneously injure yourself.[63] The injury to oneself is thought to consist in the damage done to one's character and in the fact that such damage prejudices one's chances of being rewarded with a favourable afterlife.

In addition, the Qur'ān contains an insistence that righteous behaviour does not consist in the external trappings of religious life but in belief 'in God, and the Last Day, the angels, the Book, and the Prophets'.[64] Corresponding to these five objects of faith are the 'Five Pillars' of practical doctrine that give a basic shape to the Muslim lifestyle. In the Qur'ān, a Muslim is defined as someone who has born witness in public at least once that 'There is no god but God and Muhammad is his prophet' – this formula of faith being known as the *Shahada*. Muslims are also expected: to pray (*salat*) five times a day in the direction of Mecca; to pay *zakat* – that is, the special welfare tax mentioned earlier; to fast (*sawm*) during

Ramadan;[65] and, finally, to participate in the *hajj* – the annual pilgrimage to the Ka'ba – at least once in their lifetime.

Another notable feature of the belief system that Muhammad left to his community was that it had religious toleration written into it. A central place is given in the Qur'ān to the claim that Allah has sent prophets to all peoples without exception, so that none has lacked guidance. In keeping with this, the Qur'ān states that every prophet's message has universal relevance and should be accepted by all humanity. Thus, the Qur'ān, in accordance with this belief, also claims that, at the final judgement by Allah, every people will be judged by the standards of its own prophets and sacred writings.[66] However, despite the religious tolerance seemingly on the surface of this claim, some Muslims, including Muhammad himself, used it to criticize Judaism precisely because the Jews claimed to have a special relationship with God.

While Muhammad seems to have encouraged his companions to respect all revelations and all prophets, from very early times Muslims have believed that he was the last in a long line of prophets. They came to believe that his message was the final version of a message Allah has been transmitting in fragmentary form to different peoples throughout human history. Muslims, then, typically do not regard Muhammad as on the same level as the prophets of other religions. And this is because they are convinced that his message includes and surpasses the fragmentary messages of former prophets, such as Moses and Jesus. This conviction is shored up by the inclusion in the Qur'ān of stories from the Hebrew and Christian Scriptures.

Such was the belief system that Muhammad was still shaping when he died after a short illness in the year 632. The loss of their political and spiritual leader so soon after they had taken control of Mecca left the young Muslim community in a highly vulnerable position. To make matters worse, Muhammad had not issued explicit instructions about who his successor should be. This resulted in the community soon becoming embroiled in bitter factional disputes – one immediate result of which being the breaking apart of the community into the Shi'a party and the Sunni party. This division still persists today, and it remains the source of considerable acrimony. Due to the continuing importance of this rift between the Shi'a and the Sunni, it is necessary to explain the source of this first division within the Islamic community.

Immediately after Muhammad's death, Abu Bakr was appointed by majority decision to be his successor. Abu Bakr had been a close friend and companion of the Prophet, so he must have seemed to many the obvious choice. However, not everyone in the community was prepared to accept this decision. Some felt that if Muhammad had been in a position to appoint a successor before he died, he would have named Ali ibn Abi Talib, who was both his cousin and his son-in-law. Over the next decades, the *Shiah-i-Ali*, the 'Partisans of Ali', now known simply as the Shi'a, grew more intransigent in their support of Ali. They argued that the leader of the Muslim community could only be someone who belonged to the family line of Ali. As the leadership of the community passed from Abu Bakr to Umar ibn al-Khattab, and then to Uthman ibn Affan, the Shi'a grew increasing dissatisfied. This tense situation came to a head with the assassination of Uthman in 665. Ali ibn Abi Talib was then named as the fourth caliph, or leader of the community. Unfortunately, though, the nomination of Ali as caliph came too late to heal the growing rift in the community.

After the death of Ali, contrary to widespread expectations, the caliphate was not passed on to his son Husayn ibn Ali. As the grandson of Muhammad, Husayn ibn Ali must have seemed born to the role of leader. However, another group – the Ummayads – gained control of the caliphate, and in 680 the Ummayad Caliph Yazid killed Husayn. The Shi'a, not surprisingly, refused to accept that the Ummayads should appoint the leaders of the community. Instead, they reiterated that Ali had been the first legitimate leader of the community since Muhammad, and to this day they hold firm to their belief that only his descendants are worthy of leading the community.[67] The Sunni, on the other hand, reject this view, growing as they did out of the non-Shi'a majority.

Despite this rupture at the core of the early Muslim community, under the Ummayads the Islamic conquest of new territories began in earnest. Islam first engulfed the Middle East, and then rapidly spread in all directions, penetrating north Africa, southern Europe, central Asia, and what is now known as Pakistan. Under the Ummayads, however, conquered peoples were not encouraged to convert to the new faith. Islam was perceived as an Arab religion. As such, it was thought to be inappropriate for adoption by non-Arabs. It seems fair to assume, therefore, that the principal motive for early Islamic expansion was political and/or economic rather than religious.

Just as the political situation of the early Muslim community was fraught with internal strife, so too was the intellectual development of the movement. One of the earliest intellectual groups to form was the Mu'tazilah. In their efforts to rationalize the Muslim belief system, scholars associated with this group found themselves embroiled in a controversy that soon issued in violence. The controversy was not about any of the major propositions of Muslim faith, nor did it concern any of Islam's political claims. Rather, the question in dispute was whether or not humans have free will. Thinkers belonging to the Mu'tazilah movement held that humans do indeed have free will and that they can exercise it to obey, or disobey, Allah's commands. They also claimed that there is a standard of justice independent of Allah, and that Allah's actions could not be just if they did not conform to this independent standard.[68]

Both of these Mu'tazilite claims turned out to be the foci of controversy. Many Muslims perceived in them a denial of the sovereignty of Allah. Indeed, if Allah is all-powerful, as the Qur'ān asserts, then the notion of free human agency becomes problematic, as does the idea that Allah is obliged to conform to an independent standard of justice. A mass response to the Mu'tazilah rapidly developed among the non-Shi'a majority. In fact, Sunni Islam took shape precisely as such a response. The leading figure was a theologian called Abu al-Hasan al-Ash'ari (d. 935). Against the Mu'tazilah, al-Ash'ari denied that we have free will; arguing that, as Allah is the creator of everything that exists, he must be the creator of all actions, and hence the direct cause of everything that takes place. On this view, then, we do not directly cause our own actions. Al-Ash'ari does not seem to have been worried by his position entailing that causation, as it is usually understood, is illusory.[69] Nevertheless, al-Ash'ari realized that he had to explain how we could be held responsible for 'our' actions. His ostensible solution was to claim that, while Allah alone acts, the actions are imputed to us. In other words, Allah regards the actions as if we had caused them. With regard to the Mu'tazilah's second claim – that if Allah is to be just, then he must conform to an independent standard of justice – al-Ash'ari baldly proposed the counter-claim that whatever Allah does is just.[70]

Al-Ash'ari's response to the Mu'tazilah initiated the tradition of Ash'arite theology – a theological school that was to become dominant within medieval Islam. It was vehemently anti-rationalist, premised as it was on al-Ash'ari's belief that the Mu'tazilah movement had gone astray by trying to conform Muslim beliefs to reason. The Ash'arite movement was also deeply traditional, for it was committed to accepting statements in the Qur'ān at face value, even when they seemed contrary to reason.

Eventually, Ash'arite theology became closely associated with the Sufi movement that had been slowly developing since the eighth century AD.[71] The link uniting them was their shared distaste for the rationalist approach to Islam that had been the hallmark of the Mu'tazilah. Sufism can be described as the mystical stream within Islam. During its first three centuries it was a small movement, and Sufis tended to be regarded as a spiritual elite. However, largely due to the influence of the theologian and philosopher Sheikh Abu Hamid al-Ghazali (1058–1111), from the twelfth century it became a mass movement, playing a significant role in attracting converts to the Muslim faith.

Al-Ghazali was a child prodigy who, in his youth, was convinced that truth was available, and that it was possible to adjudicate between the competing doctrines of his day. Hence, as he recounts in his autobiography, he embarked on the quest for 'certain knowledge' – that is, 'knowledge in which the object is known in a manner which is not open to doubt at all'.[72] At first glance, there appeared to be two candidates for

such apodictic knowledge: first, knowledge based directly on sense experience; and, second, knowledge of self-evident propositions or axioms.
Eventually, however, al-Ghazali concluded that neither of these forms of
knowledge was indubitable. Knowledge derived from sense experience
was ruled out because of the many cases in which we make faulty inferences on its basis. He took as an example the case of a distant planet in
order to illustrate how our senses are prone to deceive us: our senses tell
us that the planet is the size of a small coin; however, we have good astro-
nomical evidence that the planet is considerably larger than that.[73] Thus,
al-Ghazali concluded, on the basis of this and many other examples, that
the senses could not provide us with indubitable knowledge.

What about knowledge of self-evident propositions or axioms, then?
Al-Ghazali argues that what we obtain from self-evident propositions
is a feeling of psychological certainty. But, he asked, in what way does
this feeling of certainty differ from the feeling that typically results from
the inferences we draw from our sense-experience? Observing through
introspection that there was no subjective difference, he concluded that,
as one case had proved unreliable, the other was likewise tainted with uncertainty. In other words, he realized that mere psychological certainty,
which is what he had set out to find, was not in fact a reliable indica-
tor that one knew the truth. The problem is that psychological certainty
bears no necessary connection to possession of the truth. Even if one's
reasoning about self-evident propositions appears to be flawless, there
is always the possibility that, as al-Ghazali writes, there 'exists beyond
reason a higher authority, which would, upon its manifestation, show
the judgment of reason to be invalid, just as the authority of reason had
shown the judgment of sense to be invalid'.[74]

According to al-Ghazali, then, neither the senses nor reason can
provide us with certain knowledge. In his autobiography, he describes
how this conclusion made him ill for several months. In a word, he appears to have suffered a nervous breakdown. Eventually, what cured
him was not better arguments or different conclusions but, what he
vividly perceived to be, the direct intervention of Allah; referring in the
autobiography to a 'light that Allah infused into his heart'.[75] The result
of this religious experience was that he recovered from his illness and
became the most important advocate of Islamic orthodoxy of his era.
His task became that of refuting the many conflicting philosophical
and theological doctrines that had led to his illness, and which he now
perceived to be standing in the way of truth. One group of thinkers that
al-Ghazali singled out as particularly dangerous were the rationalist
philosophers of his day. For he came to regard any philosopher who
thought that knowledge and truth could be derived from reason alone
as an enemy both of truth and Allah. Hence, he set out to discredit their
philosophical tradition, and in *The Incoherence of the Philosophers*[76]

he attempted to show that their arguments, even if their premises are accepted, lead to incoherence.

Despite the popular appeal of al-Ghazali's form of Ash'aritism, by no means all post-Mu'tazilah Muslim philosophers adopted the critical view of reason characteristic of the Ash'arites. The history of Islamic philosophy is peppered with the names of outstanding philosophers who greatly valued reason. Many of these rationalist philosophers had a lasting impact on the tradition in spite of their often controversial views. Ibn Rushd, known in the West as Averroes (1126–98), was the last in this line of rationalist Islamic philosophers – his most famous work, *The Incoherence of the Incoherence*, comprising a response to al-Ghazali.[77] Indeed, the aim of this book was to rehabilitate rationalist philosophy within Islam in the wake of al-Ghazali's powerful attack on it.

Many regard ibn Rushd as the most sophisticated of the early Islamic philosophers. He lived in Andalusia (in southern Spain), which was then a Muslim territory. There, having spent much of his philosophical career writing commentaries on the works of Aristotle, he acquired the reputation for being single-handedly responsible for the dissemination of Aristotle's virtually forgotten ideas throughout Western Europe, with his Arabic commentaries having been first translated into Hebrew and then into Latin. Ibn Rushd believed that his philosophical predecessors had taken the wrong turn by using Neo-Platonic rather than Aristotelian philosophy as the basis of their rational approach to Islam. He was convinced that if Aristotelian philosophy were to be properly understood, it would prove to be entirely compatible with the Muslim faith. His life's goal, then, was to demonstrate that, contrary to al-Ghazali's belief, philosophy and religious faith could be united in essential harmony.

In developing his response to al-Ghazali, ibn Rushd proposed what is now known as the 'doctrine of double truth'. According to this doctrine, philosophical discourse can be true in its own philosophical way, and, simultaneously, theological discourse can be true in its own theological way. For example, the theological account of the afterlife in the Qur'ān can be regarded as theologically true, and the philosopher's somewhat sparser account of the afterlife can also be true, notwithstanding the fact that the two accounts appear on the surface to contradict one another. Ibn Rushd hoped to use the theory of double truth to show that philosophy and theology – reason and faith – are not incompatible but are just two irreducibly different ways of talking about the same things.[78] On the whole, however, ibn Rushd's Muslim contemporaries did not enthusiastically embrace the theory of double truth. They seem to have suspected it of undermining the integrity of the theological language used in the Qur'ān. However, the theory of double truth had an enormous effect on subsequent European philosophy. Some recent philosophers, such as Oliver Leaman, go so far as to claim that this theory led to the separation between religion and reason in modern European thought – adding that this separation marked the birth of modern philosophy.[79]

Despite ibn Rushd's huge influence on philosophy in medieval Europe, the Islamic philosophical tradition in Andalusia came to a sudden stop after his death. This was the direct result of the changing political fortunes of the Muslim community in Spain, although the success of al-Ghazali's critique of philosophy also contributed. Ironically, ibn Rushd's philosophy was more influential upon European Jewish and Christian philosophers, such as Maimonides and Aquinas,[80] than it was upon Muslim thinkers. The tradition of Islamic philosophy continued to develop in Persia, however; reflecting the fact that Europe became less important as a centre of Muslim culture and learning. Despite the continuous development of the Islamic philosophical tradition, philosophy was less prominent in Muslim culture after the sixteenth century than it had been previously.

Along with Ash'arite theology, Sufism, and the climax of the rationalist philosophical tradition in the work of ibn Rushd, another major development took place in the medieval period. The codification of Islamic law, known to Muslims as shari'ah, had a huge impact on Islam.[81] The elaboration of a system of law had become necessary as the Muslim community encountered novel situations that would have been unthinkable to Muhammad, and hence which had not been addressed in the Qur'ān. In fact, several rival systems of shari'ah were developed almost simultaneously, each more or less based on the tradition of hadith that had evolved in the centuries after the Prophet's death. Hadith are collections of sayings which are thought to be either the words of Muhammad unrecorded in the Qur'ān, or descriptions of Muhammad's behaviour or that of his close associates.[82] A complex theological discipline evolved within the Muslim world with the sole aim of establishing which hadith were authentic and which were not. Differences between the various systems of shari'ah often reflect a more fundamental disagreement concerning which hadith are trustworthy.

While Islam changed rapidly in its first few centuries, the belief system, along with the legal framework, had stabilized by the twelfth century, and an orthodoxy was thus established – although, due to the huge geographical area into which Islam spread, a rich diversity of practices, beliefs and laws continued to evolve. On the whole, however, Islam did not go through any major periods of further change until the eighteenth century, when a 'fundamentalist'[83] revival got under way in Arabia. The leader was Muhammad ibn 'Abd al-Wahhab (1703–92), and the movement became known as Wahhabism.[84] This movement became hugely influential in the worldwide Muslim community when al-Wahhab became affiliated, through marriage, with the house of Saud – the ruling elite of Saudi Arabia.

This eighteenth-century form of Islamic fundamentalism in its Arabian homeland paved the way for a number of reforming movements which sprang up in many Muslim territories during the following century.[85] These movements, although otherwise diverse, shared the aim of freeing Islam from what they perceived to be its medieval accretions. Each was a reaction to what can be referred to as customary Islam: that is, Islam as it had come to be diversely practised, interwoven, as it was, with various regional folk traditions and superstitions, and overlaid with medieval theology and law. The reformers claimed that it was possible to rediscover the original, pure form of Islam by applying *ijtihād* (reason) to the founding texts of the tradition. Reason was not to be unbridled, though. For the reformers sought to keep it firmly anchored to *taqlid* (the authority of tradition).[86] These first reformers were, therefore, pre-modern in the sense that they wanted to recreate the early years of Islam before the complications of conquest, theology and law had obscured the original message of the Prophet. This simple vision soon proved inadequate to the modern era, which, in its own way, turned out to be at least as complex as the medieval period had been. And many Muslims began to think that modernity required a form of Islam different from that practised in both the early and the medieval periods.

In the late nineteenth century, then, a new movement began to distinguish itself from the fold of the Wahhabi-inspired reformers. The new movement – liberal Islam – was also a reforming movement and, like the form of reformism considered above, also defined itself in contrast to customary Islam. Liberal Muslims shared with other reformers the goal of returning to the sources of the Islamic tradition in order to revitalize the religion. They differed from the other reformists, however, in their appreciation of modernity and their assessment that it was fundamentally consistent with Islam. To underscore this crucial difference between liberal Islamic reformers and Wahhabi-inspired ones, only the latter are usually described as 'reformists'. The liberals, like the reformists, advocated *ijtihād*, but, unlike the reformists, they sundered the traditionally established connection between *ijtihād* and *taqlid*. Thus, the critical assessment of the tradition was no longer the exclusive preserve of those who claimed to represent traditional authority. Rather, those in the liberal camp encouraged all Muslims to pursue an education that would enable them to engage in *ijtihād* themselves. An appropriate education, moreover, would include a large measure of secular learning. The goal of *ijtihād*, according to proponents of this movement, was to modernize Islam and to do so by taking advantage of all that modernity, and, in particular, modern education, had to offer. Their emphasis on modernity came to define the major stream within liberal Islam during the late nineteenth and early twentieth centuries; so much so that this stream of the movement came to be known as Islamic modernism.

As the nineteenth century gave way to the twentieth, the pre-modern reform movements seemed to be losing ground to Islamic modernism. The modernizers seemed to be succeeding in their project of bringing Islam more into line with modern ideas, such as the primacy of reason over tradition and notions of human rights. Inevitably, though, some found modernism too threatening, accusing modernists of eroding what was distinctive about Islam in their efforts to accommodate modern thought. In the following chapters, some of these tensions, as exemplified by Muslim thinkers in the West since the close of the nineteenth century, are examined in greater detail. As we shall see, both reformist Islam and liberal Islam survived the twentieth century, and remain important movements at the beginning of the new millennium.

Conclusion

We have now completed our brief, historical overview of the main developments in Judaism, Christianity and Islam from their origin to the beginning of the twentieth century. We have seen the Abrahamic traditions to be continuously evolving, rather than fixed by some blueprint laid down in their long-distant past. The following chapters now take up the ongoing story of these traditions by examining some of the remarkable ways in which they have adapted and reacted to twentieth-century intellectual trends and cultural movements.

Study questions

1 What is distinctive about rabbinic Judaism? In what ways is rabbinic Judaism a precursor of Judaism in modern times?

2 In what ways does Reform Judaism differ from Modern Orthodox Judaism, and how do they both differ from Conservative Judaism?

3 How similar are the beliefs of Christians in the first three centuries of the common era to those of Christians in the West today? Identify the main similarities and the main differences.

4 How much influence should the creeds formulated at the Councils of Nicea and Chalcedon exert on Christian belief today? What arguments could you give to support your answer?

5 Is it possible to reconcile the belief that Muhammad is the last of the prophets with the claim that all genuine revelations and authentic prophets are to be respected?

6 Ibn Rushd and al-Ghazali held very different views about the relationship between religious beliefs and philosophical claims. To whose view do you feel most sympathetic, and why?

Select bibliography

Cohen, A., 1995, *Everyman's Talmud: The Major Teachings of the Rabbinic Sages*, New York: Schocken Books.

Cohn-Sherbok, D., 1996, *Modern Judaism*, Basingstoke: Macmillan.

Ehrman, B., 2005, *Lost Christianities: The Battles for Scripture and the Faiths we Never Knew*, Oxford: Oxford University Press.

Esack, F., 2002, *The Qur'ān: A Short Introduction*, Oxford: Oneworld.

Fakhry, M., 1983, *A History of Islamic Philosophy*, New York: Columbia University Press.

Hayes, J. H., and J. Maxwell Miller (eds), 1977, *Israelite and Judean History*, London: SCM Press.

Leaman, O., 1999, *A Brief Introduction to Islamic Philosophy*, Cambridge: Polity Press.

Maimonides, M., 1963, *The Guide of the Perplexed*, trans. by S. Pines, Chicago: University of Chicago Press.

Neusner, J., 1995, *Judaism in Modern Times: An Introduction and Reader*, Cambridge, Massachusetts: Blackwell.

Rahman, F., 1970, *Islam*, Chicago: University of Chicago Press.

Sanders, E. P., 1993, *The Historical Figure of Jesus*, London: Penguin Books.

Stevenson, J., (ed.), 1978, *A New Eusebius: Documents Illustrative of the History of the Church to A.D. 337*, London: SPCK.

Westerlund, D., and I. Svanberg (eds), 1999, *Islam Outside the Arab World*, New York: St Martin's Press.

Notes

1 A good modern edition is *JPS Hebrew–English Tanakh*, Philadelphia: The Jewish Publication Society, 1999.

2 See, particularly, Genesis 12—50.

3 Although today, as in antiquity, the former land of Canaan is disputed territory. See Chapter 8.

4 See Exodus 20.1–17.

5 See John H. Hayes and J. Maxwell Miller (eds), 1977, *Israelite and Judean History*, London: SCM Press.

6 The Pentateuch is the name given to the first five books of the Hebrew Scriptures: Genesis, Exodus, Leviticus, Numbers and Deuteronomy. The Pentateuch is also known as the Torah, or, alternatively, as the Law.

7 Deuteronomy 6.4–9 JPS. See also Deuteronomy 11.18–21 and Exodus 13.9, 16.

8 The first mention of phylacteries occurs in a text dated between the third and first centuries BC, and Deuteronomy pre-dates this.

9 For example, the rabbinic period also saw the establishment of the Jewish calendar. Even today, Jews adhere to a calendar that begins with the year that the rabbis calculated to be the year of creation. The year 5767 in the Jewish calendar overlaps with 2007 in the Gregorian calendar (that is, the calendar used in the West).

10 The Talmud is widely available in fairly accessible editions, such as Abraham Cohen, 1995, *Everyman's Talmud: The Major Teachings of the Rabbinic Sages*, New York: Schocken Books.

11 Despite their firm belief that the Jewish people were separated from all other peoples on account of being chosen by the Lord, the rabbis nevertheless believed that all human beings stem originally from the first human pair, Adam and Eve. Hence, they held that all humans were part of a family created by God. They further believed that the Lord has a sort of rudimentary covenant with the entire human family. This covenant was symbolized in the so-called Noahic commandments that, according to the rabbis, were incumbent upon all the nations.

12 The two main streams of Judaism to emerge were the Sefardic tradition and the Ashkenazic.

13 Throughout the later medieval period, the tendency was for Jews to move further and further east into Poland and the Ukraine. These areas did not have anti-Semitism written into their legal systems. Tragically, the slaughter of European Jews in the Second World War was facilitated by the concentration of the Jewish community in Eastern Europe.

14 Though this claim has been cast into doubt by Bat Ye'or's study (1985), *The Dhimmi: Jews and Christians Under Islam*, London: Associated University Presses.

15 See below, pp. 71f.

16 Moses Maimonides, 1963, *The Guide of the Perplexed*, trans. by S. Pines, Chicago: University of Chicago Press.

17 However, as we shall see in Chapter 5, his views on religious language are an important exception.

18 The following principles of belief, with the exception of 7, 9 and 12, are also adhered to by traditional Christians and Muslims. This is just one indication of the doctrinal affinity between the three Abrahamic faiths.

19 See Moses Maimonides, 1965, *Mishneh Torah: The Book of Knowledge*, Commentary on the Tenth Chapter of the Mishnah on the Tractate Sanhedrin, trans. by M. Hyamson, Jerusalem: Boys Town Jerusalem Publishers.

20 See Dan Cohn-Sherbok, 1996, *Modern Judaism*, Basingstoke: Macmillan, p. 75.

21 Cited in James G. Heller, 1965, *Issac M. Wise: His Life, Work and Thought*, New York: The Union of American Hebrew Congregations, pp. 464f.

22 In the light of certain twentieth-century events, however, Reform Judaism rescinded this judgement.

23 Jacob Neusner, 1995, *Judaism in Modern Times: An Introduction and Reader*, Cambridge, Massachusetts: Blackwell, p. 74.

24 See Neusner, *Judaism*, pp. 78f.

25 Eli Ginzberg, 1966, *Keeper of the Law: Louis Ginzberg*, Philadelphia: Jewish Publication Society of America, p. 145.

26 Neusner, *Judaism*, p. 88.

27 No one knows with any certainty exactly when Jesus was born. By convention the year of his birth is regarded as the year 0 in the Gregorian calendar. See E. P. Sanders, 1993, *The Historical Figure of Jesus*, London: Penguin Books, pp. 11f.

28 George A. Wells, for example, developed the 'Christ-myth' theory that attempts to account for the origins of Christianity without reference to a supposedly historical Jesus. See G. A. Wells, 1996, *The Jesus Legend*, Chicago: Open Court.

29 The real names of the authors of these Gospels are unknown. The names 'Matthew', 'Mark', 'Luke' and 'John' are used in accordance with a convention established by the early Church.

30 It took some time before there was wide agreement about what was to be included in the Christian Scriptures. Athanasius' thirty-ninth Festal Letter of AD 367 is the first official document to stipulate that the New Testament is composed exclusively of the 27 books that Christians today regard as canonical.

31 The title 'Christ' is actually a hellenization of the Hebrew term 'messiah'. Nowadays, Christian authors often shift between using the name 'Jesus' and the title 'Christ'. Christian theologians often use the name 'Jesus' to refer to the historical man who lived in first-century Palestine, and they reserve the title 'Christ' for when they want to refer to the historical man as he is understood within the Christian tradition of interpretation.

32 John 3.16 NRSV.

33 The doctrines that emerged from this period are of great significance to Christianity not least because they were the result of a collaborative effort of both Eastern and Western branches of the Christian community.

34 During this period, Christianity expanded rapidly throughout the Roman Empire. A consequence seems to have been that many of those in power began to perceive this movement as a threat. This perceived threat resulted in two centuries of brutal persecution of Christians.

35 See Justin Martyr, 1912, *The First Apology of Justin Martyr: Addressed to the Emperor Antonius Pius*, ed. John Kaye, Edinburgh: John Grant. For a comprehensive selection of extracts from works of this period, see J. Stevenson (ed.), 1978, *A New Eusebius: Documents Illustrative of the History of the Church to A.D. 337*, London: SPCK.

36 Ebionitism was held by a community of Jewish Christians who called themselves 'ebionites'. The term 'ebionite' is derived from the Hebrew word meaning 'the poor'. Some scholars of early Christianity speculate that the ebionites may have been the community of 'Christians' that remained closest to the spirit of the historical Jesus – which is more than a little ironic, given their condemnation. See, for example, Henry Chadwick, 1978, *The Early Church*, Harmondsworth: Penguin Books, p. 23.

37 The Council of Nicea was the first in a series of so-called 'ecumenical councils'; the Council of Chalcedon was the fourth. In terms of their influence on the Christian tradition, these two Councils are by far the most significant.

38 The 'Nicene Creed' is reprinted in Peter Hodgson and Robert King (eds), 1995, *Readings in Christian Theology*, London: SPCK, p. 205. The Creed was written in a form of Hellenistic Greek that is unfamiliar to most Christians today. How, exactly, it should be translated into modern languages is a matter of ongoing scholarly dispute. In particular, there is a wide variety of possible translations into English of the key term *homoousios*. The version given above translates *homoousios* as 'of the same reality'. However, other translators prefer 'of the same substance' or 'of the same essence'. The differences are substantive.

39 Hodgson and King, *Readings*, p. 205.

40 On various possible interpretations of this statement, and the controversy to which it gave rise within the Christian community, see Anthony Baxter, 'Chalcedon and the Subject in Christ', *The Downside Review*, 107 (1989), pp. 1–21.

41 'The Chalcedonian Definition', reprinted in Hodgson and King, *Readings*, p. 210.

42 On the transformation that the notion of 'the end of the world' has undergone in Christian thought, see Victoria S. Harrison, 'The Metamorphosis of "the End of the World": From Theology to Philosophy and Back', *Philosophy and Theology*, 17 (2005), pp. 33–50.

43 Constantinople is now called Istanbul.

44 From the fifteenth century, however, Moscow increasingly became the spiritual and administrative centre of Eastern Christianity, becoming known as 'the third Rome'.

45 Although there are other contenders for this position – the 'Old Catholics', for example.

46 As the traditional form of Christian faith, Roman Catholicism, lost its position as the dominant form of Christianity in many parts of Europe, the discovery of the New World provided a new locus for it. Even today, by far the majority of Roman Catholic Christians are in South and Latin America.

47 Though it can be argued that the impetus for this movement had a more popular base than is usually assumed, and that intellectuals took up the cause only after the movement was under way. See S. J. Barnett, 2003, *The Enlightenment and Religion: The Myths of Modernity*, Manchester: Manchester University Press.

48 See Chapter 7 for a further discussion of this.

49 See the selection of essays in David Westerlund and Ingvar Svanberg (eds), 1999, *Islam Outside the Arab World*, New York: St Martin's Press, for accounts of the Muslim presence in various European countries and in North America.

50 See Frederick M. Denny, 1998, 'Church/Sect Theory and Emerging North American Muslim Communities: Issues and Trends' in Earle H. Waugh and Frederick M. Denny (eds), *The Shaping of an American Islamic Discourse: A Memorial to Fazlur Rahman*, Atlanta, Georgia: Scholars Press, p. 235.

51 It should be noted that many Muslims would object to this way of putting things because they regard Muhammad as the conveyor of Islam from God, rather than as the founder of a new religious movement.

52 Qur'ān, Sura (Chapter) 96.1–5. I have used the translation by Arthur J. Arberry. See A. J. Arberry, 1998, *The Koran*, Oxford: Oxford University Press, p. 651.

53 The word 'qur'ān' simply means 'recitation'.

54 Because traditional Muslims believe that the Qur'ān is the speech of Allah in written form, and that this speech was merely mediated through the Prophet, it is not surprising that, even today in the West, many Muslims resist any suggestion that the Qur'ān did not always possess the exact form it takes today. However, the fact that there are variant versions of the Qur'ān does not square happily with this traditional view. Moreover, there is substantial evidence that the text of the Qur'ān was fixed at a much later date than the traditional account

would have us believe. To be precise, it is unlikely that a definitive version of the text was established prior to the ninth century AD. See Farid Esack, 2002, *The Qur'ān: A Short Introduction*, Oxford: Oneworld, chapter 4.

55 See Esack, *Qur'ān*, chapter 5.

56 AD 622 is the first year of the Islamic calendar – the *hijra*, or 'emigration'. 1428 AH (*Anno Hegira*) overlaps with AD 2007.

57 See Chapters 8 and 10, below.

58 One implication of their incorporation, however, is that conclusions drawn from the findings of archaeology and the application of modern biblical criticism to the Hebrew Scriptures also extend to the Qur'ān.

59 Sura 3.78. Arberry, *Koran*, p. 57.

60 I have given the traditional account of Muhammad's biography and the origin of Islam. For a radically different account of Muhammad and the origins of Islam, see Michael Cook and Patricia Crone, 1977, *Hagarism: The Making of the Islamic World*, Cambridge: Cambridge University Press.

61 Sura 36.82f. Arberry, *Koran*, p. 455.

62 See Sura 9.60.

63 See, for example, Sura 2.231.

64 Sura 2.172. Arberry, *Koran*, p. 22.

65 Ramadan is the ninth month of the Islamic lunar year.

66 See Sura 4.41 and Sura 16.84. For the claim that God's teaching forms a continuous whole, and that the teaching received by the Jews and Christians must therefore be regarded as still valid, see Sura 33.40 and Sura 42.10–19.

67 Most Shi'a are now to be found in Iran.

68 For a detailed account of Mu'tazilah doctrines, see Majid Fakhry, 1983, *A History of Islamic Philosophy*, New York: Columbia University Press, pp. 44–65.

69 Denial of causation rendered Ash'arite theology deeply inimical to the practice of science. Natural science is premised on the notion that there is a regular relation between cause and effect, and that this can be discovered. In effect, Ash'arites denied that there are any natural laws for scientists to study.

70 The problem of whether God prescribes standards of justice, goodness and so on, or whether these standards exist independently and have to be followed by God is an old one. It is known as the Euthyphro Dilemma, after Plato's *Euthyphro* dialogue, where it was first raised. This dilemma continues to vex monotheists to this day.

71 See the excellent account of the origin and evolution of the Sufi movement contained in Fazlur Rahman, 1970, *Islam*, Chicago: University of Chicago Press, chapters 8 and 9.

72 Quoted in Fakhry, *History*, p. 245.

73 See Fakhry, *History*, p. 246.

74 Quoted in Fakhry, *History*, p. 246.

75 See Fakhry, *History*, p. 246.

76 Al-Ghazali, 1997, *The Incoherence of the Philosophers*, trans. by M. Marmura, Provo, Utah: Brigham Young University Press. The Arabic title of this work is *Tahāfut al-falāsifah*.

77 Ibn Rushd, 1978, *Averroes' Tahāfut al-Tahāfut*, trans. by S. Van Den Bergh, London: Luzac.

78 In Chapter 6, we shall see that this idea has also been prominent in the work of many twentieth-century thinkers.

79 See Oliver Leaman, 1999, *A Brief Introduction to Islamic Philosophy*, Cambridge: Polity Press, pp. 144–50.

80 Thomas Aquinas (1225–74), a Dominican monk, has come to be regarded as the most prominent Christian philosopher of the medieval period. Many of his views continue to be held in high esteem by Christian academics.

81 On the development of shari'ah, see Rahman, *Islam*, chapters 4 and 6.

82 For an accessible English translation of selected parts of a collection of Hadith known as the *Sahih Bukhari*, see Maulana Muhammad Ali, 1941, *A Manual of Hadith*, Lahore: Ahmadiyya Anjuman Ishaat Islam.

83 On the difficulties of employing the term 'fundamentalism' with respect to Islam, see Chapter 10.

84 See Rahman, *Islam*, pp. 196–201.

85 In the twentieth century, the form of Islam that has evolved from this movement is variously described as Islamism, Islamic fundamentalism, revivalism, reformism or Wahhabism.

86 However, there was something of a paradox involved in the reformer's attempt to judge tradition by means of tradition: it required that a clear distinction be drawn between the inauthentic traditions that had developed since the time of Muhammad and the pure tradition before it became adulterated.

4

The Challenge of Reason

Despite their diversity, traditional forms of Judaism, Christianity and Islam are united by a common message: an omnipotent, omniscient and benevolent God exists – a God who not only created the universe, but who also takes a continuing personal interest in the lives of 'his' human creatures. Upon the bedrock of faith in one particular God stand all the other religious (and, arguably, ethical) convictions of traditional Jews, Christians and Muslims. In subjecting belief in the existence of God to rational examination, philosophers have thus threatened to undermine the Abrahamic faiths at their common root. As we shall see in this chapter, the hub around which the modern philosophical challenge to religious faith revolves concerns what evidence, if any, a believer may adduce in support of the claim that God exists. Are there good reasons for belief in God, and hence for adherence to one of the faiths that worships a specific divinity? There is no doubt that the search for, and analysis of, reasons for belief preoccupied many during the twentieth century, and perhaps none more so than professional philosophers.

It would be naïve to assume, however, that traditional religious beliefs went unchallenged by philosophers until the modern period. While we should not underestimate the influence of political and social forces on the transformations the Abrahamic faiths have undergone throughout their respective histories, many of these changes have, undoubtedly, occurred as a response to the pressure brought to bear on traditional beliefs by philosophers. Indeed, philosophers seem to have always probed and questioned the religious beliefs of their day.[1] The focus of this chapter is the challenge that philosophers posed to religion in the twentieth century. We shall examine some of the most important and influential twentieth-century philosophical movements, and consider their evaluation of religious claims.[2] Singled out for attention are those movements that look set to have had a serious and lasting impact on religious thought.

During most of the twentieth century, academic philosophers of religion in the West were predominantly Christian intellectuals – thus, they were principally concerned with the God portrayed in Christianity. A few self-proclaimed atheists, such as Antony Flew and John L. Mackie, broadened the discussion in the 1950s and 1960s. Only in the closing decades of the century, however, did philosophers of religion begin to take seriously the need to consider non-Christian religions. This development was prompted by the increasing prominence at this time of Jewish and Muslim intellectuals within the West, as well as by the growing trend towards religious plurality within Europe and North America. Because of the common ancestry of the concept 'God' within the Abrahamic faiths, philosophers of religion have found it relatively easy to assimilate Judaism and Islam within their range of concerns. Moreover, philosophers typically analyse a generic concept 'God'. Thus, their arguments apply to the core beliefs of traditional Judaism, Christianity and Islam. Consequently, despite the dominance of Christian thinkers in the debates that we shall consider in this chapter, the intellectual developments described are relevant to adherents of each of the Abrahamic faiths. While these debates had an immediate effect on many Jews and Christians, they also had a less direct, though no less profound, effect on many within the Muslim community in the West. Furthermore, modern Muslim thinkers have to find their niche in an intellectual scene that has been shaped by these debates. Hence, the intellectual history surveyed in this chapter seems poised to be just as relevant to twenty-first-century Muslims as it has been to their Jewish and Christian contemporaries.

Before turning to the twentieth century, however, we need to look further back in history if we are to understand the philosophical developments of recent times. Hence, I provide a brief account, first, of the relation between philosophy and religion in the period immediately prior to the European Enlightenment, and, second, of this relation during the eighteenth – the heyday of the philosophical open season on religion – and the nineteenth centuries.

Faith and philosophy prior to the Enlightenment

In the centuries immediately prior to the Enlightenment, the population of Europe was predominantly Christian, and the intellectual climate was not one that was amenable to the essential teachings of the faith being publicly challenged.[3] For Christianity had been so assimilated into the fabric of Western European culture that few seriously questioned its credentials as the one, true religion.[4] Nevertheless, a swell of doubt slowly began to form in intellectual circles, but it did not break until well into the eighteenth century.

Judaism was likewise experiencing what may be called a pre-critical period. The minority status of Jews within Western Europe had been reinforced by the mass expulsions of the fifteenth and sixteenth centuries. Those communities that remained suffered many forms of social and political persecution on account of their adherence to Judaism. Far from being troubled by abstract philosophical problems, many within these communities sought solace in the mysticism that left few Jewish communities untouched at this time. Preoccupied with the survival of their culture and religion, and oppressed by social and political discrimination, Jewish intellectuals were hardly in a position to enter into serious intellectual debate with their Christian counterparts.[5] On the other hand, the majority of European Jews were not well educated, and their traditional lifestyles did not encourage them to question the faith of their ancestors.

After the Muslims evacuated southern Europe at the end of the fifteenth century, Islam's influence on Western European intellectuals was greatly reduced.[6] Immediately prior to the Enlightenment, then, Muslim intellectuals had little or no direct impact on intellectual life in Western Europe. Christian thinkers no longer felt pressurized to defend their beliefs against Muslim philosophers and theologians, as they had in the Middle Ages. This situation no doubt encouraged intellectual complacency. The Muslim withdrawal from southern Europe was widely perceived, by Christians, as divine vindication of their faith – a perception that is likely to have contributed to their confidence in the superiority of their own version of monotheism over other varieties.

During this period, then, Jews and Muslims were not perceived as an urgent threat to Christian hegemony within Western Europe. One might thus have expected this to be an era characterized by peace between people of different religious persuasions. This expectation is, however, belied by the facts. In the aftermath of the Reformation, Western Europe was the site of a long string of religious wars. The wars were fought by Christians of different sectarian affiliations, and continued, with few interruptions, from 1562 (when fighting broke out in France) until 1648 (when the Treaty of Augsburg was signed). One effect of these protracted wars was that many people became extremely reluctant to argue about religion. Religious beliefs were increasingly regarded as personal beliefs – as convictions to be kept out of the social and political arena.[7] Moreover, in the wake of the wars of religion, a spirit of religious toleration[8] was widely encouraged in order to reduce the risk of further conflict.

Despite the fact that to challenge religious belief publicly was a potentially dangerous undertaking during this pre-critical period, some courageous thinkers did ponder the reasons for and against religion. Given that religious beliefs had been the source of so much strife, it is hardly surprising that some began to wonder if there were good reasons for continuing to hold them at all. Insofar as people attempted to show that religious belief was justified belief, they generally engaged in what is called 'natural theology'. According to this traditional approach to religious belief, reflection about the natural world legitimately leads to particular beliefs about God. Theologians who followed this method thought that they could establish that God exists, and has a certain character, from the evidence available by observation of the natural world.[9] The complexity of nature, for example, was taken to be evidence of the existence and intelligence of the deity. A variety of arguments for the existence of

God was generated by this popular way of thinking. They each relied on an inference from some feature of the natural world to a conclusion about the existence of a God who is responsible for that particular feature. Such arguments, which are now known as 'arguments from design', gave many adherents confidence in their religious beliefs – a confidence that remained intact until philosophers active in the European Enlightenment began to undermine their foundations.[10]

Natural theology was an integral component of the pre-modern worldview shared by Jews, Christians and Muslims. Within this worldview, God was conceived as the all-powerful, all-knowing, benevolent overseer of the world – a world, moreover, that had been created for a specific purpose. Throughout the ages, generations of believers assumed that this benevolent deity controlled all that occurred in the world, and directed all things according to divine will. Although the will of God was no doubt regarded as inscrutable by many, its activity in the world was seldom openly questioned. Even in the face of great calamities, believers tended to rationalize their suffering as a deserved punishment from their God.[11] Ultimately, though, this seemingly *ad hoc* rationalization was insufficient to dispel the mounting tension between the conception of God as a benevolent overseer and – what was increasingly construed as – God's failure to attend adequately to the urgent needs of the faithful. Given belief in God's omnipotence, such failure could hardly be explained by the suggestion that God was *unable* to intervene in order to prevent terrible things from happening.[12] Inevitably, philosophers began to question the plausibility of the traditional worldview. Such questioning gathered unprecedented momentum during the eighteenth century, to which we now turn.

The growing tension between faith and reason

Voltaire (1694–1778), the French satirist and man of letters, was a germinal thinker during the early stages of the European Enlightenment, and his experience is surely representative of that of many in his era. Voltaire's confidence in the religious faith of his ancestors was shattered[13] in 1755 by an earthquake that devastated Lisbon, the capital of Portugal, and a bastion of the Roman Catholic faith. Ironically, what is now widely regarded as the first major disaster of modern times occurred on All Saint's Day, an important religious festival for Roman Catholics. Voltaire's response to this calamity was to write *Candide, ou l'optimisme* – a relentless satire on the view that everything that happens is the result of God directing events to bring about the best possible outcome.[14] Published in 1759, *Candide* had a huge impact on Voltaire's generation. Banned by the Roman Catholic Church, it captured the scepticism with which many had come to regard the idea of God promoted by the traditional Abrahamic faiths.

Natural theology, and the religious worldview within which it belongs, were further challenged by the eighteenth-century Scottish philosopher, David Hume (1711–76). In his *Dialogues Concerning Natural Religion*,[15] Hume crystallized the challenge posed by the intellectuals of his day to the traditional beliefs of their ancestors. Hume disagreed with the natural theologians; however, his disagreement was not founded upon dissatisfaction with their method. A committed empiricist himself, Hume agreed that evidence was of prime importance, and that to justify one's beliefs one should examine the world. He thought, then, that the natural theologians were correct in seeking to establish the existence of God through consideration of whatever evidence there might be for it in the natural world. He simply disagreed with their assessment of the evidence. Even if it seemed that there was evidence of a creator, such evidence did not establish the existence, never mind the continued existence, of the God of the Abrahamic faiths. Given that the world seems less than perfect, it might have been the work of an inferior God, whose creation was laughed at by greater Gods. Or the world might have been made by an extremely old God, who died shortly after half-finishing the job. Moreover, and contrary to the natural theologians, Hume thought that the natural world provided evidence against the existence of an omnipotent, omniscient and perfectly good God – the suffering of the innocent, for example.

Hume's contemporary, Immanuel Kant, attempted to shield what he regarded as the essential core of religious faith from Hume's criticisms. In *Religion Within the Bounds of Mere Reason*,[16] Kant – a pietist – distinguishes 'historical faith' from 'pure religious faith'.[17] He concedes that 'historical faith' – faith based on purported revelation – could and should be subjected to criticism; in other words, when assessing the claims of 'historical faith' one must test them against one's experience. But Kant, nevertheless, proposes that 'pure religious faith' could be supported by reason regardless of experience. His defence of religion, then, rests on the claim that evidence is irrelevant to 'pure religious faith', and thus to our acceptance of the essential truths of religion. But then, if it is not based on empirical evidence, what exactly is the content of religious knowledge, in Kant's view? The believer can know that knowledge of whether or not God exists is beyond the capacity of the human intellect. This is because God, if God exists, is necessarily transcendent to the world of our experience, and our intellect can only apply itself to what is given in experience. Kant thus denies that substantive knowledge of God is possible in order to demonstrate that religious *faith* is necessary, even in the age of reason.

During his lifetime, Kant, like Hume, was notorious for his criticisms of the traditionally accepted 'proofs' of the existence of God.[18] However, as we have seen, the conclusion Kant drew from the inadequacy of the traditional arguments was different from Hume's. Kant was convinced that 'pure reason' (that is, reason unaided by experience) could neither prove nor disprove the existence of God. The only recourse, then, was to what he terms 'practical reason'. Kant argues that, as human beings with a particular mental structure, we can arrive at the concept 'God' solely through our practical reasoning abilities. Kant claims that unless we suppose that God exists, we undermine the rational foundation of our ethical behaviour. For only the assumption that God exists can give us confidence that our moral actions will achieve their ultimate goal – an eschatological[19] state referred to as the *summum bonum* – and, unless we have such confidence, it will be irrational for us to follow the moral law. Moreover, in order to enjoy the *summum bonum*, we will require eternal life. Thus, practical reason requires the assumption that there is such a thing. Lastly, we must also assume that we are free to act as we decide, otherwise, according to Kant, our actions will have no moral value. Kant uses this argument to generate what he calls the three 'postulates of practical reason': namely, the three things we must assume if we are to be able to act according to reason, which comprise the existence of God, eternal life and human freedom. In Kant's view, then, 'religious knowledge' is an oxymoron. Religious *faith*, however, can be supported by attending to the requirements of practical reason, and can thus legitimately retain its place in the life of an enlightened thinker.

Kant's argument ensured that the concept 'God' retained a place within post-Enlightenment thought – although this place was somewhat diminished in comparison to the centrality of the concept within pre-Enlightenment intellectual life. The primary source of the diminished importance of the concept 'God' was the separation engineered by Kant between the philosophical concept and the descriptions of God found within the sacred texts and traditions (these descriptions having been rejected by Kant as part of 'historical faith'). Kant argues that this separation is necessary if the very notion of 'God' is to have any place within a purely rational religion that has, purportedly, dispensed with superstition.

Kant's strategy of demarcating a domain of faith within which Hume's criticisms of religion had no bite was enthusiastically embraced by many. One of Kant's admirers was the German Protestant theologian Friedrich Daniel Ernst Schleiermacher, who is now widely regarded as the founder of modern Protestant theology. Taking his lead from Kant's claim that knowledge of God was impossible, Schleiermacher was the first theologian to attempt to base theology primarily on religious feeling.[20] He revolutionized theology by distinguishing between religion as something felt in the inner core of one's being and religion as a system of doctrinal statements. Through Schleiermacher, Kant's influence penetrated to the heart of Protestant theology, and contributed to the distinctive character of much twentieth-century Protestantism.

Thus, eighteenth-century philosophers had a profound effect on religious thought in the West. Their influence was not only confined to Christian thinking, however, but also had a deep impact upon Judaism. Participants in the *Haskalah* – the Jewish Enlightenment – were responsible for spreading modern European culture among European Jews.[21] The German philosopher Moses Mendelssohn (1729–86) was, perhaps, the most influential figure in this movement.[22] Among many other achievements, he translated the Pentateuch into German in order to facilitate the integration of the German Jewish community into its adopted homeland. The study of modern philosophy led Mendelssohn, like Locke before him, to advocate freedom of conscience in religious matters, arguing that the only reasonable attitude one could take towards different religious opinions was one of tolerance. Consequently, he encouraged his co-religionists to

> [p]ave the way for a happy posterity toward that height of culture, toward that universal tolerance of man for which reason still sighs in vain! Reward and punish no doctrine, tempt and bribe no one to adopt any religious opinion! Let everyone be permitted to speak as he thinks, to invoke God after his own manner or that of his fathers, and to seek eternal salvation where he thinks he may find it, as long as he does not disturb public felicity and acts honestly toward the civil laws, towards you and his fellow citizens. Let no one in your states be a searcher of hearts and a judge of thought; let no one assume a right that the Omniscient has reserved to himself alone! If we render unto *Caesar* what is *Caesar's*, then do you yourselves render unto *God what is God's! Love truth! Love peace!*[23]

Like his contemporary, Kant, Mendelssohn did not believe that it was possible to argue cogently for the veracity of any particular religious tradition. But, also like Kant, he was convinced that there were reasons for adherence to one's own particular historical faith-tradition. Religious faith, in his view, remained viable even though religious knowledge (that might be publicly debated) did not. It is not surprising, then, that he was an energetic defendant of religious toleration.

Although many Jews and Christians accepted the separation between knowledge and faith with relief rather than trepidation, it soon became apparent that it opened the way for the marginalization of the concept 'God' from European intellectual life. In fact, largely as a result of the success and influence of Kant's restriction of the concept 'God', from the nineteenth century onwards God was increasingly conceived as a 'God of the gaps' within Western European intellectual circles – a God whose role in our thinking is to explain the otherwise inexplicable. In other words, 'God of the gaps' is only invoked when a phenomenon lacks a rational explanation. Prior to Darwin's theory of evolution, for example, a God of the gaps was needed to account for the otherwise unexplained fact of how well animals are suited to their various environments. But once God had been reduced to a God of the gaps, there became less and less need for the concept 'God' in human thinking as – due to the increasing success of science in the nineteenth and twentieth centuries – more and more explanatory gaps were quickly filled in.

Despite what many religious believers might have been expected to view as the encroachment of science into what had previously been regarded as an exclusively religious domain, many of them perceived reason in the eighteenth and nineteenth centuries as promising liberation from unhealthy superstitions. Many believers, taking their lead from Kant, Schleiermacher and Mendelssohn, regarded this as a positive development; for philosophical criticism of superstition allowed pure religious faith to emerge – faith that stood its ground independently of the old superstitions.[24] However, as the nineteenth century moved towards the twentieth, many began to regard the relationship between philosophy and religion in a rather different light: they denied that religious faith could remain credible to one who had accepted the methods of modern philosophy.[25] This reassessment of the relationship between philosophy and religion was spurred on by the increasing prominence of positivism within philosophy. Positivists were concerned to avoid all metaphysical speculation, and to confine their thought exclusively to what was given 'positively' in sense experience. This turn to a strict form of empiricism was taken even further in the early twentieth century by a group of philosophers known as the logical positivists. As we shall see, they were convinced that religious belief is contrary to reason. Indeed, in their view, religious discourse is mere nonsense. But before examining the claims of logical positivism, let us briefly consider the views of an influential advocate of the idea that philosophy is the noble enemy, not the liberator, of religion – a thinker whose life spans the shift from the nineteenth to the twentieth centuries.

Russell's attack on the concept 'God'

Bertrand Russell (1872–1970) was an empiricist in the tradition of David Hume. Like Hume, he believed that philosophy conclusively demonstrates that religious beliefs are intellectually disreputable. Russell's essay 'Why I am Not a Christian: An Examination of the God-Idea and Christianity'[26] serves as an archetypal expression of the attitude towards religion held by many intellectuals in the early decades of the twentieth century. Russell surveys the main arguments for the existence of God advanced by believers through the centuries: the first cause argument, the natural-law argument, the argument from design, the moral argument, and the argument for the remedying of injustice. He claims that they all fail and, moreover, represent an intellectual decline from stronger arguments to weaker ones. Russell, however, does not believe that the failure of these arguments has had a significant impact on the majority of religious people. For, in his view, the arguments are so bad that no one capable of fully understanding them could possibly use them as a basis for faith. The real motivation for religious faith must, according to Russell, lie elsewhere. In his assessment, most people embrace religion to allay fear caused by 'the terror of the unknown'.[27] As he puts it: 'Fear is the basis of the whole thing – fear of the mysterious, fear of defeat, fear of death.'[28] After arguing that religion is an ineffective response to fear, Russell counsels that a superior response is at hand: science. Moreover, he was firmly convinced that as science progressed, and shed light on what was previously regarded with fear, religious faith would become less compelling. Opining that once their fear was diminished people would clearly recognize that religion was merely a vestigial belief from an age characterized by ignorance of the natural world, Russell concludes:

> The whole conception of God is a conception derived from the ancient Oriental despotisms. It is a conception quite unworthy of free men. When you hear people in church debasing themselves and saying that they are miserable sinners, and all the rest of it, it seems comtemptible and not worthy of self-respecting human beings.[29]

While Russell's arguments perhaps captured the mood of many of his contemporaries, it was left to those in the logical positivist movement (a movement with which Russell had sympathies) to formulate a more focused challenge to religious belief.

Logical positivism and the analytic/synthetic distinction

At the heart of the challenge philosophers posed to religion in the early twentieth century lay a distinction between analytic and synthetic propositions.[30] An analytic proposition is tautologous, and can be known to be true merely by analysing the terms employed. A synthetic proposition cannot, for in being non-tautologous, it contains some further information beyond the predicates of the sentence merely restating what is contained in the subject of the sentence.[31] Commitment to a hard and fast distinction between these two types of proposition was a central feature of logical positivism – arguably the most influential Western European philosophical movement during the first half of the twentieth century.[32] The main contention of logical positivism was that every genuine proposition is either analytic or synthetic, and that synthetic propositions have to be, at least in principle, if not in fact, verifiable in order to be meaningful. As we shall see, this seemingly innocuous claim has far-reaching implications for the assessment of religious beliefs. For logical positivists judged the utterances of religious believers to be non-analytic,[33] and to belong to the class of meaningless synthetic pseudo-propositions. Not surprisingly, this judgement had a devastating effect on the philosophy of religion. A direct result of the success of logical positivism was that the philosophy of religion ceased to be regarded, in many Western universities, as a serious branch of philosophy.

To appreciate fully why logical positivism had such radical implications for the analysis of religious beliefs, it is necessary to be clear on the distinction between analytic and synthetic propositions. Consider:

a All bachelors are unmarried.
b All swans are white.

Proposition (a) is analytic. It is true by definition. One does not need to examine the world in order to know that it is true. For it is impossible to imagine a situation in which (a) is false. If you encountered some group conducting a survey of the residents of their city in order to ascertain whether or not there were any married bachelors living there, you would immediately realize that they had misunderstood what the term 'bachelor' means.

Proposition (b), on the other hand, is synthetic. If it were true, it would be so because of how the world happens to be, and not because of what 'swan' means. There is no conceptual contradiction involved in imagining a swan that is not white, which tells us that there is no logically necessary relation between swans and whiteness.[34] Indeed, Europeans once believed that all swans were white. But when certain large, black birds were discovered in Australia, the response was not that they could not possibly have been swans, which would have been the only appropriate response if (b) were analytic. Rather, the response was that some swans are actually black, which shows that (b) was not true by definition, but was synthetic. It was falsified by experience, whereas no experience could have falsified (a). And had there just happened to have been no black swans anywhere in the world, then (b) would have been true. Put another way, it follows from the meaning of the word 'bachelor' that any bachelor is *necessarily* unmarried. Analytic propositions, then, are true because of the meaning of the words the sentences expressing them contain, and their truth is established through consideration of what the words mean. The truth of synthetic propositions is arrived at quite differently: it can only be established through empirical observation of the world.

Synthetic propositions clearly make substantive claims that presuppose the existence of the entities to which they refer. Analytic propositions make no such claims. For example, from the analytic truth that 'All unicorns have a single horn' we cannot infer that there are any unicorns. On the other hand, if a synthetic proposition such as 'This dog is dirty' is true, we can infer that the world contains at least one dirty dog. This explains the logical positivist's claim that analytic propositions are 'trivial' (they make no claim about the world, merely about our concepts), whereas synthetic propositions are 'informative' (because they make some claim about the world, even if that claim is false).

Logical positivists advise us, then, that if we are to acquire genuine knowledge about the world, we must concentrate on synthetic propositions. But not all propositions that contain two logically distinct concepts give us information about the world. The logical positivists insist that only those propositions that can be verified (or falsified) by observation are genuinely informative. The claim that only such propositions are meaningful follows from the logical positivist's novel theory of meaning, according to which the meaning of a proposition just is the method of its verification. Logical positivism is thus premised upon what is known as the 'verification principle': a proposition is factually significant, and hence meaningful, only if we know how to verify (or falsify) it. In other words, logical positivists employ the verification principle as a test to determine if a synthetic proposition is genuinely informative about the world. Only meaningful propositions pass this test, and are thus shown to be genuine synthetic propositions.[35] All purportedly informative propositions, therefore, were required to pass the test of being in principle, if not in practice, empirically verifiable before they were admissible, by the logical positivists, as meaningful. 'The universe is shrinking uniformly' is an example of a proposition that fails the test.[36] This proposition fails the logical positivists' test because it is unverifiable in principle – no possible observation could confirm that the universe is shrinking uniformly. All observers, along with their measuring devices, would be shrinking at the same rate as anything being measured. Hence, no universal shrinkage could be detected. Contrast 'The universe is shrinking uniformly' with the proposition 'There are intelligent life-forms in other galaxies'. The propositions may seem similar because they both refer to situations outside of our immediate experience. But, nevertheless, there is a crucial difference between them. Unlike 'The universe is shrinking uniformly', the second proposition is verifiable in principle. We do have some ideas about what observations would confirm it. The conceivability of empirical observations – potential, not actual, verification – relevant to the truth or falsity of a proposition is enough to render it meaningful according to the logical positivists' theory of meaning.[37]

Why were the logical positivists led to posit the verification principle? The hyperbolic doubt of René Descartes (1596–1650) was a major impetus behind the development of modern philosophy. Indeed, Descartes is widely regarded as its founder. He argued that we might be mistaken about virtually anything we currently think we know. Our apparent 'knowledge' could be the result of illusion or a dream-state, or it could even be caused by an evil demon.[38] The logical positivists responded to Descartes' scepticism by claiming that we can at least be certain that we are having the experience of seeing particular colours and shapes, and of hearing particular sounds. In short, we can be certain of our own 'sense data'. But if we can only be certain of sense data, then our knowledge of the world needs to be understood in terms of such sense experience. What, then, of things we are not currently experiencing? We can refer to things in the world by means of the sense data we would have if we were to engage in certain actions. So, we can refer to the wall in front of us by means of the colours and shapes that we associate with that wall, but we can also refer to an object behind that wall by means of the sense data we would have as a result of climbing over the wall. Hence, saying that a ball is on the other side of the wall is really to say that there are certain experiences one would have were one to go over the wall. In other words, the meaning of 'There is a ball on the other side of the wall' consists in the experiences one would have in seeing or touching that ball. The method of verification of that statement consists, then, in what one would need to do in order to have the appropriate experiences. If there were no experiences that one could possibly have that would verify a statement, then that statement is not referring to anything. For reference is constructed out of actual and possible experiences. And in failing to refer, such a statement would be meaningless.

At the root of logical positivism, then, was the fundamental conviction that to exist is to make an empirically observable difference. Perhaps one reason for the astounding popularity of logical positivism was that its fundamental conviction struck many as intuitively plausible. Few would deny that empirical verification is, and ought to remain, central among our means of gaining knowledge about the world. Furthermore, the astonishing scientific advances that occurred during the twentieth century convinced many of the efficacy of pursuing knowledge through empirical investigation of the natural world.

Verification and religious belief

However, the price of adopting the verification principle as the sole criterion of meaning proved to be a high one. Not only were religious claims consigned to the set of meaningless propositions – for many religious claims seem immune to verification or falsification – but aesthetic and ethical claims met the same fate. Consider, for example, what possible experience could verify the claim 'Murder is morally wrong'. We might be able to verify that people say that murder is morally wrong, and we might be able to verify that they behave as if they believe it to be so. But how do we verify that it really is morally wrong? Purported ethical properties, such as rightness and wrongness, are not, logical positivists claim, given in sense data. We cannot experience, say, wrongness, in the way that we can experience, say, hotness or coldness. Because it appears that religious, aesthetic and ethical claims are incapable of verification by any possible experience, such claims were widely thought to be incapable of either truth or falsity.[39] Hence, many came to regard the very idea of religious, aesthetic, or ethical knowledge as vacuous.

On the other hand, this also led some to conclude that something must be amiss with the verification principle. Nevertheless, many were reluctant to give up the idea that if beliefs are true, there ought to be something within our possible experience that can, at least in principle, confirm their truth. The worry is that to give up the verification principle seems tantamount to admitting that the relationship between knowledge and experience is unimportant, and that fantasy or wish-fulfilment are no less legitimate as sources of knowledge than is veridical experience. Consider the following well-known parable:

> Once upon a time two explorers came upon a clearing in the jungle. In the jungle were growing many flowers and many weeds. One explorer says, 'Some gardener must tend this plot.' The other disagrees, 'There is no gardener.' So they pitch their tents and set a watch. No gardener is ever seen. 'But perhaps he is an invisible gardener.' So they set up a barbed-wire fence. They electrify it. They patrol with bloodhounds. (For they remember how H. G. Wells's 'Invisible Man' could be both smelt and touched though he could not be seen.) But no shrieks ever suggest that some intruder has received a shock. No movements of the wire ever betray an invisible climber. The bloodhounds never give a cry. Yet still the Believer is not convinced. 'But there is a gardener, invisible, intangible, insensible to electric shocks, a gardener who has no scent and makes no sound, a gardener who comes secretly to look after the garden which he loves.' At last the Sceptic despairs, 'But what remains of your original assertion? Just how does what you call an invisible, intangible, eternally elusive gardener differ from an imaginary gardener or even from no gardener at all?'[40]

Antony Flew employs this parable to demonstrate the process of adding *ad hoc* qualifications by which the claims of religious believers become increasingly detached from experience, and hence from all possible verification or falsification. At the end of the parable, the Sceptic accuses the

Believer of claiming nothing at all. If the existence of the gardener can make no observable difference to the universe, then one may as well admit that the claim that the gardener exists is neither true nor false. Now, consider the claim 'God exists'. The Sceptic will challenge the Believer as follows: what observable difference does it make to the universe whether the claim 'God exists' is true or not? What actual, or possible, observable evidence would either verify or falsify this claim?

Flew argues that as theists are extremely reluctant to accept that observation of the world can falsify their belief that God exists,[41] they should be equally reluctant to accept such observation as verifying that belief. But reluctance to take observation into account renders their claim 'God exists' neither verifiable nor falsifiable. And if their claim is neither verifiable nor falsifiable, then, from the point of view of someone who accepts the verification theory of meaning, it is neither true nor false. In other words, the claim 'God exists' is not a meaningful claim at all.[42] But, continues Flew, theists do regard 'God exists' as meaningful, therefore they cannot avoid the responsibility of specifying some observation which would be relevant to its verification or falsification.

Defusing the verificationist's challenge

One possible response a theist might offer to a verificationist relies on the distinction between 'direct' and 'indirect' verification. A theist will probably not even try to argue that, during this life, at least, 'God exists' can be verified or falsified by the kind of *direct* observation that would satisfy a logical positivist. This is because the qualities typically ascribed to God by monotheists (infinite, perfectly good, eternal, for example) are not the sorts of qualities that finite, morally weak and mortal human beings are likely to be able to observe directly. Indeed, John Hick argues that while the method of direct verification is appropriate for physical objects, it is not appropriate for a wider range of phenomena – specifically, but not exclusively, religious phenomena. To illustrate this point, consider the claims you might make about the character of one of your best friends. Are claims about your friend's character directly verifiable in the same way as your claims about medium-sized physical objects? Can you *directly observe* that your friend is honourable, just, kind, and so on? On the other hand, can you *directly observe* anything that contradicts these claims about your friend, and thus falsifies them?[43]

To account for your mooted knowledge of your friend's character, without abandoning the basic verificationist insight that claims should have some relationship to experience, one might appeal to the notion of *indirect* verification. Claims, like those about a person's character, might be progressively confirmed through the accumulation of a variety of observations. The notion of indirect verification thus may enable one to explain how it is that claims that cannot be directly verified nevertheless have some connection to experience. Such claims might include those concerning religion, morality, aesthetics and even large-scale scientific theories (as such theories typically cannot be confirmed by means of direct observation). With regard to the core claim of monotheism – namely, that God exists – Hick posits that the 'experiential confirmation of God's existence will not ... consist in a direct observation of God but in experiencing features of the universe, as it changes through time, which trace the difference that the existence of God makes.'[44]

What features of the universe might we experience that 'trace the difference that the existence of God makes', and thus provide indirect verification of God's existence? Hick advises us to attend to all those 'features of the universe' which 'constitute the fulfilment of the divine purpose for the creation'.[45] For, as Hick points out, the Abrahamic religions portray time as linear. Time flows in one direction from the beginning to the end of the universe. Moreover, this linear conception of time is combined with the view that the universe is moving towards a final state. And the achievement of this state was the reason why God created the universe. This final state is variously conceived as the kingdom of God, paradise, or heaven and hell. Hick suggests that we call it the 'eschatological state' or 'escaton'. And if the universe is indeed becoming closer to the final state as time passes, then we should be able to observe it slowly changing for the better. Such observations will count as indirect evidence for the existence of God. In addition, Hick claims that in the eschatological state we will be able to experience God with a new clarity that is not possible here and now:

> Whereas in this life the sense of God's presence occurs in tension with experiences of pain and suffering, of injustice and the triumph of evil, which continually challenge its authenticity, in the eschatological state there will be no such tension. Our God-consciousness will be unimpeded and free from any seeds of doubt.[46]

Hick's strategy to meet the verificationist's challenge, then, is to propose that religious claims can be indirectly verified by careful observation of the world in its current state, and that these claims will be directly verified in the eschaton – the final state of the universe. At the end of time, then, our observations will either verify or falsify religious claims, particularly the claim 'God exists'. Relating this to the examples used earlier, Hick would claim that 'God exists' is like the proposition 'There are intelligent life-forms in other galaxies' (because it is verifiable in principle, if not in practice), and unlike the proposition 'The universe is shrinking uniformly' (because the latter *is* unverifiable in principle).

Although Hick's argument is couched in the language of an (albeit qualified) verificationist, still a verificationist might not be entirely convinced. The cogency of Hick's response hinges on whether or not we can coherently imagine an eschatological state in which we are in a position to make observations. If a philosopher denies that such a state of affairs is coherent, then he or she will not find Hick's argument satisfying. And there is at least one good reason why someone might question the coherence of this state of affairs: observation is a process that takes place in time. However, time is supposed to have ended in the escaton. If there is no time, there can be no observation, and without observation neither verification nor falsification can take place. Perhaps, then, Hick's attempt to immunize religious beliefs from the challenge of verificationism rests on a logical inconsistency.

An alternative response to the verificationist's challenge, adopted by some theists, involves biting the bullet, and conceding that religious claims are not propositions and do not convey information. The philosopher R. M. Hare employs this strategy when he proposes that the content of religious belief is a distinctive attitude to the world.[47] In Hare's view, being a religious believer centrally involves commitment to a particular religious attitude, not to a set of propositions. If he is correct, the verificationist challenge to religious belief is misguided because it relies on a false theory concerning the nature of religion. But does Hare's characterization of religion as an attitude genuinely capture religion's essence and allow the theist to evade the challenge posed by verificationism? Perhaps Hare has rashly conceded too much to verificationism? The claim that religious beliefs are non-informative and merely express a particular religious attitude struck many twentieth-century theists as far too drastic a response to the threat of verificationism. Rather than opt for this purported solution, other philosophers who were sympathetic to religion confronted the verificationist's philosophy head-on. They proposed that verificationists were simply mistaken in their claim that unverifiable (and unfalsifiable) propositions are meaningless.

Brian Davies, for example, objects that people do, in fact, 'seem to be able to understand statements without being able to say what available sense experience would make it likely or unlikely that they are true' – an ability which adherents of the verification theory of meaning cannot explain.[48] Richard Swinburne illustrates this ability by means of the following example:

A man can understand the statement 'Once upon a time, before there were men or any other rational creatures, the earth was covered by sea', without his having any idea what geological evidence would count for or against this proposition, or any idea of how to establish what geological evidence would count for or against the proposition.[49]

On the face of it, the ability to understand the meaning of statements without having any idea how they might be verified does not augur well for the verification principle and its associated theory of meaning. Like the person who says he understands the proposition in Swinburne's example, a theist might claim that she understands the proposition 'God exists' despite the fact that she has no idea what sense experience would count for or against its truth. If we are prepared to admit that the theist could be right about her own ability to understand the proposition 'God exists', then, Davies and Swinburne argue, the verification principle and the verificationist theory of meaning must be discarded.

However, Swinburne's example might be accused of missing the significance of the logical positivists' insistence that verification or falsification of a proposition need only be possible *in principle* for it to count as meaningful. Consider the following: had, counterfactually, there been humans around when 'the earth was covered by sea', then we have no difficulty envisaging what kind of experiences they would have enjoyed. This could be taken to provide some meaningful content for claims about the prehistoric past. But we do not have even the slightest idea of what kind of experience might verify the claim that murder is morally wrong, rather than that people say that it is morally wrong or that they act as if they believe it to be so. In other words, there are certain propositions, logical positivists could insist, that are of a quite different order to those concerning the distant past. And religious claims, they could further insist, are of this different order.

Nevertheless, despite the wide success initially enjoyed by logical positivism and the seeming abundance of its resources for answering objections to it, many simply rejected the verificationist principle out of hand because it appeared to rule out meaningful talk about far too many vitally important aspects of our lives – aspects which many insist we are able to talk about meaningfully. As we have seen, above, by means of the verification principle, the logical positivists had denied meaning not only to religious claims but also to ethical and aesthetic ones. All such assertions were consigned to the realm of the meaningless. To many, this was simply beyond the pale. But more importantly, serious philosophical problems with this extreme form of empiricism were evident to many from the late 1940s onwards. For example, Willard van Orman Quine (1908–2000) famously came to challenge the cogency of the analytic/synthetic distinction (for he argued that any proposition is, in principle, revisable, and hence not simply true by definition), and, as we shall see in Chapter 11, offered in its place a more holistic theory of meaning. In doing so he dealt, what many philosophers regarded as, a fatal blow to logical positivism.[50]

Moreover, some philosophers began to wonder how the logical positivists could establish that the verification principle was itself meaningful:

for it does not seem to be analytically true, yet what observations could possibly establish the truth or falsity of logical positivism's key principle? As Davies points out, it seems unlikely that there is any sense experience that would 'count in favour of the claim that a [proposition is only] ... meaningful if some sense experience or observation statement makes it probable or counts in its favour'.[51] In which case, it would appear that, by their own lights, logical positivists base their philosophy upon a meaningless claim. On the other hand, if, as seems likely, the verification principle, while being neither analytically true nor in principle empirically verifiable or falsifiable, is nevertheless not meaningless, how can logical positivists be justified in confidently rejecting certain other propositions that are neither analytically true nor empirically verifiable as meaningless (such as religious, moral or aesthetic ones)?

As the limitations of logical positivism became increasingly apparent, its popularity waned. And once the grip of verificationism had loosened, philosophers began to experiment with new ways of characterizing the relationship between reason and religion. Consequently, the debate between atheists and theists began to exhibit fresh dimensions. The key figure in this new development was Ludwig Wittgenstein.

Wittgenstein on the proper role of philosophy

As a young man, Wittgenstein had strong ties to the Vienna circle. He later broke with them, however, and developed a radically different style of philosophizing. In several works, posthumously published during the 1950s and 1960s,[52] Wittgenstein presented novel views on a wide range of philosophical topics: principally the theory of knowledge, the theory of meaning, philosophy of language and philosophy of mind. Despite the fact that Wittgenstein wrote very little explicitly on the topic of religion, his ideas have had a tremendous impact on the philosophy of religion, as well as on academic theology.[53]

In his later works, Wittgenstein claims that the only legitimate role that philosophy may perform is to enable the philosopher to acquire a sympathetic understanding of the views ordinary people express in language. Criticism of these views lies outside the scope of philosophy's purpose, Wittgenstein famously iterates. Underlying this claim lies a radical break with the modern Western philosophical tradition. Prior to Wittgenstein, philosophers had viewed their *raison d'être* as the shedding of light on superstitious, irrational beliefs in the hope of freeing people from them. We saw, above, that the logical positivists regarded religious beliefs as nonsense and, as such, not worthy of serious consideration. They thought that philosophers were performing a great service to humanity by exposing all metaphysics as meaningless nonsense.

Moreover, philosophers sympathetic to logical positivism lamented the undisciplined use of language that resulted in the utterance of wholesale gibberish. Some, Bertrand Russell, for example, went so far as to propose reforms of spoken languages in order to bring them more into line with the findings of modern philosophy. Clearly, Wittgenstein's insistence that the only legitimate role of philosophy was to understand the views of ordinary people is tantamount to rejecting all of these claims outright. With this rejection, he ushered in a new stage in the history of Western philosophy – a stage characterized by a preoccupation with 'ordinary language'. Here, we consider several key features of Wittgenstein's theory of language, as well as the theory that he attempts to replace.

Wittgenstein shared a central concern with the philosophy he set out to reject: namely, how best to explain the nature of linguistic meaning? Many modern philosophers, including, as we have seen, the logical positivists, had also attempted to provide an account of meaning. Most followed the proposals of John Locke.[54] Locke argues that non-mental objects are never directly accessible to the mind, and hence that the mind can never apply words to them directly. He then considers what is directly available to the mind if it is not non-mental objects, and concludes that it must be 'ideas'.[55] If only ideas are available to the mind, he reasons, then it must be these that words signify. Our language, concludes Locke, is thus connected to things in the world through the mediation of our ideas. Locke's basic thesis, then, is that while ideas are signs of things, words are signs of ideas:[56]

> For since the Things, the Mind contemplates, are none of them, besides it self, present to the Understanding, 'tis necessary that something else, as a Sign or Representation of the thing it considers, should be present to it: And these are *Ideas*. And because the Scene of *Ideas* that makes one Man's Thoughts, cannot be laid open to the immediate view of another, nor laid up any where but in the Memory, a no very sure Repository: Therefore to communicate our Thoughts to one another, as well as record them for our own use, Signs of our *Ideas* are also necessary. Those which Men have found most convenient, and therefore generally make use of, are articulate Sounds.[57]

Locke describes the relation between ideas and things as a natural relation. Specifically, he construes it as a relation based on a causal connection: things cause the particular ideas associated with them. In contrast, he considers the relation between words and ideas as an arbitrary relation. To be precise, the association between particular words and particular ideas is entirely a matter of convention. The meaning of words, then, is a function of their ability to signify ideas that represent things. So, at the most fundamental level, the representative power of our ideas underlies the meaning possessed by our words.

While this theory of language has proved attractive to many, it has certain disadvantages. The chief disadvantage is the distance the theory posits between our language and the things to which we attempt to use language to refer. According to Locke, our language is far removed from the things that we usually assume ourselves to be talking about. For example, when I see my neighbour's dog and I say 'I see my neighbour's dog', the word 'dog' is not used as a sign for the dog in the world but as a sign of an idea in my mind.

Locke's theory of language left an important puzzle unresolved. Many subsequent philosophers found its account of the relationship between ideas and things particularly unsatisfactory. How exactly do our ideas represent things? Locke's failure to provide a convincing answer to this question left a crucial lacuna in his theory. Wittgenstein's rejection of the Lockean theory was prompted by his conviction that it left the link between ideas and things ultimately mysterious. Wittgenstein proposes that meaning will always be inexplicable as long as it is thought to depend on a mysterious link between ideas and non-verbal objects. As a solution to the mystery of meaning, Wittgenstein argues, instead, that we should concentrate on language in its everyday use rather than on seemingly fixed relations between words, ideas and things. Hence, a major theme of Wittgenstein's later writings is that a viable theory of language cannot explain meaning by appeal to the representative function of ideas. In opposition to the older representational theory of language, Wittgenstein proposed a new theory; the central idea being expressed in the slogan 'meaning is use'.[58]

Clearly, if the meaning of a locution is its use, then to ascertain the meaning of any statement, one should examine the way that people ordinarily employ it. If Wittgenstein is correct, meaning will be exhibited in ordinary linguistic practice. The theory of meaning proposed by Wittgenstein, then, is aligned with his new conception of the role of philosophy: 'Philosophy may in no way interfere with the actual use of language; it can only describe it. For it cannot give it any foundation either. It leaves everything as it is.'[59] Practised thus, philosophy would emerge, Wittgenstein famously claims, as a form of therapy – a therapy that he regarded as a remedy for the puzzles generated by the former way of doing philosophy.

But what if a philosopher heeds Wittgenstein's advice, and attends to the way that ordinary speakers use language, only to find that they do not always use language consistently? Wittgenstein argues that correct use is to be judged by the standards of the linguistic community. Even if linguistic practices prove to be inconsistent, the mere fact that language is employed in a social context is enough to dignify it with meaning. If a locution has a use, it has a meaning; and if it has more than one use, it has more than one meaning. In short, it is the linguistic community that establishes what meanings statements have. Language is public, and its use is governed by socially accepted standards. One implication of this is that a private language is incoherent. Language has its meaning because of its public use. Yet in attempting to apprehend the world on the basis of personal sensations (sense data), the logical positivists seemed to require language to be able to refer to purely private experiences. If Wittgenstein's claims are correct, then logical positivism seems to be premised upon a mistaken view of language.

Wittgenstein's new theory of linguistic meaning had a profound effect on the attitude of many philosophers towards religious belief. Clearly, people do have religious beliefs and they typically express these beliefs in language. According to Wittgenstein, the mere fact that religious language is used establishes that it has meaning. The philosopher has no business questioning such meaning, or claiming that propositions expressing religious beliefs are somehow deficient in meaning. Instead, the philosopher should simply examine the meaning given in the language religious believers use, and attempt to describe that language: 'Philosophy simply puts everything before us, and neither explains nor deduces anything. – Since everything lies open to view there is nothing to explain.'[60] In other words, philosophers should focus their attention on the things that believers actually say. And in doing so, criticism is out of place.

Wittgenstein's theory of meaning proved to be immensely popular among European and North American philosophers in the analytical tradition, and his influence long outlasted that of the logical positivists. His distinctive personality attracted a number of devoted students, who spread and popularized his ideas.[61] The effect of these ideas on the way that many philosophers viewed the relationship between reason and religion was almost immediate. It was as if the siege under which modern philosophy had placed religion since the eighteenth century had suddenly been lifted.

Malcolm on the groundlessness of religious belief

As we have seen, according to Wittgenstein, philosophy could not legitimately be deployed to criticize religious beliefs but only to understand them. This view has an important implication that Wittgenstein did not emphasize: namely, that it is also beyond the legitimate function of philosophy to support religious beliefs. A philosopher would exhibit a misunderstanding of the scope of philosophy if he or she were to seek rational grounds for such beliefs. In other words, philosophers should not seek foundations for beliefs of a religious nature. Norman Malcolm (1911–90), a former student of Wittgenstein, elaborates on this idea by claiming that religious belief is groundless. This claim assumed huge importance within the philosophy of religion in the second half of the twentieth century. Moreover, its prominence within academia ensured that its impact was felt in the world at large. What, then, does Malcolm mean when he claims that religious belief is groundless?

Malcolm's non-foundationalism was inspired by an entry in one of Wittgenstein's last notebooks: it is difficult 'to realize the groundlessness of our believing'.[62] Wittgenstein's point seems to have been that we hold a huge proportion of our beliefs on the basis of no evidence whatsoever. In other words, we accept a vast number of beliefs simply on trust or without giving them much thought. Moreover, it rarely, if ever, occurs to us to doubt most of these beliefs – unless, that is, our thinking has been contaminated by malpractised philosophy. As an example of a fundamental belief that most of us simply accept without reflection, Malcolm proposes 'the belief that familiar material things (watches, shoes, chairs) do not cease to exist without some physical explanation',[63] adding that

> [o]ur attitude in this matter is striking. We would not be willing to consider it as even improbable that a missing lawn chair had 'just ceased to exist'. We would not entertain such a suggestion. If anyone proposed it we would be sure he was joking. It is no exaggeration to say that this attitude is part of the foundation of our thinking. I do not want to say that this attitude is *un*reasonable, but rather that it is something that we do not *try* to support with grounds. It could be said to belong to 'the framework' of our thinking about material things.[64]

The key claim is that significant proportions of our beliefs are embedded within a framework composed of fundamental beliefs that cannot be seriously questioned. Beliefs supported by the framework can be questioned, however, and we may seek justification for them by appealing to the fundamental beliefs themselves. The latter cannot be justified but must be simply accepted. Moreover, according to Malcolm, it is largely our upbringing within a particular human community that determines which beliefs are fundamental to us: 'The framework propositions that we accept, grow into, are not idiosyncrasies but common ways of speaking and thinking that are pressed on us by our human community.'[65] The sense in which our fundamental beliefs are thought to be groundless should now be clear. They are groundless insofar as they form part of the framework within which non-fundamental beliefs are embedded. Groundless beliefs, unlike the non-fundamental ones, are not dependent on evidence and do not require justification.

Malcolm applies this analysis to religious beliefs, claiming that these fall into two categories: the fundamental and the non-fundamental. Beliefs in the first category are insensitive to evidence. They are simply accepted, and hence form the framework that supports beliefs in the second category (which are sensitive to evidence). This analysis of religious belief adheres to Wittgenstein's stipulations about the legitimate scope of philosophy. Malcolm thus purports to describe two kinds of religious belief that ordinary people hold, even though they may not be aware of the distinction before a philosopher succeeds in pointing it out to them.

Now, Malcolm is occasionally misunderstood when he claims that belief is groundless, for his distinction between the two kinds of belief is often overlooked. His view is that non-fundamental religious beliefs are grounded upon fundamental ones, but the latter are themselves groundless. The significance of this is that, even if it were legitimate for philosophy to criticize certain everyday assumptions, it would be illegitimate for it to criticize fundamental religious beliefs on the basis of their groundlessness. All fundamental beliefs are groundless, on Malcolm's Wittgensteinian view. Fundamental religious beliefs, like any fundamental belief, should simply be accepted because they are not in need of justification and are not candidates for doubt. People can, of course, still argue about, criticize, and doubt non-fundamental religious beliefs. But to do so presupposes that they first accept the framework that makes possible these critical activities.[66] So, if Malcolm is right, fundamental religious beliefs have a special status that protects them from criticism: they are groundless, insensitive to evidence and lacking ultimate justification.

However, not all philosophers find this acceptable. Many feel that religious discourse is not solely justified by its use within a particular community. Rather, in their view, it rests upon a genuine foundation: an omnipotent, omniscient, perfectly good God. And for those who hold that there are genuine foundations for religious claims, it is irrational to hold religious beliefs that are groundless, insensitive to evidence and unjustified. And surely, many would argue, believers are not completely mistaken in seeking some rational grounds for their religious beliefs. For if they were to allow that there could, in principle, be no such grounds, would they not be implicitly conceding an inability to distinguish between beliefs that genuinely tell us something about reality and those that might not? However, a global non-foundationalist could reply that even science is ultimately without foundations. Scientific discourse equally obtains its meaning by its use. Hence, religion no less tells us the truth than science. Nevertheless, a serious problem would seem to remain. If religious beliefs are not rationally grounded, it can seem that there can be no rational grounds for adhering to one consistent set rather than another – a conclusion that would trouble many believers. Admittedly, Malcolm thought that we were only entitled to accept without justification the beliefs that formed part of the framework of thought in which we had grown up. But where does that leave those who have not been brought up to accept any religious framework? Just as the logical positivists, perhaps, went too far in the evidential demands they laid on religious belief, it may be that

Malcolm has also gone too far towards the other extreme. I now turn to a position that attempts to occupy a middle ground.

The middle ground: reformed epistemology

During the last two decades of the twentieth century, a new movement emerged within academic philosophy of religion. The central conviction motivating this movement was that it could be rational to hold religious beliefs *regardless* of whether or not arguments in favour of them, or evidence in support of them, are available. This conviction was reminiscent of the ideology of the sixteenth-century Christian reformers, specifically John Calvin. Hence, the movement took the name 'reformed epistemology'. Reformed epistemologists embrace their link with the reformers of the past, given that they, too, are Protestant Christians. Key figures in the movement are William P. Alston,[67] Nicholas Wolterstorff,[68] and Alvin Plantinga.[69] In the following, we shall principally be concerned with the latter's views.[70]

As we have seen, Malcolm's claim that religious beliefs are not rationally grounded is unacceptable to many believers. And many epistemologists[71] assume that evidence in support of a belief is required if it is to be deemed rational for someone to hold that belief. It is precisely this assumption that Plantinga rejects in an attempt to avoid the worries raised by Malcolm's theory. Plantinga, like Malcolm, questions the cogency of traditional foundationalist epistemology, according to which all beliefs that it is rational to subscribe to fall into one of two categories: they are either (a) self-evident or incorrigible; or (b) derived from, and hence justified by, beliefs that are in category (a). Clearly, religious beliefs fall into neither category. Hence, according to this epistemological theory, it is not rational to hold them. Traditionally, category (a) is taken to provide the foundations for category (b). The solution, Plantinga claims, is not to reject foundationalism, as Malcolm does, but to modify it so that a broader range of beliefs can be regarded as foundational, or as he puts it: 'properly basic'.[72] And Plantinga hopes to persuade us that religious beliefs can be properly basic under certain conditions. But first he has to offer a plausible theory about how we might identify properly basic beliefs. Rejecting the idea that a criterion of proper basicality is required before we can begin assessing particular beliefs, he proposes that we

> must assemble examples of beliefs and conditions such that the former are obviously properly basic in the latter, and examples of beliefs and conditions such that the former are obviously *not* properly basic in the latter. We must then frame hypotheses as to the necessary and sufficient conditions of proper basicality and test these hypotheses by

reference to those examples. Under the right conditions, for example, it is clearly rational to believe that you see a human person before you: a being who has thoughts and feelings, who knows and believes things, who makes decisions and acts. It is clear, furthermore, that you are under no obligation to reason to this belief from others you hold; under those conditions that belief is properly basic for you.[73]

Notice that, according to Plantinga, under normal circumstances it would be incorrect to claim that the belief that there is a human person in front of one is groundless. Under the right conditions, this belief is grounded in the experience one has had of the person in front of one. So, in Plantinga's view, properly basic beliefs may lack justification in other beliefs while being neither groundless nor irrational.[74] The important point is that, if Plantinga is right, a belief can be properly basic even though it is neither self-evident (or incorrigible), nor justified by a self-evident (or incorrigible) belief.

Plantinga, then, attempts to broaden the class of propositions that can be regarded as properly basic to include beliefs that are generated by personal experience. He does not argue that highly abstract beliefs are properly basic, because they are not directly related to our experience. Plantinga concedes that the proposition 'God exists' is abstract, and hence is not a candidate for proper basicality. He proposes, however, that other important religious beliefs should be regarded as properly basic because they are typically generated by the experience of those who hold them. Plantinga provides the following examples:

God is speaking to me.
God has created all this.
God disapproves of what I have done.
God forgives me.
God is to be thanked and praised.[75]

Because such beliefs are generated by experience, in Plantinga's view, they can be properly basic. There is a qualification, however. Such beliefs can only be properly basic to whomever has the relevant experience. Nevertheless, if the proper basicality of such beliefs is conceded, then the abstract proposition 'God exists' should be regarded as justified (at least to those people for whom the other beliefs are properly basic). 'It is not', writes Plantinga, 'the relatively high-level and general proposition *God exists* that is properly basic, but instead propositions detailing some of his attributes or actions.'[76] Upon this claim stands Plantinga's attempt to find a middle ground between the logical positivists' charge that religious beliefs are meaningless because they are insensitive to observation, and Malcolm's claim that religious beliefs (at least the fundamental ones) are groundless and not appropriate subjects for rational debate. The middle ground occupied by Plantinga purports to view a significant number of religious beliefs as grounded in experience (contra the verificationists), and as rational (contra Malcolm) because properly basic.

Although Plantinga's variety of reformed epistemology has been enormously influential, his account of religious belief raises significant problems. One concerns the religious propositions that Plantinga regards as basic for those who have the relevant experience. It may be that the gap between an experience and its interpretation as, say, 'God speaking to me', is wider than Plantinga would allow. The more tenuous the relation between experience and interpretation is thought to be, the less plausible will seem Plantinga's claim that propositions expressing purported religious experiences are properly basic. Moreover, if the same experience could have a religious and a non-religious interpretation (for example, a psychological one), then Plantinga's claim will seem even less persuasive. Another mooted problem is that Plantinga's account of religious belief can be used to support a number of different and competing religious belief systems. Plantinga's characterization of proper basicality would seem to commit him to holding that the beliefs of a variety of religious faiths may be rational.[77] This is not a conclusion that Plantinga, as a Christian exclusivist,[78] would be willing to accept. Malcolm's position left no grounds for rationally preferring one religion to another (one was expected to embrace whichever tradition within which one was brought up); it seems that Plantinga has arrived at the same impasse. How is one to judge between rival religious belief systems?[79] Plantinga must surely resort to arguments if he wishes to promote his own religion – Christianity – as rationally preferable to others. But then, it would seem that philosophers of religion, in an effort to produce pertinent arguments, must once more resort to natural theology.

Conclusion

We have examined some important criticisms of religious belief advanced by twentieth-century philosophers. The most powerful criticism was mounted by empiricist philosophers who argued that experience does not (or never could) support rational belief in the existence of God. The fact that many believers claim to have a personal religious experience was widely thought to be irrelevant as a defence against this criticism. Because of the possibility of hallucination, and because mere appearances can be deceptive, empiricists are only prepared to accept as justifiable evidence those experiences which are in principle available to anyone who is in relevantly similar circumstances. Religious experience is typically unrepeatable and, moreover, is subject to various interpretations. It is not, therefore, the sort of experience that an empiricist would regard as capable of yielding genuine knowledge.

Consequently, most twentieth-century philosophers of religion were preoccupied with the pursuit of the sort of religious knowledge that might be available to a neutral observer. In an effort to break away from the characterization of religious belief as inferior to such knowledge, Malcolm – following Wittgenstein – claimed that religious belief was groundless. Many, however, found this position unsatisfactory because it entailed that the holding of religious belief could not be rationally justified; a conclusion that flies in the face of most traditional religious teaching. And such attempted truce between philosophy and religion thus came with too high a price attached: religious belief could be neither criticized nor ultimately supported. This conclusion was unwelcome to many religious thinkers who feared that religion would simply cease to be relevant if it could not be rationally defended.

It is clear that, at the end of the twentieth century, the relationship between religion and philosophy was no longer constituted simply by the open conflict typical of the earlier part of the century.[80] For philosophy has also been deployed in an attempt to push religious thought forward. In Chapter 6, we examine how a similar shift has taken place with respect to the relationship between science and religious belief. However, in the following chapter, we consider the impact on their belief systems of changing views about the language used by religious believers.

Study questions

1 What reasons did Immanuel Kant give for his claim that 'religious knowledge' is an oxymoron? Do you agree with his position?

2 How did the separation between knowledge and faith promoted by eighteenth-century thinkers such as Immanuel Kant prepare the way for the marginalization of the concept 'God' within European intellectual life?

3 Should reason be used to assess religious belief?

4 Norman Malcolm claims that religious belief is a system which we do not choose to accept on the basis of evidence or grounds, but within which doubts can arise and questions can be asked. Rationality operates within the system, but cannot be used to justify the system itself. Do you agree? If not, why not?

5 Does doubt presuppose belief?

6 Do you agree with Ludwig Wittgenstein and Norman Malcolm that the role of philosophy is not to justify or undermine religious belief, but to understand it?

7 Alvin Plantinga and Norman Malcolm disagree about the nature of religious belief. In your view, which thinker gives the more accurate account?

Select bibliography

Alston, W. P., 1991, *Perceiving God: The Epistemology of Religious Experience*, Ithaca, New York: Cornell University Press.

Ayer, A. J., 1978, *Language, Truth and Logic*, Harmondsworth: Penguin.

Cohen, H., 1972, *Religion of Reason Out of the Sources of Judaism*, New York: Ungar.

Feiner, S. and D. J. Sorkin (eds), 2001, *New Perspectives on the Haskalah*, London: Littman Library of Jewish Civilization.

Hick, J., 1989, *An Interpretation of Religion: Human Responses to the Transcendent*, London: Macmillan.

Hume, D., 1970, *Dialogues Concerning Natural Religion*, Indianapolis: Bobbs-Merrill Company.

Kant, I., 1996, 'Religion Within the Bounds of Mere Reason' in *The Cambridge Edition of the Works of Immanuel Kant, Religion and Rational Theology*, trans. and edited by Allen Wood and George di Giovanni, Cambridge: Cambridge University Press, pp. 55–215.

Mitchell, B. (ed.), 1971, *The Philosophy of Religion*, Oxford: Oxford University Press.

Plantinga, A., 2000, *Warranted Christian Belief*, New York: Oxford University Press.

Schleiermacher, F. D. E., 1996, *On Religion: Speeches to Its Cultured Despisers*, trans. and edited by Richard Crouter, Cambridge: Cambridge University Press.

Swinburne, R., 1981, *Faith and Reason*, Oxford: Clarendon Press.

Wittgenstein, L., 1966, *Lectures and Conversations on Aesthetics, Psychology & Religious Belief*, Oxford: Blackwell, pp. 53–72.

Wittgenstein, L., 1988, *Philosophical Investigations*, trans. by G. E. M. Anscombe, Oxford: Blackwell.

Wynn, M., 1999, *God and Goodness: A Natural Theological Perspective*, London: Routledge.

Notes

1 Philosophy and religion have long been intimately related. In fact, in many cultures the origins of philosophy seem to lie in scepticism about religion. This is as true of ancient Chinese and Indian philosophies as it is of ancient Greek philosophy (from which the Western philosophical tradition sprouted).

2 Many of the ideas discussed in this chapter may appear somewhat abstract and, as such, unlikely to have had much impact on the religious faith of the majority of believers in the West. Indeed, many of the ideas only had a direct impact on a small minority – those educated in universities. This minority has, however, enjoyed a disproportionate influence. And via the twentieth-century media, the majority of the population has been given indirect access to these ideas.

3 Certain aspects of Christianity were, of course, challenged in the sixteenth century during the Reformation. However, in taking issue with the Church authorities, the mainstream reformers did not subject the core beliefs of the faith to criticism.

4 Moreover, during this period, Christians were engaged in colonizing the New World. Many devoted a great deal of effort to establishing Christianity in their new homeland. This enterprise involved spreading the faith to Native Americans, some of whom encountered European culture for the first time in the 1600s. Needless to say, this missionary environment did not facilitate deep questioning of the core beliefs of the faith.

5 One important exception was the rationalist philosopher Baruch de Spinoza (1632–77). Initially a member of the relatively successful Dutch Jewish community, Spinoza's unorthodox beliefs – for example, that there is no separation between God and the world – led to his excommunication. Despite this ostracism, his views had a significant impact on subsequent Jewish philosophers as well as on later gentile thinkers. He is regarded by many as the founder of the *Haskalah* – the Jewish Enlightenment.

6 In fact, as I remarked in the previous chapter, the Islamic intellectual tradition that formerly flourished in Andalusia enjoyed its final great representative, ibn Rushd, in the twelfth century. He was the last in a line of distinguished Muslim philosophers who each had a profound impact on Jewish and Christian thought.

7 In Chapter 8 I examine some ramifications, especially important in the twentieth century, of the restructured relationship between religion and politics that was a direct result of the European wars of religion.

8 This was famously given intellectual expression by a British philosopher, John Locke (1632–1704). See John Locke, 1983, *A Letter Concerning Toleration*, edited by James H. Tully, Indianapolis: Hackett Publishing Company.

9 Thomas Aquinas, for example, thought that the existence of God could be proved in five ways. Each 'way' is based on an examination of features of the natural world. See Thomas Aquinas, 1998, *Selected Philosophical Writings*, trans. by Timothy McDermott, Oxford: Oxford University Press, pp. 200ff.

10 I do not mean to suggest that natural theology lacks practitioners today. As we shall see in Chapter 6, arguments from design once more assumed a prominent place within religious philosophy in the late twentieth century. Richard Swinburne, one of the most illustrious philosophers of religion in recent times, contributed much to the ongoing tradition of natural theology. See Richard Swinburne, 1977, *The Coherence of Theism*, Oxford: Clarendon Press; Richard Swinburne, 1979, *The Existence of God*, Oxford: Clarendon Press; and Richard Swinburne, 1981, *Faith and Reason*, Oxford: Clarendon Press. For a more recent example of natural theology, see Mark Wynn, 1999, *God and Goodness: A Natural Theological Perspective*, London: Routledge.

11 The notion that suffering is a divinely inflicted punishment for sin has been particularly prominent within Judaism. Traditional Jews have appealed to this idea in an effort to explain calamities such as the destruction of the Second Temple in Jerusalem in AD 70 and the Nazi death-camps of the twentieth century.

12 In Chapter 8 we shall consider the form this problem (which is technically known as 'the problem of evil') took in the face of twentieth-century atrocities.

13 Interestingly, Voltaire did not entirely renounce belief in God. Rather than embrace atheism, he merely rejected Christianity (specifically Roman Catholicism), and declared himself a deist. To be precise, he believed that a creator God had originated the universe, and then took no further interest in it.

14 See Voltaire, 1991, *Candide, or, Optimism*, trans. and edited by Robert M. Adams, New York: W. W. Norton & Company. *Candide* was a parody of the views of the philosopher Gottfried Wilhelm Leibniz (1646–1716), who famously argued that this is the best of all possible worlds.

15 David Hume, 1970, *Dialogues Concerning Natural Religion*, Indianapolis: Bobbs-Merrill Company.

16 Immanuel Kant, 1996, 'Religion Within the Bounds of Mere Reason' in *The Cambridge Edition of the Works of Immanuel Kant, Religion and Rational Theology*, trans. and edited by Allen Wood and George di Giovanni, Cambridge: Cambridge University Press, pp. 55–215.

17 Kant declares: 'historical faith (which is based upon revelation as experience) has only particular validity, namely for those in contact with the history on which the faith rests, and, like all cognition based on experience, carries with it the consciousness not that the object believed in *must* be so and not otherwise but only that it *is* so; hence it carries at the same time the consciousness of contingency. This faith can therefore indeed suffice as an ecclesiastical faith (of which there can be several); but only the pure faith of religion, based entirely on reason, can be recognised as necessary and hence as the one which exclusively marks out the *true* church.' 'Religion', p. 146.

18 His books were banned by the Roman Catholic Church until 1929.

19 This term is derived from 'eschatology', which refers to the part of theology that is concerned with death and final destiny, or 'the end times'.

20 In an early work, one that surprisingly retains its relevance today, Schleiermacher defends religion to his educated, cultured contemporaries, who tended to believe it to be intellectually redundant. See F. D. E. Schleiermacher, 1996, *On Religion: Speeches to Its Cultured Despisers*, trans. and edited by Richard Crouter, Cambridge: Cambridge University Press.

21 For an excellent selection of essays on the *Haskalah*, see Shmuel Feiner and David J. Sorkin (eds), 2001, *New Perspectives on the Haskalah*, London: Littman Library of Jewish Civilization.

22 See Allan Arkush, 1994, *Moses Mendelssohn and the Enlightenment*, Albany: State University of New York Press.

23 Moses Mendelssohn, 1983, *Jerusalem: Or, on Religious Power and Judaism*, trans. by Allan Arkush, Hanover: Brandeis University Press. *Jerusalem* was first published in 1783, just two years after Emperor Joseph II issued an edict of toleration which, among other things, abolished the practice of forcing Jews to wear distinctive clothing and allowed them to attend imperial universities for the first time.

24 The impulse to separate genuine religion from redundant superstitions led to the development of Reform Judaism. See Chapter 3, pp. 48f.

25 There were notable exceptions, of course. Hermann Cohen (1842–1918), for example, applied Kant's philosophy to Judaism at this time. See Hermann Cohen, 1972, *Religion of Reason Out of the Sources of Judaism*, New York: Ungar.

26 Bertrand Russell, 1957, 'Why I am Not a Christian: An Examination of the God-Idea and Christianity' in P. Edwards (ed.), *Why I am Not a Christian, and Other Essays on Religion and Related Subjects*, New York: Simon and Schuster, pp. 3–23.

27 Russell, 'Why', p. 22.

28 Russell, 'Why', p. 22.

29 Russell, 'Why', p. 23.

30 'Proposition' is a technical term used by philosophers to denote whatever it is that a sentence expresses.

31 Shortly, I explain in more detail what this means.

32 The core group within this movement, which was led by Moritz Schlick (1882–1936), was known as the 'Vienna circle'. Their ideas were widely popularized by A. J. Ayer (1910–89). Although logical positivism dominated Western philosophy for a number of years, and had a profound impact on many other disciplines (such as economics and political science), by the 1950s the movement was beginning to lose ground among professional philosophers. By then, however, the movement had become widespread – with influential proponents throughout Europe and in the United States. The speed at which logical positivism spread can in part be attributed to the rapid exodus of intellectuals out of Austria and Germany in the 1930s and 1940s.

33 Theists, however, frequently claim that 'God exists' is true by definition, and thus is analytic.

34 Synthetic propositions are the result of a *synthesis* of two logically distinct things – for example, 'This *dog* is *dirty*'. Because dogs and dirtiness are conceptually distinct, we have no difficulty imagining a clean dog. Hence, if we are to find out if there is a dog that has the property of dirtiness, then we need to look for one.

35 Various philosophers active in the logical positivist movement attempted to formulate the verification principle more precisely. One of the most well-known attempts was by A. J. Ayer. According to Ayer, a proposition will be non-analytically significant to a given person if and only if that person knows how to verify the claim it expresses. In other words, that person must know what observations would lead him or her under certain conditions to accept the proposition as true, or reject it as false. See A. J. Ayer, 1978, *Language, Truth and Logic*, Harmondsworth: Penguin.

36 Moritz Schlick originally proposed this example.

37 For a discussion of the logical positivists' empiricist criteria of meaning, see William P. Alston, 1964, *Philosophy of Language*, Englewood Cliffs, New Jersey: Prentice-Hall, chapter 4.

38 See René Descartes, 1986, *Meditations on First Philosophy*, trans. by John Cottingham, Cambridge: Cambridge University Press. There is a notable parallel between Descartes' methodological doubt and al-Ghazali's scepticism. See Chapter 3, p. 70.

39 Ayer: 'to say that "God exists" is to make a metaphysical utterance which cannot be either true or false. And by the same criterion, no sentence which purports to describe the nature of a transcendent god can possess any literal significance'. Ayer, *Language*, p. 152.

40 In Antony Flew's contribution to Antony Flew, R. M. Hare and Basil Mitchell, 1971, 'Theology and Falsification: A Symposium' in B. Mitchell (ed.), *The Philosophy of Religion*, Oxford: Oxford University Press, p. 13. The parable was originally presented in John Wisdom, 'Gods', *Proceedings of the Aristotelian Society*, 45 (1944–45), pp. 185–206.

41 In particular, many theists are reluctant to accept the evidence of evil in the world as counting against the existence of a good, omnipotent God.

42 The verificationist's charge is thus that religious utterances are nonsense-utterances and not significant claims at all. When the challenge is put in this form, one obvious way for a theist to respond is to offer some explanation of how religious utterances might succeed in being meaningful. We consider a range of possible explanations in Chapter 5.

43 One way a verificationist might respond is by reducing things like character traits to observable behaviour, or dispositions to behave. See Gilbert Ryle, 1949, *The Concept of Mind*, New York: Barnes & Noble. But this seems to lead to some odd implications. Consider happiness. Whereas it might be plausible to construe another's happiness in terms of how lively they are, how often they smile, and so on, it would be strange indeed to reduce one's own happiness to outward manifestations.

44 John Hick, 1989, *An Interpretation of Religion: Human Responses to the Transcendent*, London: Macmillan, p. 178.

45 Hick, *Interpretation*, p. 178.

46 Hick, *Interpretation*, p. 179.

47 See R. M. Hare's contribution to Antony Flew, R. M. Hare and Basil Mitchell, 'Theology' in Mitchell, *Philosophy*, p. 17.

48 Brian Davies, 1986, *An Introduction to the Philosophy of Religion*, Oxford: Oxford University Press, p. 5.

49 Swinburne, *Coherence*, p. 28.

50 See Willard van Orman Quine, 1961, 'Two Dogmas of Empiricism' in Willard van Orman Quine, *From a Logical Point of View*, New York: Harper & Row, pp. 20–46.

51 Davies, *Introduction*, p. 5.

52 The most important are: Ludwig Wittgenstein, 1988, *Philosophical Investigations*, trans. by G. E. M. Anscombe, Oxford: Blackwell; and Ludwig Wittgenstein, 1972, *On Certainty*, edited by G. E. M. Anscombe and G. H. von Wright, New York: Harper & Row. Of especial interest with regard to Wittgenstein's views on religious belief are his 'Lectures on Religious Belief' in Ludwig Wittgenstein, 1966, *Lectures and Conversations on Aesthetics, Psychology & Religious Belief*, Oxford: Blackwell, pp. 53–72.

53 For an example of an explicitly post-Wittgensteinian Christian theology, see Fergus Kerr, 1986, *Theology After Wittgenstein*, Oxford: Blackwell.

54 See John Locke, 1979, *An Essay Concerning Human Understanding*, edited by Peter H. Nidditch, Oxford: Clarendon Press. First published in 1690, Locke's *Essay* is one of the greatest works of its century. Moreover, it proved to be one of the most influential books of the following three centuries. A selection of essays on Locke's theory of language can be found in I. C. Tipton (ed.), 1977, *Locke on Human Understanding: Selected Essays*, Oxford: Oxford University Press.

55 See Locke, *Essay*, pp. 720f. (IV, xxi, 4). In Book I, chapter I, section 8, Locke explains that he uses the word 'idea' 'to stand for whatsoever is the Object of the Understanding when a Man thinks', using the word 'to express whatever is meant by *Phantasm, Notion, Species*, or whatever it is, which the Mind can be employ'd about in thinking ...' Locke, *Essay*, p. 47.

56 Locke attempts to establish this thesis in *Essay*, Book II, chapters I and II. Realizing that his theory of language would be implausible if he attempted to explain every kind of word as a sign of an idea, Locke wisely limits his thesis to the claim that nouns, or names, signify ideas.

57 Locke, *Essay*, pp. 720f. (IV, xxi, 4).

58 'For a *large* class of cases – though not for all – in which we employ the word "meaning" it can be defined thus: the meaning of a word is its use in the language.' Wittgenstein, *Philosophical*, p. 20 (paragraph 40). The definition of meaning as use is in stark contrast to the logical positivists' claim that the meaning of a proposition is its method of verification.

59 Wittgenstein, *Philosophical*, p. 49 (paragraph 124).

60 Wittgenstein, *Philosophical*, p. 50 (paragraph 126).

61 Wittgenstein was something of a twentieth-century cultural icon. Moreover, he is unique among twentieth-century philosophers in being the subject of a film that bears his name: 'Wittgenstein' directed by Derek Jarman and Ken Butler (UK, 1993).

62 Wittgenstein, *Certainty*, p. 24 (paragraph 166).

63 Norman Malcolm, 1977, 'The Groundlessness of Belief' in Stuart C. Brown (ed.), *Reason and Religion*, Ithaca, New York: Cornell University Press, pp. 143f.

64 Malcolm, 'Groundlessness', p. 145.

65 Malcolm, 'Groundlessness', p. 147.

66 See Malcolm, 'Groundlessness', p. 152.

67 See William P. Alston, 1991, *Perceiving God: The Epistemology of Religious Experience*, Ithaca, New York: Cornell University Press.

68 See Nicholas Wolterstorff, 1983, 'Can Belief in God be Rational if it has no Foundations?' in Alvin Plantinga and Nicholas Wolterstorff (eds), *Faith and Rationality: Reason and Belief in God*, Notre Dame: University of Notre Dame Press, pp. 135–86.

69 Plantinga has contributed a trilogy to reformed epistemology: *Warrant: The Current Debate*, New York: Oxford University Press, 1993; *Warrant and Proper Function*, New York: Oxford University Press, 1993; and *Warranted Christian Belief*, New York: Oxford University Press, 2000.

70 Plantinga's main arguments are presented in Alvin Plantinga, 1983, 'Reason and Belief in God' in Plantinga and Wolterstorff, *Faith*, pp. 16–93.

71 Epistemologists are philosophers who focus on theories of knowledge. They are particularly interested in concepts such as 'belief', 'certainty', 'rationality' and 'justification'.

72 Plantinga provides a self-referential refutation of the form of foundationalism he wants to reject. He claims that the thesis stating that all beliefs fall into one or other of these two categories itself falls into neither – thus there must be at least one other category into which beliefs can be classified. See Plantinga, 'Reason', pp. 75f.

73 Plantinga, 'Reason', p. 76.

74 In his early work, Plantinga regards properly basic beliefs as being justified by, for example, the experience that gave rise to the belief. In his later work, however, he emphasizes a distinction between justification and warrant – arguing that beliefs can be warranted even though we are not in a position to recognize

that they are justified. Whether a belief is warranted or not is thought to depend on the mechanism for belief-formation through which it was arrived at.

75 See Plantinga, 'Reason', p. 81.

76 Plantinga, 'Reason', p. 81.

77 Plantinga might appeal to the Calvinist notion that we have a God-given disposition to believe certain propositions, adding that we are disposed towards the beliefs of one tradition rather than those of another. There would, however, seem to be little evidence to support this claim. Moreover, even if we have such a disposition, it is unlikely to be fine-tuned enough to allow us to discriminate among religions that share a significant number of beliefs, as do Judaism, Christianity and Islam. See Plantinga, 'Reason', p. 80.

78 See Chapter 7 for a discussion of religious exclusivism.

79 In Chapter 7 we examine some alternative solutions to the problems posed by what are often perceived as rival religious belief systems.

80 Pope John Paul II's confidence in the harmony between philosophy and religious faith showed no signs of diminishment as the twentieth century drew to a close. In fact, despite the buffeting religion had received at the hands of philosophers, he restated the traditional Roman Catholic view: 'There is ... no reason for competition of any kind between reason and faith: each contains the other, and each has its own scope for action'. Karol Wojtyla, 1998, *Encyclical of Pope John Paul II on Faith and Reason, Fides et Ratio*, 15 October 1998, New Hope, Kentucky: Urbi et Orbi Communications, p. 10, paragraph 17.

5

New Conceptions of Religious Language

During the early twentieth century, as we saw in the previous chapter, many educated people in the West were influenced by logical positivism. As was previously discussed, at the heart of that philosophical movement lay a theory of language according to which meaningful propositions were either analytic or synthetic. Propositions that were neither analytic nor synthetic were, correspondingly, held to be meaningless because they were regarded as incapable of truth or falsity; or put another way, because they lacked any truth-value. Given the popularity of this theory of language, the burning question of the era – as far as those interested in religious language were concerned – was whether or not religious propositions were meaningful. Many of the religious thinkers we considered in the previous chapter responded directly to this question.

By the mid-twentieth century, two typical forms of response to the question of whether or not religious propositions were meaningful had been developed by religious thinkers. The first, adopted, for example, by John Hick, claimed that religious propositions were indeed meaningful – in the logical positivists' sense of having truth-value – and strove to explain how this might be the case. A second form of response, inspired by the work of Ludwig Wittgenstein, conceded that religious propositions lack truth-value, yet denied that this entailed that they were meaningless. What distinguishes these responses from each other is their stance vis-à-vis the logical positivists' theory of language. The first response accepts that theory, while challenging what logical positivists had perceived to be its implications for religious propositions. The second response, by contrast, rejects a central part of the logical positivists' theory – the part that ties meaning exclusively to true analytic propositions and potentially true synthetic propositions. In short, the second form of response was premised upon the radically new idea that linguistic meaning can be independent of the aptness of propositions for truth or falsity.[1]

The idea that the notion of meaning can be separated from the concepts of truth and falsity opened the way for fresh ways of thinking about language. In the second half of the twentieth century, then, new approaches to the study of language were explored by thinkers within both the anglophone analytic and the continental philosophical traditions. Although otherwise diverse, these approaches were united in rejecting the theory of language that had motivated the question: 'Are religious propositions meaningful?' Indeed, this question was rapidly made redundant by the new avenues to understanding language that were opened by, for example, the movement of hermeneutical philosophy, on the one hand, and the analysis of metaphor on the other.[2] As we shall see, by the late twentieth century, those working in these areas had revolutionized the way that many people in the West thought about language. And as we shall also see, these new approaches to the study of language in turn spawned new analyses of religious language, which proved much friendlier to theists than the analysis of religious language that had been proffered by logical positivism.

But why did a focus on language play such a central role within twentieth-century scholarship? Yet again, the impetus would seem to have come from the discipline of philosophy. A great deal of Western philosophy struggled with metaphysical questions, as philosophers had sought to comprehend the nature and structure of reality. The shift of focus from metaphysics to linguistic philosophy was initiated, albeit unwittingly, by Immanuel Kant, who became convinced that we cannot answer questions about the nature of reality without first inquiring how *we can know* reality. From the claim that the first task of a philosopher is to understand how we are able to know things, and where the boundaries of knowledge lie, it is but a short step to the further claim that we cannot understand the processes of knowing, or of even thinking at all, unless we first understand the nature of language, for it is within language that our knowledge and thought are expressed. And this latter claim – that we must understand the nature of language before we can understand what is involved in knowing and thinking – lies behind the profound interest of twentieth-century scholars in the philosophy of language.

In this chapter, we are, of course, principally concerned with the religious language employed by Jews, Christians and Muslims. Before we can proceed, however, some clarification is required of how the term 'religious language' is used. 'Religious language', as employed by religious scholars in the everyday sense, refers to the written and spoken language typically used by religious believers when they talk about their religious beliefs and their religious experiences. The term also covers the language used in sacred texts and in worship and prayer.[3] Use of the term 'religious language' might suggest that there is a special 'religious' component of natural languages, which is clearly distinct from the normal, secular component of these languages. This, however, is obviously not the case. For when believers employ 'religious language', they do not use completely different words from those uttered by their non-religious contemporaries.[4] While certain words may be uttered by believers with greater frequency than by atheists, nonetheless, the words that feature in 'religious language' are the same words that are used in 'non-religious language'.[5] Even a word as quintessentially religious as 'God' appears in the language of many non-religious people in the context of a variety of commonly used curses. Moreover, if one were to open a page of the Scriptures of Judaism, Christianity or Islam most of the words on that page would seem to bear the same mundane meaning as they do in ordinary, 'secular' discourse. In short, it would seem that the religiosity of language cannot lie in the actual words used but must be found in something else. I suggest that the 'something else' consists principally, although not exclusively, in two factors: first, the 'religious' purpose some language serves; and, second, the overtly 'religious' context of some linguistic uses. The term 'religious language', as used below, then, should be regarded as shorthand for 'language that is used either to serve a religious purpose or in a religious context, or both'.[6]

Given how much 'religious language' and 'ordinary language' have in common, it should not surprise us that, at the level of theory and interpretation, many people tend to regard them as on a par. So, for example, in a culture in which ordinary language is regarded as primarily descriptive of what is 'literally' the case, it is likely that religious language will be viewed as similarly oriented. Indeed, it seems that whichever theory of ordinary language is popular at any given time effects the way that religious language is conceived. This notwithstanding, throughout the ages religious thinkers have found it necessary to develop distinctive theories of religious language. What is it, then, about religious language that seems to require a special account? A significant portion of the religious language used by traditional Jews, Christians and Muslims concerns a God that is conceived to be transcendent to the world. How can human languages, which seem better suited to describing the mundane world of our everyday experiences, purport to describe or refer to something that transcends this world? Many religious thinkers, both traditional and modern, have been deeply puzzled by this question, and their theories of religious language attempt to provide an answer to it.

In this chapter, before considering the new directions that religious thinkers have taken in their attempt to account for the language used by religious believers, I shall briefly review three traditional theories of religious language. As we shall see, these traditional theories continue to influence thought about religious language even in the light of the distinctive new approaches to language that opened up in the twentieth century.

Traditional theories of religious language

It has become increasingly common in the modern period for religious believers to regard much of their language about God as literally true – that is, as accurately representing the way things are. Many, no doubt, believe that in taking religious language to be literally true, they are being faithful to their religious tradition, and they might therefore regard those believers who depart from a purportedly literal understanding of religious language as breaking with that tradition.[7]

Despite this modern trend, the view that religious language, particularly the language used in sacred texts to refer to God, should be interpreted literally was by no means the only, or even always the dominant, theory entertained within the monotheistic traditions. In antiquity, both Jewish and Christian thinkers typically recognized various levels of meaning in their Scriptures. In the Christian tradition, such recognition became explicit in the so-called 'fourfold method of exegesis', which was prominent from the medieval period until the sixteenth century. According to this method, understanding the text required taking into account not just the literal meaning but also three 'higher' levels of meaning.[8] The non-literal meaning of the text was thought to become accessible when the interpreter allowed his or her imagination to engage with the symbolism of the language used.

One result of distinguishing between the spiritual meanings of a sacred text and the literal sense of the words that constitute it was that an enormous number of different, and sometimes rival, interpretations of the same texts became possible. The interpretations of sacred texts proffered by those within the Gnostic movement, for example, presented a particular problem to the early Christian Church, which sought an interpretation agreed by all. In response to the Gnostics' claim that they possessed esoteric spiritual knowledge, purportedly gained by going beyond the literal meaning of the Christian texts, the idea was promoted that only bishops – recognized church leaders – could provide authoritative interpretations of Scripture. This attempt to control what were to be considered acceptable interpretations of the sacred texts perhaps prepared the ground for the idea that there was only *one* meaning that could be read out of the text – an idea that became popular in sixteenth-century Europe.

But, in addition to the view that religious language should be interpreted literally, two alternative theories of religious language that had developed within the traditional monotheisms were still regarded as live options by many at the beginning of modernity. According to one theory, language about God should not be understood literally, and all terms applied to God must be negated lest one run the risk of misrepresenting the divine. This theory is known to theologians as the *via negativa* (the negative way). A rival theory holds that we can make statements about God without negating them, but that such statements are not to be understood literally, but as analogical claims. More specifically, according to the latter theory, words that are applied to God do not carry exactly the same meaning as they bear when applied to other things, but nor do they have a completely different meaning. Let us briefly consider each of these three rival theories.

Religious language as literal language

Martin Luther, who, as we have seen, was a principal figure in the reformation of Christianity in Europe, is held by many to be responsible for the increased prominence given, from the onset of the modern period, to the literal meaning of religious texts. Indeed, the 'fourfold method of exegesis' fell out of use in the sixteenth century largely due to the emphasis Protestants placed on the literal meaning of Scripture. This emphasis on literal meaning was required because imaginative interpretation of the text went against the assumption that the meaning of the Bible was directly accessible to all – a key principle of early Protestantism, which sought to liberate believers from any reliance on a priestly elite. In a characteristic statement, Luther writes:

> No violence is to be done to the words of God, whether by man or angel; but they are to be retained in their simplest meaning wherever possible, and to be understood in their grammatical and literal sense unless the context plainly forbids, lest we give our adversaries occasion to make a mockery of all the Scriptures.[9]

There is no doubt that the emphasis placed on the literal meaning of the Christian Scriptures by Luther and his contemporary reformers was part of a wider agenda. The intention was to shift the responsibility for interpreting the sacred texts away from the established Church and onto the individual (male) Christian. Instead of the Church evaluating the meaning of the Scriptures, the reformers hoped that the Scriptures could be used to judge what was of value in the Church. Luther held that ordinary literate people should be able to read and understand the Bible without the help of the interpretation authorized by the religious establishment. Consequently, he argued that the words of the Bible are to be understood in their literal sense; that is, in the sense that they possess in other areas of discourse. On this view, when the Bible refers to God as 'Father', for example, then the word 'Father' means exactly what it means when it is used with reference to a non-divine patriarch.

The view of religious language popularized by Luther became dominant in the Protestant churches of Northern Europe, from where it eventually spread to the Protestant churches of North America. And in North America, particularly, and despite growing recognition that some interpretation is inevitable even when one is committed to reading the Bible as literally as possible, this view remained influential throughout the twentieth century. Its popularity notwithstanding, biblical literalism (as, within the context of Christianity, this view is often called today) has been subjected to vigorous criticism. Russell McCutcheon, for example, remarks that 'it should be apparent that, when reading a document that reflects the entrenched cultural and historical context of people half a world away and reaching back thousands of years, it is utterly impossible to take the entire document literally'.[10] Furthermore, in the twentieth century, there was increased sensitivity to what appeared to many as the hypocrisy of those claiming to interpret the Bible literally while nevertheless being highly selective in the parts they chose to take seriously. As McCutcheon observes:

> In spite of the fact that the Hebrew text calls for a regular and total redistribution of debt, property, and goods every fifty years (known as the Jubilee year in Leviticus 25.8ff.), and the Christian Scriptures routinely make judgments on the imminent end of the world and a radical renunciation of property and wealth, Jews and Christians throughout the world are somehow able to thrive in capitalist economies. In other words, when Jesus says that Peter is his 'rock', literalists do not maintain that Jesus mistook Peter for inert, inorganic material. Somehow, readers are able to negotiate this metaphor smoothly and are able to distinguish this text from those that, to them at least, are most certainly not metaphoric. Those Protestant groups who handle rattle snakes during their services of worship, groups that can be found in some areas of the Appalachian region of the United States, are some of the few groups who take literally certain (but, once again, not all) portions of the Christian text. In this case, they put great emphasis on a certain portion of the Gospel of Mark (16.18) where true believers are distinguished not only by their ability to speak in tongues and to heal, but also by their ability to drink poison without being harmed and to handle deadly snakes. ...[11]

Despite the problems that a religious group exposes itself to when it claims to interpret the Bible literally, the view that Scripture, as the word of God, does not stand in need of interpretation dies hard. Moreover, emphasis on the literal meaning of religious language has not been limited to Protestant Christians. It has also been the dominant view of religious language in the Muslim tradition, as well as having enjoyed some popularity among certain sectors of the Jewish community. Indeed, in segments of each of these traditions it remained a powerful force at the end of the twentieth century. We shall consider some of the ramification of this in Chapter 10, when we examine religious fundamentalism.

The claim of some Jews, Christians and Muslims that their respective religious texts require no interpretation, and can be understood in a literal sense, is aligned to a particular view of revelation. According to this view, the Scriptures are the word – literally, the direct speech – of God put into writing; as such, they are thought to be invested with ultimate authority and are regarded as inerrant and unchangeable. Moreover, those who hold this view are likely to regard as impertinent the claim that God's words are in need of interpretation. In effect, an adherent of this view expects to be able to open any page of their Scriptures and encounter the direct speech of God. Given that this view of revelation has, at various times, been important within each monotheism, it is not surprising that each tradition provides an account of how God's word came to be put into writing. The traditional Islamic account is typical: God commanded Muhammad to 'recite' what was dictated by the Angel Gabriel. Similarly, according to the traditional Christian account, God, through the agency of the Holy Spirit, 'inspired' those humans who wrote down God's words. Traditional Judaism, limiting its claims to the Torah (the first five books of the Hebrew Scriptures), claimed that revelation was transmitted in written form on Mount Sinai. All of these accounts, clearly, have one aim: to impress upon believers the divine origin of the sacred texts.

This literalist, propositional model of revelation was severely criticized in the twentieth century, both by thinkers within and without the Abrahamic traditions. Textual and historical criticism of the documents in question further undermined the traditional accounts of the origin of the sacred texts. By the close of the twentieth century, few academic religious thinkers in the West, within any of the monotheisms, supported an unqualified version of any of the traditional accounts of Scripture and its link to revelation. Few Western religious scholars or educated believers would now deny that the Scriptures are historical documents, and that their interpretation requires an awareness of the context in which they were written. The shift from traditional approaches to the sacred texts to a view tempered by modern scholarship has been profound, one result being that many twentieth-century theologians came to regard human experience as the new locus of revelation.[12] According to this new view of revelation, Scriptures continue to be regarded as important religious documents – but only because they are records, albeit partial and inaccurate, of the human experience of encounters with God. In particular, they record the experiences of early communities of Jews, Christians and Muslims – communities that strove to live according to the religious visions which inspired their respective traditions.

For many who reject traditional accounts of the relation between Scriptures and revelation, the vehicle of revelation is no longer thought to be the actual propositions which constitute the Torah, Bible or Qur'ān; rather, it is the experience that underlies them. Thus, for such believers, the integrity of revelation no longer hinges on whether the texts require interpretation or can be read literally; no strict correspondence is thus required between the speech of God and the words on the page.[13] And it is the conviction that there is such a correspondence that motivates the view that the literal meaning of the language used in religious texts is of paramount importance.

However, it is not exclusively a specific view about the relation between revelation and the words in which it is expressed that motivates a purportedly literal understanding of religious language. A particular theory of language and meaning also provides powerful motivation. According to this theory, words carry meaning independently of the context in which they are used. A word is conceived, then, as if it were a container, with the content of the container being the word's meaning. We consider this view of language in more detail, below. Suffice it to say for now that this theory underlay certain practices traditionally found within Judaism, Christianity and Islam – each of which having what is regarded by its adherents as a sacred language: namely, Ancient Hebrew, Latin and Classical Arabic, respectively. Moreover, for much of its history, each tradition insisted on the use of these sacred languages during worship, despite the fact that they were incomprehensible to the majority of believers.[14] The language itself was clearly thought to be more important than human understanding. Indeed, merely learning creeds and prayers verbatim was often regarded as religiously sufficient, even if one failed to comprehend a word. For in reciting them, one could still transmit the meaning of the words uttered to other worshippers. As we shall see later, the view of language which such practices implied was undercut by the new theories of language developed in the twentieth century.

In the previous chapter, we saw the result of logical positivists confronting a literalist understanding of religious language: religious language, along with other significant linguistic domains, was declared to be meaningless, and hence judged to be unworthy of serious consideration. All of the criticisms of religious language that were considered in the previous chapter are premised upon a literal understanding of it, according to which it either corresponds to reality, and hence is literally true, or fails to correspond to reality, and hence is literally false. But, as we have seen, this is not the only – and certainly not the dominant – way that religious language has been viewed by religious believers themselves. In fact, all the theories of language we shall consider below, ancient and modern, are united in undermining the view that religious language should, or even could, be taken literally.

The *via negativa*

There is, undeniably, a certain oddity about the claim that religious language, particularly language that purports to refer to a world-transcendent God, literally describes the way things are, and that the words used have the same literal meaning as they do when applied to things that are 'of this world'. The oddity is caused by the fact that language which purports to be about God inevitably involves words whose meaning would seem to derive from the world of our experience; whereas a world-transcendent God is not within the range of what we can possibly experience. When theists claim to use language about God literally, then, how can they avoid undermining the firm conceptual distinction between God and the world – a distinction maintained by all the traditional forms of Abrahamic monotheism? The claim that language can be used literally in a religious context can easily give the impression that the God which theists believe in is just like us, only better: more knowledgeable, more powerful, and so on.

Some theists are more alert to this danger than others. Those who are most sensitive to it tend to adopt some form of *via negativa*, an extreme form of which was popularized in the Middle Ages by the influential Jewish philosopher Moses Maimonides.[15] Maimonides claimed that statements predicating 'positive attributes' to the divine being – that is, statements of the form 'God is ...' – are theologically illegitimate, and should never be employed. Only statements of the form 'God is not ...' are, Maimonides argues, legitimate. In a famous passage he declares:

> There is no necessity at all for you to use positive attributes of God with the view of magnifying Him in your thought. ... I will give you ... some illustrations, in order that you may better understand the propriety of forming as many negative attributes as possible, and the impropriety of ascribing to God any positive attributes. A person may know for certain that a 'ship' is in existence, but he may not know to what object that name is applied, whether to a substance or to an accident; a second person then learns that a ship is not an accident; a third, that it is not a mineral; a fourth, that it is not a plant growing in the earth; a fifth, that it is not a body whose parts are joined together by nature; a sixth, that it is not a flat object like boards or doors; a seventh, that it is not a sphere; an eighth, that it is not pointed; a ninth, that it is not round shaped; nor equilateral; a tenth, that it is not solid. It is clear that this tenth person has almost arrived at the correct notion of a 'ship' by the foregoing negative attributes. ... In the same manner you will come nearer to the knowledge and comprehension of God by the negative attributes. ... I do not merely declare that he who affirms attributes of God has not sufficient knowledge concerning the Creator ... but I say that he unconsciously loses his belief in God.[16]

At first sight, it may seem strange that adherents of the *via negativa* should attempt to speak about God at all. If one cannot say anything about God except regarding what God is not, then why not remain silent? Maimonides, however, clearly believes that language can play a role in leading to an understanding of God. In the passage quoted above, he states that by considering God's negative attributes 'you will come nearer to the knowledge and comprehension of God'. How precisely, though, does religious language work? In Maimonides' view, language about God is valuable only insofar as it is capable of evoking an experience of the divine. The purpose of religious language is not, then, to provide a definite description of God or to convey information about the divine in propositional form. Rather, it is to facilitate religious experience and to inspire prayer. Furthermore, as we have seen, Maimonides does not merely claim that one would be mistaken if one were to make statements predicating 'positive attributes' of God; he also claims that one would thereby lose one's belief in God. What might motivate this extraordinary claim? What is the connection, in his view, between predicating 'positive attributes' of God and losing one's belief in God? The idea would seem to be that the result of predicating 'positive attributes' of God is that one arrives at an image of God that is formed by compiling together a number of concepts that denote finite qualities – and the 'God' represented by such limited concepts could not inspire belief.[17] Thus, only by limiting one's claims about God to statements about what God is not can one preserve a concept 'God' that is both responsible to the purported reality and, at the same time, credible.[18]

Attractive as the *via negativa* has seemed to many, it has at least one significant drawback. As Brian Davies explains:

> only saying what something is not gives no indication of what it actually is, and if one can only say what God is not, one cannot understand him at all. Suppose I say that there is something in my room, and suppose I reject every suggestion you make as to what is actually there. In that case, you will get no idea at all about what is in my room. Going back to the quotation from Maimonides ... it is simply unreasonable to say that someone who has all the negations mentioned in it 'has almost arrived at the correct notion of a "ship"'. He could equally well be thinking of a wardrobe.[19]

Thus, in their efforts to avoid misrepresenting God, those who adopt this approach seem to court another danger – that of saying nothing at all about God. Moreover, if all one can say is that God is not this, that, or the other, it may well be difficult for one's interlocutor to resist the conclusion that God is nothing at all. Despite this danger, the *via negativa* has struck many religious thinkers as the best available theory of religious language. Indeed, it enjoyed something of a renaissance in the twentieth century.

Ian Crombie, for example, adheres to a form of *via negativa*.[20] In response to the critic's claim that religious statements do not refer to the real world, Crombie aims to provide a sense in which theological statements are indeed meaningful. The critic claims that although some religious statements seem to make reference to the real world, as a matter of fact they do not. And they fail to do so because all key religious statements are defined by reference to each other. They form a circular system of mutual definition (or, a network of meaning) which cannot be broken into from outside that circle. Crombie illustrates the mooted problem by means of the Christian concept 'grace'.[21] One might think that this concept would allow us to break into the circle because, surely, if there is one religious phenomenon that really touches human reality, it must be the one to which 'grace' refers. However, we soon discover, instead, that we cannot find out what 'grace' refers to without reference to 'God'. And we only wanted to know what 'grace' meant in order to break into the theological system of meaning which, we hoped, might provide us with some content for the concept 'God'.

However, this objection seems to presuppose that there is some straightforward referential relationship between religious language and religious entities. Hence, in response to this problem, Crombie observes that religious statements, particularly theological statements, are, instead, 'elusive'. They are elusive because they are all, ultimately, about God, and God is not part of the spatio-temporal world. Thus, the elusiveness of theological statements follows directly from the purpose which they are meant to serve: that is, to refer to a being, God, who, on the one hand, is not part of the spatio-temporal world, and, on the other hand, is intimately involved with the world. As Crombie writes:

> If one is to talk about these matters, one has to do so by making use of statements governed by apparently conflicting rules. The formal properties of theological statements (that is to say, the rules determining how they are to be taken and how they are supposed to be related to statements of other kinds) have to be, at first sight, mutually contradictory if they are to do their proper work.[22]

Hence, Crombie argues that religious language supposedly referring to God cannot possibly specify its object exactly; but that is because of the nature of its object. But this does not make religious language pointless, for it can point us towards God. So, the elusiveness of religious language 'derives', writes Crombie, 'not from the natural shiftiness of persons who make theological statements, but from the uses for which such statements are devised'.[23] In a nutshell, although the theist cannot say precisely what the characteristics of God are, religious language can nevertheless be used to point us in the right direction:

> When we speak of God as an infinite being we are not, of course, using the word; 'infinite' in its strict mathematical sense. We mean, negatively that he is unlimited; or, more positively, that, being the source of

all limitation, there is nothing whatsoever to which he is conformed, or to which he must conform himself. 'Infinite', therefore, comes to very much the same thing as 'necessary', 'omnipotent', 'creator of all things' and other words of the same kind which we use about God. For, since we do not know God, they cannot acquire a precise sense by reference to his properties; if then they have a precise sense they must acquire it from reference to the properties of something else; and, since nothing else can be an adequate model for God, in so far as they have a precise sense, it cannot be applied to him. Suppose we say then, that what we mean is something rather loose and vague, loosely and vaguely connected with the normal uses of these words. ...[24]

But the 'looseness' and 'vagueness' of such religious language might be thought to render the concept 'God' far too inscrutable. Is there anything that could be added to this approach that might ease the burden of incomprehensibility? One possibility might be found in the work of a philosopher of Jewish descent, Hilary Putnam – who also supports a form of the *via negativa*. Putnam argues that philosophical theories cannot contribute much towards illumining the concept 'God' because

> [t]rying to assimilate God to one or another philosophical construct ... is like trying to improve the appearance of gold by covering it with tinsel. Yet that does not mean that the notion of 'God' is self-explanatory; rather it means that how you understand the notion can only be shown by how you live. Metaphysics is, so to speak, too *superficial* to be of help here.[25]

Thus, in Putnam's view, it is not enough simply to state what God is not; nor should the theist simply rely on the hope that the concept 'God' is self-explanatory. Rather, as Putnam claims, the theist's understanding of the concept 'God' can only be elaborated by the way he or she lives. We shall return to this claim in Chapter 11. But now we turn to what is arguably the most important of all the traditional theories of religious language.

Religious language as analogical

Thomas Aquinas, who was a contemporary of Maimonides, developed an account of religious language that became, for a while, the dominant view in the West, and which remains highly influential within Roman Catholic circles to this day.

Aquinas was convinced that, because the divinity is radically different from all other beings, little of our language could be applied univocally (or, literally) to God. However, Aquinas felt compelled to reject the obvious alternative: namely, the view that most of the words used in religious language are equivocal, having an entirely different meaning from the one they possess when employed in non-religious discourse – these two different meanings being as unrelated as, for example, the various meanings of the word 'bat'. The problem with this alternative view is that, if religious language were simply equivocal, then it seems that we could never know whether or not we were describing God correctly. For, whereas we can certainly acquire the mundane meanings of words, what would enable us to grasp the religious meanings? And if we do not understand the religious meanings, we would not be able to make true statements about God. And hence, we would lack all knowledge of the divinity. But we do possess some knowledge of God through revelation. Therefore, Aquinas concluded that when we refer to God, we cannot be employing words equivocally.

As an alternative both to the view that religious language was univocal and to the view that it was equivocal, Aquinas proposed that religious discourse was analogical, placing particular emphasis on a variety of analogy that he terms 'analogy of attribution'. Aquinas illustrates analogy of attribution with the following example. Consider the word 'health'. When we think of healthy people we attribute health to them in a literal sense. But we might also think of medicine as healthy. However, it is clear that medicine is not healthy in the same way in which people are healthy. By means of this example, Aquinas identified a use of words that he believed falls somewhere between the univocal and the equivocal. And it is by speaking in this manner – by employing analogies of attribution – that, Aquinas holds, we can talk meaningfully about God. As he writes:

> some words are used neither univocally nor purely equivocally of God and creatures, but analogically, for we cannot speak of God at all except in the language we use of creatures, and so whatever is said both of God and creatures is said *in virtue of the order* that creatures have to God as to their source and cause in which all perfections of things pre-exist transcendentally.[26]

Aquinas conceived of God as the first, or uncaused, cause of everything that is. He also believed that causes must bear some similarity to their effects – or, in other words, that whatever quality an effect possessed had to be present in its cause. As an example, he thought that whatever causes goodness in the world must itself be good. Because God is the cause of everything that exists, we can, therefore, correctly attribute to the divinity properties of worldly things – goodness, for example.

Of course, there is an obvious problem here, which Aquinas anticipated. His theory would seem to allow that all our terms are equally applicable to God, and it would therefore appear to provide no grounds for deciding what may, and what may not, be correctly said of God. Thus, there would be no significant difference between saying 'God is a rose' and saying 'God is a father', because God is the cause of both roses and fathers. Aquinas attempted to sidestep this difficulty by arguing that, since God is infinite, terms that are capable of referring to the infinite are the ones most suitable for applying to the divine. While this excludes words like 'rose', it allows words like 'good' to be used in describing God. However, this strategy also excludes words like 'father' – words that Aquinas clearly is interested in retaining. So, he further modifies the theory to include metaphors, which he regarded as a valuable means of genuinely saying something about God. Nevertheless, he maintained that metaphor was not as important within religious language as analogy. Because of the primacy he accorded to analogy over metaphor, he failed to develop a detailed account of the way that metaphor functions in religious language. In fact, a fuller exploration of the use of metaphor in theology was not undertaken until the twentieth century. And we shall consider these developments below.

Unfortunately, there appears to be a serious flaw in Aquinas' account of analogy. The problem lies in Aquinas' understanding of causation – a notion that plays a key role in his theory. For the reason why certain terms can be applied to God analogically, he argues, is because God is the *cause* of all things. In short, Aquinas assumes that whatever qualities an effect had must be present transcendentally in the cause of that effect. And he took this to entail that effects must bear some likeness to their causes. Consequently, given his belief that God is the cause of everything that exists, Aquinas held that there is a certain qualified likeness between God the creator and God's creatures. In technical theological terms, this likeness is known as the *analogia entis*. It is because of this special likeness between God and 'his' creation that, according to Aquinas, we are able to use words analogically in order to speak about God. So, Aquinas' theory of analogy depends upon a specific understanding of what causation involves. Clearly, if one rejects this view of causation, and most people today would reject the assumption that whatever qualities an effect possesses must be present transcendentally in its cause, then Aquinas' theory loses its power to explain how words can be used analogically to refer to God. Indeed, in the twentieth century, the theory of religious language as analogical struck many people as unpersuasive precisely because they no longer shared Aquinas' beliefs about causation, and hence no longer subscribed to a worldview that recognized the *analogia entis*. The apparent failure of Aquinas' theory of analogy led many twentieth-century religious thinkers to search for alternatives. As we shall now see, this search was facilitated by developments within twentieth-century philosophy of language in both the continental and the analytical philosophical traditions.

Shifting the ground of the problem

Each of the three traditional theories of religious language was developed as a response to the question: how can religious language meaningfully refer to a God who, if such exists, is radically different from everything else to which our language refers? Both Aquinas' analogical theory of religious language and the *via negativa* were attempts to find a middle way between the twin dangers of misrepresenting God, on the one hand, and failing to talk meaningfully on the other. The fear underlying this seeming dilemma is that the gap between God and any human conceptual scheme is so great that anything we might attempt to say about God would be either meaningless or a complete misrepresentation. Moreover, the avoidance of one danger seems to lead to the other: for in order to prevent language about God appearing meaningless, some have felt the need to try to make it as precise as possible. But the more precise religious language becomes, and as a result, the more specific becomes one's conception of God, the greater is the risk of misrepresenting the divinity. Theories of religious language, both traditional and modern, have thus been shaped by their framer's perception of where the greatest danger lies.

Aquinas clearly feared that meaninglessness posed the greatest danger to religious belief. And while avoiding the pitfall of possible misrepresentation by pointing out that language is not univocal (or literal), he set about trying to show how non-literal language can nevertheless be meaningful: it can convey meaning through analogy. Thus his theory of religious language served to explain the way in which it could be meaningful without appealing to the univocal commitments of those who understood religious language literally. Advocates of the *via negativa*, in contrast, took misrepresentation to be the greatest danger. While seeking to avoid the pitfall of meaningless talk – though how successfully is moot – by making literally true claims (such as 'God is not material'), they avoided misrepresenting God by refusing to say anything positive about the divine. From the perspective of the history of ideas, it is notable how the problem of religious language, as it persisted within twentieth-century philosophy of religion, retained the same basic form that it held during the Middle Ages: how one can meaningfully use language about God without wholesale misrepresentation of the divine.

The charge that all language purporting to refer to God was meaningless, advanced in the early twentieth century by the logical positivists, stimulated a renewed interest in theories, such as that of Aquinas, which attempted to explain how religious language could, nevertheless, be meaningful. However, given that Aquinas' theory is unacceptable to many modern people because of its seemingly antiquated metaphysical presuppositions, a number of religious believers began to search for alternative ways of understanding the language they employed to talk about their religious beliefs and experiences. Developments within the philosophy of language gave new impetus to the search for an appropriate theory of religious language. On the one hand, 'ordinary language philosophy', advanced in the mid-twentieth century by philosophers such as Ludwig Wittgenstein (and discussed in the previous chapter), had a profound influence on many whose primary concern was with religious language. The focus of ordinary language philosophy was on the function of words – the roles in which language users employed them.[27] As we shall now see, this focus was shared by hermeneutical philosophy – a philosophy that became prominent in continental Europe at the same time that ordinary language philosophy became dominant in England and the United States.

Hermeneutics

Martin Heidegger (1889–1976) and his former student Hans-Georg Gadamer (1900–2002) made hermeneutical philosophy an important intellectual movement among continental European philosophers. In the late twentieth century, this movement spread to the United States, where many thinkers, such as Paul Ricoeur (1913–2005), explored its potential for yielding fruitful accounts of religious language. Despite the novelty of the philosophy developed by Heidegger and Gadamer, hermeneutics – which is principally concerned with the interpretation of texts – was not a new discipline. In fact, in its modern form, it was initiated by a theologian closely associated with German Romanticism, namely, Friedrich Schleiermacher.[28]

In opposition to what he perceived as the overly rationalist approach to religious knowledge promoted by philosophers such as Immanuel Kant, Schleiermacher averred that feeling (or emotion) and imagination were important sources of such knowledge. He thus argued that the appropriate method to employ when reading a text such as the Bible would accord a central place to these affective faculties. Specifically, he argued that feeling should be used to stimulate the imagination; the latter being the key to understanding the text. According to Schleiermacher, reading the Bible in the way he prescribed, and by its means acquiring religious knowledge, was to participate in revelation. It was, therefore, a religiously significant undertaking, in his view. And by emphasizing the psychological dimensions of reading and understanding a text, and of revelation,

Schleiermacher developed the idea of a 'hermeneutical circle'. As we shall now see, this idea was of the utmost importance to later thinkers in the hermeneutical philosophical tradition.

The phrase 'hermeneutical circle' denotes the process through which, according to those who follow this approach, one comes to understand a text. During this process, the reader's understanding of the text develops incrementally. First, a preliminary understanding of the text's individual parts is acquired; then, in the light of that understanding, the reader strives to understand the text as a whole. The next step involves reassessing the understanding of the parts of the text that has been acquired in the light of the newly acquired understanding of the whole. This process is regarded as a 'hermeneutical circle' because, once a new understanding of the parts of a text has been reached, a new understanding of the whole is generated, and the latter is then thought to lead to a new understanding of the parts, which in turn leads to a more refined understanding of the whole – a process of interpretation that is, in principle, without end.

Schleiermacher believed that the 'hermeneutical circle' was not vicious but – in virtue of the necessary involvement of the reader's feelings and imagination – could lead to an adequate understanding of what the author meant. Many later thinkers in the hermeneutical tradition, however, came to regard an author's intentions as of little relevance to the meaning of a text. The meaning that can be gleaned from the text itself, irrespective of the author's intentions, thus became the focus of concern for later hermeneuts. Moreover, the activity of understanding a text came to be viewed as a creative activity – that is, as an activity that is productive of meaning. Gadamer, for instance, asserts: 'Not just occasionally but always, the meaning of a text goes beyond its author. That is why understanding is not merely a reproductive but always a productive activity as well.'[29]

Emphasis on the creative nature of the act of understanding a text is clearly of particular relevance with regard to religious texts. As Schleiermacher realized, viewing the interpretation of texts – especially biblical texts – as an imaginative activity suggests a novel view of revelation. And clearly, Schleiermacher's theory of revelation constitutes a radical alternative to the literalist's view, discussed above, that God's revelation is given in the words of the religious text without any need for human acts of interpretation or understanding. Indeed, rather than being portrayed as the mere passive recipients of revelation, the readers of religious texts could now be thought of as active participants in the revelatory process. This idea has been adopted by thinkers within each of the Abrahamic monotheisms.[30]

Moreover, if one accepts, along with many twentieth-century hermeneuts, that an author's intentions do not determine the meaning of a text, then the recognition that a sacred text is not the product of an individual writer will not seem as threatening to believers as it might otherwise have done. Both the consideration that understanding is creative and the presumption that authors do not determine meaning suggest that a reader's personal judgement should be accorded a far greater role in the interpretation of religious texts than most previous theories had allowed. I say 'most previous theories' because the 'fourfold method of exegesis', which was discussed above, seems to bear striking similarities to this new approach. The 'fourfold method', which, as we have seen, fell out of favour during the Middle Ages, seemed to place a great deal of importance on the individual reader's imaginative engagement with the sacred text. Hermeneutical philosophy's emphasis on active interpretation, then, is not entirely novel but would appear to have been anticipated by much earlier thinkers.

The contribution of hermeneutical philosophy to twentieth-century religious thought has not, however, been limited to reminding religious thinkers of the reader's role in the interpretation of texts. Indeed, in the twentieth century the scope of the discipline of hermeneutics was considerably extended. This was a result of Heidegger's claim that every act of understanding, not just textual interpretation, was hermeneutical. In other words, he believed that all understanding involves a 'hermeneutical circle' in which the interpreter's personal judgement plays a key role. The natural sciences, in his view, were no less in need of hermeneutical understanding than were works of literature. By arguing that hermeneutics was relevant to all acts of understanding, Heidegger strove to undermine the traditional scholarly distinction between the arts and the sciences. According to a popular way of construing this distinction, the arts (or humanities) involve a high degree of subjective judgement and contested interpretation, and hence do not yield knowledge in the same way that the supposedly more objective sciences do. Throughout modernity, this distinction had been problematic from the perspective of many religious thinkers because religion, or theology, was typically assigned to the 'arts' rather than to the 'sciences' – an association which many thought to be derogatory, given that it seemed to undermine religion's, or theology's, claim to provide genuine knowledge. In arguing that both the arts *and* the sciences necessarily involve hermeneutics, Heidegger is claiming that, with respect to their ability to yield knowledge, all branches of human study are on a par. And certain religious thinkers – the Roman Catholic theologian Hans Urs von Balthasar (1905–87), for example – appropriated this idea in an attempt to enhance the respectability of theology as an academic discipline within modern educational institutions.[31]

After Heidegger, then, those philosophers who were engaged in the hermeneutical project were no longer exclusively concerned with interpreting texts but had much broader ambitions. Indeed, philosophers such as Gadamer perceive themselves as offering a hermeneutical account of nothing less than 'the whole human experience of the world'.[32] And Gadamer regards the totality of human experience as 'hermeneutical' because, in his view, the hermeneutical process is

> repeated continually throughout our familiar experience. There is always a world already interpreted, already organized in its basic relations, into which experience steps as something new, upsetting what has led our expectations and undergoing reorganization itself in the upheaval. Misunderstanding and strangeness are not the first factors, so that avoiding misunderstanding cannot be regarded as the specific task of hermeneutics. Just the reverse is the case. Only the support of the familiar and common understanding makes possible the venture into the alien, the lifting up of something out of the alien and thus the broadening and enrichment of our own experience of the world.[33]

In short, Gadamer argues, one cannot provide an accurate account of how humans understand new experiences without taking into account their 'familiar and common understanding' of what has already been experienced. Indeed, according to Gadamer, any new act of understanding always takes place in the context of one's 'preunderstandings'; that is, of what one already understands. In Gadamer's view, it is such 'preunderstandings' that make possible one's understanding of anything new. Prior to the development of hermeneutical philosophy in the twentieth century, such 'preunderstandings' had been portrayed derogatively as prejudices. Many philosophers had argued that such prejudices should play no part in acquiring knowledge, particularly scientific knowledge – the quest for which was widely thought to require an objective attitude, often perceived as the antithesis of one coloured by prejudice. In arguing that 'preunderstandings' make a positive and essential contribution to human understanding, Gadamer therefore rejects the paradigm of objective knowledge that was so central to the way that many people have thought about human understanding ever since the Enlightenment.

Gadamer's theory of 'preunderstandings' has far-reaching implications for the way that religious knowledge might be conceived. For if religious faith is an essential component of a person's 'preunderstanding', then it may be regarded as a legitimate starting point for successful inquiry, contrary to widespread assumptions from the time of the Enlightenment. Moreover, if greater understanding is always premised upon one's 'preunderstanding', then everyone's final assessment of the intellectual issues at stake will inevitably be coloured, and there is simply no way around it. But then, why rule out in advance one kind of 'colouration' in preference to some other kind? In short, if Gadamer is correct about the central role played by 'preunderstandings' in gaining any new understanding, then it would seem to be acceptable for a believer to make his or her faith-stance an explicit part of a quest for greater understanding. Indeed, it would seem to be a mistake to try, arbitrarily, to bracket out religious beliefs in an effort to attain 'objectivity'.

Now, the possible understandings that become open to a person – that individual's own 'horizon' of understanding – depends upon that individual's preunderstandings, or so Gadamer argues. But a text will also have been written at a specific time and within a specific context; a time and context with different preunderstandings from those of the reader. In a sense, then, the text will have its own 'horizon' of understanding. So, if we are to understand a text, Gadamer claims, our horizon of understanding must 'fuse' with the horizon of understanding represented by the text. Clearly, the resulting understanding, which is the creative product of the 'fusion' of these two horizons, could not have been anticipated by the author of the text, for he or she could not possibly have anticipated every reader's preunderstandings. Moreover, because an individual's preunderstandings, and hence his or her horizon of understanding, is historically conditioned, the understanding achieved by, say, a late twentieth-century reader will differ from that arrived at by a reader from any previous or future era. One implication of this is that the process of interpreting a text can never be completed definitively. Thus, the meaning of any text should not be regarded as established once and for all, but should rather be seen as continually arising afresh as an interpreter's own preunderstandings evolve in response to his or her changing situation,[34] and as new interpreters with different historical and cultural situations take over the task. As all understandings will involve a fusion of horizons, it follows that it is illegitimate to regard any single understanding of a text's meaning as objectively correct – that is, correct for all people at all times and in all places.

Gadamer's account of what is involved in the understanding of a text soon encountered a seemingly telling objection lodged by his contemporary Jürgen Habermas (b. 1929). Habermas argued that Gadamer's account of preunderstandings allows too little scope for criticism.[35] For if, within the creative process of understanding, we must simply accept our preunderstandings as given, then what scope is there for recognizing them as inadequate and in need of criticism? Gadamer's response is reminiscent of Schleiermacher's idea of the benign hermeneutical circle: there is always a critical interaction between the horizons that are fused in the act of interpretation. Hence, the preunderstandings of the interpreter may be challenged, criticized and changed by his or her encounter with the alien horizon of understanding present in the text.[36]

As Gadamer was well aware, his ideas have far-reaching implications for the way religious texts are understood. According to his form of hermeneutics, it is no more possible to understand the New Testament, or any ancient religious text for that matter, in an objective, purely historical–scientific manner than it is to understand any other ancient document. For understanding the New Testament in the twenty-first century requires fusing a twenty-first-century horizon of understanding with the horizon represented by the text, and thus creating the meaning of the text anew.

But there is a further aspect of the religious text that Gadamer highlights: with regard to the New Testament, he insists that it 'does not exist in order to be understood as a merely historical document, but to be taken in such a way that it exercises its saving effect'.[37] In his view, creative engagement with the 'meaning' of the religious text reveals its salvific nature. In short, according to Gadamer, religious texts have an additional component: their ability to lead one to salvation. And hence, one who does not allow the text to impact him or her in a soteriological manner cannot legitimately claim to have understood it.

Gadamer's proposal clearly impacted upon the theory developed by the Muslim scholar Fazlur Rahman (1919–88), although, as we shall see below, Rahman is critical of some aspects of Gadamer's approach. Rahman outlines a new method for Qur'ānic hermeneutics, key to which is an understanding of the text as a totality. He criticizes previous methods of interpretation because, in his view, they fail 'to understand the underlying unity of the Qur'an' and insist on interpreting individual verses in isolation from the whole.[38] Rahman seeks to replace this 'atomistic' approach with the conviction that the Qur'ān possesses a 'deeper unity' which yields a 'definite weltanschauung' (that is, a worldview).[39] To appreciate the worldview that the Qur'ān makes available, one must, argues Rahman, engage in a method of interpretation that 'consists of a double movement, from the present situation to Qur'anic time, then back to the present'.[40] The first step, then, is for the modern interpreter to consider the text of the Qur'ān in its original socio-historical context. This context is important, Rahman avers, because, far from being an ahistorical document, the Qur'ān is 'a divine response, through the Prophet's mind, to the moral-social situation of the Prophet's Arabia, particularly to the commercial Meccan society of his day'.[41] Earlier interpreters had failed to realize, he argues, that the Qur'ān responds to specific historical problems, and that one cannot simply apply the solutions it proposes to these problems to the very different problems confronting later generations of Muslims. In order to apply the Qur'ān's message to contemporary problems, one must first understand the various parts of the Qur'ān in the context of their origin, and then one must seek to understand specific verses in the context of the whole. Only then can one enunciate 'statements of general moral-social objectives that can be "distilled" from specific texts in the light of the sociohistorical background …'.[42] Once this has been accomplished, the next interpretive 'movement' begins in which one seeks to apply the Qur'ānic worldview to the present time. Like Gadamer, Rahman argues that both stages of the hermeneutical process are complementary; either one taken alone, he claims, would be incomplete. The intellectual effort involved in this double movement should be regarded, Rahman argues, as a form of *ijtihād* – that traditional form of Islamic reasoning which seeks to extend one's understanding of the Qur'ān in order to apply its principles to novel situations.[43]

The importance that Rahman assigns to the first part of the hermeneutical process is what, in his view, distinguishes his theory from Gadamer's. On Rahman's reading of Gadamer, the facts required to get what Rahman identifies as the first stage of the interpretive process under way are in principle unavailable because we can never distance ourselves enough from our current worldview in order to arrive at an objective perspective. But Rahman, to the contrary, claims that it

> seems reasonable to hold ... that all conscious responses to the past involve two moments that must be distinguished. One is the objective ascertaining of the past (– which Gadamer does not allow), which is possible in principle provided requisite evidence is available; the other is the response itself, which necessarily involves values and which is determined (not predetermined) by my present situation, of which effective history is a part but of which my conscious effort and self-aware activity also constitute an important part. For Gadamer these two movements are utterly inseparable and indistinguishable.[44]

Clearly, Rahman has much more confidence in our ability to reach an objective understanding of the text in its original context than does Gadamer. And given Rahman's belief that it is God's response (through the mind of Muhammad) to the situation of the time that the Qur'ān makes available, then such an understanding of the text is clearly of vital importance.[45]

But while Rahman emphasizes the objectivity required of an interpreter when engaged in the first part of the hermeneutical process, he also gives due weight to the conditional nature of the interpretation arrived at as a result of the second part of the process. Indeed, he argues that this latter aspect of Qur'ānic hermeneutics should be recognized as open-ended. An interpretation of the Qur'ān cannot, in his view, be established as definitive precisely because the situation in which interpretation takes place will never be permanent.[46] Thus, Rahman is able to argue that acknowledging the contingency of the situation in which the Qur'ān is interpreted at any given time can free Muslims from the tendency to attempt to impose features of the original context of the Qur'ān onto the modern world. Some have argued, for example, that because the Qur'ān mentions the poor, some people must remain in poverty so that Muslims can continue to fulfil the religious obligations towards the poor that are stipulated by the text. Clearly, Rahman regards such reasoning as a *reductio ad absurdum* of the form of traditional Qur'ānic interpretation that he has labelled 'atomistic'.[47] The result of reading the Qur'ān atomistically is, he argues, not even a genuinely Islamic interpretation of the text. An authentically Islamic interpretation, in his view, must be consistent with 'the total teaching of the Qur'an and the Sunna'.[48] Moreover, he claims that a variety of interpretations can simultaneously be authentic insofar as they meet this criterion. Indeed, Rahman argues that the existence of a variety of interpretations is of positive value, 'for it is only through confrontation of different and opposing views that truth *gradually* emerges'.[49]

Now, Rahman is well aware that the idea of a gradually emerging truth might appear shocking to those who are used to regarding each individual passage of their religious text as imbued with absolute certainty because each is a direct revelation from God.[50] In fact, he is explicit that his hermeneutical method implies nothing less than a radical change in the received Muslim view of revelation. For the particular verses in which Qur'ānic teaching is conveyed are subject to changing interpretation, and are thus not the proper objects of certainty. But what Muslims can be certain about, and which are revealed through study of the religious text, are the principles or values upon which the teaching of the Qur'ān converges.

Rahman's work inspired a new generation of Western Muslim intellectuals to explore and take further the approach to interpreting the Qur'ān that he pioneered. Ebrahim Moosa is one such example, emphasizing the crucial role played by the audience in any interpretive reading of the sacred text:

> the Qur'an itself prefigures a community of listeners and participants: without this audience it ceases to be the Qur'an. Let me explain. Literally the word *qur'an* means a 'recitation'. As a revelation it is recited by the human voice and heard by the human ear. In the final instance the message must both be heard and understood by the 'heart', as the Qur'an literally puts it. In all this a fundamental presumption persists: the Qur'an as revelation requires an audience of listeners and speakers. In other words, a community is integral to it being a revelation. If one does not take that audience and community seriously, implicitly one has not taken revelation seriously. This audience is not a passive audience, but an interactive audience that engages with a performative revelation.[51]

Moosa is aware, however, that many modern Muslim audiences fail to play their role as well as they might, for they exhibit

> little sensibility for the complex ways a revealed and performance text like the Qur'an is interpreted. The fact is that how the interpretation of

the Qur'an is to be approached is not as easily available as free copies of the holy book. Instead many people read it like one reads a medical textbook or an engineering manual. So the Qur'an has been turned into a sovereign, passive, non-interactive text. In other words, it ceases to be a revelation that melts the heart of the reciter and/or listener. It no longer makes the reverent reader's skin shiver in awe of the Divine.[52]

Hermeneutical philosophy has not only had an impact on Muslim thinkers it has also profoundly influenced the theology of at least one central branch of Christianity: namely, Roman Catholicism. The German Jesuit theologian Karl Rahner (1904–84) is widely regarded as one of the most important Roman Catholic theologians of the twentieth century, and it was he who assimilated many of the ideas of hermeneutical philosophy into the theology of his church. Rahner was concerned that Christian faith, and Christian doctrines, had become largely unintelligible to his contemporaries, and thus struck many of them as unacceptable. His response to this situation was to attempt to show that the faith and the church's doctrines were intelligible when they were situated within a modern horizon of understanding. Thus, Rahner reinterpreted traditional doctrines, such as the doctrine of Christ's double-nature and the doctrine of grace, from within a perspective that had assimilated much of the modern, twentieth-century scientific worldview.[53] Rahner's genius, and the key to his popularity within institutional Roman Catholicism, was to convince many of his co-religionists that, what at first sight appeared to be radically new interpretations of traditional Christian doctrines, were in fact orthodox.

There is no doubt, then, that hermeneutical philosophy has contributed a great deal to twentieth-century religious thought. But has it succeeded in providing religious thinkers with a way of understanding religious language that avoids the twin perils of meaninglessness and misrepresentation? With respect to meaning, hermeneutical philosophers would claim that the only meaning that religious language can possess is the meaning invested in it by those who employ it, with the onus lying on religious believers, themselves, continually to project meaning into traditional religious idioms. Consequently, hermeneutical philosophers do seem to have provided an account of how religious language can be meaningful. Unfortunately, their approach would seem to fare less well as a response to the problem of misrepresentation. Once the meaning of language is viewed as the product of a creative activity, it would seem to be impossible to provide guidelines for determining whether or not a purported 'understanding' is a valid interpretation of the mooted religious object. And this may well be regarded as a serious problem within a domain in which contested meanings can lead to intolerant attitudes and, sometimes, even to violence. However, hermeneutical philosophers could reply that intolerance is precisely what follows when one mistakenly assumes that a text has a single, authoritative meaning. But this reply is unlikely to satisfy anyone, including the great majority of believers, who thinks that the word of God is not open to limitless interpretations.

Despite this seeming difficulty, the idea that understanding, or gleaning meaning from, a text is a creative activity became a recurrent theme within late twentieth-century theories of religious language. The principal advantage of theories that emphasize this idea is, perhaps, the obverse of its main difficulty: many people have, no doubt, found liberating the idea that they are responsible for the meaning of traditional religious texts. One who endorses the general approach of hermeneutical philosophy will be less inclined to accept as authoritative any one supposedly 'orthodox' interpretation of a text's meaning. During an age in which religious authorities are widely regarded with suspicion, many religious people no doubt find it advantageous to have the meaning of religious texts in their own hands, or, at least, in the hands of the interpretive community to which they belong.

But there is an additional way of understanding religious language that might avoid the twin perils of meaninglessness and misrepresentation, and that is to construe religious discourse as metaphorical. As we shall see, this approach has certain affinities with the main ideas of hermeneutical philosophy; hence they should, perhaps, not be seen as rivals but as complementary theories of language.

Metaphor

Metaphor is a figure of speech in which we speak about one thing in terms that are usually employed to talk about something else.[54] Although metaphor is ubiquitous within ordinary, as well as within explicitly poetic, speech and writing, until the twentieth century metaphorical expressions were commonly regarded as inferior to non-figurative ones. The belief that only literal language is capable of being true, which is commonly attributed to Plato (427–347 BC), has been held responsible for the view that metaphors only play a minor linguistic role. Until recently, most philosophers assumed that metaphors were merely ornamental, and were, moreover, translatable into literal language without loss of meaning. In other words, they subscribed to the 'substitution theory', according to which, in metaphorical uses of language, certain figurative words are substituted for other non-figurative words. Thus, the metaphor can be eliminated by simply substituting back the original word.

It was only in the twentieth century, when people began to think about language in new ways, that certain philosophers began to develop more adequate theories of metaphor. Given the importance of metaphor within religious texts, it is no surprise that these new theories were employed to shed light on the nature of religious language.

Richards and Black on metaphor

I. A. Richards was the first to reconsider the role that metaphors play in language, and hence the first to reject the substitution theory,[55] with Max Black following his lead. Both insist that, far from being merely ornamental and reducible to literal language (as the substitution theory claimed), metaphors can be used to say things that cannot be said in any other way. Consequently, they play an irreplaceable role in our language.[56] In arguing against the substitution theory, both Richards and Black reject the view that individual words are the bearers of meaning. Instead, the relationship between words and meaning is far more complex, which Richards seeks to elucidate by means of what he calls an 'interanimative' theory of metaphor.

Rather than construe individual words as possessing a meaning that is fixed independently both of the way they are used and of the context of their utterance, Richards proposes that the meaning of words can only be arrived at through considering 'the interplay of the interpretive possibilities of the whole utterance' in which the words are lodged.[57] In the case of metaphor, the interpretive possibilities are extended. Consider the use of 'pig' as a metaphor for 'glutton'. When we call someone a pig, we elicit both the thought of a pig and the thought of a glutton. In Richards' view, 'when we use a metaphor we have two thoughts of different things active together and supported by a single word or phrase, *whose meaning is the result of their interaction*'.[58] A metaphor, then, does not work simply by bringing together two words, each with its own fixed meaning, and thereby somehow producing a meaning that is a fusion of the two original meanings. Rather, a successful metaphor, in Richards' view, creates a new meaning from the interaction, or 'interanimation', of the two original meanings. In other words, metaphors operate by drawing together pairs of meanings that are not usually thought of together. Richards' key idea is that both are essential to the success of the metaphor as a generator of meaning.

Black develops a similar theory, which he calls the 'interactive theory of metaphor', but adds that metaphors make certain features prominent, and that this then shapes our perception. As he argues, by means of the metaphor 'Man is a wolf': 'Any human traits that can without undue strain be talked about in "wolf-language" will be rendered prominent, and any that cannot will be pushed into the background. The wolf-metaphor suppresses some details, emphasizes others – in short, *organizes* our view of man.'[59] Hence, Black holds that, in bringing together the complex frameworks of meaning invoked by the terms 'man' and 'wolf', the metaphor works in a much more subtle way than the traditional substitution theory acknowledges. In forcing us to select which aspects of talk about wolves can be applied to man and which cannot, the metaphor changes the way in which we think about man. If the metaphor succeeds, henceforth the meanings associated with the word 'man' will, in part, be structured by the meanings associated with wolves. Thus, an important change will have taken place in the way we think about men – a change that cannot be irreducibly expressed in literal language. Moreover, our thinking about wolves will not remain unchanged for, 'if to call a man a wolf is to put him in a special light, we must not forget that the metaphor makes the wolf seem more human than he otherwise would'.[60]

Soskice on metaphor and religious language

Janet Martin Soskice has employed the theories of both Richards and Black to develop what is, perhaps, the most influential account of metaphor and religious language to appear to date. Like Richards and Black, she rejects the substitution theory of metaphor, and emphasizes the role that metaphors play in generating new perspectives capable of increasing our understanding. In her view, by generating new perspectives, successful metaphors expand our descriptive powers in a way that other types of linguistic expressions do not.[61] In short, metaphors 'disclose' to view what has not been previously available.[62] Consider the following example:

> When we speak of the camel as 'the ship of the desert', the relational irreducibility of the metaphor lies in the potentially limitless suggestions that are evoked by considering the camel on the model of a ship: the implied corollaries of a swaying motion, a heavy and precious cargo, a broad wilderness, a route mapped by stars, distant ports of call, and so on. Saying merely 'camel' does not bring in these associations at all.[63]

Thus, the metaphor of the camel as 'the ship of the desert' genuinely tells us something about camels that we would not have been able to learn without the help of the metaphor. The range of associations evoked by metaphors such as this is, then, one of their principal advantages and, according to Soskice, one of the chief reasons why they are indispensable. Moreover, the evocative function of metaphors can, she stresses, be particularly important within religious language, where it might serve to facilitate a new range of experiences – ones for which there may be no established literal description.

This might suggest that Soskice regards the principal function of metaphor as evocative. However, she argues strongly that it is a mistake to view metaphors and models (in other words, extended metaphors) as having a primarily evocative function. Rather, a

> model in religious language may evoke an emotional, moral, or spiritual response but this does not mean that the model has no cognitive or explanatory function. In fact the reverse is true; the model can only be affective because it is taken as explanatory. ... The cognitive function is primary.[64]

Soskice further claims that in order to explain the cognitive function of metaphors and models within religious language, we must consider the way in which they are actually employed. So, using the model of God as 'father', which is so prominent within Christianity, to illustrate how models function in religious language, she points out that those who use this particular model implicitly base further convictions upon it.[65] For example, the use of this model presumes that 'if God is our father, he will hear us when we cry to him; if God is our father, then as children and heirs we come to him without fear; if God is our father, he will not give us stones when we ask for bread'.[66] Such convictions are, she argues, action-guiding – and therein lies their cognitive content.

Soskice also argues that metaphorical terms can 'be seen as denoting candidates for real existence', and that such terms can be reality depicting despite the fact that they are not 'exhaustively descriptive'.[67] Indeed, metaphorical terms are characteristically vague, and this, Soskice argues, is one of their virtues. In both religion and science, Soskice avers, metaphorical terms are indispensable precisely because they are vague. Without this vagueness, there would be a tendency for people to regard the terms as expressing a complete understanding of the aspect of reality in question. They would thus be prone to dogmatism and resistant to any proposed changes to the theory expressed by these terms. In consequence, their theories might cease to be responsive to any new knowledge which comes to light. Thus, the great virtue of metaphor in the context of religious and scientific theories is that it allows us to refer to what really exists, while conceding that our knowledge of the relevant aspects of reality might be incomplete. Metaphor makes this possible because it is a way of using language that allows us to refer to things without defining them. Soskice:

> This is the fine edge at which negative theology and positive theology meet, for the apophatic insight that we say nothing of God, but only point towards Him, is the basis for the tentative and avowedly inadequate stammerings by which we attempt to speak of God and His acts. And, as we have argued, this separation of referring and defining is at

the very heart of metaphorical speaking and is what makes it not only possible but necessary that in our stammering after a transcendent God we must speak, for the most part, metaphorically or not at all.[68]

The great advantage of metaphor, then, is that it allows people to refer to God without their having to define 'God'. Thus, metaphorical uses of language would seem to allow religious believers to talk meaningfully about God (supposing that they do in fact succeed in referring), while simultaneously avoiding the danger of misrepresentation. For example, a theist might employ the phrase 'God is a rock'. A statement such as this, if Soskice is correct, can refer to God but should not be understood as either defining or describing the divine. Thus, it can be true that 'God is a rock', without having to be literally true. The claim can be true insofar it tells us something about God's supposed characteristics – but we should not understand it as the claim that God is literally a rock.

Promising as this approach has seemed to many, there is a difficulty with the claim that religious language is metaphorical. When we use metaphor to talk about everyday things – for example, using 'pig' to refer to gluttons – both are not usually too far removed from our experience. But in the case of religious language this is not so. Consider again the example, 'God is a rock'. Clearly, we know what a rock is. But does this really tell us anything at all about God? The problem is that what one of the terms refers to is unknown.

Soskice responds to this objection by pointing out how important metaphor has been in the development of scientific theories. Let me give an example. When people started using the word 'electron', they did not know much about electrons or their properties. And clearly, electrons are not accessible to our experience in the way that rocks are. Initially, scientists referred to an electron as a particle, despite the fact that electrons are, in a number of crucial respects, not at all like the particles we encounter in our immediate experience. In certain respects, electrons are nothing like grains of sand, for example. Other scientists then began referring to electrons as waves. But again, the use of 'wave' was clearly metaphorical. In several crucial respects, an electron is nothing like the surface of the sea. Seemingly worse, what, exactly, is a wave-particle supposed to be? Yet the metaphors of wave and particle were indispensable in enabling scientists to pick out the objects they wished to study. The term 'wave-particle' was able to refer to electrons without literally describing them. And once those particles were referred to, they could be studied empirically.

So, electrons provide an example of how metaphors allow us to refer to things outside of our immediate experience without literally describing them. If scientists can do that with respect to things like electrons, surely believers can do the same with respect to God. In short, metaphors can enable us to refer to entities that we would be unable to refer to were our uses of language exclusively literal.

This seems a very strong response because, if Soskice is right, it implies that theologians are not doing anything significantly different, in a sense, from what scientists are doing. Both require metaphors to refer to the objects that concern them. However, it could be objected against Soskice that scientists can conduct experiments that give us some reason for thinking that the phenomena they are able to study directly are caused by electrons. New data often requires some revision in what we take electrons to be. And this suggests that we are learning more about electrons. But what is the parallel evidence that suggests we are successfully referring to God? Soskice argues that the theist's confidence in the existence of that to which his or her 'God-talk' aims to refer is grounded in religious experience.[69] Moreover, she believes that the experience of saintly individuals is likely to carry the most weight.[70] Such people may be the best placed to instil in others confidence that their talk about God has a real referent. Moreover, there is a sense in which a religious tradition embodies the cumulative experiences of its participants through the ages. It is a tradition of experience and of interpretation, against the background of which metaphorical religious language is used and understood. Soskice argues, then, that religious traditions, Scriptures and the experience upon which they are based can provide sufficient background information to give us an idea of that for which the unknown term in religious language stands. But this response clearly presupposes some degree of faith, and is therefore of little use to a sceptic. Moreover, any reliance on private experiences, as religious experiences tend to be, seems to make religious claims immune to public testability. Yet it is surely the public testability, at least in principle, of certain of the claims made about electrons that appears to justify our ever-increasing confidence that we are successful in referring to them.

Nevertheless, in drawing attention to the relation between metaphor and religious experience, Soskice has pointed to a possible explanation of the vital importance of metaphors within religious language. We now turn to a theory of metaphor that offers the prospect of according a central role to this relation.

An alternative approach to metaphor

George Lakoff and Mark Johnson, like Soskice, have developed a theory of metaphor that builds on the work of Richards and Black. They accord metaphors a far greater role in our cognitive structure than do any of the theories examined so far. For they argue not only that metaphors play a significant and irreplaceable role in the way we think, but also that huge areas of our language are structured by them. Hence, in their influential book entitled *Metaphors We Live By*,[71] they aim to undermine the view that literal language is primary and that metaphorical language is dependent upon it. Indeed, they go so far as to argue that what many people regard as literal language only functions within a context that is deeply structured by metaphor: 'Our ordinary conceptual system, in terms of which we both think and act, is fundamentally metaphorical in nature', they aver.[72] With this claim, Lakoff and Johnson go far beyond the views of metaphor we have thus far considered. Soskice, Richards and Black regarded metaphor as a figure of speech, albeit a potent one that enables the creation of meaning. Lakoff and Johnson clearly regard metaphor as much more than this, for, in their view, it is constitutive of our thought. Moreover, they argue that the claim that our conceptual experience is pervasively metaphorical has two further implications. First, given the widely accepted view that our conceptual system affects our experience, and given that our conceptual system is structured by metaphor, then if we are to understand our experience, we must understand how the metaphors we employ function. Second, given that reality is presented to us only in our experience, and given that our experience is shaped by our conceptual system, then metaphors play a crucial part in defining what is to count as reality. Given these convictions, it is unsurprising that Lakoff and Johnson argue that the notion of metaphor should be recognized as a central philosophical concept. It is the key, they claim, to comprehending how conceptual systems are related to our experience, and to how understanding emerges from this relationship.

The primary focus of interest within the work of Lakoff and Johnson is on our conceptual systems – in other words, on the 'concepts that structure what we perceive, how we get around in the world, and how we relate to other people'.[73] They take it for granted, however, that we cannot simply look inward and thereby study our conceptual system. Put another way, we cannot make it an object of direct knowledge. Nevertheless, they assume that our conceptual system can be studied; namely, by means of the language we use. Because our language, they claim, is based upon our conceptual system, then the structure of our language provides evidence regarding the structure of our conceptual system. And the linguistic evidence, they maintain, establishes 'that most of our ordinary conceptual system is metaphorical in nature'.[74]

The force of the argument that Lakoff and Johnson present derives from the many examples they provide in support of their case. One of the most persuasive of these, which is often referred to by subsequent authors, is the metaphor 'argument is war'. Lakoff and Johnson use this metaphor as an illustration of a 'conceptual metaphor', which is a metaphor that exercises a structural effect both on our thought and on our everyday activity. They begin by drawing attention to a variety of metaphors that are subsidiary to the conceptual metaphor 'argument is war', and which, themselves, form part of our ordinary way of talking about arguments. Consider, for example: 'Your claims are *indefensible*', 'He *attacked every weak point* in my argument', 'His criticisms were *right on target*', 'He *shot down* all of my arguments'. Commenting on these common metaphorical ways of speaking, they claim:

> It is important to see that we don't just *talk* about arguments in terms of war. We can actually win or lose arguments. We see the person we are arguing with as an opponent. We attack his positions and we defend our own. We gain and lose ground. We plan and use strategies. If we find a position indefensible, we can abandon it and take a new line of attack. Many of the things we *do* in arguing are partially structured by the concept of war. Though there is no physical battle, there is a verbal battle, and the structure of an argument – attack, defense, counterattack, etc. – reflects this. It is in this sense that the ARGUMENT IS WAR metaphor is one that we live by in this culture; it structures the actions we perform in arguing.[75]

In understanding arguments in terms of war, then, we thereby stipulate what arguments consist in within our culture. And anyone who did not employ the metaphor 'argument is war' would not experience 'arguments' in the way that those who accept the metaphor clearly do. In fact, such a person would be unable to engage in arguments as they are conceived within our culture. Hence, the activity of arguing, and the experience one has while doing it, are, Lakoff and Johnson aver, metaphorically structured. Without the metaphor, one cannot engage in the activity, and hence one cannot have the experience that goes with it. Because conceptual metaphors, like 'argument is war', have the function of structuring our thought, activity and experience, metaphor cannot simply constitute the peripheral feature of our language use that traditional theorists had presumed. Rather, conceptual metaphors consist in structuring concepts that control whole networks of our thought and activity. Moreover, there are numerous conceptual metaphors, and together they structure most of what we think, say and do. And only *within* such networks, Lakoff and Johnson argue, does literal language function.

Metaphors, then, can structure not only our thinking but also our activities. And Lakoff and Johnson insist that a large number of our activities are 'metaphorical'; in other words, our performance of those activities is structured by metaphor. Indeed, there is a very real sense in which our use of metaphorical concepts has created these 'metaphorical' activities. Thus, as Lakoff and Johnson argue:

> New metaphors have the power to create a new reality. This can begin to happen when we start to comprehend our experience in terms of

a metaphor, and it becomes a deeper reality when we begin to act in terms of it. If a new metaphor enters the conceptual system that we base our actions on, it will alter that conceptual system and the perceptions and actions that the system gives rise to.[76]

So, consider love – an example frequently deployed by Lakoff and Johnson to illustrate the extent to which metaphors can shape our experience. Most people would surely agree that love, like most, if not all, of our emotions, defies full conceptualization in non-metaphorical terms. In order to talk and think adequately about love, we therefore require conceptual metaphors. Lakoff and Johnson provide as examples: 'Love is a physical force'; 'Love is patient'; 'Love is madness'; 'Love is magic'; and 'Love is war'.[77] Each of these conceptual metaphors structures a possible way of thinking and talking about love. Thus, by adopting the 'Love is a physical force' conceptual metaphor, we are able to say things like: 'I could feel the *electricity* between us'; or 'His whole life *revolves* around her'. Adopting a different conceptual metaphor would enable us to talk in a very different way about love. We could, instead, adopt the 'Love is war' conceptual metaphor, and thus say such things as: 'He is known for his many rapid *conquests*'; 'He *won* her hand in marriage'; or 'He *overpowered* her'.

But if Lakoff and Johnson are correct, these conceptual metaphors do more than merely allow us to think and talk about love in novel ways. A new conceptual metaphor will also enable us to experience love in a new manner. In other words, the alteration in our conceptual system caused by the introduction of a new conceptual metaphor is such as to change what we experience. Consequently, when people began to think of love as war, Lakoff and Johnson argue, they also began to experience love as war – their reality had begun to change. Therefore, when different people come to diverge in the conceptual metaphors they employ to structure their thought, language and experience, then there is a sense in which they will no longer share the same reality. And this way of understanding how it might be that different people experience different 'realities' may shed light on cultural diversity, given that many striking differences between conceptual metaphors can be found across cultures.[78]

As users of metaphor, then, we can transform 'reality', at least in the sense of bringing about significant changes to the 'perceptions, conceptualizations, motivations, and actions that constitute most of what we experience'.[79] And, as Lakoff and Johnson point out, this makes metaphor a political concern.[80] For people in power – and in the twentieth century, those in control of the media might be thought to have become some of the chief wielders of power – can control which metaphors become dominant, and hence can strongly influence how we experience our world.[81] Once a metaphor has become accepted, people will experience the world in the terms it suggests, and thus will view what it entails as true. Consequently, those who shape the metaphors dominant within a culture will thereby exercise a disproportionate influence on what is regarded as true within that culture.

Despite the tremendous significance of this conclusion, Lakoff and Johnson regard issues concerning truth as secondary to what they consider to be the deeper issue: namely, that conceptual metaphors structure our understanding of our experience, and, through that experience, they structure our understanding of the world. Hence, those who can persuade us to adopt their metaphors will, if Lakoff and Johnson are right, be able to lure us into accepting their worldview. And it is this that Lakoff and Johnson take to be of prime importance. We shall consider the relevance of this for religious language shortly. But first, it is worth noting that this is not the only danger inherent in the use of successful conceptual metaphors.

As we saw earlier, the substitution theory held that metaphors were incapable of communicating anything that could not equally be said by means of non-figurative language. But Lakoff and Johnson argue that the account of non-figurative language presumed by the substitution theory is itself based upon a conceptual metaphor: namely, that of a 'conduit'.[82] This conceptual metaphor has three subsidiary metaphors: 'ideas (or meanings) are objects'; 'linguistic expressions are containers'; and 'communication is sending'. According to Lakoff and Johnson, these metaphors structure the way in which many people think about language.[83] And the image this pattern of metaphors yields is that '[t]he speaker puts ideas (objects) into words (containers) and sends them (along a conduit) to a hearer who takes the idea/objects out of the word/containers'.[84] Obvious examples of this way of thinking are 'It's hard to *get* that idea *across* to him', 'I *gave* you that idea', 'It's difficult to *put* my ideas *into* words', and so on.[85] Such common linguistic expressions, which seem to be structured by the conduit metaphor-complex, would appear to provide considerable support for the theory that Lakoff and Johnson defend.

So, thinking about language in terms of the conduit metaphor would seem to present us with a structured pattern for understanding what it is that we do with words. But, as Lakoff and Johnson argue, this particular metaphor well illustrates how powerful conceptual metaphors can be so successful in structuring our experience that they leave us quite unaware of what is omitted from the worldview they shape – a further feature of conceptual metaphors that should cause us to be wary of them. In other words, through entailing, for example, that words and sentences bear meaning independently of the speaker or context, the conduit metaphor can effectively blind us to the role that speakers and contexts play in the process of communication. Hence, this particular metaphor leaves us without any resources for explaining, or even recognizing, situations in which the meaning is not carried by the words used but by the context in which they are uttered. Furthermore, the conduit metaphor may structure our understanding of language in such a way that we become insensitive to cases in which the same sentence will mean entirely different things to different people because of their different backgrounds, expectations, and so on. Thus, in structuring our thought, action and language, metaphors also screen out various alternatives.[86] The important moral that Lakoff and Johnson draw from this feature of conceptual metaphors is that such metaphors only ever provide us with a partial 'reality' – but one that, fortunately, may be extended by the use of complementary metaphors. Clearly, the claim that a conceptual metaphor can hide aspects of reality as well as reveal them is of tremendous relevance to an adequate theory of religious language, even though this implication of the work of Lakoff and Johnson has not been pursued to date.

How might this thought be developed, then? As we have seen, conceptual metaphors, according to Lakoff and Johnson, are essential if we are to talk and think about things that defy conceptualization in straightforwardly non-metaphorical terms. Many theists, of course, with the obvious exception of the literalists, are in agreement that the divine – the mooted object of much religious discourse – defies all such conceptualization. God is, therefore, a prime candidate for conceptualization through metaphor. Moreover, analysis of what religious believers actually say about God would appear to bear out the claim that the content of their thought and speech regarding this mooted object is structured by organizing, or conceptual, metaphors. Think of 'God is love'. Not only does this particular conceptual metaphor shape a 'reality' in which God stands as divine carer for all creation but it also excludes a whole host of alternatives, such as everything that is implied by conceptualizing the world as ruled by a vengeful God. And this, if the theory propounded by Lakoff and Johnson is correct, shapes the experiences that the faithful have of their relationship to God.

Now, as we have seen, Lakoff and Johnson claim that people who use different conceptual metaphors may actually experience different 'realities'; for, by structuring speech, thought and activity, conceptual metaphors create their own possibilities of experience, thereby potentially creating new 'realities'. It may well be, then, that a new metaphor within religious language would enable people to experience the divine in ways that were unavailable prior to the introduction of that metaphor. Consider, again, the metaphor 'God is love'. By utilizing the analysis advanced by Lakoff and Johnson, we could argue that when people first began to think of God as love they also began to experience a loving God – in short, their 'reality' had changed. But a similar 'change in reality' may have occurred when the metaphor 'God as father' was introduced into Semitic monotheism by Jesus. Likewise, the metaphors employed in the Hebrew Scriptures and the Qur'ān could be regarded as opening up new ways of experiencing the divine, and hence as generating new 'realities'.

However, this way of thinking about metaphor in religious language also highlights a problematic facet of religious experience. As we have seen, metaphors work, according to Lakoff and Johnson, by drawing our attention to certain features of things, while simultaneously screening certain other aspects from our attention. Thus, the conceptual metaphor 'God as father' draws attention to certain features of God (power, providential care, and so on), while screening from us certain other purported features that cannot so easily be associated with fatherhood (God as nurturer, for example). The metaphor 'God as father' may, then, facilitate a certain way of experiencing the divine, while closing off numerous other possibilities. These observations would seem to converge with the analyses of religious language developed by those feminist theologians who have pointed to the negative consequences of the almost exclusive use of male metaphors for God within the monotheistic traditions[87] – which is one reason for not relegating the study of metaphor within religious language to the exclusive, abstract concern of a few scholars. For if Lakoff and Johnson are correct, then we have grounds for thinking that specific conceptual metaphors have shaped whole religious traditions. We would have reason to think that such metaphors have determined how religious people experience what they take to be the divine, and how they understand the language that they use in their attempts to talk about it. And a wariness with respect to how specific conceptual metaphors have shaped whole religious traditions could have far-reaching consequences for how the divine is conceived in the future.

Conclusion

Each of the three traditional approaches to religious language considered earlier in this chapter continued to find advocates into the twenty-first century.[88] However, during the last few decades of the twentieth century, an increasing number of religious thinkers turned to hermeneutics and theories of metaphor in their efforts to provide a theoretical account of their religious discourse.

Certainly, there are some advantages to be gained from regarding the interpretation of sacred texts as an ongoing process – as hermeneutical philosophers argue it inevitably must be. For it discourages dogmatism, while encouraging tolerance towards diverging interpretations. Moreover, the view that religious language is principally metaphorical rather than literal also offers significant advantages to religious believers; one being that it facilitates regarding a range of metaphors or models of the divine as possessing equal value, even if, at first sight, they appear to be mutually exclusive (for example, the metaphors of father and mother when applied to the deity). And drawing attention to the range of possible metaphors makes it harder for one construal of God to trump all others, especially when each may be regarded as having something to contribute to a fuller religious understanding. This observation would seem to pave the way for appreciating just how much religious people might stand to gain from exploring the metaphors deployed in a range of religious traditions. Judaism, Christianity and Islam all attempt to refer to God using distinct, but overlapping, metaphors and models. Viewing these as complementary, rather than as rivals, becomes a more acceptable option once religious language is regarded as functioning in the manner outlined above. And clearly, this would be of considerable advantage to the denizens of an increasingly multicultural world.[89]

As we noted, this emphasis on metaphor arose, in part, from an increasing awareness that science had progressed through employing metaphors as a means of referring to theoretical entities. Whereas the logical positivists had sought to drive a wedge between scientific and religious claims, there was a growing appreciation through the second half of the twentieth century of the similarities between religious and scientific discourse, as both were increasingly recognized to contain a larger component of non-literal, metaphorical language than many had previously assumed. Given the view of language that dominated the early decades of the century – central to which being the conviction that scientific discourse was language *par excellence*, and that it set the standard which religious language must strive to meet and of which it seemingly fell far short – the growing emphasis on metaphor was all the more significant. By the closing decades of the century, difficulties that had formerly seemed peculiar to religious language came to be widely perceived as afflicting all language, including scientific discourse. But this also implied that religious discourse need no longer be regarded as a poorer relative. Some of these issues will resurface in the following chapter, as we turn to consider the interface between science and religion in modern thought.

Study questions

1 Why did many twentieth-century philosophers believe that it was important to determine whether or not religious statements were meaningful?

2 What is religious language? Can it be clearly distinguished from non-religious language? What problems can arise when we try to make this distinction?

3 Which, if any, traditional theory of religious language most closely describes the way that you think about religious language? How might you defend your chosen theory against criticism?

4 What kinds of problems arise when one tries to read an ancient religious text, such as the Torah, the New Testament or the Qur'an, literally?

5 What purpose does the *via negativa* serve in our thinking about religious language?

6 Why does Aquinas believe that we need a theory of analogy to understand religious language? Is he correct?

7 Do you agree with hermeneutical philosophy that all interpretation is conditional? If the hermeneutical view is correct, what are some of the implications for religious language, particularly the language used in sacred texts?

8 Could religious communities adopt the view that truth gradually emerges from a variety of interpretations without undermining their claim to possess religious knowledge?

9 Could accepting a hermeneutical approach to religious language encourage religious believers to be more tolerant of the beliefs held by adherents of other faiths?

10 Does metaphor succeed in allowing people to refer to God without their having first to define 'God'? If so, why is this important for modern religious believers?

11 What do George Lakoff and Mark Johnson mean by their claim that metaphors play a crucial part in defining what is to count as reality? Do you agree with their view?

12 To what extent is being a religious person about experiencing a reality that is shaped by specific religious metaphors? Does this view of the relationship between metaphor and experience give us any real insights into what it is to be religious?

Select bibliography

Bleicher, J., (ed.), 1980, *Contemporary Hermeneutics: Hermeneutics as Method, Philosophy, and Critique*, London: Routledge and Kegan Paul.

Gadamer, H.-G., 1977, *Philosophical Hermeneutics*, edited and trans. by David Linge, Berkeley and Los Angeles: University of California Press.

Gadamer, H.-G., 1991, *Truth and Method*, trans. by Joel Weinsheimer and Donald G. Marshall, New York: Crossroad.

Johnson, M. (ed.), 1981, *Philosophical Perspectives on Metaphor*, Minneapolis: University of Minnesota Press.

Kepnes, S., P. Ochs and R. Gibbs, 1998, *Reasoning After Revelation: Dialogues in Postmodern Jewish Philosophy*, Boulder: Westview Press.

Lakoff, G. and Mark Johnson, 1980, *Metaphors We Live By*, Chicago: University of Chicago Press.

Lindbeck, G. A., 1984, *The Nature of Doctrine: Religion and Theology in a Postliberal Age*, Philadelphia: The Westminster Press.

McFague, S., 1982, *Metaphorical Theology: Models of God in Religious Language*, Philadelphia: Fortress Press.

Rahman, F., 1982, *Islam and Modernity: Transformation of an Intellectual Tradition*, Chicago: The University of Chicago Press.

Schleiermacher, F. D. E., 1986, *Hermeneutics: The Hand-written Manuscripts*, trans. by James Duke and Jack Forstman, Atlanta, Georgia: Scholars Press.

Soskice, J. M., 1985, *Metaphor and Religious Language*, Oxford: Clarendon Press.

Stiver, D. R., 1996, *The Philosophy of Religious Language: Sign, Symbol & Story*, Oxford: Blackwell.

Notes

1 As we saw in the previous chapter, Wittgenstein's theory of 'meaning as use' was independent of any theory of truth. Once the meaning of a proposition was distinguished from that proposition's capacity for truth or falsity, a new pair of terms gained importance. Meaningful propositions that are capable of being true or false came to be described as 'cognitive', whereas the term 'non-cognitive' was applied to meaningful propositions that are not truth-apt. Using these terms, we can say that Hick's theory of religious language was a cognitivist theory, while Wittgenstein (at least in his later works) advocated a non-cognitivist theory.

2 In this chapter, I do not examine the influence of structuralism or poststructuralism on understandings of religious language. While they had a considerable influence on European intellectual life in the mid-twentieth century, they now seem to have been somewhat ephemeral intellectual fashions. Here I focus on intellectual movements whose impact looks set to last.

3 It is common to distinguish between what we might call 'general religious language' on the one hand, and, on the other hand, a specialized category of religious language called 'theological language'. General religious language includes the language used in religious texts (parables, stories, myths and so on), as well as the language employed by believers in prayer and worship, etc. Such language tends to be replete with images and metaphors, and is sometimes referred to as 'first-order' language. Theological language, by contrast, tends to contain a high proportion of abstract concepts; that is, concepts that are far removed from our direct experience. Thus, it is sometimes referred to as 'second-order' language. In what follows, we shall be concerned principally with general religious language.

4 For example, compare the word 'passion' employed in the phrase 'the passion of Christ' to its usage in the phrase 'the passion of Henry for Annaïs'. Notice that even if 'passion' has two quite different meanings (or more), it is nevertheless one word.

5 The shared vocabulary of 'religious' and 'secular' language can, however, be camouflaged by the fact that the 'languages' of Judaism, Christianity and Islam are peppered by antiquated terms and expressions that have long since passed out of everyday parlance.

6 It would, of course, be a further matter to stipulate exactly what constitutes 'a religious context'. Indeed, to attempt to do so would return us to the discussion in Chapter 2, concerning how religion is to be defined. Nevertheless,

perhaps we can suggest that a 'religious context' typically includes references to such things as Scripture, prayer, worship, religious experiences, and so on.

7 This is somewhat ironic given the view, accepted by many scholars, that scriptural literalism is a product of modernity. See, for example, George A. Lindbeck, 1984, *The Nature of Doctrine: Religion and Theology in a Postliberal Age*, Philadelphia: The Westminster Press, p. 51.

8 The levels of interpretation were: literal, allegorical, tropological (moral) and anagogical (referring to the future life). See Karlfried Froehlich (ed.), 1984, *Biblical Interpretation in the Early Church*, Philadelphia: Fortress Press, p. 28.

9 Martin Luther, 1982, *The Babylonian Captivity of the Church*, Works of Martin Luther, Grand Rapids, Michigan: Baker Book House, vol. 2, pp. 189f.

10 Russell T. McCutcheon, 2001, *Critics not Caretakers: Redescribing the Public Study of Religion*, Albany: State University of New York Press, p. 51.

11 McCutcheon, *Critics*, p. 51.

12 See, for example, Ignaz Maybaum, 1973, *Trialogue between Jew, Christian and Muslim*, London: Routledge & Kegan Paul, pp. 148f.

13 Traditionally, such correspondence had been regarded as of the utmost importance. Within traditional Islam, for example, there remains a prohibition on translating the original Arabic of the Qur'ān into any other language – lest the correspondence be lost. Mohammed Arkoun argues that this attitude results from a failure to distinguish appropriately between the written Qur'ān and what he terms the 'Qur'ānic discourse' (the discourse that was heard by the Prophet). In his view, the Qur'ānic discourse is the locus of revelation, not the text of the Qur'ān. See Mohammed Arkoun, 1994, *Rethinking Islam: Common Questions, Uncommon Answers*, trans. and edited by Robert D. Lee, Boulder: Westview, pp. 30 and 39.

14 Replacing Ancient Hebrew as the language of worship with the vernacular was the principal agenda item of those who initiated Reform Judaism in nineteenth-century Germany. Roman Catholics had to wait until the late 1960s for such an innovation. The shift from using a language that few understood to using vernacular languages was accompanied by a wide range of other major changes within each tradition.

15 Within the Christian tradition, Pseudo-Dionysius is a key early exponent of the *via negativa*. See Pseudo-Dionysius Areopagite, 1940, *The Divine Names and the Mystical Theology*, trans. by C. E. Rolt, New York: Macmillan. The German mystic Meister Eckhart (1260–1327) was another well-known proponent of this approach to religious language.

16 Moses Maimonides, 1936, *The Guide for the Perplexed*, trans. by M. Friedlander, London: Dover, pp. 86f.

17 Expressing similar sentiments to Maimonides, Karen Armstrong claims: 'Once the Bible begins to be interpreted literally instead of symbolically, the idea of its God becomes impossible.' Karen Armstrong, 1999, *A History of God: From Abraham to the Present: The 4000-year Quest for God*, London: Vintage, p. 326.

18 Maimonides did, however, allow that a partial conception of God can be arrived at through considering God's manifestations in the world; even though it may be the case that not everyone is able to achieve knowledge of God this way. Ehud Ben-Or interprets Maimonides as claiming that God's manifestations in

the world could only be recognized as such by the virtuous. If this is right, then Maimonides believes that the conception a person might form of God is limited by that person's character. See Ehud Ben-Or, 1995, *Worship of the Heart: A Study of Maimonides' Philosophy of Religion*, Albany, New York: SUNY.

19 Brian Davies, 1986, *An Introduction to the Philosophy of Religion*, Oxford: Oxford University Press, p. 12.

20 See Ian Crombie, 1971, 'The Possibility of Theological Statements' in B. Mitchell (ed.), *The Philosophy of Religion*, Oxford: Oxford University Press, pp. 23–52.

21 'Grace' is a translation of the term *charis*, which is used in the Christian Scriptures to refer to God's favour towards certain men and women – favour that is often unmerited.

22 Crombie, 'Possibility', p. 29.

23 Crombie, 'Possibility', p. 29.

24 Crombie, 'Possibility', p. 48.

25 Hilary Putnam, 1997, 'God and the Philosophers' in Peter A. French, Theodore E. Uehling, Jr and Howard K. Wettstein (eds), *The Philosophy of Religion*, Midwest Studies in Philosophy, vol. 21, Notre Dame, Indiana: University of Notre Dame Press, p. 185.

26 Thomas Aquinas, 1964, *Summa Theologiae*, trans. by H. McCabe, London: Blackfriars, vol. 3, 1a, 13, 5. My italics.

27 One key idea within ordinary language philosophy is best clarified by means of one of Wittgenstein's analogies: 'Think of the tools in a tool-box: there is a hammer, pliers, a saw, a screw-driver, a rule, a glue-pot, glue, nails and screws.' As he remarks: 'The functions of words are as diverse as the functions of these objects.' Ludwig Wittgenstein, 1959, *Philosophical Investigations*, trans. by G. E. M. Anscombe, Oxford: Blackwell, paragraph 11.

28 See Friedrich Daniel Ernst Schleiermacher, 1986, *Hermeneutics: The Hand-written Manuscripts*, trans. by James Duke and Jack Forstman, Atlanta, Georgia: Scholars Press.

29 Hans-Georg Gadamer, 1991, *Truth and Method*, trans. by Joel Weinsheimer and Donald G. Marshall, New York: Crossroad, p. 296.

30 See, for example, Steven Kepnes, Peter Ochs and Robert Gibbs, 1998, *Reasoning After Revelation: Dialogues in Postmodern Jewish Philosophy*, Boulder: Westview Press, p. 140.

31 See Chapter 11.

32 Hans-Georg Gadamer, 1977, *Philosophical Hermeneutics*, edited and trans. by David Linge, Berkeley and Los Angeles: University of California Press, p. 15. And see Gadamer, *Truth*, p. 296.

33 Gadamer, *Philosophical*, p. 15.

34 Mohammed Arkoun makes a similar claim: 'Meaning is no longer stable, forever rooted in transcendence, but is rather exposed to the continued genesis of destruction. Meaning is generated by semantic creativity, the inventiveness of the subject under the pressure of new existential demands that necessitate destroying, transforming, or surpassing previous meanings.' Arkoun, *Rethinking*, p. 84.

35 See Jürgen Habermas, 1980, 'The Hermeneutic Claim to Universality' in J. Bleicher (ed.), *Contemporary Hermeneutics: Hermeneutics as Method,*

Philosophy, and Critique, London: Routledge and Kegan Paul, pp. 181–211.

36 See Gadamer, *Truth*, p. 295.

37 Gadamer, *Truth*, p. 309.

38 Fazlur Rahman, 1982, *Islam and Modernity: Transformation of an Intellectual Tradition*, Chicago: The University of Chicago Press, p. 2.

39 Rahman, *Islam*, p. 3.

40 Rahman, *Islam*, p. 5.

41 Rahman, *Islam*, p. 5.

42 Rahman, *Islam*, p. 6.

43 See Chapter 3, p. 73.

44 Rahman, *Islam*, p. 10.

45 See Rahman, *Islam*, pp. 8f.

46 See Rahman, *Islam*, p. 11.

47 See Rahman, *Islam*, p. 19.

48 Rahman, *Islam*, p. 23.

49 Rahman, *Islam*, p. 158. Rahman's argument is clearly reminiscent of John Stuart Mill's. See John Stuart Mill, 1978, *On Liberty*, Indianapolis: Hackett Publishing Company.

50 See Rahman, *Islam*, p. 20.

51 Ebrahim Moosa, 2003, 'The Debts and Burdens of Critical Islam' in O. Safi (ed.), *Progressive Muslims: On Justice, Gender, and Pluralism*, Oxford: Oneworld, p. 124.

52 Moosa, 'Debts', p. 124.

53 See Karl Rahner, 1984, *Foundations of Christian Faith: An Introduction to the Idea of Christianity*, London: Darton, Longman & Todd. I consider Rahner's views further in Chapter 6, see p. 172.

54 See Janet Martin Soskice, 1985, *Metaphor and Religious Language*, Oxford: Clarendon Press, p. 15.

55 See I. A. Richards, 1936, *The Philosophy of Rhetoric*, Oxford: Oxford University Press.

56 See the essays in Mark Johnson (ed.), 1981, *Philosophical Perspectives on Metaphor*, Minneapolis: University of Minnesota Press.

57 Richards, *Rhetoric*, p. 55.

58 Richards, *Rhetoric*, p. 93. My italics.

59 Max Black, 1981, 'Metaphor' in Johnson, *Philosophical*, p. 75.

60 Black, 'Metaphor', p. 77.

61 Soskice, *Metaphor*, p. 66.

62 See, for example, Soskice, *Metaphor*, p. 89.

63 Soskice, *Metaphor*, p. 95.

64 Soskice, *Metaphor*, p. 109.

65 Sallie McFague also employs 'God the Father' as an example of a model within religious language, which she regards as a dominant metaphor that has established itself as a model through its staying power. 'As a model,' she writes, 'it not only retains characteristics of metaphor but also reaches toward qualities of conceptual thought. It suggests a comprehensive, ordering structure with impressive interpretative potential. As a rich model with many associated common-places as well as a host of supporting metaphors, an entire theology can be worked out from this model. Thus, if God is understood on the model of

"father", human beings are understood as "children", sin is rebellion against the "father", redemption is sacrifice by the "elder son" on behalf of the "brothers and sisters" for the guilt against the "father" and so on'. Sallie McFague, 1982, *Metaphorical Theology: Models of God in Religious Language*, Philadelphia: Fortress Press, p. 23. Ironically, as McFague points out, it is the very comprehensiveness of successful models that leads people to take them too literally.

66 Soskice, *Metaphor*, p. 112.

67 Soskice, *Metaphor*, p. 133.

68 Soskice, *Metaphor*, p. 140.

69 See Soskice, *Metaphor*, pp. 139f.

70 Hans Urs von Balthasar argues extensively in favour of the type of position advanced by Soskice. He claims that the experience of the saints should be used as a primary resource within Christian theology. On this aspect of von Balthasar's thought, see Victoria S. Harrison, 2000, *The Apologetic Value of Human Holiness: Von Balthasar's Christocentric Philosophical Anthropology*, Dordrecht: Kluwer Academic Publishers.

71 George Lakoff and Mark Johnson, 1980, *Metaphors We Live By*, Chicago: University of Chicago Press.

72 Lakoff and Johnson, *Metaphors*, p. 3.

73 Lakoff and Johnson, *Metaphors*, p. 3.

74 Lakoff and Johnson, *Metaphors*, p. 4.

75 Lakoff and Johnson, *Metaphors*, p. 4.

76 Lakoff and Johnson, *Metaphors*, p. 145.

77 See Lakoff and Johnson, *Metaphors*, p. 49.

78 See Chapter 7.

79 Lakoff and Johnson, *Metaphors*, p. 146.

80 See Lakoff and Johnson, *Metaphors*, pp. 157f.

81 Michel Foucault has also written extensively about the close ties between language and power.

82 Here Lakoff and Johnson are indebted to Michael Reddy. See Michael Reddy, 1979, 'The Conduit Metaphor: A Case of Frame Conflict in our Language about Language' in A. Ortony (ed.), *Metaphor and Thought*, Cambridge: Cambridge University Press, pp. 164–201.

83 See Lakoff and Johnson, *Metaphors*, chapter 3.

84 Lakoff and Johnson, *Metaphors*, p. 10.

85 Lakoff and Johnson, *Metaphors*, p. 11.

86 For one illustration of such screening, see McFague, *Metaphorical*, p. x.

87 See Chapter 9.

88 As is well known, many Jews, Christians and Muslims support some form of scriptural literalism – a position we consider further when we turn to religious fundamentalism in Chapter 10.

89 We return to the issue of religious plurality in Chapter 7.

6

The Impact of Science

The discussion of metaphor in the previous chapter suggests that each of the Abrahamic monotheisms provides its adherents with a distinctive conceptual framework for understanding the world they inhabit: in other words, with a worldview. In the modern era, religious worldviews have been faced with a new competitor – the scientific worldview (or, more precisely, scientific worldviews). The worldviews of traditional religion and that of modern science are often thought to be irreconcilable because modern science appears to contradict at least some of the core beliefs of each of the Abrahamic faiths. At the very least, the credibility of traditional beliefs concerning the creation of the world,[1] the special place of humans in the created order, and God's ability to act upon the world[2] all appear to be undermined by scientific claims. Moreover, given the emphasis placed on science within modern education and by mainstream Western culture, it has been difficult for many to avoid the challenge that science presents to their religious belief system. It should not surprise us, then, that scientific ideas have had a significant transformative impact upon traditional religious worldviews.[3]

The success enjoyed by many branches of science in the twentieth century is no doubt largely responsible for the role it has come to play within modern intellectual life.[4] Few would deny that one of the most remarkable features of the twentieth century was the unprecedented success of scientific method in providing explanations for many things that had previously seemed inexplicable. The results yielded by scientific method, which primarily involved the testing of theories by means of empirical experimentation, were often so impressive that many people came to regard science as the only reliable source of knowledge.[5] A significant number, moreover, would seem to have drawn the further conclusion that religious beliefs should be abandoned in those cases where they conflict with the findings of the natural sciences. Indeed, throughout much of the twentieth century, religion, in contrast to the advance of the sciences, seemed to be making a corresponding forced retreat. As Don Cupitt observes:

> the development of an immense body of objective knowledge of the world about us in modern times seems directly connected with the decline of religion. The difference between a medieval bestiary [a moralising medieval treatise on real and imaginary beasts] and a

modern work of zoology is that symbolic and religious ways of looking at animals have been replaced by cool and intense observation of
natural fact.[6]

Not surprisingly, Cupitt argues that scientific knowledge *replaces* religious ways of understanding the world, and that the expansion of the
former is thereby directly responsible for the decline of the latter. In support of this view, Cupitt appeals to the undeniable fact that, throughout
the modern era, scientific knowledge has caused massive disruption to
systems of religious belief,[7] which had survived basically unchanged for
centuries. Nevertheless, although traditional religious beliefs have often
been retracted as a result of scientific claims,[8] it may be too hasty simply
to assume – as Cupitt clearly does – that a further retreat of religious
belief is inevitable in the face of modern science.[9]

Indeed, construals of the purported threat that science poses to religion would appear to depend upon how the relationship between them
is conceived. By the end of the twentieth century, those who were alert
to these issues had come to occupy one of three positions. According to
those who hold the first position, science and religion are in inevitable
competition and co-exist in a state of outright conflict. In short, science
and religion are antagonistic. Those holding the second position aver that
science and religion are fundamentally different to a degree that not only
rules out genuine conflict but also makes it impossible for them to contribute anything to each other. Put another way, science and religion are
non-antagonistically incommensurable. Finally, advocates of the third
position hold that science and religion are compatible domains of inquiry
– they share some common ground and can influence each other, but
serious disagreement between their respective claims should not arise. In
other words, science and religion are complementary.

In this chapter, I provide an overview of these positions before
focusing on a cluster of arguments exemplifying the third position: in
particular, so-called 'new design arguments' for the existence of God.
We shall see that science has the potential both to undermine religious
belief and to support it. Let us now turn, then, to the view that science
and religion are competitors locked within an inevitably conflictual
struggle.

Scientific materialism and its critics: the antagonistic relationship view

Many people, both religious and non-religious, hold not only that traditional religious beliefs and the claims of modern science are in direct
conflict but also that the respective presuppositions of religion and

science are fundamentally opposed. One critic of Islam, ibn Warraq, for example, claims that science

directly conflicts with Muslim religious beliefs on a number of issues. But the more fundamental difference is a question of methodology – Islam relies on blind faith and the uncritical acceptance of texts on which the religion is based, whereas science depends on critical thought, observation, deduction, and results that are internally coherent and correspond to reality.[10]

While many would no doubt object to Warraq's self-avowedly polemical characterization of Islam, his stance, nevertheless, exemplifies the first position: science and religion are in direct conflict. For religion, Warraq claims, involves 'blind faith' and the 'uncritical acceptance of texts', whereas science is based on 'critical thought', 'observation' and 'deduction', and yields 'results that are internally coherent' and which 'correspond to reality'. The implication, clearly, is that religious beliefs are not the product of critical thought, observation or deduction, are mutually incoherent and fail to correspond to reality. When the contrast between science and religion is conceived in this light, it is no surprise that they are thought to be in direct conflict, and that many plump for science.

Despite the fact that many in the twentieth century rejected this implied characterization of religion, the notion of an irreconcilable conflict between religion and science remained a commonly held one. Moreover, the popular image of the modern scientist who sets at naught traditional religious 'wisdom' in relentless pursuit of 'objective' scientific knowledge[11] invites the conclusion that science and religion are locked in unremitting conflict. While this image might be thought something of a caricature, it is, nevertheless, reminiscent of those early twentieth-century scientists who – convinced of positivism – held that science is the only reliable source of knowledge, and that all religious claims should be shunned because they are based on groundless superstition. These opinions have commonly been entertained alongside the assumption that fundamental reality is material, and that, consequently, only the objects of science are 'real' – a position usually termed 'scientific materialism',[12] and which constituted a significant challenge to religion during the twentieth century (as it continues to do in the twenty-first).

Curiously, scientific materialism has a certain affinity with another stance which, at first sight, appears to be very different: namely, scriptural literalism. The latter holds that the claims of some specific set of religious Scriptures are true, and that where these claims contradict the purported findings of modern scientists, the claims of the scientists are to be rejected as false. The feature common to both of these stances is to be found in their account of what is required for knowledge. For both assert that knowledge must be based on certain, or indubitable, foundations. Early twentieth-century scientific materialists generally claimed that the foundations of knowledge are logic and sense-data, whereas scriptural literalists tended to hold that the only secure foundation for knowledge is revelation within its Scriptures. And both parties tended to assume that there is a direct conflict between their respective claims. Having already examined scriptural literalism in the previous chapter, we now consider scientific materialism.

Scientific materialism has taken a variety of forms, and has been endorsed by a wide range of thinkers.[13] In the late twentieth century, scientific materialism – principally, in the form of a new discipline called sociobiology – had a huge impact on the intellectual life of the West. Sociobiologists, such as Edward O. Wilson, popularized the idea that it is only a matter of time before everything that is as yet unexplained by science will be so explained. Holding that the human sciences (such as sociology and religious studies) will all ultimately be reduced to biology,[14] Wilson predicts that when religion is fully explained in terms of biology, it will lose much of its power. He believes, nevertheless, that '[t]he predisposition to religious belief is the most complex and powerful force in the human mind and in all probability an ineradicable part of human nature'.[15] One conclusion that Wilson draws from this assessment of religious belief is that '[r]eligion constitutes the greatest challenge to human sociobiology and its most exciting opportunity to progress as a truly original theoretical discipline'.[16] Wilson's ambition is, therefore, to explain religion by means of general sociobiological principles. In other words, he aspires to explain religion by providing an account of the role that religious beliefs and practices play in furthering our self-interested biological ends. Hence, he argues that the

> highest forms of religious practice, when examined more closely, can be seen to confer biological advantage. Above all they congeal identity. In the midst of the chaotic and potentially disorienting experiences each person undergoes daily, religion classifies him, provides him with unquestioned membership in a group claiming great powers, and by this means gives him a driving purpose in life compatible with his self interest.[17]

Wilson thus sets great store by the claim that a religion confers a biological advantage upon its adherents, insisting that, if this claim can be supported, scientific naturalism will have successfully explained religious phenomena, and will thus be established as the superior worldview.[18] Clearly, Wilson assumes that if one can explain some phenomenon as biologically advantageous, then this explanation says all that need be said about that phenomenon. In particular, such an explanation is taken to foreclose the question of whether or not any beliefs underlying the phenomenon in question might be true. The philosopher, theologian and scientist Holmes Rolston III, whose own ideas we discuss below, challenges Wilson's assumption by analysing its apparent logical structure:

Premise 1:   If B (biologically advantageous), then not T (true).
Premise 2:   B.
Conclusion: Therefore not T.[19]

As Rolston points out, this argument is formally valid (the conclusion follows from the premises), but we have no reason to judge that it is sound (for we have no reason to assume that both the premises are true). The first premise certainly does not seem to be established so much as assumed by Wilson, given that he fails to provide any compelling argument for the implicit claim that if acting on a certain belief is biologically advantageous, then that belief cannot also be true.

The uncompromising stance of scientific materialists such as Wilson would seem to be motivated by the assumption, mentioned above, that the natural sciences alone are capable of yielding genuine knowledge because they alone study 'real' objects. This assumption is supported by the conviction that only scientific claims can be publicly verified. Scientific experiments are repeatable by anyone who has the correct equipment, the argument might go; and thus the results of science are reliable because they are reproducible. The public and reproducible nature of scientific conclusions might then be contrasted with religious beliefs, which do not seem to be based on the kind of public data which could verify them. Religious beliefs, scientific materialists are keen to point out, are thus not public in the sense that they cannot be checked by empirical investigation whose results could be reproduced by anyone. Thus, science is thought to be 'objective', whereas religion is considered to be 'subjective'.

In criticizing scientific materialism, Keith Ward summarizes its basic tenets as follows: 'the only things that exist are material things in space. There is no purpose or meaning in the universe. Scientific principles are the only proper forms of explanation.'[20] He then argues that, contrary to the impression scientific materialists seek to convey, these tenets 'are not scientific theories or assertions. They do not belong to physics or chemistry or psychology or biology. They are certainly statements of faith.'[21] This characterization of the, purportedly, non-scientific foundations of scientific materialism suggests to Ward that it should be regarded as a worldview rather than as a scientific theory. One holds such beliefs, according to Ward, not on the basis of evidence but 'because they seem to form the basis for a coherent, adequate and consistent description of the world which fits one's fundamental value-judgements and attitudes'.[22] In emphasizing the status of scientific materialism as a worldview, Ward hopes that we will regard its adoption, in preference to other candidates, as a choice, and not as inevitable. And once we see this, Ward argues, the next step will be to ask the question: which type of worldview, the scientific materialist one or the theistic one, has the most power to explain the universe we inhabit? As we shall see, when we consider the argument from design, Ward argues that the theistic worldview is the most rational one for us to adopt. Interestingly, Wilson would probably agree with the way that Ward has framed this question. For he, too, holds that scientific materialism is a worldview that we should adopt, or not, on the basis of its explanatory power. His disagreement with Ward concerns which worldview, a scientific materialist one or a religious one, has superior explanatory power, and thus is the rational one to choose. What gives scientific materialism the edge, in Wilson's view, is that, as explained above, its conclusions can be supported by publicly verifiable data, and thus are 'objective'; whereas religious beliefs are not supported in this way, and are, therefore, 'subjective'.

Wilson is, therefore, typical of those who hold that science and religion are in conflict because they have nothing in common – the former being founded upon reason, and the latter being founded upon superstition. However, this assumption, although extremely popular during the first half of the twentieth century, was seriously questioned later in the century by many who argued that that there is a continuum between science and religion: for science, as Ward insists, involves *both* reason *and* faith, just as religion involves *both* faith *and* reason. The well-known philosopher of religion, Basil Mitchell, for example, argues for such a continuum on the grounds that an element of faith is an essential requirement of all rational enquiry.[23]

In support of this conclusion, Mitchell avers that the conception of reason presupposed by those who contrast rationality with faith implies that, in order to be rational, one must: (i) 'have sufficient evidence for what one believes'; (ii) 'be prepared to produce the evidence on demand'; and (iii) 'proportion one's confidence in the truth of the belief to [the weight of] the evidence as it stands at the time of speaking'.[24] In order to demonstrate that it is unlikely that there is any sharp contrast between faith and reason, Mitchell points out that what we ordinarily consider to be instances of rational thought rarely satisfy these criteria. Instead, as Mitchell, borrowing from John Henry Newman (1801–90), observes: (a) 'much of our reasoning is tacit and informal'; (b) 'most arguments are cumulative in form'; (c) 'in estimating the force of the evidence and in deciding what is to be believed on the strength of it we are rightly influenced by considerations other than those provided by the evidence itself'; that is, 'we bring to the evidence assumptions which inevitably' and rightly 'affect our interpretation of it'; and (d) systems of belief require stability over time in order to develop, and, once developed, they tend to persist.[25]

Thus, Mitchell hopes to persuade us that the contrast 'between the entirely open-minded approach of the scientist and the committed nature of religious faith is, at the very least, overdrawn'.[26] For example, stubbornness, as he notes, can be a virtue with respect to finding truth in science, and this seems to suggest that an element of faith is a requirement of scientific procedure. Hence, Mitchell concludes that faith is not confined to theology but is a feature of all intellectual endeavours.[27] However, 'as one moves from the natural sciences, through the biological to the psychological and social sciences and on to the humanities, the role of faith becomes steadily more apparent'.[28] In other words, instead of a sharp divide we have a continuum, in Mitchell's view.

Given these arguments against scientific materialism, with its core assumption that only science can yield 'objective' knowledge of 'real' objects, what might explain its widespread adoption in the early twentieth century? Clearly, the views of the logical positivists, which we examined in Chapter 4, provided a philosophical underpinning for the central ideas of scientific materialism, and persuaded many to adopt its approach. As we have seen, members of the logical positivist movement were convinced that the only meaningful propositions (analytic propositions of logical form excepted) were synthetic propositions which could be publicly verified through scientific experimentation. All synthetic propositions that could not be verified (metaphysical, ethical and religious 'propositions', for example) were, therefore, said to be meaningless. Thus, all meaningful propositions were thought to belong to the category of what could be expressed in instrumental statements about what experiences we would have were we to perform certain actions.

However, as we noted in Chapter 4, although logical positivism captivated the minds of many philosophers and scientists for at least two decades, it soon became clear that, as a theory of meaning, it was inadequate as an account of the full spectrum of human experience. Moreover, as many philosophers argued, it also failed to take sufficient account of the interplay between factual and evaluational judgements within our reasoning processes.[29] Critics of logical positivism further pointed out that sense-data could not be foundational in the sense which logical positivists and scientific materialists assumed. In fact, it became increasingly apparent to many that sense-data are simply not available in the raw state which the logical positivists and scientific materialists supposed. Rather, the act of gathering information, or of experiencing sense-data, already involves interpretation, because human consciousness does not seem to have access to sense-data that are prior to some preliminary conceptualization. In short, the case can be made that to experience something is already to interpret it. Later theorists would therefore stress the degree to which sense-data were influenced by prior theory and by the interaction of the observer with the observed. So, despite the undoubted influence which logical positivism had earlier exercised in shoring up the convictions of the scientific materialists, by the end of the twentieth century few believed it justified the view that there is no reliable route to knowledge outside of science. And many critics of scientific materialism agreed that, just as logical positivists have an idealized view of meaning, scientific materialists have an idealized view of science.

Consequently, many religious thinkers came to believe that to conceive the relationship between religion and science as one of direct conflict is to distort the nature of both domains. Hence, some began to explore alternative conceptions of their relationship. Nevertheless, as we shall now see, many, perhaps understandably, remained reluctant to give up the distinction between the two domains.

No genuine conflict is possible: the incommensurability view

Those adhering to some version of the second position on the relationship between religion and science – the non-antagonistic incommensurability view – typically argue that science and religion are autonomous domains of human understanding, each focusing on different objects of enquiry. Stephen Jay Gould (1941–2002), for example, argues that, because science and religion have different subject matter, there can be no genuine conflict between their respective claims. Indeed, the view that science and religion do not make claims about the same aspects of reality is fairly common. One motivation for this view is the widespread conviction that, whereas science is concerned with supposedly value-neutral facts about the objective world, religion is concerned with evaluation. The famous biologist John Maynard Smith (1920–2004), for example, expresses this conviction when he asserts that scientific theories have nothing to say 'about the value of human beings',[30] adding that such 'theories say nothing about what is right but only about what is possible, and we need some other source of values'.[31] Mordecai Kaplan (1881–1983), the founder of Reconstructionist Judaism,[32] offers a similar view:

> The so-called conflict between religion and science is actually a conflict only between religion, conceived as theurgy [that is, a supernatural means of controlling the world], and science, conceived as a method based upon experience and experiment. There can be no quarrel between religion conceived as a source of values and meanings, and science, as a description of objective reality.[33]

According to this stance, then, science and religion are concerned with different domains: science with 'objective reality', and religion with 'values and meanings'. Hence, the argument goes, provided that each respects the boundary of the other's territory, no genuine conflict should arise.

The non-antagonistic incommensurability view has, in fact, an extremely long history. Commonplace in the medieval period was a distinction between 'revealed knowledge' and 'natural knowledge'. The latter was thought to be the product of human discovery through natural as opposed to supernatural means; while the former was thought to have a supernatural origin, and was believed to be discovered within sacred texts and, in some versions of the distinction, in the wisdom inherent within a religious tradition. While earlier proponents of this view, ibn Rushd and Thomas Aquinas, for example, claimed that there is some overlap in the content of these two types of knowledge,[34] modern advocates tend to emphasize the complete disjunction between 'revealed' and 'natural' knowledge. Thus, many modern thinkers, such as the Protestant theologian Karl Barth (1886–1968), deny that there is any 'natural knowledge' of God at all.[35] And this entails that discoveries and advances within natural science cannot, even in principle, contribute anything to our knowledge of God. Scientific, or 'natural', knowledge is therefore thought to have no relevance whatsoever to religious belief. Likewise, 'revealed knowledge' – the preserve of faith – is thought to have no bearing on scientific knowledge.

The nineteenth-century Danish philosopher, Søren Kierkegaard (1813–55), was another influential modern thinker who held this position.[36] In his view, if it were the case that reason or empirical investigation, unaided by revelation, successfully proved religious beliefs to be true, then religious faith would be redundant. In other words, he holds not only that 'natural knowledge' can contribute nothing of importance to a person's religious beliefs but also that if, *per impossibile*, it could do so, then it would constitute a danger to faith. Consequently, he argued that science should stay within the boundaries of its own domain, and not seek to intrude into domains where it can contribute nothing.

However, it is clear that, as science developed, scientific knowledge came to cover more and more ground. Features of the world that had previously been 'explained' by religion now seem better explained by scientific theories, for these theories enable us to make reliable predictions that were not facilitated by religious explanations. Hence, religious belief has been obliged to withdraw its claims in the face of the advancing frontier of science – a process that seems to have occurred at an unprecedented pace during the nineteenth and twentieth centuries. Indeed, modern theologians who adopted the non-antagonistic incommensurability view soon found that the only apparently secure domain in which religious knowledge was not threatened by the growth of scientific explanations was that of human subjectivity. Here, at least, or so it seemed, the scientific outlook could not reach. Hence, following Friedrich Schleiermacher, theologians sought to found theology on human feeling. However, the failure of this strategy soon became apparent in the early twentieth century, when science – in the form of psychology – staked its claim on the domain of human subjectivity.

As a result of the unprecedented advance of science, a variant of the non-antagonistic incommensurability view became prominent during the second half of the twentieth century. Science and religion, according to this modified view, both make claims about the real world, but they do so from radically different and irreducible perspectives. Inspired by the philosophy of Ludwig Wittgenstein, what this view amounts to in practice is the belief that the scientist and the religious believer, in effect, speak different languages. These languages are construed as fulfilling different but equally legitimate functions – and, because the languages are so different, there can be no genuine conflict between their respective claims.

As we saw in Chapter 4, Wittgenstein came to regard human discourse as a series of language games, each with its own rules determining the various meanings of the statements made within them. As we have also seen, his theory of language games emphasizes the way that language is used, and insists that the 'rules' of each language game can only be discovered from within the language game itself. Thus, on this view, it would be a mistake to judge the statements made in one language game by the standards of a quite different language game. Applying this to the relationship between science and religion, the implication is that it would be illegitimate to judge religious claims – such as, for example, the claim that God created the world in six days – from a scientific standpoint: for to do so would be to miss the point of the religious claims, and to confuse the discrete discourses of science and religion.

According to this approach, then, we should examine the different functions of these two language games: the scientific and the religious. And if we do, we shall see that scientific language functions in that particular area of inquiry which deals with natural phenomena, for which it is a useful tool that allows us to describe such phenomena. Likewise, we shall discover that the function of religious language is to promote values and, perhaps, a whole philosophy of life which binds together a human community. On this view, therefore, the dispute between a religious believer and a scientist is not really a disagreement over the nature of reality at all. As Wittgenstein remarks: regarding the denial of the religious belief that illness is a punishment from God, 'you can call it believing the opposite but it is entirely different from what we normally call believing the opposite. I think differently, in a different way, I say different things to myself. I have different pictures.'[37] The religious believer and the scientist, then, are engaged in different language games that correspond to what Wittgenstein calls their different 'forms of life'.

Wittgenstein's theory of language has been elaborated and applied specifically to the philosophy of religion by D. Z. Phillips. Emphasizing the uniqueness and autonomy of the religious form of life, Phillips, like Wittgenstein, claims that each language game has its own internal criteria of truth and falsity, and, therefore, cannot legitimately be evaluated on the basis of external criteria. It follows, according to Phillips, that the meanings of terms such as 'true', 'false', 'real', 'unreal', 'rational' and 'irrational' differ from context to context. And as religious statements cannot be understood or appraised on the basis of criteria external to the religious language game, such as that of science, then it follows that religious beliefs cannot conflict with scientific claims.[38]

While this Wittgensteinian strategy for maintaining the distinction between scientific and religious claims is ingenious, it nevertheless incurs difficulties that, some would claim, vitiate its appeal. One problem is that it seems to leave us with a plurality of irreducibly different and unrelated language games, each with its own 'true' claims. Thus, it would seem to rule out the possibility of a monistic, overarching explanation of the diversity of human experiences, which many thinkers, even today, continue to seek. Apparently presupposing the possibility of such a unified theory, one Christian theologian, Harold A. Netland, writes:

> Since ultimately there is unity and consistency to truth, we would expect that what is true in religion is consistent with what is true in other domains such as science, history, and archaeology. Glaring inconsistency between what is asserted in a given religious worldview and what has been established in, say, history indicates that either the religious claim or the conclusion from history is in error.[39]

Although, as we shall see in the following chapter, there may be good reasons in favour of a pluralistic conception of truth (and it may be that the idea of a unified theory is a chimera), this is not a conception that achieved a consensus amongst the majority of twentieth-century religious thinkers. Consequently, many found the Wittgensteinian strategy unpersuasive as an explanation of the relationship between science and religion.

A further difficulty incurred by this approach is that, were it correct, it would seem unlikely that scientific claims and religious claims should have a noticeable impact on one another. However, as we shall shortly see, the facts would appear to be otherwise. A final problem with this view, which we touched on in Chapter 4, is that it seems inherently conservative. The view that religion is for the philosopher to study and to seek to understand, but not to criticize, and certainly not to seek to change in the light of knowledge acquired from other domains of inquiry, would appear to encourage the intellectual fossilization of religion.

In light of these difficulties, many thinkers felt unsatisfied with the non-antagonistic incommensurability view in its modified Wittgensteinian form; and this dissatisfaction led some to occupy the third position, to which we now turn. From the perspective offered by this position, religion and science are complementary domains of inquiry. They share some common ground, and are able to influence each other; moreover, serious conflict between their respective claims need not arise.

A fruitful alliance: the complementarity view

In the eleventh century, al-Ghazali argued that those who deny the findings of science in an attempt to defend their religious beliefs do religion more harm than good.[40] In so arguing, he set a precedent for those twentieth-century thinkers who held that a religion cannot remain credible if it retains beliefs in the face of scientific knowledge which appears to refute them decisively. Many of those who believe that science cannot be safely ignored by religious believers adopt some version of the complementarity view, according to which science and religion will, ideally, form part of an integrated worldview within which each contributes to the other. Clearly, according to this position, scientific theories will not be viewed as alternative accounts of reality that rival religious ones. The claim is not, therefore, that scientific theories are substitutes for religious theories, or vice versa. Rather, scientific and religious theories are regarded as leaving room for (and even requiring) one another. It is no surprise, then, that proponents of this view characteristically focus on what have been called 'boundary questions': religious questions that purportedly arise at the boundaries of science.[41]

The hope of those adopting this particular approach is that the claims of modern science and those of traditional religion can be rendered mutually coherent. Thus, the ambition of those endorsing this position is subtler than that of earlier thinkers who sought to demonstrate that religious doctrines directly support the findings of modern science, or vice versa. Their position is also in sharp contrast to the two positions we have reviewed above. Consider, for example, the religious doctrine that God created the universe and the scientific theory that the universe originated in a Big Bang. Those holding the antagonistic relationship view would regard the religious doctrine and the scientific theory as in deep conflict. In contrast, those holding the non-antagonistic incommensurability view might claim that the religious doctrine concerns the value and meaning of the universe, while the scientific theory explains the objective facts about it. According to the complementarity view, however, one might interpret the religious doctrine not as a theory of cosmogenesis but as a claim about the world's ultimate dependence on God. God might then be envisaged as providing the conditions under which the Big Bang took place. In such a manner, the claims of scientists and those of religious believers might be rendered mutually coherent.

This type of position became increasing popular as the twentieth century approached its close. Indeed, its attractions are easy to identify, for it claims to offer the religious believer a worldview that harmoniously embraces both scientific and religious claims. The pressure of the need to choose one or the other is released, while the cognitive dissonance involved in the effort to keep both within rigidly defined limits is avoided. Furthermore, on the face of it, this position might not require any substantive change to certain religious views. However, as we shall see, this may only be an appearance – an appearance, moreover, which disguises a serious problem inherent within this position. But, before we consider problems with the complementarity view, let us review what has contributed to its success.

The complementarity view has received support from new conceptions of the nature of science that emerged during the second half of the twentieth century. Indeed, since the demise of logical positivism in the mid-century, conceptions of science have changed enormously. Few scientists or philosophers of science now endorse an unqualified version of a positivist conception of science. Some, notably Karl Popper (1902–94), argue that understanding the world scientifically is a creative activity in which the imagination of the scientist plays a crucial role.[42] Others stress the role of paradigms, models and analogies within scientific thinking.[43] The common factor behind each of these new ways of thinking about science is a re-evaluation of scientific language. Earlier positivist theories were committed to the possibility of pure 'observation statements'.[44] These were supposed to report what was present to the senses without the aid of theory or interpretation. The goal was to base scientific theories on the indubitable foundation of such statements. As science advanced in the late twentieth century, however, this goal began to appear increasingly elusive. The theories of quantum mechanics that were so prominent within late twentieth-century science, for example, strained the imagination in an effort to found them on indubitable observation statements which reported basic sensory experiences. It was difficult for many to avoid the conclusion that scientific theories were radically underdetermined by raw observations. Moreover, in an effort to describe the understanding of our world that emerged from increasingly sophisticated experiments, scientists were forced to resort to non-literal language. Indeed, all of the substantial scientific theories of the late twentieth century relied upon metaphor for their articulation. Scientific language, like religious language, came to be recognized as loaded with imagery and interpretation, rather than just comprising a literally true description of the 'facts' grounded in observation.[45] By the end of the twentieth century, it had become common to emphasize how theory-laden are the data of science. Many theorists argued quite plausibly that what was regarded as scientific data depended to a large extent upon the theory that was assumed. In other words, they claimed that scientific theories determine what one will regard as salient, and hence what one will identify as a potential 'fact'.

This new perspective on the relationship between theory and interpretation within science suggested further similarities between it and religion. John Polkinghorne, who is both a professionally trained physicist and an Anglican priest, argues that religion, like science, has data that are shaped by theory.[46] Religious doctrines, he claims, both determine what is to count as data and provide a framework for interpreting it, just as scientific theories do within their domain. And what we can therefore learn from considering the similarities between science and religion, Polkinghorne avers, is that 'each is corrigible, having to relate theory to experience, and each is essentially concerned with entities whose unpicturable reality is more subtle than that of naive objectivity'.[47]

Religious thinkers have, then, quickly apprised themselves of the new, more flexible views of science and scientific language that flourished in the late twentieth century. Not everyone who is sympathetic to religion, however, has unreserved confidence in this approach. Ian Barbour, for example, while recognizing the advantages of theories like Polkinghorne's, expresses reservations:

> In the attempt to legitimate religion in an age of science, it is tempting to dwell on similarities and pass over differences. Although science is indeed a more theory-laden enterprise than the positivist had recognized, it is clearly more objective than religion. ... The kinds of data from which religion draws are radically different from those in science, and the possibility of testing religious beliefs is more limited.[48]

One danger, then, facing those who argue for an alliance of science and religion based on their supposed similarities is that they may overlook important differences between the two domains.

Moreover, those thinkers who emphasize the similarities are, perhaps, motivated by the hope that if science and religion can be shown to be similar in the relevant respects, then the challenges which scientific claims would seem to pose to religious claims need not be regarded as being as devastating as they would have to be if science were thought to be methodologically superior to religion. And if science and religion can be shown to be on a par, then religious believers would no longer be compelled – on pain of irrationality – simply to defer to scientific claims. Scientific claims would need to be made consistent with religious claims no less than the obverse. Nevertheless, most thinkers who endorse some version of the complementarity view do not tend to draw attention to what strikes many as their devaluation of science. Rather, they primarily strive to show how the claims of science can be rendered consonant with the claims of religion. Some go even further, though, and employ scientific theories to provide new interpretations of traditional religious ideas. Pierre Teilhard de Chardin is one.

Chardin (1881–1955) synthesizes scientific theory and Christian religious belief with the specific aim of arriving at a comprehensive worldview.[49] And his understanding of one of the major scientific theories of his day – the theory of evolution – led him to regard God as immanent in a world that, Chardin believes, should be conceived as incomplete; and this constitutes a striking departure from the traditional Christian conception of God. Another example of how Chardin's religious ideas were altered as a result of his scientific views is his theory of the Omega point. Chardin thought that the theory of evolution was somehow parallel to the Christian belief that all things will be fulfilled in Christ. Thus, the culmination of the process of evolution, he believed, was identical with what in traditional Christianity was regarded as the 'Cosmic Christ', the 'Omega' or goal of creation. Needless to say, this view of Christ diverges quite dramatically from that held by traditional Christians. But such modifications to traditional religious ideas were required, in Chardin's view, in order to 'baptize' evolutionary theory by explaining its place within a wider religious worldview.

Another Christian thinker exemplifying the complementarity view is Karl Rahner, who also employs the theory of evolution, but who does so in order to provide a novel interpretation of the Christian doctrine of the incarnation.[50] Portraying the incarnation as simultaneously the climax of the evolutionary process and the climax of God's self-expression, he regards it as a continuation of the salvific process that was begun in creation. Many Christians object to this reformulation of the doctrine, however, because they believe that, in portraying Christ as emerging naturally from the evolutionary process and not as the result of a unique act of God, it underplays the element of discontinuity with the past that was central to the traditional account. Despite Rahner's claim that his interpretation is faithful to the spirit of the original doctrine, the result is a startling example of the type of doctrinal modification that the complementarity view might demand.

Thus, perhaps the main problem with approaches such as Chardin's and Rahner's lies in the extent to which traditional religious ideas are transformed in the attempt to make them fit within a worldview that is primarily shaped by scientific theories. And religious believers might legitimately fear that if the scientific theories came to be superseded, then the religious beliefs that had been shaped by them would simultaneously be undermined. In short, the religious beliefs may come to appear as indefensible as the superseded scientific ones. To be fair, however, this is not a problem that uniquely afflicts thinkers who adopt the approach exemplified by Chardin and Rahner: it is merely a reformulation of a problem that has been addressed by many religious thinkers, Jewish, Christian and Muslim, throughout the centuries. The problem has arisen whenever a religious thinker has appropriated the concepts of any philosophy in order to articulate his or her religious beliefs. The classic example is the assimilation of Greek philosophy during the medieval period as a vehicle for expressing and clarifying the beliefs of the Abrahamic monotheisms. Given the difficulty of elucidating religious beliefs without the aid of any kind of philosophy whatsoever, the outcome of those medieval debates was on the side of those who claimed to employ a philosophy (such as Aristotelianism) without allowing it to distort too profoundly the content of their religious beliefs. In the case of Chardin and Rahner, we can readily see that they attempt to elucidate their Christian beliefs by interpreting them with the aid of scientific theory. However, in so doing, they clearly go well beyond what many of their co-religionists would find acceptable, and are thus frequently accused of changing the substance of traditional Christian belief past recognition.[51]

Despite this problem, it does seem that the view that science and religion are complementary has at least one significant advantage over the other positions we have considered. Namely, it aspires to provide a unified worldview that is sensitive to the claims of both science and religion. And, surely, such a worldview, if available, would be superior to one in which scientific and religious claims were held despite their obvious contradictions. Given this, it is no surprise that many religious thinkers have been attracted to the view that science and religion are complementary. Let us, therefore, turn to consider a cluster of arguments exemplifying this position: 'new design arguments' for the existence of God. These arguments rely directly on developments within late twentieth-century natural science in attempting to establish their conclusions. One question that needs to be addressed, therefore, is: To what extent are they susceptible to the criticism that they only succeed by distorting the religious beliefs they claim to champion? But before we can examine new design arguments, we must first consider traditional arguments from design, and note some of the problems they face.

Traditional design arguments for the existence of God

Arguments from design consist in deducing the existence of God on the basis of evidence that the world must have been designed by an intelligent being. Traditional design arguments rely upon our ability to recognize the place that particular natural objects purportedly occupy within the context of the providential design of the whole.[52] Such arguments are developments of an idea that appears in the Scriptures of each of the Abrahamic faiths. In the Hebrew Scriptures, for example, one reads: 'The heavens declare the glory of God, the sky proclaims His handi-work.'[53] Likewise, the Qur'ān proclaims:

> Surely in the creation of the heavens and the earth
> and the alternation of night and day
> and in ships that run in the sea with profit
> to men, and the water God sends down from heaven
> therewith reviving the earth after it is dead
> and His scattering abroad in it all manner of
> crawling thing, and the turning about of the winds
> and the clouds compelled between heaven and earth –
> surely there are signs for a people having understanding.[54]

Such passages would seem to foreshadow the later development of sophis-ticated design arguments, and they have ensured that arguments from design have been important to many Jews, Christians and Muslims.

Design arguments were particularly popular in the Middle Ages. Dur-ing this period Thomas Aquinas, for example, developed an argument from design that was based upon his observation that natural objects appear to be oriented towards goals. As he writes:

> Goal-directed behaviour is observed in all bodies of nature, even those lacking awareness; for we see their behaviour hardly ever varying and practically always turning out well, which shows they truly tend to goals and do not merely hit them by accident. But nothing lacking awareness can tend to a goal except it be directed by someone with awareness and understanding: arrows by archers, for example. So everything in nature is directed to its goal by someone with under-standing, and this we call *God*.[55]

Aquinas' argument, then, seeks to explain a purportedly observable fea-ture of the natural world – goal-directed behaviour – by invoking an intelligence that directs those things exhibiting it. Aquinas assumes this intelligence to be God. Design arguments like Aquinas' are examples of natural theology and, as such, have an obvious affinity with natural sci-ence in its most basic form; for both seek to explain observable features of our world. Hence, it is no surprise that design arguments were also popular in the seventeenth and eighteenth centuries – an era when develop-ments within natural science were revealing more about the structure of the natural world.

Prominent scientists Robert Boyle (1627–92) and Isaac Newton (1642–1727) both advanced design arguments. It was William Paley (1743–1805), however, who drew the attention of a wider public to this genre of argument.[56] Paley invites us to imagine that, while walking on a heath, we suddenly come across a watch lying on the ground.[57] Upon examination we notice the complexity of the various parts of the watch and the remarkable way in which they all fit together to serve the purpose of time-keeping. Such observations, argues Paley, compel us to conclude that this object cannot have come into being by chance, and that it must, therefore, be the product of an intelligent designer – in this case a watchmaker. In short, we make an inference to the existence of the watchmaker from the observable features of the watch. The crucial step in Paley's argument, however, lies in his further claim that we are entitled to draw a similar inference from the observable qualities of natural objects, such as the eye, to the existence of an intelligent designer: namely, God. Paley holds that when we infer the existence of the watchmaker from the watch, or the existence of God from the eye, we thereby arrive at the best explanation for what we encounter in the world. This is an argument, then, which aims to track the relationship between effects and their causes; and it purports to do so by seeking the best explanation for whatever effect we are examining, irrespective of whether we are considering human-made or natural objects. Paley, then, thought that by positing God as the, so to speak, 'grand designer', we arrive at the best explanation of certain features of the natural world.

There is no doubt that the appeal of design arguments like Paley's is that they offer an explanation for what might otherwise have seemed totally inexplicable. However, in the nineteenth century an alternative explanation emerged as a rival to Paley's. For Charles Darwin's (1809–82) theory of evolution by natural selection also purports to explain why plants and animals 'work' so well in being highly adapted to their surroundings, and it does so without bringing God into the account. The core issue, then, for those seeking to prove the existence of God is which theory provides the best explanation for our observations.[58] Unfortunately for such theists, the explanatory power of the Darwinian account came to appear to many as rendering the presumption of a designer redundant.

A further difficulty with Paley's argument is that it will only seem plausible if one agrees that human artefacts (for example, watches) and natural objects (for example, eyes) are relevantly similar, and thus require a similar explanation. In other words, the argument will only be cogent if a clear analogy between human-made and natural objects is granted. For one may well agree that Paley's inference from the watch to the watchmaker is reasonable, while balking at the inference from natural objects to the existence of a divine designer. Paley assumes that, for example, watches and eyes are sufficiently similar – in view of the complexity they both exhibit, and the way that they appear to be functional for a particular purpose – to justify one in drawing a similar conclusion about the nature of their origin.

The argument is based, then, on the assumption that there is a similarity, or analogy, between particular instances of two kinds of things: natural objects and human artefacts. Essentially, then, Paley's argument is an argument from analogy; such arguments relying on the assumption that if two objects are similar in some respects, then they are likely to be similar in others. But are natural objects, such as eyes, relevantly similar to undisputed instances of the artefactual, such as watches? Whether this mooted similarity obtains is one of the things in dispute between those who advocate traditional forms of design argument and those who reject them. And the more one notices dissimilarities between human-made and natural objects, the less plausible does Paley's argument appear. As Philo, one of David Hume's characters in the *Dialogues Concerning Natural Religion*, comments:

> That a stone will fall, that a fire will burn, that the earth has solidity, we have observed a thousand and a thousand times; and when any new instance of this nature is presented, we draw without hesitation the accustomed inference. The exact similarity of the cases gives us a perfect assurance of a similar event, and a stronger evidence is never desired nor sought after. But wherever you depart, in the least, from the similarity of the cases, you diminish proportionably the evidence; and may at last bring it to a very weak *analogy*, which is confessedly liable to error and uncertainty.[59]

But, as Hume points out, natural objects are far from being exactly similar to human-made objects. Therefore, our experience of the way that human artefacts are produced does not entitle us to infer that natural objects result from a similar type of cause – namely, that they are the products of intelligent design. Furthermore, the argument from design relies on an even more tenuous analogy than that which its advocates suppose to exist between what is known to be artefactual, such as a chair, and natural objects. For not only do theists sympathetic to natural theology infer a divine designer in order to explain the existence and character of particular natural objects, but many also believe that consideration of the totality of natural objects – particularly, of the way they cohere into a whole – merits the conclusion that the universe itself is the product of intelligent design. In this version of the argument, it is assumed that the universe as a whole is like a gigantic watch: it appears to be just like a large and complex machine, the features of which only being explicable by positing intelligent design. But as Philo argues:

> If we see a house … , we conclude, with the greatest certainty, that it had an architect or builder; because this is precisely that species of effect which we have experienced to proceed from that species of cause. But

surely you will not affirm that the universe bears such a resemblance to a house that we can with the same certainty infer a similar cause, or that the analogy is here entire and perfect. The dissimilitude is so striking that the utmost you can here pretend to is a guess, a conjecture, a presumption concerning a similar cause. ...[60]

In the *Dialogues*, Hume expounds several other criticisms of traditional design arguments, many of them undermining the use of analogy, with others challenging the specific conclusions that proponents of such arguments claim can legitimately be drawn from them.[61]

Notwithstanding the vigorous philosophical criticism which arguments from design attracted in the eighteenth and nineteenth centuries, design arguments enjoyed a renaissance in the late twentieth century. So-called 'new design arguments' are typically based on recent discoveries in science, particularly in the fields of biology, physics and biochemistry, and the hope of those who develop them is that they will be invulnerable to the criticisms that afflicted traditional forms of the argument from design.

New design arguments

One new argument from design is advocated by the physicist Paul Davies, who argues that traditional design arguments and other forms of natural theology fail because they rely on there being some natural facts which science has failed to explain. (In the case of Paley's argument, for instance, one relevant natural fact would be the complexity of the eye, which seemed inexplicable prior to Darwin.) The problem with this strategy is that, in the long run, as Davies argues, scientists do eventually explain these natural facts; and when they do, God can no longer be regarded as the best explanation for them. But while it might seem that God is threatened by redundancy as scientists increasingly explain what had formerly been the preserve of theologians, Davies avers that this is not really the case, because the idea of God still has explanatory power at a deeper level. Consider the example of physics, which is regarded by many as the most fundamental of the natural sciences. What twentieth-century physicists have done, according to Davies, is discover the laws that govern natural phenomena. But, this notwithstanding, they have failed to explain why one set of laws governs the physical world rather than another. Thus, the idea of God can still be invoked as the best explanation for the particular configuration of natural laws that physicists have discovered.[62]

In response to arguments like Davies', scientific materialists would resist the suggestion that we should seek to explain why the universe is governed by just that set of natural laws which modern physics has described. They conceive the role of scientists as the investigation of what actually is the case in the universe, rather than in speculating about *why* the universe is the way it is. Theologians, however, tend to regard the refusal of scientists to ask the latter question as, at best, faint-heartedness and, at worst, a failure to acknowledge a real question that cannot be answered by science alone. Some argue, moreover, that, with respect to this question, scientists are simply being unreasonable in not considering the contribution that religion might make towards providing an answer. Keith Ward, for example, argues that the existence of a universe such as this one – one that exhibits structural simplicity, mathematical elegance and integration – is so improbable that it

> would be reasonable to accept any postulate that would make it more probable. The postulate that raises its probability to the highest degree is the postulate that some mind ... intends to bring into existence a physical realm which actualises a subset of elegant possibilities. That would explain with complete adequacy the extraordinary precision of the Big Bang that began this universe.[63]

According to Ward, then, the more that science reveals about the structure of the universe, the more improbable the existence of the universe becomes, and, hence, the more it stands in need of a theological explanation.

Moreover, the feature of the universe that is most improbable is 'the precision of the mathematical structure needed to produce conscious life',[64] and this, Ward argues, would seem to demand an explanation involving the idea of design. Ward therefore argues that the theory of evolution by natural selection on its own does not allow us to conclude that the existence of sentient life-forms is more probable than not. Adding the hypothesis of a God who sets up the process of mutation with the intention of bringing sentient life into being does, however, make the existence of such life-forms probable. And, as it is the mark of a good theory that it makes the facts to be explained probable, the God-hypothesis, argues Ward, is superior to the hypothesis of natural selection considered alone. Thus, Ward claims that

> one could hold that God has designed the basic laws so that, in the long run, in one way or another, conscious beings would come to exist. One would see natural selection as the way in which God works, without interference in the laws of nature, to realise the divine purposes in creation. God would not be needed to explain why natural selection moves in the direction it does, when it could easily have moved in some other direction (or in no direction at all). But God would still have an

explanatory role, in providing a reason why this set of physical laws exists, and in assigning a goal (of conscious relationship to God) to the process of evolution.[65]

In other words, Ward argues that a religious perspective can complement a scientific one by providing a higher-level explanation of the facts discovered by science. The scientific account alone, in his view, would be unsatisfactory insofar as it could only provide a description of the universe and not an explanation of it. The God-hypothesis, then, is not only compatible with the scientific account of the universe but also supplements that account by making it more reasonable to believe (that is, by showing it to be more probable).

Now, it might seem that, if Ward's argument is successful, then the traditional concept 'God' can make an important contribution to scientific theory. This appearance may, however, be deceptive. A closer look at Ward's argument reveals that the key religious concept 'God' at work within his theory has undergone a startling transformation in response to a certain scientific worldview, and the role that God is thought to play in our world, in Ward's view, is itself constrained by what is possible according to the scientific worldview in question. In short, Ward conceives God as 'the sustainer of a network of dynamic interrelated energies', and, as such, God 'might well be seen as the ultimate environing non-material field which draws from material natures a range of the potentialities which lie implicit within them.'[66] Thus, in explaining how religion and science can be complementary, Ward has been compelled to re-conceptualize 'God'.

Ward's theory, then, can be seen as an imaginative encounter between science and religious ideas. In this encounter, as Ward conceives it, science must surrender its claim to provide an exclusive account of the universe (which constitutes a significant transformation in the modern conception of natural science), while the religious concept 'God' must undergo radical transformation in response to the scientific worldview. Though intriguing, theories like Ward's are likely to be highly controversial because, if they are to succeed, both scientists and religious believers must be sufficiently persuaded of their merits to accept the radical transformations required within both domains. As we shall see, other proponents of new design arguments require no less radical conceptual transformations.

While Ward, like Davies, focuses on the role God can play in explaining the general physical laws that govern the universe, other thinkers, such as Michael J. Behe,[67] William A. Dembski[68] and Holmes Rolston III,[69] have attempted to revitalize design arguments by concentrating on the findings of the biological sciences.[70] Behe and Dembski base their respective arguments upon the mooted impossibility of explaining the genesis of complex biological systems without appeal to the notion of intelligent design. Rolston, on the other hand, offers a theory that is structurally similar to Ward's. We first consider the work of Rolston, before turning to the theories of Behe and Dembski.

Like Ward, Rolston argues that a purely scientific account of evolution lacks explanatory power. In his view, simply to assert that the mechanisms of evolution are immanent within nature explains nothing. A satisfying explanation, he claims, would provide 'an account of the setup, an account of the generating processes; of how possibilities get actualized, of how possibility spaces come to be; of the depth sources of creativity'.[71] Once science has said all that it can say about evolutionary history, there remains, according to Rolston, an intellectual challenge that must be met on a philosophical, metaphysical and theological level. In essence, the challenge is to explain the origin of the information transferred across generations by means of DNA. But all that science seems able to say on this matter, Rolston avers, is that the information spontaneously appears.[72] But this is clearly unsatisfactory, in his view, for

[i]n the course of evolutionary history, one would be disturbed to find matter or energy spontaneously created, but here is information floating in from nowhere. For lack of better explanations, the usual turn here is simply to conclude that nature is self-organizing (autopoiesis), though, since no 'self' is present, this is better termed spontaneously organized. ... More comes from less, again and again.[73]

The question for which Rolston seeks an answer – namely, how can we explain the origin of genetic information? – is one that it is only possible to ask because of advances within twentieth-century biology. And it is a question that, according to Rolston, demands a religious response.[74]

This might seem to be a paradigmatic case of religion being called upon to contribute to a scientific understanding of the world. However, as with Ward's theory, science has also impacted on, and thereby transformed, the key religious concept 'God', which is employed by Rolston in answering the question science has raised. For Rolston claims that a 'more plausible explanation' of the origin of genetic information than that offered by science alone 'is that ... there is a Ground of Information, or an Ambience of Information, otherwise known as God'.[75] Clearly, by characterizing God as the 'Ground' or 'Ambience of Information', Rolston has adapted the traditional concept 'God' in order to present it as a plausible explanation of the facts discovered by science. Moreover, as was also the case with Ward's theory, Rolston's conception of the way that God acts is shaped by the scientific worldview that he accepts. For he posits

God as a countercurrent to entropy, a sort of biogravity that lures life upwards. God would not do anything in particular but be the background, autopoietic force energizing all the particulars. The particulars would be the discoveries of the autonomous individuals. God would be the lift-up (more than the setup) that elevates creatures along their paths of cybernetic and storied achievement. God introduces new possibility space along the way.[76]

So, while there are substantial differences in the content of Ward's and Rolston's theories, they share a similar structure. Both argue that certain questions raised by science can best be answered by appealing to religious ideas. Both, moreover, are prepared to transform the traditional religious concept 'God' dramatically in order to answer the questions that science raises. Perhaps it is because Ward and Rolston are both philosophers, as well as theologians,[77] that they have exercised a significant amount of freedom in creatively transforming religious ideas and in arguing for, what can be seen as, an integration of scientific and religious thinking. Michael Behe and William Dembski differ from Ward and Rolston in being primarily scientists rather than philosophers or theologians, and both Behe and Dembski have been vigorously criticized for what has been seen as their willingness to compromise the integrity of their scientific discipline by appealing to religious ideas in order to explain natural facts.[78]

Behe and Dembski argue respectively not only that the biological sciences provide evidence for the universe being the product of intelligent design but also that a key structural feature of biological systems can only be explained as the product of such design. The feature they have focused upon is termed 'irreducible complexity' by Behe and 'specified complexity' by Dembski. Both claim that the theory of evolution by natural selection is incapable of explaining the origin of this prominent feature of the natural world. Behe deploys the system of blood coagulation as an example of 'irreducible complexity'. In his view, it is an irreducibly complex system insofar as we simply could not explain how all the required individual elements came together to form such a complex biochemical system. The argument is that unintelligent, or 'blind', evolutionary change cannot explain how such complex systems originate. There is, Behe argues, a critical point of development only after which complex systems function, and prior to this the system would be unable to function at all. What could explain the evolutionary development up to this critical point? Yet, Behe argues, many complex biochemical systems are irreducibly complex. This means that we cannot explain their development by explaining the development of the individual parts. The problem is that the parts which make up these complex systems seem to have no function apart from their role within the system, and natural selection cannot operate on a part which has no function. We could only explain such irreducibly complex systems by giving an account of how and why the parts came together in just the way they did. But in order to give such an account, Behe insists, we need to talk about purpose and intelligent design.

Dembski regards 'irreducible complexity' as a special case of 'specified complexity', claiming to identify the latter in a wide range of natural phenomena. The theory of evolution by natural selection is powerless to explain 'specified complexity', he claims, because, according to the principles of the theory, we would expect natural selection to favour simplicity. The more complex a phenomenon, the more improbable it is, and, thus, the less susceptible to explanation by the theory of natural selection. The best explanation, then, of complex natural phenomena is not that they are the product of evolution by natural selection but that they are the product of an intelligent designer: God. Dembski clearly believes that the reason why more scientists do not agree with his conclusion is that they have been infected by scientific naturalism (that is, scientific materialism), which he regards as 'the intellectual pathology of our day'.[79] Naturalism, according to Dembski,

> artificially constricts the life of the mind and shuts down inquiry into the transcendent. ... The fundamental tenet of naturalism in the West (or what is typically known as scientific naturalism) is the sufficiency of undirected natural causes to account for all of reality. The only way naturalism can be proved false is if reality is in fact a much richer place than naturalism allows. Specifically reality must include intelligent causes that neither reduce to nor emerge out of undirected natural causes. Moreover the only way to refute naturalism is to show that intelligent causes are empirically detectable. In short, if we're going to show that naturalism is false, we need to locate observable features of the world that demonstrate design.[80]

Dembski, then, and Behe along with him, go further than the other thinkers considered insofar as they believe that it is not merely the best explanation of the facts to claim that the universe is the work of an intelligent designer but, further, that intelligent design is actually empirically observable. We observe it, they insist, when we study biological systems that exhibit complexity.[81] Thus, their case ultimately rests on a phenomenological claim. One can observe that certain features of the natural world are designed, they assert, and those who claim not to *see* this misrepresent the facts (perhaps because they are suffering from the pathology of scientific naturalism).

From a traditional religious perspective, arguments such as Behe's and Dembski's may be more appealing than those of Ward and Rolston, for, unlike the latter pair, the former do not explicitly transform the concept 'God' in their efforts to provide an explanation of natural facts. But, as we shall see, this nevertheless leaves a large gap between the intelligent designer they posit and God as conceived by traditional theists. This gap will become apparent as we assess the various new design arguments we have considered.

Criticisms of new design arguments

Neither of the new forms of argument from design proposed by Ward and Davies, respectively, seems to be principally based on analogy. They are not, then, vulnerable to one of the key Humean criticisms to which traditional design arguments appeared susceptible. Yet they are able to conclude that the only cogent explanation of certain features of the world is that they are the product of intelligent design. This suggests that (at least some) new design arguments represent a completely different type of argument to traditional arguments from design, which, as we have seen, hinge on there being a similarity between natural and human-made objects.[82] If these new design arguments are indeed invulnerable to the criticism of being based on an unacceptable analogy, do they succeed, or are there other criticisms that they face? One major difficulty that proponents of new design arguments seem to encounter, and which also tells against the traditional argument, arises from the presence of what might be described as 'flaws' in our world (traditionally known as 'evil').

Someone who regards the natural world as the work of God may well be embarrassed by certain features of the world that would appear to indicate that it falls far short of perfection. Indeed, nature has struck many thinkers as wantonly cruel, if not indifferent to the plight of humans and other animals. As John Stuart Mill (1806–73) observes:

> nearly all the things that men are hanged or imprisoned for doing to one another are nature's everyday performances. Killing, the most criminal act recognized by human laws, nature does once to every being that lives, and in a large proportion of cases after protracted tortures such as only the greatest monsters whom we read of ever purposely inflicted on their living fellow creatures. ... Next to the taking of life (equal to it, according to a higher authority) is taking the means by which we live; and nature does this too, on the largest scale and with the most callous indifference. A single hurricane destroys the hopes of a season; a flight of locusts, or an inundation, desolates a district; a trifling chemical change in an inedible root starves a million people.[83]

Such considerations seem to weigh heavily against traditional arguments from design. But the problem to which Mill draws attention was not new, and theists have long sought a solution to the so-called 'problem of evil'.[84] But Mill recognized what others, such as Paley, had failed to acknowledge: namely, that features of the world commonly described as 'evil' vitiate arguments from design. While Mill advanced this objection against traditional forms of design argument, it would seem that it is equally forceful against new design arguments. For if we were to accept that the universe is the product of intelligent design, then we would expect some explanation for what would then appear to be the design flaws that result in so much suffering. Worse still, what would sober consideration of the natural world allow us to infer about the character of the purported designer? Surely such consideration would not justify the conclusion that the designer possessed the attributes of omnipotence, omniscience and omnibenevolence – attributes ascribed to God by traditional monotheism. In fact, as we shall now see, there are problems with all of these qualities.

First, if an omnipotent and omniscient God had designed our world, then we would expect it to be a flawless creation. While an omnipotent being would have the power to create a perfect world, an omniscient being would have the knowledge required to do so. Thus, any apparent flaws in design would suggest that the designer lacks at least one of these qualities. Are there such seeming design flaws? Many people believe that there are features of the natural world that, if they were designed, are evident design failures. Inadequacies in the human eye, a useless but potentially dangerous human appendix, weaknesses in the human spine and the pain of childbirth are clear candidates for design flaws. Indeed, Richard Dawkins, a critic of design arguments, argues that if natural objects like the eye have been designed, then we can only laugh at the absurd design exhibited (and which, it would seem, makes a mockery of the designer).[85] At the very least, it is hard to deny the oddity of the claim that an omnipotent, omniscient designer has deliberately designed humans to exhibit these particular features. Not surprisingly, then, Mill concludes that if the world is the product of an omnipotent and omniscient designer, then that designer must be a demon.[86]

Even if we were to accept that the evidence points to a designer, then, the sort of designer who emerges from consideration of the natural world is, at best, a somewhat limited one – limited in power and in knowledge. And a God limited in this way is not the God of traditional theism, but is more akin to the demiurge envisaged by Plato: a limited god who puts the world together out of various materials already at hand. Alternatively, a theist might claim that the designer is omnipotent and omniscient but is not perfectly good (and is thus not concerned to minimize the suffering caused by a failure to design the world in a manner that would be optimal for our well-being). Either choice would clearly constitute a departure from traditional Abrahamic monotheism.

Now, an advocate of design arguments might attempt to resist this conclusion by claiming that God's goodness differs substantially from human goodness. And as we do not know what it is for God to be 'good', we cannot claim to know that God is not 'good' simply on the basis of empirical observations. Mill, however, anticipates this reply:

> If in ascribing goodness to God I do not mean what I mean by goodness; if I do not mean the goodness of which I have some knowledge, but an incomprehensible attribute of an incomprehensible substance, which for all I know may be a totally different quality from what I love and venerate ... [, then] what do I mean by calling it goodness and what reason have I for venerating it? ... To say that God's goodness may be different in kind from man's goodness, what is it but saying, with a slight change in phraseology, that God possibly may not be good?[87]

It would seem that this argument has equal bite on both traditional and new versions of the argument from design. If any design argument is to be compelling, then it must respond to these objections. One possible response would be to argue that, despite 'evil' and suffering, this is, nevertheless, the best possible world; this approach having been adopted by Wilhelm Gottfried Leibniz. As we have seen, in Chapter 4, Leibniz's theory was the subject of a relentless satire by Voltaire in *Candide*. But while Voltaire has discredited Leibniz's view, it would, nevertheless, remain open to advocates of new design arguments to present a modified version of Leibniz's view. They might argue, for example, that once we take into account what the new science of ecology teaches us about the interrelationships between ecosystems and the organisms that inhabit them, we will see that what used to be regarded as unnecessary suffering (and hence as 'evil') is in fact a necessary component of nature.[88] In short, an appropriately sophisticated understanding of the natural world discloses that all things are indeed arranged in the best possible way; what appears to be pointless suffering actually playing a role in the greater scheme of things. The designer is then to be admired for the ecological efficiency of the world, rather than to be blamed for what, only from a short-sighted and purely anthropocentric view, appear as deficiencies.

While this response shows promise (and would, incidentally, constitute another instance of scientific ideas contributing to religious ones), it has one drawback that may prevent many traditional theists from adopting it: namely, it implies that God's omnipotence is limited to the ability to do anything that is *causally* possible. The image becomes that of a God who arranges the natural world in the best possible way given certain causal limitations. Many theists in the Abrahamic traditions, however, understand 'omnipotence' much more widely. They claim that genuine omnipotence is only limited by an inability to do the logically impossible. And the merely causally impossible should present no obstacle to an omnipotent being, for such a being could have established different causal laws. So, acceptance of the ecological solution to the difficulties we have raised against design arguments would entail a weaker conception of omnipotence than many theists would be prepared to accept. In other words, this sort of attempt at making religion and science complementary requires some revision in how God is to be conceptualized.

It would seem, then, that even if some version of the argument from design had been conclusive, its conclusions would have been extremely limited. For one thing, the argument would fall short of establishing the existence of an omnipotent, omniscient and omnibenevolent God.[89] Indeed, it would rather seem to have shown that God is not omnipotent, omniscient and simultaneously omnibenevolent. So, such an argument could not prove the existence of the sort of God who continually cares for the universe. Hence, advocates of both new and traditional design arguments tend to concede that their arguments do not establish that the designer is the God of any traditional monotheism. And as we have seen, some advocates of new design arguments, such as Ward and Rolston, arrive at a conception of God that diverges dramatically from that entertained by traditional theists. Others who favour design arguments might claim, however, that, even though no content for the concept 'God' is provided by design arguments, such arguments still have value insofar as, once a designer is accepted, appeal can then be made to revelation and other purported sources of religious knowledge. Together these can fill out the conception of God.

Needless to say, those not already committed to a traditional conception of God will have little reason to accept this move. But more importantly, if there is a designer, it would appear that our less than perfect anatomy must then be described as a result of 'design flaws'. And this must restrict the plausible interpretations of both Scripture and revelation. Indeed, because design flaws would provide evidence of a flawed designer, any reliance by traditional theists on arguments from design could be regarded as somewhat self-defeating – which seems ironic, given the hostility that a number display towards Darwinism. Indeed, if one wishes to believe in a benevolent deity, it might be wiser to allow a Darwinian evolutionary process to take the blame for anatomical imperfections.

We have examined a cluster of arguments premised upon the conviction that scientific and religious ideas are fundamentally compatible, and that science and religion can make positive contributions to each other. It is noteworthy that, in the closing years of the twentieth century, design arguments achieved a popularity that they had not enjoyed since the mid-nineteenth century. This, perhaps, indicates that a growing number of educated religious people are shunning the antagonistic relationship and the incommensurability views considered earlier in this chapter and, instead, are seeking a *rapprochement* between their religious beliefs and a scientific worldview. If the project of *rapprochement* is consistently carried through, however, the result, as we have seen, is likely to be not only a scientific worldview transformed by religious ideas but also a radical transformation of traditional religious concepts – particularly the concept 'God'. The *rapprochement* at issue, then, appears to offer believers the opportunity of locating both science and religious belief within a coherent worldview, but only at the cost of transforming both. Not surprisingly, by the end of the twentieth century, many religious people were still uncertain about whether to regard science as an ally or as a foe.

Conclusion

The relationship between science and religion has clearly evolved over the twentieth century. At the start of the century, it looked as if science was set to replace religion completely. Science seemed to be capable of providing a reductive explanation of why people held religious beliefs, as well as offering a worldview that was capable of explaining numerous facts about our world, and ourselves, in a much more coherent way than traditional religious worldviews had appeared able to do. However, as the century unfolded, those sympathetic to religious ideas rose to the challenge, and explored various strategies for maintaining the integrity of religious beliefs in a world increasingly dominated by science. As time passed, many scientific claims themselves came under threat, and were superseded. In addition, many people became increasingly sensitive to what they took to be the destructive potential unleashed by science when it became divorced from established cultural and religious values. These developments spurred religious thinkers on in their search for a way of holding together scientific and religious worldviews. Thus, by the end of the twentieth century, the view that science was on the verge of replacing religion was far from being universally held. Instead, there has been a significant trend in certain quarters towards approaches that sought to integrate these two domains of inquiry.

In the meantime, however, another change had taken place. Whereas, at the beginning of the twentieth century, Western Europe and North America were overwhelmingly dominated by one religious tradition – Christianity – by the end of the century this homogeneity no longer prevailed. Thus, instead of one religious worldview seeking to retain its credibility in an increasingly scientific and secular culture, several sought to maintain a niche. In addition, some rejected all moves to bring their religious beliefs into conformity with the claims of science. (We discuss religious fundamentalism in Chapter 10.) This has meant that different groupings adhering to seemingly incompatible systems of belief now find themselves living within the same society. We discuss the political implications of this in Chapter 8. But first, in the next chapter, we consider how we might best conceptualize the relationship between a plurality of faiths.

Study questions

1 What are the key presuppositions of the scientific worldview? Are they necessarily opposed to all religious worldviews?

2 Do you think that it is possible that religion conferred a biological advantage upon its adherents in the past? Might holding religious beliefs be biologically advantageous today? Assuming that at some time it has been biologically advantageous to hold religious beliefs, would it follow that those beliefs could not be true?

3 Is Keith Ward right to claim that scientific materialism is a worldview in the same way that religions are worldviews? If so, what are the implications of this for our understanding of the relationship between science and religion?

4 To which of the three views considered about the relationship between science and religion do you feel most sympathetic? What are the advantages of your favoured view over its competitors? Which view do you think would have most appeal to modern religious believers, and why?

5 How can we tell the difference between a case of altering the core meaning of a religious belief by expressing it in a scientific idiom, and a case of merely expressing that belief in a novel way? Consider, for example, Karl Rahner's account of the incarnation.

6 Can any form of the design argument, either traditional or new, successfully establish that it is rational for us to believe that God exists?

7 Are new design arguments susceptible to any of the same problems as traditional forms of the argument from design?

8 What might explain the resurgence in popularity of design arguments, especially given the criticism they have received since the eighteenth century?

9 Is science more aptly portrayed as an ally to the religious person, or as a foe?

Select bibliography

Barbour, I. G., 1990, *Religion in an Age of Science*, London: SCM Press.

Behe, M. J., 1998, *Darwin's Black Box: The Biochemical Challenge to Evolution*, New York: Simon and Schuster.

Behe, M. J., W. A. Dembski and S. C. Meyer (eds), 2000, *Science and Evidence for Design in the Universe*, San Francisco: Ignatius Press.

Chardin, P. T. de, 1959, *The Phenomenon of Man*, New York: Harper & Row.

Davies, P., 1993, *The Mind of God: Science and the Search for Ultimate Meaning*, Harmondsworth: Penguin.

Dawkins, R., 1996, *The Blind Watchmaker: Why the Evidence of Evolution Reveals a Universe Without Design*, New York: W. W. Norton & Co.

Dembski, W. A., 2002, *No Free Lunch: Why Specified Complexity Cannot be Purchased without Intelligence*, Lanham: Rowan & Littlefield.

Hume, D., 1970, *Dialogues Concerning Natural Religion*, Indianapolis: Bobbs-Merrill Company.

Kuhn, T., 1962, *The Structure of Scientific Revolutions*, Chicago: University of Chicago Press.

Phillips, D. Z., 1970, *Faith and Philosophical Enquiry*, New York: Schocken Books.

Polkinghorne, J., 1987, *One World: The Interaction of Science and Theology*, Princeton: Princeton University Press.

Rachels, J., 1990, *Created from Animals: The Moral Implications of Darwinism*, Oxford: Oxford University Press.

Rahner, K., 1984, *Foundations of Christian Faith: An Introduction to the Idea of Christianity*, London: Darton, Longman and Todd.

Rolston, H., III, 1999, *Genes, Genesis and God: Values and Their Origins in Natural and Human History*, Cambridge: Cambridge University Press.

Ward, K., 1996, *God, Chance & Necessity*, Oxford: Oneworld.

Ward, K., 1999, *God, Faith and the New Millennium: Christian Belief in an Age of Science*, Oxford: Oneworld.

Wilson, E. O., 1975, *Sociobiology: The New Synthesis*, Cambridge: Harvard University Press.

Notes

1 For the traditional Hebrew account of creation, see Genesis 1—2 (this account also plays an important role within the traditional Christian belief system). For an account of creation in the Qur'ān, see, for example, Sura 41.9–12.

2 Traditionally each of the monotheisms has assigned great importance to beliefs concerning God's action upon the world on behalf of their respective faith-communities. Miracles (incidents in which God is thought to intervene in the world by breaking natural laws) have been invoked by each tradition in support of its claims.

3 This would be more than a little ironic if, as some have argued, the three Abrahamic faiths provided the initial conditions under which modern science developed. For example, Steve Bruce argues that, by reducing a plethora of divinities to one God, and regarding that one God as distant from the universe, the monotheisms encouraged people 'to explore that universe and elaborate theories of its operations that paid only lip-service to the creator'. Steve Bruce, 2000, *Fundamentalism*, Cambridge: Polity, p. 23.

4 Nevertheless, not all twentieth-century intellectuals have adopted a sanguine attitude towards the success of the natural sciences. For example, Bertrand Russell remarks that the results of developments within the sciences 'have been by no means wholly beneficial. ... [T]hey have increased the destructiveness of weapons of war, and the proportion of the population that can be spared from peaceful industry for fighting and the manufacture of munitions.' Bertrand Russell, 1935, *Religion and Science*, London: Oxford University Press, p. 246.

5 Notwithstanding this popular view, philosophers were well aware that scientific method could not yield absolute certainty. Thus, science fell far short of the standards Western philosophers, such as René Descartes, expected knowledge to meet. Some have argued that scientific claims fall short of certainty because they appear to be derived from a reasoning process called induction: after one has seen many swans, and each one seen thus far has been white, one comes to believe that all swans are white. But as David Hume pointed out in the eighteenth century, no matter how many particular observations one has made, one can never be absolutely certain that the next one will be similar. In the twentieth century, Bertrand Russell illustrated the problem of induction thus: the chicken, having been fed every morning, expects the same thing to happen every day – only to have its head chopped off at Christmas time! See Bertrand Russell, 1967, *The Problems of Philosophy*, London: Oxford University Press. Karl Popper, however, has argued that, strictly speaking, the problem is not that of induction. When puppies, for example, sniff a cigarette, they run away from it, and will not return. They do not draw the conclusion from several unpleasant experiences that the next one, too, will be unpleasant. One such experience is quite enough. On Popper's preferred account, one moves from particular observations to the formulation of a general theory that can explain these observations. Good scientific practice, in Popper's view, consists in attempting to refute by experiments the theory that has been proposed to explain the observations. The best theory is the one that withstands such testing. However, in Popper's view, this does not establish that the best theory is therefore true. The experimental data to date will always support both the best theory and some other, conceivable theory. And for all we know, the next set of data will support the alternative theory and not our preferred one. This problem is generally referred to as the 'underdetermination' of scientific theories.

6 Don Cupitt, 1976, *The Worlds of Science and Religion*, London: Sheldon Press, p. 86.

7 The view that the earth was stationary and was the centre of the universe, around which all the planets and stars moved, was one of the first religious views to be challenged by modern science and eventually superseded. This geocentric view occupied a central place in how medieval religious people understood the world. It was challenged by Copernicus (1473–1543) in the early sixteenth century and, later, by Galileo (1564–1642). The alternative heliocentric view put forward by Copernicus and Galileo – namely, that the earth went round the sun, and was not, therefore, the centre of the universe – was thought to be so threatening to Christianity that Galileo was imprisoned and forbidden to publicize his work. It took a long time for the religious authorities to admit defeat, but eventually they lost the battle, and adopted the Copernican view themselves. On the religious reaction to the heliocentric theory, see Richard Tarnas, 1996, *The Passion of the Western Mind: Understanding the Ideas that Have Shaped our World View*, London: Pimlico, pp. 251–4.

8 For example, the religious belief that God created the world in a finished state has, by and large, been retracted in the light of evolutionary theory.

9 Any such assumption is surely vitiated by the fact that the majority of religious believers in the West seem to have no difficulty in adhering to their faith while having enjoyed an education that prioritizes the sciences. Given this situ-

ation, the assumption that religion and science are in inevitable conflict begins to seem less plausible.

10 Ibn Warraq, 1995, *Why I Am Not a Muslim*, New York: Prometheus Books, p. 7.

11 Epitomized, perhaps, by Mary Shelley's Dr Frankenstein.

12 'Scientific materialism' is alternatively known as 'scientific naturalism'.

13 Among the more prominent scientific materialists are numbered: Francis Crick, Stephen Hawking, Richard Dawkins and Jacques Monod, each with a best-selling book to his credit – which is indicative of the considerable interest scientific materialism has stimulated at the level of popular culture.

14 See Edward O. Wilson, 1975, *Sociobiology: The New Synthesis*, Cambridge: Harvard University Press, chapter 4. Also, see Edward O. Wilson, 1978, *On Human Nature*, Cambridge: Harvard University Press, chapters 8 and 9.

15 Wilson, *Human*, p. 169.

16 Wilson, *Human*, p. 175.

17 Wilson, *Human*, p. 188.

18 Wilson adds that 'theology is unlikely to survive as an independent intellectual discipline'. *Human*, p. 192.

19 Adapted from Holmes Rolston III, 1999, *Genes, Genesis and God: Values and Their Origins in Natural and Human History*, Cambridge: Cambridge University Press, p. 335.

20 Keith Ward, 1996, *God, Chance & Necessity*, Oxford: Oneworld, p. 99.

21 Ward, *God*, p. 99.

22 Ward, *God*, p. 100.

23 See Basil Mitchell, 1994, *Faith and Criticism*, Oxford: Clarendon Press, p. 10.

24 Mitchell, *Faith*, p. 11.

25 See Mitchell, *Faith*, pp. 12–17.

26 Mitchell, *Faith*, p. 19. In a similar vein, Michael Polanyi claims that all knowledge requires the personal participation of the knowing subject, and that the assessment of evidence – in science or in religion – is always, at bottom, an act of personal discretion. Objectivity is secured, he avers, by participation in a community of inquiry, be it scientific or religious. See Michael Polanyi, 1958, *Personal Knowledge*, Chicago: University of Chicago Press.

27 Mitchell, *Faith*, p. 18.

28 Mitchell, *Faith*, p. 22.

29 See, for example, Hilary Putnam, 'The Impact of Science on Modern Conceptions of Rationality', *Synthese*, 46 (1981), p. 365.

30 John Maynard Smith, 'Science and Myth', *Natural History*, 93 (1984), p. 11.

31 Smith, 'Science', p. 24.

32 Kaplan founded Reconstructionist Judaism in the 1920s with the intention of 'reconstructing' Jewish lifestyles and beliefs to cohere with modernity. He argued that Judaism is an evolving civilization, and that it is now time for it to evolve in ways conducive to its survival within the modern culture of the twentieth-century West. This form of Judaism advocated more radical changes to the tradition than any of the forms of Judaism that developed in the nineteenth century. Reconstructionist Judaism was, for example, explicitly atheistic

(although it retained a non-supernatural conception of God as a power immanent within the Jewish community).

33 Modercai Kaplan, 1958, *Judaism Without Supernaturalism*, New York: The Reconstructionist Press, p. 48.

34 While the medieval proponents of natural theology maintained that full knowledge of God could only be arrived at by revelation, they also held that there was at least some knowledge of God that could be arrived at by natural means – for example, knowledge of God's existence. Thus, there was thought to be some overlap in what could be learned from the two means of acquiring knowledge.

35 See Karl Barth, 1975, *Church Dogmatics*, vol. 1/i: *The Doctrine of the Word of God*, edited by G. W. Bromiley and T. F. Torrance, Edinburgh: T. & T. Clark; and Karl Barth, 1957, *Church Dogmatics*, vol. 2/i: *The Doctrine of God*, edited by G. W. Bromiley and T. F. Torrance, Edinburgh: T. & T. Clark.

36 See Søren Kierkegaard, 1974, *Concluding Unscientific Postscript*, trans. by D. F. Swenson, Princeton, New Jersey: Princeton University Press.

37 Ludwig Wittgenstein, 1966, *Lectures and Conversations on Aesthetics, Psychology, and Religious Belief*, edited by C. Barrett, Oxford: Oxford University Press, p. 55.

38 See D. Z. Phillips, 1970, *Faith and Philosophical Enquiry*, New York: Schocken Books.

39 Harold A. Netland, 1991, *Dissonant Voices: Religious Pluralism and the Question of Truth*, Leicester: Apollos, p. 187.

40 See Sheikh Abu Hamid Al-Ghazali, 1997, *The Incoherence of the Philosophers, Tahāfut al-falāsifah: a parallel English-Arabic text*, trans., introduced and annotated by Michael E. Marmura, Provo, Utah: Brigham Young University Press, pp. 5f.

41 The Christian theologian Thomas Torrance, for example, points out that through scientific enquiry we can establish exactly what conditions were present when the universe began, although we cannot determine why just those initial conditions obtained. The latter question, according to Torrance, requires a religious answer. See Thomas Torrance, 1981, *Divine and Contingent Order*, Oxford: Oxford University Press.

42 See Karl Popper, 1959, *The Logic of Scientific Discovery*, London: Hutchinson.

43 See, for example, Thomas Kuhn, 1962, *The Structure of Scientific Revolutions*, Chicago: University of Chicago Press. Kuhn argues that scientific paradigms are highly resistant to falsification. Religious thinkers have pointed out the apparent parallel with the resistance of core religious beliefs to falsification.

44 See Chapter 4.

45 See, for example, Ian G. Barbour, 1974, *Myths, Models and Paradigms*, New York: Harper & Row; Sallie McFague, 1982, *Metaphorical Theology: Models of God in Religious Language*, Philadelphia: Fortress Press; and Janet Martin Soskice, 1985, *Metaphor and Religious Language*, Oxford: Clarendon Press.

46 The data of religion, according to Polkinghorne, are its Scriptures and the religious experiences of past and present believers.

47 John Polkinghorne, 1987, *One World: The Interaction of Science and Theology*, Princeton: Princeton University Press. Quoted in Ian G. Barbour,

1990, *Religion in an Age of Science*, London: SCM Press, p. 23. For a similar view, see Holmes Rolston III, 1987, *Science and Religion: A Critical Survey*, New York: Random House.

48 Barbour, *Religion*, p. 23.

49 See, for example, Pierre Teilhard de Chardin, 1959, *The Phenomenon of Man*, New York: Harper & Row.

50 See Karl Rahner, 1984, *Foundations of Christian Faith: An Introduction to the Idea of Christianity*, London: Darton, Longman and Todd, chapter 6.

51 Another potential problem is that if a religion is identified too closely with a particular scientific theory, or metaphysical system, it becomes susceptible to the undesirable consequences of that theory, or system. Thus, Chardin's position led him to argue for the racial and cultural superiority of Europeans – something that was not implied by traditional Christianity.

52 Design arguments are sometimes known as 'teleological arguments' (from the Greek word *telos*, meaning 'end' or 'goal').

53 Psalm 19.2. *JPS Hebrew–English Tanakh*, Philadelphia: The Jewish Publication Society, 1999.

54 Sura 2.158–9. Arthur J. Arberry, 1998, *The Koran*, Oxford: Oxford University Press. See, also, Sura 88.17–20.

55 Thomas Aquinas, 1998, *Selected Philosophical Writings*, trans. by Timothy McDermott, Oxford: Oxford University Press, pp. 201f. This argument is the last of Aquinas' celebrated five ways 'proving' the existence of God.

56 See William Paley, 1802, *Natural Theology; or, Evidences of the Existence and Attributes of the Deity: Collected from the Appearances of Nature*, Philadelphia: H. Maxwell.

57 Paley took the example of a watch from Boyle, who ruminated on the cathedral clock in Strasbourg.

58 Notice that accepting Darwin's theory of evolution by natural selection does not imply that one must deny that God exists. God may still be conceived as the one who set the process of evolution in train. Nevertheless, as James Rachels points out, Darwin's theory prevents the design argument from providing *conclusive proof* of God's existence. See James Rachels, 1990, *Created from Animals: The Moral Implications of Darwinism*, Oxford: Oxford University Press.

59 David Hume, 1970, *Dialogues Concerning Natural Religion*, Indianapolis: Bobbs-Merrill Company, p. 23.

60 Hume, *Dialogues*, pp. 23f.

61 See, particularly, Hume, *Dialogues*, Parts II–VIII. Ironically, Hume's arguments were already relatively well known long before Paley published his *Natural Theology*.

62 See Paul Davies, 1993, *The Mind of God: Science and the Search for Ultimate Meaning*, Harmondsworth: Penguin.

63 Ward, *God*, p. 46.

64 Ward, *God*, p. 52.

65 Ward, *God*, p. 77. Ward does not, however, advocate some form of what is known as the 'anthropic principle'. This principle asserts that the laws and constants of nature (for example, the chemical properties of the carbon atom and the thermal properties of water) seem to be finely tuned to support just the kind of life which we find in the cosmos – specifically, our own humanoid life-form. The

conclusion drawn by exponents of this principle, such as Michael Denton, is that the evolution of our humanoid life-form must have been the intended purpose of the universe. Ward demurs from this conclusion when he acknowledges the possibility of our current life-form evolving into something better – one which we cannot currently conceive. See Ward, *God, passim*. Also, see Michael J. Denton, 1998, *Nature's Destiny: How the Laws of Biology Reveal Purpose in the Universe*, New York: Free Press.

66 Ward, *God*, p. 57.

67 See Michael J. Behe, 1998, *Darwin's Black Box: The Biochemical Challenge to Evolution*, New York: Simon and Schuster.

68 See William A. Dembski, 1998, *The Design Inference: Eliminating Chance through Small Probabilities*, Cambridge: Cambridge University Press; William A. Dembski, 1999, *Intelligent Design: The Bridge Between Science and Theology*, Downers Grove: InterVarsity Press; and William A. Dembski, 2002, *No Free Lunch: Why Specified Complexity Cannot be Purchased without Intelligence*, Lanham: Rowan & Littlefield.

69 Rolston, *Genes*.

70 For an article critical of their approach, see David B. Myers, 'New Design Arguments: Old Millian Objections', *Religious Studies*, 36 (2000), pp. 141–62.

71 Rolston, *Genes*, p. 297.

72 See Rolston, *Genes*, p. 297.

73 Rolston, *Genes*, p. 359.

74 See Rolston, *Genes*, p. 296.

75 Rolston, *Genes*, p. 359.

76 Rolston, *Genes*, p. 364.

77 Rolston also enjoys a considerable reputation as a biologist.

78 For a response to methodological criticisms of the approach adopted by Behe and Dembski et al., see Stephen C. Meyer, 2000, 'The Scientific Status of Intelligent Design: The Methodological Equivalence of Naturalistic and Non-Naturalistic Origins Theories' in Michael J. Behe, William A. Dembski and Stephen C. Meyer (eds), *Science and Evidence for Design in the Universe*, San Francisco: Ignatius Press, pp. 151–211. Also, see Michael J. Behe, 2000, 'Answering Scientific Criticisms of Intelligent Design' in Behe, Dembski and Meyer, *Science*, pp. 133–49.

79 Dembski, *Intelligent*, p. 120.

80 Dembski, *Intelligent*, p. 120.

81 See, for example, William A. Dembski, 2000, 'The Third Mode of Explanation: Detecting Evidence of Intelligent Design in Science' in Behe, Dembski and Meyer, *Science*, pp. 17–51; and Michael J. Behe, 2000, 'Evidence for Design at the Foundation of Life' in Behe, Dembski and Meyer, *Science*, pp. 113–28. For criticisms of this type of view from a scientific perspective, see Elliot Sober (with Branden Fitelson and Christopher Stephens), 'How Not to Detect Design – A Review of William Dembski's *The Design Inference*', *Philosophy of Science*, 66 (1999), pp. 472–88.

82 Although it could be argued that new design arguments rely on analogy no less than do traditional ones, for any understanding of what it means for the universe to exhibit 'design' must surely depend on an analogy between the work of a transcendent 'designer' and the work of a human designer.

THE IMPACT OF SCIENCE

83 John Stuart Mill, 1958, 'Nature' in John Stuart Mill, *Nature and Utility of Religion*, edited by George Nakhnikian, New York: Bobbs-Merrill, pp. 20f.

84 We return to this problem in Chapter 8.

85 See Richard Dawkins, 1996, *The Blind Watchmaker: Why the Evidence of Evolution Reveals a Universe Without Design*, New York: W.W. Norton & Co, p. 93.

86 Mill, 'Nature', p. 40.

87 John Stuart Mill, 1999, 'The Infinite Goodness of God' in Paul Helm (ed.), *Faith and Reason*, Oxford: Oxford University Press, p. 250.

88 Robin Atfield develops such an argument in 'Evolution, Theodicy and Value', *Heythrop Journal*, 41 (2000), pp. 281–96. See, also, Rolston, *Genes*, pp. 303–7.

89 Indeed, as Hume pointed out, the argument from design does not even support the view that there is only one God, as it is also consistent with the idea that a group of gods created the world.

7

Religion in a Pluralist World

Religious plurality is a pervasive feature of the modern world. Today, in the cities of Western Europe and North America, it is not unusual for adherents of diverse religious traditions to live side by side. Indeed, for the majority of people living in the West, it is no longer possible simply to take for granted a homogeneous religious tradition. This means that they cannot assume, as many of their ancestors probably did, that the key events of their lives – in particular, birth, marriage and the death of their loved ones – are to be interpreted within a religious conceptual framework that is unquestioningly accepted by the vast majority in their society.

At least since the mid-nineteenth century, a growing number of religious believers have been struggling to come to terms with religious plurality and the theological, philosophical and social problems it raises. Many have found that their own religious convictions are put to the test by the awareness that people in similar situations to themselves hold very different religious views. Whatever their faith-tradition, people who live in societies characterized by religious plurality often find it difficult to accept the claims of any one religious tradition exclusively and uncritically. As Paul Heelas writes:

> With components from different cultures becoming more and more available in any particular cultural setting, the cultural realm becomes more pluralistic. Cultures come to contain a fragmented, variegated range of beliefs and values. Faced with diversity, it is then suggested, people lose faith in what has been traditionally sustained by way of socialization within a closed environment. The choices afforded by multivocal culture serve to confuse. Differentiation serves to undermine the exclusivistic claims and credibility of what was previously homogeneous and therefore unquestioned. In sum, 'plausibility structures' loses their credibility – even collapse.[1]

Religious plurality has, indeed, proven to be problematic for adherents of each of the Abrahamic faiths. Within the Christian tradition, the main problem is usually perceived to lie in the difficulty of reconciling traditional claims about Christianity constituting an exclusive path to salvation with an appreciation of non-Christian belief systems. The central problem that concerns Muslim thinkers is quite different. It is the more immediately practical issue of how a Muslim can live in a modern, religiously plural, non-Islamic state without his or her sense of religious identity being undermined. This problem arises from the traditional Islamic conviction that a Muslim can only live a fully Muslim life within an Islamic state.[2] Many Jewish intellectuals are also concerned with the issues raised by religious plurality.[3] However, for traditional Jewish thinkers, the main problem concerns how to regard the theological claims made by gentiles in the light of the fundamental belief that the Jewish people have been uniquely selected for a special relationship with God.

Although Western European and, to a lesser extent, North American societies have been religiously plural for some time, it is only since the mid-1960s that religious plurality has engendered what some perceive as a religious crisis. This chapter examines a variety of intellectual responses to this problem. We shall see that many thinkers have devoted considerable attention to the religious and philosophical issues raised by religious plurality. While the specific questions raised by religious plurality differ across traditions, the more general problem that faces all religious intellectuals is how to provide a compelling theoretical account of the relationship between the various religions of the world. The theories devised by philosophers and theologians generally fall under one of the following three rubrics: religious exclusivism,[4] religious inclusivism and religious pluralism.[5]

According to exclusivist theories, only the theorizer's own religious tradition is to be regarded as possessing value – because only it is thought to offer 'salvation', as well as being the sole preserve of religious truth. Religious exclusivism is now somewhat out of fashion (at least within intellectual circles), and a cause of embarrassment to many religious believers, as we shall see. Nevertheless, this type of theory still elicits vigorous support. Jewish, Christian and Muslim fundamentalists tend to be enthusiastic advocates of some form of exclusivism.[6] Harold Netland, to take just one example, has argued forcibly for a form of Christian exclusivism.[7] Netland defines 'Christian exclusivism' as adherence to the following four propositions:

(a) Jesus Christ is the unique incarnation of God, fully God and fully man; (b) only through the person and work of Jesus Christ is there the possibility of salvation; (c) the Bible is God's unique revelation written, and thus is true and authoritative; and (d) where the claims of Scripture are incompatible with those of other faiths, the latter are to be rejected as false.[8]

Netland goes on to characterize 'Christian inclusivism' as any position which 'maintains that the central claims of Christian faith are true', while simultaneously adopting 'a much more positive view of other religions than does exclusivism'.[9] In particular, according to Netland, inclusivists hold: (1) that 'God has revealed himself definitively in Jesus Christ'; and (2) that while Jesus is 'central to God's provision of salvation for humankind', salvation is nevertheless possible through other religions.[10] Christian inclusivism, then, is distinguished from Christian exclusivism by the former's 'attempt to strike the delicate balance between the affirmation of God's unique revelation and salvation in Jesus Christ and openness to God's saving activity in other religions'.[11]

As we shall see, nowadays a significant number of scholars prefer some form of religious inclusivism to religious exclusivism. And according to religious inclusivists, all religions have value insofar as they facilitate arrival at the religious goal – although their value is derivative upon the greater value of the theorizer's own religious tradition. This type of theory has wide appeal among educated European Christians. The theologian Karl Rahner, to whom we shall shortly turn, is a prominent example of a scholar who adopts this type of approach. And while the discussion has tended to be dominated by Christian thinkers, religious inclusivism is, nevertheless, a position that is available to adherents of any religious tradition. Netland's characterization of 'Christian inclusivism' could be de-Christianized to fit the case of Islam simply by substituting 'the Qur'ān' for the name 'Jesus'.[12] According to a modified characterization of inclusivism, then, a Muslim inclusivist might hold: (1) that God has revealed Godself definitively in the Qur'ān; and (2) that while the Qur'ān is central to God's provision of salvation for humankind, salvation is nevertheless possible through religions other than Islam.[13] Moreover, Islamic inclusivism would indeed seem to be distinguished by an attempt to strike a delicate balance between, on the one hand, the affirmation of God's unique revelation and salvation in the Qur'ān and, on the other, openness to God's saving activity within other religions.

Finally, there are also exponents of religious pluralism. Theories that fall under this rubric consider all religions to have *prima facie* value in their own right. Each religion is regarded as a viable path to the religious goal. Moreover, each is thought to provide knowledge about the ultimate nature of reality. According to religious pluralists, then, we would never, in principle, be in a position to identify any one religion as the singularly correct one. Although religious pluralism has so far enjoyed less popular support than either exclusivism or inclusivism, it is, not surprisingly, important to those who participate in inter-faith dialogue. Furthermore, theories of religious pluralism became increasingly important as a focus of, often heated, intellectual debate during the closing decades of the twentieth century. Perhaps the most famous advocate of this type of theory is the widely respected Christian philosopher of religion John Hick[14] – whose theory is considered in detail later.

Religious pluralism developed as a response to what are often taken to be the inadequacies of religious exclusivism and religious inclusivism. In particular, it seeks to provide a theory of religious plurality that better meets the needs of those living in the multicultural societies of today. There is no doubt that religious pluralism is the most quintessentially modern of the theories available. Hence, it will be given greater prominence below. But before we examine religious pluralism in greater detail, we need first to consider religious exclusivism and then religious inclusivism.

Religious exclusivism and its decline

For a complex mixture of social, political and theological reasons, adherents of Judaism and Islam have been much less inclined to embrace religious exclusivism than have their Christian counterparts. In Chapter 3 we saw that an open attitude to people of other faiths has been endorsed by the Muslim tradition since the time of the Prophet, and is explicitly counselled in the Qur'ān. There were no such scriptural impediments to the official adoption of religious exclusivism within Christianity. Moreover, Christianity's dominant position within Western Europe throughout much of the common era might help to explain the appeal exclusivism exerted on many Christians.

Christian exclusivism, as it was traditionally understood, is graphically summed up in the following statement ratified by the Council of Florence (1438–45):

> [The Council] firmly believes, professes and proclaims that those not living within the Catholic Church, not only pagans but also Jews and heretics and schismatics, cannot participate in eternal life, but will depart 'into everlasting fire which was prepared for the devil and his angels,' unless before the end of life the same have been added to the flock. ...[N]o one, whatever almsgiving he has practised, even if he has shed blood for the name of Christ, can be saved, unless he has remained in the bosom and unity of the Catholic Church.[15]

Why, though, would anyone rationally subscribe to such an ostensibly extreme, exclusivist position? While some might presume that religious exclusivism is simply the result of a proclivity towards dogmatism, there are seemingly cogent, philosophical reasons for rejecting its obvious alternative: religious inclusivism. Perhaps the most compelling reason is provided by Netland, who argues that

> Christian exclusivism is based upon the assumption that two or more incompatible assertions cannot all be true. Where there are contradictory claims being advanced by various religions, not all of them can be

true. At least one must be false. This, of course, is simply an application of the principle of noncontradiction – two contradictory statements cannot both be true.[16]

We shall later discover that, although this seems *prima facie* compelling, some philosophers of religion have nevertheless advanced reasons for doubting Netland's core assumption that 'two or more incompatible assertions cannot all be true'. Indeed, it is precisely the rejection of this apparently obvious assumption that lies at the heart of religious pluralism.

This notwithstanding, until well into the nineteenth century some form of exclusivist position – like the one displayed in the above quotation from the Council of Florence – dominated mainstream Christianity. Even in eighteenth-century Europe, however, there were lone voices, such as Gotthold Lessing's,[17] that promoted a less exclusivist approach towards other religions. Momentum against Christian exclusivism gradually picked up speed in the nineteenth century due to two principal factors. One factor was that, by and large, Western European Christian intellectuals experienced increased contact with, and hence acquired greater knowledge of, other religious traditions.[18] Another factor was, in part, a result of the first, and came from developments within liberal Protestant Christianity. In spirit of critical inquiry fostered by the Enlightenment, new methods of historical and literary criticism were applied to the New Testament, with startling results. Prior to this pioneering work, the dominant view within the Christian world was that the Scriptures were authored directly by God. This view became increasingly improbable in the light of new academic techniques which appeared to show not only that the New Testament was composed of a variety of different types of literary material, but also that it was written by different authors over a considerable period of time. While Christian thinkers were trying to come to terms with these new discoveries regarding their sacred text, Jewish thinkers were at work applying the same techniques to the Hebrew Scriptures. In short, within both Judaism and Christianity, the Scriptures came to be recognized by numerous scholars as being far more the product of human work than had previously been presumed.

Within Christian circles, what came to be known as 'the quest for the historical Jesus' was closely linked with this new way of thinking about the Scriptures. The quest was principally undertaken by German theologians associated with the liberal Protestant movement in nineteenth-century German theology. Their agenda was to discredit the New Testament (and later Christian) portrayal of Jesus by emphasizing the discontinuity between that portrayal and the historical Jesus.[19] Those involved in the quest, like the famous German Protestant Albrecht Ritschl (1822–89), hoped to discover the historical Jesus as he existed prior to the accounts of him proffered by biblical writers and theologians. Ultimately, they aimed to establish a new version of Christianity that would be based on their discoveries about the real Jesus, and they firmly believed that this new version of Christianity would be better, because more credible, than any form of Christianity that had existed prior to their work.

In the end, this ambitious project proved to be unrealizable, because the historical figure of Jesus turned out to be more elusive than those seeking him had anticipated. Critics of the quest complained that the 'real Jesus' ostensibly being discovered was nothing more than an idealized image of the seekers.[20] They also remarked that those on the trail of the historical Jesus seemed prone to discover the kind of Jesus they needed – one who was, incidentally, the only kind acceptable to them: namely, an enlightened moral teacher. Despite these criticisms, the theologians involved in the quest were to exercise a lasting impact on Western Christianity. In effect, they prepared the way for its modernization.

One direct result of the work of the nineteenth-century pioneers of biblical criticism was seriously to undermine confidence among Western Christians that their religion was innately superior to all others. Many began to doubt that Christianity was above suspicion as the one true, revealed religion, divinely authorized by God as the only route to human salvation. This doubt about Christianity's privileged status was augmented by prolonged contact with adherents of other religious traditions. And together, these factors contributed to a gradual softening of the traditional exclusivist position. Some, like Netland, for example, think that Christian attitudes have softened far too much. They believe that the gradual shift towards inclusivism is an unnecessary mistake, perceiving in it a compromise of the fundamental claims of Christianity – particularly claims about Jesus Christ. Nevertheless, the dominant tendency, among Christian thinkers at least, has been to respond to the perceived need to modify the old exclusivist position. The extent to which even the official Roman Catholic position has softened away from outright exclusivism and towards inclusivism is palpable in the following extract from the documents of the Second Vatican Council:

> Those who[,] through no fault of their own, do not know the Gospel of Christ or his Church, but who nevertheless seek God with a sincere heart, and, moved by grace, try in their actions to do his will as they know it through the dictates of their conscience – those too may achieve eternal salvation. Nor shall divine providence deny the assistance necessary for salvation to those who, without any fault of theirs, have not yet arrived at an explicit knowledge of God, and who, not without grace, strive to lead a good life. Whatever good or truth is found amongst them is considered by the Church to be a preparation for the Gospel and given by him who enlightens all men that they may at length have life.[21]

A comparison of this position, as set out in the documents of Vatican II, with that endorsed by the Council of Florence, discloses the radical shift in attitude that has taken place in the intervening years. While the official Roman Catholic position would not appear to be a thoroughgoing inclusivism, it has certainly moved away from the earlier, rigidly exclusivist stance. For Vatican II's position, unlike that of the Council of Florence, does not entail that other religions have no value. Nor does it imply that people who are not *bona fide* members of the Roman Catholic Church are condemned to eternal damnation. In fact, the position can be interpreted as inclusivist about salvation and exclusivist regarding knowledge. In other words, regardless of religious affiliation, anyone can be saved if they 'seek God with a sincere heart' and try 'to do his will'. However, 'explicit knowledge of God' is only available within the Roman Catholic Church.

The retreat of the Roman Catholic Church from hard-core exclusivism is symptomatic of the declining credibility of religious exclusivism.[22] Such exclusivism is becoming less and less attractive an option to religious people today, many of whom feel the pull of two, apparently opposing, impulses: the impulse to remain faithful to their religious tradition, and the impulse to respect other religious traditions. It is, perhaps, not surprising, therefore, that religious inclusivism should have gained many adherents.

Religious inclusivism

At least in its modern form, religious inclusivism, perhaps surprisingly, owes much to the popularity of evolutionary theory among nineteenth-century intellectuals. The result of bringing the notion of evolution to bear on the study of religions was the development of what has been called a 'fulfilment theory' of religion. To many in the Christian West, the theory of evolution suggested that the relationship of Christianity to the other world religions might be understood as one of fulfilment – Christianity being thought to fulfil the potential latent in other religions. In other words, the other world religions were often portrayed as being in a lesser state of development, and as gradually evolving towards a closer approximation to Christianity. Christianity was thus construed as the superior, or 'absolute' religion, in the sense that it was considered to be the peak of human religious achievement.[23] Within the conceptual framework offered by this type of theory, then, potentially all religions could be regarded as having value. How much value they had was thought to be determined by how closely they approximated to Christianity.

This way of thinking about the relationship of the world religions was elaborated in the twentieth century by a number of religious thinkers – as mentioned earlier, Karl Rahner being one of the most prominent

Christian intellectuals to adopt and develop this approach. Rahner, to whose views we now turn, was perhaps the single most influential religious inclusivist of the twentieth century.

Rahner's inclusivism is rooted in his conviction, derived from the Christian Scriptures, that God has a 'universal' will directed towards the salvation of all human beings.[24] On the basis of this conviction, he surmises that everyone is open to the possibility of experiencing God (or what he calls the Holy Mystery). Accordingly, he claims that even certain false beliefs can result in lifestyles that are capable of mediating an experience of God. And all such experience, according to Rahner, is mediated, for it takes place not in a vacuum but within the context of particular societies, histories and cultures – the natural diversity of which accounts for the variety of religions. In Rahner's view, then, one's culture shapes one's experience. But if God has a universal salvific will, then salvation must be possible in all cultures, regardless of how false the beliefs at the heart of the culture in question may be. To an inclusivist, this approach has the obvious merit of regarding each religion as a more or less legitimate response to the Holy Mystery; thus allowing all religions to be viewed as vehicles through which human beings can attain salvation.[25]

Rahner's theory appealed to a large number of Christians in the twentieth century because it offered an explanation – one that many found convincing – of the spiritual and moral values instantiated in non-Christian religions. Moreover, in holding that the detailed claims of other religions were false, while those of Christianity were true, Rahner offered a theory that did not involve rejecting the principle of non-contradiction. Indeed, many found the theory particularly attractive because it was exclusive regarding truth while being inclusive with respect to salvation. Notwithstanding this seeming advantage over exclusivism, critics of Rahner's theory noted that it is unreservedly Christian, for it holds that Christianity sets the standard by which all religions should be judged. Furthermore, his theory was developed to answer the question: How can people subscribing to non-Christian religions be saved? Clearly, this specific question is being asked from within a Christian conceptual framework, for the very concept 'salvation' is a Christian one.

Not surprisingly, then, Rahner's answer to the question is biased towards Christianity, which he is therefore led to view as fulfilling the potential latent within all other religions. By focusing upon the Christian notion of salvation, he claims that the salvific experience of God, or the Holy Mystery, that is available in Christianity is explicit; whereas in non-Christian religions, the salvific experience is only implicit. But in being implicit, it is striving towards what is realized only in Christianity. It is in this sense that Rahner's is a fulfilment theory. Christianity actualizes what is a mere potential in other religions. Thus, concludes Rahner, Christianity is the supreme religion to which all the other religions (to the extent that they are legitimate) are merely partial approximations. Adherents of non-Christian religions are thus referred to as 'anonymous Christians' because they are presumed to share implicitly the salvific experience of God that is available explicitly in Christianity.[26] Of course, if one were to begin with a religious notion other than salvation – say, nirvana – then Christianity would have to be viewed as striving to realize what is explicit in some other religion.

It should come as no surprise, therefore, that Rahner's specifically Christian form of religious inclusivism has had limited appeal to non-Christians. Nevertheless, some adherents of non-Christian faiths have adapted his theory to their own traditions. For example, Adnan Aslan has proposed an Islamic version of Rahnerian inclusivism, suggesting that: '[e]very revealed religion can be named as islam, when it is seen as "a state of submission to God" (literally islam)'.[27] Moreover, Aslan is able to quote from Hasan Askari: '[W]hoever among Jews and Christians and the people of other religions, surrenders to God, the One and only God, and does not explicitly and implicitly associate gods (race, religion and any other "signs" and "manifestations" of) with God, is a "muslim".'[28] Furthermore, the term 'anonymous Muslims' has been adopted by, for example, Syed Vahiduddin.[29]

Rahner's own religious tradition is, of course, Roman Catholicism. And despite the inclusivist strain found in some of the documents endorsed at Vatican Council II,[30] the exclusivist doctrine of extra ecclesiam nulla sallus (no salvation outside the Church) has never been officially repealed. However, many modern Roman Catholics feel that Rahner's theory has outmanoeuvred the old doctrine. For in viewing devout adherents of other faiths as anonymous Christians, Rahner has, in effect, included them within the Church. Indeed, a post-Vatican Council II encyclical seems to endorse Rahner's theory when it states that 'every man without exception has been redeemed by Christ', and that Christ is united with every man, 'even when [a] man is unaware of it'.[31]

There is no doubt that Rahner's theory has been instrumental in reshaping the way that many people, both within and without Christianity, think about the relationship between religions. Nevertheless, several important criticisms have been levelled against the theory. On the one hand, the theory has been accused of being patronizing to adherents of non-Christian religions. Muslims, for example, are more likely to be offended than gratified by the title 'anonymous Christian'. On the other hand, some Christians have accused the theory of undermining the uniqueness of Christianity. Moreover, many Christian theologians, not surprisingly, accuse the theory of undermining the value of membership within the Christian Church (for if one can be sufficiently Christian without being a member of the institutional Church, why should anyone feel the need to join it?).

However, perhaps the major problem with Rahner's theory, as with all Christian-based inclusivist and exclusivist theories of religion, is that, unless one is already a Christian, there seems to be no good reason for accepting it. In other words, Rahner's theory appears to presuppose the conviction that Christianity is better than the other world religions.[32]

Religious pluralism and relativism

What, then, about the alternative to both religious exclusivism and religious inclusivism: namely, religious pluralism? Are theories that are premised upon the equal value of more than one religious tradition any more compelling than the theories discussed so far? Perhaps the most influential early advocate of a pluralist theory was the German philosopher and theologian Ernst Troeltsch (1865–1923). Troeltsch was a historian of religions, and one of the first scholars to regard them as developing phenomena located within specific historical contexts.[33] Proposing that all religions were finite expressions of the transcendent Divine reality, Troeltsch, in his earlier work, advances a form of Christian inclusivism – portraying Christianity as the culmination of human religious effort. In his later work, however, he goes far beyond inclusivism, arguing that Christianity is only one stage in God's continuing revelation. Thus, he came to accept the possibility that Christianity could, in principle, be superseded by another, more highly developed, and hence more adequate, religion.

Influenced by Troeltsch's pioneering ideas, and no doubt also as a result of the social and political upheavals experienced in the twentieth century, many religious thinkers adopted what came to be identified as a relativist stance towards religious ideas and values. This trend towards a relativist interpretation of religions gathered pace from the 1960s. By the late twentieth century, relativism had impacted religious thought to an unprecedented degree. Moreover, there was a marked tendency – among intellectuals as well as the general public – to confuse religious pluralism with relativism about religion. Due to the close connection between religious pluralism and relativism that is assumed by many, let us examine relativism in more detail before considering religious pluralism.

In the second half of the twentieth century, relativism swept across the social sciences and humanities in Western Europe and North America. Consequently, relativism, as a general attitude as well as a theory, became ingrained within popular opinion. Many came to regard relativism as the only intellectually viable theory with which to respond to what they found to be a bewildering experience of religious and cultural plurality. Apart from the option of rejecting religion entirely, there appeared to be only three possible standpoints for religiously inclined intellectuals to choose between. The first was to retreat back to religious exclusivism, asserting that one's own tradition was correct, and that, insofar as other traditions conflicted with it, they were in error. The second option was to accept a form of religious inclusivism that explained other religions away by characterizing them as inferior to one's own – and claiming that whatever was of value in them came from their relationship to one's own religion. Finally, the third option was to adopt a relativist position which asserts that my own religion can be 'true for our group' while a different religion can be equally 'true' for another group. Only the third option seemed to accord adequate respect to other faiths in a multicultural world.

The allure of the third option proved to be a strong one. It is by no means unusual for people today simply to accept that something can be right or 'true' for us, while simultaneously being wrong or 'false' for others; and this is particularly the case in matters of morality and religion. Philosophical relativism takes this view seriously, and is characterized by the core conviction that all claims are to be judged true or false relative to some conceptual scheme.[34] Philosophical relativists typically elaborate that core conviction by stipulating that what it means for a claim to be true in any conceptual scheme is just that the claim is warranted or justified within that scheme. Basic norms of rationality are also thought to be relative to some conceptual scheme. Put another way, such relativists typically hold that there is no truth or standard of rationality which is independent of any conceptual scheme. Extreme philosophical relativists may also hold that conceptual schemes are incommensurable.[35] In other words, the meaning of statements is so conceptual-scheme dependent that there can be no mutual understanding between people who think within differing conceptual schemes, and thus there can be no translation of truth-claims from one conceptual scheme into another.[36] As D. Z. Phillips claims:

> If I hear that one of my neighbours has killed another neighbour's child, given that he is sane, my condemnation is immediate. ... But if I hear that some remote tribe practices child sacrifice, what then? I do not know what sacrifice means for the tribe in question. What would it mean to say that I condemned it when the 'it' refers to something I know nothing about? If I did condemn it, I would be condemning murder. But murder is not child sacrifice.[37]

A relativist about religious language, then, might regard the key propositions of each religion as being true within the conceptual scheme of that religion. Thus, within the Christian conceptual scheme, 'Jesus is the Son of God' could be correctly regarded as a true proposition; while within, for example, a Jewish conceptual scheme, the claim that 'Jesus is the Son of God', could, equally correctly, be regarded as false or even meaningless.

But despite its popular appeal, relativism, as a philosophical position, has attracted vigorous criticism, especially since the 1980s.[38] For example, critics of relativism have pointed out that the proposition 'the correct application of "true" and "false" is perspective-dependent' would have to be, if taken seriously, itself either true or false depending upon one's perspective. And what is to prevent one from adopting the perspective according to which it is false? The relativist seems to want to assert that all claims are perspective-dependent, while denying the perspective-dependence of *that* claim. Thus, one powerful criticism of philosophical relativism is that it cannot be stated without contradiction.[39] If it is simply asserted that 'true' and 'false' are perspective-dependent and, therefore, that all claims are relative, then that claim seems to be a non-relative one, which appears to show relativism to be, at best, paradoxical.

Now, it should be noted that there is an important distinction that can be drawn between philosophical, or what is often called 'cognitive', relativism, on the one hand, and cultural relativism,[40] on the other. Cultural relativism is the recognition that certain beliefs and practices (which can differ both temporally and geographically) derive their meaning or significance from particular societal contexts.[41] One can be perfectly consistent in accepting cultural relativism while rejecting philosophical relativism. Moreover, the criticisms of philosophical relativism mentioned above have no bite against cultural relativism.[42]

In the above discussion, our concern was limited to philosophical relativism. And not everyone who argues that there are incommensurable religious conceptual schemes, each with their own set of true and false propositions, would accept the label 'philosophical relativist'. For there are at least two possible ways of construing the relationship between conceptual schemes and the world. Either there is no common, mind-independent reality underlying the incommensurable religious conceptual schemes, or there is such a reality underlying them. If one were to adopt the latter position, it might be because one holds that mind-independent reality is intrinsically inaccessible to the human mind – for all that is accessible to our minds are the conceptions we have, and not reality itself. Only those subscribing to the first position would be happy to call themselves philosophical relativists. Those who believe in a mind-independent reality might hold that there are truth-claims outside our conceptual schemes, but they are not available to us. Philosophical relativists usually hold that there can be no truth-claims outside a conceptual scheme.

In their theorizing about religion, some philosophers have relied on the first possibility (that there is no mind-independent reality underlying the differing religious conceptual schemes), while others have relied on the second (that there is a mind-independent reality inaccessible to the human mind). The first possibility tends to appeal to thinkers who advocate some form of naturalistic theory of religion[43] – that is, those who subscribe to the view that the various religious traditions have evolved through natural (as opposed to supernatural) causes.[44] In their view, there is no mind-independent, 'supernatural' reality to which religious claims can refer. The second possibility has appealed to thinkers, such as Hick, who are convinced that all the religions of humankind obliquely point to some transcendental, inaccessible, ultimate reality.

Phillips is a prominent example of an influential twentieth-century philosopher of religion who argues that there is no mind-independent, ultimate religious reality underlying the various conceptual schemes employed by religious people. Phillips is a genuine philosophical relativist, and goes so far as to propose that people employing different conceptual schemes actually perceive different worlds. Given that different worlds are being perceived, and that they are conceptual-scheme dependent, it makes no sense, according to Phillips, to argue about whether or not there are any ultimate religious realities.[45]

John Hick's transcendental pluralism

In contrast to D. Z. Phillips, John Hick embraces the second possibility – arguing that there is an ultimate ground to the religious experiences facilitated by the various religious traditions, but that we can have no direct access to it. In other words, we can have no cognitive access to the reality underlying the various conceptual schemes that, in Hick's view, shape the experiences available to religious believers. According to Hick, then, we can never be in a position to find out with certainty whether conflicting religious truth-claims arise from false descriptions of the same reality, or whether the apparently conflicting claims are not about the same thing at all, and hence are not genuinely conflicting. In view of this lack of certainty, Hick suggests that we revise our conception of religious truth. We should abandon the notion of literal truth – as it is applicable to only a very small number of religious statements – in favour of what he terms 'mythological truth'.[46]

Hick holds that we should not regard religious propositions as literally true, not because they are false or meaningless, but because the 'Real'[47] in itself cannot be experienced. Thus, it would, in principle, be impossible to check any purportedly literally true propositions about the Real against that to which those propositions were thought to refer. Hick takes it to follow that

[n]one of the descriptive terms that apply within the realm of human experience can apply literally to the unexperiencable reality that under-

lies that realm. All that we can say is that we postulate the Real *an sich* as the ultimate ground of the intentional objects of the different forms of religious thought-and-experience. Nevertheless perhaps we can speak about the Real indirectly and mythologically. For insofar as these gods and absolutes are indeed manifestations of the ultimately Real, an appropriate human response to any one of them will also be an appropriate form of response ... because the Real is perceived in a range of ways, but it will nevertheless be *an* appropriate response.[48]

Hick is probably the most innovative and influential twentieth-century philosopher of religion to have concentrated on the issues raised by the conflicting claims of the various world religions.[49] By distinguishing between the intentional objects of religious thought and the Real-in-it-self, Hick has been able to develop a hypothesis which would explain both how the various world religions could all be equally valuable and how they could all make justifiable truth-claims. Although Hick is a Christian, his theory does not give any one of the world religions pride of place. Thus, his theory differs from most previous theories of religion, which had interpreted all other religions from the perspective of the theorizer's religion – usually Christianity. Before describing Hick's pluralistic theory of religion, though, it might first be useful to note what motivated the construction of his theory.

Hick realized that the majority of human beings do not choose their religion, but are, instead, *born* into a religious tradition. Whichever tradition a person belongs to, observes Hick, is almost entirely dependent upon where and when that person is born.[50] Thus, if one is born into a devout Muslim family in Pakistan, one is very likely to be a Muslim; likewise, if one is born into a devout Christian family in New England, one is very likely to be a Christian; and so on. As Hick puts it:

We are left, then, with the conclusion that in the great majority of cases – I would guess well over 95% – the tradition within which a religious person ... [is located], depends to a very great extent upon where and when she or he is born. For normally, in the world as a whole, the faith that a person accepts is the only faith that has been effectively made available to him or her. We can refer to this manifest dependence of spiritual allegiance upon the circumstances of birth and upbringing as the genetic and environmental relativity of religious perception and commitment. And it is an extraordinary, and to some a disturbing, thought that one's basic religious vision, which has come to seem so obviously right and true, has been largely selected by factors entirely beyond one's control – by the accidents of birth. It is not that one cannot move from one stream of religious life to another, but that this is a rare occurrence, usually presupposing privileged educational

opportunities; so that the great majority of human beings live throughout their lives within the tradition by which they were formed. In view
of this situation, can one be unquestioningly confident that the religion which one happens to have inherited by birth is indeed normative
... ? Certainly, it is possible that one particular religious tradition is
uniquely normative, and that I happen to have had the good fortune to
be born into it. And indeed, psychologically, it is very difficult not to
assume precisely this. And yet the possibility must persistently recur
to any intelligent person, who has taken note of the broad genetic and
environmental relativity of the forms of religious commitment, that to
assess the traditions of the world by the measure of one's own tradition
may merely be to be behaving, predictably, in accordance with the con-
ditioning of one's upbringing.[51]

Hick concludes from this observation that it is appropriate to adopt, what
he calls, a 'hermeneutic of suspicion' with regard to all beliefs that one
holds which are due to such influences.[52]

According to Hick, then, both religious exclusivism and religious inclusivism ignore the 'genetic and environmental relativity of religious
perception and commitment'. They are also inadequate because they fail
to account convincingly for the relationship of the world religions to one
another and to any ultimate, mind-independent, religious reality. In response to what he regards as the failure of both religious exclusivism
and religious inclusivism, Hick advances the pluralist hypothesis that the
various world faiths are embodiments of 'different perceptions and conceptions of, and correspondingly different responses to, the Real from
within the major variant ways of being human; and that within each
of them the transformation of human existence from self-centredness
to Reality-centredness is taking place.'[53] Accordingly, he regards these
traditions as 'alternative soteriological "spaces" within which, or "ways"
along which, men and women can find salvation/liberation/fulfilment'.[54]

Thus, beginning in the 1960s, a new paradigm has come to prominence – one which does not take just one tradition as the starting point of
theorizing about religions, but rather adopts a global perspective regarding the relationship between the world faiths. This paradigm shift may
be regarded as analogous to the shift from a Ptolemaic to a Copernican
worldview.[55] As Michael Barnes observes, Hick likens all inclusivist and
exclusivist theologies

to the Ptolemaic map of an earth-centred universe. In theology Christianity is seen as the centre of the universe of faith with all the other
religions revolving around it and being graded in value according to
their distance from the centre. Such theories as the Anonymous Christian are not so much a redrawing of the map of the universe, more

another 'epicycle' – an attempt to accommodate growing knowledge of other faiths by drawing a more complicated, but still thoroughly Christianity-centred map. Sooner or later, says Hick, we have to face the fact that more is needed than another version of the old; we have to find a new paradigm, a shift from a Christianity-centred or Jesus-centred model of the universe of faiths, 'to the realisation that it is *God* who is at the centre, and that all the religions of mankind, including our own, serve and revolve around him'. Hence the *Copernican* model: all religions are relative not to a static Christianity but to God or, as Hick puts it in order to accommodate non-theistic religions like Buddhism, the Real.[56]

From within this Copernican paradigm, as it were, it is illegitimate to presume the superiority of any one religion, and to use that religion as the starting-point from which to theorize about other religions, just as it is now considered inadequate to view the earth as the centre of the universe. Moreover, such a Copernican theological paradigm differs from the Ptolemaic in the former's insistence that one's theorizing about religions must start from a principle of charity which assumes that all the world's major religions are of equal worth and value.

But does the Copernican paradigm, as some of its critics have claimed, actually imply that all so-called religious truth is merely tradition-relative? Critics often assume that Hick is vulnerable to the objections levelled against philosophical relativism, for he argues that the adherents of the various religious traditions can each be justified in holding the beliefs associated with those traditions, and that there is nothing to stop equal degrees of justification being offered to religious traditions whose beliefs are mutually contradictory.[57] Hick attempts to rebut the charge of philosophical relativism by employing a Kantian argument. Immanuel Kant argued that our minds structure the phenomena we perceive, and that whatever it is – the noumenon (or the thing in itself) – that is 'prior' to being structured by our minds is in principle unknowable to us. So, according to Hick, if we were to assume that there is a noumenon of religion that is in principle unknowable to us, then it would provide the background postulate for very different religious phenomena.[58] As Hick argues:

> the divine noumenon is a necessary postulate of the pluralistic religious life of humanity. For within each tradition we regard as real the objects of our worship or contemplation. If ... it is also proper to regard as real the objects of worship within the other traditions, we are led to postulate the Real *an sich* [in itself] as the presupposition of the veridical character of this range of forms of religious experience. Without this postulate we should be left with a plurality of *personae* and *impersonae*

each of which is claimed to be the Ultimate, but no one of which can be. We should have either to regard all the reported experiences as illusory or else return to the confessional position in which we affirm the authenticity of our own stream of religious experience whilst dismissing as illusory those occurring within other traditions. But for those to whom neither of these options seems realistic the pluralistic affirmation becomes inevitable, and with it the postulation of the Real *an sich*, which is variously experienced and thought as the range of divine phenomena described by the history of religion.[59]

But how, precisely, does Hick account for the truth or falsity of religious propositions? As we have seen, Hick holds that their truth or falsity should not be understood as literal. As we also noted, Hick instead refers to, what he calls, 'mythological' or 'practical' truthfulness.[60] To be precise, religious language is 'true' insofar as it enables people to relate to the Real in a way that furthers the religious quest for salvation/liberation/fulfilment. Moreover, in Hick's assessment, religious worldviews are primarily expressed in myths, and it is these myths which can be (metaphorically) true or false. Religious myths are thus 'true' insofar as they succeed in evoking 'in us attitudes and modes of behaviour which are appropriate to our situation in relation to the Real'.[61]

Hick does, of course, recognize that many religious believers currently hold a much more literal view of the truth of religious propositions than the one he proposes.[62] Nevertheless, he believes that there are good grounds for the expectation that, over time, his view of religious truth will gradually come to be accepted and even to be taken for granted by the majority of people.[63] But if most of the world's religious believers come to accept a Hickean view of truth, as well as a Hickean form of religious pluralism, would that result in the various religions merging to form a single religion?[64] In other words, is Hick's vision for the future one of increasing religious syncretism? Religious syncretism is often conceived as an inevitable outcome of any theory seeking to find a common strand among, and which purports to justify, the various positions within a world of religious plurality. But it is not, in fact, an outcome that Hick foresees:

> What we are picturing here as a future possibility is not a single world religion, but a situation in which the different traditions no longer see themselves and each other as rival ideological communities. A single world religion is, I would think, never likely, and not a consummation to be desired. For so long as there is a variety of human types there will be a variety of kinds of worship and a variety of theological emphases and approaches. ... But it is not necessary, and it may in a more ecumenical age not be felt to be necessary, to assume that if God is being

truly worshipped by Christians he cannot also be truly worshipped by Jews and Muslims and Sikhs and by theistic Hindus and Amida Buddhists; or even that if the Ultimate Divine Reality is being validly experienced within the theistic streams of religious life as a personal presence, that Reality may not also be validly experienced within other streams of religious life as the infinite Being–Consciousness–Bliss (*Satchitananda*) of some forms of Hinduism, or as the ineffable cosmic Buddha-nature (the *Dharmakaya*) of some forms of Buddhism.[65]

So, within Hick's vision for the future, religious pluralism is accepted, but without undermining the worth and integrity of the various religious traditions.[66] Instead, it enables religious adherents of different faiths to respect each other's views, and to avoid perceiving themselves as members of rival ideological communities.

Hick's theory strikes many today as quintessentially modern, and Hick himself is often regarded as a paradigm of a twentieth-century intellectual liberal. However, we should bear in mind that many of his ideas would not have seemed novel to some earlier religious thinkers, such as the celebrated Muslim mystic ibn al-Arabi (AD 1165–1240).[67] Ibn al-Arabi was a religious pluralist who declared himself to be equally comfortable in the places of worship of each of the Abrahamic faiths. Moreover, he counsels believers thus:

> Do not attach yourself to any particular creed exclusively, so that you may disbelieve all the rest; otherwise you will lose much good, nay, you will fail to recognise the real truth of the matter. God, the omnipresent and omnipotent, is not limited by any one creed, for, he says, 'Wheresoever ye turn, there is the face of al-Lah' (Qur'an 2:109). Everyone praises what he believes; his god is his own creature, and in praising it he praises himself. Consequently he blames the beliefs of others, which he would not do if he were just, but his dislike is based on ignorance.[68]

Some criticisms of Hickean pluralism

Despite the continuities between Hick's theory of religious pluralism and ideas that circulated in what was, perhaps, a more tolerant phase of monotheistic history, Hick's views have struck many of his contemporaries as unacceptable innovations to the tradition, and hence have attracted considerable criticism. Harold Netland, for example, criticizes Hick's theory on the grounds that the notion of truth it employs departs too violently from how religious truth has always been understood by religious people.[69] Hence, against Hick, Netland argues that an adequate understanding of religious faith must centrally include the notions of propositional and exclusive truth. If our understanding of religious faith does not include these notions, he insists, then any purported revelation cannot be genuinely informative.[70] Many traditional Muslims would be inclined to agree with this criticism, as the notion of literal truth has always played a large role in the way that Islam has been understood by its adherents[71] – particularly with respect to the Qur'ān, which many take to be literally true. In response to this objection, however, it would be open to Hick to propose that revelation does not need to be informative in the sense of providing us with literally true propositions about facts. Rather, it is sufficient for revelation to be practically useful in furthering the human quest for salvation/liberation/fulfilment.

A further criticism of Hick's theory is that its adoption would entail the abandonment of traditional forms of Judaism, Christianity and Islam. Critics of Hick point out that an essential component of the Abrahamic faiths is that they are each regarded by their adherents as *uniquely* privileged in being founded on a special revelation from God. On the basis of this purported special revelation, traditional Jews, Christians and Muslims each believe that they possess knowledge of God that is superior to that available in other religions. If they gave up this belief, so the argument goes, they would lose something essential to their religious identity.[72] Hick's form of religious pluralism, then, according to its critics, relativizes this key religious claim, and thus critically undermines traditional religions. Hick does not dispute that, if religious pluralism is adopted, religions will be conceived differently from how the majority of their adherents have conceived them in the past. However, in response to his critics, he argues that the change in viewpoint he recommends does not, in fact, require the loss of anything genuinely essential to any of the religious traditions. Put another way, in Hick's view, if pluralism were widely adopted, traditional religions would not be left unchanged, but the changes undergone would not be so extreme as to entail that the original religions were no longer practised.[73]

However, some would reply that if such a pluralist approach were to be adopted, then it would inevitably undermine the ability of religious belief-systems to enable people to reach the ultimate religious goal of salvation/liberation/fulfilment. Some of Hick's critics assume that if religions are to fulfil their function within human life of allowing people to achieve salvation/liberation/fulfilment, then it is necessary that religious claims be believed, and that they be held as literally true. Belief in the literal truth of religious claims is regarded by them as psychologically necessary for moral and spiritual motivation. Thus, one recent critic concludes that '[e]ven if Hick's Kantian understanding of Reality is right, he should just keep it to himself'.[74] Such views demonstrate how dangerous Hickean religious pluralism can appear to those who are committed to what Hick would regard as a pre-Copernican way of thinking.

Indeed, many religious believers find Hick's form of pluralism some-what suspect. Christians tend to be particularly concerned about the extent to which the traditional understanding of the identity and signifi-cance of Jesus[75] would have to change in order to fit in with Hick's re-interpretation of Christianity. Hick's theory of religious pluralism would seem to require a radical toning down of Christian claims about Jesus. The traditional Christian belief in the incarnation – as God and man literally being united in Jesus – would have to be modified so that it was viewed simply as mythical. Hick's Christology would therefore seem, in its implications, to be more akin to Arius' than to the Christology that came to be accepted as 'orthodox' by the majority of post-Chalcedonian Christians.[76] In point of fact, Hick does accept that the traditional Christ-ian concept 'incarnation' could no longer be taken literally were his theory accepted, but he maintains that this would not necessarily prevent Christians from regarding Jesus with reverence. In short, Hick endorses a portrayal of Jesus as a person who was

> intensely and overwhelmingly conscious of the reality of God. He was a man of God, living in the unseen presence of God, and addressing God as *abba*, father. His spirit was open to God and his life a continu-ous response to the divine love as both utterly gracious and demanding. He was so powerfully God conscious that his life vibrated, as it were, to the divine life; and as a result his hands could heal the sick, and the 'poor in spirit' were kindled to new life in his presence. ... Thus in Jesus' presence, we should have felt that we are in the presence of God – not in the sense that the man Jesus literally *is* God, but in the sense that he was so totally conscious of God that we could catch something of that consciousness by spiritual contagion.[77]

Here, on such an interpretation, we can see how Christian language about the incarnation is to be understood as mythically, rather than as literally, true. But, despite this, Jesus is no less the motivating source of the Christian way of life.

Commenting on the type of Christology seemingly entailed by reli-gious pluralism, Netland remarks that in such theories there is nothing 'unique or normative about the person of Jesus. He is simply one of many great religious leaders who have been used by God to provide salvation for humankind.'[78] Perhaps the most important question facing Christian thinkers who are inclined to adopt some form of religious pluralism, then, is whether or not such an interpretation of Jesus could be adequate within a Christian worldview. Do Christians have to think of Jesus in the terms laid down by traditional Christology?[79] Many theologians today argue that they do not. Perhaps the crux of the issue is whether what is of ultimate significance are literal truths about Jesus, or whether his life should primarily be viewed as an exemplar showing Christians how, practically, to live. If the latter, then the mythical truth of the incarnation would likely suffice.

But it is an empirical question whether or not one must believe in the incarnation in the way it has been understood in the classical Christian tradition in order to be motivated to live the kind of life that has been presumed to lead towards salvation/liberation/fulfilment. Perhaps it is worth recalling that countless Buddhists do not have to believe in the divinity of Gautama Sakyamuni in order for them to live as he recommended with the goal of their attaining enlightenment.

Religious pluralism from the perspectives of liberal Judaism and traditional Islam

We have seen that, for Christian thinkers, perhaps the most serious complaint against Hick's theory is that its acceptance would demand major changes in the way that Jesus is to be understood. Obviously, from the perspectives of Judaism and Islam, this constitutes no problem at all.[80] Muslims have always held that Jesus was simply a prophet. Neither the Jewish nor the Islamic traditions contain a figure about whom claims are made that are comparable to those that Christians characteristically make regarding Jesus. So, neither Jews nor Muslims would be likely to object to Hick's theory on these grounds.

Indeed, it would seem that both the Jewish and the Islamic traditions contain fewer internal impediments to the acceptance of some form of religious pluralism than does Christianity. Dan Cohn-Sherbok is one influential, liberal Jewish rabbi who takes this view. In fact, Cohn-Sherbok advances a theory of religious pluralism similar to Hick's.[81] He claims that, typically, Jews have extended a tolerant attitude to adherents of other religions. To substantiate this claim, he appeals to the common Jewish belief that, regardless of whether or not they held any religious beliefs, people could live well in the sight of God if they observed these seven precepts:

1 Do not worship idols.
2 Do not commit murder.
3 Do not commit adultery or incest.
4 Do not eat a limb torn from a living animal.
5 Do not blaspheme.
6 Do not steal.
7 Have an adequate system of law and justice.[82]

Paralleling Christian accounts of exclusivism, inclusivism and pluralism, Cohn-Sherbok contrasts three models of the relationship between

Judaism and the other world religions. On the first model, Judaism is portrayed as absolutely and exclusively true. God's revelation has been directed to the Jewish people alone; so, the truth-claims of other religions can all be judged by how well they cohere with those of Judaism. The problem with this model, as Cohn-Sherbok sees it, is that '[i]f God is the providential Lord of history, it is difficult indeed to understand why He would have hidden His presence and withheld His revelation from humanity – except for the Jews'.[83] The second model portrays God's revelation as having been bestowed on Jews as well as on other peoples – the only significant difference being that the Jews have received more of it. As Cohn-Sherbok points out, on this second model, the truth-claims of other religions would still be judged with reference to those of Judaism. The problem with this model is that there seems to be no good reason for adopting it. It is far more likely, urges Cohn-Sherbok, that a third model is correct – a model according to which 'in each and every generation and to all peoples of the world, God has disclosed Himself in numerous ways. Thus, neither in Judaism, nor for that matter in any other religion, has God revealed Himself completely.'[84] Consequently, Cohn-Sherbok prefers the third model of representing the relationship between Judaism and the other world faiths. Moreover, he claims that the conception of God implicit in the third model is consistent with the Jewish faith, while the conception of God implied by the other models is not. This is because the third model assumes that God is benevolent and generous, while the other models portray a God who withholds revelation from all but the Jewish people, which hardly seems either benevolent or generous.

Hick's theory of religious pluralism has not only had an impact on scholars within the Jewish community, it has also received considerable attention from Muslim intellectuals. Adnan Aslan, for example, provides a detailed critique of Hick's form of religious pluralism from an Islamic perspective. The core of his critique is the claim that, far from being tradition-neutral, as Hick claims, his theory is in fact both 'implicitly Christian and explicitly "modern-secular"'.[85] Aslan advances this critique of Hick's theory while, at the same time, expounding another form of religious pluralism – that of the highly influential Muslim intellectual Seyyed Hossein Nasr.

Nasr's form of religious pluralism is premised upon his conception of, and commitment to, perennial philosophy. In other words, he holds that there is a 'Primordial Tradition', the *sophia perennis*,[86] which is essentially unchanging and contains within it all the truths of the various religions. And *sophia perennis* is, Nasr believes, expressed variously in the different religions of the world. So, according to Nasr, all traditions are 'earthly manifestations of celestial archetypes of the Primordial Tradition in the same way that all revelations are related to the Logos or the Word which was at the beginning and which is at once an aspect of the Universal Logos and the Universal Logos as such'.[87] As Aslan explains, in Nasr's view, 'since all religions stem from the same origin, they share a substance, that is, the Primordial Tradition, which binds religions not only to the Source but also to each other'.[88] Nasr further claims that the Primordial Tradition does not change, although its expressions in history can. And Aslan believes that consideration of the problems faced by Hick's theory demonstrates that Nasr's form of religious pluralism is superior.

What problems does Aslan have in mind here? He criticizes Hick's theory on the grounds that, unlike Nasr's, it fails to provide a religiously adequate account of revelation. As we have seen, Hick argues that the Real in itself is unknowable. This view would seem to commit Hick to the position that it is in principle impossible for the Real intentionally to communicate knowledge about itself to a mere mortal. On Hick's view, then, the Qur'ān would be a product of Muhammad's mind rather than the result of the Real's intention to communicate certain specific religious truths. As Aslan points out, the failure of Hick's theory to accommodate the traditional Muslim view of Islam as founded on a revelation to the Prophet renders his theory unacceptable to many Muslims.[89]

Aslan is also critical of Hick's distinction between 'fact-asserting' religious statements and 'myth-asserting' ones. Hick, as we have noted, believes that most religious statements are mythological, and only a few, minimally controversial, statements are fact-asserting. But Aslan argues that a hidden criterion allows Hick to distinguish ostensibly factual and mythical statements. In Aslan's assessment, what Hick regards as mythical and what he regards as factual is determined by his liberal education and Western scientific way of thinking. Aslan attempts to substantiate this claim by analysing how Hick would classify the statement 'the Qur'ān is the word of God': because of certain views that Hick already holds, he cannot conceive of the Real speaking. Hence, he has to classify this statement as mythical. However, as Aslan points out, if Hick shared the prior beliefs of those Muslims who understand this statement literally, then the claim that God speaks is by no means absurd. So, in order to make the distinction between fact and myth that Hick relies on, we would have to assume Hick's 'liberal values and his trust in science'.[90]

There is another aspect of Hick's theory that, Aslan believes, would be unacceptable from an Islamic point of view. Aslan has in mind Hick's belief that religious traditions change over time as a result of the interaction between human cultural creativity and religious experiences. Hick and others, such as Wilfred Cantwell Smith, have popularized an image of religions as rather like growing organisms that change through time. Aslan holds that this image of organic growth cannot be applied to Islam without distorting its genuine character; his principal reason for this claim being that Islam is founded on an 'unchanged sacred text, the Qur'an, which contains the Sacred Law, the *Shariah*' – and he takes this to imply that the 'concept of permanence is central to Islam'.[91] As we have seen, however, Aslan cannot speak for all Muslims when he makes these assertions.[92]

Aslan's study has effectively contrasted two very different ways of conceptualizing religious traditions: the Hickean view that emphasizes organic growth, and that of Nasr. What, then, is Nasr's view of the nature of religion?

> Religion in its earthly manifestation comes from the wedding between a Divine Norm and a human collectivity destined providentially to receive the imprint of that Norm. From this wedding is born religion as seen in this world among different peoples and cultures. The differences in the recipient are certainly important and constitute one of the causes for the multiplicity of religious forms and phenomena, but religion itself cannot be reduced to its terrestrial embodiment. If a day would come when not a single Muslim or Christian were to be left on the surface of the earth, Islam or Christianity would not cease to exist nor lose their reality in the ultimate sense.[93]

In short, Nasr believes that each world religion is the earthly 'imprint' of a celestial divine norm. This leads him to embrace religious pluralism, arguing that each religion ought to be respected as valuable insofar as it constitutes such an imprint. Thus, Nasr believes that we should not regard any religion as intrinsically superior to any other. Hence, Nasr's form of religious pluralism accords each religion equal respect without compromising belief in the divine origin of any religion.[94] And, as Aslan points out, Nasr seems to offer a genuinely *religious* form of religious pluralism that, unlike Hick's theory, does not involve reinterpreting religious traditions or doctrines to make them fit in with a particular theory of religions that has been developed without a commitment to any religious tradition.

In a nutshell, then, Aslan holds that Hick's version of religious pluralism will be unacceptable to many religious believers because it fails to provide a religious explanation of the diversity of religious belief systems. In fact, Aslan suggests that Hickean pluralism is actually an ideological rather than a religious 'solution' to the problem of religious plurality. He is also critical of Hick's 'ideological' theory because, unlike Nasr's, it tends to smooth out the differences between religions rather than accepting each tradition for what it is. Indeed, Aslan goes so far as to allege that the danger inherent in Hick's view is that it 'is not unreasonable to envisage that "ideological pluralisms" such as Hick's have been promoted by a global power in order to settle potential religious conflicts'.[95] In other words, Hick's form of religious pluralism can be construed as serving a particular political vision of what the world ought to be like: a global village, with a global market and a global theology.[96]

In Aslan's view, the main weakness of Hick's theory, however, lies in his commitment to the claim that the Real *an sich* is ineffable. It is, as we have seen, central to Hickean transcendental pluralism that the ineffable Real is the ground of the various – and often conflicting – images of God within the world's religions. Aslan is not alone in objecting that Hick has failed to provide a convincing explanation of how we know that there is an appropriate connection between the Real and its varying manifestations. The extreme ineffability of the Real seems to undermine all the various cognitive claims made by religious believers.

It is here where the crucial difference in the approaches of Hick and Nasr is to be found. While Hick stresses the ineffability of the Real *an sich*, Nasr insists that knowledge of ultimate reality is possible. In a word, Nasr claims that unmediated metaphysical knowledge comes through revelation. So, according to Nasr, the world religions provide different contexts within which knowledge of the ultimate reality becomes available. Hence, the 'ultimates' of the various religions are all genuine, Nasr would have us believe, in the sense that they are all revelations of the same ultimate reality – they are 'relative absolutes'.

In Nasr's view, then, God is the sole cause of religious variety, without human conceptual schemes bearing any responsibility. One problem with this approach is that it seems odd that God should have chosen to create such different religious archetypes. Indeed, religions that believe in reincarnation appear to be so different from the Abrahamic monotheisms that it seems bizarre that God should have created such archetypes at all. Or are we to exclude Buddhism and Hinduism from the class of acceptable religions? But this would seem to go against the principal motivation for developing a theory of religious pluralism: namely, the sincerity of the adherents of diverse faiths.

Non-transcendental religious pluralism

Given the significant problems faced by Hick's form of religious pluralism and the seeming limitations of Nasr's theory, some, who are otherwise sympathetic to the pluralist agenda, have been driven to seek an alternative version. We shall now consider a form of religious pluralism that is based on Hilary Putnam's theory of internal realism[97] – hence, we shall refer to it as 'internalist pluralism'.[98] Let us begin, then, by considering the general philosophical approach that underlies internalist pluralism.[99]

Putnam famously contrasts 'internal realism' with 'metaphysical realism'. The core claims of the form of metaphysical realism targeted by Putnam are:

1 The world consists of a fixed totality of mind-independent objects.
2 There is exactly one true and complete description of the way the world is.
3 Truth involves some sort of correspondence.

Internal realism rejects all three doctrines. In rejecting metaphysical realism, the internal realist aims to break away from the dichotomy between 'objective' and 'subjective' notions of truth and reason as they have been traditionally construed. The aim is to find a way of holding on to the objectivity of truth, while denying that there is a correspondence between statements and some mind-independent reality.

Why is this view referred to as '*internal* realism'? Because it holds that the question 'What objects does the world consist of?' is only intelligible *within* a conceptual scheme.[100] Moreover, not only is it the case that the objects which the world contains differ according to which scheme is employed, but also what is true of those objects equally depends upon the particular scheme. Hence, 'truth' does not consist in correspondence to some pre-given objects, for the objects that are deemed to exist are, in some sense, conceptual-scheme dependent. Rather, 'truth' is to be understood as 'idealized rational acceptability' – that is, 'some sort of ideal coherence of our beliefs with each other and with our experiences *as those experiences are themselves represented in our belief system*'.[101]

So, truth is not simply rational acceptability – that is, what is true is not reducible to what it is rationally acceptable to believe at any given time. Putnam's argument for rejecting any such identification is that truth, while being a property of certain statements, is supposed to be one that cannot be lost, whereas justification may be forfeited. (For example, the acquisition of further information might render it no longer rational to accept a claim that one was formerly rational in accepting.) Therefore, truth and justification cannot be identical.[102] So, a commitment to the characterization of truth as a property that cannot be lost by any statement that possesses it is enough by itself to avoid the conflation of truth and rational acceptability. Thus, while rejecting traditional versions of realism, Putnam's theory nevertheless reserves the right to be viewed as a variety of realism, because it retains the distinction between truth and justification. And the hallmark of realism is often held to be precisely a distinction between truth and justification.

Putnam then proceeds to reject the view that truth is somehow independent of all conceptual schemes or that it is tied to one, and only one, conceptual scheme – the supposedly correct one. How, then, is the distinction between truth and rational acceptability to be maintained within any conceptual scheme? As we have noted, it can be preserved by regarding truth as an *idealization* of rational acceptability. In other words, truth is to be viewed as inhabiting epistemically ideal conditions, of which, unfortunately, there are none. Nevertheless, even though this might suggest that truth is unattainable, the idealization theory of truth incorporates two key features that allow us to make truth-claims. The first is that truth is independent of justification here and now, but not, in principle, independent of all justification. Rather, to claim that a statement is true is to claim that it could, in principle if not in fact, be justified. The second is that the truth-claims within a particular conceptual scheme that are most likely to be true will be those that are stable or 'convergent'.[103]

Moreover, an internal realist holds not only that objects are dependent upon the conceptual scheme employed but also that the very notion of 'existence' is equally conceptual-scheme dependent. For consider Putnam's original example of a world comprising three coloured 'atoms'. Within the conceptual scheme of 'the Carnapian logician', they constitute all the objects that exist. However, within the conceptual scheme of 'the Polish logician' – one that counts aggregates along with atoms – seven objects exist: three individual atoms, three pairs of atoms and one trio. Hence, not only is it the case that what counts as an 'object' is conceptual-scheme dependent, but it must equally be the case that what counts as 'existing' is dependent upon the conceptual scheme employed. In a word, reality is conceptual-scheme dependent. And thus it makes no sense to talk of anything existing outside all conceptual schemes.

This implies that there is no way of discussing what exists in a manner that is conceptual-scheme neutral. What happens when we apply this to religion? A thoroughgoing internal realist should, to be consistent, recognize that the existence of purported religious realities can only be meaningfully discussed within a particular conceptual scheme or, what we might call, a 'faith-stance'.[104] For it would make no sense to talk of the Real existing outside any faith-stance. But given different faith-stances – given different conceptual schemes – this suggests different realities and different truths.

In short, just as the truths within the conceptual scheme of 'the Carnapian logician' differ substantively from those within the conceptual scheme of 'the Polish logician', the truths within one religious tradition differ substantively from those within another. But as with the case of the two logicians, this does not entail that either set of religious claims fail to be genuine truths. Moreover, they would remain truths without any form of correspondence to some reality outside all religious or secular belief systems. Indeed, from the standpoint of internal realism, there is no reality outside our conceptual schemes. A religious belief system is thus a self-contained world. And there is a plurality of such belief systems. Thus, internal realism applied to the issue of religious plurality – internalist pluralism – constitutes a form of religious pluralism that is neither 'Ptolemaic' nor 'Copernican'.

Internalist pluralism could thus allow one to say, for example, that within Shaivite Hinduism, Shiva is a real, objectively existing God; while within Christianity, the Trinity of Father, Son and Spirit objectively exists. But what one could not do is intelligibly discuss the qualities of, say, the Shiva of a Hindu from within a conceptual framework in which Shiva has no place. This is because the meaning of the term 'Shiva' is dependent upon the conceptual scheme that regards Shiva as a possible object.[105]

Consequently, internal realism generates a radical form of religious pluralism. However, this form of pluralism – internalist pluralism – does not simply amount to philosophical relativism with respect to religious beliefs. For such a relativist denies objective truth. The internalist pluralist, on the other hand, can talk about objective truths. Notwithstanding the caveat that they remain true only within a specific conceptual framework, religious claims are objectively true if they would be rationally assertable in ideal epistemic circumstances. And any particular faith-stance may come with its own set of objective truths that are non-commensurate with those of other belief systems. It follows that there can be no legitimate dispute between those within different belief systems about the objectivity of certain of their respective claims. For example, consider the case of a Christian asserting that Jesus is the Son of God, and a Muslim replying: 'No, he isn't!' They may not, in fact, be disagreeing, but merely talking past each other (just as 'the Polish logician' is not actually contradicting 'the Carnapian logician' in denying that there are only three objects).

Moreover, internalist pluralism claims to take all religious beliefs much more literally and far more seriously than do other approaches to the problems posed by religious plurality. And it does so by discarding any notion of the religious noumenon. It requires nothing that is transcendent to whichever religious conceptual scheme is in question. It is in a position to acknowledge the genuine differences between religious traditions because it is able to accept that some statements are false within one faith-stance while being true within another. Indeed, internalist pluralism goes so far as to accept that religious statements can be objectively true within the relevant faith-stance. Moreover, the religious phenomena of all traditions are given equal weighting, and none need be re-described in a manner that brings them closer to other traditions. Nor does internalist pluralism have any need to re-describe the core concepts or the goals of any religious tradition.

Internalist pluralism thus claims to avoid the major problems that currently beset Hickean transcendental pluralism. In addition, the existence of morally motivated atheists seems to provide further reason for adopting an internalist version of pluralism in preference to Hick's Kantian variety. For an adherent of internalist pluralism can take the beliefs of all morally motivated individuals equally seriously, whether their belief systems are religious or secular. And this is because, in contradistinction to metaphysical realism, internalist pluralism does not presume that some noumenon, never mind that the *same* noumenon, must ultimately lie behind all moral and religious phenomena. Consequently, internalist pluralism has no difficulty in regarding the conceptual schemes of atheists as being on a par with those of religious believers. And nor is it compelled to re-describe or put in question atheistic moral motivation, which both Hick's and Nasr's approaches seem compelled to do.

Conclusion

The growing appeal of religious pluralism in the late twentieth century reflects a significant change in the way that many in the West conceptualize the ideal form of a liberal democratic society. During the 1960s and 1970s, the ideal society was seen as an integrated one in which originally diverse cultural, religious and ethnic groups were all assimilated into the whole. Given this ideal, it is understandable that many religious thinkers would favour some form of religious inclusivism. However, by the end of the 1970s it had become clear to many that the goal of integration was both elusive and problematic. It was elusive in the sense that it proved to be extraordinarily difficult to formulate public policies that effectively encouraged integration. And it was problematic because not everyone was equally enthusiastic about the envisaged outcome. In particular, members of minority groups tended to resent efforts to assimilate them within the dominant social group in such a way as to undermine their traditions. Such efforts were often perceived as attempts to force them to adopt alien cultural, religious or ethnic values. When the problems associated with integrationism began to appear overwhelming, it was replaced by a new organizing idea: multiculturalism. According to this notion, the ideal society would be one in which diverse cultural, religious and ethnic groups were woven together into a cohesive society within which their genuine differences were not only accepted but were each regarded as contributing to the good of the whole. By the end of the twentieth century, multiculturalism was still an ideal rather than a reality in many parts of the West, and there is no consensus that the project of finding a suitable theoretical base for it has been satisfactorily completed.

Clearly, though, in societies that hold multiculturalism to be the ideal form for society to take, theories of religious exclusivism and religious inclusivism would appear to be sorely out of place. Indeed, some theory of religious pluralism would seem to be required within a workable multicultural society. This may explain why, since the late twentieth century, a growing number have adopted some form of religious pluralism. But one question that multiculturalism gives rise to, given that it involves a plurality of belief systems, is: If each worldview is internally consistent, are there any cogent grounds for rejecting some of them? Human beings are natural creatures living within a natural world. While the nature of human beings does not seem to determine that only one form of life is conducive to human flourishing, certain aspects of their nature – for example – their natural physiology, mean that some forms of life cannot be conducive to genuine human flourishing. Hence, while a criterion of conduciveness to human flourishing does not identify a single, exclusive form of life as fit for humans, it would allow us to reject those worldviews that are part and parcel of forms of life that are restrictive of human flourishing.[106] And if one were to adopt this criterion, then surely any form of life that is conducive to genuine human flourishing should be tolerated and, indeed, is such as to merit a measure of respect. And this would seem to imply that multiculturalism is itself of some value. In short, a criterion such as conduciveness to human flourishing can be combined with a theory of religious pluralism in such as way as to ensure that the theory does not result in the conclusion that, with respect to the various forms of life and their respective belief systems, anything goes.

However, while it is undoubtedly the case that an increasing number of educated people are favouring some form of pluralist theory of religion over exclusivism and inclusivism, there has also been a significant movement in the opposite direction: for a number have felt the need to resist liberal religious tendencies. Religious fundamentalism is an unmistakable feature of the modern world, and religious fundamentalists are far from accepting pluralist theories of religion. In some quarters, even religious inclusivism is rejected as far too liberal, with religious exclusivism remaining the official position. We turn to religious fundamentalism in Chapter 10.

In the next chapter, however, we consider some of the responses that those within the Abrahamic traditions have produced to a changing political climate, including the political aftermath of significant religious conflicts – an aftermath that has precipitated the development of the kinds of multi-faith societies that would seem to require an adequate theory of religious pluralism.

Study questions

1 What challenges does religious diversity pose to religious people? Which of these challenges particularly concern philosophers of religion?

2 For what reasons might someone adopt religious exclusivism? Are these reasons strong enough to withstand the criticisms of thinkers such as John Hick?

3 During the nineteenth century, how did changing views about the origin and nature of religious scriptures begin to affect the way that people thought about religious diversity? To what extent is the impact of such views about religious scriptures still felt today?

4 Is it an advantage or a disadvantage for Karl Rahner's form of religious inclusivism that his theory of the anonymous Christian can so easily be employed by theorists within non-Christian religious traditions? Think, for example, of anonymous Muslims and anonymous Jews.

5 The relativist position asserts that one religion can be 'true for one group' while a different religion can be equally 'true' for another group. What problems confront someone who holds this view? Is this form of relativism a coherent philosophical position?

6 Can one adopt a 'hermeneutic of suspicion' with respect to one's own religious beliefs and yet remain committed to those beliefs?

7 Do you agree with John Hick that the divine noumenon, or the Real, is the best explanation for religious diversity? If not, which explanation do you find superior, and why?

8 Is a future in which all religious people shared one syncretic world religion desirable? What, if anything, do you find appealing about such a future? What negative consequences might it have?

9 Is Seyyed Hossein Nasr's form of religious pluralism a more *religious* theory of pluralism than Hick's, as Aslan claims? If so, why might it matter, and to whom?

10 Does internalist pluralism constitute a superior theory of pluralism to the other theories of pluralism considered? Are there any special problems raised for someone who adopts this explanation of religious diversity and yet remains committed to just one religious faith?

Select bibliography

Aslan, A., 1998, *Religious Pluralism in Christian and Islamic Philosophy: The Thought of John Hick and Seyyed Hossein Nasr*, Richmond: Curzon.

Barnes, M., 1989, *Religions in Conversation: Christian Identity and Religious Pluralism*, London: SPCK.

Boghossian, P., 2006, *Fear of Knowledge: Against Relativism and Constructivism*, Oxford: Clarendon.

Cohn-Sherbok, D., 1991, *Issues in Contemporary Judaism*, London: Macmillan.

Cohn-Sherbok, D. (ed.), 1991, *Islam in a World of Diverse Faiths*, London: Macmillan.

Harrison, V. S., 'Internal Realism and the Problem of Religious Diversity', *Philosophia*, 34 (2006), pp. 287–301.

Hick, J., 1980, *God Has Many Names*, London: Macmillan.

Hick, J., 1989, *An Interpretation of Religion: Human Responses to the Transcendent*, London: Macmillan.

Netland, H. A., 2001, *Encountering Religious Pluralism: The Challenge to Christian Faith and Mission*, Leicester: Apollos.

Phillips, D. Z., 1988, *Faith After Foundationalism*, London: Routledge.

Putnam, H., 1992, *Reason, Truth and History*, Cambridge: Cambridge University Press.

Quinn, P. L. and K. Meeker (eds), 2000, *The Philosophical Challenge of Religious Diversity*, Oxford: Oxford University Press.

Rahner, K., 1969, 'Anonymous Christians' in Karl Rahner, *Theological Investigations*, vol. 6, Baltimore: Helicon Press, pp. 390–8.

Senor, T. D. (ed.), 1995, *The Rationality of Belief and the Plurality of Faith: Essays in Honor of William P. Alston*, Ithaca, NY: Cornell University Press.

Notes

1 Paul Heelas, 1996, 'Introduction: Detraditionalization and its Rivals' in P. Heelas, S. Lash and P. Morris (eds), *Detraditionalization: Critical Reflections on Authority and Identity*, Oxford: Blackwell, p. 4.

2 Islamic scholars traditionally distinguish three realms: the Abode of Islam (*dar al-Islam*), which is under Muslim rule; the Abode of Peace (*dar al-sulh*), which covers territories that Muslims have entered into peace treaties with; and the Abode of War (*dar al-harb*), which is everywhere else.

3 Franz Rosenzweig (1886–1929) is an important example of a modern Jewish philosopher and theologian who was especially concerned with religious plurality and its theological implications. For Rosenzweig's approach, and other modern Jewish accounts of the relationship between Judaism and Christianity, see Fritz A. Rothschild (ed.), 1996, *Jewish Perspectives on Christianity: Leo Baeck, Martin Buber, Franz Rosenzweig, Will Herberg, and Abraham J. Heschel*, New York: Continuum.

4 Exclusivism is sometimes referred to as particularism.

5 It should be noted that despite the widespread adoption of this typology, Gavin D'Costa has nevertheless argued that it does not serve to identify any distinctions useful to the debate on religious diversity. See Gavin D'Costa, 'The Impossibility of a Pluralist View of Religions', *Religious Studies*, 32 (1996), pp. 223–32. John Hick has ably come to the defence of the tripartite typology in 'Religious Pluralism: A Reply to Gavin D'Costa', *Religious Studies*, 33 (1997), pp. 161–66.

6 See Chapter 10.

7 See Harold A. Netland, 1991, *Dissonant Voices: Religious Pluralism and the Question of Truth*, Leicester: Apollos; and Harold A. Netland, 2001, *Encountering Religious Pluralism: The Challenge to Christian Faith and Mission*, Leicester: Apollos.

8 Netland, *Dissonant*, p. 34.

9 Netland, *Dissonant*, pp. 9f.

10 Netland, *Dissonant*, pp. 9f.

11 Netland, *Dissonant*, p. 10.

12 Alternatively, for a version of Jewish inclusivism one could substitute 'the Torah' for 'Jesus'.

13 Interestingly, this is not an inaccurate characterization of the view held by many Muslims, both traditional and modern.

14 The most detailed presentation of Hick's religious pluralism is in John Hick, 1989, *An Interpretation of Religion: Human Responses to the Transcendent*, London: Macmillan.

15 *Enchiridion Symbolorum*, trans. by R. J. Deferrari, in Henry Denzinger (ed.), 1957, *The Sources of Catholic Dogma*, St Louis: Herder, p. 230.

16 Netland, *Dissonant*, p. 142.

17 See Gotthold E. Lessing, 'Parable of the Rings', quoted in Don Cupitt, 1984, *The Sea of Faith: Christianity in Change*, London: BBC, p. 163.

18 With respect to Eastern religions, this process is described and analysed in John Clarke, 1997, *Oriental Enlightenment: The Encounter Between Asian and Western Thought*, London: Routledge.

19 This quest for the historical Jesus is now referred to as 'the original quest' in order to distinguish it from the so-called 'new quest' for the historical Jesus. These two quests had opposite agendas – the agenda of the latter being to disclose the ostensible continuity between the New Testament portrayal of Jesus and the historical figure. Those involved in the new quest believed that if this continuity were established, it would lend credibility to post-New Testament Christianity, as well as to Christianity in its modern forms. The new quest began in the 1950s, with the work of the German New Testament scholar Ernst Käsemann (1906–98). However, the quest was short-lived due to the difficulty of demonstrating the sought-after continuity. The new quest has now been overtaken by the so-called 'third quest'. The third quest focuses on Jesus' actions (for example, his performance of exorcisms), as these are portrayed within the New Testament and within extra-canonical sources such as the Gospel of Thomas. Third 'questers' attempt to understand these actions in the overall context of our knowledge about the society within which Jesus lived. For a comprehensive introduction to the 'third quest' by one of its leading participants, see Marcus Borg, 1993, *Jesus in Contemporary Scholarship*, Valley Forge: Trinity. Those involved in the third quest benefited from the discovery of the Dead Sea Scrolls in 1947–56. The scrolls gave new impetus to scholarly inquiry into the wider historical context of Jesus' life and the early Christian movement.

20 See, for example, John Dominic Crossan, 1991, *The Historical Jesus: The Life of a Mediterranean Jewish Peasant*, San Francisco: HarperSanFrancisco.

21 A. P. Flannery (ed.), 1975, *Vatican Council II: The Conciliar and Post Conciliar Documents*, Leominster: Fowler Wright Books Ltd, pp. 367f. See also the conciliar document '*Nostra aetate*' in which the relation of the Church to non-Christian religions is addressed. Flannery, *Vatican*, pp. 738–42.

22 This is certainly not to say that religious exclusivism lacks supporters. Alvin Plantinga, for example, defends a form of religious exclusivism. See Alvin Plantinga, 1995, 'A Defense of Religious Exclusivism' in Thomas D. Senor (ed.), *The Rationality of Belief and the Plurality of Faith: Essays in Honor of William P. Alston*, Ithaca, New York: Cornell University Press, pp. 191–215.

23 It does not seem to have occurred to the Christian thinkers who adopted this stance that the idea of religions evolving towards more perfect states can be deployed, perhaps with more plausibility, by the devotees of Islam. Traditional Muslim thinkers have always argued that the revelation in the Qur'ān was superior to and fulfilled all previous revelations. If Christianity is indeed at the

apex of the evolution of religion, it is difficult to explain the evolution of another monotheism – Islam, which is similar to Christianity in so many respects – some 600 years later.

24 See, for example, Karl Rahner, 1978, *Foundations of Christian Faith: An Introduction to the Idea of Christianity*, London: DLT, p. 313.

25 See Rahner, *Foundations*, p. 314.

26 See Karl Rahner, 1969, 'Anonymous Christians' in Karl Rahner, *Theological Investigations*, vol. 6, Baltimore: Helicon Press, pp. 390–98.

27 Adnan Aslan, 1998, *Religious Pluralism in Christian and Islamic Philosophy: The Thought of John Hick and Seyyed Hossein Nasr*, Richmond: Curzon, p. 190.

28 Quoted in Aslan, *Religious*, p. 190.

29 See Syed Vahiduddin, 'Islam and Diversity of Religions', *Islam and Christian-Muslim Relations*, 1 (1990), pp. 3–11.

30 For example, *Lumen Gentium*, paragraph 8, suggests that the Catholic Church has a wider extension than the Roman Catholic communion – an extension so wide, in fact, that it goes far beyond the boundaries of the visible Church. Flannery, *Vatican*, p. 357.

31 *Redemptor Hominis* (1979), paragraph 14. Quoted in John Hick, 2000, 'Religious Pluralism and Salvation' in Philip L. Quinn and Kevin Meeker (eds), *The Philosophical Challenge of Religious Diversity*, Oxford: Oxford University Press, p. 64.

32 John Hick famously assesses whether or not there are any good reasons to think that Christianity is better than other world religions. His conclusion is that we are not in a position to make a considered judgement. See John Hick, 1991, 'On Grading Religions' in Ann Loades and Loyal D. Rue (eds), *Contemporary Classics in the Philosophy of Religion*, La Salle: Open Court, pp. 449–70. Dan Cohn-Sherbok disagrees by arguing that 'viability' is the best criterion for assessing a religion's value, thus concluding that the more viable a religion the better it is. See Dan Cohn-Sherbok, 1991, *Issues in Contemporary Judaism*, London: Macmillan, pp. 135–45.

33 See Ernst Troeltsch, 1972, *The Absoluteness of Christianity and the History of Religions*, London: SCM Press.

34 'Conceptual scheme' is a term of art within twentieth-century philosophy. Most philosophers would agree that a conceptual scheme can be defined as the 'general system of concepts with which we organize our thoughts and perceptions'. Simon Blackburn (ed.), 1996, *Dictionary of Philosophy*, Oxford: Oxford University Press, p. 72.

35 Peter Winch is a clear example of someone holding this view. See Peter Winch, 'Understanding a Primitive Society', *American Philosophical Quarterly*, 1 (1964), pp. 307–24.

36 However, not all relativists go that far. For a particular thinker might be relativist about a certain class of statements without being committed to relativism about other classes of statements.

37 D. Z. Phillips, 1970, *Faith and Philosophical Enquiry*, London: Routledge & Kegan Paul, p. 237.

38 See Paul Boghossian, 2006, *Fear of Knowledge: Against Relativism and Constructivism*, Oxford: Clarendon.

39 See Maurice Mandelbaum, 'Subjective, Objective, and Conceptual Relativisms', *The Monist*, 62 (1979), pp. 403–23.

40 The origin of the idea of cultural relativism in the modern European history of ideas is to be found in Michel de Montaigne's essay 'Of Cannibals' (published 1580).

41 As an example of a practice that changes its significance with a change in its cultural context, consider presenting one's raised thumb while standing at the side of the road. Within one culture it signifies that one is asking for a lift. Within another, one is being extremely insulting to passing motorists.

42 Philosophical relativism, as we have seen, seems committed to the assertion and the denial that all claims are perspective-dependent. Cultural relativism does not imply a similar self-contradiction. If, because of differing societal contexts, one person were to mean one thing by 'cultural relativism' and another person were to mean something else by the term, there would not be a self-contradiction. It would not be a case of one person asserting and denying the same thing, but of two people asserting different things.

43 See Chapter 2.

44 An example of a natural cause, in this context, would be the fear of death.

45 See D. Z. Phillips, 1988, *Faith After Foundationalism*, London: Routledge; and D. Z. Phillips, 'Religion and Epistemology: Some Contemporary Confusions', *Australasian Journal of Philosophy*, 44 (1966), pp. 316–30.

46 As Hick explains: 'A statement or set of statements about X is mythologically true if it is not literally true but nevertheless tends to evoke an appropriate dispositional attitude to X.' Hick, *Interpretation*, p. 348.

47 Hick uses the term 'the Real' to refer to whatever constitutes the ultimate reality which underlies the world's religions. The term has the advantage of being tradition-neutral, and it can be used with regard to both theistic and non-theistic religions.

48 Hick, *Interpretation*, pp. 350f.

49 For a sympathetic and clear exposition of the philosophical structure of Hick's theory, and an outline of some of the most important criticisms, see Sumner B. Twiss, 2000, 'The Philosophy of Religious Pluralism: A Critical Appraisal of Hick and His Critics' in Quinn and Meeker, *Philosophical*, pp. 67–98.

50 One might think of this in terms of 'spiritual luck'.

51 Hick, 'Grading', pp. 455f.

52 See, also, John Hick, 'The Epistemological Challenge of Religious Pluralism', *Faith and Philosophy*, 14 (1997), p. 281.

53 Hick, *Interpretation*, p. 240.

54 Hick, *Interpretation*, p. 240.

55 See John Hick, 1973, *God and the Universe of Faiths*, London: Macmillan, pp. 120–32; and John Hick, 1980, *God Has Many Names*, London: Macmillan.

56 Michael Barnes, 1989, *Religions in Conversation: Christian Identity and Religious Pluralism*, London: SPCK, p. 73. Barnes is here quoting from Hick, *Universe*, p. 131.

57 Hick, *Interpretation*. See particularly, pp. 210–30.

58 Indeed, within many world religions, believers claim that ultimate reality is ineffable. Hick takes this to support his thesis, as it is consistent with various

claims about ineffability being about *the same* ineffable reality. Keith Ward, however, argues that this assumption is unjustified. See Keith Ward, 'Truth and the Diversity of Religions', *Religious Studies*, 26 (1990), p. 5.

59 Hick, *Interpretation*, p. 249.

60 Hick, *Interpretation*, p. 248. Hick's appeal to 'practical truthfulness' echoes William James' pragmatic approach to religious truth.

61 Hick, *Interpretation*, p. 248.

62 However, it could easily be argued that given a lack of contact with adherents of other faiths, people would be likely to presume that the metaphorical truths of their own faith were literal truths.

63 See Hick, *Interpretation*, p. 377.

64 See Hick, *Christian*, pp. 123f.

65 Hick, *Names*, p. 58.

66 See *Christian*, pp. 134–9, for Hick's speculative account of the relations between the world religions in the year 2056.

67 Ibn al-Arabi is only one example from the Muslim tradition which has, historically, been particularly rich in religious pluralists.

68 Quoted in Reynold A. Nicholson (ed.), 1969, *Translations of Eastern Poetry and Prose*, New York: Greenwood Press, p. 148.

69 Hick discusses and responds to this objection in *Names*, pp. 45–9.

70 See Netland, *Dissonant*, p. 126.

71 This being the case despite the fact that Muslim philosophers have repeatedly cautioned against the notion.

72 With respect to Christianity, Peter van Inwagen has argued this in his 'A Reply to Professor Hick', *Faith and Philosophy*, 14 (1997), p. 300.

73 A parallel would be that certain changes in values would surely mean that a society's morality had changed rather than that it had been undermined. Cf. Hart's famous critique of Lord Devlin in H. L. A. Hart, 1963, *Law, Liberty, and Morality*, London: Oxford University Press, pp. 51f.

74 Kelly James Clark, 'Perils of Pluralism', *Faith and Philosophy*, 14 (1997), p. 319.

75 The traditional understanding is the one agreed upon by the Council of Chalcedon in AD 451. See Chapter 3.

76 Again, see Chapter 3.

77 John Hick, 1977, 'Jesus and the World Religions' in John Hick (ed.), *The Myth of God Incarnate*, London: SCM Press, p. 172.

78 Netland, *Dissonant*, p. 10.

79 On this issue, see the collection of essays in Hick, *Myth*.

80 Hick's Christology has been well received by many Muslim thinkers, for it is consonant with the traditional Muslim view of Jesus. Dan Cohn-Sherbok analyses this convergence of views in 'Incarnation and Trialogue' in Dan Cohn-Sherbok (ed.), 1991, *Islam in a World of Diverse Faiths*, London: Macmillan, p. 18.

81 See Dan Cohn-Sherbok, 1991, *Issues in Contemporary Judaism*, London: Macmillan, chapters 11 and 12.

82 It is significant that following these precepts is part of what it means to be a Muslim. Moreover, all except (4) – and arguably, (7) – are enjoined by most forms of Christianity.

83 Cohn-Sherbok, *Issues*, p. 132.

84 Cohn-Sherbok, *Issues*, p. 133.

85 Aslan, *Religious*, p. 38.

86 For Aslan's account of the *sophia perennis*, see Aslan, *Religious*, pp. 43–6.

87 Seyyed Hossein Nasr, 1989, *Knowledge and the Sacred*, Albany: SUNY, p. 74.

88 Aslan, *Religious*, p. 50.

89 See Aslan, *Religious*, p. 33 and pp. 61–73.

90 Aslan, *Religious*, pp. 76f.

91 Aslan, *Religious*, p. 41.

92 As we saw in Chapters 3 and 4, the view of the Qur'ān held by Aslan is now widely regarded as false.

93 Cited in Aslan, *Religious*, pp. 51f. From Seyyed Hossein Nasr, 1993, *The Need for a Sacred Science*, London: Curzon Press, pp. 56f.

94 Nasr presents his version of religious pluralism in 'Islam and the Encounter of Religions' in Seyyed Hossein Nasr, 1991, *Sufi Essays*, Albany: SUNY. There, he argues that the best response to religious plurality lies in Sufism for Muslims, and in the perennial philosophy for those of other faiths.

95 Aslan, *Religious*, p. 100. Also see p. 103.

96 Kenneth Surin has also criticized Hick's form of religious pluralism on these grounds. See Kenneth Surin, '"A Certain Politics of Speech": "Religious Pluralism" in the Age of the McDonald's Hamburger', *Modern Theology*, 7 (1990), pp. 67–100.

97 See, for example, Hilary Putnam, 1992, *Reason, Truth and History*, Cambridge: Cambridge University Press. For a discussion of the relevance of internal realism to religious epistemology, see Victoria S. Harrison, 'Putnam's Internal Realism and von Balthasar's Religious Epistemology', *International Journal for Philosophy of Religion*, 44 (1998), pp. 67–92.

98 Internalist pluralism has some affinities with George Lindbeck's 'cultural–linguistic' approach to religion, according to which religions are 'comprehensive interpretive schemes, usually embodied in myths or narratives and heavily ritualized, which structure human experience and understanding of self and world'. George A. Lindbeck, 1984, *The Nature of Doctrine: Religion and Theology in a Postliberal Age*, Philadelphia: The Westminster Press, p. 32.

99 See Victoria S. Harrison, 'Internal Realism and the Problem of Religious Diversity', *Philosophia*, 34 (2006), pp. 287–301.

100 See Putnam, *Reason*, p. 49.

101 Putnam, *Reason*, pp. 49f.

102 See Putnam, *Reason*, pp. 49f. In so arguing, Putnam is distancing his internal realism from the anti-realism of Michael Dummett. Dummett reduces truth to what one is warranted in asserting. But if 'truth' is equated with 'warranted assertibility', then because there are some claims that one is neither warranted in asserting nor warranted in denying, they are neither true nor false. This constitutes the basis of semantic anti-realism. See, for example, Michael Dummett, 1978, 'The Reality of the Past' in Michael Dummett, *Truth and Other Enigmas*, London: Duckworth, pp. 358–74.

103 See Putnam, *Reason*, p. 56.

104 See Victoria S. Harrison, 2000, *The Apologetic Value of Human Holiness: Von Balthasar's Christocentric Philosophical Anthropology*, Dordrecht: Kluwer, chapters 5 and 6.

105 From the perspective of his cultural–linguistic approach to religion, Lindbeck makes a similar claim with regard to religious language: 'Meaning is constituted by the uses of a specific [religious] language rather than being distinguishable from it. Thus the proper way to determine what "God" signifies, for example, is by examining how the word operates within a religion and thereby shapes reality and experience rather than by first establishing its prepositional or experiential meaning and reinterpreting or reformulating its uses accordingly. It is in this sense that theological description in the cultural-linguistic mode is intrasemiotic or intratextual.' Lindbeck, *Nature*, p. 114.

106 See, for example, Joseph Raz, 1988, *The Morality of Freedom*, Oxford: Clarendon Press.

8

Religion, Politics and the Environment

In the twentieth century, both political ideas and political events had a significant impact upon religious thought. During this time, two opposing views regarding the ideal relationship between the religious and the political domains were the subject of vigorous debate. While some held that the separation between religion and politics prevailing in most parts of the West was a positive development, others argued that it was not. In other words, some religious thinkers objected to the liberal democratic forms of government adopted within many Western countries which relied on the principle that religion and politics should be kept separate – a principle that many believers reject.

Given the overwhelming religiosity of the majority within their populations, it might seem odd that Western societies, especially modern European ones, have come to accept a form of government that seeks to minimize the direct influence of religion upon political affairs. Hence, we consider what is, perhaps, the most influential explanation for why modern Western countries have chosen this course, despite opposition from numerous adherents of the Abrahamic faiths. And we shall see that, notwithstanding the desire of many to separate religion and politics, each has, in practice, exerted a significant impact upon the other from the Reformation onwards. This is particularly evident with respect to the impact that two major political events – the two world wars – had upon religion and religious ideas. In this regard, we examine the new forms of Judaism that matured during this period of international conflict, before focusing on the 'post-holocaust' Jewish theologies that emerged after the Second World War.

But 'post-holocaust' theology was not the only form of religious thought to appear as a response to the impact of political events and ideas upon the religious domain during this period. Liberation theology, black theology and eco-theology each developed as adherents of the Abrahamic faiths reacted to the political circumstances of the twentieth century. The aftermath of the Second World War was a world divided along two axes: on the one hand, between an Eastern bloc claiming adherence to Marxism and a Western bloc espousing the twin values of private property and a free market; and on the other, between a wealthy 'north' and a seemingly internationally exploited, impoverished 'south'. And whereas it might be presumed that Marxism would be wholly at odds with religion, it actually came to exert a significant influence on it through its incorporation into liberation theology. Black theology, too, was prompted by a perception of exploitation – in this case, racial – while eco-theology arose out of a perception of the 'exploitation' of nature that appeared to accelerate as a result of the untrammelled workings of the free market and a growing perception of a resulting environmental threat. But before examining these later political and religious movements, we must first consider the two opposing views that came to prominence regarding the ideal relationship between the religious and the political domains.

Religion, liberalism and authority

Many in the West have grown up within a culture that appears to be dominated by secular values; so much so, that it is now widely viewed as axiomatic that religious institutions should not directly determine political affairs. Moreover, in a pluralist world, the very idea that one set of religious beliefs should shape public policy is viewed by many as an anachronism – a throwback to the pre-modern era. In Chapter 10 we examine in detail the standpoint of certain Jews, Christians and Muslims who, in contradistinction, vehemently oppose the divide between the political and religious domains. But for now, suffice it to note that many feel that religion is far too important to be consigned to a minor role, for it has been argued that religion and politics are two of the most fundamental human concerns. Not surprisingly, a number of those holding this view also claim that a person's religious convictions inevitably, and appropriately, affect his or her political orientations, and *vice versa*.

The view that religion and politics are both fundamental human concerns may help explain why many people have found a separation of religion and politics undesirable, and why, within an avowedly secular society, questions about the relationship of these two domains continue to elicit heated debate. Even in late-modern Britain – one of the most secularized countries in the West – a wide range of views coexist concerning the appropriate relationship between religion and politics. Some argue that it is a mark of progress that religious justifications for the actions of government are increasingly no longer sought, and some therefore hold that religious people should concentrate on individual salvation, while leaving the state to deal with the civic community.[1] Others argue that a healthy society requires a religious tradition to unite its people and to underpin its moral values, and some therefore counsel that politicians should welcome the contribution that religion can make to society.[2]

Such disagreement often comes to public attention when particular issues are at stake. Whether or not abortion should be legal is one such issue. In concerning what the legislature ought to enact, it is clearly a political issue, although it is one about which many religious people have strong views. As is well known, most of the political pressure to make or keep abortion illegal comes from Christian groups, whose members are motivated by their religious belief in the sanctity of life.[3] Indeed, this belief constitutes a clear example of a religious conviction that is likely to impinge upon the political realm. And when religious people who hold certain beliefs live within a society whose laws do not reflect them, then they usually feel morally obliged to reshape legislation; and sometimes by violent means.

However, not all issues that stimulate religious people to become politically engaged would seem to concern beliefs of such a fundamental nature as the sanctity of life. For example, legislation preventing children from wearing clothes in school that reveal their religious identity has also caused many religious people to protest, and consequently has attracted considerable public attention.[4] The vigour of the debates provoked by issues such as abortion and schoolchildren's clothing is a strong indication that a great deal of disagreement persists in the modern West concerning the appropriate relationship between religious beliefs and political decisions. In short, there would seem to be little consensus regarding the extent to which religious beliefs should shape the shared political world.

Notwithstanding the ongoing nature of this debate, religion has, as a matter of fact, continued to enjoy a significant impact on political affairs within many Western countries throughout the modern era. The extent of this impact has led some to question the once prevalent view that the modernization of Western societies has pushed religion to a marginal and uninfluential position within the modern world.[5] Within Western Europe, one reason why religion maintained its considerable influence upon politics in the modern era may well lie in the conception of nation that has been widely accepted. Nations are often defined primarily in terms of the ethnic and cultural identities of those occupying a particular territory; and, inevitably, religious traditions contribute to these identities, with possession of a common culture often including a shared religion. Moreover, the link between nationhood and religion was especially transparent in Western Europe from about 1750, when the modern Western European nations were developing.[6] And the predominantly Christian identity of those comprising these nations remained difficult to overlook in the twentieth century. It might seem odd, therefore, that such religiosity is not reflected in the liberal democratic forms of governments which the populations of Western European countries typically prefer. But an explanation for this seeming oddity may be found in the Protestant Reformation of the sixteenth century, and in the subsequent religious wars, which shattered the religious unity of Western Europe – a region that had previously been dominated by the Roman Catholic Church.[7] All of a sudden, Western Europe came to be characterized by religious plurality, and it has retained this feature ever since.

John Rawls (1921–2002), a prominent political philosopher, has famously noted that one result of medieval Christianity splitting into a variety of groups was that – instead of one authoritative religion dominating Western Europe – a plurality of Christian confessions emerged, each claiming to be authoritative.[8] And Rawls argues that this situation engendered the wars of religion. Hence, it was not, as some had claimed, the purported fact that people had lost sight both of the certainties that religion had previously afforded them and of what constituted 'the good life' that lay behind the conflict. Rather, in Rawls' view, the different Christian confessions had different certainties of their own and, hence, different conceptions of the good life. Given such fundamental disagreements, Rawls concludes that the key political questions of the era became: How is society even possible between those of different faiths? What can conceivably be the basis of religious toleration?[9]

Rawls' thesis is that the search for answers to these two questions frames the early history and the ostensible justification of the tradition now known as political liberalism. After claiming that 'the historical origin of political liberalism (and of liberalism more generally) is the Reformation and its aftermath, with the long controversies over religious toleration in the sixteenth and seventeenth centuries',[10] Rawls proceeds to argue that here, in its origins, lies the explanation for the predominance of liberalism in twentieth-century Western Europe. In a nutshell, liberalism takes for granted the fact of religious plurality; holding as a central presupposition the claim that one should tolerate other people's views as long as they are prepared to tolerate one's own. Another feature of political liberalism, according to Rawls, is that it refuses to endorse any particular conception of the good life, thereby making it possible for people of different religions, as well as for atheists, as long as they display tolerance, to accept its principles, and so be on an equal footing with regard to government and legislation. And in manifesting these features, political liberalism seems to offer the only realistic prospect of an end to deep-rooted conflict. Modern liberalism, therefore, is constituted by the realization that the only way one can live without inevitable conflict is by tolerating other views – and, hence, by taking the fact of plurality seriously. Essentially, then, Rawls argues that the horror of the religious wars in Western Europe forced Western Europeans to become liberals, for only by tolerating those of other faiths was the potential for conflict attenuated. And this both resulted in, and ultimately justifies, a form of state that is neutral with respect both to religious convictions and to conceptions of the good life.

Bernard Lewis also regards the Reformation as the key to comprehending the political culture of modern Western European societies. In his view, the violent conflicts between different groups of Christians that flared up during and after the Reformation led to the emergence of secularism.[11] At the core of secularism, according to Lewis, lies the 'notion that religion and political authority, church and state, are different and that they can and should be separated'.[12] Given this, Lewis argues that it is understandable that secularism took root in precisely those Western European countries that had been most affected by the wars of religion.[13] Moreover, Lewis claims that secularism is a Christian notion insofar as it can be traced back to the following verse from the Christian Scriptures: 'Give therefore to the emperor the things that are the emperor's, and to God the things that are God's.'[14] In his view, the purported link between Christianity and secularism made it all the more likely that the latter would flourish in countries with predominantly Christian populations. Conversely, he argues that it should not surprise us that secularism did not emerge or become established in non-Christian lands that (in his view) were unaffected by such inter-religious conflict.[15]

The arguments of Rawls and Lewis may shed light on why Western European societies have, by and large, accepted some form of political liberalism that includes the secularist separation between religion and political authority. Such mechanisms of government allow different religious views to be given equal consideration while, purportedly, at least, keeping them all equally distant from government and legislation. These ideas were first put into legislative form not, however, in Europe but in the United States. And in 1790, George Washington explained the legislative principles at the core of the new republic in a letter to a Jewish community leader, wherein Washington claims that all 'citizens of the United States of America'

> possess alike liberty of conscience and immunities of citizenship. It is now no more that toleration is spoken of, as if it was by the indulgence of one class of people that another enjoyed the exercise of their inherent natural rights. For happily the Government of the United States, which gives to bigotry no sanction, to persecution no assistance, requires only that they who live under its protection, should demean themselves as good citizens, in giving it on all occasions their effectual support.[16]

Put another way, within a territory that accepts a separation between religion and government, religious tolerance is not supposed to be granted by special favour to members of minority religious groups by those within the dominant one. Rather, those belonging to all religious groups are supposed to enjoy equal protection by law. The price of such protection is that members of different religious groups must concede that political authority is independent of religious sanction. Clearly, this conception of political authority differs considerably from an alternative conception, prominent in pre-modern Europe, that regarded God as bestowing political authority upon selected individuals (choosing them to be emperors, for example). According to this older view, the source of political authority was, ultimately, supernatural – or, in other words, religious.

Moreover, there is another sense in which the re-conceptualization of the nature of political authority that took place within the West has its roots in the Reformation. For the Reformers argued for the 'priesthood' of all believers. On the basis of the claim that the ultimate source of authority in religious matters was the Holy Spirit, whose dictates were known through each individual's own conscience, they concluded that there could be no legitimate distinctions of rank among people. Certain radical Protestant groups (such as the Anabaptists) drew out the implications of this new conception of religious authority more consistently than did most other confessions. Each member of these radical congregations was thought to be endowed by God with equal dignity and value – hence, in principle, at least, all were regarded as possessing the same level of authority within the religious community. Clearly, this was a radical departure from the traditional conception of ecclesial authority, according to which authority is wielded over the laity from 'above' by the bishops and priests. And, of course, the bishops and priests had been thought to acquire their authority from even further 'above': from the pope in Rome and, ultimately, from God. In conceiving of God's authority as lodged within each individual, the radical Christian confessions subverted this traditional order. The new conception of religious authority they promoted thus had no place for a privileged ecclesial class possessing special rights and privileges above those enjoyed by ordinary people.

It can be argued that, from the theological view that all members of the religious community are equal, it was only a short step to the conviction that all people should be politically equal. Thomas Paine (1737–1809) is a prominent example of an advocate of political equality from an explicitly religious standpoint – in his case, Quakerism. Moreover, when it occurred, the political change in the conception of authority mirrored the prior religious one. As we have seen, according to the traditional Christian conception, authority came from God through bishops and priests, and was then wielded over the general populace. Similarly, according to the previously dominant political conception, political authority came from God through a divinely appointed leader, and was then imposed on the people. The later religious conception, on the other hand, regarded authority as coming directly from the people (albeit insofar as they were thought to mediate God's own authority). Likewise, the later political conception held that authority was based in the people who freely chose a government to represent them, and who were not subject to laws unless their representatives had so decreed. In short, like religion, politics came to focus on individual consent rather than on blind obedience to a special class of people who were thought to be in exclusive possession of the authority to rule.

These considerations might suggest that, far from inhibiting new political developments, some forms of Christianity have – at least in the early modern period – exercised a progressive influence upon the political life of many Western European countries. However, we should note that not every Christian confession joined the more radical Protestants in moving away from a top-down, authoritarian structure, and some Christian churches have exerted an extremely conservative influence within late-modern Western societies. It would seem, then, that there are grounds for viewing Christianity as having acted both as a progressive and as a conservative force within modern Western societies.

Let us now turn to some aspects of the influence that certain key political events of the previous century have had upon traditional religion in the West.

Political theology

The last century proved to be a time of major political turmoil. Few areas of the globe escaped violent conflict during the twentieth century – a century in which an estimated 109,655,500 people lost their lives as a result of war, with two world wars having been fought in the first half of the century. The estimated death toll of the First World War (1914–18) was 6,383,000, most of whom were civilians. The Second World War (1939–45) was even more destructive of human life, with a staggering estimate of 9,708,000 causalities (8,723,000 of whom were civilians).[17] In addition to the colossal number of fatalities, many people were displaced from their lands and suffered from disruption to, if not the destruction of, their communities. Europe was especially ravaged by the two world wars. And one consequence was the undermining of traditional lifestyles in many parts of Europe. It would have been astonishing if these events had failed to exercise a major impact on the religious beliefs of those affected by them, as they struggled to come to terms with an unpredictable and violent world. In this chapter, we consider some of the more noticeable features of the influence these events exerted upon religion and upon religious ideas.

It is interesting to note that, in the first half of the twentieth century, the percentage of the European population claiming to belong to one of the Abrahamic faiths appears to have risen significantly.[18] Perhaps this religious resurgence was a direct result of what appeared to many as the failing credibility of certain non-religious worldviews, given the devastation those worldviews seemed to have caused in unleashing two world wars. Perhaps disillusionment with rationalism and scientific materialism, in particular, led some to reconsider a religious faith that they had earlier rejected. Whatever the actual explanation, the devastating political events of the first half of the twentieth century certainly appear to have contributed to an increased level of religiosity within Western Europe.

But no less considerable an effect of the two world wars was the politicization of many religious thinkers, one direct result of which was the 'political theology' developed within West Germany by certain religious thinkers. Political theology emerged when Christian theologians re-evaluated their religious commitments in the light of the sheer amount of human suffering experienced by many during the wars. The genocide of Europe's Jewish community by the Nazi regime, for example, seemed too great a horror to be addressed adequately by the theologies of the pre-modern era. Theologians such as Jürgen Moltmann (b. 1926) and Johann Baptist Metz[19] (b. 1928) therefore argued that it was essential that a political dimension be introduced into theological discourse if it is to speak at all relevantly to such events.

Moltmann identifies five points that, in his view, both define political theology and differentiate it from other twentieth-century theologies. First, '[p]olitical theology is not a purely academic theology. It is a theology which is related to the expectations and experiences of action groups and protest movements among ordinary people in the countries of Europe.'[20] Second, political theology differs from liberal Protestant theology insofar as the latter is 'the theology of the established middle classes. Political theology has its Protestant roots in Karl Barth's anti-bourgeois theology, and in the experiences of the Confessing Church in its resistance to National Socialism.'[21] Third, '[p]olitical theology in the countries of the industrial West has always critically challenged the self-justifications of the people in power', and political theologians 'have grappled critically with political religion; with civil religion; and with the ideologies of patriotism, the "the Christian West" and anti-communism'.[22] Fourth,

> political theology has always tried to act as spokesman for the victims of violence, and to become the public voice of the voiceless: in socialist theology for the workers; in the theology of peace for the (potential) victims of a nuclear war in Europe, as well as for the (actual and present) victims of rearmament and arms exports in the Third World; in the theology of human rights for people robbed of their dignity and their rights under the East European dictatorships; in feminist theology for women who are imposed upon and maltreated; and in ecological theology for the exploited creation. ... [T]he point is always liberation of the victims and criticism of the perpetrators.[23]

And, finally: 'Political theology lives in the shared action groups, and brings into contemporary life the revolutionary traditions of the Bible and Christian history.'[24]

Clearly, political theology has an extremely wide-ranging agenda. Nevertheless, Moltmann claims that, as it matured, it focused on two related tasks: on publicly criticizing capitalism on behalf of those who suffered because of the market economy; and on 'creating justice for human beings and nature through appropriate social and environmental policies'.[25] Thus, Moltmann argues that the mandate of political theology is to criticize modern Western society from within. And one key target of this criticism is, he avows, the catastrophic effect of the market economy on the environment. We return to this later, when we consider Moltmann's own contribution to eco-theology. First, however, we turn to another major development wrought by political events in the first half of the twentieth century: namely, the transformation within Judaism that resulted from the extreme anti-Semitism that climaxed in Europe during the Second World War.

Zionism

It is estimated that six million Jews were murdered in Europe between 1939 and 1945.[26] Most of those who escaped death fled the continent, settling primarily in the Americas and the Middle East. This catastrophe not only had a profound effect upon the religious life of Europe but also left its mark on the various forms of Judaism (and of Jewish theology) that emerged later in the twentieth century – forms of Judaism that were, as Jacob Neusner argues, all in radical discontinuity with the Judaisms that developed during the previous century.[27] As we saw in Chapter 3, the nineteenth century had seen the birth of Reform Judaism, Modern Orthodox Judaism (which developed in reaction to what were perceived as the excesses of Reform Judaism), and Conservative Judaism (which attempted to occupy a position between the other two schools of thought). Neusner describes each of these as 'Judaisms of the dual Torah' because each claimed direct continuity with pre-modern Judaism which, as we noted, was premised upon a dual source of revelation: the written and oral Torah. In the twentieth century, however, many Jews found these forms of Judaism wholly inadequate when it came to understanding the extreme degree of victimization and suffering they had experienced. Thus, new forms of Judaism were developed that aspired to meet this need, each of which rejected the tradition of the dual Torah. Not surprisingly, several of these new forms of Judaism were overtly political: Zionism, Jewish Socialism and Yiddishism.[28] We shall consider the first two of these, focusing in particular on Zionism, for it is the form of Judaism that, during the twentieth century, would seem to have had the deepest impact upon the Jewish community as a whole. Yiddishism, which was a movement that emphasized Jewish cultural identity, spread rapidly in Eastern Europe, but then quickly died out, leaving little lasting impression.

Both Zionism and Jewish Socialism originated in 1897, long before the two World Wars. The institutional origin of the former lies in the creation of the World Zionist Organisation in Basel; whereas the origin of the latter can be traced to the formation of the Bund (a Jewish union organized in Poland). Jewish Socialism comprised an international network of Jews who sought the implementation of socialist policies within whichever state they happened to live. Zionism, on the other hand, is a political movement that had as one of its major goals the creation of a Jewish state governing its own homeland, for only in the creation of such a state could its adherents envisage a solution to the discrimination that Jews had historically encountered. Both of these movements – Zionism and Jewish Socialism – arose in response to the pressing social and political problems of the day, and it was to the resolution of these problems that they were specifically directed. We can thus observe the radical discontinuity between these Judaisms and pre-modern Judaism in this particularly, and exclusively, modern orientation. Moreover, as Neusner argues, Zionists and Jewish Socialists, for the most part, seemed simply to ignore the system of pre-modern dual-Torah Judaism, given that they did not even bother to respond to it.[29] Indeed, some have concluded that this degree of discontinuity with the Judaic tradition makes it tenuous to regard Zionism and Jewish Socialism as forms of Judaism at all. In addition, many Zionists and Jewish Socialists were adamantly secular, with the concept of a transcendent God, or of God's revelation in the Torah, playing no role within their intellectual systems. In short, for these twentieth-century secular Jews, being Jewish was not a matter of religious belief but of belonging to the Jewish community.

Despite Zionism's claim to be a secular Jewish movement, its attractiveness to a large number of Jews was, however, due in large measure to its skilful deployment of traditional religious ideas and symbols. Not only was a core goal of Zionism the creation of a Jewish homeland, as we have noted, but this goal was also the explicit motive behind the formation of the World Zionist Organisation. From the early days of the movement, this envisaged homeland – Zion – was portrayed as the spiritual centre of the Jewish people.[30] The religious vision of a spiritual homeland, then, developed alongside the purely secular aspirations of many Zionists, and it became increasingly important as the movement, in the face of the sheer cultural diversity within the Jewish people, sought some common cultural and ideological foundation for the Jewish 'nation' that was to occupy the land of Zion. Increasingly, Zionists were driven to refer back to the ancient Jewish tradition in order to find some commonality between the diverse populations of Jews to whom their message was targeted. One effect of this was a renewed interest in Judaic studies on the part of many Zionists, as well as a preoccupation with archaeology. As Neusner claims:

> In its eagerness to appropriate a usable past, Zionism, and Israeli nationalism, its successor, dug for roots in the sands of history, finding in archaeology links to the past, even proofs for the biblical record to which, in claiming the Land of Israel, Zionism pointed. So in pre-State times and after the creation of the State of Israel in 1948, Zionist scholars and institutions devoted great effort to digging up the ancient monuments of the Land of Israel, finding in archaeological work the link to the past that the people, one people, so desperately sought. Archaeology uncovered the Jew's roots in the Land of Israel and became a principal instrument of national expression, much as, for contemporary believers in Scripture, archaeology would prove the truths of the biblical narrative.[31]

Essentially, then, Zionism drew upon the ancient history of the Jews in order to lend credibility and an air of antiquity to nascent Jewish nationalism. The Jewish religious heritage thus came to acquire a high profile within the Zionist project. Another facet of this retrieval of the ancient past was the reappropriation, in a modified form, of the ancient language of the Jewish people. Consequently, Hebrew was to become the national language of the new state – the State of Israel – once the Zionists had attained their political goals. Moreover, 'aliyah' – the Hebrew term that the Zionists chose in order to denote immigration into the new homeland – also had significant religious connotations, originally referring to a mystical ascent to a higher state of being.

The strategy of appealing to an ancient religious heritage in an attempt to bind together the new nation was not, unsurprisingly, without drawbacks. By glorifying the distant past, Zionists undermined the value of the Jewish traditions that had developed within the Diaspora. Thus, the version of Judaism that they promoted was one divested of the rich intellectual heritage that had emerged during the common era (that is, since the Jews had been dispersed throughout the world). Some Zionists attempted to fill the intellectual and cultural gap which this strategy had produced by emphasizing the spiritual benefits of the Zionist way of life – a way of life that many appear to have experienced as nothing short of salvific. In effect, then, Zionism sought to replace the traditional religious vision of salvation through the actions of a long-awaited messiah with the promise of utopia in the here and now. As Amos Elon writes: 'Its myth of mission was the creation of a new and just society. This new society was to be another Eden, a Utopia never before seen on sea or land. The pioneers looked forward to the creation of a "new man".'[32]

There is no doubt that this Zionist project resonated with many post-war Jews, and that they came to regard the founding of the State of

Israel as a religious event.[33] This event, moreover, appears to have helped many of them to come to terms with the holocaust. For, it seemed to many, the holocaust demanded the State of Israel; and it may well be that without the subsequent founding of the State of Israel many would have felt utterly defeated by the sheer scale of the genocide their people had suffered. Thus, to a large extent, the holocaust might be thought responsible for the success of Zionism and the persuasiveness of its mythology. And not surprisingly, the connection between threats to the State of Israel and threats to the Jewish people as a whole remained a powerful one in the minds of many Jews into the twenty-first century. As Neusner argues, many have come to regard the continued existence of the State of Israel as a 'metaphysical necessity'; that is, as a necessary counter-balance to the forces of anti-Semitism that climaxed in the holocaust.[34]

Ironically, though, notwithstanding Zionism's success in achieving its goal, and despite the continued importance of the State of Israel to many Jews, the establishment of the State of Israel brought about the end of the original Zionist movement.[35] For the creation of the State of Israel in 1948 deprived Zionism of its *raison d'être*, and hence of its motivating force. Jewish Socialism, likewise, did not survive as a significant movement into the second half of the twentieth century. It had exercised wide appeal among the Yiddish-speaking population of Europe. But most of these Jews had been murdered by the end of 1945. And Jewish Socialism, like Yiddishism, did not survive the loss of its constituents, although socialism remained politically dominant within the State of Israel until the election of the Likud party in 1978 under the leadership of Menachem Begin.

Clearly, then, political events in the twentieth-century West had wide-ranging effects on Judaism. We now turn to 'post-holocaust theology' – a form of theology that also emerged out of the horrific experience that Jews had endured.

God and evil: post-holocaust theologies

Neusner and others have argued that, intellectually, the twentieth century contributed nothing of lasting significance to Judaism. The reason they adduce for this surprising claim is that most of Judaism's intellectual centres were located within the European Jewish communities that were destroyed during the genocidal campaign of the Nazi regime. Those Jews who survived, moreover, were more interested in the practical matter of establishing a Jewish state than in developing theological or philosophical systems. Indeed, Neusner concludes that, in '[c]onfronting the urgent and inescapable questions of the twentieth century, the system-makers of

Judaisms in the end came up with no self-evident, enduring answers. The twenty-first century inherits much from the nineteenth, nothing from the twentieth, in Judaisms.'[36] While it may, perhaps, be the case that the lasting intellectual contribution of Zionism, Jewish Socialism and Yiddishism to twenty-first-century Judaism will turn out to be negligible, it seems extremely premature to dismiss the contribution of all Jewish theologians outside of these movements, some of whom have developed theologies that do appear to have contributed significantly to the ongoing Jewish tradition. In this section, we consider several of these 'post-holocaust theologies'.

As the twentieth century unfolded, both Jewish and Christian thinkers displayed a steadily increasing level of interest in the problem of evil. Essentially, the problem concerns how an omnipotent, all-knowing and beneficent God could exist given the degree of evil present in the world.[37] An omnipotent God would surely have the power to prevent evil, and a beneficent God would wish to do so. Yet few will deny that our world exhibits a vast array of different forms of misery and suffering – evil, in other words. In the second half of the twentieth century, Jewish theologians such as Richard Rubenstein, David Birnbaum and Emil Fackenheim confronted this problem directly. When they did so, it was principally the evil of the holocaust that they felt compelled to address theologically. As Rubenstein, a rabbi in the conservative tradition, writes:

> Although Jewish history is replete with disaster, none has been so radical in its total import as the holocaust. Our images of God, man, and the moral order have been permanently impaired. No Jewish theology will possess even a remote degree of relevance to contemporary Jewish life if it ignores the question of God and the death camps. That is *the question* for Jewish theology in our times.[38]

In grappling with this question, Rubenstein came to espouse a theology that, echoing Friedrich Nietzsche (1844–1900), proclaimed the 'death of God'.[39] Contrary to what this phrase may suggest, however, Rubenstein's theology is not a form of atheism. As he explains: 'No man can really say that God is dead. How can we know that? Nevertheless, I am compelled to say that we live in the time of the "death of God". This is more a statement about man and his culture than about God. The death of God is a cultural fact.'[40] By the phrase 'the death of God', then, Rubenstein means that a particular conception of God has, in the light of modern experience, come to be untenable. The conception he rejects portrays God as the omnipotent author of all historical events. While this has been the traditional picture of God accepted by Abrahamic monotheists, Rubenstein believes that it has become impossible for moderns to accept it. Jews especially, he argues, can no longer embrace this traditional image of

God. The problem, as Rubenstein sees it, is essentially this: if God is the omnipotent author of all historical events, then God is directly responsible for (indeed, God no less than desired) the murder of six million Jews by the Nazis. For a traditional theist, it is not possible to draw any other conclusion. The only acceptable theological solution, argues Rubenstein, is to admit that 'God', as traditionally conceived, does not exist.[41] The 'myth of the omnipotent God of history' must be rejected, Rubenstein declares, along with 'its corollary, the election of Israel'.[42]

As we noted above, however, Rubenstein does not think that rejecting the 'God' of traditional Western monotheism compels him to embrace atheism. Instead:

> It is precisely because human existence is tragic, ultimately hopeless, and without meaning that we treasure our religious community. It is our community of ultimate concern. In it, we can and do share in a depth and dimension which no secular institution can match. ... We have turned away from the God of history to share the tragic fatalities of the God of nature.[43]

Rubenstein, then, seeks to displace the God of traditional theism, and to reorder Jewish religious life around the value of the religious community. And he hopes that the Jewish religious community can survive the death of the traditional God by drawing strength from the 'God of nature', with this latter God, or so Rubenstein argues, having been latent within the Jewish tradition. Unfortunately, in Rubenstein's view, this tradition came to be dominated by the conception of God as the 'omnipotent God of history'.

Moreover, Rubenstein believes that, because the God of nature is latent within the Jewish tradition, a transition to a more appropriate conception of God can be accomplished without losing the traditional elements of Jewish life. With regard to the role of the Torah within the Jewish community, for example, Rubenstein proclaims that Jews can 'recapture for the first time in the modern period the entire Torah as our decisive religious text';[44] his justification for this assessment resting on the assumption that, because the religious community is of ultimate religious value, anything which contributes to the historical identity of that community must also be of value. In other words, as there can be no doubt that, throughout history, the Torah has been crucial in the formation of the identity of the Jewish community, then the Torah should retain its central place, even though it is no longer to be regarded as revealing the will of God. Thus, paradoxically, although Rubenstein's theology proclaims the death of God, it supports a traditional, religious Jewish lifestyle – albeit, a lifestyle that can no longer claim legitimacy by appealing to God and revelation.[45] Furthermore, according to Rubenstein, the State of Israel provides an unprecedented opportunity for Jews to live according to their traditions and to rediscover their cultural roots. Indeed, Rubenstein links the return of a least a portion of the Jewish community to their ancestral homeland with the rediscovery of the God of nature, which he believes many of them to be experiencing.[46] Most importantly, he emphasizes that this is not a departure from the Jewish tradition, but a return to some of its most ancient sources:

> tradition and history alike have emphasized the pagan character of our earliest ancestors. ... [W]e look today with increasing respect for and sense of community with our pagan origins. It was inevitable that, with the return of the Jewish people to their ancestral earth, there would be a renewed interest in, if not contact with, the old gods of that land.[47]

This notwithstanding, Rubenstein does not envisage pagan deities such as Baal and Astarte replacing Yahweh within the Jewish religious consciousness. Rather, his expectation is that 'the earth's fruitfulness, its vicissitudes, and its engendering power will once again become the central spiritual realities of Jewish life, at least in Israel'.[48] As we shall see, Rubenstein's emphasis on the spiritual value of the environment reveals an affinity between his theology and the so-called eco-theologies that were developed in the late twentieth century.

As we noted above, Rubenstein's radical theology was motivated by a form of the 'problem of evil'. And as we have seen, the presence of evil in the world challenges the theist to provide some account of how an omnipotent and beneficent God can exist and yet not prevent its occurrence. Philosophers who have considered this problem, such as John Mackie,[49] typically argue that the theist must either give up belief in God or provide some explanation of why God (as traditionally construed) allows so much evil in the world. Theologians, however, tend to concede what philosophers assume they cannot: for many have been quite prepared to alter the concept 'God' in response to this problem.[50] And this manoeuvre is perhaps most clearly evident in the case of post-holocaust Jewish theologians.

We have seen that Rubenstein's response to the problem of evil was to reject the conception of an omnipotent God that has been dominant within traditional theism. His co-religionist, David Birnbaum, proposes a similarly radical re-conceptualization of God in the face of this seemingly insurmountable difficulty, with Birnbaum formulating the problem of evil as follows: 'How can we affirm the validity of sincere religious commitment in a world where we ourselves have witnessed such prevalence of gratuitous, gross evil?'[51] And Birnbaum explicitly acknowledges that we can only retain such commitment if we are able to provide a rationally acceptable account of God and God's dealing with the world. In developing such an account, however, he finds himself compelled to depart dramatically from the traditional concept 'God'. For Birnbaum goes so far as to argue that God's failure to intervene in the world and the deity's seeming refusal to prevent the massive suffering inflicted in Nazi Germany is to be explained by the claim that 'God has contracted His here-and-now consciousness'.[52] Put another way, God was not aware of the suffering inflicted, claims Birnbaum, and hence could not have prevented it. In support of this far-from-traditional claim, Birnbaum insists that God had a very good reason for contracting 'His here-and-now consciousness'; the reason being that only by leaving humanity alone could God provide the freedom necessary for humanity to realize its full potential. As Birnbaum sums up the core of his argument:

1. The purpose of men and women is to quest for their potential.
2. The greater a person's freedom, the greater the ability to attain his or her potential.
3. Freedom requires privacy, responsibility, and selfhood.
4. In order to yield human persons greater freedom (along with greater privacy, responsibility, and selfhood), God's here-and-now consciousness has contracted, in correlation to humankind's ascent in knowledge.
5. With the Divine consciousness increasingly contracted from the here-and-now, in which there is evil, humanity is increasingly forced to confront evil on its own.[53]

In short, Birnbaum claims that it was for our own good that God chose to withdraw from any direct involvement in human affairs. For if God had not done so, it would have been impossible for us to fulfil our human potential.

Birnbaum's proposed solution to the problem of evil is, then, a form of response known as 'the free-will defence'. What is interesting about Birnbaum's version of this defence, however, is the specific conception of God that it requires. For God, in Birnbaum's view, was omnipotent once upon a time, but is now no longer so. Why does Birnbaum make this assumption? Because in limiting 'His' consciousness, God inevitably also limited 'His' omnipotence. For if God is unaware of the events that are now occurring, then 'He' cannot be in direct control of them. In fact, Birnbaum regards his theory as consistent with traditional religious beliefs about God's past interventions on behalf of 'His' people. But his theory has the added advantage of also being consistent with the modern experience of God's absence. Moreover, Birnbaum views his proposal as a positive one. That the God worshipped by traditional Jews does exist, but, for their own good, no longer intervenes in history as 'He' formerly did is actually inspiring because, rather than feeling despondent, '[m]an ... should be uplifted by the awesome potential he has been given in trust; by the confidence placed in him by his Deity; by the magnitude of his personal freedom'.[54]

However, the cost to a theist of accepting Birnbaum's solution to the problem of evil is far from negligible. He or she must not only renounce any expectation that God will act on his or her behalf but also relinquish the idea that God is fully aware of his or her existence. As Gwen Griffith-Dickson comments, the God that Birnbaum's theory leaves one with seems indifferent to human suffering. Moreover, as she also observes, what leads Birnbaum to posit such a restricted God is his belief that there is an inevitable opposition between divine attentiveness and our ability to realize our potential. But why should we accept that there is such an opposition?[55] Consider how a parent might facilitate her child's realizing his potential. If she is too attentive and too controlling in attempting to ensure that the child never experiences any harm, then the child will fail to develop to the full. But equally, if the child is simply left to his own devices from birth, then he will probably fail to achieve any potential at all. Surely the parent is not faced with only two choices: total attentiveness or total indifference? Why, then, should God's choices be limited to these two options alone? Would that not make God more limited than we are?

Both of the Jewish theologians considered above feel compelled to depart from the traditional conception of God as an omnipotent actor within history not only as a means of responding to the problem of evil but also in order to account for the seemingly palpable absence of God that many experienced during the twentieth century. However, as we have seen, neither Rubenstein nor Birnbaum counsels atheism, and each provides an alternative conception of God which, they argue, was far more appropriate for those living within a century that had confronted radical evil. But are these attempts to reformulate the concept 'God' relevant to what people actually believe, or are they merely the result of academic exercises? Rubenstein suggests that such re-formulations are, indeed, highly relevant to those who wish to retain a religious identity in the post-holocaust world. Moreover, he is persuaded that, in such a world, the survivors of the holocaust are the ones best placed to judge the value of theological ideas. Hence, philosophers and theologians should be especially responsive to the needs of these survivors.[56]

Nevertheless, as Rubenstein is well aware, the theologian who has perhaps had the deepest impact upon Jewish thought in the post-holocaust era is Emil Fackenheim, whose insistence that traditional Jewish beliefs must be maintained has struck a deeply emotional chord with many Jews. For Fackenheim argues that if a Jew gives up his or her belief in Yahweh as a result of the holocaust, then Hitler will ultimately have been proven victorious. Rather, in the post-Auschwitz world, a new commandment (or, perhaps more accurately, a new cluster of commandments) has been discovered, thereby adding to the 613 recognized by traditional Judaism. Fackenheim declares:

> We are, first, commanded to survive as Jews, lest the Jewish people perish. We are commanded, second, to remember in our very guts and bones the martyrs of the holocaust, lest their memory perish. We are forbidden, thirdly, to deny or despair of God, however much we may have to contend with Him or with belief in Him, lest Judaism perish. We are forbidden, finally, to despair of the world as the place which is to become the kingdom of God lest we help make it a meaningless place in which God is dead or irrelevant and everything is permitted. To abandon any of these imperatives, in response to Hitler's victory at Auschwitz, would be to hand him yet another posthumous victory.[57]

Whereas Fackenheim has sought to defend the traditional conception of God, many Jewish theologians in the second half of the twentieth century, while simultaneously arguing for the retention of Judaism, nevertheless argued, as we have seen, for the rejection of the traditional view of an omnipotent being who acts directly in history. At the same time, many Christian theologians responded to the tangible evils of injustice and oppression by developing a new form of theology – liberation theology – which, while not denying the possibility that God might act in the world, emphasized the active part that believers should play in bringing about God's kingdom on earth. Perhaps ironically, given the developments in Jewish theology considered above, liberation theologians looked back to the accounts in the Hebrew Scriptures of God's intervention within history on behalf of the Israelites to support their claim that God favours the oppressed and marginalized.

Liberation theology

Liberation theology originated in the 1960s as a response to poverty, deprivation and political repression in Latin America. Despite its local origins, it quickly came to exert a global influence, achieving an extremely high profile worldwide. Moreover, it has not remained an exclusively Christian theology but has also appeared within Judaism and Islam, as well as within other major faiths. Liberation theologians, within whichever religion they are found, are united in the conviction that religion and politics must not be separated. The factors that led the first liberation theologians to this conviction were integral to the troubled social and political environment within which liberation theology originated.

It is no accident that liberation theology developed in Latin America at a time during which it is estimated that at least two-thirds of the population faced constant hunger. As is well known, the principal reason for this terrible situation was not that the continent lacked resources; it was rather that, then as now, the resources were under the control of a tiny proportion of the population. Thus, extreme poverty was endemic to the region. Impoverishment went hand in hand for many people with a lack of political rights, as the governing bodies of the region were constituted by a rich and powerful minority. Moreover, in some cases, the position of these governing bodies was maintained due to the policies of foreign governments, particularly that of the United States. It was within this bleak social and political environment that liberation theology developed, growing out of the reflection of the Christian poor on their social and political situation in the light of the Bible and their Christian faith. From these simple origins, liberation theology grew to challenge both national and international governments, as well as the Roman Catholic Church both locally and in Rome.[58]

Needless to say, the claim that liberation theology stemmed from the experience of the poor does require some clarification. After all, the really poor do not usually write theology. The explanation is that, in the 1950s, something quite unusual happened within Latin America. Small communities of economically poor and socially deprived people started to form with the intention of living according to Christian principles. These communities were inspired primarily by a passage in the Book of Acts which depicts one of the earliest Christian communities as sharing everything and, in consequence, ensuring that no real poverty was present within the community. So, in the mid-twentieth century, small communities sprang up with the intention of living like these early Christians. Such communities came to be known as 'base Christian communities'. And they were soon to have an extraordinary impact throughout much of the Christian world and beyond.

Because of a critical shortage of Roman Catholic priests in the area, people within these base Christian communities found that they were forced to interpret the Bible for themselves.[59] They began reading the Bible as if it specifically addressed their own social position – in other words, they began to read it politically. And the direct result of this was a revolutionized way of life. When, for example, they read passages about God's concern for the poor, they understood this concern personally. Moreover, they understood the New Testament prophecy 'The poor shall inherit the earth' quite literally. This style of biblical interpretation gave rise to a vivid sense among the poor that God was on their side rather than on the side of the rich Christian elite who enjoyed control of most of the wealth and power in the region.

Before long, these base communities were regarded by many as the Church of the Poor; the obvious connotation being that they were distinct from the 'Church of the Rich'. Consequently, issues concerning which 'Church' was the most authentically Christian soon arose. It was perhaps as a result of this debate about authenticity that some Latin American theologians became involved. These theologians elaborated on some of the insights of those who had formed the base Christian communities, and began to develop a new theology – one that was destined to make a huge impact on Christianity in Latin America, as well as in Western Europe, Africa and India.

The Peruvian theologian Gustavo Gutiérrez was the first to publish a version of liberation theology in a book that was simply entitled *A Theology of Liberation*;[60] a book that remains the most widely read text within the movement. The other principal text in the first phase of Christian liberation theology – *Jesus Christ Liberator*, by the Brazilian theologian Leonardo Boff – soon followed.[61] Both theologians share the same core presupposition: namely, that theology cannot, even in principle, be socially or politically neutral. In other words, it must serve either the poor or the rich. And Gutiérrez and Boff considered the life of Jesus to show that if one side had to be taken, then Christianity must side with the poor. Moreover, both argue that theology should serve the poor by providing them with the intellectual and spiritual resources that could contribute to the betterment of their social position. Latin American liberation theology is thus practical theology in the sense of attempting to offer a practical response to the experience of the poor and marginalized. Indeed, 'option for the poor' became the popular slogan expressing the chosen orientation of liberation theology.

In theologizing about poverty, Latin American liberation theologians were also concerned to expose the causes of poverty and oppression. This kind of theology sought, then, to raise awareness of the political assessment that poverty does not just occur spontaneously but is, rather, caused (or, at the very least, encouraged) by particular social, economic and political structures and institutions. Furthermore, liberation theologians accused mainstream Christianity, as it had come to be practised by the economically privileged within Latin America, of fostering precisely those structures and institutions that engendered poverty. In contrast to such a distorted form of Christianity, liberation theologians sought to promote what they regarded as a far more authentic form of Christianity: namely, one that was constituted by a way of life geared towards both material and spiritual liberation.

But liberation theology clearly does much more than promote a religiously inspired social programme; for it also proposes a new theological methodology within which hermeneutics plays a central part. Liberation theologians argue that when someone reflects upon his or her faith and upon God, that person does so from the standpoint that is afforded by his or her own experience. This implies, according to liberation theologians, that reflection on faith and on God by the poor and socially marginalized in Latin America is bound to lead to very different theological results from those obtained by the process of reflection conducted by relatively wealthy Europeans. The emphasis on hermeneutics within liberation theology was, clearly, heavily indebted to certain of the new theories of language that emerged during the twentieth century – specifically to those theories that stressed the centrality of interpretation to understanding, as well as the importance of the interpreter's cognitive environment (or 'horizon of understanding') within the process of understanding.[62] Liberation theologians also held that previous theology had gone astray in being too disengaged from the actual experience of most people, particularly the widespread experience of social disempowerment and political oppression. Only a theology that engaged with these kinds of experiences, they argued, could be relevant to the many, many Christians who were living in poverty within Latin America.

Liberation theologians also sought a new way of criticizing the elite living within the poorer countries, many of whom, while professing Christian faith, acted in ways that appeared to be in blatant contradiction to that faith. General Pinochet, the former military leader of Chile, is often cited as an example, for he is commonly regarded as one of the twentieth century's most notorious murderers, and is widely held to be responsible for the 'disappearance' of innumerable Chilean civilians. This notwithstanding, he was also a practising Roman Catholic, attending church regularly, and professing orthodox Roman Catholic beliefs. Liberation theologians refused to accept that, what they regarded as, such a radical disjunction between behaviour and belief was even plausibly compatible with any authentic form of Christianity. Hence, in their efforts to explain why such people should not be regarded as good Christians, despite their orthodox beliefs, liberation theologians came to value Christian *practice* or orthopraxy (right action, or action in accordance with faith) more highly than doctrinal orthodoxy.[63]

From the perspective of liberation theology, then, one problem with traditional theology was precisely its emphasis on orthodoxy rather than orthopraxy.[64] Because of that emphasis, traditional theologians lacked the religious grounds for criticizing those who acted in 'unchristian' ways as long as the perpetrators of such deeds held orthodox beliefs. And liberation theologians further claimed that, in failing to criticize such behaviour, traditional theology implicitly supports those orthodox believers who directly or indirectly contribute to the misery of others.

Liberation theology was clearly a unique development within Christian theology, and its uniqueness lay in its novel claim to be a theology that originated from the experience of the socially marginalized.[65] Traditionally, within Christianity at least, theology was the product of those who were socially privileged: namely, those members of the clergy who enjoyed the luxury of literacy, combined with relative wealth and the leisure that allows extended periods of study. The theology of the privileged was then handed down to the less privileged – specifically, the illiterate and the poor. Liberation theologians changed the face of theology worldwide by pointing to the connection between the theology of the socially privileged and the tendency of that theology to support, or at least not to challenge, the *status quo* within society. Additionally, they claimed that this theology had been dispensed to the poor and marginalized of society as if it were objective theology; whereas, far from being objective, it was actually premised upon the subjective standpoint of the privileged and dominant social group, with such theology functioning to support the very social structures and institutions through which the privileged are able to enjoy their benefits. For example, if the poor majority believe that they can expect justice in the next life, they will be more likely to accept their impoverished place in this life and correspondingly less likely to become politically active. By exposing the connections between certain theological ideas and behaviour within the political domain, liberation theologians strove to sever the link between theology and social privilege.

The notion that theology either supports the existing social structures or undermines them is often regarded as one of the central insights of the first liberation theologians. And this presupposition is also one of the reasons why liberation theology suffered such vigorous criticism from a number of quarters. On the one hand, the government of the United States took a very dim view of liberation theology because it seemed to be a direct challenge to that government's foreign policy. In exposing the socio-economic causes of poverty and oppression, liberation theologians found themselves criticizing the foreign policy of the United States. Many liberation theologians believed that this policy deliberately supported repressive regimes in Latin America to further the political and economic goals of the United States, and was thus responsible for many of the social and political problems experienced by the poor majority within Latin America.

On the other hand, the Roman Catholic authorities were also alarmed by the new social awareness associated with liberation theology. This was perhaps because, in advocating the cause of the poor, many of the clergy in Latin America became outspoken in their condemnation of the rich. And the rich were, of course, chiefly those with political power in the region. Certain of the leaders of the Roman Catholic Church thus perceived a threat to the Church's place within the Latin American establishment – an establishment within which it had long held significant vested interests. Furthermore, many of the rich and privileged in Latin America were also influential members of the Roman Catholic Church, and some Church leaders may have been very reluctant to offend their rich patrons.

At the same time, many critics of liberation theology claimed that it threatened to turn Christianity into the unwitting tool of Marxists – a criticism motivated by the extensive employment of Marxist philosophy within Gutiérrez's work. Indeed, Gutiérrez deployed Karl Marx's theory of history, as well as certain key Marxist concepts, to provide a theoretical framework within which to analyse and criticize social conditions and institutions. For example, he analysed poverty and underdevelopment in terms of the Marxist notion of worldwide class struggle. Moreover, Gutiérrez's account of the theological importance of the experience of the poor and marginalized rested upon a variant of Marxist epistemology.[66] Despite the fact that other liberation theologians did not rely exclusively on Marxist philosophy and social analysis, the purported connection between liberation theology and Marxism was enough to damn it decisively in the view of both the government of the United States and the Roman Catholic religious authorities within Europe.

At the same time as liberation theology faced mounting criticism, the political situation in many parts of Latin America deteriorated. The 1970s was a time of right-wing governments enjoying power throughout much of Latin America. Civilians in Nicaragua, El Salvador and Guatemala, for example, were terrorized by the so-called national security forces. Many priests, nuns, local church leaders and members of the base Christian communities were among their victims. Probably the most famous victim during this period was Archbishop Oscar Romero, who was gunned down on the steps of his cathedral in El Salvador on 24 March 1980. Romero was a high-profile martyr who had been outspoken in his support of indigenous peoples and the poor.[67] A few weeks before his assassination, he had written to President Carter requesting that the military aid from the United States to the Salvadorian government be withdrawn. The murder of Archbishop Romero secured liberation theology considerable media attention, effectively making its suppression impossible. From Latin America it spread to other parts of the world, notably to South Africa where many people were struggling against the racism of apartheid.[68] Liberation theology also began to exert a significant influence on other forms of theology, such as feminist theology and African theology, each of which was the product of a group of people – women and black Africans, respectively – who had previously been excluded, on the whole, from writing theology.

But perhaps the main legacy of liberation theology is to have popularized a political interpretation of the Bible, as well as the view that theology is integral to public life rather than merely concerned with individual salvation. The relevance of this legacy to other religious traditions did not go unnoticed. Given that the novelty of Christian liberation theology is to be located primarily in its reinterpretation of the Bible as stemming from the perspective of the poor, it is perhaps not surprising that liberation theology also emerged within the other Abrahamic faiths, given that they also possess sacred texts and are not short of poor followers.[69] So, let us turn to an example of Muslim liberation theology – a form of theology inspired by Christian liberation theology.

Farid Esack has developed what he calls a Qur'ānic theology of liberation.[70] Clarifying what he understands by 'liberation theology', Esack claims: 'A theology of liberation ... is one that works towards freeing religion from social, political and religious structures and ideas based on uncritical obedience and the freedom of all people from all forms of injustice and exploitation including those of race, gender, class and religion.'[71] This definition of liberation theology brings to the fore an idea that was, perhaps, not sufficiently emphasized by previous liberation theologians: namely, that religion itself may need to be liberated. In other words, not merely the oppressed of the world, but religion, too, needs to be freed from the control of the rich and powerful. Hence, Esack is also emphatic in his belief that religion can be co-opted by social, political and, indeed, 'religious' structures that make it collusive in oppression. But Esack is distinctive in arguing that one of the first tasks for a theology of liberation is to liberate religion, and part of that task consists in exposing the alliance between religion as co-opted and the privileged elites.

But, surely, one might object, liberation theology within any faith tradition must attend to this task – so what makes Esack's theology a distinctively *Islamic* theology of liberation? According to Esack, 'an Islamic liberation theology derives its inspiration from the Qur'ān and the struggles of all the prophets. It does so by engaging the Qur'ān and the examples of the prophets in a process of shared and ongoing theological reflection for ever-increasing liberative praxis.'[72] So, Esack claims that the crucial difference between Christian and Islamic liberation theology is that they are inspired by different sacred texts. This fact alone gives a distinctive flavour to these respective theologies. However, as Esack is well aware, it is not just a matter of which text is being interpreted by a theologian. The deeper issue concerns what guides a theologian's interpretation of the sacred text in question. This will be of crucial importance to a liberation theologian who, in rejecting much traditional theology as complicit in the co-option of the religion, must bypass many received understandings of the sacred text, as well as many of the theological concepts that have traditionally been employed to interpret it.[73] In short, a liberation theologian cannot avoid interpreting the Scripture anew in the context of a specific struggle for liberation. Moreover, according to Esack, such reinterpretation is justified by one of the central insights of all liberation theology: 'All theological categories, no matter how authentic an air has been afforded them by the passing of time, are always the product of ideology, history and seemingly apolitical reflections.'[74]

Given the need for new interpretations of the sacred text and of traditional theological concepts, what methodological principles should guide politically responsible interpretation? Esack argues that Islamic liberation theology should interpret the Qur'ān by means of six 'hermeneutical keys',[75] which, he explains, emerged from reflection on the Qur'ān and the Muslim tradition by those who were engaged in the struggle against the injustice of apartheid in South Africa. The hermeneutical keys are: *taqwa* (integrity and awareness in relation to the presence of God); *tawhid* (divine unity); *al-nas* (the people); *al-mustad'afun fi'l-ard* (the oppressed on the earth); *'adl* and *qist* (balance and justice) and *jihad* (struggle and praxis).[76] Esack claims that deploying these concepts in order to guide one's interpretation of the Qur'ān can lead Muslim liberation theologians towards an interpretation that draws out the resources of the sacred text for aiding the struggle against oppression and injustice. When the Qur'ān is read in the light of these hermeneutical keys, Esack claims, it becomes clear that the text 'singles out a particular section of humankind, the marginalized, and makes a conscious and deliberate option for them against neutrality and objectivity, on the one hand, and the powerful and oppressors, on the other'.[77]

Esack recognizes that Islamic liberation theology, as he has described it, is radically different in three respects from previous Islamic theologies. First, it emphasizes that, 'in conditions of oppression and marginalization, Islam can only truly be experienced as the liberative praxis of solidarity'.[78] Hence, liberation theology refuses to separate religious faith from the way one responds to the context within which one lives. One cannot, on this view, limit one's religious life to the narrow scope of personal piety. Rather, to experience religion genuinely, one must engage with others in actions that serve to alleviate the condition of the oppressed and marginalized. Second, unlike traditional theology, liberation theology recognizes that action comes first and theology second. Theological reflection must thus be driven by 'liberative praxis'.[79] This is clearly a radical departure from traditional Muslim theology, which, as in the Christian tradition, emphasized orthodoxy rather than orthopraxy. Finally, in contrast to traditional theology, liberation theology accepts that 'truth, for the engaged interpreter, cannot be absolute'.[80] And truth cannot be absolute because the circumstances in which one exercises 'liberative praxis' continuously change, which entails that the process of interpretation and theologizing will yield different results on different occasions and within different contexts. Nevertheless, '[a]s one's hermeneutic continuously moves on', writes Esack, 'one is pushed towards ever-increasing and authentic truth; truth which, in turn, leads to greater liberative praxis. There is no point at which God has disclosed the truth to the interpreter, but it continues to be disclosed, for there is no end to *jihad* and thus no end to His promise to disclose.'[81]

By the close of the twentieth century, Esack's theology had begun to exert a significant influence on a number of Islamic activists and scholars within the West, as well as in other parts of the world. The influence of his ideas can be clearly seen, for example, in a document produced by the Progressive Muslim Network (a group numbering Esack as one of its members), which defines 'Progressive Islam' as

> that understanding of Islam and its sources which comes from and is shaped within a commitment to transform society from an unjust one where people are mere objects of exploitation by governments, socio-economic institutions and unequal relationships. The new society will be a just one where people are the subjects of history, the shapers of their own destiny in the full awareness that all of humankind is in a state of returning to God and that the universe was created as a sign of God's presence.[82]

Wherever liberation theology is found, then, it espouses the same essential ideas: the option for the poor and marginalized; the necessity of re-interpreting the sacred text; and the claim that religion either aids or abets positive social change. As we shall now see, many of these themes are also present within another theological movement: namely, black theology, which developed at the same time and on the same continent as liberation theology.

Black theology

In the second half of the twentieth century, many people became increasingly disillusioned with social policies that aimed to further the goal of social integration by suppressing ethnic and cultural differences, for many had come to feel that, contrary to the integrationist's assumptions, ethnicity was uniquely important. This focus on ethnic identity was one of the motivations behind the emergence of the black theology movement: a movement that soon became prominent in the United States.[83] Whereas liberation theology had focused on the relevance of class to theology, black theology was fundamentally concerned, instead, with issues to do with race. Just as liberation theology viewed Christian theology as the preserve of a rich elite, black theology viewed it as the preserve of white Europeans and Anglo-Americans. Thus, the fundamental intellectual aim of the movement was, by promoting the contribution of black people to Christian theology, to address, and in some cases to reverse, the traditional domination of theological discourse by whites. And while the black theology movement enjoyed its heyday during the 1960s and 1970s, it remained significant throughout the rest of the twentieth century and into the third millennium.

The origin of the black theology movement in the United States was clearly linked with the rise in 'black consciousness' that occurred in North America during the 1960s – a time when the black liberation movement was an important social force. This was a period during which both the Christian minister, Martin Luther King, Jr (1929–68), and the Muslim leader, Malcolm X (1925–65),[84] were prominent political figures. While King argued for social justice for blacks and for non-violent resistance to oppression, Malcolm X argued for 'black power' consolidated within a Muslim community that would insist on its rights by force if need be. Both of these public figures met violent deaths: Malcolm X was assassinated in 1965 and King was assassinated in 1968. Followers of both Malcolm X and King had a huge impact on the internal politics of the United States from the 1960s onwards.

King's assassination, however, seems to have contributed to a widespread disenchantment with the non-violent approach he had espoused. Towards the end of the 1960s, then, the aggressive call to Islam associated with the late Malcolm X held considerable appeal for those in the young black community. Malcolm X, the son of a Christian minister, had argued powerfully that Christianity was a religion specifically for white people. It was the religion of the oppressor, he claimed, not of the oppressed. Thus, he urged blacks to abandon Christianity and embrace Islam.[85] The attraction of Islam was perhaps reinforced, for many blacks, by their own ambivalent attitude to Christianity, for many black Americans agreed with Malcolm X in regarding Christianity as the religion of the race who had stolen their cultural heritage and their identities by enslaving their ancestors and transporting them to an alien continent. Islam had no such connotations for the black community, and so, not surprisingly, to many it appeared a more attractive form of monotheism. Consequently, during the late 1960s, significant numbers of young blacks started to leave the Christian churches and join the Muslim community. Losing the youth to Islam made many black church leaders realize that they needed a stronger statement of black Christian identity – one to which the young could more easily relate. They agreed, to some extent, then, with Malcolm X's analysis of Christianity, but disagreed that the solution to the problem was to become Muslim. The challenge for black Christians was, therefore, to develop a distinctively black theology that could not legitimately be denounced as the religion of their oppressors.

In some ways, then, the origin of the black theology movement lies in the attempt of black church leaders to make themselves and their message both more attractive and more relevant to an increasingly disaffected young black population. Given the discrimination which blacks suffered in the United States and their experience of oppression, many black church leaders, clearly, felt that they could not simply stand by and allow

Malcolm X and his Muslim associates to appear as the only ones fighting for blacks on social and political issues. As a result, black theology became intimately linked with the burgeoning civil rights movement.

The first visible evidence of the emergence of a self-consciously black theology was the publication, in 1964, of Joseph Washington's *Black Religion*.[86] Washington argues that if you examine the religious practice and beliefs of black Christians in North America, then what you discover is that they subscribe to a quite distinctive 'black religion'. On the basis of this observation, he argued that there was an urgent need to integrate the theological insights of black people with the theology of the mainstream Protestant churches. Washington's call to integrate 'black theology' and 'white theology' was, however, rapidly superseded by the message of the next major publication in black theology: Albert Cleage's *Black Messiah*.[87] Cleage, pastor of the Shrine of the Black Madonna in Detroit, explicitly urged black Christians to liberate themselves from the oppression of white people's theology. In his view, any black theology that was written with the aim of integrating it with white theology could not meet the needs of the black Christian community. In short, he argued that the kind of theology advocated by Washington is one designed to be as acceptable as possible to whites while only paying lip-service to black interests, and not the sort of theology that is genuinely consistent with the experience of black Christians.

With the aim of placing Afro-American experience at the centre of black Christianity, Cleage proceeded to argue that the Bible was actually written by black Jews, and that the gospel was really that of the Black Messiah. He further claimed that the gospel had been perverted by St Paul in an attempt to make it acceptable to white Europeans. In reinterpreting the Christian tradition in this radical manner, the book became hugely influential among black-American Christians. And it was perceived by many as a clarion call for them, by seeking liberation from white oppression, to discover and assert their distinctive identity both as Christians and as blacks.

The theme of liberation was central to Cleage's theology, as it was for the many other black Christians who subsequently became involved in the black theology movement. In 1969, the National Committee of Black Churchmen issued a statement in which they emphasized the connection between black theology and black liberation:

> Black Theology is a theology of black liberation. It seeks to plumb the black condition in the light of God's revelation in Jesus Christ, so that the black community can see that the gospel is commensurate with the achievements of black humanity. Black Theology is a theology of 'blackness'. It is the affirmation of black humanity that emancipates black people from white racism, thus providing authentic freedom for

both white and black people. It affirms the humanity of white people in that it says No to the encroachment of white oppression.[88]

This statement was formulated at the time when the civil rights movement in the United States was beginning to disintegrate. And it marks a transition point, before which black theology was largely the product of pastors within the black community, and after which black theology became the preserve of academic theologians primarily based in seminaries.

Thus, the 1970s saw black theology enter a period of exceptional creativity. Theological analyses of liberation, oppression and the reality of suffering came to the forefront of concern. The leading figure in this second phase in the development of black theology was James Cone, whose book, *A Black Theology of Liberation*,[89] proved to be hugely influential, and established his stature as the academic guru of black theology. The next generation of theologians involved in the black theology movement were mainly taught by Cone, and much of their work is a continuation of his.

Cone's central idea was that God was deeply concerned about, and directly involved with, the black struggle for liberation. Like the Latin American liberation theologians, Cone draws attention to Jesus' preference for the oppressed and his identification with them. On the basis of this, in what is perhaps his most polemical theological claim, Cone, following Cleage, describes Jesus as the 'Black Messiah'. But by this, Cone did not mean to imply that Jesus was biologically black. Rather, the suggestion is that he is a sort of honorary black. For a parallel reason, Cone declares that God is black.

Despite the appeal of Cone's theology to black-American Christians, it was not without its critics. Some complained that it was premised upon an uncritical and, hence, unacceptable, attitude to the Bible.[90] Cone was undoubtedly not alone among black Christians in reading the Hebrew Scriptures and the New Testament as if they offered a direct description of the black experience in the modern world. But this approach meant, in practice, that no effort was made to understand the historical context of particular passages in the Bible. And the perceived similarity between the oppression recounted in the Bible[91] and that experienced by modern Afro-Americans led Cone to conclude that it must have been written by blacks for the benefit of blacks. But in the view of several scholars, Cone's reluctance to take cognizance of the historical-critical methods of reading and interpreting the biblical texts that had by then become standard among academics made his theological conclusions seem unsubstantiated. Black theologians who came after Cone have attempted to rectify this.[92]

Black theology, then, like Latin American liberation theology, claims that the experience of oppression suffered by a particular group of marginalized people should be regarded as a religious experience and, hence, as theologically relevant. Both black theology and liberation theology emphasize that theology must respond to the needs of oppressed individuals and communities. But in concentrating exclusively on humans and on the specific problems they encounter, both of these theological movements, some have argued, miss something of vital importance. In an age that many had come to regard as one of growing environmental crisis, theologies that focus exclusively on the liberation of humans have been sharply criticized for only attending to part of the problem. The final variety of theology that we examine in this chapter – eco-theology – claims to incorporate the insights of earlier theologies while also addressing broader environmental concerns.

Eco-theology

One of the most significant political issues of the late twentieth century was, undoubtedly, the degradation of the environment. The deleterious changes observed in the natural world, particularly in the second half of the century, were a direct consequence of the development of industrial societies during the modern period. By the end of the century, the extent of the impact of modern humans upon the environment had reached such proportions that many were persuaded that our planet was heading towards an environmental crisis. Symptoms of such a crisis are commonly thought to include the critical depletion of non-renewable resources, anthropogenic pollution (which appears to be changing the chemical balance of the planet's atmosphere, and which could result in global warming that, in turn, might melt the polar icecaps and raise sea levels), depletion of the ozone layer (which protects the earth from dangerous levels of ultra-violet radiation), and the loss of genuine wilderness areas on the planet, which has led to an accelerating loss of biodiversity. Furthermore, all of these symptoms are exacerbated by the human population explosion. By the end of the twentieth century, many had come to believe that this situation posed an immediate threat to the continuation of life on the planet.[93] Given the possible magnitude of this threat, it is not surprising that religious thinkers from each of the Abrahamic faiths felt the need to address some of these issues.[94] The result was eco-theology, which consists in an attempt to develop a theology that can respond to the environmental crisis.

Many people have argued that a typically Western attitude to the natural world lies at the root of the environmental crisis: specifically, an attitude shaped by the Judaeo-Christian tradition. Lynn White first drew attention to a connection between the ecological crisis and the Western religious tradition in an article published in 1967.[95] White lays much of the blame for the crisis on the Judaeo-Christian creation myths, which have often been read as depicting God to have endowed humans with the right to dominate and subdue a natural world whose only value is to provide for human needs. White argues that it was this aspect of the religious tradition more than any other single factor that encouraged humans to exploit and, ultimately, degrade the planet. Thus, if we are to deal adequately with the environmental crisis, he avers, we must fundamentally change the view of the natural world that has caused that crisis. In other words, we must change those religious beliefs that have shaped the view of nature dominant within Western culture. Because the environmental crisis was caused by religion, the solution to it must, he argues, be a religious one. Any other 'solution', White claims, will merely address isolated aspects of the environmental problem and not its root cause, and thus will fail to prevent the looming crisis.[96]

But how should religious beliefs be altered? White does not claim that new, environmentally friendly religious beliefs should be invented, but rather that they are already latent within the Western religious tradition. His religious solution to the environmental crisis consists, then, in emphasizing those beliefs – embedded within the tradition – that encourage people to think and act in ways that do not damage the environment, while de-emphasizing ways of thinking and acting that do contribute to the degradation of the environment. In particular, those elements of the tradition that portray nature as spiritual, rather than as material, hold the key to a new, environmentally benign form of Western religion. For, according to White, if people were to regard nature as spiritual, they would come to believe that it possesses intrinsic value. And once they accept this belief, they will cease to treat the natural world as merely instrumental to their needs. In short, they will give up their environmentally destructive behaviour.

By questioning previously accepted ideas about its causes, White challenged many people's perceptions of the environmental crisis. Prior to the publication of his article, most people who thought about the problem had believed that the solution lay in a better, more efficient use of resources. They had concentrated on particular aspects of the crisis and how they might be solved, without looking at the problem holistically. When White argued that the basic cause of the crisis lay in our fundamental attitudes to nature, he encouraged people to look at the problem as a whole, and as requiring a comprehensive solution.[97] Interestingly, White does not claim that the whole Christian tradition is inherently inconsistent with a benign relationship with the natural world, for he explicitly proposes St Francis of Assisi as a model for an alternative Christian tradition. His criticism is, rather, that the main form that the Christian tradition has taken espouses a dominating attitude towards the natural world, and this has principally shaped the Western European view of nature. Moreover, it is a view that appears to endorse environmental exploitation.

However, critics of White have argued that it is highly implausible to place all the blame for the environmental crisis on a major strand within the Judaeo-Christian tradition, given that humans were dramatically altering their environment long before this particular religious tradition came to prominence within the Western world. But it is worth noting that White was not claiming that all environmental damage was the fault of Jewish and Christian beliefs; merely that these beliefs were peculiarly well suited to justifying environmental exploitation.

White convinced many that Judaeo-Christian attitudes to nature had, at the very least, contributed to the laying waste of our environment. And some theologians, in regarding White's analysis as basically correct, therefore felt that the situation called for a serious response by religious thinkers.[98] Many Jewish and Christian theologians thus began to consider the theology of their traditions from the perspective of its potential effect on the environment. They looked back over the theologies developed in the previous 300–400 years, and noticed an extraordinary omission. During the critical time when the face of the planet had been changing to an unprecedented degree due to human activities, religious thought had been exclusively concerned with the salvation of individuals and the health of religious communities. There had been no interest at all in the future of the planet, or in the fate of the non-humans that share it with us. In short, the planet, insofar as it was noticed at all by earlier theologians, was simply perceived as the stage for human salvation. Because theologians had been exclusively preoccupied with spiritual and with other-worldly concerns, the understanding of the natural world had been left to scientists, who quickly developed a mechanical conception of nature. This mechanistic view of the natural world went hand in hand with the view that nature lacks intrinsic value. The natural world was thus perceived to have value only insofar as it was useful to humans. In keeping with this view, non-human animals were also regarded as machines lacking souls, as well as any capacity for thought and feeling. If they had any value, it was exclusively instrumental.

By way of a response, a number of books appeared in the 1970s and 1980s that endorsed what, in the context of Christianity, came to be called 'creation theology'. One aspect of traditional Christian theology that eco-theologians thus brought into question was its exclusive emphasis on individual human salvation. According to Christianity, each individual human being had been created in the image of God. This was a radical departure from the Jewish belief that the whole people – as a community – was God's people. In short, it seemed that Christianity had promoted individualism in religious matters, and that this had led to a strong current of individualism within society. Indeed, individualism was emphasized by both Luther and Calvin during the Reformation. Within Protestant territories immediately after the Reformation, there appears to have been a marked change in society away from more communal, traditional forms of social organization, and towards more individual patterns of life – a shift that has been linked with the origins of capitalism. And capitalism, of course, with its emphasis on uninhibited economic growth, appears to be one of the main causes of the current state of the environment.

Once theologians became sensitized to these issues, many of them began to accord the notion of creation more prominence in their work. As White had advocated, rather than presupposing that the natural world only possesses value insofar as it is instrumental to the meeting of human needs, some theologians instead drew attention to the value with which God had endowed creation. And they did so by emphasizing, far more than had previous Christian thinkers, the idea of the supposedly *ongoing* action of the Holy Spirit within creation. These theologians pointed out that, according to Christian belief, God did not merely create the natural world and then step back in order to let it run its course unaided by any ongoing divine care. For this would be a deist view, not a Christian one. Instead, according to Christianity, God sent the Holy Spirit into the world so that the divine presence would remain within creation. Previous Western theologians had failed to emphasize this idea sufficiently because they had linked the Spirit within their conceptuality too closely to Christ, the result being that the action of the Spirit was thought to be limited to wherever Christ was actually present. This seemed to entail that, as Christ came to be thought of as exclusively present within the Church, the Spirit was present and, hence, active only within the Church. By, so to speak, releasing the Spirit from its confinement within the Church, theologians were able to portray God's involvement in the natural world as much more intimate than had formerly been possible. The entire natural world could now be seen as subject to the action of the Holy Spirit.

As we have noted, many late twentieth-century Christian theologians came to challenge the view that salvation only concerns human beings. Instead, given that they had come to see nature as infused with the Spirit, some proposed that a more accurate conception of salvation would include the whole of creation. Jürgen Moltmann, in particular, has argued for a more holistic view of salvation,[99] suggesting that the culmination, or completion, of God's plan for the world will involve the renewal of all creation. In this way, Moltmann regards the whole of creation, and not just humans, as having significance within God's providential plan. Moreover, a further reason for regarding nature as being far more important than previous theologians had assumed is because the kingdom of God will not, in Moltmann's view, be a kingdom of disembodied souls but rather a kingdom of embodied people living in a physical world.[100]

Taking their cue from White, then, theologians such as Moltmann have argued that to understand the Judaeo-Christian Scriptures as endorsing an exploitative use of the natural world is to have a very partial construal of what these sacred texts actually say. Furthermore, eco-theologians insist that the Scriptures are quite explicit in asserting that creation belongs to God alone, as well as in claiming that humans are only one part of God's creation – a part, moreover, that, according to the Book of Genesis, is made directly out of the earth. Nevertheless, while eco-theologians have sought to change our perception of nature to one that accords it far greater value, they have still insisted that humans occupy a special place within creation. For notwithstanding our affinity with the rest of the natural world, humans are made, according to Christian belief, in the image of God. And eco-theologians have deployed this tenet of Christian thought in order to identify the special role that humans must be deemed to play in the natural world.

In a nutshell, eco-theologians have pointed out that being made in the image of God has certain responsibilities attached to it. Some of these responsibilities are to the rest of the world that God has created. On this view, any claim by humans to possess, and have mastery over, the world, is idolatrous because it seeks to put humans in the place of God. Consequently, eco-theologians have argued that the role of humans within nature should, on a balanced Christian view, consist in assuming a certain responsibility for creation and for ensuring that God's will for all creatures is respected. The paradigm of the role that humans should play within nature is found within the story in Genesis that portrays the first human couple as tending the Garden of Eden. Humans ought to continue in the role that God had originally assigned to humanity: namely, that of stewards of the natural world. Thus, the concept 'stewardship' has come to occupy a central place within eco-theology, with a steward or a stewardess being regarded as a co-worker with God in creation. In short, the steward or stewardess is there to implement God's will, not to serve his or her own ends. Hence, the natural world is not an object for humans to dominate and exploit, but rather a valuable garden to be lavished with loving care.

Eco-theologians have also deployed the well-known biblical stories concerning the Fall and the Tower of Babel in order to reorientate human attitudes to nature. The former story is portrayed as illustrating the terrible consequences that ensue when humanity oversteps its limits, and reaches out for knowledge which it is not supposed to possess. The latter story is interpreted as depicting what happens when humanity develops technology beyond what is required to fulfil the role of God's steward on earth. The problem in each case, eco-theologians have argued, is not knowledge and technology *per se*, but rather that humans often attempt to use them in order to usurp God's role as the ultimate authority within creation. And, the argument proceeds, it is precisely this that has brought us to the environmental crisis we now face.

This notion of responsible stewardship has been used by ecologically minded Christians as the criterion by which to measure the acceptability of certain economic and social proposals for responding to the environmental crisis. For a genuine steward would, first of all, inquire of any proposal whether it would be in accordance with the true owner's will – in this case, God's. And that would involve assessing the proposal from the standpoint of its effect upon the whole of creation rather than upon just a small part of it – namely, that of exclusively human interests. The responsible steward would also be critical of policies that undermined the long-term viability of the land, such as those that are motivated by a desire for economic growth pursued for its own sake. So, the notion of stewardship can be readily employed to provide an alternative perspective from which to criticize views that formerly went unchallenged by theologians: for example, the view that any economic development is always good, and that the worth of things can be measured solely in terms of their cash value.

Conclusion

In this chapter we have considered a wide range of theological movements that have responded to political events or issues that were highly significant in the twentieth century. As a result of these movements, political considerations are now well and truly embedded within religious thought. And each of these movements has already had a profound affect upon the way that many adherents of the Abrahamic faiths think about God and their faith. For example, the new vision of what theology is – or should become – as propounded by liberation theologians has already had an enormous impact on other theological movements. In particular, it has paved the way for feminist theology – a movement we discuss in the next chapter. And in the case of eco-theology, there has been a major reassessment of the theological significance of the natural world. Each of these movements is likely to have a continuing impact well into the twenty-first century; and if the environmental crisis continues to worsen, as many expect, then eco-theology is especially likely to grow in importance. We return to certain aspects of eco-theology in the next chapter, when we consider the ecofeminist theology developed by theologians concerned with both feminism and the environment.

Study questions

1 What reasons might someone give for the claim that the separation between religion and politics currently prevalent in most parts of the West is a positive development? Do you find these reasons persuasive?

2 What are some of the ways in which religious beliefs and values have impinged on the political realm in the West in recent times?

3 How is twentieth-century political theology different from earlier forms of theology? In what ways might the theological perspective it offers make a valuable contribution to religious thought in the new millennium?

4 Do you agree with Richard Rubenstein that the conception of God as the omnipotent author of all historical events has become untenable for those living after the holocaust? Which conception of God, if any, might serve to replace the old one?

5 What do liberation theologians mean by the claim that theology cannot, even in principle, be socially or politically neutral? How might their claim be criticized? How strong are the criticisms?

6 Farid Esack has argued that Islamic liberation theologians should interpret the Qur'ān by means of six 'hermeneutical keys'. If you were to apply this approach to the Jewish or the Christian Scriptures, what hermeneutical keys would you propose?

7 Can 'black theology' provide white Christians with any theological insights? Is it reasonable to expect that it would?

8 In what ways might eco-theology contribute to a lessening of the environmental crisis? Should religious thinkers prioritize the development of such theologies or are there other forms of religious thought more urgently required today?

Select bibliography

Birnbaum, D., 1989, *God and Evil: A Jewish Perspective*, New Jersey: Ktav.

Boff, L., 1980, *Jesus Christ Liberator: A Critical Christology of Our Time*, London: SPCK.

Cobb, J. B., 1995, *Is It Too Late? A Theology of Ecology*, revised edition, Denton: Environmental Ethics Books.

Cohn-Sherbok, D., 1991, *Issues in Contemporary Judaism*, London: Macmillan.

Cone, J. H., 1970, *A Black Theology of Liberation*, Philadelphia: Lippincott.

Esack, F., 1997, *Qur'ān, Liberation & Pluralism: An Islamic Perspective on Interreligious Solidarity Against Oppression*, Oxford: Oneworld.

Fackenheim, E., 1982, *To Mend the World: Foundations for Future Jewish Thought*, New York: Schocken Books.

Griffith-Dickson, G., 2000, *Human and Divine: An Introduction to the Philosophy of Religious Experience*, London: Duckworth.

Gutiérrez, G., 1985, *A Theology of Liberation: History, Politics and Salvation*, London: SCM Press.

Lewis, B., 1993, *Islam and the West*, New York: Oxford University Press.

Mackie, J. L., 'Evil and Omnipotence', *Mind*, 64 (1955), pp. 200–12.

Metz, J. B., 1980, *Faith in History and Society*, New York: Seabury Crossroad.

Moltmann, J., 1985, *God in Creation: An Ecological Doctrine of Creation*, trans. by Margaret Kohl, New York: HarperSanFrancisco.

Moltmann, J., 1999, *God for a Secular Society: The Public Relevance of Theology*, Minneapolis: Fortress Press.

Rubenstein, R. L., 1966, *After Auschwitz: Radical Theology and Contemporary Judaism*, Indianapolis: Bobbs-Merrill Company.

Rubenstein, R. L. and J. K. Roth, 1987, *Approaches to Auschwitz: The Legacy of the Holocaust*, London: SCM Press.

Safi, O. (ed.), *Progressive Muslims: On Justice, Gender, and Pluralism*, Oxford: Oneworld.

White, L., 1996, 'The Historical Roots of Our Ecological Crisis' in Roger S. Gottlieb (ed.), *This Sacred Earth: Religion, Nature, Environment*, New York: Routledge, pp. 184–93.

Notes

1 See, for example, Edward Norman, 1992, 'Christian Politics in a Society of Plural Values' in Dan Cohn-Sherbok and David McLellan (eds), *Religion in Public Life*, London and Basingstoke: Macmillan, pp. 17–28.

2 See, for example, Keith Ward, 1992, 'Is a Christian State a Contradiction?' in Cohn-Sherbok and McLellan, *Religion*, pp. 5–16.

3 We should note, however, that by the 'sanctity of life' Christians usually mean the sanctity of *human* life. For few of them are vegetarian.

4 Muslim schoolgirls wearing head-coverings and Sikh boys wearing traditional Sikh headgear are cases in point.

5 See George Moyser (ed.), 1991, *Politics and Religion in the Modern World*, London and New York: Routledge.

6 See MaryAnne Perkins, 1999, *Nation and Word, 1770–1850: Religious and Metaphysical Language in European National Consciousness*, Aldershot: Ashgate.

7 See p. 83.

8 Rawls: 'When an authoritative, salvationist, and expansionist religion like medieval Christianity divides, this inevitably means the appearance within the same society of a rival authoritative and salvationist religion, different in some ways from the original religion from which it split off, but having for a certain period of time many of the same features. Luther and Calvin were as dogmatic and intolerant as the Roman Church had been.' John Rawls, 1996, *Political Liberalism*, New York: Columbia University Press, p. xxv.

9 Rawls, *Political*, p. xxvi.

10 Rawls, *Political*, p. xxvi.

11 Bernard Lewis, 1993, *Islam and the West*, New York: Oxford University Press, p. 179.

12 Lewis, *Islam*, p. 179.

13 See Lewis, *Islam*, chapter 11.

14 Matthew 22.21b, NRSV.

15 Modern countries in which Muslims form a majority have not typically comprised secular liberal democracies. Nevertheless, in the late nineteenth as well as the twentieth century, many Muslim intellectuals argued that the Qur'ān advocates democracy in enjoining that political decisions be made through con-

sensus. A key text cited as evidence of this is Sura 42.38 in which Allah approves of those whose affairs are decided by mutual consultation.

16 George Washington's letter to the Hebrew congregation in Newport, Rhode Island. Reprinted in David Goldenberg (ed.), 1988, *To Bigotry No Sanction: Documents in American Jewish History*, Philadelphia: Annenberg Research Institute, pp. 57–9. The American Bill of Rights, which claims to defend religious freedom by a commitment to the separation of religion and state, was proposed in 1789 and ratified in 1791. Unfortunately, the Bill did not succeed in eliminating prejudice (consider, for example, its failure to protect the rights of indigenous peoples to practise their various religions). Moreover, despite the assurances of George Washington and the ratification of the Bill, anti-Semitism persisted in the United States well into the modern era. For a graphic portrayal of anti-Semitism in the post-Second World War United States, see the film *Gentleman's Agreement* (directed by Elia Kazan, 1947, USA). Gregory Peck stars as a writer who, in order to get an 'angle' for a feature on anti-Semitism, poses as a Jew for several weeks. The character played by Peck rapidly experiences the various forms taken by an invidious and ubiquitous anti-Semitism.

17 These estimates are by the Peace Pledge Union, a British non-governmental organization.

18 The *World Almanac* for 1901 estimates that 66.81 per cent of the European population were monotheists, whereas the *World Almanac* for 1953 puts that figure at an estimated 87.95 per cent.

19 See, for example, Johann Baptist Metz, 1980, *Faith in History and Society*, New York: Seabury Crossroad.

20 Jürgen Moltmann, 1999, *God for a Secular Society: The Public Relevance of Theology*, Minneapolis: Fortress Press, p. 57.

21 Moltmann, *God*, p. 57.

22 Moltmann, *God*, pp. 57f.

23 Moltmann, *God*, p. 58.

24 Moltmann, *God*, p. 58.

25 Moltmann, *God*, p. 60.

26 Several important films vividly acquaint many who were born after the Second World War with the horrors of the period. See, for example, *Sophie's Choice* (directed by Alan J. Pakula, 1982, USA); *Schindler's List* (directed by Steven Spielberg, 1993, USA); and *The Pianist* (directed by Roman Polanski, 2002, France, Germany, UK and Poland). For a cinematic portrayal of the outbreak of the overt manifestations of anti-Semitism that ultimately led to the genocide, see *Jew Boy Levi* (directed by Didi Danquart, 1998, Germany). The novels of the Italian author, and survivor of Auschwitz, Primo Levi (1919–87) have also contributed to an awareness of this period on the part of later generations.

27 See Jacob Neusner, 1995, *Judaism in Modern Times: An Introduction and Reader*, Cambridge, Massachusetts: Blackwell.

28 For a comprehensive account of these movements, see Neusner, *Judaism*. Two other forms of Judaism that emerged in the twentieth century were Reconstructionist Judaism and Humanist Judaism. These movements resembled Zionism, Jewish Socialism and Yiddishism in rejecting the Judaism of the dual Torah, but they were not overtly political.

29 See Neusner, *Judaism*, chapter 5.

30 For example, by the Zionist writer Ahad HaAm. See Neusner, *Judaism*, p. 160.

31 Neusner, *Judaism*, p. 164.

32 Amos Elon, 1971, *The Israelis: Founders and Sons*, New York: Holt, Rinehart & Winston, p. 39.

33 Richard Rubenstein, whose theology we consider in the following section, writes: 'Death and rebirth are the great moments of religious experience. In the twentieth century the Jewish phoenix has known both: in Germany and in eastern Europe, we Jews have tasted the bitterest and the most degrading of deaths. Yet death was not the last word. ... Death in Europe was followed by resurrection in our ancestral home.' Richard L. Rubenstein, 1966, *After Auschwitz: Radical Theology and Contemporary Judaism*, Indianapolis: Bobbs-Merrill Company, p. 128; see, also, chapter 7 and p. 141. Although, as Rubenstein himself admits, as time went on, he, like many of his contemporaries, became less sanguine about the religious value of the State of Israel. See the autobiographical note on p. 130.

34 See Neusner, *Judaism*, chapter 8.

35 Although there is a huge amount of support for the State of Israel on the part of Jews who do not reside there, it would be a mistake to view their support as a form of Zionism, because many of them disagree with one of Zionism's key principles: the necessity of immigration into the State of Israel. See Neusner, *Judaism*, p. 215.

36 Neusner, *Judaism*, pp. 126f.

37 For a comprehensive discussion of the problem of evil and an analysis of some of the responses to it that have been developed by thinkers within a range of religious traditions, see Gwen Griffith-Dickson, 2000, *Human and Divine: An Introduction to the Philosophy of Religious Experience*, London: Duckworth, Part III.

38 Rubenstein, *After*, pp. ix–x.

39 See Friedrich Nietzsche, 2001, *The Gay Science: With a Prelude in German Rhymes and an Appendix of Songs*, Cambridge: Cambridge University Press, sections 108 and 125.

40 Rubenstein, *After*, p. 151.

41 See, for example, Rubenstein, *After*, pp. 65 and 153.

42 Rubenstein, *After*, p. 69.

43 Rubenstein, *After*, p. 68. See, also, p. 119.

44 Rubenstein, *After*, p. 119.

45 See Rubenstein, *After*, pp. 152f.

46 Rubenstein, *After*, p. 68.

47 Rubenstein, *After*, p. 122.

48 Rubenstein, *After*, p. 136.

49 Mackie provided what many in the twentieth century came to regard as the paradigmatic statement of the 'problem of evil'. See J. L. Mackie, 'Evil and Omnipotence', *Mind*, 64 (1955), pp. 200–12.

50 Interestingly, it has been claimed that those who have suffered evil tend to find the theologians' response to the problem of evil more relevant to their lives than that of analytic philosophers. See Michael Levine, 'Contemporary Christian Analytic Philosophy of Religion: Biblical Fundamentalism; Terrible

Solutions to a Horrible Problem; and Hearing God', *International Journal for Philosophy of Religion*, 48 (2000), pp. 89–119.

51 David Birnbaum, 1989, *God and Evil: A Jewish Perspective*, New Jersey: Ktav, p. xx.

52 Birnbaum, *God*, p. 54.

53 Birnbaum, *God*, p. 54.

54 Birnbaum, *God*, p 159.

55 See Griffith-Dickson, *Human*, p. 191.

56 See Richard L. Rubenstein and John K. Roth, 1987, *Approaches to Auschwitz: The Legacy of the Holocaust*, London: SCM Press, chapter 10.

57 Emil Fackenheim, 1982, *To Mend the World: Foundations for Future Jewish Thought*, New York: Schocken Books, p. 13.

58 It should be noted, of course, that liberation theology developed within communities that were Roman Catholic rather than Protestant. Indeed, during this period, a large majority of Latin American Christians were Roman Catholic.

59 This process was probably facilitated by the decision of Vatican Council II to allow the Bible to be read in vernacular languages during Roman Catholic religious ceremonies rather than in Latin.

60 Gustavo Gutiérrez, 1985, *A Theology of Liberation: History, Politics and Salvation*, London: SCM Press. This was published in Lima in 1971, and the first English edition appeared in 1974.

61 Leonardo Boff, 1980, *Jesus Christ Liberator: A Critical Christology of Our Time*, London: SPCK.

62 See Chapter 5.

63 One text in the New Testament that many take to justify prioritizing action in accordance with faith over mere orthodox belief is Matthew 25.

64 See, for example, Boff, *Jesus*, pp. 46f.

65 The uniqueness of liberation theology notwithstanding, many of the themes that it considers important seem to have some historical precedent in the 'social gospel movement' – an early twentieth-century Protestant movement that was influential in the United States until about 1930. For a perceptive account of the theology of the social gospel movement, see William McGuire King, 1991, 'An Enthusiasm for Humanity: The Social Emphasis in Religion and its Accommodation in Protestant Theology' in Michael J. Lacey (ed.), *Religion & Twentieth-century American Intellectual Life*, Cambridge: Cambridge University Press, pp. 49–77.

66 For a concise account of the form of Marxist epistemology that seems to have been presupposed by Gutiérrez, see Alison M. Jaggar, 1983, *Feminist Politics and Human Nature*, Brighton: The Harvester Press, pp. 358ff.

67 Romero's life and martyrdom are celebrated in the film *Romero* (directed by John Duigan, 1989, USA).

68 The 'Kairos document' was composed by South African Christian activists, and stands as a powerful testament to the impact of liberation theology upon them. See 'The Kairos Document' reprinted in David McLellan (ed.), 1997, *Political Christianity: A Reader*, London: SPCK, pp. 120–5.

69 For one example of the Jewish appropriation of liberation theology, see Dan Cohn-Sherbok, 1991, *Issues in Contemporary Judaism*, London: Macmillan, pp. 107–27.

70 See Farid Esack, 1997, *Qur'ān, Liberation & Pluralism: An Islamic Perspective on Interreligious Solidarity Against Oppression*, Oxford: Oneworld. Esack developed his views during his involvement in the struggle against apartheid in his native South Africa.

71 Esack, *Qur'ān*, p. 83.

72 Esack, *Qur'ān*, p. 83.

73 See Esack, *Qur'ān*, p. 84.

74 Esack, *Qur'ān*, p. 85.

75 See Esack, *Qur'ān*, chapter 3.

76 Esack, *Qur'ān*, p. 83.

77 Esack, *Qur'ān*, p. 97. Cf. Sura 107.1–3.

78 Esack, *Qur'ān*, p. 110.

79 Esack, *Qur'ān*, p. 110.

80 Esack, *Qur'ān*, p. 111. Note the convergence between Esack's view and that of Fazlur Rahman, which we considered in Chapter 5. Moreover, like Esack, Rahman believes that 'the basic élan of the Qur'an' is 'the stress on socioeconomic justice and essential human egalitarianism'. Fazlur Rahman, 1982, *Islam and Modernity: Transformation of an Intellectual Tradition*, Chicago: The University of Chicago Press, p. 19.

81 Esack, *Qur'ān*, p. 111.

82 'Progressive Islam – A Definition and Declaration' cited in Farid Esack, 2003, 'In Search of Progressive Islam Beyond 9/11' in O. Safi (ed.), *Progressive Muslims: On Justice, Gender, and Pluralism*, Oxford: Oneworld, p. 80.

83 At the same time as this form of theology was developing, other ethnic groups in the United States also began to elaborate distinctive theologies. Native American Christian theology is a case in point. See, for example, Vine Deloria, Jr, 1973, *God is Red: A Native View of Religion*, New York: Grosset & Dunlap.

84 Malcolm X is known to Muslims as El-Hajj Malik El-Shabazz. His conversion from Christianity to Islam, and his subsequent activities on behalf of his new faith, have been sensitively portrayed in the film *Malcolm X* (directed by Spike Lee, 1992, USA).

85 He did so by encouraging young blacks to join an organization called the 'Nation of Islam'. This movement was founded by Elijah Muhammad (1897–1975), and, for a time at least, united black Muslims under one banner.

86 Joseph Washington, 1966, *Black Religion*, Boston: Beacon Press.

87 Albert B. Cleage, 1969, *The Black Messiah*, New York: Sheed and Ward.

88 Extract from the Statement by the National Committee of Black Churchmen, 13 June 1969. Reprinted in G. S. Wilmore and James H. Cone (eds), 1979, *Black Theology: A Documentary History, 1966–1979*, New York: Orbis, pp. 100–2.

89 James H. Cone, 1970, *A Black Theology of Liberation*, Philadelphia: Lippincott.

90 Cone was also criticized for being insufficiently sensitive to the special issues that face black women. In the final decades of the twentieth century, women constituted an estimated two-thirds of the black Christians in the United States. Cone failed to realize that a black theology developed by males might not adequately meet the needs of these women, who often suffer oppression not

only from whites but also from black males. To counter this perceived deficiency in Cone's original theology, black women theologians developed what has been termed 'womanist theology', with Jacquelyn Grant becoming one of the most prominent of the womanist theologians. See, for example, Jacquelyn Grant, 1989, *White Woman's Christ and Black Women's Jesus: Feminist Christology and Womanist Response*, Atlanta: Scholars Press. Womanist theology has been characterized as playing the same role within the black Christian community that feminist theology plays within the white Christian community. Despite this similarity in function, it would, nevertheless, be a mistake to regard womanist theology and feminist theology as equivalent.

91 Consider, for example, the account in the Hebrew Scriptures of the Israelites' slavery in Egypt, and their ultimate rescue by divine intervention.

92 See, for example, Robert A. Bennett, 1989, 'Black Experience and the Bible' in G. S. Wilmore (ed.), *African American Religious Studies*, Durham: Duke University Press, p. 130.

93 For one account of the extent of the environmental problem, see Alan Carter, 1999, *A Radical Green Political Theory*, London: Routledge, pp. 2–19.

94 The following focuses principally on the development of eco-theology by Christian thinkers. However, most of the issues these thinkers address are of equal concern to Jews and Muslims. For one Muslim perspective on the theological and philosophical issues raised by the new environmental awareness, see Seyyed Hossein Nasr, 1990, *Man and Nature: The Spiritual Crisis in Modern Man*, London: Mandala Unwin Paperbacks. And for a Jewish one, see Sherwin Wine, 1995, *Judaism Beyond God*, New York: KTAV.

95 Lynn White, 1996, 'The Historical Roots of Our Ecological Crisis' in Roger S. Gottlieb (ed.), *This Sacred Earth: Religion, Nature, Environment*, New York: Routledge, pp. 184–93.

96 See White, 'Historical', p. 186.

97 Green political parties and other environmental movements were later to develop more comprehensive policies, rather than simply treat the environment as a special interest group concern, as the mainstream parties had done. Moreover, it became increasingly common for members of the wider public to argue that it was necessary to change fundamentally our lifestyles rather than simply tinker with minimizing the level of certain pollutants in the atmosphere and re-distributing resources within the old political and economic framework.

98 One of the first theologians to address environmental issues seriously, and formulate a theological response to them, was John B. Cobb. See John B. Cobb, 1995, *Is It Too Late? A Theology of Ecology*, revised edition, Denton: Environmental Ethics Books.

99 See, for example, Jürgen Moltmann, 1985, *God in Creation: An Ecological Doctrine of Creation*, trans. by Margaret Kohl, New York: HarperSanFrancisco.

100 It should be noted, however, that Moltmann does not think that the kingdom of God will include the natural world as it is presently, for the natural world will ultimately be transformed.

9

Modern Women and Traditional Religion

The confrontation between the ideas of modern women and the beliefs and practices of traditional religion stands out among the various encounters between religion and modern thought. It does so because, for the most part, it has not been experienced as a challenge coming from outside each tradition. Rather, the challenge comes from within as Jewish, Christian and Muslim women have become increasingly conscious of what they perceive as sexism within their respective traditions.

Precisely because this challenge comes from within the religious traditions, it is perhaps the most difficult one for traditionally inclined religious adherents to ignore. Moreover, modern women challenge traditional religions on a number of fronts, which penetrate deeply into all aspects of those religions. We shall see that time-honoured interpretations of important scriptural texts have not been left undisturbed, and even the concept 'God', which lies at the heart of the monotheisms, has been probed, stretched, and, in some cases, rejected. In addition, religious institutions, laws, customs and practices have been critically analysed in the light of the insights offered by women's studies and feminist theory.

This assault on traditional religion gathered pace and momentum as it swept through Europe and North America during the twentieth century.[1] The first signs, however, that the challenge of women to traditional religion was set to become a mass movement are seen at the close of the nineteenth century in the work of the North American feminist Matilda Joslyn Gage (1826–98):

> Looking forward, I see evidence of a conflict more severe than any yet fought by reformation or science; a conflict that will shake the foundations of religious belief, tear into fragments and scatter to the winds the old dogmas upon which all forms of Christianity are based. It will not be the conflict of science upon church theories regarding creation and eternity; it will not be the light of biology illuminating the hypothesis of the resurrection of the body; but it will be the rebellion of one half of the church against those theological dogmas upon which the very existence of the church is based.[2]

The claim that the coming conflict between male and female in the Church 'will shatter the foundations of religious belief' was no doubt regarded with incredulity by many of those who heard Gage speak or who read her work when it was first published. Yet her prediction proved accurate, and no religion has escaped the impact of the increased public prominence and empowerment of women, which was one of the more laudable achievements of the twentieth century. Since Gage's time, religious institutions have been increasingly perceived as a substantial force behind sexual inequality. Moreover, religious doctrines are nowadays routinely blamed for promoting derogatory views of women – caricatures which have had far-reaching social, economic and political consequences right through to the present day. Indeed, in seeking the same social recognition, economic opportunities and political rights as men typically enjoy, women have often found that the greatest stumbling blocks are established religious traditions and the seemingly misogynist religious anthropologies upon which they are premised.

How is it that women came to criticize their religious traditions? One reason is the increasing access to education in the twentieth century, which helped many women to identify what they took to be a systematic link between their social, economic and political oppression on the one hand, and the way that they were de-valued by traditional religion on the other. Many women came to perceive the extent to which religious views had been, and continued to be, shaped by what they came to identify as patriarchy. Moreover, as we shall see, certain religious views clearly exacerbated women's inequality with men. Women responded to their growing awareness of this in different ways. One response was to analyse their religious traditions from the various perspectives offered by the feminist movement. Women scrutinized the origins and development of their religious traditions, and examined the role of these traditions in underpinning the state legislation that institutionalized the oppression of women. Examples of such legislation are the property laws in Europe which, until the twentieth century, forbade married women to own property, or the Islamic divorce laws which, in many Muslim countries even today, make it much easier for a man to divorce a woman than it is for a woman to divorce a man.[3] In both cases, this discriminatory legislation can be traced back to the derogatory views of women that have been sanctioned by religion.

Throughout the twentieth century, women persistently challenged traditional religions in many ways. Jewish, Christian and Muslim women provoked their more conservative co-religionists into taking notice of what the former viewed as the androcentric biases within their traditions, and into defending them against the challenges this posed. In this chapter, we examine some of the main expressions that the various feminist challenges to traditional forms of Judaism, Christianity and Islam have taken. In addition to surveying some of the strategies that feminists have employed in their attempt to reshape their religious traditions, we consider the standpoints of some of those who completely reject the feminist critique of religion. In doing so, the work of thinkers from all three monotheistic traditions is discussed together because, as we shall see, feminists from each tradition are, by and large, responding to remarkably similar problems.

But, as we have already noted, the challenge of modern women to traditional religion did not suddenly emerge in the twentieth century, and the pace at which it blossomed in that century would not have been possible without the pioneering efforts of earlier thinkers. And key among these was Matilda Joslyn Gage.

The beginning of the rebellion

Of all the religious thinkers active in the West at the close of the nineteenth century, Matilda Joslyn Gage was one of the few to see the magnitude of the challenge that the rapidly developing women's movement posed to traditional Christianity.[4] She was a groundbreaking figure because she not only campaigned for women's equality with men in public life but also worked hard to expose a systematic link between women's social, economic and political oppression and traditional Christianity – the faith which had dominated her culture. She saw clearly that many of the features of public life that women found oppressive – the laws regarding inheritance, marriage or birth control, for example – stemmed from Christian beliefs. Recognizing that these beliefs had evolved through the centuries, she argued that in many cases their evolution had been manipulated by men for their benefit as opposed to that of women. Moreover, Gage was convinced that some of the central doctrines of Christianity – particularly those to do with God's creation of men and women, and the Fall[5] – were directly responsible for the persecution and oppression of women during the Christian era. Indeed, Gage's seminal importance lies in her explicitly linking this oppression to the direct influence of Christian beliefs – particularly the belief that women were not created equal to men.

Interestingly, despite her attempt at a devastating exposure of sexism, patriarchy and androcentricity within Christianity, Gage did not regard herself as opposed to religion. Rather, she declared herself to be opposed to the usurpation of Christianity by those men who had deployed certain religious beliefs in order to further their own interests. She clearly believed that, if purged of male distortions, Christianity could regain its original value. Consequently, she remained a committed Presbyterian, respecting what she called 'true religion' as opposed to 'theology'.[6] As we shall see, in this continued allegiance to her religious tradition, she broke a path that has been followed by many subsequent religious feminists.

It has, of course, been commonly argued that Christianity has been such a powerful force for good in the world that it cannot possibly be as bad as some of its critics have claimed. And, clearly, Gage must have encountered this argument, for she begins her book by dismantling this defence of Christianity, proposing instead that it has been the source of grave immorality, having destroyed much of what was good in the world prior to its ascendance. To substantiate this charge, Gage provides a detailed description of the condition of women prior to the Christian era, and proceeds to contrast it with their later oppression.[7]

Consider, for example, marriage – an institution upon which Gage repeatedly focuses. Marriage within what she judges to have been the formerly matriarchal family-system stands in stark contrast to marriage within the later patriarchal one. In her assessment, marriage within the former system was profoundly less oppressive to women than under the latter. And this is because women were free to choose their husbands without any coercion, never being sold as brides.[8] The contrast between the lives of women under the original matriarchal system and their condition throughout most of the Christian era is thus marked, for the women of Europe living in the latter era were regarded as household and political slaves. And this was chiefly due to their not being allowed to own, or to inherit, property – an inequality with men that prevailed for much of recorded Christian history. In other words, instead of being regarded as property holders in their own right, women came to be viewed as a commodity owned first by their father, then by their husband, or failing that, by their own sons or eldest (even if younger) brother. Not surprisingly, this resulted in women being severely oppressed.

In Gage's view, the origin of such patriarchal subordination – and the concomitant oppression of women that had persisted to her day – can be traced to the time when Judaism was forming.[9] Patriarchal Judaism subsequently influenced the way in which Christianity developed; and, after describing the historical transmutation of Christianity into a patriarchal religion, Gage proceeds to analyse the specific means by which Christian institutions reduced women's freedom. So, focusing on marriage, she observes that it was commonly held in poor regard during the early Christian centuries, this negative view of marriage chiefly having been promoted by St Paul who, in the first century, urged Christians to remain celibate rather than marry. In his view, marriage was greatly inferior to virginity or celibacy, and should only be entered into in order to prevent the couple from enjoying sexual intercourse outside marriage, and thereby sinning. Because marriage came to be seen as a lesser good than celibacy, married people came increasingly to be perceived as inferior to the unmarried. But why was marriage so looked down upon? As Gage correctly notes, in the background to Paul's advice lay the widely held belief that the end of the world was imminent. And with the prospect of the final judgement, what everyone should have been spending all their time doing was praying. However, even after this eschatological expectation had faded, Paul's advice continued to be taken seriously. It might seem incredible now, but in the early centuries of Christianity some even denied that salvation was available to married people at all.

Gage proceeds to argue that this negative view of marriage was combined with the view that woman not only was created inferior to man but also was ultimately responsible for the Fall. According to traditional Christian doctrine, because of one woman's purported role in the Fall, all women are in the process of undergoing God's punishment. One aspect of this supposed punishment is the pain of childbirth; the other is marriage, where each woman is subjected to a man, whose task it is to punish her for her responsibility for the Fall.[10]

Moreover, an 'explanation' is provided in the Book of Genesis for why it was the woman, and not the man, who first succumbed to temptation. This explanation is to be found in one account of the creation of Adam and Eve, where Eve is portrayed as derived from Adam:

> The Lord God formed man from the dust of the ground, and breathed into his nostrils the breath of life; and the man became a living being. [And then] the Lord God caused a deep sleep to fall upon the man, and he slept; then he took one of his ribs and closed up its place with flesh. And the rib that the Lord God had taken from the man he made into a woman and brought her to the man. Then the man said, 'This at last is bone of my bones and flesh of my flesh; this one shall be called Woman, for out of Man this one was taken.'[11]

This version of the creation myth has long been taken to imply that, as woman was created out of man, she must be inferior to him. Moreover, the rest of the story emphasizes that woman was created in order to fulfil a need in man: namely, to be his helper and his wife.[12] Gage was perhaps the first to observe that the important role ascribed within the Judaeo-Christian tradition to the creation myth is responsible for the widespread perception that the human race can be neatly divided into two groups along gender lines, and that one group is innately inferior to the other.

Although one cannot hold later religious thinkers responsible for the presence of such passages in their sacred writings, one can, as Gage chides, reproach them for choosing to give continued prominence to them and for thereby condoning the gender inequalities they seem to endorse. And according to Gage's interpretation of the history of Christianity, St Paul is indeed blameworthy for precisely this. Moreover, in selecting the particular aspects of the tradition that he chose to emphasize, Paul

> gave to the Christian world a lever long enough to reach down through eighteen centuries, all that time moving it in opposition to a belief in a

woman's created and religious equality with man, to her right of private judgement and to her personal freedom. His teaching that Adam, first created, was not first in sin, divided the unity of the human race in the assumption that woman was not part of the original creative idea but a secondary thought, an inferior being brought into existence as an appendage to man.[13]

In Gage's view, it is this deeply misogynistic and dualist theological anthropology that has been the cause of much of the suffering endured by women throughout the Christian era. This particular anthropology, which became enshrined in the teaching of the Christian Church, was subsequently used to justify the formulation of different rights for women and for men in both Church and state. It was also used to justify the existence of two moral codes: one code for women and another for men. Thus, in concluding her historical account, Gage argues that the nineteenth-century social order, justly challenged by the women's movement of her day, was built on these religiously dubious patriarchal theories; and she concludes that once this is recognized, then women's struggle for social and political equality with men will be considerably easier.[14]

But what is perhaps most important for our concerns, Gage, in going straight to what many later religious feminists would take to be the heart of the problem, proceeds to criticize the exclusively male conception of God that dominates Christianity. As she writes: 'To the theory of "God the Father," … shorn of the divine attribute of motherhood, is the world beholden for its most degrading beliefs, its most infamous practices.'[15] And in Gage's analysis, one of the most serious consequences of the concept 'God the Father' is that it has led to the exclusion of women from leadership roles within the Christian Church. As she points out, during the early centuries of the common era women occupied prominent and important roles within the Christian community, and it took several hundred years before they were totally ousted, before their capacity to represent God was denied, and before the all-male priesthood was ensconced.[16]

Not only was confidence in the capacity of women to represent God critically undermined by the concept of the 'Father God', but this capacity also came to be denied of men who had intimate contact with women. Thus, from the early centuries, pressure mounted for leaders of the Western Christian Church to be celibate. However, it was some time before married people were totally excluded from roles of leadership. Nevertheless, the rules were gradually tightened to exclude married men from the priesthood; their ability to represent God being, supposedly, somehow impaired by the tainted contact that marriage was held to involve. However, the real reason behind the stated theological one may have been, as Gage cynically suggests, that married priests could be expected to have children. And they would inherit the priest's property. If the priest had no children, on the other hand, then the Church would inherit everything.

Of course, one response to the seeming venality of the Church was the Reformation. But Gage questions whether it did anything to correct these seemingly misogynistic traits, which had firmly taken root within Western Christianity as a whole. Ultimately, she judges that the condition of women remained substantially unchanged as a result of the Reformation, noting that Luther's famous 90 Theses, which he nailed on the church door in Wittemberg, failed to include any call whatsoever for the equality of women with men – which is perhaps not surprising when one considers Luther's assertion that it was unbecoming for a woman to be wise. Indeed, the lack of progress on this score is evident in the reformers' belief that, while a man could approach God directly without the mediation of a priest, a woman could only do so through a man, usually her father or husband. In other words, the Reformation sought to liberate men, but not women, from an authority imposed upon them from without. And in keeping with this, women in England, for a long time after the Reformation, were forbidden to read the Bible.[17] For reading the Bible for oneself was one of the means by which one was to be liberated from control by a priesthood. Yet women were explicitly denied this route to emancipation. Instead, they were required to submit to men, who were portrayed as the direct representatives of God.[18] From this it was concluded that a woman who was disobedient to her husband was thereby disobedient to God – a form of disobedience punishable by the state.[19]

Another indication, in Gage's view, that the reformers were no more kindly disposed towards women than were members of the Roman Catholic Church, is their equally relentless condemnation of witches. The persecution of women suspected of witchcraft persisted in many parts of Europe and North America until the nineteenth century.[20] Yet all the burnings and hangings, writes Gage, were meted out as punishments for 'a crime that never existed save in the imagination of those persecutors and which grew in their imagination from a false belief in woman's extraordinary wickedness, based upon a false theory as to original sin'.[21]

In Gage's view, then, the persecution of those suspected of witchcraft was to be explained by the widely held belief that women were inherently wicked. In other words, it was yet another result of the core Christian convictions that women were created inferior to men and that a woman was the first to sin. So, the persecution of witches had the same basic cause as the legal inequalities that still plagued women in Gage's time. And these legal inequalities were considerable:

[E]ven in this year 1892, within eight years of the Twentieth Christian century, we find the largest proportion of the United States still giving the husband custody of the wife's person; the exclusive control of the children of the marriage; of the wife's personal and real estate; the absolute right to her labor and the products of her industry.[22]

Gage was well known during her lifetime for her involvement in the struggle for women's rights. And in the course of this struggle she was often confronted with this view of women having been created inferior to men. In fact, she found that the most vigorous opposition to women's claims to be granted equal rights came from the clergy who, more than most, were committed to this dogma. Consider a sermon preached in 1880 by an English clergyman to a largely female audience in Philadelphia:

> God made himself to be born of woman to sanctify the virtue of endurance; loving submission is an attribute of woman; men are logical, but women lacking this quality, have an intricacy of thought. There are those who think that women can be taught logic; this is a mistake, they can never by any power of education arrive at the same mental status as that enjoyed by man, but they have a quickness of apprehension, which is usually called leaping at conclusions, that is astonishing. There, then, we have distinctive traits of a woman, namely: endurance, loving submission and quickness of apprehension. Wifehood is the crowning glory of a woman. In it she is bound for all time. To her husband she owes the duty of unqualified obedience. There is no crime which a man can commit which justifies his wife leaving him or applying for that monstrous thing, divorce. It is her duty to subject herself to him always, and no crime that he can commit can justify her lack of obedience. If he be a bad or wicked man, she may gently remonstrate with him, but refuse him, never.[23]

Gage observes that while this sermon was preached during 'the full blaze of the nineteenth century',[24] which saw itself as so progressive, the view of women it expresses is drawn directly from the dark ages. Incredibly, this kind of argument was still being deployed well into the twentieth century in order to deny women equal rights. As we saw in the previous chapter, many Christians nowadays cultivate an image that projects the power for liberation within the Christian message. But at the end of the nineteenth century, the Church could hardly be viewed as standing out as a power for the liberation of women.

Summing up her conclusions, Gage declares: 'All the evils that have resulted from dignifying one sex and degrading the other may be traced to one central error, a belief in a trinity of masculine gods, in one from which the feminine element is wholly eliminated. ...'[25] And yet, continues Gage, this happened despite a scriptural account of creation in which male and female were declared to be created equal, as we shall shortly see.

Appropriating sacred texts

Gage bequeathed twentieth-century religious feminists a penetrating diagnosis of the problem that traditional religion posed to modern women. However, it was left to later feminists to develop solutions to this problem. One popular strategy was to reclaim sacred texts from what they took to be the gendered interpretations placed on them by men. Even at the beginning of the twenty-first century, Christian and Jewish women still frequently have to remind their co-religionists that there are two creation stories within the Hebrew Scriptures. The first to appear, although not the most ancient, is found in Genesis 1.1–2.3.[26] Within this alternative account can be found the following 'description' of how God created humans:

> Then God said, 'Let us make humankind in our image, according to our likeness...'
>> So God created humankind in his image,
>> in the image of God he created them;
>> male and female he created them.[27]

In contrast to the more famous creation story, mentioned in the previous section, the noteworthy feature of this version of the myth is that *both* male and female are declared to be created in the image of God. This might be taken to suggest that there is some sense in which God is both male and female. Consequently, this particular text cannot be so easily used to support an anthropology that portrays women and men as intrinsically unequal. Jewish and Christian feminists, therefore, argue that this account, which they have taken to emphasize gender equality, ought to be given priority within their traditions.

This attempt to take control of sacred texts is typical of what happened in the twentieth century when, for the first time, large numbers of women began to read the texts for themselves, and to read them critically. Once they were no longer dependent upon males for an interpretation of the sacred texts, women claimed to notice a selective bias lying behind the choice of texts emphasized within their traditions. In the Christian Scriptures, for example, God is depicted by a rich array of metaphors and parables. Yet only a small selection of these have been adopted by the Christian tradition and allowed to play a significant role in the way that Christians conceptualize God. Feminists have pointed out that those metaphors and parables that have been selected for extensive use are invariably ones drawn from male rather than female experience. In the Gospel of Luke, chapter 15, for instance, two parables are presented: the parable of the lost sheep; and the parable of the woman and the lost coin. Each attempts to illustrate the joy felt by God over a sinner's repentance.

The Christian tradition, however, has given a central place to only one of these parables – that of the shepherd and the lost sheep. This parable is based on the male figure of the shepherd, and it is this which has entered into the Christian imagination – as can be seen from the many works of Christian art depicting the scene. The parable of the woman and the lost coin, by contrast, has not been elaborated by the tradition, and is not represented by an extensive body of painting. One aim of feminist readings of Scripture is to identify such neglected texts, and to begin building a tradition of interpretation around them. Indeed, the twentieth century witnessed the burgeoning of a whole industry of feminist interpretations of the sacred texts.

Jewish feminists, in contrast to their Christian counterparts, have devoted considerable attention to Exodus 19.15, in which Moses gives this warning to his people: 'Be ready for the third day; do not go near a woman.' This verse has troubled many Jewish women, for 'the third day' is when the Israelites are to receive the covenant. As Judith Plaskow writes, this text is particularly disturbing because

> here, at the very moment that the Jewish people stands at Sinai ready to receive the covenant – not now the covenant with individual patriarchs but with the people as a whole – at the very moment when Israel stands trembling waiting for God's presence to descend upon the mountain, Moses addressed the community only as men. ... At the central moment of Jewish history, women are invisible. Whether they too stood there trembling in fear and expectation, what they heard when the men heard these words of Moses, we do not know. It was not their experience that interested the chronicler or that informed and shaped the Torah.[28]

We have seen in Chapter 3 that traditional Jewish identity is intimately bound to a consciousness of membership within a community that is unique in having entered into a covenant with God. Many Jews regard the experience of living within this covenant as the core religious experience of Judaism. Plaskow, however, observes that, from the beginnings of the tradition, this experience has been presented as available only to men – as women were not included in the official account of the giving and receiving of the covenant. Moreover, she charges that this exclusion of women from the original covenant led to a pattern in which women's invisibility became endemic throughout traditional Judaism.[29]

Plaskow's observations seem warranted, as any survey of the trajectory of Jewish tradition from its earliest days to the present appears to confirm. When the rabbis codified *halakah* (Jewish law),[30] they legislated as if the requirements of the covenant rested principally on the male members of the community. The majority of the 613 commandments, which the covenant requires Jews to keep, are only binding on adult males.[31] It is also significant that the commandments which women are typically not required to fulfil are those that concern public religious worship and study.[32] In addition, the tradition appears to suffer from an overwhelming tendency to portray women as less than persons.[33]

All of this has led some Jewish women to question seriously whether they are actually included in the covenant with God. 'Are women Jews?', thus asks Rachel Adler.[34] Nevertheless, Plaskow speaks for many Jewish feminists when she asserts that

> [t]o accept our absence from Sinai would be to allow the male text to define us and our connection to Judaism. To stand on the ground of our experience, on the other hand, to start with the certainty of our membership in our own people is to be forced to re-member and recreate its history, to reshape Torah. It is to move from anger at the tradition, through anger to empowerment. It is to begin the journey toward the creation of a feminist Judaism.[35]

In Plaskow's analysis, then, a key aim of Jewish feminism is 'to reshape Torah'. Within the Jewish tradition, this is the issue for which the challenge of modern women to traditional religion is at its most intense. Plaskow is well aware that there will be a great deal of resistance to the claim that the reshaping of Torah is a legitimate intention. Torah is traditionally regarded as the product of a direct revelation from God, providing the blueprint for a divinely sanctioned lifestyle, which is thought to be valid for all time. Any Jew who wants to participate in the feminist project must reject this traditional view of Torah. But, as Plaskow also counsels, rejecting the traditional view is not enough; if the feminist wishes to remain within the Jewish tradition, then she must provide an alternative conception of the link between Torah and revelation.

Plaskow looks for an alternative in the ancient Jewish kabbalistic tradition. There, she finds a distinction between the primordial Torah, which is identified with God's essence, and the incomplete and partial expression of this, which has been codified by men. It is a short step to the idea that each person, through study and prayer, can gain a unique perspective on the primordial Torah. 'But', declares Plaskow, as she presses this kabbalistic idea into the service of Jewish feminism,

> this image of the relation between hidden and manifest Torah reminds us that half the souls of Israel have not left for us the Torah they have seen. Insofar as we can begin to recover women's experience of God, insofar as we can restore a part of their history and vision, we have more of the primordial Torah, the divine fullness, of which the present Torah is only a fragment and a sign.[36]

This view of the original Torah as transcending the seemingly andro-centric document that has been passed down through the generations and enshrined in the tradition gives Jewish feminists a new freedom to challenge and 'reshape' the text. This new freedom in dealing with the written form has converged with the rising tide of scepticism regarding any insistence that the Scriptures of Judaism, Christianity and Islam are a literal record of God's direct speech. Over the course of the twentieth century, areas of scholarship as diverse as palaeontology, particle physics and biblical criticism have made it increasingly difficult for educated moderns to regard the Scriptures of the various traditions as literally true. In particular, serious doubts have been cast on the historical veracity of the Sinai narrative, and few well-educated people today regard the creation stories as literal accounts of what happened. Consequently, debates about the interpretation of Scripture can no longer be settled simply by appealing to a purportedly neutral reading of the text as ostensibly offered by traditional rabbis, priests or mullas. Feminists from all three Abrahamic faiths have been claiming the right to interpret sacred texts for themselves.

The texts, however, present undeniable obstacles to women's efforts at interpreting them. Women can easily find themselves embroiled in a battle with the representatives of a tradition of interpretation that typically claims to hold a pedigree traceable back to the early days of the religious community. Some feel that this is a battle that women cannot win. As Ibn Warraq, for example, opines when commenting on the situation within Islam:

> to do battle with the orthodox, the fanatics, and the mullas in the interpretation of these texts is to do battle on their ... terms, on their ground. [For] every text that you produce they will adduce a dozen others contradicting yours. The reformists cannot win on these terms – whatever mental gymnastics the reformists perform, they cannot escape the fact that Islam is deeply antifeminist. *Islam is the fundamental cause of the repression of Muslim women and remains the major obstacle to the evolution of their position.* Islam has always considered women as creatures inferior in every way: physically, intellectually, and morally. This negative vision is divinely sanctioned in the Koran, corroborated by the hadiths and perpetuated by the commentaries of the theologians. ...[37]

Many religious feminists, regardless of their particular faith, would agree, at least to a certain extent; claiming that a negative vision of women is ingrained not only in the Qur'ān but within the sacred texts of each of the monotheisms. However, aware of the important place occupied by these texts within the 'religions of the Book', they realize that they have no option, if they want to remain within their traditions, but to confront these texts. One of the main problems with the sacred texts of Judaism, Christianity and Islam is the excessive and all-but-exclusive use of male images within their respective religious symbolism. This problem is mitigated, however, once an obligation to interpret these texts literally is no longer felt.

Many Jewish, Christian and Muslim women have thus been exercising a new sense of freedom in interpreting the texts of their Scriptures, noting that, as Fatima Mernissi remarks: '[d]epending on how it is used, the sacred text can be a threshold for escape or an insurmountable barrier. It can be that rare music that leads to dreaming or simply a dispiriting routine. It all depends on the person who invokes it.'[38] In accordance with this realization, there are abundant examples of creative rewriting of Scriptures, prayer books and liturgies in order to give greater prominence to women.[39] For example, religious feminists have striven to insert feminine imagery into these documents in an attempt to balance out the masculine. However, this strategy of altering the balance between male and female imagery within sacred texts is, of course, closed to all those within religious communities who are wedded to a literal interpretation of such texts, be they Jewish, Christian or Muslim. But excepting such religious literalists, throughout the twentieth century, as we saw in Chapter 5, there has been a growing acceptance that all texts are interpreted to a greater or lesser extent. The question is: Who is responsible for the interpretation?

Women have become increasingly aware that, due to many factors, perhaps chief among which being access to education, the interpretation of sacred texts has been the preserve of men. This has meant, according to many feminists, that the traditional interpretations of these texts are far from 'neutral' or 'objective' but are, instead, gendered. For if the meaning of a text is not automatically provided by the words on the page, but is, rather, the result of a process whereby the text is interpreted through the lens of the reader's experience, and if the readers of the text are male, then the interpretation which is arrived at will likely be masculinist.

One notable example of an attempt at reinterpreting a sacred text from a woman's perspective is that of Amina Wadud-Muhsin, an African-American Muslim feminist, who construes interpretation as a product which 'reflects, in part, the intentions of the text, as well as the "prior text" of the one who' performs the interpretation.[40] By 'prior text' she means the 'perspectives, circumstances, and background of the individual' interpreter.[41] On the basis of this understanding of what is involved in interpreting a text, she specifically aims to provide an interpretation of the Qur'ān that will be 'meaningful to women living in the modern era'.[42] In her view, traditional interpretations of the Qur'ān are not meaningful to modern women precisely because they 'were generated without the participation and firsthand representation of women'.[43] Nevertheless, the exclusion of women from an interpretive role should not be equated with their exclusion from the message within the text, and Wadud-Muhsin proposes that women's 'voicelessness during critical periods of development in Qur'anic interpretation has ... been mistakenly equated with voicelessness in the text itself'.[44]

Wadud-Muhsin clearly believes that present within the Qur'ān, and waiting to be deployed, are the resources for an interpretation that will prove liberatory for modern women. As a Muslim wanting to reclaim rather than abandon her religion, she emphasizes the importance of the relationship between the core text – namely, the Qur'ān – and her own liberatory interpretation of it. Most importantly, it is neither, in her view, the core text nor the principles which it propounds that change, but only the 'prior text' – that is, the 'perspectives, circumstances, and background of the individual' interpreter. The onus, then, is on each historically and culturally located individual to assimilate the revelation contained within the Qur'ān. Such assimilation will involve developing new interpretations that allow the core principles of the Qur'ānic revelation to be expressed in a manner appropriate to each particular time and place. Indeed, Wadud-Muhsin goes so far as to accuse Muslims who deny the necessity for developing new Qur'ānic interpretations of contradicting Islam's claim to be a universal religion. For, in her view, Islam succeeds in being universal not by having a single, canonical formulation but by being assimilable in different ways by different cultures.

Having made the case for the legitimacy, indeed necessity, of a variety of interpretations of the Qur'ān, Wadud-Muhsin proceeds to argue that the interpreter's specific conception of gender difference will be part of her or his 'prior text'. In other words, how any particular person views the differences between women and men is not, in her view, an essential component of the message contained in the Qur'ān. And this implies that it is perfectly acceptable to interpret the text from the standpoint offered by an alternative perspective on gender – say, a feminist one.

Wadud-Muhsin's argument thus has far-reaching implications, for it challenges the religious anthropology that many Muslims have taken to be fundamental to Islam. According to this traditional anthropology, there are essential differences between men and women. These differences are often expressed in claims regarding women falling short of men in important respects: they are weaker, less intelligent, more prone to evil, and spiritually inferior. Moreover, these differences are thought to have been deliberately created by Allah. Hence, they are taken to justify the de-valuing of women which, many accuse, is endemic within traditional forms of Muslim society. This religious anthropology has also been used in an attempt to justify a denial of basic freedoms to Muslim women, such as the freedom to choose whom to marry, to get an education, to pursue a career, or even to leave the house.

But if an androcentric anthropology is external to the essential revelation and is, instead, a product of the cultural background of those who have interpreted it, then, as Wadud-Muhsin argues, Islam could, in principle, escape the burden of misogyny. For if she is right, then the only reason why Islam and the Qur'ān have been perceived to be androcentric and patriarchal is that those who claimed for themselves the exclusive right to interpret the text, and thus shape the tradition, were imbued with the vice of misogyny.[45] But not everyone need be so prejudiced. Wadud-Muhsin would, therefore, no doubt agree with this heartfelt exclamation from Nazira Zein-ed-Din, a Muslim feminist active in the 1920s:

> I only wish that those who pretend to protect Islam and raise its banners would look in the same way as I do and see what I see. I wish they did not look at Islam through the narrow vision of commentaries and interpretations which interpret Islam in ways they want to see it. Islam is far beyond that. It is much greater.[46]

Feminists from each of the Abrahamic religions, then, are united in their claim that (what they denounce as) patriarchal religious traditions have systematically excluded women from contributing to traditionally accepted interpretations of the sacred texts. As we have noted, feminist theologians, faced with this situation, have attempted to interpret the Scriptures of their traditions from the standpoint provided by their own experience as women.[47] And twentieth-century religious feminists were quick to realize that, once women began to interpret sacred texts for themselves, they would have a powerful tool with which to mount a critique of the theological traditions that had excluded them. For example, writing within a Christian context, Rosemary Radford Ruether – one of the first twentieth-century religious feminists to produce a 'feminist theology' – makes a point of expressing the radical potential of using the experience of women as a source of scriptural interpretation and theology:

> The use of women's experience in feminist theology ... explodes as a critical force, exposing classical theology, including its codified traditions, as based on *male* experience rather than on universal human experience. Feminist theology makes the sociology of theological knowledge visible, no longer hidden behind mystifications of objectified divine and universal authority.[48]

Feminists have thus argued that, even today, Judaism, Christianity and Islam depend upon a background theological framework that is inherently patriarchal. As Daphne Hampson succinctly observes: 'theology, as we have known it, has been the creation of men; indeed men living within a patriarchal society. As women come into their own, theology will take a different shape.'[49]

Battle lines are drawn

An increasing number of people have thus begun to agree that each of the monotheisms, with its sacred text and theological tradition, is essentially patriarchal. The overload of male-inspired images of the divine has prompted some feminists to go so far as to argue that such imagery is indicative of traditions so pervasively patriarchal that they cannot be salvaged. Therefore, some thinkers urge the complete rejection of monotheism on feminist grounds. Not all thinkers who are alert to the ostensible androcentric bias within the monotheisms would go this far, though. As we shall see, some believe that, notwithstanding the view that sexist bias 'is like a buried continent whose subaqueous pull has shaped all currents of the theological enterprise',[50] it ought to be possible to retain what is valuable within each tradition, while shedding undesirable elements. These religious feminists labour to reclaim and reshape the monotheisms in a way that, while remaining faithful to their traditions, is not inimical to women's dignity. Yet others believe that all such feminist claims ought to be vigorously resisted, and the traditional forms of Judaism, Christianity and Islam preserved. In what follows, we survey a spectrum of views ranging from the conservative to what could be described as post-Jewish, post-Christian and post-Muslim feminism.

We have seen that the appropriation by women of the sacred texts of the traditional monotheisms has led to an awareness of the power that can be unleashed when feminine experience is allowed to shape theology. Inevitably, this potential power for change has led to a demand for reform within Judaism, Christianity and Islam. In Judaism and Christianity, the call for reform has principally been expressed as a demand for the right to participate equally within the religious community. More specifically, women have demanded the opportunity to serve their communities as rabbis or priests. Many of the conservative positions are staunchly opposed to granting women any such opportunities.

Conservative stances and their limitations

Conservatives are so named because they see an overriding value in conserving their tradition in the form in which it has been handed down through time, with the way that believers acted in the past typically being regarded as normative for all subsequent generations. In other words, conservatives believe that the criteria by which the present should be judged are to be found in the past. Within the Christian tradition, for example, St Paul's view – which is expressed in the Christian Scriptures – that women should be silent in church has come to represent a standard by which the desires of modern women to preach may be condemned.[51] Analogues to this use of Scripture, where the past is taken as providing the yardstick, as a means of judging women's aspirations in the present are also abundant within Judaism and Islam.

This conservative attitude is often supported by a belief that Scripture should be interpreted literally. It is also typically aligned with a model of revelation in which the propositions contained in the sacred texts are regarded as the unalterable word of God. As we have seen, both the tendency to interpret Scripture literally and the propositional view of revelation came under increasing strain as the twentieth century unfolded.

Most of the opposition to women assuming roles of leadership within their faith-communities took, and still takes, this conservative form. Moreover, conservatives, on the basis of their reading of Scripture, tend to argue that God has given men and women distinct and clear-cut roles within the religious community, and that these roles are unchangeable. Furthermore, the present arrangements are often described as 'natural' because they are taken to have been established by God; hence, they are not regarded as products of human social organization. Not too long ago, of course, similar views were commonly held about women's social roles in general.

A prominent example of this kind of conservative stance is the Roman Catholic Church's response to the mounting pressure to ordain women as priests.[52] Its main line of defence against this pressure is to cite what it regards as a paradigm from the Christian Scriptures. According to the official Roman Catholic position, if Jesus had wanted women priests, he would have instituted them himself. But he did not. Instead, he chose 12 male disciples, and instituted them as priests. The trouble with this argument, though, is that it is now well known that 'priests' did not exist at this stage of Christian history. In fact, the male, unmarried, Roman Catholic priest, as we now know him, was only really established during the late Middle Ages. Moreover, thanks to the work of Elisabeth Schlüsser Fiorenza,[53] it is now widely accepted that women were prominent figures within the early Christian community, only being ousted by their male counterparts when Christianity increasingly transformed itself in order better to fit in with the Greco-Roman society it was, in effect, infiltrating.

It is perhaps not surprising that the purest expressions of the conservative position tend to be formulated by men. Louis Bouyer, in his book *Woman in the Church*,[54] sums up what he takes to be the traditional Roman Catholic view of women and their role within the Church. In this book, which contains an enthusiastic epilogue by the eminent Roman Catholic theologian Hans Urs von Balthasar, Bouyer attempts to confront the arguments that feminists have advanced for women's admittance into the Roman Catholic priesthood. The core of Bouyer's argument is that allowing women into the priesthood would 'annihilate' their 'originality' and identity as women.[55] And the history of early Hebrew, then later Jewish and Christian, religious practice establishes that the difference between women and men has always been respected by these traditions. From the supposed fact that women have always been excluded from enjoying responsibility for public religious practice in the Judaeo-Christian tradition, Bouyer thus concludes that 'one can no longer assume that we are dealing with a fortuitous phenomenon, explicable by virtue of transitory contingencies, but corresponding to no intrinsic necessity in the nature of man and woman'.[56] In other words, given that the Judaeo-Christian tradition has, it is claimed, always been structured so as to exclude women from the public realm of religious practice, we must assume that this exclusion is not accidental but grounded in a necessity arising from the way that God has deliberately made men and women. Bouyer recognizes that the exclusion of women would be 'both incomprehensible and unjustifiable' if 'it were not substantiated by a fundamental principle'.[57] Unfortunately, he neglects to spell out the fundamental principle in question. Perhaps this omission is the result of his conviction that 'the mystery of woman ... is ... the final mystery of creation'?[58] But one must wonder if women would appear so mysterious if the perspective were not exclusively male.

Nevertheless, accusing of myopia those who refuse to recognize the necessity of the continued exclusion of women from public roles in the religious domain, Bouyer cites the following in support of the *status quo*: the consensus which, he claims, has persisted within the Christian tradition throughout its history, the authority of the Scriptures, and the testimony of Christian spiritual experience.[59] Here, Bouyer rests his case on precisely the three elements on which feminist critiques of religion have also focused. First, regarding the consensus of the faithful, feminists have pointed out that women have been excluded from expressing their opinions and contributing to a consensus. Hence, the celebrated *consensus fidelium* is actually a consensus of only part of the Church's membership – specifically, it represents the views of males in positions of power. Second, as we have seen, feminist biblical interpretation has revealed the degree to which the sacred texts are the 'literary precipitate'[60] of a community deeply affected by sexism. In other words, the Scriptures themselves must be treated with a 'hermeneutic of suspicion' because they reflect the silencing of women at an early stage of the Christian movement. Third, feminists have recently been exploring whether, and to what extent, the spiritual experiences that have been taken as paradigmatic within Christianity have actually been masculine. And they have sought to expose the degree to which the experiences of women have been marginalized from, rather than integrated into, the tradition.[61] Given these foci of feminist theory, feminists would, no doubt, respond to Bouyer's accusation by accusing him of myopia.

Bouyer was writing in the mid-1970s and, clearly, the form of feminism that he had encountered was one that demanded an equality between women and men, and that was usually expressed in terms of equality of opportunity. Applied to Roman Catholicism, this cashed out in a demand for women's admittance into the priesthood on exactly the same terms as men. Bouyer describes the situation thus:

> We find ourselves ... in the presence of a form of feminism which, well-intentioned as it might be, can only be destructive of true liberation of women. For equality which is confused with pure and simple identity with another (while he is, of course, your equal, but for all that, not identical with you) could not possibly be anything but a delusion. It could only result, for those who insist upon it, in the loss of their own identity.[62]

Many feminists would be prepared to concede that Bouyer is making a valuable point here, but they would part company with him when he draws his conclusion. The point of agreement would be that simply inserting women into institutions that have been formed by men, and dominated by androcentric ideology, will fail as a strategy for promoting equality between women and men. But from the fact that women will not fit well into male institutions, Bouyer attempts to conclude that no woman should be ordained,[63] claiming further that we 'should avoid crushing her femininity through the conferring of a ministry for which she is not fitted'.[64] Feminists would, no doubt, respond by suggesting that the problem may well lie in the structure of the ministry rather than in the nature of women.

Before we consider further how feminists have responded to arguments like Bouyer's, there is another figure who deserves mention, a short essay by whom having been appended to Bouyer's volume.[65] C. S. Lewis was one of the most widely read Christian authors of the twentieth century, and his work continues to exert a great influence on many Christians in the present century. He begins his essay on the ordination of women with the casual remark that he has just 'heard that the Church of England was being advised to declare women capable of Priests' Orders'.[66] Regarding this as a preposterous suggestion, Lewis was clearly pleased to be 'informed that such a proposal is very unlikely to be seriously considered by the authorities'.[67] And because he assumes that the institution of women priestesses could never happen, he views the question of women's ordination as a merely theoretical one, and hence treats it as such.

Lewis does recognize that the distaste which many Christians feel when called upon to consider women as priests provides insufficient reason for denying them holy orders. So what is the real reason justifying the rejection of women's ordination? The reason, according to Lewis, is quite simple: an essential part of a priest's function is to represent God to the people. But a woman cannot represent God because God is male.[68] As Lewis explains:

> a priest is primarily a representative, a double representative, who represents us to God and God to us. Our very eyes teach us this in church. Sometimes the priest turns his back on us and faces the East – he speaks to God for us: sometimes he faces us and speaks to us for God. We have no objection to a woman doing the first: the whole difficulty is about the second. But why? Why should a woman not in this sense represent God? ...
>
> Suppose the reformer stops saying that a good woman may be like God and begins saying that God is like a good woman. Suppose he says that we might just as well pray to 'Our Mother which art in heaven' as to 'Our Father'. Suppose he suggests that the Incarnation might just as well have taken a female as a male form, and the Second Person of the Trinity be as well called the Daughter as the Son. Suppose, finally, that the mystical marriage were reversed, that the Church were the Bridegroom and Christ the Bride. All this, as it seems to me, is involved in the claim that a woman can represent God as a priest does.[69]

And Lewis believes that if these linguistic changes were instituted, the resulting religion would no longer be a form of Christianity. On his view, then, Christianity is a religion that cannot survive any diminishment in its androcentric manner of symbolizing and representing God. We will shortly see how other, more imaginative, thinkers deal with the claim that Christianity could not survive any feminization.

Clearly, Lewis, like Bouyer, is arguing against a form of feminism that presses for equal opportunities and equal rights. While this was indeed the primary focus of many feminists during the 1960s and early 1970s, from the mid-1970s onwards many feminist theorists began to suspect that this approach was inadequate by itself. This led to what has been termed the 'second wave' of the feminist movement.[70] The second wave was enormously influential in shaping the thought of many religious feminists during the final decades of the twentieth century. It focused more on women's liberation rather than being exclusively concerned with women's rights. This shift of interest was facilitated by a growing awareness that many of the social structures that women found oppressive were such precisely because of real differences between the genders. In stressing the need for equality, feminists involved in the 'first wave' tended to ignore gender differences, with one consequence being a neglect of the special problems that women could be expected to encounter should they ever be treated in exactly the same way as men within the existing workplace. For example, the life-cycle of men does not necessitate any time off work for pregnancy. If women are treated as if they do not require any time off either, then special problems arise. In cases such as this, feminists argue, equality of opportunity and equal rights will not be provided simply by treating women and men identically within extant institutions.

Feminists involved in the second wave, therefore, addressed some of the issues that had been omitted in the original demand for equal opportunities. Second-wave feminist theory is thus characterized by the challenge it poses to social and political institutions that are structured to favour male rather than female participants. In the context of religious institutions, they strongly criticize thinkers such as Bouyer and Lewis, who fail to see that the problem might well lie in the specific way in which these institutions are structured. Bouyer had seen the problem in terms of women's unsuitability for the priesthood; second-wave feminists would see the problem as lying in the priesthood not being suited to women. And whereas it might be the case that women cannot change to fit the present priesthood, there is no cogent reason to assume that the priesthood cannot change to fit women better. Hence, one solution proposed by second-wave feminists is to restructure the priesthood into an institution that is not tailored to fit one sex alone.

This new analysis of the problem facing women within both secular and religious society was a fundamental breakthrough in feminist theory, and it entailed a whole new way of looking at the difficulties women faced, thereby generating novel, potential solutions. And once the second wave of feminism got under way, the challenge it posed to traditional ways of thinking about, and ordering, society became more profound than many conservative thinkers were able to recognize. For Bouyer, Lewis and other conservatives clearly thought that they were doing women a favour by protecting their innate female dignity from the well-meaning but misguided demands of feminists. But this was surely because of their inability even to conceive of a restructured Church that was more suited to female needs.

The traditional appeal to women's dignity has exerted a powerful pull within Judaism and Islam, as well as within Christianity. And the treatment of women within the Abrahamic faiths has often been portrayed as being in accordance with their special value in God's eyes. Moreover, the lifestyles that traditional forms of Judaism, Christianity and Islam offer to women are presented as ideally suited to their God-given nature and desires. This is widely perceived to be in sharp contrast to the lifestyles pursued by women within modern secular societies, in which their female nature is often presumed to be fatally compromised. Indeed, the appeal that such traditional religious lifestyles exert upon many women should not be underestimated. Many Modern Orthodox Jewish women, for example, find the place they occupy within a traditional Jewish home to be intensely satisfying; and many formerly secularized Jewish women have turned to this form of life as a matter of deliberate choice.[71] Tamar

Frankiel, for one, has written extensively on the compatibility between women's spiritual needs and the traditional roles available to them within Judaism.[72]

Conservatives within Judaism[73] thus argue that the place of women in the religious and ethnic community should remain the same as it has always been, while Jewish feminists respond by insisting that the traditions be modernized in keeping with more enlightened views of women. This debate between conservatives and modernizers has been unfolding within Judaism since the early nineteenth century, when the Jewish reformers saw a need to break with tradition, especially in regard to the role of women within the faith community. Only in 1972, though, did Reformed Jewish congregations ordain their first woman rabbi in the United States. Since then, Reconstructionist and Humanist Jews have followed suit. In addition, many within the Conservative Movement have now come to accept women rabbis.

There are striking parallels between the debate over the ordination of women within Christianity and the debate within Judaism concerning the possibility of women rabbis.[74] There is no clear parallel within Islam, for there is no direct equivalent of priests or rabbis within the Muslim community. However, within Islam, the body of scholars, or mullas, does enjoy certain privileges akin to those enjoyed by, and shares some notable similarities with, the rabbis within Judaism and the priests within Christianity. Thus, the admittance of women in 1961 to the University of al-Azhar, one of the bastions of scholarship in the Muslim world, can be seen as a breakthrough.

There remains, however, a strong tendency for many Muslims to adopt a conservative stance when they reflect upon the tension between Islam and feminism. Many Muslim women, as well as men, perceive feminism to be a peculiarly Western vice – one that has developed within an alien culture, and which might be foisted onto them as yet another aspect of Western imperialism. Sachiko Murata, for example, clearly regards feminism as posing such a threat to Islam when she argues that feminists

> base their positions upon a worldview radically alien to the Islamic worldview. Their critique typically takes a moral stance. They ask for reform, whether explicitly or implicitly. The reform they have in view is of the standard Western type. Among other things, this means that there is an abstract ideal, thought up by us or by our leader, which has to be imposed by overthrowing the old order. This reform is of the same lineage as the Western imperialism that originally appeared in the East as Christian missionary activity.[75]

Presumably, Murata would have no corresponding grounds for discomfort with a feminism that had developed directly out of Islam. But any such development may be hard to identify, given that the boundary between 'the Islamic worldview' and the products of a Western 'moral stance' which she perceives to be so well defined has become increasingly opaque to many other Muslims. Does a Muslim scholar necessarily depart from 'the Islamic worldview' if he or she applies to the Qur'ān a form of textual criticism developed in the universities of Western Europe? Murata, it seems, would believe that he or she must. But other Muslims would find the scholar's use of new techniques a perfectly legitimate way of proceeding, and would, moreover, feel that the spirit of the Qur'ān itself condones such scholarship. For the Qur'ān encourages critical study of its revelation. What is more, many Western universities are, nowadays, well stocked with Western Muslim scholars. Who is able to say with any certainty, then, precisely which components of their learning are 'Western' and which 'Muslim'?

It may be that a significant part of what anti-feminists, such as Murata, find distasteful about feminism is not intrinsic to feminism as such, but is, rather, the product of a conflation between feminists and a particular vision of Western women in general. Many Western women have little or nothing to do with the feminist movement explicitly, although they may well have benefited from its achievements. And it is well known that stereotypes of Western women as immoral in general, and promiscuous in particular, abound within some sections of the Muslim community. Perhaps such a stereotypical impression of Western women feeds the image which many Muslims form of feminism. Their distaste for the former may tend to colour their view of feminists, even when the latter may be equally critical of the kind of promiscuity that Muslims typically condemn.

Feminists, for their part, tend to regard conservative religious thinking as unacceptable because it fails to take women's criticisms of their traditions seriously. Indeed, many conservative thinkers show only a superficial knowledge and limited understanding of feminism, and many of them demonstrate no knowledge of feminist theory as it has developed since the mid-1970s. In fact, one may wonder if the conservative position responds to the feminist challenge at all. Hence, it comes as no surprise that the conservative standpoint fails to appeal to many educated modern women.

Recent feminist stances

In the early days of the feminist religious movement, many felt that the solution to the problem that traditional monotheisms posed to modern women lay simply in the elimination of male bias within religious language. More recently, however, there has been a growing feeling that the real problem is far more acute. As one woman who has been extensively involved in the reformulation of traditional Jewish prayers puts it: 'Unfortunately, the rather obvious gender problem in our God-language is the surface manifestation of a deeper and more complex difficulty.'[76]

In order to meet this deeper difficulty head-on, women have begun to reappraise the core concepts within their tradition, particularly the concept 'God' – which is, of course, the organizing concept within the belief system of each monotheistic faith. Insisting that the real problem lies deeper than androcentric texts and patriarchal institutions, the new wave of religious feminists clearly cut right to the heart of Judaism, Christianity and Islam when they go so far as to reject many of the central concepts of these religions. Like earlier religious feminists, many of the new wave have claimed to notice a symbiotic relationship between the conception of God employed in their tradition and an androcentric religious anthropology. But they go further in claiming that, when the particular conception of God and its attendant anthropology are rejected, entire theological systems can be re-figured in the light of feminist principles.

Elizabeth Johnson attempts such a re-figuration in her prize-winning book *She Who Is*.[77] Johnson emphasizes that many of her ideas about the concept 'God' within the Christian tradition also apply to the concept 'God' within Judaism.[78] And, like other Christian feminists, she has no doubt that God is conceptualized as male within the Christian tradition. This is of the utmost importance because, Johnson claims, the conception of God dominant within a religious community provides religious believers with an

> ultimate point of reference for understanding experience, life, and the world. Hence the way in which a faith community shapes language about God implicitly represents what it takes to be the highest good, the profoundest truth, the most appealing beauty. Such speaking [of God], in turn, powerfully molds the corporate identity of the community and directs its praxis.[79]

Agreeing with other religious feminists that the particular conception of God dominant within the monotheisms supports an androcentric religious anthropology, she thus argues that this conception should be challenged and replaced with a new one. Moreover, it is imperative, in her view, that the new conception of God be dissociated from any dualist anthropology that portrays women as inferior.[80]

Johnson believes that a powerful argument supports her radical proposal. First, she points out that historical study reveals the substantial transformations that each religious tradition has undergone. Indeed, it is simply not credible that Judaism, Christianity and Islam have remained unchanged since their origin. Second, what underlies the transformations undergone by these traditions is, in many cases, a shift in core religious concepts. Indeed, Johnson argues that the key concept 'God' has been particularly prone to change, as can be seen by the different ways in which people have talked about God through the centuries. As she remarks: 'there has been no timeless speech about God'.[81] Given, then, that the traditions and their conceptions of God have changed and continue to change, what objection could there be to women now directing such change? In particular, given a history of change, if God has come to be viewed as male, what objection could there be to coming to view God as female, instead?

Well, of course, there are objections. What they boil down to, according to Johnson, is the claim that conceptualizing God as female is just not fitting. For many – perhaps the majority – of those who have been brought up within a tradition that identifies God as 'Father', there is something deeply jarring about using the term 'Mother' in its place. For example, C. S. Lewis refers to the 'horror' aroused by 'the idea of turning all our theological language into feminine gender'.[82] Indeed, many people find that, even after years of practice, it can still feel somewhat strained. But what conclusion should we draw from this experience? Surely not that the term 'Mother' is inappropriate to use with respect to God; but rather that, as Johnson in fact suggests, the term 'Father' has become a dead metaphor. People now understand it far too literally. As a result of the persistent and exclusive use of this symbol through the ages,[83] many appear to have the impression of a masculine God deeply imprinted on their minds. And it is this male image of God firmly lodged in the mind that the term 'Mother' jars against. Looked at in this light, the fact that the term 'Mother' has a grating effect stands in its favour as a religious symbol. For it is a radical and necessary reminder, argues Johnson, that all words used of God are intrinsically inadequate. Any characterization of God can only be metaphorical or analogical.[84] Thus, all that dead metaphors do is mislead.

In Johnson's analysis, then, patriarchal traditions have failed to respect the non-literal character of religious language. One consequence of this is that they have been deeply affected by idolatry:

> insofar as male dominant language is honored as the only or the supremely fitting way of speaking about God, it absolutizes a single set of metaphors and obscures the height and depth and length and breadth of divine mystery. Thus it does damage to the very truth of God that theology is supposed to cherish and promote.[85]

Johnson's challenge to traditional monotheisms is thus presented as a medicine needed to restore their health. Moreover, by supplementing her argument with a detailed account of the way in which talk about God was regarded as provisional within the early Judaeo-Christian tradition, she is able to emphasize the degree of sensitivity that the theologians of antiquity displayed to the consideration that language about God could never be literally true.[86]

Like Gage, then, Johnson also believes that over-literalness with respect to God, which overtook the common understanding of religious language after antiquity, supported particular forms of civil and religious institutions. And a key problem with any symbol of God that is modelled on a solitary ruling male is that it lends legitimacy to social structures within which a single man dominates everyone else, with a prime example being the way in which the Father God's singular position is still thought to legitimize the patriarchal structure of the Roman Catholic Church to this day – a structure within which the pope is envisaged as the powerful representative of the heavenly patriarch 'above'.

The masculinity of God is, as Johnson and many other Christian feminists have pointed out, exacerbated within the Christian tradition by the significance commonly accorded to Jesus' gender.[87] As Johnson acutely observes: 'when Jesus' maleness, which belongs to his historical identity, is interpreted to be essential to his redeeming christic function and identity, then the Christ serves as a religious tool for marginalizing and excluding women'.[88] Within the Christian tradition, Jesus is regarded as the revelation of God in human flesh. And given the maleness of Jesus, it comes naturally to many people (including, as we have seen, C. S. Lewis),[89] to assume that masculinity must have a greater affinity with God than femininity. Thus, as Johnson remarks:

> What androcentric anthropology already holds as a basic assumption, Christology confirms: men are not only more truly theomorphic but, in virtue of their sex, also christomorphic in a way that goes beyond what is possible for women. As stated in an official argument against women's ordination, for example, men, thanks to their 'natural resemblance' enjoy a capacity for closer identification with Christ than do women.[90]

Johnson develops a two-pronged response to this assumption. She argues, first, that it is a mistake to accept the polarity between male and female that this style of anthropology assumes.[91] Second, she points out that Jesus' gender is one of several 'historical particularities' of his person, others being his 'racial characteristics, linguistic heritage, [and] social class'.[92] But as, in her view, no one regards these other characteristics as having any particular relevance to Jesus' capacity to represent God,[93] she concludes that there is no reason to settle on his gender as having special significance. Furthermore, Jesus the historical figure has been transformed into the body of Christ, which incorporates all Christians.

Thus, Johnson argues that whatever is actually significant about Jesus-conceived-as-the-Christ can equally well be captured by thinking of him in female terms as in male, proposing that the term *Christa* be adopted to refer to those female Christians whose lives reveal something about God. Interestingly, Ruether also reaches a similar conclusion regarding how the ongoing link between Christ and the Christian community should be conceptualized:

> Christ, as redemptive person and Word of God, is not to be encapsulated 'once-for-all' in the historical Jesus. The Christian community continues Christ's identity. As vine and branches Christic personhood continues in our sisters and brothers. In the language of early Christian prophetism, we can encounter Christ *in the form of our sister*. Christ, the liberated humanity, is not confined to a static perfection of one person two thousand years ago. Rather, redemptive humanity goes ahead of us, calling us to yet incompleted dimensions of human liberation.[94]

What has stood in the way of women's aspirations within the Christian community, then, is a form of religious anthropology that has portrayed them as intrinsically inferior to men. Likewise, within Judaism and Islam, the traditionally dominant religious anthropology has portrayed women and men as having essentially different natures – natures that have been taken to determine their unchangeable roles within the religious community. The result has been that an army of male rabbis, priests and mullas have been thought to represent the Father God's authority to those disqualified by gender from rising up the religious hierarchy or from having access to the sacred texts. Not only have Christian and Jewish women confronted such religious sexism, but Muslim women, too, have challenged the misogynistic religious anthropology by means of which, they believe, male interpreters have corrupted Allah's revelation. But before we conclude that misogynistic religious anthropologies are the sole cause of the problems that modern women face in their confrontation with traditional religion, we need to examine another theory that, at first sight, appears to provide an alternative explanation.

Fatima Mernissi, an influential Muslim feminist, develops a feminist critique of Islam that is very different from any we have considered thus far.[95] For she argues that the problems that Islam poses for women are quite unlike those which Christianity presents. She has two reasons for this claim: first, women are portrayed as having a very different nature within each tradition; and second, Islam should not be understood as anti-women, in the sense that she takes Christianity to be, but rather as opposed to intimacy between women and men. It is in her elaboration of this second point that Mernissi's ideas are distinctive. For she insists that

the Muslim system is not so much opposed to women as to the heterosexual unit. What is feared is the growth of the involvement between a
man and a woman into an all-encompassing love satisfying the sexual,
emotional and intellectual needs of both partners. Such an involvement constitutes a direct threat to man's allegiance to Allah, which
requires the unconditional investment of all his energies, thoughts and
feelings in his God.[96]

In Mernissi's analysis, therefore, the threat which modern women, such
as herself, are seen to pose to Islam is not primarily due to their demand
for equality or for political rights but, rather, lies in their demand for a
transformation of male–female relationships and in their altered expectations regarding such relationships. It is the pressure for a change in the
relations between the sexes that, in her view, constitutes the most significant threat to Islam to have emerged over the course of the twentieth
century.

The real issue for women, Mernissi insists, is not an ideology within
which women are portrayed as inferior; rather, it is the laws and customs
that institutionalize their subjugation. Laws relating to the family, for
example, promote just such an institutionalized subjugation of women.
For family law in traditional Muslim societies is still based on oppressive seventh-century Islamic family law, which was simply carried over
into modern legislation. Mernissi explains that, in the seventh century,
Muhammad created the institution of the Muslim family – an institution
that was, apparently, quite unlike anything that had existed in Arabia
prior to that time. Indeed, Muhammad made the Muslim family the central unit of the community of believers. And because the Muslim family
was a radical departure from the past, it had to be supported by an intri-
cate web of legislation. Thus, the Qur'ān contains a great deal of precise
legislation on marriage, the family and sex. But because all this detail is
in the Qur'ān, and because traditional Muslims believe that the Qur'ān
is valid for all time, the institution of marriage within Islam is preserved
in a form that strikes modern women as archaic. This has given rise to a
great deal of debate between, on the one hand, traditionalists who argue
that the laws to do with marriage, the family and sex cannot be altered,
and, on the other hand, those who argue that it would be consistent with
Islam to modernize these laws.[97]

Mernissi observes that those on both sides of this debate simply assume
that Islam should constitute the foundation of society. But in her view, by
relying on this assumption, they both show themselves to be mistaken.
For the problem is not simply that Islam happens to have laws relating to
women which are hopelessly outdated and which unacceptably subjugate
and oppress women. Rather, the problem is that these laws are fundamental to the Muslim view of God and of the relation of human beings

to the divinity, which is one of complete submission. Thus, in arguing that the problem is deeper than both sides of the debate realize, Mernissi claims that there is a fundamental contradiction between enforcing an Islamic society and pursuing an official policy of sexual equality. And, in her view, this contradiction is generated because '[s]exual equality violates Islam's premiss, actualized in its laws, that heterosexual love is dangerous to Allah's order'.[98]

One might assume that the link between women's subjugation and Islam was caused by viewing women as inferior to men, as in the case of Christianity. But as I have already intimated, Mernissi believes that this is not so. For she argues that the assumption that women are powerful and dangerous beings is what is fundamental to Islam, and that the sexual institutions of the religion, like polygamy and sexual segregation, should be understood as devices for containing this power. To be precise, women are viewed as having the power to distract men both from God and from the work needed to hold society together. Hence, the Islamic institutions regarding sexual relationships are specifically designed to prevent women and men from forming any partnership that might exclude God. So, what actually lies behind the subjection of women is the viewing of them as potentially destructive and dangerous. Thus, as Mernissi comments: 'The whole Muslim organization of social interaction and spatial configuration can be understood in terms of women's ... power. The social order then appears as an attempt to subjugate her power and neutralize its disruptive effects.'[99] Clearly, this is not a case of viewing women as inherently inferior to men.

Mernissi, therefore, provides a very different analysis of the root of the subordination that modern women experience within traditional Islam. However, there remains an important similarity between her account and that of the other feminist thinkers we have considered. For she, too, acknowledges that the key problem lies in religious anthropology.[100] And although Mernissi claims that Islamic anthropology is not intrinsically denigratory of women, she nevertheless admits that it has given rise to societies in which women are seriously oppressed and discriminated against in the name of Allah.

Perhaps two comments are in order at this juncture. First, it is not clear that Christianity is as different from Islam as Mernissi claims. One reason why priests and nuns are traditionally kept separate is so that they may devote all their time to God without distraction. Moreover, there is a tradition within Christianity that sees women as powerful temptresses. Second, if women are not viewed as inferior to men, but as equally powerful, and if men and women distract each other from their religious pursuits whenever they are together, then the obvious solution is to keep them apart, just as nuns are kept apart from priests. To subjugate one sex to the other is a bizarre 'solution' unless there is also some additional derogatory view of the subjugated sex. In fact, in a later work, Mernissi appears to have reconsidered her analysis when she postulates that the sexist practices of Muslim societies have not developed out of Islam but have been smuggled in as remnants of pre-Islamic cultures.[101] Nevertheless, she remains in agreement with all of the feminists considered above that such institutions cannot be tolerated and must be fought.

In sum, what the religious feminists surveyed thus far in this chapter envisage is the more or less radical reassessment of religious ideas and institutions. Some of them have formulated a criterion to guide this reassessment. According to Johnson, the criterion ought to be 'the emancipation of women toward human flourishing'.[102] Application of a criterion such as this would result, or so religious feminists believe, in the transformation of traditional religions – a transformation that would involve a rejection of former ways of characterizing gender differences, as well as a revolution in the conception of God central to these traditions. But would the transformed monotheistic traditions and their altered conception of God still be recognizable as Judaism, Christianity and Islam? It may be that the result of applying a feminist criterion, such as the one formulated by Johnson, in order to shape the future of any Abrahamic faith would be the wholesale demise of the original tradition. C. S. Lewis, for one, is unable to contemplate a 'Christianity' in which God is not conceptualized as 'Father' and the priesthood is not composed entirely of males.[103] Maybe this is simply a failure of imagination, which would be surprising coming from the author of *The Chronicles of Narnia*. Nevertheless, some feminist thinkers agree with Lewis' assessment. They argue that the monotheisms are so deeply patriarchal that none of the strategies devised can save them. Religious feminists, if they succeed in carrying out their proposals, will inevitably end up with something very different from traditional Judaism, Christianity or Islam. Some, therefore, have argued that religious feminists ought to accept this, perhaps unwelcome truth, and unashamedly develop post-Jewish, post-Christian and post-Islamic traditions and theologies.

The exodus

Those who, as a result of feminist analysis, have opted to go beyond the boundaries of their inherited religious traditions claim that feminists who remain within the traditions are fighting a losing battle. The former regard the monotheisms as simply too patriarchal, their heritage of patriarchal, tribal Judaism condemning them from the start. Moreover, in the final assessment, many feminists judge Judaism, Christianity and Islam to be intrinsically inimical to women. This harsh conclusion has led many women to walk out of their synagogues, churches and mosques.[104]

However, not all thinkers who judge that Judaism, Christianity or Islam ought to be rejected on feminist grounds want to go so far as to give up all claim to being religious. For some feminists, religion seems to be too deeply connected to their sense of self-identity and personal well-being for them to abandon it – and many find atheistic secular humanism unattractive. The challenge for such thinkers is to construct a new religious identity that is uninfected by the sexism which they see as afflicting the traditional monotheisms.

Thinkers who respond to feminism's critique of religion in this way typically argue that one can freely select from the old traditions whatever seems spiritually beneficial, and reject the rest. At this point, post-Jewish, post-Christian and post-Islamic feminists join company with others who have rejected traditional forms of monotheism, yet who, nevertheless, wish to retain some form of spiritual life. However, what guides a feminist's choice of an alternative spirituality is quite distinctive. Religious feminists typically seek access to a religious experience that is not distorted from the start by a male view of reality.

The two most popular forms that such alternative spiritualities began to take at the close of the twentieth century were Goddess worship and witchcraft.[105] Through both of these routes, women attempt to unearth the resources they believe may be found in what they take to be pre-patriarchal spirituality. And they do so with the specific aim of retrieving female symbols of the divine. Although some modern women find these symbols, ostensibly retrieved from the ancient past, very difficult to assimilate, others argue that it is, nevertheless, essential to use such symbols if the old androcentric ones are not to slip back into their traditional place and fill the gap left in women's religious consciousness by their absence.[106]

Daphne Hampson is a post-Christian and a clear example of someone who, in rejecting her former tradition, refuses to reject all religious values.[107] Like many radical feminists who are also religious, she insists that new myths and ceremonies can be invented – ones that better meet the needs of women. She thus attempts to distinguish between being a religious person and being a religious person trapped within a specific religious tradition. In this she is reminiscent of Gage, who also wanted to discard the Christian tradition, which she perceived as the source of women's oppression, in order to be genuinely religious.

Finally, in this chapter, we return to Rosemary Radford Ruether. We shall see that she goes even further in rejecting traditional Judaeo-Christian conceptions of God than most other religious feminists are prepared to go. For Ruether claims not only that it is appropriate to criticize traditional conceptions of God from a feminist perspective but also that there are compelling environmental reasons for challenging traditional religious beliefs.

Ecofeminist theology

Ecofeminist theology arose from the idea that the problems feminist theology and eco-theology each address are not as unrelated as might at first appear. Indeed, ecofeminists such as Ruether go so far as to argue that the problems are, in point of fact, deeply interrelated. Hence, ecofeminist theology aims to integrate the insights of both eco-theology and feminist theology in order to provide a combined approach to the problems of social injustice and the domination of nature.[108]

Ruether's ecofeminism has led her to advocate radical changes within Christian theology, including changes in the way that Christians think about themselves, God and the world. Her hope is that these transformations will lead to radical changes in their social relations and in their lifestyles – changes that will be both friendly to women and benign to the environment. However, Ruether is careful not to assume that changes in the social and environmental situation will automatically follow from changes in religious ideas. Instead, she argues that theological or spiritual changes are just one aspect of a more comprehensive programme for change, which must also include explicit proposals for restructuring society as a whole. And being a theologian does not prevent Ruether from making numerous suggestions regarding the practical changes to social relations that she believes are necessitated by the quest for what she terms 'ecojustice'. And in demanding ecojustice, she rejects both capitalism and communism, opting instead for a form of social communitarianism.

Ruether became an ecofeminist in the 1970s, when she became aware that two distinct revolutions were under way, each developing under the impetus of a different social movement: one social movement is environmentalism, which campaigns for changes in human lifestyles in order to make them less environmentally destructive; the other is the third-world development movement, which aims at the liberation of the poor and oppressed in the south. The first of these movements, Ruether claims, is the more elitist of the two, being supported by a minority within the rich world. The latter movement, however, has tended to regard the environment as exclusively the concern of the rich, and pushes for technological progress within the underdeveloped world. The irony is that the progress called for by the third-world development movement is often environmentally destructive. Hence, these two movements often work at cross-purposes, and the revolutions in our thinking and lifestyles that they demand seem to push in different directions.

Ruether's core claim is that the women's movement is uniquely placed with regard to solving the problems that preoccupy the environmental and the third-world development movements. For, by developing a feminine perspective that can easily be made consistent with environmental and social justice concerns, the aims of both movements might be rendered compatible. Indeed, she goes further in arguing that the environmental movement cannot ultimately achieve success without the simultaneous success of the women's movement, because on its own, the perspective of environmentalism is too restricted to solve the problems it has set itself the task of solving. This is because women are often driven through the oppression they encounter to engage in environmentally destructive actions, and without a feminist solution, these actions will continue. But neither can the third-world development movement ultimately succeed without the simultaneous success of the women's movement, because those who suffer most in the underdeveloped world are usually women. Hence, a feminist perspective is required to solve their problems.

Ruether argues not only that the environmental and the third-world development movements on their own provide inadequate solutions, but also that the women's movement is incomplete by itself. And she does so by pointing out that two issues that had previously been regarded as separate are, in fact, connected: namely, the human domination of nature and the domination of women by men. As she writes:

> Women must see that there can be no liberation for them and no solution to the ecological crisis within a society whose fundamental model of relationships continues to be one of domination. They must unite the demands of the women's movement with those of the ecological movement to envision a radical reshaping of the basic socioeconomic relations and the underlying values of this society.[109]

This is a common theme within ecofeminism, but Ruether applies these ideas to theology, claiming that any theology adequate to the problems of today must address both the issue of environmental degradation and the issue of social injustice, particularly the injustice suffered by the vast majority of women. But most traditional theology is unsuited to the task, because, in her view, it has been androcentric and anthropocentric. In other words, it has been developed primarily from a male standpoint and from a human one; the latter failing to see humans as part of the web of nature. And because of the limitations of the perspective adopted by traditional theology, it has encouraged what Ruether calls 'a double domination': the domination of men over women, and the domination of humans over nature. Moreover, these two dominations, in her judgement, both have a common cause: namely, the dualistic worldview adopted by the early Christians, which emphasized a purportedly radical discontinuity between spirit and matter, God and nature, and men and women.

Notwithstanding these theological claims, a significant proportion of Ruether's work has fallen within the realm of cultural history rather than within Christian theology – although she does deploy what she has discovered about ancient cultural history within a critique of modern

Christianity and its theology. As part of her study of Western culture, Ruether has explored in detail the developing perception of women as objects to be dominated. In seeking to establish that this negative perception of women began to emerge at a very early stage in human history, she refers us to the Babylonian creation story (dating from the third millennium BC). In this myth,

> Marduk, the warrior champion of the gods of the city states, is seen as creating the cosmos by conquering the Mother Goddess Tiamat, pictured as a monstrous female animal. Marduk kills her, treads her body underfoot, and then splits it in half, using one half to fashion the starry firmament of the skies, and the other half the earth below. The elemental mother is literally turned into the matter out of which the cosmos is fashioned (not accidentally, the words *mother* and *matter* have the same etymological root). She can be used as matter only by being killed; that is, by destroying her as 'wild', autonomous life, making her life-giving body into 'stuff' possessed and controlled by the architect of a male-defined cosmos.[110]

This myth, and others like it, seems to confirm that a dualistic way of thinking about the differences between women and men had developed by a very early stage in human cultural history. In particular, the tendency to identify women with matter, and to view men as those who had control over matter, would appear, Ruether argues, to be an ancient one. And this early dualistic worldview gradually developed in a specific form that portrays reality as constituted by soulless matter (regarded as female) on the one hand, and by transcendent consciousness (regarded as male) on the other. And it is precisely this form of dualism, Ruether opines, that has given rise to both the degradation of the environment and the oppression of women. Consequently, Ruether believes that if these problems are to be effectively tackled, then it is crucial to understand the intimate connection between them. And such understanding, she insists, requires attending to the plight of women, for the '[d]omination of women has provided a key link, both socially and symbolically, to the domination of the earth'.[111]

The way forward, then, must involve rejecting such dualisms in order to rediscover our genuine place within the natural world. And if we focus upon our present relation to nature, then we will soon discover that we are currently living as parasites on the food chain, taking far more from the world than we ever give back. But once we discover that our behaviour is parasitical, we will seek to correct the situation. Ruether claims that the first step will consist in the recognition of our utter dependence upon 'the great life-producing matrix of the planet'.[112] And this recognition will allow us to 'reintegrate our human systems of production, consumption, and waste into the ecological patterns by which nature sustains life'.[113] Moreover, as she also argues, an essential part of this reintegration will involve re-conceptualizing the place of human consciousness, or mind, within nature. For within Western culture, there has been a tendency to perceive mind as something transcending nature and originating outside it. It is often perceived as that which distinguishes humans from the rest of the natural world. But a more accurate image of the mind, Ruether avers, will perceive it as 'the place where nature itself becomes conscious'.[114] And this change in how we perceive the human mind within nature will also, she argues, impact upon our conception of God. Rather than

> modelling God after alienated male consciousness, outside of and ruling over nature ... [,] God, in ecofeminist spirituality, is the immanent source of life that sustains the whole planetary community. God is neither male nor anthropomorphic. God is the font from which the variety of plants and animals well up in each new generation, the matrix that sustains their life-giving interdependency with one another.[115]

In an ecofeminist vision of reality, then, there are no hierarchies or dualisms. Instead, mutual dependency provides the principal model for construing the relationships that obtain between all beings. And Ruether argues that if we employ this model of mutual dependency, then we will have a tool with which to transform the social injustices of our world, as well as to stem environmental degradation. Hence, she offers the adoption of this model as an alternative to the Christian response to the environmental crisis that emphasizes stewardship, excoriating the latter because of its tendency to disregard social injustices and its advocacy of a merely conservationist ethic. The alternative perspective developed by Ruether focuses, instead, on the notion of a covenant between God and creation. This covenant she understands as including both humans and non-human nature. Moreover, the covenant is such as to entail humans having ethical obligations not only to other humans but also to non-humans. Air, soil and water pollution, among other things, are thus seen to be violations of this covenant. And Ruether is well aware of the radical implications of her view. For she is explicit in pointing out that the changes to the Christian vision of reality that she advocates would involve nothing less than a 'conversion' regarding the way in which Christians think about themselves, their culture, their social relationships and, crucially, God.[116]

Conclusion

As we have just seen, Ruether claims that adopting an ecofeminist vision of reality involves a radical transformation of the Christian conception of God. We have also seen that many other religious feminists have been driven to a similar conclusion. Thus, their work stands in continuity with that of many other twentieth-century religious thinkers who, as we saw in earlier chapters, also find traditional ways of construing God unsatisfactory and inappropriate in late modernity. Nevertheless, not all religious thinkers share this appraisal. And as we shall see in the chapter that follows, religious fundamentalism – which vigorously opposes the sorts of changes to religious beliefs and practices endorsed by religious feminists – also emerged as a powerful current within twentieth-century religious thought.

Study questions

1 To what extent are Matilda Josyln Gage's criticisms of nineteenth-century Christianity also applicable to Christianity in both the twentieth and twenty-first centuries?

2 Why do religious feminists claim that it is so important that women and not just men interpret sacred texts? Are they right to be concerned that only the interpretations of men have shaped the religious traditions that we have today?

3 What does it mean to claim that traditional interpretations of sacred texts are gendered? Do you think it is possible to arrive at a non-gendered interpretation? If so, how might this be achieved?

4 What exactly was so radical about the idea of using the experience of women as a source of scriptural interpretation and theology?

5 How might the arguments of Louis Bouyer and C. S. Lewis be made more convincing? What are the main weaknesses of their positions?

6 In what ways can particular religious anthropologies influence conceptions of God? Does the direction of influence also go the other way? Should it? Can the concept 'God' ever be fully independent from a religious theory of the nature of humans, both men and women?

7 Do religious feminists within Islam face problems that are not encountered by Jewish or Christian feminists? If so, what are these problems?

8 If you were asked to formulate a criterion to guide the reassessment of religious ideas and institutions, what would you propose? What would be the main goals of your proposal?

9 How does ecofeminist theology differ from eco-theology? What distinctive contribution does the former hope to make to our global situation?

Select bibliography

Adler, R., 1997, *Engendering Judaism*, Philadelphia: Jewish Publication Society.

Engineer, A. A., 1992, *The Rights of Women in Islam*, London: C. Hurst & Company.

Gage, M. J., 1980, *Women, Church and State: A Historical Account of the Status of Woman through the Christian Ages: With reminiscences of the matriarchate*, Watertown, Massachusetts: Persephone Press.

Hampson, D., 1996, *After Christianity*, London: SCM Press.

Jaggar, A. M., 1983, *Feminist Politics and Human Nature*, Brighton: The Harvester Press.

Jantzen, G. M., 1999, *Becoming Divine: Towards a Feminist Philosophy of Religion*, Bloomington and Indianapolis: Indiana University Press.

Johnson, E. A., 1994, *She Who Is: The Mystery of God in Feminist Theological Discourse*, New York: Crossroads.

McFague, S., 1993, *The Body of God: An Ecological Theology*, Minneapolis: Fortress Press.

Mernissi, F., 1985, *Beyond the Veil: Male–Female Dynamics in Modern Muslim Society*, London: Al Saqi Books.

Mernissi, F., 1991, *The Veil and the Male Elite: A Feminist Interpretation of Women's Rights in Islam*, trans. by Mary Jo Lakeland, Reading, Massachusetts: Addison-Wesley Publishing Company.

Plaskow, J., 1990, *Standing Again at Sinai: Judaism from a Feminist Perspective*, New York: HarperCollins Publishers.

Ruether, R. R., 1983, *Sexism and God-Talk: Towards a Feminist Theology*, London: SCM Press.

Ruether, R. R., 1993, *Gaia & God: An Ecofeminist Theology of Earth Healing*, London: SCM Press.

Schüssler Fiorenza, E., 1983, *In Memory of Her: A Feminist Theological Reconstruction of Christian Origins*, New York: Crossroads.

Wadud-Muhsin, A., 1992, *Qur'an and Woman*, Kuala Lumpur: Penerbit Fajar.

Notes

1 A similar movement was simultaneously gathering force in the Arab world, particularly within Egypt and Turkey. Some of the core texts of the Arab feminist movement are available in English translation in Margot Badran and Miriam Cooke (eds), 1992, *Opening the Gates: A Century of Arab Feminist Writing*, London: Virago Press.

2 Matilda Joslyn Gage, 1980, *Women, Church and State: A Historical Account of the Status of Woman through the Christian Ages: With reminiscences of the matriarchate*, Watertown, Massachusetts: Persephone Press, p. 544.

3 For a graphic portrayal of some of the problems which these archaic divorce laws generate today, see the documentary film *Divorce: Iranian Style* (directed by Kim Loninotto and Ziba Mir-Hosseini, 1998, UK).

4 Although Gage applied her ideas exclusively to the Christian tradition, many of them are equally relevant, as we shall see, to the Jewish and Muslim traditions.

5 'The Fall', where Adam disobeys God under Eve's prompting, and which is recounted in Genesis 3.1–7, has played a major role within the Christian tradition. Augustine (AD 354–430), an enormously influential Latin theologian, developed the original myth by adding to it the concept 'original sin'.

6 Gage, *Women*, p. 11.

7 This strategy of comparing the oppression of women under a religious tradition with their more favourable situation prior to the dominance of that tradition has also been adopted by Muslim writers. See, for example, Fatima Mernissi, 1985, *Beyond the Veil: Male–Female Dynamics in Modern Muslim Society*, London: Al Saqi Books, chapter 3.

8 See Gage, *Women*, p. 20.

9 See Gage, *Women*, p. 43.

10 See Genesis 3.16. For a Muslim account of women's ongoing punishment for Eve's misbehaviour, see al-Ghazali's list of its 18 forms in his *Book of Council for Kings*. Cited in Ibn Warraq, 1995, *Why I Am Not a Muslim*, New York: Prometheus Books, p. 300.

11 Genesis 2.7 and 21–23 NRSV.

12 Each of the monotheistic traditions has developed this legend, reinforcing the impression it gives of woman having been created inferior to man. Muslim tradition, for example, ascribes to Muhammad the following saying: 'Be friendly to women for womankind was created from a rib, but the bent part of the rib, high up, if you try to straighten it you will break it; if you do nothing, she will continue to be bent.' Cited in Warraq, *Why*, p. 295. Many apparently misogynistic hadiths, such as this one, are regarded as authentic by traditional Muslims. But see Fatima Mernissi, 1991, *The Veil and the Male Elite: A Feminist Interpretation of Women's Rights in Islam*, trans. by Mary Jo Lakeland, Reading, Massachusetts: Addison-Wesley Publishing Company.

13 Gage, *Women*, p. 54.

14 See Gage, *Women*, pp. 62f.

15 Gage, *Women*, p. 69.

16 See Elisabeth Schüssler Fiorenza, 1983, *In Memory of Her: A Feminist Theological Reconstruction of Christian Origins*, New York: Crossroads.

17 See Gage, *Women*, p. 355.

18 A remarkably similar view prevailed in the Muslim world. This attitude towards women is encapsulated in a well-known hadith which many Muslims believe records Muhammad's words: 'If it had been given me to order someone to prostrate themselves in front of someone other than God, I would surely have ordered women to prostrate themselves in front of their husbands. ... A woman cannot fulfill her duties towards God without first having accomplished those that she owes her husband.' Cited in Warraq, *Why*, p. 298.

19 See Gage, *Women*, p. 314.

20 And continues in some non-Western countries even today.

21 Gage, *Women*, p. 228.

22 Gage, *Women*, p. 329.

23 Quoted in Gage, *Women*, pp. 492f. This chilling sermon might fruitfully be compared with the disturbing film *10 Rillington Place* (directed by Richard Fleischer, 1971, UK), which is based on a true story. Upon discovering that her husband (played by Richard Attenborough) is a brutal serial killer, a down-

trodden housewife in 1940s Britain feels compelled to respect and defer to the unexpected tastes of her spouse – even to the extent of lying to the police on his behalf.

24 Gage, *Women*, p. 493.

25 Gage, *Women*, pp. 521f.

26 Genesis 1.1–2.3 is dated at about 400 BC; while Genesis 2.4–3.24, which provides the better-known account, is dated at approximately 900 BC.

27 Genesis 1.26a and 27 NRSV.

28 Judith Plaskow, 1990, *Standing again at Sinai: Judaism from a Feminist Perspective*, New York: HarperCollins Publishers, p. 25.

29 See Plaskow, *Standing*, pp. 25f.

30 See Chapter 3, p. 45, above.

31 Many Jewish feminists now claim that if women are to participate fully in Judaism, then it is essential for *halakah* to be reformed. The work of Rachel Adler attempts precisely such a reformation. See Rachel Adler, 1997, *Engendering Judaism*, Philadelphia: Jewish Publication Society.

32 Moses Maimonides, seeking to clarify the Mishnah's somewhat counter-intuitive stance on women's study of the Torah, writes: 'A woman who studies Torah will be recompensed, but not in the same measure as a man, for study was not imposed on her as a duty, and one who performs a meritorious act which is not obligatory will not receive the same reward as one upon whom it is incumbent and one who fulfills it as a duty, but only a lesser reward.' Moses Maimonides, 1965, *Mishneh Torah: The Book of Knowledge*, Laws Concerning the Study of the Torah, chapter 1.13, trans. by Moses Hyamson, Jerusalem: Boys Town Jerusalem Publishers, p. 58a.

33 See Judith Romney Wegner, 1988, *Chattel or Person? The Status of Women in the Mishnah*, New York: Oxford University Press.

34 Rachel Adler, '"I've Had Nothing Yet So I Can't Take More"', *Moment*, 8 (September 1983), p. 22.

35 Plaskow, *Standing*, pp. 27f.

36 Plaskow, *Standing*, p. 34.

37 Warraq, *Why*, p. 293.

38 Mernissi, *Veil*, p. 64.

39 An early example was the *Woman's Bible* by Elizabeth Cady Stanton (1815–1902), published in 1895.

40 Amina Wadud-Muhsin, 1992, *Qur'an and Woman*, Kuala Lumpur: Penerbit Fajar, p. 1.

41 Wadud-Muhsin, *Qur'an*, p. 12, note 1.

42 Wadud-Muhsin, *Qur'an*, p. 1. Wadud-Muhsin is not, of course, the only Muslim who reads the Qur'ān from a critical feminist perspective. See also Asma Barlas, 2002, *'Believing Women' in Islam: Unreading Patriarchal Interpretations of the Qur'an*, Austin: University of Texas Press.

43 Wadud-Muhsin, *Qur'an*, p. 2.

44 Wadud-Muhsin, *Qur'an*, p. 2.

45 Similarly, Benazir Bhutto claims that the distinctions routinely made between women and men by traditional Muslims are not found in the Qur'ān. In her view, it 'is man and it is the *mullas* … who make these discriminations and who give the wrong impression of our religion not only to the outside world but

to Muslims ourselves'. Benazir Bhutto, 'Politics and the Muslim Woman', Cambridge, Massachusetts: unpublished audio recording, Rama Mehta Lecture, Radcliffe College Archive, 11 April 1985. Quoted in Charles Kurzman (ed.), 1998, *Liberal Islam: A Sourcebook*, Oxford: Oxford University Press, p. 110.

46 Nazira Zein-ed-Din, 'Removing the Veil and Veiling: Towards Women's Liberation and Social Reform', trans. by Salah-Dine Hammoud in *Women's Studies International Forum*, 5 (1982), pp. 223–6. Cited in Kurzman, *Liberal*, p. 104.

47 Early feminists tended to refer to 'women's experience'. Late twentieth-century feminists, however, came to feel that 'women's experience' is an overly abstract concept. Consequently, later feminist works emphasize that the experience of women is not homogenous but richly varied, being dependent upon factors such as social status and racial/ethnic background. Distinctive forms of theology have developed from this recognition of difference, one of the most prominent being 'womanist theology', which draws on the experience of black women Christians.

48 Rosemary Radford Ruether, 1983, *Sexism and God-Talk: Towards a Feminist Theology*, London: SCM Press, p. 13.

49 Daphne Hampson, 1990, *Theology and Feminism*, Oxford: Blackwell, p. 1.

50 Elizabeth A. Johnson, 1994, *She Who Is: The Mystery of God in Feminist Theological Discourse*, New York: Crossroads, p. 29.

51 See 1 Corinthians 14.34.

52 The Roman Catholic Church's official arguments against the ordination of women to the priesthood are contained in its 'Declaration on the Question of Admission of Women to the Ministerial Priesthood' (Vatican City, 15 October 1976). There is a website devoted to an examination of the case for and against the ordination of women in the Roman Catholic Church. Arguments based on tradition, Scripture and theology are summarized, and an impressive range of books, articles and documents is available. See http://www.womenpriests.org.

53 See Schüssler Fiorenza, *Memory*.

54 Louis Bouyer, 1984, *Woman in the Church*, trans. by Marilyn Teichert, San Francisco: Ignatius Press.

55 Bouyer, *Woman*, p. 16.

56 Bouyer, *Woman*, p. 21.

57 Bouyer, *Woman*, p. 21.

58 Bouyer, *Woman*, p. 28.

59 Bouyer, *Woman*, p. 23.

60 This is Elizabeth Johnson's phrase. See *She Who Is*.

61 See Victoria S. Harrison, 'Feminist Philosophy of Religion and the Problem of Epistemic Privilege', *Heythrop Journal*, forthcoming.

62 Bouyer, *Woman*, p. 24.

63 Bouyer introduces this argument by first considering the campaign for racial equality within the United States. According to his analysis, when blacks were admitted to the political echelons of white society, they quickly noticed that their new situation was worse than South African apartheid. Blacks found that the integration into white society that they had been offered was not a benefit but rather undermined their identity as blacks. Bouyer does not conclude that

the problem may have been with the society that the blacks were invited to join; instead, he opines that it was a mistake to have allowed them to join in the first place. See *Woman*, pp. 24f.

64 Bouyer, *Woman*, p. 27.

65 C. S. Lewis, 'Priestesses in the Church?' in Bouyer, *Woman*, pp. 123–32.

66 Lewis, 'Priestesses', p. 124.

67 Lewis, 'Priestesses', p. 124.

68 This argument is accepted by many conservatively inclined Anglicans. See, for example, John Saward, 1977, *Christ and His Bride*, London: Church Literature Association.

69 Lewis, 'Priestesses', pp. 127f.

70 For an excellent anthology guiding the reader through the main developments within the second wave, see Linda Nicholson (ed.), 1997, *The Second Wave: A Reader in Feminist Theory*, London: Routledge.

71 A sympathetic portrayal of this phenomenon is given in the film *The Return of Sarah's Daughters* (directed by Marcia Jarmel, 1997, USA).

72 See Tamar Frankiel, 1990, *The Voice of Sarah: Feminine Spirituality and Traditional Judaism*, New York: Biblio Press.

73 'Conservatives' in the sense used here should not automatically be equated with Jews belonging to the Conservative Movement, which is a particular branch of Judaism. See Chapter 3.

74 For a study of this debate within Judaism, see Pamela Susan Nadell, 1998, *Women Who Would Be Rabbis: A History of Women's Ordination, 1889–1985*, Boston: Beacon Press.

75 Sachiko Murata, 1992, *The Tao of Islam: A Sourcebook on Gender Relationships in Islamic Thought*, Albany: SUNY, p. 4.

76 Marcia Falk, 'Towards a Feminist Jewish Reconstruction of Monotheism', *Tikkun: A Bi-Monthly Jewish Critique of Politics, Culture and Society*, 4 (July/August 1989), p. 53.

77 Johnson, *She*.

78 Unfortunately, she does not consider how her work might apply within Islam.

79 Johnson, *She*, p. 4.

80 Marcia Falk, within Judaism, and Rosemary Radford Ruether, within Roman Catholic Christianity, each offer a penetrating analysis of the concept 'God', and both provide an account of how they consider the concept to have been misused. In both cases, their attempt to retrieve the concept 'God' from misuse leads them towards an ecofeminist theology. Ruether's later work, in particular, is increasingly focused in this direction. See Falk, 'Towards'; and Rosemary Radford Ruether, 1993, *Gaia & God: An Ecofeminist Theology of Earth Healing*, London: SCM Press. We consider ecofeminist theology later in this chapter.

81 Johnson, *She*, p. 6.

82 Lewis, 'Priestesses', p. 128.

83 This continues both in the Creed that many Christians confess weekly in their churches, which begins with the statement 'We believe in God, The Father almighty', and in the prayer that the majority of Christians are taught as children which begins by addressing God as 'Our Father'. The long tradition of Christian

art, which typically portrays God the Father as a still-vigorous, elderly gent, also continues to reinforce this male stereotyping of the divinity.

84 See Chapter 5.

85 Johnson, *She*, p. 18.

86 A similar sensitivity has also been characteristic of many Muslim theologians through the ages.

87 See, for example, Ruether, *Sexism*, chapter 5.

88 Johnson, *She*, p. 151.

89 Cf.: 'it is an old saying in the army that you salute the uniform not the wearer. Only one wearing the masculine uniform can represent the Lord to the Church. ... We men often make very bad priests. That is because we are insufficiently masculine.' Lewis, 'Priestesses', p. 131.

90 Johnson, *She*, pp. 152f.

91 See Johnson, *She*, p. 156.

92 Johnson, *She*, p. 166.

93 Johnson seems to be unaware that black Christians, such as the Zulu Zionists, challenge the image of Jesus as white precisely because it fails adequately to represent God to non-whites.

94 Ruether, *Sexism*, p. 138.

95 Mernissi is a Moroccan, educated in France and the United States. Her maternal grandmother was kidnapped as a child, and spent the rest of her life in a harem. Mernissi herself grew up in a harem in Fez. Her autobiography contains a colourful and fascinating account of childhood. See Fatima Mernissi, 1997, *The Harem Within: Tales of a Moroccan Girlhood*, London: Bantam Books.

96 Mernissi, *Beyond*, p. 8.

97 For one example of a Muslim making the case for modernization, see Asghar Ali Engineer, 1992, *The Rights of Women in Islam*, London: C. Hurst & Company.

98 Mernissi, *Beyond*, p. 19.

99 Mernissi, *Beyond*, p. 33.

100 Religious feminists unanimously reject what they see as androcentric anthropologies favoured by patriarchal religious traditions. However, there is less agreement on what form of anthropology to put in its place. Different forms of feminism tend to have their own favoured anthropologies. For a detailed treatment of the variety of views of human nature that are aligned with some of the most important forms of feminism, see Alison M. Jaggar, 1983, *Feminist Politics and Human Nature*, Brighton: The Harvester Press.

101 See Mernissi, *Veil*, p. 81.

102 Johnson, *She*, p. 30.

103 See Lewis, 'Priestesses', p. 128.

104 With respect to Christianity, it has been argued that the Church's resistance to feminism is the principal cause of the dramatic decline in church attendance documented in Britain since the 1960s. See Callum G. Brown, 2000, *The Death of Christian Britain*, London: Routledge.

105 For a brief survey of some of the many forms in which women's spirituality is currently expressed, see Marie Tulip, 1990, 'Religion' in Sneja Gunew (ed.), *Feminist Knowledge: Critique and Construct*, London: Routledge, pp. 253–63.

106 See Carol P. Christ, 1979, 'Why Women Need the Goddess: Phenomeno-logical, Psychological, and Political Reflections' in Carol P. Christ and Judith Plaskow (eds), *Womanspirit Rising: A Feminist Reader in Religion*, New York: Harper & Row, pp. 273–87.

107 See Daphne Hampson, 1996, *After Christianity*, London: SCM Press.

108 The work of Rosemary Radford Ruether is, by and large, representa-tive of ecofeminist theology. However, she is by no means its sole proponent. Sallie McFague, for example, is also a prominent ecofeminist theologian. See Sallie McFague, 1987, *Models of God: Theology for an Ecological, Nuclear Age*, Philadelphia: Fortress Press; and Sallie McFague, 1993, *The Body of God: An Ecological Theology*, Minneapolis: Fortress Press.

109 Rosemary Radford Ruether, 1975, *New Woman/New Earth: Sexist Ideologies and Human Liberation*, San Francisco: Harper and Row, p. 204.

110 Rosemary Radford Ruether, 1996, 'Ecofeminism: Symbolic and Social Connections of the Oppression of Women and the Domination of Nature' in Roger S. Gottlieb (ed.), *This Sacred Earth: Religion, Nature, Environment*, New York: Routledge, p. 325.

111 Ruether, *Gaia*, p. 3.

112 Ruether, 'Ecofeminism', p. 330.

113 Ruether, 'Ecofeminism', p. 330.

114 Ruether, 'Ecofeminism', p. 330.

115 Ruether, 'Ecofeminism', p. 330.

116 See Ruether, *Gaia*, p. 86.

10

Religious Fundamentalism and Modernity

In this chapter we finally turn to a subject that we have touched upon many times throughout this book: religious fundamentalism. Previous chapters have emphasized the adaptations undergone by religious beliefs as those who hold them adjust to, and assimilate, various aspects of modern thought. We have seen that what on the surface can appear as a conflict between religion and modern ideas can also be seen as a tension-ridden, but nevertheless creative relationship in which traditional religious ideas are transformed for appropriation by new generations of believers. Now, however, we turn to those whose reaction to modernity appears to consist in a self-conscious refusal to adjust, or to assimilate, their religious ideas to its demands: an attitude, in other words, that appears characterizable by rejection. As we shall see, those who reject modernity also tend to reject vigorously the religious thought that has developed as a constructive response to it. To what extent, though, do those who seek to reject modern ideas succeed in sustaining pre-modern religious worldviews within the modern world? I will argue that, ironically, and as implausible as it might initially seem, the systems of religious belief promoted by those who seek to reject modern thought are no less the product of modernity than are the explicitly modern religious ideas that we have considered thus far.

Here, I shall follow the common practice of referring to those who seek to reject modernity and to preserve traditional religious views as 'religious fundamentalists', although this term cannot be employed without considerable qualification. Many writers avoid the term 'religious fundamentalism' (along with the term 'religious extremism') because of its supposedly negative connotations, preferring alternative terms such as 'religious revivalism' or 'religious resurgence'. The difficulty encountered in selecting the term that most accurately identifies the phenomenon under consideration is compounded by the diversity of the religious traditions in which it is apparent. Nevertheless, despite the difficulties, the term 'religious fundamentalism' enjoys wide currency. It is commonly used to refer to groups within the Jewish, Christian and Muslim traditions (as well as to groups within other, non-monotheistic faiths) who, despite their obvious differences, would appear to share a similar approach to their respective faith-traditions, and who, moreover, would also seem to espouse a similar assessment of modernity. Throughout this chapter, then, I shall use the term 'religious fundamentalism', and I will reserve the term 'religious extremism' to refer to those individuals and groups within each of the Abrahamic faiths whose religious commitments lead them to endorse acts of violence.

Religious fundamentalists can often be recognized by their distinctive perspective on many of the issues treated in this book. They tend to prescribe strict limits, for example, to the scope of human reason in criticizing religious beliefs. They also emphasize a view of the meaning of religious texts that minimizes – or even excludes – the need for interpretation. They accept science only insofar as it does not threaten their religious beliefs. They reject religious pluralism, typically preferring some form of religious exclusivism. They tend to resist the separation of religion from politics, and, unlike more liberal religious thinkers, are inclined to side with the political right rather than with the left. And, finally, they are prone to adopt a negative attitude towards feminism in general and, in particular, towards demands by women that religion be reformed in order to accommodate gender equality. This set of views is clearly opposed to many of the positions on these issues defended by the religious thinkers considered in earlier chapters. To the extent that religious fundamentalism is a reaction to the more liberalizing ideas that this book has focused on so far, it might be viewed, to borrow Jungian terminology, as the 'shadow side' of those developments within religious thought. Clearly, this book would have been both incomplete and misleading had we only considered liberal adaptations to modern thought on the part of religious believers, and neglected the other, arguably less progressive, dimension of the religious response to modernity.

While all the themes treated thus far provide connections to religious fundamentalism, it is perhaps the topic of religious exclusivism that brought us nearest to it. In Chapter 7 we considered the increasing receptivity of many religious thinkers to non-exclusivist views of religion. We saw that one does not have to embrace Hickean transcendental pluralism or, alternatively, internalist pluralism in order to be sympathetic to the view that religious traditions other than one's own possess value. For many who remain deeply committed to their own faiths nevertheless seek *rapprochement* with adherents of other traditions. But religious plurality does not exist solely at the level of world faiths; it has also arisen within religious traditions themselves, as different groups have tried to differentiate themselves from each other. Within Christianity, for example, the ecumenical movement arose within the post-war West as Christians sought to enhance understanding and fellowship between the various Christian denominations that had grown increasingly estranged in the course of the twentieth century. This resulted in the founding of the World Council of Churches in 1948. Many saw the Council as a force for progress. Christian fundamentalists, however, were unanimous in their condemnation of it. Two key fundamentalist leaders – Ian Paisley, a Northern Irish Protestant minister, and Bob Jones, a North American evangelical pastor – founded a rival organization: the World Congress of Fundamentalists. In 1999, at a meeting of the Congress, a delegation ratified the following resolution:

> We deplore and denounce the ecumenical movement in all its forms and ramifications, exhorting each other to a greater fidelity to the Word of God, to a more vigorous preaching of the Gospel of Christ, and to a thoroughgoing exposure of the satanically inspired movement which is producing the worldwide confederation of religions of the end time.[1]

The resolution also makes clear that what these fundamentalists particularly object to is the ecumenical dialogues taking place between evangelical Protestants and Eastern Orthodox Christians on the one hand, and evangelical Protestants and Roman Catholics on the other. Not only are fundamentalists opposed to all forms of religious pluralism, then, but they are also opposed to all efforts at enhancing relations between different Christian denominations.

This opposition highlights an important feature of all fundamentalist movements: they thrive by demarcating themselves from others within their own faith-tradition. A clear distinction between true believers (the 'saved' in the language of Christian fundamentalism) and inauthentic believers (the 'unsaved') lies at the core of all forms of religious fundamentalism. Fundamentalists, moreover, believe that it is essential to the religious integrity of their community that they distance themselves from those who have been deemed to have strayed from the one and only correct form of the faith. Thus, fundamentalist groups, irrespective of their religious tradition, tend to form exclusive communities within which only those who share their beliefs and their lifestyle are welcome.

Moreover, religious fundamentalists, while not necessarily in possession of a unique religious worldview that enables them to be clearly distinguished from non-fundamentalists of the same religion, tend to focus primarily on selected aspects of their religion – religious law, for example. And because fundamentalists emphasize selected facets of a religious tradition, they thereby isolate themselves from those of their co-religionists who do not share their particular emphasis. Thus, what to an outsider can appear to be a minor theological disagreement may be the cause of a group of fundamentalists consolidating a sub-culture that separates them not only from the wider secular world but also from others within the same religious tradition. This process of isolation from those holding different views encourages the development of a distinctive atmosphere within such groups, and this, in turn, reinforces the fundamentalists' sense that their particular interpretation of their faith-tradition is exclusively correct. For as Don Cupitt remarks:

> Vivid religious faith often tends to shut one up in a sub-culture of like-minded people. Within that world the truth of the faith seems obvious and unquestionable, so much something taken for granted that it is rarely mentioned. A tacit consent of this kind creates a strong and distinctive atmosphere that works to exclude sceptical outsiders and their uncomfortable questions. And the more we are able to assume that our truth is *the* truth and our world *the* world, the less we shall be aware of any world outside our own world.[2]

Furthermore, religious fundamentalists characteristically perceive what they tend to think of as the 'outside world' as extremely threatening. The nature of the perceived threat does, however, vary according to the religion in question and to the local circumstances with which its adherents are attempting to cope. Jonathan Sacks identifies what appears to be a common pattern when he observes that Jewish fundamentalists fear assimilation, Christian fundamentalists fear secularity, and Islamic fundamentalists fear Westernization.[3] Despite these different objects of fear, trepidation is, in each case, a response to some aspect of modern life – and it frequently results in an attempt to isolate the religious community from the impact of the modern world. Such distinctive communities form discrete pockets that co-exist in tension with modern secular culture. In the twentieth century, such communities demonstrated that they had the power to unsettle and influence the world outside the boundaries of their own particular group. In this chapter, we shall take a closer look at some of these communities, and consider the impact they have made in recent times on modern secular culture. And we shall see that religious fundamentalism in the Abrahamic faiths has exercised a growing influence worldwide since the 1970s, with its increasing prominence challenging at least one central assumption within modern thought concerning religion.

We begin by looking at the origins of the term 'religious fundamentalism', and briefly consider the distinctive character that fundamentalism exhibits within twentieth-century Judaism, Christianity and Islam, respectively. We then turn to the 'secularization thesis' – the theory that predicts that, as societies modernize, they inevitably become less religious – and examine its failure to account for patterns of religious commitment in the late twentieth century. These patterns are illustrated in the following three sections in which we consider examples of fundamentalism in each of the monotheistic faiths. Finally, in the concluding section, some general conclusions are drawn; in particular, conclusions concerning the link between religious fundamentalism and modernity.

The origins of 'religious fundamentalism' and the character of fundamentalist movements

The term 'religious fundamentalism' was coined shortly after the publication of a series of pamphlets called *The Fundamentals* in the United States between 1910 and 1915.[4] The authors of these pamphlets were evangelical Christians[5] from a range of Protestant denominations, who expounded what they regarded as the 'fundamentals' of Christian belief, as well as responding to the threats they perceived that modernity posed to those beliefs. One especial focus of the pamphlets was the defence of the Bible against those who would interpret it by means of the so-called 'higher criticism' promoted at that time by more liberal Christians. The authors rejected higher criticism and, instead, advocated an approach to the Bible grounded in what they regarded as common sense. For only such an approach, they argued, was genuinely rational and scientific. Moreover, one of the key concerns of many of the authors was to defend the inerrancy of the Bible – some appealing to 'dictation theory' in support of this claim.[6] In addition to this defence of a pre-critical reading of the Bible, there was also a marked emphasis on 'soul saving' and on the importance of personal religious experience, with discussion of ethical, social or political issues being conspicuous by its absence.

The huge impact of these pamphlets was largely due to the substantial financial backing behind them, which allowed them to be widely, and freely, distributed throughout the anglophone world. The high public profile they achieved made them the reference point by which the evangelical Christian fundamentalist movement within the United States initially came to be recognized. However, this movement soon developed far beyond its original roots. Hence, while the term 'religious fundamentalism' was first used to refer to those evangelical Christians within the Protestant churches who were associated with the views promoted in these pamphlets,[7] its reference became much broader in the last quarter of the twentieth century, expanding eventually to include movements within every major religious tradition. Judaism, Christianity and Islam are now each recognized as host to their own fundamentalist groups.

Irrespective of which religion we consider, fundamentalists are united in urging their co-religionists to return to the original sources of their tradition. They aim to revitalize their tradition so that it can become the foundation of society. For example, when the original pamphleteers argued for a return to the fundamentals of the Christian religion, they tended to portray this as a return to the past – in other words, to the era prior to modernity when Christian belief was relatively unchallenged, and when Christian moral principles were the foundation of Western society. However, given the common orientation towards a better *future* that is to be shaped by the revitalized religious tradition, it is perhaps misleading to regard religious fundamentalism simply as aspiring to reinstate the past and as an attempt to resist modernity. In fact, as we shall see, within each of the Abrahamic faiths religious fundamentalism displays features that suggest that it is a distinctively modern phenomenon.

Because fundamentalists feel compelled to resist secular culture, they are often involved in an ongoing struggle with its most visible representatives (for example, with government officials and educators within secular institutions). Hence, Sacks claims that, at root, religious fundamentalism is simply the 'common-sense defence of Orthodoxy in a highly secular age, a reaction against what is seen as a liberal intelligentsia's subversion of established beliefs'.[8] Ironically, though, this defensive engagement actually requires fundamentalists to present their faith and values in a way that will appeal to those immersed in modern secular culture, which, of course, implies some change to the tradition. Indeed, this dynamic was already evident in the United States during the first decades of the twentieth century when evangelical Protestant fundamentalism was first evolving. For, as Karen Armstrong argues, the attempt to return to the 'fundamentals' of faith undertaken by those involved within this movement was 'in line with other intellectual and scientific currents in the early twentieth century', with those behind this attempt being 'as addicted to scientific rationalism as any other modernists'.[9] Why is this so? Because going back to the fundamentals was perceived as a way of grounding religious faith upon facts rather than upon mere speculation. These facts, it was believed, could be arrived at by anyone if they were sufficiently observant and used their God-given reasoning powers. And this project, if successful, would have modernized theology, and thereby demonstrated that it was no less legitimate than any other science. Clearly, then, the fundamentalists' programme, as originally conceived, was actually a response to modern standards of science and of knowledge, more generally. Similarly, 'fundamentalist' movements within nineteenth-century Islam, such as Wahhabism, were attempts at rendering faith more rational, and hence more modern, by returning to its sources without the aid of centuries of commentary and interpretation.

It is interesting that fundamentalists, irrespective of their religious tradition, insist that sacred texts and 'tradition' can be appropriated without interpretation. In previous chapters, we have considered a variety of arguments that suggest that this aspect of the fundamentalist project is doomed to failure.[10] Indeed, if one considers the uses to which fundamentalists press sacred texts and traditions – uses that we shall later consider – it soon becomes evident that their approach relies just as much on a specific interpretation of them as does that of any of the more explicitly progressive thinkers we considered earlier. This would not, moreover, seem to be the only inconsistency in the fundamentalist worldview.

A further seeming inconsistency lies in the stark contrast between the emphasis fundamentalists place upon an unmediated reading of their Scriptures and their tendency to rely on the guidance of their religious leaders for detailed instructions regarding an acceptable lifestyle – this reliance being another common tendency exhibited by most fundamentalist groups. And the ease and frequency of contact with a religious leader that one might enjoy in the modern world is likely to exacerbate any tendency that members of fundamentalist groups might show towards relying on that leader's advice and guidance rather than on their own judgement.[11] Not only does this increasing tendency sit uneasily with the fundamentalists' insistence that the 'truth' can be accessed by each individual by means of a literal reading of the Scriptures and without the aid of religious experts, but it also clearly runs counter to what might be thought of as one of the most important injunctions of modern thought: namely, the injunction to think for oneself. And thinking for oneself, at the very least, would seem to imply that one must not let one's opinions and choices be determined exclusively by others.

As we noted in Chapter 1, the intellectual tradition that developed from the Enlightenment stressed that a refusal to think for oneself, and thus an unquestioning deference of one's opinions to those of others or to one's religious tradition, constitutes a lapse of personal responsibility. And during the nineteenth century, as we saw in Chapter 4, many Jewish, Christian and Muslim religious thinkers took to heart the injunction to think for oneself. They were led to reassess their religious traditions and to change many of the facets of those traditions that the light of reason showed to be inappropriate, especially given the changing circumstances of the modern world. Such transformations were undertaken most thoroughly within the Jewish Reformed tradition and the Christian Liberal Protestant tradition.[12] The modernist tradition within Islam, which we briefly consider later in this chapter, also proposed such reforms. However, it was less successful than the reform movements within Judaism and Christianity insofar as it failed to attract any large following, remaining a 'movement' of somewhat isolated intellectuals. Nevertheless, such prominent figures as Fazlur Rahman have ensured that modernism remains an important intellectual movement within Islam. Not surprisingly, fundamentalists within each of the Abrahamic faiths find themselves at odds not only with non-religious thinkers but also with those religious thinkers from within their own faith-traditions who endorse progressive views.

Given that all religious believers in the West have to cope with the encounter between their religious beliefs and secular culture, it seems that some explanation is required for why some religious groups are more prone to embrace fundamentalism than others. Steve Bruce argues that, if fundamentalism is to develop, there is one basic requirement that the religious group must meet: it must be at least plausible for them to claim to be the genuine guardians of an orthodoxy from which their co-religionists have strayed. As he remarks, this condition is met in many evangelical Protestant denominations but not, or at least not easily, in Roman Catholicism, for example (where a centralized ecclesial hierarchy determines orthodoxy for an international institution). In this respect, he argues, evangelical Protestantism and Islam are two of a kind insofar as they 'both suppose that authoritative knowledge is democratically available. Any right-spirited person can discern God's will by reading the Scriptures or studying the Qur'an.'[13] But this can easily lead to a plethora of rival 'orthodoxies', and each could then evolve into a form of fundamentalism, thereby giving rise to a potentially fractious situation.

Perhaps surprisingly, fundamentalists of all traditions also regard their conservative non-fundamentalist co-religionists in much the same light as they regard the more liberal religious groups. For in the fundamentalists' view, all but their own group have made far too many concessions to modern times. This polarity between fundamentalists and the rest can be clearly seen in the case of their divergent responses to scientific claims. For example, a mainstream Christian who was either liberal or conservative would probably have no major difficulty in accepting Darwin's theory of evolution, while a fundamentalist Christian might be prepared to go to court to prevent the theory being taught to her child. One reason for this extreme difference is that, unlike religious fundamentalists, non-fundamentalists often hold that certain religious doctrines are provisional, and that they can change as the human understanding of the world and of history advances. Consequently, many believe that revelation has to be interpreted anew by each successive generation, albeit in the light of the past tradition.

At bottom, then, it is this view of revelation and interpretation that the fundamentalist refuses to accept. For fundamentalists assert that revelation is timelessly true, and is thus not relative to historical epochs or cultures. Everything that God is believed to have said in the Scriptures is presumed to be valid for all time, with the prevalent Islamic view of the Qur'ān being typical of this conception of revelation. Traditional Muslims believe that the Qur'ān is eternal. It has always been with God in its present form – the form in which it was dictated to the Prophet Muhammad, who simply recounted what he had heard. Fundamentalist Christians similarly believe in the literal truth of the 'Old' and 'New' Testaments. The Jewish fundamentalists' version of this literalism applies it not only to the Hebrew Scriptures but also to a whole tradition of commentary, as well as to the sayings of sages stretching from the distant past into the present. Given such a view, it is not surprising that fundamentalists resist any attempt to alter the text of their Scriptures. Some Christian fundamentalists, for example, claim that even altering the pronouns used in the text in order to make them gender-neutral is nothing short of falsifying the word of God.[14] Not surprisingly, feminists and fundamentalists tend to be at odds.

Because of their view of revelation as timelessly true, religious fundamentalists not only seek to read their Scriptures literally but also, and not surprisingly, display a deeply conservative attitude – one that tends to make them very resistant to social change. And this is particularly evident with regard to the position of women within society. Fundamentalists in each tradition are, moreover, inclined to want their own reading of Scripture to dictate government policy. Thus, the connection between religious fundamentalism and political conservativism is often a function of the fundamentalists' theory of revelation.

Another common feature of fundamentalist groups, which is linked both to their distinctive theory of revelation and to their particular manner of responding to modernity, is that they claim to provide clear and unambiguous answers to metaphysical and moral questions. In short, they claim to offer certainty in the midst of a modern world that many experience as riddled with uncertainty.[15] This may explain the edge that fundamentalism came to acquire over more liberal forms of faith as the twentieth century advanced. In an increasingly uncertain world, many people began to look to religion to provide the security missing elsewhere in their lives. The qualified and changing faiths of more liberal religious thinkers appear hard pressed to satisfy this particular psychological need. If their views are correct, why do they need to keep changing them in the light of new scientific discoveries and other intellectual developments? The conservativism of fundamentalist thinkers adds to their projected image as defenders of the one and only truth. Thus, the trend in the late twentieth century was that, while the more (intellectually and politically) liberal groups within the Abrahamic religions continued to decline in numbers – a decline that had begun earlier in the century – those groups that were less accommodating to modern society grew in strength. As we shall now see, the fact that the religious movements which made no effort to keep pace with modernity should have been the ones to flourish flies in the face of the secularization thesis – a thesis that had become almost axiomatic within academic circles by the mid-twentieth century.[16]

Religious fundamentalism and the secularization thesis

Many have found it puzzling that, while Western society has become increasingly secular, in the sense that religion has lost the influence on civic life that it traditionally enjoyed, there seems to have been a simultaneous increase within it of religious fundamentalism. For the secularization thesis had predicted that religion would disappear as society modernized. Until the closing decades of the twentieth century, few intellectuals doubted that as societies became more modern, they simultaneously became more secular – in other words, less religious. A corresponding transformation was envisaged on the individual level: the more an individual was exposed to modern secular culture, the less religious that person would be. Prior to the 1970s, these assumptions had seemed to be corroborated by the facts. Whatever form secularization took (a Marxist form in Eastern Europe that sought to eliminate religion or, in Western Europe and North America, the institutional separation of Church and state), the results seemed to be the same. Religious beliefs seemed to drop away the more that people were assimilated into modern, secular society. Moreover, the shedding of religious beliefs could be witnessed vividly in the case of immigrants into Western cultures during the early to mid-twentieth century. Each successive generation seemed to retain fewer of the religious beliefs held by the generation that preceded it. This observation led many thinkers to predict that, before long, religion would die a natural death.

This prediction, however, has not been fulfilled.[17] Nor has the related assumption that modernity is synonymous with secularization been borne out. It now seems that those who supported the secularization thesis failed to anticipate the force of the religious counter-movements that would develop in response to secularization. In fact, after a period of decline, the Abrahamic religions would seem to have recovered in strength. In many cases, religious believers appear to have been stimulated to reassert their faith aggressively. Instances of what we might call a 'religious resurgence', such as that which took place within London's Jewish communities towards the end of the twentieth century, provide striking counter-examples to the claim that modern societies are secular ones in which religion has no place. Again, contrary to the secularization thesis, fundamentalism within Islam has been most prominent in the more Westernized states, such as Egypt and Iran. What is more, rather than people losing their religious faith after moving into modern urban environments, it now seems that they are no less likely to become more religious than they were before.[18]

Those who held the secularization thesis also assumed that the forms of religion that were most antithetical to modernity would be the first to disappear, while those that were prepared to adapt to modernity would be those most likely to survive longest. The first signs that these predictions were inaccurate were observed in the 1960s. And in 1965, Charles Liebman challenged the assumption that Jewish Orthodoxy was in terminal decline.[19] As he pointed out, Ultra-Orthodox Jewish groups, contrary to what the secularization thesis had led people to expect, were growing at the expense of those forms of Judaism that had made significant concessions to modernity (that is, Modern Orthodox, Conservative and Reform groups). A similar phenomenon to that noticed by Liebman in the Jewish community was subsequently recorded in the Christian community. While the decline of mainstream Christian groups, both Protestant and Roman Catholic, continued as predicted, there was a notable resurgence of groups such as the Southern Baptists, Pentecostalists, Seventh Day Adventists, Jehovah's Witnesses and Mormons. In contrast to what advocates of the secularization thesis had predicted, therefore, those religious movements that took an uncompromising stand against modernity were the ones to flourish, while those that compromised and adapted their claims and institutions to modern values went into decline (at least in terms of numbers).[20] Indeed, since the 1960s, fundamentalist religious groups seem to have been going from strength to strength.[21]

It is possible to regard the surprising resurgence of religion in modern times as a temporary deviation from the trajectory predicted by the secularization thesis. However, in view of the increasing prominence of fundamentalist religious groups within all of the major world religions, it seems more plausible to conclude that the standard view of the relation between modernity, secularization and faith ignores something important. Hence, by the end of the twentieth century, many scholars had come to reject the secularization thesis, and to seek new ways of explaining the relationship between religion and modernity. Liebman, for example, proposes an alternative theory, claiming that, in the modern world, religious fundamentalism is the norm, and religious moderation is, rather, the phenomenon requiring explanation.[22] He attempts to support this thesis by means of a study of Judaism within Israel (although he believes that his account of religious fundamentalism also applies to other religions elsewhere). According to Liebman,

> a propensity to religious extremism does not require explanation since it is entirely consistent with basic religious tenets and authentic religious orientations. It is religious moderation or religious liberalism, the willingness of religious adherents to accommodate themselves to their environment, to adapt their behavioral and belief patterns to prevailing cultural norms, to make peace with the world, that requires explanation. ... If our description of the extremist orientation is correct, then extremism is a tendency to which every religiously oriented person is attracted.[23]

Essentially, then, Liebman argues that all religion tends to push people towards fundamentalism. In pre-modern societies, this tendency was counterbalanced by the many interconnections that existed between culture, communal life and religion. After the Enlightenment, however, these connections were broken as religion became increasingly isolated from other aspects of life. Thus, argues Liebman, the attraction of religious believers towards fundamentalism was no longer balanced by other factors, and was therefore allowed to attain its full expression. Moreover, religious fundamentalism is typically expressed in the drive to expand religious law, in the desire to increase the social isolation of the religious community, and, conversely, in the rejection, cultivated by the fundamentalist group, of the dominant culture. Let us consider each of these dimensions of religious fundamentalism in turn.

Religious law does seem to be an especially attractive focus for many fundamentalists within the major religious traditions.[24] This might be for the reason that law is traditionally conceived as objective, unambiguous and authoritative. In discussing several aspects of the Jewish fundamentalists' focus on Jewish Law (*halakah*),[25] Liebman notes that the two most important are the desire to expand the scope of religious law, and the desire to elaborate on its details. Regarding this first aspect, religious fundamentalists seek to expand the scope of religious law because they want it to legislate over all aspects of public and private behaviour. Furthermore, expanding the scope of religious law would provide the fundamentalist group with its own social standards by which to criticize existing social institutions. Religious fundamentalists may then try to impose their programme on the whole of society. And their effort to impose religious law on society as a whole often embroils religious fundamentalists in political conflict. However, in some cases, their primary political demand may simply be for political autonomy.

The second important aspect of the religious fundamentalists' focus on religious law concerns their preoccupation with the details of the law. Liebman provides the example of the *halakhic* requirement that people, particularly women, dress modestly. This requirement is, as it stands, fairly vague, for it leaves open the possibility that each community, or individual, can decide what would count as modest. Jewish religious fundamentalists, however, prefer not to leave this question open. Instead, they elaborate on the law in order to specify the exact length of sleeves or hemline, say, that is consistent with modesty. A similar tendency is prevalent within Islamic fundamentalism.

These two aspects of the religious fundamentalists' attitude to religious law are linked by a common thread, for they both seek to emphasize the overriding priority of law over the individual's choice and judgement. And in so doing, both seek to limit personal authority, expecting the individual to defer to religious leaders in even, what appear to outsiders to be, the smallest and most trivial matters – such as the length of one's sleeves or hemline.

Whereas religious law constitutes the first dimension of religious fundamentalism discussed by Liebman, the second dimension, as we noted above, consists in a tendency towards isolation from the rest of society. For a characteristic response of religious fundamentalists to those who do not accept their religious values is to separate themselves from them.

This attitude may be tempered by a desire to convert others, in which case fundamentalists may go to considerable lengths in order to mitigate the dangers of contact with those perceived as outsiders. This trend towards increasing social isolation is particularly evident in the case of religious education. Religious fundamentalists usually insist on their children being educated in their communities' own schools. Typically, these schools give their pupils only as much secular education as is deemed necessary in order to remain within the law of the land. In the case of Hasidic schools, most of the pupil's time is spent learning the Scriptures from memory (and traditional Muslim schools display a similar preoccupation with learning Scripture by rote). One result is that children who have been educated in this way enjoy few points of intellectual or physical contact with children from non-religious schools.

The third dimension of religious fundamentalism, according to Liebman, is the tendency of religious fundamentalists to reject all cultural forms and cultural values that are not perceived to be intrinsic to their religious tradition. In practice, this often means that religious fundamentalist leaders forbid members of their group to watch television, to go to the cinema, or to read newspapers, magazines and other secular literature. In short, all exposure to forms of media not controlled by the religious group is forbidden. This ban on the secular media is imposed in conjunction with a demand to engage in so many other activities within the community that the individual is unlikely to have the time to miss secular forms of entertainment. Male Ultra-Orthodox Jews, for example, are expected to spend all their available time studying the sacred texts.

Liebman argues that these three dimensions of religious fundamentalism – the desire to expand the scope of religious law, the wish to isolate their community from the rest of society, and the rejection of the dominant culture – have always been an intrinsic part of many religions. As was mentioned earlier, the fundamentalist orientation of religious believers had been restrained in the past because, Liebman claims, traditional religious communities contained other tendencies that balanced out fundamentalist ones. And the most important of these were the more conservative tendencies within society. Hence, Liebman holds that religious fundamentalism is on the increase because the breakdown of traditional religious communities has weakened any 'capacity to check extremist impulses'[26] that society might otherwise have enjoyed. Liebman's theory, then, offers one possible explanation for why religion has not simply faded away within increasingly modern societies, as had been anticipated.

If Liebman's theory is to be persuasive, though, it needs to provide some account of the factors at play within traditional societies that serve to restrain the expression of religious fundamentalism. In fact, he mentions several, with two appearing to be the most important. One is that traditional societies contained no clear distinction between the religious and non-religious aspects of social life; and the emergence of this separation within society stimulates the growth of religious fundamentalism. As Liebman explains:

> Religious institutions arise within a particular culture and society. ... Extremism is restrained when religion is an organic part of the society diffused throughout its institutions. Where differentiation has taken place, the religious institution is often impelled to worldly activity in order to maximise its autonomy, control its environment, protect itself, attract adherents, etc. The need for the approval of others and the interaction with other economic and political institutions introduces a compromising or adaptionist tendency.[27]

And religious fundamentalism is, as we have seen, a reaction against all such compromises and adaptations on the part of the traditional faith.

The second important factor that Liebman mentions is that when religious institutions were integrally connected with other cultural and social institutions within traditional societies, successful religions could benefit their leaders with status and material rewards. This would have encouraged self-interested people to become religious leaders in order to promote their own or their family's interests, with the notorious corruption among Roman Catholic leaders during the Middle Ages being a case in point. Such self-interested individuals enjoying positions of religious leadership would, Liebman maintains, have had an interest in keeping fundamentalist tendencies at bay; and within a traditional society, they would have had more power to do so.

The claim, then, is that the current rise in religious fundamentalism can be explained by the disappearance of such regulatory factors – factors that, Liebman argues, formerly restrained any fundamentalist tendencies within society. Clearly, one feature of the modern world is the compartmentalization of religion. Since the Enlightenment, religion has become increasingly distanced from other areas of public life. Consequently, religious leaders rarely attain the public status they once enjoyed, and this perhaps means that self-interested individuals are less likely to strive to become religious leaders.[28] Hence, the two factors that, if Liebman is correct, were previously paramount in checking the tendency of religious people towards fundamentalism have been significantly attenuated within modern Western society.

It may be, then, that Liebman's theory can explain why religious fundamentalism is a distinctively modern phenomenon, and not simply an expression of a desire to return to a pre-modern state of mind in which one's religious beliefs are seemingly immune from challenge. The theory also appears to offer a persuasive explanation for why religion has not died the natural death that had been predicted by twentieth-century social science.

But whether or not we should accept Liebman's theoretical explanation, the secularization thesis, which was virtually unquestioned in the 1950s and 1960s, seems to have been critically undermined by the unexpected religious revival that occurred during the second half of the twentieth century.[29] The relationship between religion and modernity is thus far more complex than the thesis allows. Even within Western Europe, in those areas – such as the United Kingdom and the Netherlands – where the thesis has come closest to being borne out, the situation is more nuanced than had been predicted. Affiliation to religious institutions has indeed dropped dramatically, as predicted by the secularization thesis. Nevertheless, as was noted in Chapter 2, religious belief still persists to a remarkable degree, even where it has become dissociated from religious institutions. What seems to have changed in parts of Western Europe, then, is the locus of religion, from institutions to the private life of the individual.

Elsewhere in the world, however, individuals have joined fundamentalist groups *en masse*. So, let us now consider the shape taken by religious fundamentalism within each of the Abrahamic religions. We begin with Judaism.

Jewish fundamentalism

In the modern West, Jewish fundamentalism, in the form of what is sometimes known as Ultra-Orthodox Jewry, has become particularly visible in recent times. The last decades of the twentieth century saw this movement steadily increase in numbers and continue to grow in strength, both in terms of its morale and its political influence.

Until the mid-1960s, no one doubted that Ultra-Orthodox Judaism was just a remnant of the Eastern European past. It then became apparent that more people were either converting, or returning, to this type of Judaism than were leaving. 'Ultra-Orthodox Jews' is, of course, a rather imprecise designation. It is employed to refer to a variety of Jewish groups, one of the most prominent being the Hasidic Jews, or the Hasidim. The word '*hasidim*' simply means 'the pious'. In the United States, these Jews are often referred to as Haredi Jews, and their movement is called Haredism. Hasidic, or Haredi Jews are more antagonistic to modernity and to non-Jews (and, indeed to non-Hasidic Jews) than are those belonging to any other branch of Judaism. Their distinctive dress, hair and customs make them easily recognizable, and set them apart from the rest of society. They seek to maintain cultural isolation, often trying to recreate the setting of their community's past in Eastern Europe.

Moreover, these Ultra-Orthodox Jews have a significant influence on other types of Jews, partly because of their reputation for piety but also because of their influence on the religious establishment within the State of Israel. Hasidic Judaism became increasingly popular as the twentieth century drew to a close. After two centuries of decline in the face of society's increasing modernization, and following the decimation of the holocaust, Hasidic Judaism began to gain ground against other forms of Judaism.

The Hasidic movement began in eighteenth-century Eastern Europe. The founder was Israel ben Eliezer (1700–60), also known as the Baal Shem Tov (which simply means 'the Master of the Good Name'). The movement stressed personal piety and a mystical type of worship, and was regarded as heterodox by those traditional Jews who remained outside the movement. Most of Europe's Hasidic Jews were killed during the Second World War. However, a remnant escaped, and the survivors gathered in the United States and, later, in the State of Israel – the two countries where their most powerful centres are now to be found. There are various sub-groups within Hasidic Jewry. Based on old Eastern European family dynasties, the most famous is the Lubavitch Hasidim, who have received a great deal of media attention because, unlike other Hasidic groups, they are active missionaries. Their missionary activities usually target secular Jews, whom they attempt to restore to what they regard as orthodox Jewish faith.

The Lubavitch Hasidim originated within Russia, where, in the early twentieth century, they experienced intense persecution at the hands of the Bolsheviks. In a pattern typical of fundamentalist movements, persecution led to resistance. Under the leadership of Joseph Isaac Schneerson (1880–1950), the Sixth Rebbe of the Lubavitch dynasty, a Jewish resistance movement was organized. The principal aim of the movement was to keep Jewish culture and learning alive in spite of the heavy persecution experienced in Bolshevik Russia – persecution that, in quintessentially fundamentalist fashion, Rabbi Schneerson interpreted as a sign of the imminent arrival of the long-awaited Messiah. The Jewish resistance movement did not go unnoticed by the Bolshevik authorities, however, and Schneerson and his court were exiled to Poland. There, Schneerson modernized his organization, consolidating a network that relied on modern communication technology in order to unite the Lubavitch Hasidim that had begun to spread throughout the world. The result was a modern, centrally controlled, international organization that evolved into one of the most successful Jewish groups in the second half of the twentieth century. The success of the Lubavitch is also due to the Rebbe's timely exit from Poland and arrival in the United States. Once established in the New World, the Lubavitch raised their missionary campaign to a new intensity in an effort to return American Jews (who, in their view, had been 'victims' of secularization) to the faith. The year before his death, Schneerson founded Kfar Habad – the first Hasidic settlement in the State of Israel. This was also part of the Lubavitch's missionary agenda, as they perceived Jews living within Israel to be in grave need of conversion for having been corrupted by the Zionists into attempting to occupy the Land in opposition to the express will of God.

Certainly, the Lubavitch Hasidim have been extremely successful in attracting secularized Jews, and Jews from other, more liberal, backgrounds, to their version of 'orthodox' Jewish faith. This has included an influx of young adults into the Lubavitch Hasidim, the majority of whom have grown up within a secular culture. We might have expected Hasidic Judaism to have been transformed and brought closer to secular culture by such an influx of young people, but this is not in the least what happened. For, as David Landau argues, joining such a group requires the complete renunciation of one's former culture rather than any attempt at synthesizing the old with the new. The converts are required to attend a *yeshiva* (a Jewish religious school), where they are expected to undergo a thorough internal metamorphosis, involving the complete renunciation of all secular culture. When they have children, they will be sent automatically to a *yeshiva*, and the children of converts usually display as little interest in secular culture as those whose parents were born into the movement.[30]

In Hasidic religious schools the Torah is the main object of study. This focus is understandable, given the strict fidelity to Scripture that is characteristic of every form of religious fundamentalism. Such fidelity, however, takes an unusual form within Hasidic fundamentalism. For Hasidim do not confine their reverence to the Pentateuch, but include a reverence for commentaries such as the Talmud, which means that the Scriptures must be read and understood through the medium of later interpretation. Indeed, the whole life of Hasidic Jews comes, as Landau writes, to be 'ruled by "the Torah", which for them is a concept that embraces God Himself, all His prophets and scribes, a vast body of legal and ethical literature, and a chain of spiritual leaders down to the rabbis of today ...'.[31] And this explains why, as Landau puts it, the Hasidic Jew's 'religious reverence is a seamless web. God Himself, the Bible, the Talmud, the rabbinical writings, the rabbis themselves – all are intertwined in an unbroken thread ...'.[32] This also partly explains the 'blind obeisance to rabbis', which, in Landau's view, is one of the most alienating characteristics of this form of Judaism in the eyes of the outside world, both Jewish and gentile.[33]

One reason for the appeal of this form of Judaism to many Jews is that it attempts to reconstitute the form of Jewish life that was lost as a result of the holocaust (or *Shoah*, as Jews name this event). The seamless web, referred to above, is a modern attempt to provide Jews with a means of living the same traditional life as their European ancestors did. Ironically, though, what was, in a sense, a natural lifestyle in pre-modern Europe is clearly not as natural to post-war Jews within the United States or within the State of Israel. For the very fact that the modern Hasidic lifestyle is consciously chosen, and not merely passively inherited, by many in the community, distinguishes it substantively from the traditional form of life that it diligently attempts to reproduce.[34] And there are at least two senses in which adoption of the Hasidic lifestyle today can be seen as a deliberate choice. First, it is an explicit choice on the part of converts to it. Second, it constitutes a choice even for non-converts insofar as they cannot but be aware of the plurality of other lifestyles available. Hence, given such awareness, remaining a Hasidic Jew is more of a choice than an unconscious commitment. And given that the choice to live in such a manner implies an explicit rejection of all other alternatives (most note-worthily, liberal religious lifestyles or secular ones), then it should come as no surprise that the Hasidic lifestyle is often perceived as a militant one. One aspect of this militancy is the anti-Zionist stance advanced by Hasidic Jews, who believe that it is God's prerogative to return the faith-ful to the Land of Israel, and that the State of Israel is an abomination because it has attempted to do what only God can rightfully accomplish. Thus, those Hasidic Jews who live in the State of Israel occupy distinct communities, and attempt to minimize their contact with non-Hasidic Jews. Considering their vehement disapproval of the State of Israel, it seems a strange twist of fate that, by the late twentieth century, they should have come to enjoy sufficient political power to determine the course of Israeli politics. The circumstances that led to this situation found the Hasidic Jews aligned with another Jewish movement that they had hitherto held in disdain – religious Zionism.

In Chapter 8 we noted how Zionism began as an aggressively anti-religious and secular organization, and that this stance was soon com-promised by the exigencies of founding a unified political community. In the second half of the twentieth century, a distinct movement developed within Zionism, one that was explicitly religious – although it did in-clude a number of secular Jews. This new movement was committed to an understanding of Zionism as a movement that was bringing about the will of God, and it crystallized in 1974 with the founding of Gush Emunin ('the Block of the Faithful'). Some of those belonging to this movement believed, as had Rebbe Schneerson, that the Messiah was about to arrive. But, unlike Schneerson, they had come to believe that the Messiah was waiting for the Jewish people to resettle the entire terri-tory of their ancient homeland. Thus, they regarded it as imperative that Zionist expansion proceed at the fastest possible pace. Obstacles to this expansion were considered to be the work of the forces of evil, working in league in order to delay the Messiah's arrival. Under these circum-stances, any means that would further the acquisition of more territory were thought to be acceptable.

Between 1974 and 1977, Gush Emunin enjoyed enormous popularity among Israeli Jews, and its success during this period contributed to a major turning point in Israeli political history. In 1977, in a rupture from Israel's socialist past, Likkud, a right-wing party, won the general elections. One of the new government's first actions was to begin a settlement programme in what were then known as the Occupied Territories. However, in the year of its election, Likkud, under the leadership of Menachem Begin, also began negotiating the Camp David Accords – an agreement which returned Sinai to Egyptian governance. Members of Gush Emunim and their sympathizers regarded this as a betrayal. Sinai had been gained by an Israeli military victory, and, in their view, the hand of God must have been behind it. Returning Sinai to Egypt was thus, they believed, against the will of God. However, in the 1980s, Israeli public opinion swung increasingly towards a negotiated peace with the Palestinians, who had previously lived in the land now occupied by the State of Israel. One result was that Gush Emunin's belligerent attitude became marginalized from Israeli political life.

But as the influence of Gush Emunin faded, its place was taken by the Hasidim, who, in the 1980s, began to acquire an unprecedented influence on Israeli politics. To cut a long and complicated story short, during the 1980s a variety of religious parties proliferated in Israel. Although there was considerable antagonism between these parties, they won, in the 1988 election, 18 seats in the Knesset (the Israeli Parliament). This, in effect, meant that the balance of power between Likud and Labour lay with the religious vote. Thus, somewhat reluctantly, and still with deep reservations about the religious legitimacy of the State of Israel, the Hasidim were drawn into political life. Moreover, they seem to have been motivated by a perception of their values and way of life being threatened by both secular and religious (but non-Hasidic) Jews, and therefore concluded that the best way to defend themselves was through a direct involvement in politics.

The 1980s also saw an upsurge in religiously motivated violence, as some of those who remained committed to the vision of Gush Emunin resorted to extreme measures in an attempt to hasten the coming of the Messiah. Some came to perceive the Dome on the Rock, the third holiest site in the Muslim world, as the place from whence emanated the evil forces of opposition to the will of God. In particular, the forces motivating negotiations for peace, such as the Camp David Accords, were thought to stem from there. Thus, a plan was hatched to blow up the Dome, and thus to cut off the evil forces that were impeding the reoccupation of Israel by the Jews, and thereby delaying the coming of the Messiah. Despite careful planning, the plot was never carried out – it came to light while the prospective perpetrators were delayed by their inability to find a rabbi who would sanction the act.[35] One result of this episode, however, was seemingly irreparable damage to the credibility of Gush Emunim in the eyes of the Israeli public. Sadly, though, this was not the end of religiously inspired violence within the State of Israel. In the mid-1990s, after the Oslo Accords had committed Israelis to returning some of the occupied territories to Palestinian control, rabbis involved with Gush Emunim raised the question of whether President Yitzhak Rabin had made himself an enemy of the Jewish people by signing away their land. If he had, then Jewish law would sanction his death. In late 1995, Rabin was assassinated by Yigal Amir, a student of Jewish law, who was convinced that, as a religious Jew, he had acted according to his duty.[36] Amir is on record as stating, immediately after the assassination, that he had acted 'on orders from God'.[37]

Clearly, it is not only within Judaism that fundamentalist thinking has led to violence. Fundamentalists have also perpetrated acts of religiously motivated violence in the name of Christianity and Islam. We now consider fundamentalism within Christianity, before turning to its expression within Islam.

Christian fundamentalism

In this section we focus on Christian fundamentalism as it appears in various non-mainstream Protestant communities within the United States. We noted earlier that the term 'fundamentalism' was originally applied to the stance of a sub-group of evangelical Christians from a number of Protestant denominations. These Christians belonged to churches which, by the second decade of the twentieth century, had become polarized between conservative and liberal constituents. The tension between these orientations resulted in the fracturing of all the major Protestant denominations, with fundamentalists breaking away from their original denominations in order to form new churches with other like-minded Christians. Because fundamentalists not only disagreed with the liberals within their original denominations but also disagreed between each other, the result was a bewildering proliferation of independent churches. But still, despite the theological disagreements between these numerous fundamentalist groups, their members could be recognized as sharing an orientation akin to that promoted by the authors of *The Fundamentals*. Religious fundamentalism, as a recognizable movement in the United States, stems from the period immediately following the fracturing of the Protestant denominations.

The newly formed independent fundamentalist churches adopted a militant pose towards secular society – that is, a society in which religious beliefs and values were, at least in principle, denied influence on public life. Members of these churches typically portrayed such a society as the work of Satan. They were also opposed to more liberal forms of Christianity which, in their view, made far too many concessions to secularism. Moreover, as we noted earlier, they were united in their desire to 'save souls' and return to what they regarded as the basics of their religion. In addition, these new fundamentalist churches, by and large, unanimously adopted 'premillennialist' beliefs about the timing of the day of judgement. In other words, their members held that the damned are to be separated from the saved during the day of judgement, which will inaugurate the 'millennium' – a thousand-year reign of the righteous.[38] They believed, what is more, that the day of judgement was imminent. Many were led by these beliefs to withdraw from society in order to prepare themselves for judgement, and await what was commonly referred to as 'the rapture' – in other words, the immense joy that the saved would experience when Christ takes them up to heaven on judgement day.

A mood of withdrawal and disengagement from secular society was characteristic of fundamentalist Christians until the 1960s. Their retreat from mainstream society was a response to the increasingly marginalized place that their beliefs and values had come to occupy within the United States. This form of Christianity did not quietly disappear, however, as advocates of the secularization thesis predicted. Instead, fundamentalist groups were remarkably successful during the mid-twentieth century in building their own culture in opposition to the dominant one. Their hope was that their culture would ultimately prove resilient enough to withstand the onslaughts of secularism, and provide the foundation for the spiritual regeneration of North America.

Key to the effort to establish a new religious culture was the formation of fundamentalist educational institutions, both at the primary and higher levels.[39] In time, these educational institutions came to be supplemented by an extensive fundamentalist-controlled media network. The purpose was both to support the new cultural movement and to regain the 'soul' of North America by means of 'televangelism'. By the 1980s, the media network had become so successful that fundamentalist broadcasting on both television and radio had become a pervasive part of North American culture.[40] Indeed, at a time when the mainstream Protestant denominations appeared to be stagnating (in terms of recruits, at least), many independent fundamentalist churches were growing at a remarkable rate.[41]

Indeed, the staggering numbers of people that fundamentalist churches were able to attract during the 1970s helped precipitate the entry of Christian fundamentalism into the arena of public life in the United States – a situation that strained the common assumption that the latter, purportedly one of the most modern countries in the world, was a genuinely secular state. It was at this time that fundamentalists began to form pressure groups in order to lobby for their favourite causes; and once mobilized, these groups were able to exert considerable influence on the politics of the United States simply by virtue of the large number of people they represented. Such political lobbying naturally proved most effective when it focused on narrow issues upon which a wide range of different fundamentalist groups could agree: for example, that there should be government funding for religious schools[42] and that abortion should not be legalized were issues on which fundamentalists could easily reach consensus.[43] Moreover, on both of these issues, fundamentalists could count on the support of other, non-fundamentalist, religious people – such as Roman Catholics and many Jews.

When Jimmy Carter, a Christian belonging to the Baptist denomination, was elected to the presidency of the United States in 1976, his election was widely thought to be due to the support of Christians who wanted their religious values to have a greater influence on North American politics. Similarly, fundamentalist voters were widely held to be responsible for Ronald Reagan's election to the presidency in 1980.[44] In the latter case, the fundamentalist electorate had been encouraged to vote according to the advice of the Moral Majority – a movement created in 1979, and spearheaded by Jerry Falwell, in order to promote the religious renewal of North America.[45] This movement enjoyed the sympathies of a large constituency, as it vied for the support of conservatives outside, as well as within, the fundamentalist movement. Even without approaching conservative Jews, Roman Catholics and Mormons, the Moral Majority could count on the sympathies of a broad sweep of the population. In 1979, a national Gallup poll revealed that one-third of all adults in the United States regarded themselves as 'born again'.[46] The claim of the Moral Majority, then, was to represent the views of all but a small minority of the population of the United States: the 'immoral minority', as Jerry Falwell named them,[47] who were regarded as a handful of secularists who had, by hook or by crook, gained control of Washington and, hence, the political machinery of the United States.

What factors contributed to the extraordinary growth of Christian fundamentalism in the United States during the twentieth century? It is not insignificant that the fundamentalist movement consolidated its position during an era when large-scale violence – or the threat of it – dominated world politics. When the United States launched a nuclear attack on Hiroshima and Nagasaki in 1945, fundamentalists in the United States regarded this as an event of cosmic significance pre-figuring the beginning of the 'end times'. Further 'confirmation' that the premillennial day of judgement was nigh was provided by contemporary events in Israel. It was central to the beliefs of many Christian fundamentalists that an unmistakable sign of the coming of the Messiah would be the return of the Jews to the Land of Israel.[48] The Balfour Declaration of 1917 had thus been a cause of great excitement. The creation of the State of Israel in 1948 was, likewise, regarded as a religious event of the utmost significance. Falwell, for example, perceived this particular event as 'the greatest ... single sign indicating the imminent return of Jesus Christ'.[49] Lest one be tempted to regard this perspective as something of a minority view, it is worth bearing in mind that, at the peak of his career, in the 1960s and 1970s, an estimated 40 per cent of all households in the United States listened to Falwell's radio station.[50] He thus had strong grounds for his claim to be the nation's leading born-again media personality, and to have the ear of the nation. The message that Falwell and his associates broadcast was depicted as presenting the 'facts' to the public – the facts being that certain important prophecies were in the process of being fulfilled. And, judging by the number of people that regularly listened to such radio shows, many were fascinated by this message.

It would seem, then, that the United States, in the second half of the twentieth century, was extremely fertile ground for the growth of religious fundamentalism. This is a striking observation, given that the United States was, at that time, widely perceived to be at the forefront of modernization. Moreover, given the numbers who regularly listened to religious fundamentalist radio programmes, the secularization thesis seems, at best, wildly premature in its predictions.

But before we can draw any general conclusions concerning the relationship between fundamentalism and modernity, we should first consider fundamentalism and Islam.

Islam and fundamentalism

As the focus of this book is upon religion in the West, Muslim thought clearly falls within our purview when it has either emerged from the West or, although originating from without, has been influential within it. Hence, we would have no reason for concentrating at this juncture on forms of Islamic fundamentalism that only exercised an influence within the Arab world. But, as we shall see, Islamic fundamentalism has had a very significant impact on Western Muslims, and, hence, clearly requires our attention.

It is often pointed out that, in a sense, Islam is a quintessentially fundamentalist religion.[51] This is because liberals, modernists and revivalists alike all look back to, and attempt to base their respective forms of Islam on, a sacred text and the examples provided by Muhammad and the early Muslim tradition. Practically all Muslims are committed to the infallibility of the Qur'ān, to the authentic prophethood of Muhammad, to regarding Muhammad's *sunna* (behaviour) as an impeccable example of how God desires that humans should live, and to the authority of the shari'ah. Moreover, Muslims are united in their adherence to the five pillars of Islam – which constitute the fundamentals of Muslim belief.[52] As Fazlur Rahman observes, it is

something of an irony to pit the so-called Muslim fundamentalists against the Muslim modernists, since, so far as their acclaimed procedure goes, the Muslim modernists say exactly the same thing as the so-called Muslim fundamentalists say: that Muslims must go back to the original and definitive sources of Islam and perform *ijtihad* on that basis.[53]

In practice, however, Islamic revivalists are more akin to the fundamentalists of other religious traditions. They aim to return to the original sources of the tradition in a way that circumvents the need for *ijtihād* – the critical interpretation of the texts. Moreover, paralleling the emergence of fundamentalism within Judaism and Christianity, what we shall call 'Islamic fundamentalism' arose in the early twentieth century as a reaction to concessions within their tradition to modernity. In the case of Islamic fundamentalism, the reaction was especially to Islamic modernism, sometimes known as Salafism, which was a reform movement developed by a number of influential figures, such as Jamal al-Din al-Afghani (1838–97), Muhammad 'Abduh (1849–1905) and Muhammad Iqbal (1875–1938). The modernist movement was uncannily like Wahhabism – an earlier reform movement – insofar as both movements emphasized the need to return to the original sources of the tradition. Both, moreover, aimed to revitalize Islam by this means. The modernists, however, were more receptive than the Wahhabists had been to the selective assimilation of aspects of modernity, arguing that the original sources of the tradition should be reinterpreted in accordance with the needs of the times. As one commentator puts it, the 'proponents of Salafism were eager to throw off the shackles of tradition, and to engage in the rethinking of Islamic solutions in the light of modern demands'.[54]

In retrospect, it is clear that thinkers engaged within the modernist movement were working on two fronts simultaneously. On the one hand, they employed the tools of modern scholarship in their attempt to reform the Muslim tradition from within, while, on the other hand, they strove to present Islam in such a way that it would not alienate modern, Western non-Muslims. With this latter agenda in mind, modernists were eager to emphasize the progressive nature of Islam, both socially and intellectually. Both of these goals would seem to reveal that these thinkers had formed an extremely positive assessment of modernity and modern ideas.[55]

More conservative thinkers, however, came to believe that the modernists were too uncritical in their acceptance of Western ideas and values, and hence, to their mind, were insufficiently Islamic. The movement that developed as a direct response to Islamic modernism is known as revivalism. The aim of those associated with this latter movement, such as Sayyid Qutb (1906–66), was to revitalize Islam without appeal to Western ideas and values; the goal being to create an authentically Islamic version of modernity by creatively drawing upon the Muslim tradition rather than upon Western culture. Revivalism has been extremely influential throughout many predominantly Muslim areas ever since the Second World War, particularly, for example, in Algeria, Iran, the Sudan, Pakistan, Saudi Arabia and Egypt. Moreover, many revivalists have engaged in missionary activities in the West (although there is no consensus about how successful they have been in propagating their form of Islam within Western Europe and North America). Islamic revivalism did, however, clearly gain considerable ground in many areas outside the West where Muslims form a majority, especially after what was widely perceived as the failure of Arab socialism and nationalism following the devastating defeat of the combined Arab forces during the six-day war against the State of Israel in 1967.

The origins of Islamic revivalism as a significant political force are often associated with the figure of Hasan al-Banna (1906–49). Appalled by the social conditions many of his contemporary co-religionists were experiencing in his native Egypt, al-Banna founded the Muslim Brotherhood in 1928. The Brotherhood was originally a non-violent movement for the reform of Islam through peaceful and constructive social and political action.[56] Al-Banna was principally motivated by the belief that the intense social problems in Egypt called for religious answers, not just political ones.[57] Thus, his religious beliefs informed his enormously successful social and political programme – a programme that was aimed at the betterment of the underprivileged in his society.

Despite its initial success, the Muslim Brotherhood failed to maintain its founder's commitment to non-violence. This seems to have been due to the intensive persecution it suffered during the 1950s at the hands of the Egyptian government under the leadership of President Gamal Abd Al-Nasir; and, in consequence, the movement became far more radical. By the time it spread to other parts of the world, it had completely lost its original commitment to non-violence, and was widely perceived to be an aggressive movement. From the 1950s onwards, the concept 'jihad' played an increasingly prominent role in the movement's rhetoric – in part, because of the influence of Sayyid Qutb, one of the Brotherhood's main public representatives.[58] Qutb was imprisoned in Nasir's Egypt only one year after joining the Brotherhood in 1953. And his experience of imprisonment clearly radicalized him. While he had formerly been enthusiastic about Western culture and sympathetic to its secular orientation, being on the receiving end of secular intolerance in Egypt led him to conclude that a conflict between secularism and religious values was inevitable. And it was during his imprisonment that he developed the ideas that made him the father of Sunni fundamentalism. Significantly, Qutb's ire was not chiefly directed at the West but rather at Westernizers within his own country, specifically Nasirites.

Qutb was executed on direct orders from President Nasir in 1966, with his execution turning him into something of a martyr in the eyes of many Sunni Muslims. As a result of his perceived martyrdom, he became a major figurehead, and his writings were widely circulated among the swelling ranks of Islamic revivalists.

Although Islamic revivalism has taken different forms wherever it has emerged, it seems to be united in its commitment to six tenets. These tenets are summed up as follows by John Esposito:

1 Islam is a total and comprehensive way of life. Religion is integral to politics, law, and society.
2 The failure of Muslim societies is due to their departure from the straight path of Islam and following a Western secular path with its materialistic ideologies and values.
3 The renewal of society requires a return to Islam, an Islamic religio-political and social reformation or revolution, that draws its inspiration from the Quran and from the first great Islamic movement led by the Prophet Muhammad.
4 To restore God's rule and inaugurate a true Islamic social order, western-inspired civil codes must be replaced by Islamic law which is the only acceptable blueprint for a Muslim society.
5 ... Science and technology are ... to be subordinated to Islamic belief and values in order to guard against the westernization and secularization of Muslim society.
6 The process of Islamization, or more accurately, re-Islamization, requires organizations or associations of dedicated and trained Muslims who, by their example and activities, call upon others to be more observant and who are willing to struggle (*jihad*) against corruption and social injustice.[59]

Despite the appeal of Islamic revivalism outside the West, it has proven less appealing to the majority of Western European and North American Muslims, many of whom favour more liberal or progressive interpretations of Islam. Indeed, the six core tenets of Islamic revivalism listed above would seem, at first sight, to be of little relevance to a Muslim whose home is located within a modern Western society, and who has no intention of emigrating to a Muslim state. Such people, not surprisingly, tend not to identify with the agenda of Islamic revivalism, even though, in a technical sense, many of them are religious fundamentalists.

One reason why Islamic revivalism might seem less appealing to Muslims living in the West is its assignment to the shari'ah of a central role in the governing of society. This is likely to be less appealing to Muslims in the West because they tend to be acculturated to life within a pluralist liberal democracy, and if they adhere to the shari'ah at all, then it is usually only to that part which governs family relations. Moreover, Muslims in the West would seem, on the whole, to be more concerned with consolidating their local religious community rather than with promoting Islam as the comprehensive blueprint for the political order.[60]

Nevertheless, Islamic revivalism has still managed to exert a significant influence on Muslims living within Western Europe and in North America. And it has exerted most influence on them through the way in which it is often portrayed as archetypal, and thus used as the standard by which to judge the beliefs and behaviour of all Muslims. Thus, many Western Muslims have felt pressurized to accede to its supposed authority; and in conceding that theirs is a corrupt form of Islam, they have also felt compelled to adopt a lifestyle more in line with 'tradition'. Many Western Muslim intellectuals are currently occupied with combating this notion of an archetypal Islam. Thus, much of their work, and particularly that of the intellectuals involved in the 'Progressive Islam' movement, is concerned to justify their opposing view of Islam to its critics outside the West.

But, clearly, they only feel compelled to engage in such self-justification because of the very real pressure that Islamic revivalism exerts. And the pressure to return to 'tradition' that many Muslims in the West experience is intensified in those parts of North America and Europe where established Muslim communities continually welcome large numbers of new immigrants from countries where Islamic revivalism predominates. These new immigrants often regard indigenous Western Muslim communities as inferior to the 'traditional' ones they left behind in their homelands – a judgement that has elicited a variety of responses from Western Muslims, with the following being representative of the growing impatience many feel when confronted with such an attitude:

> First, we have to recognize that Islam in America is probably closer to the true teaching of the Prophet Muhammad than anywhere else at any other time in the last five hundred years .... I'm saying that the access to pure Islamic teachings and the ability to live them to their fullest moral and social potential is more pronounced in America than it has been for centuries in Iraq, Turkey, Saudi Arabia, Pakistan, Afghanistan, Nigeria, or anywhere else. ... The light of Islam has been put out in the Muslim world and has been reborn in the heart of the supposedly secular, faithless West.[61]

Moreover, Islamic revivalism has encountered criticism from a number of quarters for presenting Islam as a monolithic entity. Mohammed

Arkoun, for example, claims that Islamic revivalism errs in relying on a mistaken image of Islam – one that overlooks the dynamic nature of the various Islamic traditions. Moreover, Arkoun argues further that the 'Islam' of the revivalists is actually derived from a notion of the faith that has been 'constructed by the Western scientific study of Islam', and transformed by the revivalists 'into historical and doctrinal "authenticity"'.[62] Thus, if Arkoun is correct, then the form of Islam that has come to dominate much Islamic thinking is, ironically, based on a distorted view of Islam deriving from Western orientalist scholarship. To make matters worse, Arkoun argues, the success of revivalism now serves to confirm that ideological account of the tradition both among Western scholars of Islam and among those Muslims involved within the movement.

While Islamic revivalism has made itself felt within Europe and North America, it is not the dominant form of Islam in the West. Nevertheless, it does seem to be the case that, in a global context, fundamentalism has been more prominent within Islam than within either Judaism or Christianity. One explanation for this may lie in the different ways that secularization was experienced by, on the one hand, Jews and Christians within the West and, on the other hand, Muslims outside the West. As we have seen in previous chapters, many Jews and Christians within the West experienced secularization as liberating. Many Jews benefited politically from the secularization process, and many religious thinkers of both faiths felt that they had been freed from burdensome layers of tradition, and could interpret their faiths more creatively than was possible in the past. In many parts of the world where Muslims constitute the majority, however, secularization was part and parcel of the experience of colonialism. Thus, few experienced it as a force for the good. This negative perception of secularization appears to have intensified the more that modernization was forced upon unwilling populations by the agents of colonial powers. Consequently, a resistance to secularization became closely linked with a resistance to colonialism.

One way in which Muslims outside the West were able to respond to colonialism was by emphasizing the indigenous nature of Islam, and its supposedly intrinsic connection to the local polity. Thus, popular movements developed with the aim of promoting Islam as the principal source of public policy, and insisting upon the need for Islamic scholars and jurists to occupy prominent roles within government. The most successful of these movements developed among the Shi'a Muslims of Iran. And in 1978–79, their hostility to the secular government of the Western-backed Shah culminated in a popular revolution that elevated a religious leader, the Ayatollah Khomeini, to head of state. Significantly, in the decades preceding the revolution, repressive strategies had been employed similar to those used in Egypt. Ostensibly, they had been imposed on the people in order to serve the ends of modernization. And under such a secular regime – one that sought to exclude religion from the public sphere – religious people found themselves fighting to retain their integrity. It was in this climate that the Ayatollah Khomeini was able to build his reputation and acquire a popular following.

There can be no doubt that the Iranian revolution had immense repercussions throughout many Muslim communities outside the West. People who had formerly been disempowered by the political legacies of colonialism suddenly felt that they could take control of their own political destiny, and that they could do so in a way that affirmed their traditional religious beliefs. However, in the eyes of many in the West, the Iranian revolution simply served to link the image of Islam with the notion of violence: a connection that is tragically reinforced with every widely publicized act of violence perpetrated by Muslims. The climax of this trend, of course, was reached at the beginning of the twenty-first century when pictures of the destruction of the twin towers of the World Trade Centre in New York City were broadcast across the globe.

Because Islam has now become so associated with violence in the minds of many in the West, it is necessary to point out that, despite the fact that many Muslims are fundamentalist in a technical sense, relatively few of them feel incited by their religious convictions to perpetrate acts of violence upon those who do not share their beliefs. Thus, even if religious fundamentalism should prove to be a necessary condition for religiously motivated acts of violence, it is clearly not a sufficient one. For if it is to issue in violence, other conditions (social, political and economic, for instance) would seem to be required.

Clearly, as we have seen in this chapter, religious fundamentalism has not arisen in a vacuum, but, rather, in relationship with modernity. Moreover, there seems no reason to think that, in a modern world, fundamentalist tendencies will not persist well into the future. This chapter concludes, therefore, by considering the link between religious fundamentalism and modernity in greater detail.

Religious fundamentalism and modernity

The forms of fundamentalism considered above, despite their considerable differences, bear some striking resemblances to one another. The similarities become particularly apparent when one considers the broad goals of these various fundamentalist movements. Each asserts the primacy of its own particular form of religion, and aspires to influence government policies in order to facilitate the transmission of that religion. In each case, this assertive stance is a defensive response to the tendency of modern societies to undermine the public role of religious faith and values. Moreover, as we have seen above, as secularization undermines the more liberal, or progressive, forms of religion, people are drawn to the fundamentalist varieties, which seem more resilient to the encroachments of modernity. There is no doubt, however, that, despite first appearances, forms of religious fundamentalism are not merely atavistic survivals within a modern age of traditional belief systems. Rather, they are quintessentially modern phenomena. As Steve Bruce claims, they

> arise in traditional cultures but they are not traditional in any simple sense. Enough of the old religion needs to have been preserved to provide the inspiration and the symbolism for those who wish to reassert its predominance. But fundamentalisms are not mere survivals, the past continued. ... [T]hey are radical revisions of the past provoked by changes that threaten the continuity of the tradition. In that sense, fundamentalisms are reactive.[63]

Indeed, it is difficult to study religious fundamentalism in the twentieth century without concluding that it constitutes a highly innovative response to modernity. For one can see the various forms of religious fundamentalism, as Karen Armstrong does, as 'modern religious experiments' – the legacy of which, at the end of the twentieth century, being the return of religion, in many parts of the world, to a prominent place within public life.[64] And this occurred in a century during which religion was expected to die a natural death. One consequence of the success of fundamentalist forms of Judaism, Christianity and Islam is that, as we have seen, it has caused many thinkers to re-evaluate the connection between modernity and secularity. Given the prominence of religious fundamentalism within modern societies in the closing decades of the twentieth century, it can no longer be assumed that secularity is the only possible expression of modernity.

What might explain the extraordinary popularity of fundamentalist forms of religion in the modern world? This phenomenon is all the more striking in countries that explicitly cultivate an image of modernity in the eyes of the rest of the world.[65] No doubt a range of factors contributes, but perhaps it is not insignificant that, in an era during which many religious people became more qualified about their faith,[66] the numbers confessing some form of fundamentalism rose dramatically. Those seeking psychological security from religion would no doubt be more attracted to the non-compromising commitments of the fundamentalist churches. Also, in the second half of the twentieth century, many of the more liberal religious thinkers (whether Jewish, Christian or Muslim) felt that they should not burden their children with too much religious education – an education that was often portrayed as indoctrination. Rather, such religious liberals felt that their children should be the ones to choose whether or not to be religious. Moreover, it was often held that this is a decision people should make later in life, when they might be in a better position to make a genuine choice. One result of this strategy was that many people reached young adulthood lacking any basic knowledge about religion. They were thus intellectually unequipped to take their place within the faith communities of their parents. It would not be surprising if these people turned out to be more prone than others towards conversion to fundamentalist forms of religion. As Fazlur Rahman writes:

> an intense and irrational faith in a subjective humanism among several present-day 'liberated' circles has led many to 'leave our children alone when they are young so that they can choose their own way of life when they are adults' and the like. Such statements, often made in good faith ... , in fact betray a lack of concern for the future of humanity. For, if humans could grow by themselves, highly sophisticated religious and educational systems would not have developed in the first place. And what we are seeing develop in societies whose liberals think they are the first secular liberals in human history is that, instead of growing into humans, many of the new generation are in fact growing into animals. To remedy the crudity and even cruelty of a self-righteous traditional system is one thing. To throw out the baby with the bath water is quite another.[67]

These observations would seem to be borne out by an increasing number of scholars who have noticed that the children of liberally oriented religious people often grow up to be far more religiously conservative than their parents – even to the point of overtly criticizing the religious liberalism of their parents.[68]

Thus, it may be that many people opt for fundamentalism because they do not understand, and are, perhaps, not even aware of the other possible expressions of faith. Indeed, one might say that the alternatives are not live options for them. Modern society typically fails to equip people either philosophically or theologically for an appreciation of the resources of evolving faith-traditions. Consequently, it would, perhaps, not be too far off the mark to claim that, by the late twentieth century, many in the West had grown up to be 'religiously illiterate'.[69] Such illiteracy, moreover, is bound to be cultivated in societies, such as the United States, where it is often impossible to discuss critically within state schools issues pertaining to religion.

Despite these considerations, to which we return in the next chapter, the sheer numbers of people who are attracted by fundamentalist lifestyles, and, evidently, feel the appeal of fundamentalist worldviews, continue to perplex many who do not feel this attraction. Some are puzzled as to why more liberal or progressive versions of traditional faiths do not exercise a similar attraction on equally large numbers of people. Earlier in this book we traced the development of liberal religious thinking, and we noted the striking transformations that liberal religious thinkers have worked upon traditional religious beliefs. The speed of this development in the modern period, if not the development itself, is unprecedented. Perhaps, despite the argument that fundamentalist forms of religion are just as much products of modernity as are any of the liberal or progressive forms, fundamentalism at least gives the appearance of continuity with the past in a way that other modern forms of faith are strained to do. If so, this might provide some explanation for their wide appeal. These issues raise the question of which form of faith, fundamentalist or liberal, is the oddest. As Peter Berger reflects, it is not fundamentalism that is rare in the modern world; rather, the real rarities are 'people who think otherwise'.[70] Thus, he goes on to deny the common assumption that we live in a secularized world: 'The world today, with some exceptions [particularly Western Europe], is as furiously religious as it ever was, and in some places more so than ever'.[71]

Berger's argument might be taken to suggest that fundamentalist forms of faith have remained essentially unchanged by modernity, while liberal forms have evolved in response to it. But it seems, rather, that religious fundamentalism is just as quintessentially modern as the more liberal varieties of religion. At the very least, religious fundamentalism is modern to the extent that, just like religious liberalism and secularism, it is a response to modern conditions – conditions that the fundamentalist perceives as threatening religious faith at its very core. And, as we have seen, fundamentalists tend to regard themselves as involved in a struggle to preserve their religious beliefs and way of life in the face of a social world that is increasingly structured and controlled by the policies of secular governments. Given this interpretation of political affairs, it is perhaps not surprising that the more secularism advances, the stronger the response from fundamentalists.

Conclusion

Many fundamentalist Christians in the United States understand themselves to be engaged in a war in which the enemy is the secular culture within their own country. In a sense, then, their war is a civil war. It is noteworthy that many Muslims, both within and outside the United States, also perceive themselves to be at war with the same enemy: the secular culture of the United States. The features of the United States and its culture that many Muslims find objectionable would seem to be remarkably similar to those to which many Christians object. For example, the secular images and values promoted worldwide by the United States media are as offensive to many North American Christians as they are to many Muslims – and, for that matter, to many Jews. The seeming promotion through the national media of alcohol, extra-marital sex and drugs, and licentious images then exported worldwide through Hollywood, provide examples of what is offensive to many. Again, then, and contrary to much of the rhetoric emanating from Muslim communities outside the West – a rhetoric linking the United States with Satan – both Christian fundamentalism and Islamic fundamentalism would seem to be a response to the same set of quintessentially modern 'problems'.

This suggests that the cultural forces that run contrary to the ideals that many liberals in the West espouse arise, at least in part, from within Western culture itself.[72] To deny this would be to deny that fundamentalist forms of Protestantism, for example, are a product of Western culture. And clearly, when fundamentalists are pitched against secularists within Western societies, as is the case in the United States, for example, it would seem to be symptomatic of a significant cultural clash within such societies. Two divergent streams within Western culture would thus seem to be in conflict. As we have seen in this chapter, religious fundamentalists are united in identifying secular modern culture as the enemy. Insofar as fundamentalists across different religious traditions share the same enemy, they might be thought to have more in common with each other than with liberals within their own faith-traditions. Jewish, Christian and Muslim fundamentalists clearly speak a common language, even though they disagree on particular items of belief. Moreover, all tend to find the discourse of liberal religion incomprehensible.

Finally, it is important to recognize that religious fundamentalists are surely correct to identify secular modern culture as their principal enemy. Moreover, they have not underestimated the threat to their religious worldview that such culture poses. For it would seem that what has eroded traditional religious faith within the West, more than any other single factor, is modern secular culture. The values promoted by this culture – materialism and individualism, for example – stand in stark opposition to the values celebrated by traditional faiths, and thus pose a powerful challenge to those faiths. If religious belief is to survive within modern secular cultures, it must, in one way or another, adapt to new conditions. As we have seen earlier in this book, various strategies for adaptation are available. Individual beliefs within the religious worldview can be adapted so that conflict with modern ideas and values is minimized. Or the militant path of religious fundamentalism can be employed. What would not seem to be feasible, though, would be for religious believers to ignore the problems that modernity has presented to their belief systems. Some have sought to avoid these problems, however, by claiming that modern secular culture has now expired. In the final chapter, then, we consider where the traditional Abrahamic religions stand in the light of styles of thought that many have now come to regard as 'postmodern'.

Study questions

1 Why has religious law proved to be such an important focal point of attention for Jewish and Muslim fundamentalist groups?

2 What is the best explanation for the strength of the religious counter-movements that have developed in certain parts of the West as a response to secularization?

3 Is it convincing to claim that the resurgence of religion in modern times is just a temporary deviation from the trajectory predicted by the secularization thesis? How might you support this view?

4 What might explain the difference between religious fundamentalist groups that sanction religiously motivated acts of violence and those that do not?

5 What features does religious fundamentalism in Judaism, Christianity and Islam share? How do they differ?

6 Is religious fundamentalism as much an expression of modernity as secularization? If so, what implications might this have for the future of religious fundamentalism?

7 What might explain the attraction of fundamentalism in the modern world?

Select bibliography

Armstrong, K., 2001, *The Battle for God: Fundamentalism in Judaism, Christianity and Islam*, London: HarperCollins.

Bruce, S., 2000, *Fundamentalism*, Cambridge: Polity.

Bruce, S. (ed.), 1992, *Religion and Modernization: Sociologists and Historians Debate the Secularization Thesis*, Oxford: Clarendon Press.

Huntington, S. P., 1996, *The Clash of Civilizations and the Remaking of the World Order*, New York: Simon & Schuster.

Juergensmeyer, M., 2000, *Terror in the Mind of God: The Global Rise of Religious Violence*, Berkeley: University of California Press.

Landau, D., 1993, *Piety and Power: The World of Jewish Fundamentalism*, New York: Hill and Wang.

Lee, R. D., 1997, *Overcoming Tradition and Modernity: The Search for Islamic Authenticity*, Boulder: Westview Press.

Liebman, C. S., 'Extremism as a Religious Norm', *Journal for the Scientific Study of Religion*, 22 (1983), pp. 75–86.

Marsden, G. M., 1980, *Fundamentalism and American Culture: The Shaping of Twentieth-Century Evangelism: 1870–1925*, New York: Oxford University Press.

Marty, M. E., and R. Scott Appleby (eds), *Fundamentalisms and Society: Reclaiming the Sciences, the Family, and Education*, The Fundamentalist Project, vol. 2, Chicago: The University of Chicago Press.

Rahman, F., 2000, *Revival and Reform in Islam: A Study of Islamic Fundamentalism*, edited by Ebrahim Moosa, Oxford: Oneworld.

Sacks, J., 1991, *The Persistence of Faith: Religion, Morality and Society in a Secular Age*, London: Weidenfeld & Nicolson.
Safi, O. (ed.), *Progressive Muslims: On Justice, Gender, and Pluralism*, Oxford: Oneworld.

Notes

1 Resolution of the World Congress of Fundamentalists. Internet publication http://www.itib.org/resolutions/10-ecumenical_movement.html.

2 Don Cupitt, 1984, *The Sea of Faith: Christianity in Change*, London: BBC, p. 160.

3 See Jonathan Sacks, 1991, *The Persistence of Faith: Religion, Morality and Society in a Secular Age*, London: Weidenfeld & Nicolson, p. 78. Sacks is currently Chief Rabbi of the United Hebrew Congregations of the Commonwealth (a Modern Orthodox organization).

4 *The Fundamentals: A Testimony to the Truth*, 12 vols, Chicago: Testimony Publishing, 1910–15.

5 'Evangelical Christians' are Protestants who emphasize evangelism, the 'plain' message of the Bible, and the saving power of Jesus as a personal Lord. At the beginning of the twentieth century, Christians of this type could be found in all the major Protestant denominations within the United States: Episcopalian, Lutheran, Congregational, Baptist, Methodist and Presbyterian, for example. Although evangelism had precedents in the pietist forms of Christianity that developed within medieval Europe, its modern form took shape in eighteenth-century England, from whence it spread to the United States with successive waves of immigrants. The distinction between evangelical Christians and fundamentalists has always been a difficult one to define, as many, although by no means all, evangelicals are also fundamentalists. Indeed, from the 1940s, in reaction to the fundamentalist movement, a neo-evangelical movement developed in many parts of the United States. Billy Graham is the most well-known figure associated with neo-evangelism.

6 The Bible was thought to be inerrant because it was an unmediated account of what was in God's mind, dictated by God to those who served as his agents in writing down the text. Indeed, the Bible was thought to have always existed in the mind of God (given that the divine mind is unchanging). This view explains why any notion of the Bible requiring interpretation was anathema to these thinkers. For attempting to interpret the eternal word of God is tantamount to changing the message. Moreover, strictly speaking, the whole Bible, on this view, has only one author – God. For an account of fundamentalist ideas about the Bible, see James Barr, 1987, *Fundamentalism*, London: SCM Press, chapter 3. The remarkable similarity between this view of the Bible and the view of the Qur'ān that came to dominate the Muslim tradition should not go unnoticed.

7 On the consolidation of this denominationally disparate group into a single movement, see George M. Marsden, 1980, *Fundamentalism and American Culture: The Shaping of Twentieth-Century Evangelism: 1870–1925*, New York: Oxford University Press.

8 Sacks, *Persistence*, p. 77.

9 Karen Armstrong, 2001, *The Battle for God: Fundamentalism in Judaism, Christianity and Islam*, London: HarperCollins, p. 178.

10 See, particularly, Chapter 5.

11 See David Landau, 1993, *Piety and Power: The World of Jewish Fundamentalism*, New York: Hill and Wang, p. 51.

12 Modern Orthodox Judaism and all types of conservative Christianity also made concessions to the enlightenment principle that one is enjoined to think for oneself. However, as their names imply, they did not go as far as either the Reformed Jewish tradition or the Liberal Protestant Christian tradition. Rather, they sought a compromise. And this is why the dividing line between Modern Orthodox Judaism and Ultra-Orthodox Judaism on the one hand, and conservative Christianity and fundamentalist Christianity on the other, is not always clear cut. With respect to each faith-tradition, care is needed if one is not to confuse fundamentalists with conservative believers. While there may be considerable overlap, the groups are by no means co-extensive. In fact, Jews, Christians and Muslims who might be happy to call themselves 'conservative' can feel just as threatened by fundamentalists as can liberals.

13 Steve Bruce, 2000, *Fundamentalism*, Cambridge: Polity, p. 98.

14 A resolution to this effect was passed by delegates of the World Congress of Fundamentalists in 1999.

15 Cf. 'No mariner ever entered upon a more uncharted sea than does the average human being born into the twentieth century. Our ancestors thought they knew their way from birth through all eternity: we are puzzled about the day after to-morrow.' Walter Lippmann, 1985, *Drift and Mastery*, Madison: University of Wisconsin Press, p. 112.

16 The work of the sociologist Max Weber (1864–1920) was influential in promoting this thesis.

17 See Peter Berger, 'Against the Current', *Prospect*, 17 March (1997), pp. 32–6.

18 See Will Herberg, 1994, *Protestant–Catholic–Jew: An Essay in American Religious Sociology*, Chicago: University of Chicago Press.

19 See Charles S. Liebman, 1983, 'Orthodoxy in American Jewish Life' in Reuven Bulka (ed.), *Dimensions of Orthodox Judaism*, New York: KTAV, pp. 33–105.

20 In keeping with this pattern, the Roman Catholic Church began to lose ground against other denominations in the wake of the liberalizing Second Vatican Council in the 1960s. However, later in the twentieth century, under the leadership of the conservative Pontiff John Paul II, it exhibited a greater ability to attract converts and to keep its existing members.

21 See Paul Kurtz, 1988, 'The Growth of Fundamentalism Worldwide' in The Academy of Humanism, *Neo-Fundamentalism: The Humanist Response*, Buffalo: Prometheus Books, pp. 7f.

22 Charles S. Liebman, 'Extremism as a Religious Norm', *Journal for the Scientific Study of Religion*, 22 (1983), pp. 75–86. Whereas Liebman uses the term 'extremism', here I retain the term 'fundamentalism' because of the connotation of the use of violence that is typical of the former term but not of the latter.

23 Liebman, 'Extremism', p. 79.

24 Judaism, Christianity and Islam each have their own version of religious law. Christian fundamentalists do not usually pay much attention to religious law, possibly because it is perceived as Roman Catholic law, and the majority of Christian fundamentalists reject Roman Catholicism. However, by contrast, religious law is an important focus for Jewish and Islamic fundamentalists.

25 Aspects which would also seem to be of especial significance to Islamic fundamentalists.

26 Liebman, 'Extremism', p. 79.

27 Liebman, 'Extremism', pp. 79f.

28 Although an obvious counter-example that Liebman does not anticipate is provided by the 'televangelist' media personalities that dominated Christian broadcasting in the United States during the 1970s and 1980s (about whom see, below).

29 Nevertheless, the thesis continues to stimulate vigorous debate. See, for example, the collection of essays in Steve Bruce (ed.), 1992, *Religion and Modernization: Sociologists and Historians Debate the Secularization Thesis*, Oxford: Clarendon Press.

30 See Landau, *Piety*, p. xxiv.

31 Landau, *Piety*, p. xxv.

32 Landau, *Piety*, p. 45.

33 Landau, *Piety*, p. 45.

34 Indeed, this claim also applies to other religious communities in the West. During the twentieth century, many of these communities increasingly became communities of *ascent* rather than communities of *descent*. The modern emphasis on autonomy and personal choice fuelled this development. On the distinction between these two forms of community, see Paul Morris, 1996, 'Community Beyond Tradition' in Paul Heelas, Scott Lash and Paul Morris (eds), *Detraditionalization: Critical Reflections on Authority and Identity*, Oxford: Blackwell, pp. 238f.

35 The award-winning film *Time of Favor* (directed by Joseph Cedar, 2000, Israel) vividly reconstructs a similar plot.

36 On Rabin's assassination, see Mark Juergensmeyer, 2000, *Terror in the Mind of God: The Global Rise of Religious Violence*, Berkeley: University of California Press, pp. 44–9.

37 Yigal Amir, quoted in Joel Greenberg, 'Rabin's Assassin', *New York Times*, 5 November 1995.

38 'Postmillennialist' fundamentalists, in contrast to premillennialists, believe that the thousand-year reign of the righteous will precede the day of judgement.

39 An early example is Bob Jones University, founded in Florida in 1927.

40 Indeed, Sara Diamond has argued that 'religious broadcasting has been the single most important development in the rise of the Christian Right'. Sara Diamond, 1998, *Not by Politics Alone: The Enduring Influence of the Christian Right*, New York and London: The Guildford Press, p. 13, and see Chapter 1.

41 See Mark A. Shibley, 1996, *Resurgent Evangelism in the United States: Mapping Cultural Change since 1970*, Columbia, South Carolina: University of South Carolina Press, p. 27.

42 Fundamentalists were appalled by the increasing demand in the post-Second World War United States that publicly funded schools be explicitly

non-religious. From the 1950s through to the 1970s a series of rulings was passed by the Supreme Court that forbade, among other things, the reading of the Bible in public schools. This trend was symptomatic of what many in the United States regarded as an unwarranted expansion of state interference in what they viewed as the private realm. In effect, there was wide disagreement over whether education was 'public' or 'private'. In the state's view, whatever it funded was thereby 'public'. It is probable, though, that this dispute led many who had hitherto not been inclined towards fundamentalism to join the fundamentalist movement. On the debate between government representatives and fundamentalists over education, see Susan Rose, 1993, 'Christian Fundamentalism and Education in the United States' in Martin E. Marty and R. Scott Appleby (eds), *Fundamentalisms and Society: Reclaiming the Sciences, the Family, and Education*, The Fundamentalist Project, vol. 2, Chicago: The University of Chicago Press, pp. 452–89.

43 This is not to imply that all Christians who were involved in fundamentalist churches became politically active, nor that they identified with the 'new Christian Right'. In fact, a direct correlation between affiliation to some form of fundamentalism, or evangelical Protestantism more generally, and the political Right is difficult to establish.

44 Indeed, this event is often regarded as the biggest single success of the 'New Christian Right'.

45 The Moral Majority remained influential in politics in the United States until it folded in 1987, when Falwell retired from public life. Upon Falwell's retirement, Pat Robertson, a minister in the Pentecostal tradition, attempted to fill the role of public leader of the New Christian Right. His main asset was his ownership of a broadcasting conglomerate: CBN (the Christian Broadcasting Network). In 1988, Robertson ran for the presidency – a campaign that ended in failure. Steve Bruce attributes Robertson's demise at the polls to his need to cultivate two different, and ultimately contradictory, ways of presenting himself. To the general public, Robertson presented himself as a successful businessman: someone in the business of religious television but who was still at home in the secular world. But to his co-religionists he presented a very different image, announcing to them that 'the feminist agenda is not about equal rights for women. It is about a socialist, anti-family political movement that encourages women to leave their husbands, kill their children, practice witchcraft, destroy capitalism, and become lesbians.' (Quoted in Bruce, *Fundamentalism*, p. 87.) These personas are clearly so disparate that, Bruce opines, they were far too easy to see through – and hence, Robertson's lack of support at the polls.

46 See Michael Lienesch, 1993, *Redeeming America: Piety and Politics in the New Christian Right*, Chapell Hill: University of North Carolina Press, p. 1. Lienesch cites 'The Christianity Today-Gallup Poll: An Overview', *Christianity Today*, 23 (December 1979), pp. 12–19. This poll, moreover, claims that an astonishing 50 per cent of the population of the United States regarded the Bible as inerrant.

47 Cited in Armstrong, *Battle*, p. 310.

48 This belief explains the otherwise inexplicable support, during this period, of fundamentalist Christians for the State of Israel. Because they were convinced that the Last Days could not begin until all Jews had returned to their ancestral

homeland, Christian fundamentalists were numbered among the strongest allies of the fledging Israeli state. Some of these Christians were strange 'friends' to the Jews, however. For they believed that God's purpose in gathering Jews together in the Land of Israel was to slaughter the majority of them for their resistance to the Messiah – a belief formed on the basis of a collation of texts from the Hebrew Scriptures and the New Testament. See, for example, Hal Lindsey (with C. C. Carlson), 1970, *The Late Great Planet Earth*, Grand Rapids, Michigan: Zondervan, pp. 54f.

49 Cited in Armstrong, *Battle*, p. 217.

50 See Armstrong, *Battle*, p. 275.

51 See, for example, Frederick Denny, 1987, *Islam and the Muslim Community*, San Francisco: Harper and Row, p. 117.

52 See Chapter 3, p. 66.

53 Fazlur Rahman, 1982, *Islam and Modernity: Transformation of an Intellectual Tradition*, Chicago: The University of Chicago Press, p. 142.

54 Khaled Abou El Fadl, 2003, 'The Ugly Modern and the Modern Ugly: Reclaiming the Beautiful in Islam' in O. Safi (ed.), *Progressive Muslims: On Justice, Gender, and Pluralism*, Oxford: Oneworld, p. 55.

55 This unqualified positive appraisal of modernity distinguishes early Muslim modernists from many late twentieth-century Muslim intellectuals, who, on the whole, evaluate modernity more critically. See Ebrahim Moosa, 2003, 'The Debts and Burdens of Critical Islam' in Safi, *Progressive*, pp. 118–20.

56 For an account of the genesis, development and persecution of the Muslim Brotherhood, see Dilip Hiro, 1988, *Islamic Fundamentalism*, London: Paladin, chapter 4.

57 See Hasan al-Banna: 'Politics is part of religion. Caesar and what belongs to Caesar is for God Almighty alone'. Quoted in B. B. Lawrence, 1990, *Defenders of God: The Fundamentalist Revolt against the Modern Age*, London: I. B. Tauris, p. 216.

58 For an excellent account of Qutb's thought and its relationship to contemporary Western ideas, see Robert D. Lee, 1997, *Overcoming Tradition and Modernity: The Search for Islamic Authenticity*, Boulder: Westview Press, chapter 4.

59 John L. Esposito, 1989, 'Revival and Reform in Contemporary Islam' in William M. Shea (ed.), *The Struggle Over the Past: Fundamentalism in the Modern World*, Lanham: University Press of America, p. 40.

60 For example, as Taha Jabir Alalwani, chairman of the Fiqh (Jurisprudence) Council of North America, writes: 'In all of my studies, I have never felt that Islam was too concerned about building a state. Islam, from the beginning, was working to build an *ummah*, and there is a big difference between building an *ummah* and building a state. Building an *ummah* means you have certain concepts and values. The Muslim *ummah* is based on three main values: *tawhid* (oneness of God), *tazkiya* (purification of the human being), and *'imran* (building a civilization with values). These three values are considered as the main goals of Islam.' Radwan A. Masmoudi, 2002, 'No More Simplistic Answers: An Interview with Taha Jabir Alalwani' in Michael Wolfe (ed.), *Taking Back Islam: American Muslims Reclaim Their Faith*, Emmaus, Pennsylvania: Rodale, pp. 83f.

61 Yahiya Emerick, 2002, 'The Fight for the Soul of Islam in America' in Wolfe, *Taking*, pp. 197f.

62 Mohammed Arkoun, 1994, *Rethinking Islam: Common Questions, Uncommon Answers*, trans. and edited by Robert D. Lee, Boulder: Westview, p. 1.

63 Bruce, *Fundamentalism*, p. 14.

64 Armstrong, *Battle*, p. 366.

65 One need only think of the United States, which projects a highly modern image not only through its film industry but also through its state-of-the-art weaponry.

66 For, as we have seen in previous chapters, many came to grant large concessions on core doctrines, on the status of Scripture, and on the supposed exclusive truth of their own religion.

67 Rahman, *Islam*, p. 159.

68 See, for example, Marcia Hermansen, 2003, 'How to Put the Genie Back in the Bottle? "Identity" Islam and Muslim Youth Cultures in America' in Safi, *Progressive*, pp. 306–19.

69 See Diane L. Moore, 2007, *Overcoming Religious Illiteracy: A Multicultural Approach to the Study of Religion in Secondary Education*, London: Palgrave Macmillan.

70 Berger, 'Against', p. 32.

71 Berger, 'Against', p. 32.

72 The implications of this claim clearly contradict Samuel Huntington's influential thesis that the world order has entered a new phase in which it is dominated by a clash of civilizations (notably the Islamic and the Western civilizations). See Samuel P. Huntington, 'The Clash of Civilizations?', *Foreign Affairs*, 72 (Summer 1993), pp. 22–49. Huntington regards 'Western civilization' as a relatively homogenous cultural entity embracing the two cultural units of Europe and North America ('Clash', p. 24). He does recognize that not all countries, in the sense of nation states, clearly belong to one civilization or another. But in his view, such countries, being 'torn countries', are 'candidates for dismemberment'. A torn country is one in which the population is divided in showing allegiance to different civilizations. Turkey, Huntington claims, provides an example of this phenomenon. For a significant number of the Turkish population embraces Western civilization, while the rest support Islamic revivalism ('Clash', p. 42). Curiously, Huntington does not recognize that, by his own criterion, the United States should be regarded as a 'torn country'. A large part of the population embraces secular culture, while, arguably, an equally large part advocates various forms of religious fundamentalism. As Huntington's argument would seem to apply to his own country, should he conclude that the United States is a candidate for dismemberment? See, also, Samuel P. Huntington, 1996, *The Clash of Civilizations and the Remaking of the World Order*, New York: Simon & Schuster.

Pace Huntington, it would seem to be a mistake to regard either Western civilization or Islamic civilization as homogenous cultural entities, never mind as civilizations that are locked in deep conflict. Thus, it is misguided to regard the major cultural conflicts that are currently taking place as located principally between these civilizations. Huntington's view is blind to the important conflicts that are occurring within Western culture (and, indeed, within Islamic culture).

It seems, moreover, that scholars from a range of disciplines are converging on this conclusion. With respect to Islam, Robert Hefner, for example, claims: 'There is no clash of civilizations between Islam and the West. The really decisive battle is taking place *within* Muslim civilization, where ultraconservatives compete against moderates and democrats for the soul of the Muslim public.' Robert W. Hefner, 'September 11 and the Struggle for Islam', Social Science Research Council, internet publication: http://www.ssrc.org/sept11/essays/hefner.htm. Hefner's observations would seem to apply more widely than he appears to realize. It seems appropriate to say that the 'decisive battle' has many fronts – one of which is located within the pluralist culture of United States.

11

Religion and Postmodernism

This new style of religiosity may strike one as entailing an unduly large concession to modern thought. But there is no real cause for alarm. ... Wherever we may begin, we religious thinkers can safely be trusted ... to arrive finally at God.[1]

The world of the late twentieth century, in which, as we saw in the previous chapter, various forms of religious fundamentalism have flourished, is now often described as 'postmodern'. In this final chapter, we focus upon the relationship between religion and postmodern thought. As we shall see, according to some, postmodern thought presents an intensification of the challenge posed to traditional religions by modern thought, while, according to others, it is much more amenable to religious belief than modern thought had been. Many late twentieth-century religious thinkers embrace the latter view, and claim that religious beliefs can retain a position of continuing importance for those living within a postmodern world. David Ray Griffin, for example, claims that 'the modern worldview simply has no natural place in it for God',[2] while a postmodern worldview 'makes belief in God possible again, even natural'.[3] But before we examine the relationship between religion and postmodern thought, we first need to consider some of the ways in which 'postmodernism' is construed, and how it is thought to be related to modernity.

Postmodernism and modern thought

Throughout this book we have surveyed issues concerning which there is widespread disagreement. In many of the debates we have considered, the source of disagreement clearly lies in the radically different values to which the debating parties subscribe and their differences regarding the meaning of core terms. Indeed, the late twentieth century would seem to be characterized by the wide availability of different worldviews holding incommensurable values and assigning significantly different meanings to terms. It is these features of the late twentieth century that have led some to characterize it as 'postmodern'.

Several thinkers prefer the term 'late-modern' to 'postmodern'.[4] Obviously, one's choice of term betrays a prior decision about whether to regard recent history as divided into two radically different epochs, the 'modern' and the 'postmodern', or whether to regard it as consti-tuted by one epoch – the modern – that has persisted through differ-ent phases (early modernity, mid-modernity and, now, late-modernity). Those who employ the term 'postmodern' rather than 'late-modern' seek to emphasize the discontinuity between what they regard as two distinct epochs. While those who prefer the term 'late-modern' to 'postmodern' are more impressed by the continuities between what they see as the dif-ferent phases of modernity. Despite this difference of analysis, it would seem that the term 'postmodern' refers to roughly the same time period as is referred to by the term 'late-modern': that is, the period that began at the end of the 1960s.

Unfortunately, the term 'postmodern' is used in a bewildering variety of ways. For example, it is often used to denote a particular style of thinking and writing. This style is identifiable in architecture, art and literature throughout most of the twentieth century. But it is also used, perhaps most importantly, to denote a certain philosophical style. Yet it was not until after 1968 that such 'postmodern thought' began to appear within many of the major academic disciplines such as history, sociology, philosophy, art, politics, religious studies and theology. As a result of the diversity of disciplines in which it has become prominent, postmodern-ism has now become extraordinarily difficult to define. Consequently, intellectuals (even those within the same field of study) entertain rival views about what constitutes postmodern thought.

One account of postmodernism seeks to define it by contrasting it with modern thought. Those who favour this approach associate modern thought with the Enlightenment, and further claim that postmodern thought is premised upon a rejection of the principal values it promoted (such as, for example, the valuing of reason over superstition and emo-tion, the value accorded to independent thought, and the valuing of so-called 'meta-theories', or 'meta-narratives' – theories, such as Marx-ism, that claimed to explain the totality of our experience). According to this way of conceiving the relation between postmodern and modern thought, the former is an inversion of the latter. Postmodern thinkers reject the notion that thought can be completely independent, and they stress, instead, the different contexts in which thinkers are located. They also tend to deny that the ability to use reason is the most valuable aspect of being human. And postmodern thinkers have abandoned the search for theories capable of explaining 'everything' – in other words, they reject meta-theories or meta-narratives.[5] This last point is, perhaps, the most crucial to this particular construal of postmodernism. Indeed, one self-consciously postmodern thinker, Jean-François Lyotard (1924–98), defines '*postmodernism* as an incredulity towards metanarratives'.[6] And by 'metanarratives', Lyotard clearly has in mind those supposedly comprehensive theories (such as Marxism) that were so typical of modern thought in the nineteenth and early twentieth centuries. According to this view of the relation between postmodern and modern thought, then, the former is premised upon a radical break from key aspects of the latter.[7]

Persuasive as this account of the relationship between postmodern and modern thought may initially seem, it is, nevertheless, highly contestable. For it seems to take for granted not only the assumption that postmodern thought can only arise when the key ideas and values of modern thought are rejected but also that such postmodern thought is now prevalent. But in contrast with this characterization of the fate of modern thought, perhaps a more plausible account would claim that the intellectual insights of modernity have been turned inward, and applied to modern thought itself. But this seems more of a continuity within modern thought than a radical break with it. Hence, such a process might be thought to engender 'late-modern' thought rather than 'postmodern' thought.[8]

This notwithstanding, the term 'postmodernism' now enjoys such wide currency and has become so vague in meaning that it might well be cognate with 'late-modernism' in the minds of many, even if a process whereby the assumptions of modern thought have turned back on modern thought itself would suggest the latter to be the preferable term. John Thornhill seems to describe just such a process of modern thought having turned back on itself, when he claims that modernity has been the victim of its own principal intellectual criterion, which he takes to be accountability:

> The ideology of modernity is essentially a reactionary movement. In response to the shortcoming of the intellectual climate of late medievalism, this movement established *accountability* as its essential proposition: the proper autonomy of our human existence demands that all propositions laying claim to an authority to shape the life of our cultural tradition must give a critical account of themselves before the bar of a shared understanding. ... But this proposition will inevitably find itself lost in a vicious, self-destructive circle if it does not refer to a warrant which lies beyond the ideological order. ... The ideology of modernity, calling *all* positions to critically validate themselves, inevitably finds itself 'hoisted with its own petard' unless it acknowledges a measure which is not essentially ideological.[9]

According to Thornhill, then, postmodern thought is really the by-product of modern thought, which has been self-undermining. In short, it results from the inability of modern thought to meet its own intellectual standards. So, the charge is that modern thinkers have been unable to defend cogently their intellectual principles in a way that meets their own criteria, with the result that modern thought has collapsed into postmodernism.[10]

Thornhill further argues that, if we construe postmodernism as a phase of modern thought, then we can benefit from the genuine insights of postmodern thinkers, and use them to carry forward the intellectual project begun in the Enlightenment. For example, he regards the criticisms of ideologies and meta-narratives developed by postmodern thinkers as a significant contribution to this project. Thornhill claims that the validity of such criticisms can be acknowledged without thereby giving up the key intellectual values characteristic of modern thought. This is not to say, however, that these values do not themselves stand in need of ongoing re-evaluation. But we can concede this much, Thornhill avers, without being compelled to abandon the intellectual project driving modern thought. Indeed, he argues that the continued development of modern thought is urgently required, and that 'today's talk of "the end of modernity" and of a new culture of "post-modernism" is an evasion of the real issues'.[11] To arrest the development of modern thought at this juncture, he argues, would be disastrous, as 'the essential task of modernity and the Enlightenment is still incomplete'.[12] It is only now, he claims, that modern thought is approaching a new maturity – a stage that was out of reach until it had passed through its first 'reactionary' phase.[13]

Thus, according to this view, what many perceive as postmodern thought is really modern thought on the threshold of its next phase of development. Later, we shall consider Thornhill's account of what direction the next phase of modern thought might take. At present, however, we are merely concerned with his claim that postmodern thought is actually modern thought in a state of transition. It is this transition that, he believes, has given rise to what has been widely perceived as a crisis within modern thought.

Those who, like Thornhill, aver that postmodernism is really a phase of modern thought, and those who, like Lyotard, claim that postmodernism represents a radical break with modern thought, can nevertheless agree that during the twentieth century many in the West experienced something of an intellectual crisis. Moreover, this crisis, irrespective of whether it is thought to issue in postmodern thought or in the next phase of modern thought, clearly has important, and widely recognized, cultural dimensions. In one study of the contemporary culture of the United States, the crisis is described as follows:

> There is a widespread feeling that the promise of the modern era is slipping away from us. A movement of enlightenment and liberation that was to have freed us from superstition and tyranny has led in the twentieth century to a world in which ideological fanaticism and political oppression have reached extremes unknown in previous history. Science, which was to have unlocked the bounties of nature, has given us the power to destroy all life on the earth. Progress, modernity's

master idea, seems less compelling when it appears that it may be a progress into the abyss. And the globe today is divided between a liberal world so incoherent that it seems to be losing the significance of its own ideals ... and a poor, and often tyrannical, Third World reaching for the very first rungs of modernity.[14]

The cultural dimensions of the intellectual crisis which many take to be currently afflicting modern thought are, moreover, judged by some to be so far-reaching as to suggest that the present time consists in 'a vast period of global transformation, the greatest since the coming of settled agriculture'.[15]

Thus, whichever account of 'postmodernism' we prefer, and however we understand its relation to modernity, it is clear that significant transformations have been taking place both in the intellectual and in the wider cultural domain. Next, we consider some of the characteristics assumed by the traditional Abrahamic faiths in the tumultuous world of postmodernity.[16]

Postmodernism and religion

Throughout this book, I have sought to emphasize the range of ideas explored by religious thinkers from each of the Abrahamic monotheisms as they have responded to modern thought. We have seen that many have handled the core concepts of their respective faith-traditions in ways that would seem to depart violently from the way in which those ideas were previously understood. Indeed, it would seem that religious thinkers, at least within the West, have been increasingly free to explore religious ideas more creatively than was, perhaps, possible in the past.

This can be viewed as one aspect of the ongoing process of detraditionalization. This is a process that many believe to have advanced to such an extent that traditional religious ideas (and the practices they inform) continue to exist in the postmodern world merely as fragments – moreover, fragments that have been removed from their original location within comprehensive and coherent religious worldviews. These fragments are thought to float freely, having drifted from their institutional moorings and their harbours in ways of life. In such a situation, as it has been portrayed by many theorists, individuals who wish to be religious must choose from the various religious ideas floating around within the general culture, and put together their own idiosyncratic package, thereby constructing their own unique faith and lifestyle.[17] In short, a common claim is that, in the postmodern environment, religion no longer presents itself pre-packaged in the way that it did in previous eras. Don Cupitt, whose own form of postmodern Christian thought we consider below, describes the mooted situation as follows:

In the past, all of people's ideas about reality and objectivity – their sense of life's basic *shape* – depended ultimately upon the authority of a deeply ingrained sense of religious law, and proximately upon a framework of shared philosophical assumptions. In modernity these assumptions especially concerned the human subject, consciousness, experience, reason, and language. But in postmodern times they have all broken down. Metaphysical realism has come to an end, and our whole world-view has become very much more pluralized, pragmatic, free-floating, and maintained by continual *bricolage*, or improvisation. In theological terms, this adds up ... to the Death of God, the Disappearance of the Self, the End of History, and the Closure of the Book; the end therefore of all forms of realism and supernaturalism; the end of objective Truth, and of all forms of faith in some future and hoped-for totalization of the human world.[18]

Religious ideas and practices may have been especially prone to becoming 'free-floating' in postmodernity because, in many cases, they are no longer exclusively tied to religious traditions practised in particular locales, but have, rather, become de-localized. An individual might, for example, adopt certain of the practices and beliefs of Christianity without attaching herself to any particular Christian denomination or without joining a local Christian community. She might also combine her Christian practices and beliefs with elements taken from other, perhaps very different, religious traditions, such as yoga or Tai Chi. De-localized traditions are currently maintained and transmitted through a number of channels, though the media has become especially important – particularly, television and the internet.[19] But not only have religious traditions, in many cases, become de-localized, they have also become increasingly de-personalized. In other words, a growing number of people are no longer dependent upon a local religious leader with whom they have a personal relationship for guidance in matters pertaining to religious belief and practice. And this de-localization of religious traditions, along with the de-personalization that accompanies it, contributes to the tendency of religions to be regarded as abstract packages of belief – often graspable in slogans. Thus, while, in a sense, religious traditions are made more accessible when they are de-localized and de-personalized, they are simultaneously, it can be argued, de-valued in the market place of ideas. It is such de-localized, de-personalized and de-valued religion that is often regarded as 'postmodern religion'. Paul Heelas describes this form of religion as

very much in the hands of the 'free' subject. ... The deregulation of the religious realm, combined with the cultural emphasis on freedom and choice, results in intermingled, interfused, forms of religious –

or 'religious'-cum-'secular' – life which exists beyond the tradition-regulated church and chapel. People no longer feel obliged to heed the boundaries of the religions of modernity. Instead, they are positively encouraged to exercise their 'autonomy' to draw on what has diffused through the culture. ... They – so to speak – raid the world, drawing on whatever is felt desirable: the religious (perhaps Shamanism and Christianity); the religious and the non-religious (perhaps yoga and champagne).[20]

Moreover, another characteristic of postmodern religion, according to Heelas, is the separation of religious *experience* from religious *belief* – two elements that modern thought had striven to keep firmly united. Heelas believes that 'this results in a form of relativism', for 'religion beyond belief is religion where "truth" is relative to what one takes to be involved in satisfying one's requirements'.[21] It is perhaps the disjunction between religious experience and religious belief that is quintessential to much religious thought in postmodernity. As we shall see later, by the end of the twentieth century, many different voices argued that religious experience can withstand a loss of confidence in traditional religious beliefs. Religion, the argument goes, is a way of life that offers a distinctive way of experiencing reality; and, as such, it does not require an intellectual edifice to support it. Clearly, this argument, which we later consider in more detail, is but one form of response to the stress that religious traditions have been put under in the postmodern world. As we have seen earlier in this book, however, twentieth-century religious thinkers from each of the Abrahamic faiths have been enormously creative in their development of religious *ideas*. And this testifies to the ongoing significance of such ideas during this period. Moreover, the significance of religious ideas is still apparent when we turn to consider religious thinkers who seek explicitly to engage religious thought with postmodern thought. These religious thinkers can be loosely categorized as one of two types: either 'liberal' or 'conservative' postmodernists.[22]

Both liberals and conservatives within the religious postmodernist movement tend to assume that modern thought has failed to underwrite religious belief. However, they draw very different conclusions from this supposed failure. The liberals are resigned to what they perceive as the regrettable failure of modern thought, and they accept the criticisms that postmodern theorists level against it. Nonetheless, they seek to give a rational account of religion in the face of this failure, even if it leads them to reject the core beliefs of traditional Abrahamic religion – such as, for example, belief in the existence of God. Instead, liberal postmodern religious thinkers tend to emphasize apologetics: in other words, they attempt to present their religious ideas through the medium of postmodern thought in order to render them more appealing to those within what they regard as postmodern culture. While all liberal postmodern religious thinkers seek to express their religious ideas through the cultural idioms of postmodernity, their respective intellectual projects diverge dramatically from this common base. We consider one example of this style of thought shortly.

It has been argued, however, that liberal postmodern religious thinkers are not as thoroughly postmodern as their conservative counterparts. Graham Ward, for example, claims the work of the former 'is an expression of [their liberal secular] culture, not a critique of it'.[23] By contrast, conservative postmodernists employ the methods of postmodern thought to reinterpret foundational religious texts, be they Scriptures, creeds or liturgies. They seek to develop religious ideas and, sometimes, systematic theologies by employing postmodern insights. This results in radically new ways of thinking about religion that purport to be consonant with the contours of the postmodern world.

We now briefly consider one example of liberal postmodern religious thought from the Christian tradition, before turning our attention to conservative postmodern thought in Judaism, Christianity and Islam.

Liberal postmodern religious thought

Don Cupitt provides our example of a liberal postmodern religious thinker. Particularly in his earlier works, Cupitt stands as a typical representative of this style of thought. He argues that, if religion is to be meaningful in postmodernity, then each person must arrive at a personal and highly subjective understanding of it. People can no longer be expected simply to accept purportedly objective religious 'truths' that are handed down by their traditions. Indeed, Cupitt avers that objective religious truth (in the sense of truth that is independent of what religious people think and desire), even if such were available, would not be a good thing, because it would prevent people from creatively appropriating religious ideas, thereby stunting their spiritual growth. In keeping with this assessment, he also holds that rejection of a foundationalist, or correspondence, view of truth is an advantage to religion because it opens up new possibilities of belief. For, once believers realize that their religious beliefs are without foundation in supernatural facts, and are, instead, the product of human beings like themselves, they can learn to appreciate religion for what it genuinely is. Cupitt writes:

> In the past those who came to see that religion is just human became themselves non-religious. Today this is no longer the case. The first *conscious* believers are appearing, people who know that religion is just human but have come to see that it is no less vital to us for that.

Religion has to be human; it could not be otherwise, for it would not work as religion unless it were simply human.[24]

One consequence of Cupitt's view that human beings are the architects of religion is that the notion of one unique religious truth, which is the same for everyone, seems considerably less plausible. And this, therefore, leads Cupitt to argue for a form of religious pluralism:

> There are in the human world many complete and coherent spiritual-ities or ways of life. Their values may overlap, but as wholes they are distinct; and there is no Archimedean point independent of them all from which they can be evaluated. ... Thus our most fundamental beliefs have simply to be chosen. Their 'truth' is not descriptive or factual truth, but the truth about the way they work in our lives. They are to be acted upon.[25]

Cupitt is well aware that a traditional conception of God, as an omnipo-tent, omniscient, omnibenevolent being that exists independently of the world, can have no place within the type of postmodern religious worldview that he advocates. Thus, he has been, perhaps aptly, termed an 'atheologian'. Nevertheless, he wishes to retain a conception of God within his theology – although the concept he arrives at differs consid-erably from the concept that had dominated earlier Christian thought. The revised concept that Cupitt proposes is of a 'post-Theological God who functions only to remind us that we are out-of-nothing. He is no sort of existent being, but something *prior* to being that may be called a background of radical otherness and difference against which all beings ex-ist or out-stand.'[26] Clearly, some major revision of the concept 'God' is required by Cupitt's claim that religious 'truth' has to be the product of the individual creativity of religious people. For the idea of an objectively existing God is surely inconsistent with the assumption that religious 'truth' is radically subjective insofar as it is a product of individual desires or preferences.

Cupitt's theology is typical of much liberal postmodern religious thinking. It is perhaps not surprising, then, that postmodernism of this sort characteristically issues in atheism. This is clearly so in the case of Cupitt – a later book by whom being succinctly entitled *After God*.[27] Hence, liberal postmodern religious thinkers would appear to follow the modern project of secularizing religious thought to its logical extreme. Postmodern thought is thus used by them to explain 'the death of God', and to arrive at a fully secular theology ending in what might be called 'religious atheism'.

Let us now turn to some examples of conservative postmodern re-ligious thought. As we shall see in the following three sections, such conservative thought – in contrast to its liberal counterpart – seeks to discover a religious dimension within postmodernism itself. And we shall see that it is principally the attitude taken towards religious tradition that distinguishes conservative from liberal postmodern thinkers. Whereas liberal postmodernists believe that tradition should be abandoned wherever it conflicts with modern thought, conservative postmodern religious thinkers hold that religious tradition should be retained, for it possesses an independent value of its own. We now consider some important examples of conservative postmodern religious thought from each of the Abrahamic faiths. We begin with the Jewish tradition.

Open-traditionalism: Jewish 'conservative' postmodern thought

Eugene Borowitz, a rabbi from the Reformed tradition, provides our first example of conservative postmodern religious thought. In many respects, Borowitz was well ahead of his time, when, in 1968, he declared:

> I must take my stand where I find myself and where I find a not insignificant fraction of my people gathering. We are that group who, having stampeded from Jewish tradition into general culture, now find it a higher wisdom to reclaim our stake in our traditional faith. ... Contemporary Christianity may be agog over secularity. Since we were in it up to the nostrils for several decades, we know we are men of faith precisely because we must move beyond it. We obviously do not believe as much as our grandfathers did, but we have discovered painfully that we believe far more than our society does.[28]

Here, Borowitz claims to be describing an experience common to many within the Jewish community during the second half of the twentieth century; an experience characterized by the disillusionment that many came to feel with respect to secularity and modern thought. He realizes that Jews of his era cannot simply return to the style of Judaism practised by their predecessors, but nor, in his view, can they rest content with the secularity of the general culture. Hence, Borowitz concludes that Jews who wish to retain their religious identity must 'move beyond' secular culture, and 'reclaim' their 'stake in our traditional faith'.[29] Secular culture, although it has certain advantages, has become the enemy of religiosity because, Borowitz claims, it is 'moving toward an amoral, pleasure-seeking, present-oriented human style'.[30] A significant result of which being that one can no longer 'count on educated people to be religious, or spiritual, or even moral when a real crisis occurs'.[31] This assessment of modernity leads Borowitz to advocate what he terms 'open traditionalism': namely, a commitment to tradition combined with a recognition of 'the basic importance of the free choice of human action, including, therefore, the right to conscientious dissent from what Jewish tradition once required or strongly urged'.[32]

A critical and selective appropriation of the religious tradition can, moreover, provide a standpoint, Borowitz claims, from which to evaluate modern secular culture. 'Open traditionalism' can thus, he argues, provide a way for Judaism to make a genuine and valuable contribution to modern society and culture, without Jews being compelled to assimilate that culture.[33]

Borowitz's approach seems genuinely postmodern, for he rejects the idea that modern thought and Judaism stand in an asymmetrical relationship – one within which modern thought has the right to criticize and evaluate Judaism, while Judaism lacks any such right with respect to modern thought. Thus, he argues instead for a partnership between modern thought and Judaism – a partnership in which both are regarded as equals, and in which the contribution of each to an emerging postmodern Western culture would be equally valued.[34] Moreover, Borowitz adds that, within the emergent postmodern Western culture, religious identity cannot be merely passively accepted, but must be actively chosen:

> One should choose to be Jewish and resist as nondeterminative the claims of family, history, or personal sentiment. That choice, particularly since it is a fundamental commitment of one's life, must be made autonomously to be authentic. Yet the high value attached to autonomy is no longer self-explanatory. One can explain one's seriousness about it and one's determined pursuit of it only in terms of a prior faith: for the Jew, Judaism. The tradition grounds the autonomy – but it must be the basis of affirming the tradition – and so endlessly. The circle of faith is complete and in its harmonious closing the integrity of liberal Jewish existence despite its paradoxical foundation is established.[35]

As was remarked above, Borowitz was ahead of his time.[36] His belief that Judaism should no longer seek expression exclusively within the accepted cultural idioms of the age clearly separates his thought from that of modern liberal Jewish theologians (as represented, particularly, by those within the early Reformed tradition and by the Reconstructionist thought of Moredcai Kaplan). Subsequent to Borowitz's pioneering early work, a group of younger Jewish philosophers and theologians has sought to develop Jewish thought in a self-consciously postmodern direction.[37] Borowitz's claim that Jews who wished to be genuinely religious should reappropriate their religious tradition in a spirit of 'open traditionalism' is echoed in a concept that has become extremely important within postmodern Judaism: 'teshuvah', or return.[38] However, the return to traditional Judaism advocated by postmodern Jewish thinkers is not envisaged as a return to Judaism as it was practised in the past. As Steven Kepnes writes:

> the postmodern return to Judaism by Jewish thinkers is not a simple return to premodern rabbinic Judaism. For postmodern Jews do not return to a ghettoized Judaism isolated from other cultures and faiths but to a Judaism set in the context of cultural and religious pluralism. Postmodern Jewish thinkers have grown up and live in a universe where toleration of differing worldviews, if not the actual reality, is presented as an important value of the overarching political system within which we live. Postmodern Jews, however concerned they are to resurrect and rehabilitate Judaism, do so with extremely little desire to denigrate other cultural and religious systems. In this sense, postmodern Jews are like their modern predecessors. Yet, where modern Jews placed themselves in relation to the universal everyman, postmodern Jews stand in a radically pluralized context and place themselves in relation to Christians, Muslims, Hindus, and the countless varieties of secularists.[39]

What, we might ask, lies behind this apparently widespread disillusionment with modern thought and secular culture that motivates the return to a more tradition-centred form of Judaism? Within the Jewish community, many would seem to identify the root of this disillusionment in the holocaust. As we have seen,[40] the holocaust marks a watershed in twentieth-century Jewish thought. Many view it as symptomatic of the utter failure of those forms of Judaism that sought assimilation within general, universal, Western culture, and of those forms of Jewish theology that attempted to bring traditional Judaism into line with modern thought. Because of the disastrous failure of integrationist approaches, post-holocaust Jewry completely lost confidence in the intellectual strategies employed by pre-holocaust Jewish thinkers.[41]

While many Jewish thinkers recognize a need for postmodern Jewish theologies and philosophies that are able to speak to post-holocaust Jews, the project of developing such intellectual systems is ongoing, and there would seem to be considerable scope for clarification concerning the appropriate content of these new systems. In an attempt to make constructive progress towards this end, several Jewish thinkers met to discuss the question: What is Jewish postmodern thought? Consider the following excerpt from their dialogue:

P: Yes, I think we have returned to Judaism as a system of wisdom with world-historical power, its teaching being the power of human love.

Y: What do you mean?

P: I mean that Judaism is true. Ontologically true.

...

S: But do you mean by 'truth' an abstract, universal idea?

P: No. I mean something like loyalty, or trust over time, even love.

S: Not Hellenic Truth?

P: No, of course not. I mean Jewish praxis, Jewish truth that is not based in the modernist notion of the excluded middle.

S: So you do not mean universal truth but the truth that is particular to Judaism and to living and learning in Judaism?

P: Yes, that is what postmodern Jewish philosophy is about.[42]

As we shall see, such claims about 'truth' would seem to be characteristic of all conservative religious postmodern thought. Most prominent is the idea that the notion of truth typically employed in modern thought is inadequate within the context of religion. 'Truth' is to be regarded as neither abstract nor universal, but as emerging from a religious praxis that is tied to a historical religious tradition. Religious 'truth' is therefore thought to be specific to whatever religious tradition is in question – in this case, Judaism. This 'non-Hellenic' view of 'truth', moreover, is thought to open the way for acknowledgement of the 'truth' found within other religious traditions, while inviting the recognition that other traditions have their own particular 'truth'. Thus, this form of postmodern thought, like Cupitt's version (which we considered above), does not entail that only one religious tradition is 'true'. Hence, postmodern religious thinkers, in theory, should have no difficulty in embracing religious pluralism. We shall find similar claims regarding 'truth' in the Christian form of conservative postmodern thought, to which we now turn.

Radical orthodoxy: Christian 'conservative' postmodern thought

Radical orthodoxy is a movement within Christian theology (principally, within high-Anglican and Roman Catholic theology) that constitutes a clear example of conservative postmodern religious thought.[43] It was initiated by John Milbank, whose book entitled *Theology and Social Theory: Beyond Secular Reason*,[44] became highly influential within Western European and North American Christian theology in the last decade of the twentieth century. Essentially, the intellectual strategy employed by Milbank, and those such as Catherine Pickstock and Graham Ward who followed his lead, was to agree with postmodern thinkers insofar as they criticized 'secular reason', but to disagree with the postmodern alternatives to secular reason proposed by thinkers such as Jacques Derrida (1930–2004).

Those committed to radical orthodoxy claim that, by undermining our beliefs about the relationship between experience, knowledge and value, as well as our ideas about the nature of the self, postmodernism results in intellectual and ethical nihilism. And such nihilism, they argue, is a far from desirable outcome. They further claim that radical orthodoxy constitutes a genuine alternative to 'secular reason'. But it does so both without engendering nihilism and while still remaining consistent with what they take to be the genuine insights of postmodernism. As Pickstock writes: radical orthodoxy presents a third alternative to the 'benign, universal, rationalist humanism' of liberalism and nihilistic postmodernism. Radical orthodoxy concedes 'with postmodernism, the indeterminacy of all our knowledge and experience of selfhood', while, nevertheless, construing 'this shifting flux as a sign of our dependency on a transcendent source which "gives" all reality as mystery, rather than as adducing our suspension over the void'.[45]

Milbank is especially notable in being the first to claim explicitly that modern Christian thought had become hostage to secular reason. And in arguing against the particular style of religious thinking that had dominated the anglophone theological world throughout the twentieth century, he aspires 'to overcome the pathos of modern theology, and to restore in postmodern terms, the possibility of theology as a metadiscourse'.[46] Indeed, as we have seen throughout this book, during the modern era many religious thinkers had felt under pressure to present their ideas apologetically. Consequently, they sought to accommodate religious ideas to the culture of secular modernity, thereby conceding that religious ideas could, and should, be evaluated from a non-religious perspective. This approach has shaped whole streams of thought within each of the Abrahamic monotheisms. For example, Reform Judaism, Liberal Protestant Christianity and Modernist Islam, as we saw in previous chapters, would clearly appear to have adopted it. And this approach is, moreover, the one adopted by certain postmodern thinkers – principally, those who have been described as liberal. Conservative postmodern religious theorists, on the other hand, are distinguished by their rejection of this apologetic, conciliatory style of religious thinking.

Milbank's argument is that modern religious thought (at least in the Christian case) had been reduced to a form of apologetics because theologians had, by and large, uncritically accepted the presumption that religious thought should answer to the criticisms of modern social theorists. Milbank also argues that modern Christian thought has been far too passive in the face of criticism. And this passivity proliferated as a result of theologians simply taking it for granted that social theorists had the right to 'explain' religion, and the right to treat theology as simply one of the human sciences. Against this presumption, Milbank counters that social theory is no more rational than the religious thought which it seems so ready to criticize.[47]

One implication of Milbank's claim that secular reason is no more rationally justifiable than what we might call 'theological reason' is that there are no rational grounds for preferring the secular stance of the social theorist to that of the theologian. If the choice between accepting the perspective of 'secular reason' or that of 'theological reason' is not a rational choice, then, Milbank argues, it must be decided on wholly non-rational grounds. And, in his view, the choice that any individual will actually make is most likely to be determined by which perspective he or she finds most aesthetically appealing and, on this ground, the most persuasive. Moreover, 'truth', Milbank declares, 'is available only through persuasion'.[48] This conclusion, as he well recognizes, has enormous implications for religious thought. In effect, Milbank has issued religious thinkers with an intellectual licence to ignore the claims of those employing 'secular reason'.

In support of this argument, Milbank seeks to demonstrate that 'secular reason' developed within a particular form of society; that is, an increasingly secular one. On the basis of this, he further claims that 'secular reason' can only legitimately apply within a secular society. His next claim is, perhaps, the most contentious: the religious thinker must reassert his or her right to live in a non-secular – that is, in an ecclesial – society. Christian theology will then develop as a result of the communal practices of Christians living within such an ecclesial society. Only such a theology, argues Milbank, will successfully escape the pressures of secular reason, thereby simultaneously avoiding the temptations of apologetics. And '[h]ere theology, as the theory of a new practice, the Church, can position itself as a gaze at once above, but also alongside, (with or against) other, inherited human gazes'.[49] It is precisely because, in Milbank's view, such a theology would develop out of the practice of appropriate religious communities that it would not need to claim that it was based on universal truths or rational foundations.[50]

It should be emphasized that Milbank does not assert that Christian theology constitutes a perspective that is *rationally* superior to other perspectives. Indeed, he claims that it 'is just another socio-historical gaze, just another perspective alongside other gazes, and faith, in its commitment to this gaze, constitutes a metanarrative ...'.[51] Each perspective, moreover, informs a form of life. Furthermore, only from the standpoint of some perspective or other, Milbank argues, are certain kinds of claims possible: 'Claims for objective truth, goodness and happiness can only be made by identification with a particular form of life that is claimed to participate in them – and this identification cannot be dialectically tested. Christianity can be seen as representing such a form of life.'[52] Milbank, however, then proceeds to make a claim that, at first sight, may appear to be radically at odds with the pluralist approach just intimated. 'Christianity is not', he contends, 'merely one more perspective. It is also *uniquely* different.'[53]

Thus, while Christianity, according to Milbank, is thought to be only one perspective among many, it is, nevertheless, 'not *merely* one more perspective'.[54] And in being uniquely different, it is clearly distinguishable from any other perspective. This will be evident, Milbank argues, insofar as the specific claims made by authentic Christians concerning 'object-ive truth, goodness and happiness' are uniquely related to the Christian 'form of life'. As Milbank explains: 'Christian belief belongs to Christian practice, and it sustains its affirmations about God and creation only by repeating and enacting a metanarrative about how God speaks in the world in order to redeem it.'[55] But while Milbank does not concern himself with the perspectives of other faiths, it would seem that particu-lar claims concerning objective truth, goodness and happiness will be uniquely related to whatever form of life is informed by the perspective from which they are made. So, despite the claim that 'Christianity is not merely one more perspective', Milbank's theory is, it would appear, con-sistent with the recognition that other religious traditions can make the same claim on their own behalf.

Milbank's wish is, clearly, to excoriate all forms of theology that seek to accommodate religious ideas to modern thought. His view would thus seem to be at odds with most of the religious thought surveyed in this book (the notable exception being, of course, that discussed in the pre-vious chapter). Indeed, Milbank would consider many of the ideas we have examined in earlier chapters to represent distortions of religion, and hence to derive from ersatz religious forms. In particular, he objects to the idea that either de-traditionalized or de-institutionalized religion could represent a legitimate – or even a viable – alternative to institution-alized, traditional religion. And correspondingly, he seems to regard all subjective forms of religion, such as the liberal postmodernism advocated by Cupitt, as chimeras.

Nevertheless, there is a sense in which Milbank's theory is consonant with the general trend of many of the more progressive ideas considered in earlier chapters. In particular, the notion of truth that he promotes, and the claim that rationality is intrinsically (rather than accidentally) tied to some form of life, not to mention the resultant pluralism within his theory, all link his ideas to those of many of the religious thinkers we have considered. Indeed, Milbank's thought seems to follow the contours of a wider cultural trend. As we shall see, his ideas converge with those of other religious thinkers who shared his concern regarding the state of religion at the end of the twentieth century, be the religion in question Judaism, Christianity or Islam. But first we turn to our final example of conservative postmodern thought – an example taken from Islam.

Traditions of interpretation: Islamic 'conservative' postmodern thought

Mohammed Arkoun is undoubtedly one of the most intellectually sophisticated religious thinkers of the twentieth century.[56] Moreover, he is one of the principal intellectuals in the West to have seriously considered the implications of postmodernism for the study of religion, believing that, within postmodernity, a new understanding is now required of contemporary Islam and its foundational event, which he terms 'the *Qur'ānic fact*'. The understanding he seeks is to be 'fashioned in the light of a cultural, social, and religious anthropology that has extended and reinterpreted the findings of historians, sociologists and linguists'.[57] His work, moreover, is postmodern insofar as he explicitly rejects the 'postulates, hierarchies, and cleavages together with notions of truth, progress, and civilization bequeathed by the Enlightenment'.[58] Arkoun shares the view of many late twentieth-century intellectuals that religious traditions now exist in a fragmented form. With respect to Islam, he claims that what is regarded as 'contemporary Islam' is constituted by 'the exegetical, theological, juridical, and semiotic constructs characteristic of classical Islam ... revived as fragments taken out of context ...'.[59]

Moreover, Arkoun believes that it is a grave mistake to regard a religious tradition, such as Islam, as constituting one monolithic entity. For Islam, he claims, should not be regarded as a blueprint to be instantiated in the same way in every time and place, with deviations from the plan being evaluated negatively (as, for example, Seyyed Hossein Nasr argues).[60] The Qur'ānic fact can certainly be seen as the foundational event of Islam, in the sense that it is the revelatory event that lies at the historical origin of the religious tradition. But Islam, Arkoun argues, cannot be simply identified with this fact. Islam as a historical religious tradition is, rather, a development from this fact. It is not, however, a single line of development, for different interpretive communities have interpreted the Qur'ānic fact in a rich variety of ways. The result of these interpretations is, in each case, a unique form of the Islamic tradition and a correspondingly unique form of Islamic truth.[61] Thus, Islam consists of a multiplicity of traditions that each arose as the result of a particular interpretation of the Qur'ānic fact.

Furthermore, the Qur'ān, Arkoun argues, does not possess a single meaning that gives rise to a set of doctrines that are constitutive of Islam. Rather the meaning that can be read out of the Qur'ān differs according to the character of the interpretive community. The unity of Muslims does not rest, then, on a shared understanding of the meaning of the Qur'ān, but is based on the fact that the religious experience of all Muslims is shaped by the 'Qur'ānic fact'. The Qur'ān, according to this view, should not be thought of as bearing one true meaning that is accessible to all interpreters. Rather, it serves to generate different versions of Islamic 'truth'. For this reason, Qur'ānic interpretation should be regarded as an ongoing project that should not be arbitrarily terminated at any historical juncture; to do so, Arkoun claims, would be to reduce the Qur'ān to ideology.

Like a number of the thinkers we have considered in this book, Arkoun argues that there is no access to any truth or facts that transcend experience. And experience, as he also notes, will be shaped by the social, historical, anthropological and linguistic contexts within which it takes place. Any understanding of the 'truth' of Islam must, then, be arrived at through a study of Islam as it is variously experienced in these diverse contexts. Arkoun thus proposes an ambitious programme of study that will, he hopes, eventually allow a comprehensive knowledge of what he calls the 'Islamic fact' to emerge. Such knowledge is of vital importance, he believes, because it is a precondition for the recovery of authentic Islam in an age in which both Muslims and non-Muslims have become transfixed by an abstract ideological version of the tradition.

In order to understand contemporary Islam, then, Arkoun argues that one must study the various Muslim traditions that have developed in diverse cultural and ethnic environments, without presuming that any of these are privileged and therefore represent 'genuine' Islam. The totality of interpretations of the Qur'ānic fact, Arkoun claims, constitutes Islam. Hence, none should be excluded from investigation. This may seem like a daunting task, given that Islam is practised within an enormous geographical area, and within highly diverse cultural environments. Nevertheless, Arkoun argues that such a comprehensive investigation is the only effective way to combat the reified and, in his view, false image of Islam promoted by many today. The way to proceed, then, is by focusing on the way that Islamic traditions have been elaborated within different communities.

Arkoun is well aware, however, that many Muslims would regard his project with deep distrust. This is because there is a pronounced tendency for Muslims (as, arguably, there is for believers within all of the major religions) to regard their own version of their faith as exclusively correct. Indeed, it is far from uncommon for religious people to hold that there is one authentic form of their tradition, and that they are the ones who possess it. With respect to Islam, Arkoun believes that such exclusivity is wholly misconceived, given the common origin of all forms of Islam in the Qur'ānic fact. Hence, he argues that each Islamic tradition must abandon its claim to exclusivity, and acknowledge, instead, the validity of all other forms of Islam. As no one branch of Islam can claim the status of the privileged purveyor of Islamic truth, only Islam as the totality of the 'Islamic fact' can make such a claim.[62]

Arkoun has been criticized, however, for rejecting the idea that there is any one privileged version of 'true' Islam, only to argue that his own approach – informed as it is by the social sciences and by postmodern thought – provides the privileged vantage point from which authentic Islam may be displayed. Moreover, while advocating tolerance and the non-exclusivity of all interpretations of Islam, he nevertheless seems to argue that his own perspective is superior to all others.[63] This criticism, however, misses the point of Arkoun's project. Arkoun is clearly not committed to the claim that his own interpretation of Islam is on a par with all other variants of the Islamic tradition. In fact, it would seem to be a mistake to take him as proposing a variant of the Islamic tradition at all. Rather, Arkoun has proposed a meta-theory. In other words, he has proposed a theory that (if successful) can provide a unified second-order account of all the divergent streams that together constitute Islam. Thus, he is not compelled to concede that any truth he arrives at will be just one among many of the competing 'truths' advocated by different branches of the Islamic tradition. This would be to confuse two different levels of analysis. In other words, the various branches of Islam make first-order truth-claims, while Arkoun's theory makes a second-order claim about those first-order claims. Arkoun would only be guilty of inconsistency were he, too, to be offering further first-order truth-claims.

The understanding of Islam developed by Arkoun would seem, then, to be suitably sensitive to the view that Islam is constituted by diverse traditions of interpretation. And that there are diverse traditions of Islamic interpretation is an increasingly common view among Muslims in the West. Indeed, it is a key part of the vision of Islam promoted by 'progressive' Muslims, who seek 'an *Islam bi la Hudud* – an Islam without borders – that locates itself in the present realities of the borderless, plural, multicultural, complex, unequal, and unjust world that we live in today'.[64] Like Arkoun, those involved in the progressive Muslim movement regard this vision as representing Islam within the real and complex world of postmodernity, as opposed to some supposedly archetypal 'slogan' Islam. Thus, the movement's call for 'an introspection and self-critique that will help disabuse us of some of the myths of our own making, such as the myth of a "pure," "authentic," and "uncontaminated" *umma* that appears *ex nihilo*',[65] would seem to be met, in part, by the theory of Islam that Arkoun has developed.

This completes our brief foray into conservative postmodern religious thought. As we have seen, all the thinkers considered above are united in their rejection of the particular notion of truth that they regard as central to 'modern' thought. And they all seek to develop alternative ways of thinking about religious truth that, among other things, can make sense of the apparently rival claims made both by adherents of different religious traditions and by those practising different forms of the same tradition.

Postmodernism and narrative

As we have seen in several earlier chapters, many recent thinkers hold that reducing every important religious claim to a proposition that is either literally true or literally false often misses out something of vital importance. But that the only meaningful sense in which a claim can be true or false is in its expressing a truth-evaluable proposition was a core assumption of much of modern thought. Postmodernists, 'conservatives' included, share an antipathy towards this assumption.[66] And this has led them to explore other ways in which ideas – particularly, religious ideas – might be expressed, communicated and understood.[67] Many, such as John Milbank and John Thornhill, argue that narratives – or, in other words, stories – are the most appropriate medium through which to express religious understanding, with Milbank claiming that 'narrating' is

> a more basic category than either explanation or understanding: unlike either of these it does not assume punctiliar facts or discrete meanings. Neither is it concerned with universal laws, nor universal truths of the spirit. Yet it is not arbitrary in the sense that one can repeat a text in just any fashion, although one can indeed do so in any number of fashions.[68]

Indeed, narratives form a large part of the Scriptures of Judaism, Christianity and Islam. And it has been suggested that the stories contained within these sacred texts possess universal appeal because they resonate with our common human experience.[69] It could be argued, moreover, that the preponderance of narratives within these texts was overlooked by those moderns who read them while searching exclusively for information expressible in the form of statements corresponding to mooted facts. Reading the sacred texts with the expectation of finding such information may have contributed to the loss of confidence in them that many experienced during the twentieth century. For example, when the Bible was taken to claim, literally, that God created the world in seven days, then many modern readers assumed that they had found a straightforwardly false claim in the sacred text rather than a true one. And the quite different sort of understanding that the narrative form might convey was regarded by many modern thinkers as of little value in contrast to the true statements and, supposedly, objective knowledge available by means of the methods of the natural sciences.

The re-evaluation of religious texts in terms of narratives only progressed when the view that scientific knowledge was fundamentally different in kind from knowledge obtained in the humanities was challenged. For example, Jean-François Lyotard, while holding that knowledge within the humanities is not fundamentally different in kind from knowledge within the natural sciences, proceeds to argue that a comparison of scientific knowledge with the kind of knowledge that is expressed in narratives, or stories, reveals that both

> are composed of sets of statements; the statements are 'moves' made by the players within the framework of generally applicable rules; these rules are specific to each particular kind of knowledge, and the 'moves' judged to be 'good' in one cannot be of the same type as those judged 'good' in another, unless it happens that way by chance.[70]

So, although scientific claims and narrative are on a par insofar as they are both species of discourse, nevertheless, according to Lyotard, the criteria appropriate for judging a 'move' within science differ substantially from those relevant to evaluating a 'move' within a narrative. Moreover, he claims that 'narrative knowledge does not give priority to the question of its own legitimation and ... it certifies itself in the pragmatics of its own transmission without having recourse to argumentation and proof'.[71] In other words, if our aim is to seek logical arguments or demonstrative proofs within narratives, we are approaching them in the wrong way. Hence, we should not be evaluating narratives either as forms of logical argument or in terms of their status as demonstrative proofs. Rather, their worth lies in the specific way in which they are employed.

How, then, are narratives employed in a manner that reveals their particular worth? According to Milbank, writing with respect to Christianity:

> In a rhetorical perspective, narrative really does cease to be a mere appendage, because here the story of the development of a tradition – for example, in the case of Christianity, a story of preachings, journeyings, miracles, martyrdoms, vocations, marriages, icons painted and liturgies sung, as well as of intrigues, sins and warfare – really *is* the argument for the tradition (a perilous argument indeed, which may not prove persuasive at all), and not just the story of arguments concerning a certain X (for example the nature of human virtue) lying outside the story.[72]

But if there are no extrinsic arguments supporting such narratives, one might wonder why they should be taken seriously. And, moreover, what might compel us to favour the narratives within one religion over that of another? In response to this question, some, such as Milbank, cite the attractiveness of the religious lifestyles of those who are inspired by the religious narrative in question.[73] Ultimately, Milbank claims, it is the appeal of a particular lifestyle that compels a person to prefer the narratives of that religious tradition to those of any other.[74]

The prioritizing of religious lifestyles over religious truth-claims has been a common thread uniting several of the thinkers we have studied in this book. Some have argued, in addition, that narratives are essential for a religious lifestyle. And Alasdair MacIntyre's claim that narrative is the condition of possibility for any meaningful action has been deployed in support of this conclusion. In a characteristic statement, MacIntyre asserts that

> man is in his actions and practice, as well as in his fictions, essentially a story-telling animal. He is not essentially, but becomes through his history, a teller of stories that aspire to truth. ... I can only answer the question 'What am I to do?' if I can answer the prior question 'Of what story or stories do I find myself a part?'... Deprive children of stories and you leave them unscripted, anxious stutterers in their actions as in their words.[75]

Not only is the narrative approach consistent with the view that religious knowledge is intrinsically related to meaningful forms of life, but it is also, clearly, at one with the anti-foundationalism that characterizes much religious thought in the postmodern period. Anti-foundationalism holds that there is no ultimate 'Archimedean point' upon which our knowledge may be grounded. Every premise supporting a conclusion is, ultimately, open to doubt, and hence none stands as an indubitable foundation upon which a belief system can be reliably constructed. In the specific context of religious thought, anti-foundationalism feeds the denial that a person's most basic religious beliefs and commitments are ultimately premised upon logical argumentation or demonstrative proofs, which coheres with Lyotard's view that narrative should not be assessed in such terms – an aspect of his thinking that we noted earlier.

However, such anti-foundationalism is not taken by postmodernists to imply that religious beliefs and commitments are unreasonable, but rather that the reasonableness of subscribing to them can only be appraised from inside the form of life within which they are embedded. From this, it might be thought to follow, as George Lindbeck claims it does indeed follow, that

> basic religious and theological positions, like Kuhn's scientific paradigms, are invulnerable to definitive refutation (as well as confirmation) but can nevertheless be tested and argued about in various ways, and these tests and arguments in the long run make a difference. Reason places constraints on religious as well as on scientific options even though these constraints are too flexible and informal to be spelled out in either foundational theology or a general theory of science. In short, intelligibility comes from skill, not theory, and credibility comes

from good performance, not adherence to independently formulated criteria.[76]

If a religious worldview is to acquire its credibility from exemplary instances of living the form of life within which that worldview is embedded, and if a full understanding of that worldview requires skill in living the form of life in question, and, further, if that form of life is transmitted through a deep acquaintance with the stories that shape its worldview, then narrative becomes key.

As we shall now see, however, any such account of the importance of narrative as a way of acquiring religious knowledge, and as underwriting religious lifestyles and practices, would appear to lead to a rather gloomy assessment of the situation in which traditional forms of Judaism, Christianity and Islam found themselves at the end of the twentieth century.

Postmodernism and the *jāhilīya*

As the twentieth century drew to a close, adherents of the three Abrahamic faiths could no longer assume, as their ancestors may have done, that the narratives of their particular faith-tradition informed the wider cultural and social practices, never mind the core values, of the societies in which they lived. Moreover, for those growing up within modern Western culture, socialization into a religious tradition, through familiarity with the narratives of that tradition, had ceased to be a matter of course, as it had been for many in the past. Thus, traditional religions came to lack obvious points of contact with the dominant, modern, secular culture. One consequence of this is that a large fraction of the West's population came to find traditional Abrahamic religions quite alien. Many people, although perhaps interested to some extent in religion, would, by the end of the twentieth century, seem to have lacked the necessary culturally imbued skills for a meaningful engagement with any of the faiths. Encounters with traditional religion may well have left many postmoderns simply feeling awkward and uninformed.[77] There is much evidence in popular culture to suggest that many, at the century's close, did indeed experience traditional religion to be nothing short of incomprehensible, and that many of those who did, nevertheless, enquire into it further were rewarded only with extreme cultural dissonance.

In the not too distant past, on the other hand, virtually everyone who had been brought up within Western culture had become familiar with the narratives of at least one religious tradition – which, far more often than not, was, of course, Christianity. Although many, clearly, did not subscribe to the beliefs of the religious tradition that was dominant within their culture, in many cases it nevertheless continued to inform their cultural understanding and values. In short, people by and large shared a set of religious symbols, images and values which occupied a core role within the general culture, even if many chose not to belong to any faith-community. It would seem that this situation has now changed to such an extent that many people today seem incapable of understanding the languages, symbols and imagery of religion, are unfamiliar with sacred literature, and do not share the values endorsed by the Abrahamic faiths.

In Christian terms, an increasing number of people are thus 'unchurched'. Among other things, they are ignorant of the differences between the various Christian denominations; a consideration that has, in many parts of the West, given rise to the need for a new approach on the part of institutionalized religions. Consider, for example, Alister McGrath's depiction of one of the new style of non-denominational churches flourishing in the United States at the end of the twentieth century. McGrath provides a detailed description of the Willow Creek Community Church – a massive ecclesial complex in Illinois, whose average Sunday attendance is 20,000. McGrath opines that the appeal of this church would seem to be, in large part, due to its founders' recognition that, because many North Americans were unchurched, then a new approach was now required if the Christian ministry were to deliver their message effectively. For many people simply

> had no experience of clerical robes, hard pews, collection plates and the old-fashioned hymns. They did not know the language of the Christian tradition, and the Bible was a closed book to them. Why, its leaders wondered, did newcomers to the faith have to fight their way through a jungle of obsolete Christian cultural trappings to find out about Jesus? For an unchurched person the first experience of a traditional church worship service was likely to be the last. Old-fashioned music, dusty old hymnals, uncomfortable pews and a pompous liturgy were in stark contrast to the everyday life experienced by modern Americans.[78]

In short, the founders of Willow Creek had begun to worry that many found traditional Christianity unappealing primarily because of its mootedly unessential, antiquated accoutrements. Moreover, these accoutrements were totally alien to the target audience. So, in an effort to make their church 'seeker sensitive', they chose to abandon all such features. Clearly, this constitutes one way of responding to a growing religious illiteracy on the part of the general public. And it is a response that seems to be in continuity with some of the modern forms of religion that had been promoted earlier in the twentieth century, such as Reform Judaism and Modernist Islam. However, it remains a highly contested 'solution' to the problem that religious illiteracy poses.

As we have seen, many deny that accommodating a religious tradition to the cultural expectations of postmodernity offers a genuine solution to this problem. The claim that a 'religion', such as Judaism, Christianity or Islam, has an essential form that can be clearly demarcated from its cultural expression in any particular era is one that came under increasing attack during the twentieth century. Many have argued that these religions have no essence, and that, at the deepest level, they are constituted solely by their varied cultural expressions. It follows that in order to be religious, one must be inculturated into a particular faith-community's worldview. And according to this understanding, the strategy of accommodation has come to seem unavoidable because, as George Lindbeck claims, religions 'have become foreign texts that are much easier to translate into currently popular categories than to read in terms of their intrinsic sense'.[79] However, as Lindbeck proceeds to argue, the ease of translation into current cultural idioms is more apparent than real, and can disguise the fact that 'religions, like languages, can be understood only in their own terms, not by transposing them into an alien speech'.[80]

On Lindbeck's view, then, acquiring a religion is analogous to acquiring a culture or learning a language. It is a matter of 'interiorizing outlooks that others have created, and mastering skills that others have honed'.[81] However, as Lindbeck also notes, many modern thinkers baulk at this process, because it would seem to be an affront to an individual's freedom of choice and self-expression. Indeed, as we have seen, many, such as Don Cupitt, promote a view of religion as a deeply individual affair. It is a personal quest in which people are encouraged 'to meet God first in the depths of their souls and then, perhaps, if they find something personally congenial, to become part of a tradition or join a church'.[82] If Lindbeck's account of religion is correct, however, acquiring a religion without the help of a religious tradition is, if not impossible, extremely difficult; just as mastering a language without participating in a community that speaks that language is an onerous task – and one at which many fail.[83]

Furthermore, in Lindbeck's view, 'it is necessary to have the means for expressing an experience in order to have it, and the richer our expressive or linguistic system, the more subtle, varied, and differentiated can be our experience'.[84] Analogously, he holds that the deeper one's interiorization of a religious tradition, the more 'subtle, varied, and differentiated' will be the range of religious experiences accessible to one. The real problem of religious illiteracy, then, according to this view, is that without a certain degree of religious inculturation, a person will be unable to express, and hence will be incapable of having, certain kinds of religious experience. And as beliefs and experiences are mutually reinforcing within any healthy worldview, it should be no surprise if religious beliefs that were not supported by appropriate religious experiences were found to be uncompelling. If this is an accurate account of the problem, then it would seem to follow that the strategy of accommodating religious beliefs and practices in order to meet modern cultural expectations will fail to provide a long-term solution. Indeed, the only way to ameliorate the problem would be to provide people with the cultural skills necessary for a deep understanding of religion. However, as many have remarked, the transmission of these skills had, by the close of the twentieth century, become progressively more attenuated. And this has, perhaps, been exacerbated by the steadily decreasing influence of religious thought upon Western culture as a whole.[85]

This is a trend, moreover, that shows no signs of reversal. Indeed, Lindbeck himself is far from sanguine about the future prospects of traditional religion within Western culture. For he regards this culture as having reached a stage in which 'socialization is ineffective, catechesis is impossible, and translation a tempting alternative ...',[86] adding that the 'impossibility of effective catechesis in the present situation is partly the result of the implicit assumption that knowledge of a few tag ends of religious language is knowledge of the religion ...'.[87]

While Lindbeck's focus is upon Christianity, it would seem that his analysis describes the situation of each of the Abrahamic monotheisms in the modern West. Among those who adhere to one of these faiths, as well as amongst those who do not, there is evidence of a marked lack of religious education. It is plausible to regard this as symptomatic of the marginalization that the intellectual study of religion has suffered within modern Western culture. Within academia, there would seem to be several reasons for this marginalization. I shall mention two. First, religion has become increasingly the preserve of those interested in cultural studies, specifically cultural anthropology. Many theology departments have turned into religious studies departments in a laudable effort to broaden the study of religion beyond Christianity. But many of these departments now focus upon ritual and other phenomenological expressions of religion, rather than upon religious *ideas*. Indeed, many are seemingly hostile to the study of ideas. Thus, the study of religions as intellectual systems has become increasingly less important within academia. Second, in the twentieth century, academia became increasingly driven by pragmatic interests. Funding was diverted from the human into the natural sciences and other disciplines that appeared to have immediate pragmatic value. Thus, the humanities became under-funded, and hence marginalized. The study of religious intellectual systems suffered enormously from this, as did generations of students who have become progressively deprived of any but the most superficial cultural education.

In the case of Christianity, however, the fault does not lie exclusively with the system of education favoured in the modern West. To a large extent, Christian theologians have been complicit in the process that has led to their marginalization within Western European and North American intellectual life. Throughout the twentieth century, many of them promoted a view of theology as a strictly academic discipline – one independent from the interests of Christian churches. Thus, theologians rejected their natural audience and sought, instead, the attention and respect of their secular academic colleagues. Consequently, theology became increasingly irrelevant to Christians, who found it to have little, if anything, to contribute to their spiritual lives. At the close of the twentieth century, an increasing number of Christian theologians began to acknowledge that a rift between the Christian churches and theology had taken place, which some then sought to overcome.[88] Clearly, closing the gap between theology and Christian communities will do nothing to increase theology's standing in the secular academic arena – but theology might, at least, stand to regain its audience.[89] Hence, many now accept that the way forward for Christian theology is to recognize that its intellectual responsibility is principally to one community – the Christian one – and that it should focus on fulfilling this responsibility rather than aspiring to regain, in a world now dominated by the natural sciences, its former place in Western European intellectual life as the Queen of the Sciences.

The problem of growing religious illiteracy in the West not only afflicts the Christian community, however, but would also seem to be a significant failing within Jewish and Muslim communities. The Muslim thinker Sayyid Qutb, for example, claimed that the modern era constitutes a second *jāhilīya* (age of ignorance). In other words, he regarded the ignorance of many of his contemporaries as comparable to that of those living in the time prior to Muhammad: the first *jāhilīya*.[90] And an author of a very different intellectual bent, Fazlur Rahman, argues that, while emotionally reorienting many modern-educated Muslims to Islam, the revivalist movement failed to have 'any positive effect on Islamic thinking and scholarship'.[91] Moreover, in his view, Islamic revivalists have simply substituted 'cliché mongering for serious academic endeavor'.[92] Thus, he blames the de-intellectualization of Islam on the success of revivalism within many Muslim communities during the twentieth century. But revivalism is not the only guilty party, in Rahman's view. He also blames Sufism, which became increasingly popular among Muslims in the West during the twentieth century, for popularizing an attitude that separated the cultivation of the spiritual life from intellectual development.[93] Hence, Rahman firmly believes that, if Islam is to rise to meet the challenges of modern thought, Muslims must make educational reform their top priority.

If we turn to Judaism, we find that Jacob Neusner has drawn attention to what he regards as the intellectual decline of the Jewish community within the United States, noting

> the as yet unappreciated factor of sheer ignorance, the profound pathos of Jews' illiteracy in all books but the books of the street and market-places of the day. The second generation beyond immigration to the USA received in the streets and the public press its education in Jewish existence. The third generation in a more benign age turned to the same sources and came away with nothing negative, but little positive. And by the fourth generation, the Jews in North America had attained complete illiteracy.[94]

And, in Neusner's view, one immediate consequence of this situation is that most Jews towards the close of the twentieth century had become incapable of valuing anything in the religious domain that did not lead to immediate enjoyment. Thus, they have been rendered incapable of valuing the depths and complexities of their religious tradition. Moreover, he argues that this has become equally the case regarding the adherents of other religious traditions in the West. Almost all, he avers, have been rendered virtually incapable of seeking, or understanding, anything beyond their immediate experience. The core of the problem in each case, or so he argues, is a profound illiteracy with regard to the history and literature of their respective traditions.[95]

We thus see that prominent scholars from each of the major monotheisms practised in the West have reached a remarkably similar conclusion about the main problem facing their respective forms of traditional Abrahamic faith at the end of the twentieth century: religious illiteracy. And in agreeing that the social changes and political upheavals that characterized the twentieth-century West have contributed to this ostensible defect, they are also united in identifying its main cause as the decline of an overtly religious culture in the West, hastened by the disappearance of any serious religious education. Given that Western European secular culture is now ubiquitous to a degree unimaginable even at the beginning of the twentieth century, and given that this culture is still in the ascendancy, it seems reasonable to assume that the problem that religious illiteracy poses to the traditional faiths will become progressively more intractable as time proceeds.

Some would, no doubt, argue that the passing of religious culture and the demise of religious education constitutes a positive development, and, moreover, one to be encouraged. It is certainly undeniable that many today view religious education unfavourably. However, even those who deem the decline of an overtly religious culture in the West to be progressive are likely to regard one possible result of religious illiteracy as extremely costly. For, as we have noted, many who lack early familiarity with a religious tradition become religious later in life. And when they do, lacking any grounding in a tradition that manifests different intellectual expressions and that can facilitate a wide range of religious experiences, they are often attracted to religion in one of its fundamentalist, and sometimes one of its extremist, forms. Thus, a social policy that seeks to exclude religious education from the curriculum may, ironically, be contributing towards increased levels of religious fundamentalism.[96] Perhaps, then, the kind of education most appropriate within a multicultural world is, rather than religious indoctrination or one that leads to religious illiteracy, a form (as favoured, for example, by Mohammed Arkoun) that fosters the comprehensive understanding of different traditions.

A further consequence of the dominance of Western European secular culture is that, as Sherwin Wine claims,[97] religious identity is now experienced by most Westerners today only with considerable effort.[98] This brings to the fore another characteristic of religiosity at the close of the twentieth century: namely, that assuming a religious identity – or being a religious person – has become a matter of choice, rather than hereditary. In a cultural shift that is surely not unconnected to the steadily increasing levels of religious illiteracy within Western society, religious communities have become communities of assent rather than descent. It would seem, moreover, that this change has been accompanied by similarly dramatic alterations within the belief systems of each religious tradition. This is because many people are now less inclined simply to accept all the beliefs that have, in the past, been part of what is now their tradition of choice, and are now more likely to evaluate critically each belief and to question the cogency of traditional religious concepts.

We now consider some other conclusions that we might be warranted in drawing concerning traditional Abrahamic monotheisms in the West at the beginning of the new millennium.

Conclusion: Abrahamic monotheisms at the start of the third millennium

Hans-Georg Gadamer claims that religion has become not so much a matter of belief but rather a way of being.[99] Nietzsche would seem to have anticipated this development when he claimed that, in view of the bankruptcy of Christian theology, 'only Christian *practice*, a life such as he *lived* who died on the cross, is Christian. Such a life is still possible today, for certain people even necessary: genuine, original Christianity will be possible at all times.'[100]

We have seen that the mooted bankruptcy of the Abrahamic faiths as intellectual systems appears to have been conceded by thinkers within each tradition (some of whom have been recognized religious leaders within their communities). Nevertheless, many of these thinkers have, like Nietzsche, asserted that religious lifestyles continue to be of value. Richard Holloway, a former bishop in the Scottish Episcopal Church, for example, argues that traditional Christianity as an intellectual system cannot survive into the future because, given the ideas and values that many now accept, traditional beliefs are no longer tenable. In the face of this situation, he proposes that we go beyond both belief and unbelief, and embrace, instead, a 'way of action'. It is, he argues, 'more important to follow the way of Jesus than to believe or disbelieve the traditional Christian claims about him. Above all ... the task of Christianity today is the challenge, not to go on interpreting the world in the ancient way, but to start disturbing it in a new way.'[101] Thus, the trend seems to favour orthopraxy – practice in accordance with faith – over orthodoxy.[102]

One conclusion, then, is that, while religious belief has clearly been embarrassed by modernity, much religious practice would seem to have entered the twenty-first century relatively unscathed. Many religious thinkers, from each of the Abrahamic traditions, would seem to be united in their emphasis on religious lifestyles and spirituality in preference to beliefs that are constituted by demonstrative propositions. Does this suggest that, as we enter the twenty-first century, religious *belief* has arrived at a dead end? It is, surely, still open to religious thinkers today to seek more nuanced accounts of the relationship between religious beliefs, experience and truth. Thus, it may not necessarily be the case that the focus on experience and practice so prominent in religious self-understanding at the beginning of the third millennium is incompatible with commitment to religious beliefs. And consequently, there would seem to be a legitimate task ahead for philosophers of religion and theologians who seek to examine not only these beliefs but also their relation to the experience of religious believers.

Nevertheless, the trend in favour of orthopraxy resonates with the changing conception of religious thought that is evident within each of the monotheisms. The further the twentieth century marched on, the more one can see religious thinkers turning their attention away from the metaphysics of theism and towards the human dimensions of religious experience. This change of focus can be clearly seen in, for example, the work of Richard Rubenstein, who claims that

[c]ontemporary theology reveals less about God than it does about the kind of men we are. It is largely an anthropological discipline. Today's theologian, be he Jewish or Christian, has more in common with the poet and creative artist than with the metaphysician and physical

scientist. He communicates a very private subjectivity. Its relevance lies in the possibility that he may enable other men to gain insight and clarify their religious lives in the face of common experience.[103]

Moreover, '[t]he meaning of God in human experience', adds Rubenstein 'is a variable which is inevitably altered by radical changes in that experience. Scientific arguments for or against the existence of God are far less significant that the existential matrix out of which such affirmations or denials flow.'[104]

However, despite the trend towards orthopraxy, and despite the emphasis upon religious anthropology that can be found in the work of many religious thinkers, forms of faith that can make a convincing appeal to 'orthodoxy' would still seem to stand at an advantage over those that seemingly cannot. Indeed, during the period of postmodernity, as we have seen, there would appear to have been a tendency for people to convert from the more liberal religious groups into the, ostensibly, more robust varieties. Hence, it would seem that many prefer what appear to them to be more historically grounded and tradition-imbued forms of faith, and are thus more inclined to convert, for example, from Reform Judaism to Hasidism, or from evangelical Christianity to either Eastern Orthodoxy or Roman Catholicism, or from cultural Islam to some form of revivalism.

Another aspect of this tendency is, perhaps, the steadily increasing number of converts from Christianity to Islam. Within the United States, for example, a growing number of former Christians have become spokespersons for Islam, their new faith. Those who have been members of Christian churches that express uncertainty about the status of Scripture, or about the doctrines regarding God or the incarnation of Christ, may well choose to dispense with such worries and adopt a form of non-liberal Islam, instead, where no such doubts are entertained. And Islam may well seem to be the most rationally acceptable form of Abrahamic monotheism, because it does not involve commitment to any of the more rationally taxing doctrines of Christianity (with the exception of the virgin birth of Jesus) or of Judaism (for example, the doctrine of the election of the people of Israel). And regarding Jesus as a prophet of God might come naturally to one schooled in the demythologization characteristic of liberal Protestant thought. Moreover, if one's own form of Christianity has rescinded on the claim that Christ is God incarnate, then what is to stop one simply becoming a Muslim, when that is precisely the principal Christian belief that Islam denies?[105]

But what of those who wish to remain within their original religious communities, and who wish to do so without having to renounce their aspirations to articulate meaningfully the beliefs that inform their religious practices? We have seen that many have responded to the challenges posed to their faith by certain aspects of modern thought by seeking to redefine 'God'. While the classical conception of God may have seemed plausible in a world that changed very slowly, it became increasingly alien and irrelevant to many people in the twentieth century. Thus, as we have seen, radical changes in the concept 'God' have been proposed.[106] Fazlur Rahman, for example, conceives of God as 'the ultimate source of created energy that can be appropriated by individuals and societies',[107] while Don Cupitt holds that God 'is the sum of our values, representing to us their ideal unity, their claims upon us and their creative power'.[108] Mordecai Kaplan proposes an equally radical redefinition. For 'God', he claims, 'is the Power that makes for salvation of man through the community which organizes its entire social order around the purpose of man's salvation.'[109]

It is surely no accident that, according to each of these definitions, God is impersonal – which clearly represents a dramatic conceptual shift from the conception of God that had traditionally been the organizing idea of each of the Abrahamic monotheisms. For one thing, an impersonal conception of God clearly makes a nonsense of God's authorship of the sacred texts. And such a construal of 'God' would, further, seem to make any understanding of those texts as a storehouse of literally true accounts of natural and supernatural facts quite implausible. This has paved the way for religious thinkers to experiment with alternative notions of truth to those that had typically been employed by Western philosophers. Increasingly, then, religions have come to be seen as worldviews or systems of meaning, whose 'truths' cannot be isolated from their context within extremely complex traditions, or from within the forms of life they inspire.

Willard van Orman Quine has argued that a system of meaning is like a network.[110] At the heart of the network are concepts which function to determine the meaning of those at the periphery of the network. But most importantly, while all concepts are in principle revisable, the closer a concept is to the core of the network, argues Quine, the more will it be resistant to change. Changes in the meaning of concepts, then, more usually occur among those at the periphery. And if the meaning of a concept at the periphery is adjusted, then there may well be a corresponding change in closely connected concepts also located at the periphery. But those at the heart of the system of meaning will remain unchanged.

With Quine's holistic theory of meaning as our guide, we might plausibly argue that, ever since the three Abrahamic belief systems stabilized during the first millennium of the common era, alterations in religious belief principally concerned the meaning of concepts at the periphery of those belief systems (which is not to deny that some of the concepts that underwent transformation were less peripheral than others). The meaning of the core concepts of each tradition – such as, for example, 'God' and 'revelation' – remained relatively constant, being unaffected by the alterations in the meanings of concepts at the periphery. Matters changed significantly during the twentieth century, however; and particularly in its second half. For this was a time in which, as we have seen, many thinkers from each of the Abrahamic faiths felt that some change in the concepts at the heart of their respective religious traditions was required. It is the fact that such changes to the meaning of *core* religious concepts were proposed, and, in many cases, carried through, that marks religious thought in the West during the twentieth century as quite distinct from previous religious thinking.[111]

As we have seen numerous times in the course of this book, it was precisely the core concepts of Judaism, Christianity and Islam that came to be challenged by modern thought. And many religious thinkers were able to mount a response to this challenge only by altering those core religious concepts,[112] correctly realizing that tinkering with those at the periphery of their religious belief system would do little to resolve the problem posed by the apparent implausibility and seeming incomprehensibility of the whole system, at least in the eyes of many living within the modern world.

Moreover, not only is it the case that traditional religious worldviews, or systems of meaning, have undergone dramatic shifts affecting even the core religious concepts, but it is also undeniable that entire systems of meaning have been called into question. We have seen that, in the twentieth century, thinkers from each of the Abrahamic faiths have been forced to confront the problems raised by religious plurality. As a result, many have come to accept that their own religious worldview is merely one among several – and that each is deserving of respect. This realization has motivated religious thinkers to re-conceive the status of their own worldview, and to reassess any claim to exclusive truth made from the standpoint of any worldview. In short, by the end of the twentieth century, the claim that any one religious worldview exclusively expresses the 'Truth', and is rationally superior to all others, came to be viewed by an increasing number of religious thinkers as highly implausible. And this, too, represents a radical conceptual shift from earlier ways of conceiving religious worldviews. For, previously, each theorizer had tended to take for granted the presumption that his or her worldview should be regarded as normative for everyone.

The current epoch is characterized by an especially high degree of creativity within the domain of religious ideas. Long-established religious traditions appear, to many, inadequate to the needs of the times, and new forms of religiosity are currently emerging as the old ones lose their appeal and persuasiveness. Needless to say, it is too early to judge the success of any of the proposed alterations to the Abrahamic faiths that we have reviewed. What we can do, however, is admire the creativity and the ingenuity of the religious thinkers who have risen to the challenges posed to their belief systems by modernity.

Study questions

1 Is the current epoch more aptly characterized as 'late-modern' or 'postmodern'?

2 How would you characterize the contrast between modern and post-modern thought? What are the key differences and similarities?

3 How has the media contributed to the detraditionalization undergone by the Abrahamic faiths in postmodernity? In your view, has detrad-itionalization had a positive or negative effect on Judaism, Christianity and Islam?

4 Does the separation of religious experience from religious belief inevitably lead to relativism about religion, as Paul Heelas claims?

5 Why is Don Cupitt's theology described as 'liberal postmodern religious thought'? In what key ways does it differ from so-called 'conservative postmodern religious thought'?

6 What is 'open-traditionalism'? What does Eugene Borowitz aim to achieve with this theory?

7 Why do postmodern religious thinkers often claim that the notion of truth typically employed in modern thought is inadequate within the context of religion? Do you agree with their view? What notion of truth might be appropriate within the context of religion?

8 How serious a problem does religious illiteracy pose for the Abrahamic faiths in the West? How might this problem be solved?

9 In your opinion, is it a positive or a negative development that many faith-communities have become communities of ascent rather than communities of descent?

10 Is orthopraxy – practice in accordance with faith – more important than religious belief? Is orthopaxy sustainable without orthodoxy?

11 What are some of the changes that have been proposed to the concept 'God' by twentieth-century religious thinkers? Will the concept 'God' still be recognizable by the end of the third millennium?

12 What do you imagine Judaism, Christianity and Islam will be like at the turn of the next century?

Select bibliography

Akbar, A. S., 1998, *Postmodernism and the Islamic Predicament*, London: Routledge.

Akhtar, S., 1990, *A Faith for All Seasons: Islam and the Challenge of the Modern World*, Chicago: Ivan R. Dee.

Arkoun, M., 1994, *Rethinking Islam: Common Questions, Uncommon Answers*, trans. and edited by R. D. Lee, Boulder: Westview.

Borowitz, E. B., 1968, *A New Jewish Theology in the Making*, Philadelphia: The Westminster Press.

Cupitt, D., 1987, *The Long-Legged Fly: A Theology of Language and Desire*, London: SCM Press.

Griffin, D. R., 1989, *God and Religion in the Postmodern World: Essays in Postmodern Theology*, New York: SUNY.

Harrison, V. S., 2000, *The Apologetic Value of Human Holiness: Von Balthasar's Christocentric Philosophical Anthropology*, Studies in Philosophy and Religion, vol. 21, Dordrecht: Kluwer Academic Publishers.

Kaplan, M. M., 1958, *Judaism Without Supernaturalism: The Only Alternative to Orthodoxy and Secularism*, New York: The Reconstructionist Press.

Lindbeck, G. A., 1984, *The Nature of Doctrine: Religion and Theology in a Postliberal Age*, Philadelphia: The Westminster Press.

Milbank, J., 1993, *Theology and Social Theory: Beyond Secular Reason*, Oxford: Blackwell.

McGrath, A. E., 2002, *The Future of Christianity*, Oxford: Blackwell.

Rahman, F., 1982, *Islam and Modernity: Transformation of an Intellectual Tradition*, Chicago: The University of Chicago Press.

Smith, J. K. A., 2004, *Introducing Radical Orthodoxy: Mapping a Post-secular Theology*, Grand Rapids, Michigan: Baker Academic.

Thornhill, J., 2000, *Modernity: Christianity's Estranged Child Reconstructed*, Grand Rapids: William B. Eerdmans.

Wine, S., 1995, *Judaism Beyond God*, New York: KTAV.

Wolfe, M. (ed.), 2002, *Taking Back Islam: American Muslims Reclaim Their Faith*, Emmaus, Pennsylvania: Rodale.

Notes

1 Shabbir Akhtar, 1990, *A Faith for All Seasons: Islam and the Challenge of the Modern World*, Chicago: Ivan R. Dee, p. 205.

2 David Ray Griffin, 1989, *God and Religion in the Postmodern World: Essays in Postmodern Theology*, New York: SUNY, p. 54.

3 Griffin, *God*, p. 62.

4 Anthony Giddens is, perhaps, one of the most prominent proponents of the term 'late-modern'. See, for example, Anthony Giddens, 1991, *Modernity and Self-Identity: Self and Society in the Late Modern Era*, Stanford, California: Stanford University Press.

5 As Pauline Marie Rosenau explains: 'Postmodernism challenges global, all-encompassing world views, be they political, religious, or social. It reduces Marxism, Christianity, Fascism, Stalinism, capitalism, liberal democracy, secular humanism, feminism, Islam, and modern science to the same order and dismisses them all as logocentric, transcendental totalising meta-narratives that anticipate all the questions and provide pre-determined answers.' Pauline Marie Rosenau, 1992, *Postmodernism and the Social Sciences: Insights, Inroads, and Intrusions*, Princeton: Princeton University Press, p. 6.

6 Jean-François Lyotard, 1997, *The Postmodern Condition: A Report on Knowledge*, trans. by Geoff Bennington and Brian Massumi, Minneapolis: University of Minnesota Press, p. xxiv.

7 David West, for example, supports this interpretation when he claims that '[p]ostmodernism attempts a radical break with all the major strands of post-Enlightenment thought'. David West, 1996, *An Introduction to Continental Philosophy*, Oxford: Blackwell, p. 189.

8 And if it is, indeed, more accurately conceptualized as 'late-modern' rather than 'postmodern' thought, then any book entitled *Religion and Modern Thought* would need to include some discussion of it, given its prominence towards the end of the twentieth century.

9 John Thornhill, 2000, *Modernity: Christianity's Estranged Child Reconstructed*, Grand Rapids: William B. Eerdmans, p. 51.

10 Thornhill is by no means alone in this judgement. Catherine Pickstock, a representative of radical orthodoxy (about which, see below) also supports this view when she claims that secular postmodern thought 'is only the logical outcome of the rationalism of modernity, and in no sense its inversion'. Catherine Pickstock, 1998, *After Writing: On the Liturgical Consummation of Philosophy*, Oxford: Blackwell, p. xii.

11 Thornhill, *Modernity*, p. 54.

12 Thornhill, *Modernity*, p. 55.

13 See Thornhill, *Modernity*, p. 55.

14 Robert N. Bellah et al., 1986, *Habits of the Heart: Individualism and Commitment in American Life*, New York: Harper & Row, p. 277.

15 Robert N. Bellah et al., 1991, *The Good Society*, New York: Knopf, p. 7.

16 If one were to make the meaning of 'postmodernity' more precise, then it would be necessary to describe the present tumultuous world as within the stage of either postmodernity or late-modernity, depending on one's analysis. But as long as the term 'postmodernity' remains vague and poorly defined, as is the case in common usage, that choice can be side-stepped. Hence, when, in what follows, I refer to postmodernity, that should not be taken to imply that I side with the thesis that a radical break with modernity has occurred.

17 Sociologists of religion refer to this view as the 'pick-and-mix' thesis.

18 Don Cupitt, 1998, *Mysticism After Modernity*, Oxford: Blackwell, pp. 1f.

19 See John B. Thompson, 1996, 'Tradition and Self in a Mediated World' in Paul Heelas, Scott Lash and Paul Morris (eds), *Detraditionalization: Critical Reflections on Authority and Identity*, Oxford: Blackwell, p. 99.

20 Paul Heelas, 1998, 'Introduction: On Differentiation and Dedifferentiation' in Paul Heelas (ed.), *Religion, Modernity and Postmodernity*, Oxford: Blackwell, p. 5.

21 Heelas, 'Introduction', p. 5.

22 'Conservative' postmodern religious thinkers might also be referred to as 'postliberal'.

23 Graham Ward, 1997, 'Postmodern Theology' in David F. Ford (ed.), *The Modern Theologians: An Introduction to Christian Theology in the Twentieth Century*, Oxford: Blackwell, p. 586. While Ward applied the distinction between 'liberal' and 'conservative' postmodern thought within Christian theology, it would seem to be equally useful for distinguishing between the two corresponding varieties within Jewish and Muslim religious thought, respectively.

24 Don Cupitt, 1984, *The Sea of Faith: Christianity in Change*, London: British Broadcasting Corporation, pp. 19f.

25 Cupitt, *Sea*, p. 19.

26 Don Cupitt, 1987, *The Long-Legged Fly: A Theology of Language and Desire*, London: SCM Press, p. 105.

27 See Don Cupitt, 1997, *After God: The Future of Religion*, London: Weidenfeld & Nicolson.

28 Eugene B. Borowitz, 1968, *A New Jewish Theology in the Making*, Philadelphia: The Westminster Press, p. 8.

29 Borowitz, *New Jewish*, p. 8.

30 Borowitz, *New Jewish*, p. 204.

31 Borowitz, *New Jewish*, pp. 204f.

32 Borowitz, *New Jewish*, p. 207.

33 See Borowitz, *New Jewish*, p. 208.

34 See Borowitz, *New Jewish*, p. 118.

35 Borowitz, *New Jewish*, pp. 212f.

36 For his later work, see, for example, Eugene B. Borowitz, 1999, *Judaism After Modernity: Papers from a Decade of Fruition*, Lanham, Maryland: University Press of America.

37 On Borowitz's influence upon later postmodern Jewish thought, see Peter Ochs (with Eugene Borowitz) (ed.), 2000, *Reviewing the Covenant: Eugene B. Borowitz and the Postmodern Renewal of Jewish Theology*, Albany: SUNY.

38 See Steven Kepnes, in Steven Kepnes, Peter Ochs and Robert Gibbs, 1998, *Reasoning After Revelation: Dialogues in Postmodern Jewish Philosophy*, Boulder: Westview Press, p. 25.

39 Kepnes, *Reasoning*, pp. 25f.

40 See Chapter 8.

41 See Kepnes, *Reasoning*, p. 42.

42 The participants in the section of the dialogue I have quoted are Peter Ochs, Yudit Greenberg and Steven Kepnes. See Kepnes, *Reasoning*, pp. 14f.

43 For an excellent account of this movement, see James K. A. Smith, 2004, *Introducing Radical Orthodoxy: Mapping a Post-secular Theology*, Grand Rapids, Michigan: Baker Academic.

44 John Milbank, 1993, *Theology and Social Theory: Beyond Secular Reason*, Oxford: Blackwell.

45 Pickstock, *Writing*, p. xii.

46 Milbank, *Theology*, p. 1.

47 See, for example, Milbank, *Theology*, p. 380.

48 Milbank, *Theology*, p. 398. See, also, Milbank, *Theology*, p. 330.

49 Milbank, *Theology*, p. 248.

50 See Milbank, *Theology*, p. 389.

51 Milbank, *Theology*, p. 247.

52 Milbank, *Theology*, p. 262.

53 Milbank, *Theology*, p. 262.

54 Milbank, *Theology*, p. 262. My italics.

55 Milbank, *Theology*, p. 422. Another Christian 'conservative' postmodern religious thinker, Michel de Certeau (1925–86), proposes a theory that is similar to Milbank's in many respects. De Certeau also concentrates on the experience of being a member of a religious community, and the connection between this and acquiring religious knowledge: 'The Christian faith has no security other than the *living* God discovered by communities which are alive and which undergo the experience of *losing* objective securities. ... That is the first question: no longer to know whether God exists, but to *exist* as Christian communities.'

Michel de Certeau, 'How is Christianity Thinkable Today?', *Theology Digest*, 19 (1971), pp. 344f.

56 For an introduction to Arkoun's thought, see Robert D. Lee, 1997, *Overcoming Tradition and Modernity: The Search for Islamic Authenticity*, Boulder: Westview Press. Of Berber origin, Arkoun has occupied increasingly prominent academic positions within Western Europe since 1956.

57 Mohammed Arkoun, 1994, *Rethinking Islam: Common Questions, Uncommon Answers*, trans. and edited by Robert D. Lee, Boulder: Westview, p. 3.

58 Arkoun, *Rethinking*, p. 3.

59 Arkoun, *Rethinking*, p. 2.

60 We discussed Nasr's views in Chapter 7, pp. 217–20.

61 Michel de Certeau proposes a similar understanding of the Christian tradition. In his view, the life of Jesus is the revelatory event from which a variety of Christian interpretive traditions were generated.

62 See Mohammed Arkoun, 1984, *Pour une Critique de la raison islamique*, Paris: Maisonneuve et Larose, pp. 132f.

63 See, for example, Lee, *Overcoming*, p. 170.

64 Farish A. Noor, 2003, 'What is the Victory of Islam? Towards a Different Understanding of the *Ummah* and Political Success in the Contemporary World' in O. Safi (ed.), *Progressive Muslims: On Justice, Gender, and Pluralism*, Oxford: Oneworld, pp. 331f.

65 Noor, 'What is', p. 332.

66 Friedrich Nietzsche seems to have anticipated this feature of postmodernism when he declared: 'The falseness of a judgement is not for us necessarily an objection to a judgement; in this respect our new language may sound strangest. The question is to what extent it is life-promoting, life-preserving, species-preserving, perhaps even species-cultivating ...'. Friedrich Nietzsche, 1990, *Beyond Good and Evil: Prelude to a Philosophy of the Future*, trans. by R. J. Hollingdale, Harmondsworth, Penguin, I.4. Quoted in Michael Tanner, 2000, *Nietzsche: A Very Short Introduction*, Oxford: Oxford University Press, p. 72.

67 The new approaches to the interpretation of sacred texts that we considered in Chapter 5 are in line with this view.

68 Milbank, *Theology*, p. 267.

69 With respect to the narratives contained within the Christian Scriptures, Thornhill claims that 'the biblical story which reaches its climax in the life, death, and exaltation of Jesus of Nazareth discloses a truth about human existence which is universal. In the light of the biblical story, we can find the ultimate significance of our own stories. And conversely, the story of each of us can shed light on the ongoing story of the Christian people as a whole, the church.' Thornhill, *Modernity*, p. 193. And one easily can regard the central narratives of Judaism and Islam as functioning in exactly the same way.

70 Lyotard, *Postmodern*, p. 26.

71 Lyotard, *Postmodern*, p. 27.

72 Milbank, *Theology*, p. 347.

73 Cf. George Lindbeck: 'Pagan converts to the catholic mainstream did not, for the most part, first understand the faith and then decide to become Christians; rather, the process was reversed: they first decided and then they understood. More precisely, they were first attracted by the Christian community and

form of life.' George A. Lindbeck, 1984, *The Nature of Doctrine: Religion and Theology in a Postliberal Age*, Philadelphia: The Westminster Press, p. 132.

74 On how the appeal of a particular lifestyle might compel a person to adopt a particular religious tradition, see Victoria S. Harrison, 'Human Holiness and Religious *Apologia*', *International Journal for Philosophy of Religion*, 46 (1999), pp. 63–92.

75 Alasdair MacIntyre, 1982, *After Virtue: A Study in Moral Theory*, London: Duckworth, p. 216. Anthony Giddens seems to offer a parallel analysis when he claims that '[p]ersonal meaninglessness – the feeling that life has nothing worthwhile to offer – becomes a fundamental psychic problem in late modernity. We should understand this phenomenon in terms of a repression of moral questions which day-to-day life poses, but which are denied answers. "Existential isolation" is not so much a separation of individuals from others as a separation from the moral resources necessary to live a full and satisfying existence. ...' Giddens, *Modernity*, p. 9. Although Giddens is concerned with moral knowledge, his remarks would also seem applicable to religious knowledge, a point which we develop further, below.

76 Lindbeck, *Nature*, pp. 130f.

77 See Philip Larkin, 'Church Going' in Philip Larkin, 1988, *Collected Poems*, London: The Marvell Press and Faber & Faber, pp. 97f.

78 Alister E. McGrath, 2002, *The Future of Christianity*, Oxford: Blackwell, pp. 61f.

79 Lindbeck, *Nature*, p. 124.

80 Lindbeck, *Nature*, p. 129.

81 Lindbeck, *Nature*, p. 22.

82 Lindbeck, *Nature*, p. 22.

83 As Lindbeck notes: '[T]o become religious – no less than to become culturally or linguistically competent – is to interiorize a set of skills by practice and training. One learns how to feel, act, and think in conformity with a religious tradition that is, in its inner structure, far richer and more subtle than can be explicitly articulated. The primary knowledge is not *about* the religion, not *that* the religion teaches such and such, but rather *how* to be religious in such and such ways.' *Nature*, p. 35.

84 Lindbeck, *Nature*, p. 37.

85 See, for example, Lindbeck, *Nature*, p. 124.

86 Lindbeck, *Nature*, p. 133.

87 Lindbeck, *Nature*, p. 133.

88 Hans Urs von Balthasar was a lone voice in the mid-twentieth century warning theologians of the consequences of the changed conception of theology. For a study of his analysis of the situation, see Victoria S. Harrison, 2000, *The Apologetic Value of Human Holiness: Von Balthasar's Christocentric Philosophical Anthropology*, Studies in Philosophy and Religion, vol. 21, Dordrecht: Kluwer Academic Publishers.

89 See Victoria S. Harrison, 'Theology as Revelation and *Apologia*', *Theology*, CIV (2001), pp. 248–55; and Victoria S. Harrison, 'Holiness, Theology and Philosophy', *Philosophy and Theology*, 12 (2000), pp. 53–78.

90 See Lee, *Overcoming*, p. 88.

91 Fazlur Rahman, 1982, *Islam and Modernity: Transformation of an Intellectual Tradition*, Chicago: The University of Chicago Press, p. 137.

92 Rahman, *Islam*, p. 137.

93 See Rahman, *Islam*, p. 34.

94 Jacob Neusner, 1995, *Judaism in Modern Times: An Introduction and Reader*, Cambridge, Massachusetts: Blackwell, pp. 235f.

95 See Neusner, *Judaism*, pp. 236ff.

96 Indeed, such an outcome would seem to be predicted by Charles Liebman's thesis, which we discussed in Chapter 10. See Charles S. Liebman, 1983, 'Extremism as a Religious Norm', *Journal for the Scientific Study of Religion*, 22 (1983), pp. 75–86.

97 Rabbi Wine founded Humanist Judaism in the 1960s. The movement was motivated by what he perceived as the urgent need to revise Jewish practices and beliefs in accordance with quintessentially modern values, such as gender equality and human dignity. Members of this movement do not believe in a supernatural deity, and they reject the traditional dual-Torah theory of revelation. Moreover, in contradistinction to the traditional view of Jewish identity, Wine argues that anyone who chooses to identify with the Jewish tradition can be a Jew, irrespective of that person's birth. See, for example, Sherwin Wine, 1995, *Judaism Beyond God*, New York: KTAV.

98 See Wine, *Judaism*, pp. 87f. As Wine also observes, by the end of the twentieth century, religious identity had shifted its locus from the whole of life (as in pre-modernity) to specific religious holidays and activities.

99 See Hans-Georg Gadamer, 1999, 'Reflections of the Relation of Science and Religion' in Hans-Georg Gadamer, *Hermeneutics, Religion, and Ethics*, trans. by Joel Weinsheimer, New Haven: Yale University Press, p. 127.

100 Friedrich Nietzsche, 1974, 'The Antichrist' in Walter Kaufmann (ed.), *The Portable Nietzsche*, New York: Viking Press, paragraph 50. Quoted in Tanner, *Nietzsche*, p. 91.

101 Richard Holloway, 'The Myths of Christianity', Lecture Six: The End of Religion, Gresham College, 15 March 2001.

102 See Chapter 8.

103. Richard L. Rubenstein, 1966, *After Auschwitz: Radical Theology and Contemporary Judaism*, Indianapolis: Bobbs-Merrill Company, p. x.

104 Rubenstein, *After Auschwitz*, p. 131.

105 Indeed, from a theological perspective, Islam can be seen as Arianism plus Muhammad. See Michael Wolfe, 2002, 'Jesus Through a Muslim Lens' in Michael Wolfe (ed.), *Taking Back Islam: American Muslims Reclaim Their Faith*, Emmaus, Pennsylvania: Rodale, pp. 158–62. In addition, adopting Islam allows former Christians (or Jews) to retain from their former faith much of what was especially important to them.

106 These changes would, moreover, seem to require equally radical changes in the way that religious people seek to relate to God. One symptom of this may be seen in changing fashions of prayer within Christianity. Traditional forms of prayer (vocal, petitionary, etc.) were aligned with older ways of portraying God; while contemplative, or meditative prayer is more in line with the new conceptions of the divine that are gaining ascendancy. Hence, from the 1960s onwards,

many within the West became more receptive to Eastern religious traditions and to the meditation techniques taught therein.

107 Rahman, *Islam*, p. 154.

108 Cupitt, *Sea*, p. 269.

109 Mordecai M. Kaplan, 1958, *Judaism Without Supernaturalism: The Only Alternative to Orthodoxy and Secularism*, New York: The Reconstructionist Press, p. 52.

110 See Willard van Orman Quine, 1961, 'Two Dogmas of Empiricism' in Willard van Orman Quine, *From a Logical Point of View*, New York: Harper & Row, pp. 20–46.

111 I do not mean to suggest that no religious thinker prior to the twentieth century ever proposed a radical change to the concept 'God' or to the concept 'revelation'. Such a claim would clearly be erroneous. Rather, what appears distinctive about late twentieth-century religious thought is the sheer number of thinkers willing to propose such changes, along with the way in which these proposals were greeted, which was often favourably. And this seems to indicate that such transformation in the core religious concepts met a genuine and urgently felt spiritual need on the part of many people during the second half of the twentieth century.

112 As Don Cupitt acutely observes with respect to Christianity: 'theology today finds itself doing roughly what physics and painting were doing in the first decade of the twentieth century. It is *dismantling its own objects*, changing all the rules and undoing familiar and long-established methods of representation.' Cupitt, *Long-Legged*, p. 1.

Sources and Acknowledgements

For permission to include revised versions of substantial parts of the following articles, I would like to acknowledge my gratitude to *Philosophia* with respect to 'Arguments from Design: A Self-defeating Strategy', from 33 (2005), pp. 297–317, and with respect to 'Internal Realism and the Problem of Religious Diversity', from 34 (2006), pp. 287–301 (both © Springer Academic Publishers), and to *The Heythrop Journal* with respect to 'Scientific and Religious Worldviews: Antagonism, Non-antagonistic Incommensurability and Complementarity', from 47 (2006), pp. 349–66 (© Blackwell Publishers Ltd), and to *The International Journal for Philosophy of Religion* with respect to 'The Pragmatics of Defining Religion in a Multi-cultural World' from 59 (2006), pp. 133–52 (© Springer Academic Publishers), and to *Feminist Theology* with respect to 'Modern Women, Traditional Abrahamic Religions and Interpreting Sacred Texts' from 15 (2007), pp. 145–59 (© Sage Publishers). Slightly different versions are forthcoming of sections of Chapter 2 as 'On Defining the Religious Person' in *Theology*; Chapter 4 as 'Theism and the Challenge of Twentieth-Century Philosophy' in *Philotheos: International Journal of Philosophy and Theology*; Chapter 5 as 'Metaphor, Religious Language and Religious Experience' in *Sophia* and 'Hermeneutics, Religious Language and the Qur'ān' in *Islam and Christian–Muslim Relations*; Chapter 7 as 'Theorising Religious Diversity in a Multicultural World' in *ICFAI Journal of History and Culture*; Chapter 9 as 'Representing the Divine: Feminism and Religious Anthropology' in *Feminist Theology*; Chapter 10 as 'Modernity, Religious Fundamentalism and the Secularisation Thesis' in *ICFAI Journal of History and Culture*; Chapter 11 as 'Postmodern Thought and Religion: Open-traditionalism and radical orthodoxy on religious belief and experience' in *The Heythrop Journal* and 'Narrative, Postmodernity and the Problem of "Religious Illiteracy"' in *New Blackfriars*. I am grateful for permission to include parts of these articles here.

Index